D1017153

WITHDRAWN

IN THE TRENCHES

IN THE TRENCHES

Selected Speeches and Writings
of an American Jewish Activist
1979–1999

DAVID A. HARRIS

Executive Director,
The American Jewish Committee

KTAV Publishing House, Inc.

Copyright© 2000
David A. Harris

Library of Congress Cataloging-in-Publication Data

Harris, David A.
  In the trenches : selected speeches and writings of an American Jewish activist,
  1979-1999 / David A. Harris
  p. cm.
ISBN 0-88125-693-5
  1. Jews--Politics and government--1948- 2. Jews--Soviet Union--Emigration and
immigration. 3. Arab-Israeli conflict. 4. Jews--Europe--Social conditions--20th century.
5. Antisemitism. 6. American Jewish Committee--Officials and employees--Biography.
7. Holocaust, Jewish (1939-1945)--Influence. I. Title.

DS140.H36 2001
305.892'4'009045--dc21

                                                                00-058958

Distributed by
Ktav Publishing House, Inc.
900 Jefferson Street
Hoboken, NJ 07030
201-963-9524 FAX 201-963-0102
Email ktav@compuserve.com

*To the blessed memory
of two extraordinary individuals—
Sholom Comay and Ira Silverman—
whose imprint on the American
Jewish Committee and on my own
life are indelible.*

CONTENTS

1. SOVIET JEWRY

Contents / viii

2. ISRAEL AND THE MIDDLE EAST

Contents / ix

3. EUROPE

4. THE HOLOCAUST

5. JAPAN

6. LATIN AMERICA

7. INTERNATIONAL HUMAN RIGHTS

8. INTERNATIONAL TERRORISM

9. MAKING A BETTER AMERICA

10. LOOKING TO THE FUTURE OF AMERICAN JEWRY

11. THE AMERICAN JEWISH COMMITTEE

FOREWORD

Once again, David Harris has benefited the community, both Jewish and non-Jewish. He has done so by sharing his story, his personal journey—and an extraordinary collection of his selected writings and speeches, which chronicles a defining period in the life of American and world Jewry.

Reading David's collection in the context of his recollections is at once fascinating and instructive. It is as though we have been invited to view a unique and beautiful painting on a broad canvas, which comes alive and captivates in Technicolor fashion.

The overall impact is compelling and engrossing, leaving us with a clear sense of past, present, and future.

David is a brilliant mind. He passionately couples vision with reality. In these pages you will see his humanity and his humor shine through. You will understand why we at the American Jewish Committee are blessed with a sensitive, knowledgeable, articulate, and forceful professional leader, an executive director of enormous talent, integrity, and quality.

And you will also see why I have been blessed with a friend, a partner, a teacher, a mentor, a "rabbi," and a brother whom I, together with all who have the good fortune to have David in their lives, truly treasure.

Bruce M. Ramer
President, American Jewish Committee
Los Angeles, June 2000

IN THE TRENCHES

A PERSONAL JOURNEY

I came to the American Jewish Committee in 1979. I've been there ever since, with the exception of just over two years, between 1981 and 1984, when I worked as director of the National Conference on Soviet Jewry's Washington office. It's been an extraordinary two decades, and I am grateful to AJC for much, including the publication of this book of selected writings and speeches.

I'm sometimes asked how I got into this line of work. It wasn't at all foreseeable, far from it. Unlike many of my professional colleagues, I did not go to a Jewish day school or Jewish camp. My Jewish education, such as it was, ended abruptly with my bar mitzvah. I didn't enter the heavily Orthodox Hillel building even once during my five years on the University of Pennsylvania campus, nor did I enroll in any Jewish studies courses. And regrettably, my very first Shabbat dinner did not take place until I was twenty-three—a wonderfully warm but also somewhat discomfiting event in Harrison, New York, as I didn't know the words to most of the prayers and songs.

At the same time, I grew up in an unabashedly Jewish home. My mother, with whom I lived alone from the age of eleven, was quietly proud of her identity and would no more have missed services on Rosh Hashanah or Yom Kippur than she would have voted Republican on Election Day, at least at the time. We had the same seats for the High Holy Days year after year at Congregation B'nai Jeshurun in New York—long before its current rejuvenation—even if my mother and I often struggled to know what page the rabbi was on at any given moment. We fasted on the Day of Atonement and avoided leavened foods during Pesach.

For me, being a Jew meant, more than anything else, having a story to tell. Every member of my family older than I had quite a saga, which, as often as not, would be told in some combination of English,

Russian, French, and, in the case of my father and his parents, German. (Only my paternal grandmother and maternal grandfather spoke Yiddish.)

In my class at Franklin School—a West Side private school filled with Jews but no Jewish content—I was amazed that a classmate's parents had attended summer camp in New England as children. Impossible for Jews, I remember thinking. Jewish parents weren't born in the United States, I firmly believed at the time, much less spent their summers immersed in ersatz Indian folklore and color war. There was something suspect about their Jewishness.

And there were twins in my class, whose parents were also American-born. How amazed I was that their father knew the rules of baseball and enjoyed teaching the game to his kids—and to the rest of us—in Riverside Park on weekends. Baseball, I thought, was a game that we Jewish kids tried teaching our parents, not the reverse. Could this father really be a full-blooded Jew?

I certainly was embarrassed the day my father fell asleep at Yankee Stadium on a school father-son outing. But this lack of interest in America's national pastime among Jewish parents, all of whom, in my view, were supposed to come from other lands, seemed entirely understandable. At best, I thought, they might grasp the complex rules of soccer.

I was, in fact, the first member of my extended family to be born in the United States; everyone else had been born in Europe. The "lucky ones" only had to endure the Nazi threat. The unlucky ones, my mother included, experienced, first, difficult years under communism in Russia, followed by the devastation wrought by the Third Reich.

I was hungry to hear the stories, even if few were recounted in English alone. And I actually came to believe that it was the normal state of affairs for a Jew to have lived in several countries over the course of a lifetime; to have experienced persecution, expulsion, or arrest; to be multilingual; and to have somehow survived with one's determination to go on with life intact. Some of my colleagues joke that I seem to have a familial connection with lots of countries, even more than the number of states President George Bush claimed native ties to. In fact, it's quite true.

Just the two generations of the family that preceded me had more than their share of experiences in the following countries: Russia, Hungary, Poland, Germany, France, Italy, Spain, Portugal, Yugoslavia, Austria, Algeria, Australia, China, Japan, Mandatory Palestine and later Israel, and Switzerland.

But significantly, the members of my family never saw themselves as victims. I never, not once, heard an expression of self-pity; they didn't wear their suffering on their sleeves. Indeed, many in my family had been fighters—members of the French Resistance, the Office of Strategic Services (OSS), and the Haganah—but it took years to extract their remarkable deeds out of them, as modesty was a cherished family value.

In hindsight, these traits of optimism, courage, and modesty affected me greatly. Here were relatives who had been in the fire, but adamantly refused to accept their fate passively—instead smuggling French Jewish children to Switzerland, parachuting behind enemy lines to engage in espionage, escaping successfully across the Pyrenees to neutral Spain, or moving arms clandestinely from the United States to Jewish fighters in Palestine—yet never boasting of their exploits. And in subsequent years, while ever mindful of the painful historical lessons of this century, they never allowed themselves to become prisoners of that history.

Growing up, not only did I never question my identity but I always took great pride in it. Today I often ask myself why, especially when I look around at some classmates, campmates, and even relatives of the same generation for whom being Jewish was, it seemed, an option— and not always an appealing one at that—rather than a lifelong commitment. Frankly, I wasn't always quite sure of the meaning of being a Jew, beyond the most basic rituals and holiday observances. Nonetheless, I instinctively felt the tug of a powerful tribal loyalty.

Truth be told, I was one of those, from an early age, eager to know who was a Jew—which Nobel Prize winners, politicians, Hollywood stars, athletes. I *kvelled* in their success. And I loved to walk back and forth the fourteen blocks along Broadway to the synagogue on the High Holy Days to count how many stores were closed. Moreover, I was certain that the consumption of "kosher style" pastrami, bagels, lox, seeded rye bread, Dr. Brown's black cherry soda, and egg creams was the highest gastronomic expression of Judaism because it was quintessentially New York and New York was quintessentially Jewish.

That was it, I think. It was growing up on New York's West Side, where it was so easy, so natural, so normal to be a Jew. If you weren't Puerto Rican or Italian, then, by definition, it seemed, you must be Jewish. Judaism is a religion of doing, but I didn't know that, and even if I had I would have questioned it. It was enough for me to breathe the air on Broadway, West End Avenue, Seventy-second Street, Eighty-sixth Street, and everywhere else we hung out.

And I must give a great deal of credit to my mother. Of course, it wasn't obvious to me at the time, and even had I realized it, I doubt I would have said anything. But I've often asked myself why I had this high comfort level with being Jewish if there was so little Jewish sub-stance in our family and if so many of my contemporaries became indifferent, if not hostile, to their Jewish identity. The answer, at least in part, is that my mother, unlike many, never sent mixed messages about who she was; she was clear, consistent, and certain.

At family gatherings on Jewish holidays, for example, my mother, together with her father until his death in 1964, would usually get up just before dessert, put her coat on and go the synagogue. She would always ask if I wanted to come along. Loyalty to her, far more than the tug of faith, would impel me to go, leaving behind my favorite seven-layer or chocolate whipped cream cake and the promise of a good wrestling match with my first cousins. Others at the table would implore her to stay, but she was stubborn. She couldn't read a single word in the siddur, but she firmly believed that her place was in the synagogue.

I also remember the regular door-to-door solicitations by various Orthodox, sometimes Hasidic, representatives of groups in the United States and Israel. We didn't have a whole lot in common with them, or so I thought, but my mother, who struggled financially as a divorced woman employed as a full-time secretary and bookkeeper, would never let them leave without a dollar or two. For her, it was entirely natural. We were all Jews, our fates were intertwined, and if proof were need-ed of our common destiny, she had had enough of it in Europe.

In 1970, I visited Israel for the first time. These days there are heated arguments in the Jewish world about the long-term effect of relatively short visits to Israel by American Jewish youths. Count me Exhibit A for positive impact.

I went on my own, spent time with family, and traveled the length and breadth of the country, hitchhiking or by Egged bus. I was profoundly moved by just about everything, especially the palpable sense of excitement in building and defending a Jewish state. I admired and envied my contemporaries who proudly served in the Israel Defense Forces (IDF), at a time when the U.S. military was held in disrepute because of Vietnam and many young Americans on the left were engaging in what seemed to me, notwithstanding my own antiwar views, outlandish social, cultural, and political behavior. I was drawn to the communal notion of a kibbutz, and again admired and envied those living and working there. Soldiers, kibbutzniks, bus drivers—everyone seemed to be making this country move, survive, grow.

Israel, it seemed to me, was the place where history was playing itself out, and I quickly found myself drawn to it. America was demoralized, divided, drifting. Israel, on the other hand, after its extraordinary success in the 1967 Six-Day War—a success that galvanized American Jewry and transformed our Jewish self-image and political role—was on a national roll. To my own surprise, I even began to think about aliyah. Suddenly, I wanted to be part of this bold national experiment in Jewish sovereignty, which was somehow succeeding against all the odds. I wanted to live on the edge of history. I wanted to help write that history.

If there was one moment in particular that stands out on that first visit to Israel, it was riding on a city bus in Haifa, when an elderly man boarded and stood next to me. It was, I remember, a blisteringly hot day and he was in short sleeves. I saw on his left arm a number, indicating he had been in a Nazi concentration camp. It wasn't the first time I had seen such a number, but it was the first time in Israel. I began to think about the relationship between this survivor, the Holocaust, and Israel. The thought obsessed me for several days thereafter. What if there had been an Israel before the war? Might he have avoided the suffering he surely endured? How must he feel living in a Jewish state when the very idea of such a state seemed impossibly remote just twenty-five or thirty years earlier?

Thoughts of aliyah receded as I entered graduate school at the London School of Economics. There was a wonderfully *gemütlich* reading room upstairs in the main building, where I usually entered with ambitious academic intentions only to yield within a few minutes to the luxury of an afternoon nap. One day I picked up a book entitled *While Six Million Died* by Arthur D. Morse. It chronicled the official American indifference to the fate of European Jewry during the Holocaust. I couldn't put the book down, and I was tempted on several occasions to pound the table or let out a scream. I could barely believe what I was reading. After all, even with my own family's wartime travails, those who had sought entry to the United States had eventually made it, but this powerful book revealed a whole other story largely unknown to me.

I wanted to read more. I read other, more scholarly works on America's shameful wartime refugee policy. I read about the refusal of Canada and Great Britain to admit more than a handful of Jewish refugees. I read about the ill-fated Evian and Bermuda conferences on Europe's refugees. And then I went on to read books on the roots of anti-Semitism, the pogroms in Eastern Europe, the emergence of the Third Reich, the role of Righteous Gentiles during the war, and the origins of Zionism. I couldn't devour it all quickly enough.

Not sure what to do with the prospect of a master's degree in hand, I paid a visit to the aliyah center in London to inquire about possibilities in Israel. Driven by idealism, I told the official that I was thinking of spending time in Israel and that I literally wanted to help construct the country—I wanted to become a construction worker. I'm about as mechanically challenged as they come, but I visualized myself actually participating in the building of a Jewish country, maybe even erecting homes for new immigrants from the USSR. I had visions of a deeply tanned skin, hard muscles, and membership in a very different kind of Jewish fraternity than those I had known, albeit from a distance, on the Penn campus. How shocked I was, I still recall, when the Israeli representative looked at me with surprise and said: "Why would an educated young Jew want to do this 'black work' when it can be done by the Arab laborers?" Maybe, in the final analysis, my commitment to Israel just wasn't strong enough, much as I had thought it was, but this remark soured me on my emerging dream.

To sidetrack for just a moment, I continued to harbor thoughts of aliyah for a few more years, but, as I sometimes joke, it was an Egged bus driver who, in 1976, finally settled the issue for me. My future wife, Giulietta, who was born in Libya, and I were at the Jerusalem bus station on the eve of a holiday, trying to catch the last bus to Kibbutz Geva, where a sister of hers had lived for many years. The Hebrew word *balagan*, which loosely translated means "chaos," applied to the whole scene. I was standing with Giulietta, or so I thought, on a crowded and pushy bus line when the bus door closed and the driver started to leave. No sign of Giulietta. Next thing I know, I see her frantically waving at me from inside the bus. Suddenly, the bus stops, the door opens, and the driver walks through the throng. "Are you David?" he imperiously asks me. "Your girlfriend asked me to get you. Listen, I'll do it for you this once. But take it from me, don't ever make aliyah. She'll do fine, but, as an Anglo-Saxon, you'll never survive here!"

It was 1972, I was twenty three years old, and, based on lifelong interests, I wanted to pursue a career in international politics or diplomacy. I was lucky to find work in New York with the American Field Service, a distinguished nonprofit organization that ran international educational exchange programs. Early on, though, I noticed that Israel was conspicuously missing from the roster of participating countries, while many Arab countries were included. I was new and more than a bit shy, but I began gently probing to understand Israel's absence.

There was a company line that, at first blush, sounded convincing enough. Israeli youngsters entered the army at eighteen and therefore couldn't possibly participate in a yearlong international exchange program. But over time, I came to realize that this was at best only a partial explanation; after all, Israeli youths could conceivably participate at the age of seventeen, or perhaps even postpone by one year their entry into the military. These options, however, had not even been explored. Why? In two words: Arab boycott. Were Israel included, the Arab nations, it was feared, would walk. AFS would lose Morocco, Tunisia, Jordan, Kuwait, and others.

This was a stunning discovery for me. First of all, revealing yet again my youthful naïveté, I couldn't imagine that in this greatest of Jewish cities, New York, such a blatant act of discrimination against the Jewish state could occur. Moreover, I was dumbstruck that a distinguished international agency, whose singular objective was breaking down national, ethnic, racial, and religious barriers in the pursuit of world harmony, could play along with the insidious boycott, however much it masked its inexcusable stance with glib and facile explanations of Israel's omission from the AFS family of nations.

Rather than just leave an organization I otherwise admired, I decided to see what might be done. When I left AFS in 1974, Israel had still not been admitted, but it wasn't long before the attitude toward Israel began to change and eventually it was brought in. Over time, I was to learn that there were many more such dirty, dark little secrets in the international community respecting the anomalous treatment of Israel, and that all these secrets could benefit from the spotlight of exposure. Exposure alone, however, while necessary, was insufficient; perseverance and persistence would also be required to bring about change, whether at AFS or, later, in other nongovernmental organizations, foreign ministries, and the United Nations.

During 1973, my second year at AFS, two important events occurred that propelled me further along in my "Jewish development." The first came early in the year when a colleague asked if I would substitute for him that evening at an English-as-a-second-language course he was teaching at the nearby Cambridge School. He persuaded me there was nothing to it, the students were adults and quite interesting, and the pay wasn't bad for three hours' work. I agreed to do it.

In his class, it turned out, there were a couple of Soviet Jews, along with newcomers from every continent. During the break, I sought out the Soviet Jews and began speaking with them. My mother and maternal grandparents were all from Russia, I learned Russian formally beginning in high school, and I took a number of Russian studies courses in both college and graduate school. In short, I felt a natural affinity, not to mention curiosity.

Soon after the Six-Day War, some Soviet Jewish voices began clamoring for repatriation to the national Jewish homeland, Israel, or demanding religious and language rights for Jews in the USSR. These were extraordinary acts of courage, given the repressive nature of the Soviet regime. I was transfixed by the newspaper accounts I had read and Elie Wiesel's evocative book *The Jews of Silence*, and been moved by the first street demonstrations on behalf of Soviet Jews I had attended in New York in the early '70s. And here in front of me, at this school on East Forty-second Street, were actual Soviet Jews who had somehow made it out and were starting new lives. Sounds corny, perhaps, but I felt a calling. Before me, I saw my own family members, though they had come to the United States two and three decades earlier. I sensed an immediate bond, helped by language and familiarity with Russian and Russian Jewish culture, but what could I do?

I approached the school director and asked for a chance to return. Eventually I began teaching my own evening classes three times per week. While I tried to pay equal attention to all the students, many of whom had extraordinary stories to recount about their experiences in Africa, Asia, and Latin America, I would go home on the subway with some of the Russian students and occasionally visit their apartments on weekends. I couldn't get enough details from them about their lives in the USSR, the decision to emigrate, the choice of final destination (Israel vs. the United States), the vagaries of the emigration process, the arrival in Vienna and transfer to Rome for onward processing, and their first impressions of their adopted land.

My second transformative experience at AFS occurred during the Yom Kippur War. Like many other Jews, after the miraculous thumping of the Arabs by Israel in the Six-Day War, I had allowed myself to believe in the notion of Israeli invincibility. Thus, when Israel was caught off guard by the combined assaults of Egyptian and Syrian forces on the holiest day of the Jewish calendar, I, like other friends of Israel, became alarmed. Those first days, when Israeli forces were pushed back, unthinkable questions kept coming up: Would Israel survive? In what shape? If it were defeated and destroyed, what would this mean for the Jewish people? What would it mean to me?

I became obsessed with news of the war. One day at work, I passed a colleague's desk. She had a transistor radio on. I asked her about the latest reports on the war. She looked at me with puzzlement before saying: "Which war? I'm listening to the baseball game." I looked around the room at my AFS colleagues—all devoted, idealistic individuals who truly wanted to make the world a better place—and asked what I was doing here. Israel, the Jewish home, the state Jews had longed to reestablish for nearly two thousand years, the country where part of my family lived, had its back to the wall and wasn't sure it would make it, and here I am having to explain "which war."

I rushed to my desk and, without a moment's thought, called the Israeli consulate to volunteer for something, anything, in the Israeli army. I was asked a few screening questions on the phone and, being thoroughly unprepared, blurted out the wrong answer to one key query. I revealed that I was the sole surviving son in my family. Little did I know that this would disqualify me even from consideration. I had blown it and was at a loss about what to do next. In the end, I had to content myself with participating in some rallies and modest fund-raising efforts far from the war, while all the time cursing myself for my stupidity.

But as the saying goes, when God closes a door, somewhere a window is opened. That window opened for me less than a year later when, due to my teaching experience and interest in Russia, I had the chance to participate in a government-to-government exchange program, administered by AFS, as a teacher in the Soviet Union.

To fast forward, nearly three months after arriving in the USSR, I was forced to leave by Soviet officials who notified me and the American embassy that I was no longer welcome. This came after I was detained by the Soviet militia a few blocks from the synagogue on Arkhipova Street. There I had spent Shabbat with those Jews who gathered outside weekly in quiet assertion of their national dignity, to draw strength from one another, to exchange information, and to meet sympathetic foreigners like myself—always under the intrusive eye of KGB agents who sought to blend in while monitoring conversations and contacts.

I actually went to the synagogue every Shabbat. Upon later hearing this, my mother expressed dismay—mixed, I suspect, with pride—that in New York, with a synagogue on every corner, I grudgingly went twice a year, but in Moscow, with the lone synagogue under constant surveillance by secret police, I had to discover religion.

This particular Shabbat there were some French Jews who, having trouble finding a common language with the Soviet Jews, asked if I could translate from French to Russian. These French Jews were unsubtle in the messages they conveyed, and in hindsight I was too caught up in the challenge of translating to give sufficient thought to what it was I was being asked to transmit. That may have been the last straw for Soviet officials, who, in any case, weren't very delighted to have living and working in their midst a Russian-speaking American Jew far too independent and curious for their taste. They would have been much happier had I spent my evenings and weekends enthralled by the picture-perfect ballet, circus, museums, and concerts rather than at the homes of refuseniks and dissidents or at the synagogue. In fact, I suspect they would have kicked me out much sooner were I not part of an official U.S.-USSR program during the era of détente.

My three months in the USSR were quite extraordinary in every respect. How many Americans at the time had such an opportunity to reside in the Soviet Union, teach full-time six days per week in a Soviet school, and completely avoid official tours and guides? And how many Americans could claim to have spent six weeks in a modest Moscow hotel occupied not by Western tourists but rather for decades by diehard communist veterans of the Spanish Civil War and for a year by Chilean communists who fled after Salvador Allende's overthrow in 1973? And how many Americans, armed with Russian language, felt sufficiently at ease to go just about anywhere on their own, day or night?

For me, as a Jew, these three months were very significant. I met some extraordinary Soviet Jews, brave beyond words. I grasped the importance for Soviet Jewish activists of Western radio broadcasts, smuggled books, especially Leon Uris's *Exodus*, and manuscripts, the pull of Israel, and possession of a Star of David or a menorah. I learned a great deal about pride and yearning and determination. I was also given an education in the state-sponsored practice of anti-Semitism and anti-Zionism. And I came face to face with the power of communist oppression and the suffocation of any vestige of intellectual or physical freedom. I had had an earlier memorable encounter with communism in Cluj, Romania, when I spent a few weeks in 1971 loosely connected to the university there, but the months spent in Russia took me much further along this road.

Let me mention only two personal experiences in Russia, the first in Moscow, the second in Leningrad. Simchat Torah came about a week or two after my arrival in the country, and someone in New York had suggested I visit the synagogue. I remember taking the metro to the nearest stop, walking along Khmelnitsky Street—named in memory of the seventeenth-century Ukrainian responsible for the murder of hundreds of thousands of Jews—wondering what I was doing here this evening. Surely, no one would be at the synagogue. This was, after all, the USSR and Simchat Torah must be an obscure holiday for Jews forcibly disconnected from their heritage. Imagine my surprise, then, when I came to Arkhipova Street, turned right into the block, and then stood frozen for what seemed to be several minutes as I gazed down the hill and saw literally thousands of Soviet Jews packing the street, milling about, singing and dancing. I began to cry. I couldn't stop.

Here, only a few blocks from the nerve center of the most powerful totalitarian nation on earth, Jews were gathering to send a message: We are here, we are alive, we have not forgotten, we have not bent. Fifty-five years after the Bolsheviks set out to extinguish any last trace of Judaism and Jewish identity in the USSR through every means available to them, it was clear they had failed. No, Soviet Jews were not consigned to the dustbin of history, as Soviet leaders intended, nor would they be, judging from the turnout that evening.

I began walking down the hill and was immediately pulled into the throng. It was clear to all, by dress and demeanor, that I wasn't a Soviet Jew, which made me all the more welcome. After all, if foreigners were here, whether Jews or non-Jews, then Soviet Jews weren't alone in their struggle. That meant Soviet authorities, in theory at least, might have to think twice before taking measures against them. But it certainly didn't mean those authorities were paralyzed either. Within an hour, police cars began making their way up and down the crowded street, forcing people to the sidewalks and eventually compelling them to disperse.

Two months later, I was walking along the corridor of the Leningrad school to which I was subsequently assigned, School No. 185, when a young girl passed by and slipped something into my hand. I quickly went to the nearest bathroom, found an empty stall, locked the door, and unfolded the piece of paper. The note read: "David Harris, I think you are a Jew. I feel it. If I'm right, please know that my parents are refuseniks. Would you come to our house one day after school?" I memorized the indicated address and then tore up the note and flushed it down the toilet. The next day, I saw the same girl in the hallway and simply winked as we passed one another. That night I paid the family a visit, the first of several during my five-week stay in Leningrad.

Again, I was deeply moved by the encounter. Here were parents who had lost their jobs because of a desire to establish new lives in the West and to give their children the gift of freedom as human beings and as Jews. And here were two children—fourteen and ten, if I remember correctly—who had grown up very quickly, far too quickly, as they had to endure the fear, tension, and fog of life in a refusenik family, which included the very real possibility that they would be vilified at school, perhaps even expelled.

By December 1974, I was out of the Soviet Union, having lost fifteen pounds from an already thin frame and admittedly shaken by the rough nature of my expulsion. But I was determined to act somehow on all that I had seen and experienced in the previous three months.

After a restorative month with friends in Norway—much of it spent writing letters to U.S. officials and congressional leaders involved in the struggle for Soviet Jewry—I decided to travel to Rome. I recalled those Soviet Jews in my English-language classes talking of the several months they had spent there in transit. It sounded quite enticing. Maybe there would be a job for me. It turned out there was, with HIAS—the Hebrew Immigrant Aid Society—which, together with the Joint Distribution Committee (JDC), was responsible for the care, maintenance, and migration of the thousands of Soviet Jews streaming out of the USSR and seeking permanent resettlement in the West.

In March 1975 I began as a caseworker in Rome. In the ensuing period I briefed, processed, and counseled literally thousands of Soviet Jews from every corner of the country. I quickly discovered that Soviet Jews were far more heterogeneous than the rarefied types I had met in Moscow and Leningrad. There were ex-prisoners of conscience and ex-convicts; there were top-flight scientists and high school dropouts; there were those yearning for Jewish content in their lives and those fleeing from it, believing they had paid a sufficiently high price in the USSR for their bad luck in being born Jews; and there were those grateful beyond words for the support extended by HIAS and JDC and others who simply saw us as another bureaucracy, albeit one far more naive and thus manipulable than those they were used to in the USSR.

The work was not easy. Soviet Jews were, in a real sense, living betwixt and between—in a state of suspended animation—as they waited for months in Italy until their visas came through and they could depart to start a new life. In the meantime, they were entirely dependent on the Jewish agencies, unable to work, unfamiliar with the local language, and uneasy about their children's loss of education. Tensions often ran high, as the refugees could not passively accept the fact that their fate rested entirely in the hands of others, and as the caseworkers, too few in number, sought to cope with an inherently difficult situation.

I've never been able to sit still. After only a few weeks working with the refugees in Rome, it struck me that there was a gaping hole in the HIAS and JDC programs—Jewish culture and education. Virtually nothing was being done on this score, though we had, in effect, captive and, in some cases at least, hungry audiences. After work, then, I would head for Ostia, the seaside town where many of the refugees lived while in transit, and offer informal evening programs using whatever materials, films, or expert visitors I could find.

Eventually, I decided to try something still more ambitious, again because there was a vacuum that clearly needed to be filled. I proposed the writing of a basic book on Jewish history and religion, on Zionism and Israel, and on Diaspora Jewry, targeted for the refugees and oriented to their very specific mind-set and worldview.

Actually, it was the second book prepared especially for Soviet Jews in both Russian and English. Recognizing that the refugees understandably had little, if any, accurate information about the United States—and tons of misinformation—I first wrote an introductory volume about America, *Entering a New Culture*, with the support of HIAS. To its credit, HIAS also agreed to shoulder all the publishing expenses and distribute this second book—entitled *The Jewish World*—to every refugee passing through its offices. To this day, Jews arriving in the United States from the now Former Soviet Union receive both books, since updated several times.

I was the first to acknowledge that there were people far more qualified than I to write a book on Jews and Judaism, but no one else stepped forward. The book may have been intended for Soviet Jewish refugees, but the two years spent researching and writing it opened my eyes to the vast civilization of which we Jews were the heirs and trustees. I remember feeling cheated, in fact downright angry, that so much of this information had been unknown to me for the first thirty years of my life. Why were so many of us Jews to be counted among the world's most literate people, yet so strikingly illiterate about the riches of our own heritage? What was it about ourselves and our psychology that could explain this dissonant phenomenon? It was one thing that Soviet Jews were largely ignorant about their culture; the Soviets forcibly denied them access. But what about us Western Jews, who had the information and resources at our fingertips?

In all, my years with HIAS in Rome and Vienna were exhilarating and fulfilling. I was doing something real, something tangible in the lives of fellow Jews desperately in need of assistance, and I couldn't have been happier. And yes, I felt I was participating in the writing of an extraordinary chapter in this century's history. I had found a professional niche for myself. Instead of simply imagining what I want to believe I might have done had I been alive during the Holocaust— fighting, rescuing, sabotaging—here was my chance, on my watch, to do something for Jews in need. Here was the real-life challenge posed to my post-Holocaust generation, if only we would recognize it and rise to meet that challenge. Here was the opportunity to say yes, we

Jews had learned something, however painfully, from the lessons of the Holocaust about the compelling need for Jewish self-help, skillful political organization, and abandonment, for once and for all, of our perennial fear of provoking anti-Semitism by seeking full participation in public life.

And I also found it astonishing that a little over thirty years after the war's end, Jews in Europe were once again living with a real sense of threat. Palestinian-led terrorism had prompted European governments and Jewish agencies to take extraordinary protective measures to secure potential Jewish targets, including synagogues, day schools, and highly visible agencies like HIAS and the JDC. It is difficult for Americans to understand the atmosphere in Europe at the time, but the dangers were very real.

In 1973, a train carrying Soviet refugees across Czechoslovakia to Austria was hijacked by Palestinian refugees, creating an international crisis. In 1976, the JDC offices in Rome were firebombed (only a few minutes after I left the building), together with other Western and Jewish targets. The HIAS office in Vienna received several suspicious letters, at least one of which was a bomb defused after an alert staff member notified the police. And there were any number of potentially deadly incidents thwarted by Austrian and Italian security agencies alert to possible dangers.

These Palestinian terrorists and their European sympathizers in the Italian Red Brigades and German Baader Meinhoff group sought to paralyze the European Jewish world, but they failed miserably. Admittedly under far more onerous conditions, synagogues, day schools, and Jewish agencies continued to function without missing a beat. If anything, the determination of those working in these places was only strengthened. I certainly knew that to be the case in HIAS and the JDC, as well as ORT and the Jewish Agency—the operations with which I was most familiar at the time.

Parenthetically, I witnessed the same attempt at intimidation, absent the violence, in the British university system. When I returned to the London School of Economics for a brief period at the end of 1976, I was struck by the effort of the National Union of Students (NUS) to expel the Jewish students group. UN General Assembly Resolution

3379, the infamous "Zionism is racism" resolution, had been adopted by the world body the previous year. Since the NUS opposed racism, it could not countenance any "racist" group in its midst. The Jewish students group supported Zionism; therefore, by definition, it was racist and unworthy of continued membership in the NUS and the subventions that went along with it. And later, at my Oxford college, there was a serious effort to ban the college dining room's purchase of any Israeli products, especially Jaffa oranges and grapefruits, for the very same reason.

Clearly, there was a global struggle at hand involving a multifaceted campaign to isolate and delegitimize Israel and to create a "respectable" new form of anti-Semitism known as anti-Zionism. Since this was, in effect, a war against the Jewish people worldwide, the response must also be worldwide, led by Israel itself and the largest Jewish community in the world, the American.

Until I began working at HIAS, I hadn't really thought there were any serious job opportunities in the Jewish communal world. Again, my ignorance. But my perspective had been formed by the only youthful contact I had—my maternal grandmother's Jewish organizational associations, which seemed to consist mostly of occasional social lunches and canasta circles. HIAS opened a whole new world to me, and from then on I could not have imagined a more perfect fit for me than a lifetime of Jewish communal service. Indeed, it was while I was working in the HIAS Vienna office in 1978 that an American Jewish Committee delegation came to visit. It included an individual with a magnetic personality, Ira Silverman, then director of special projects.

In those days, we had many visiting groups; everyone wanted at least a glimpse of this extraordinary movement of Soviet Jews from East to West. But what struck me about the AJC delegation was that the members somehow seemed different, more worldly, more sophisticated in their manner and approach, more probing in the questions they asked, and more sincere in their interest and less concerned with simply bringing back photos of themselves with the refugees. And so when Ira, at the end of the visit, suggested we get together sometime in New York, I chose to take it as a sincere invitation and not just one of those typical American throwaway lines.

I made plans to visit New York in January 1979. Just before going, however, Giulietta, Wade Goria, a friend from Oxford, and I decided to spend a weekend in Salzburg. En route, we saw a sign for Mauthausen, the site of the infamous Nazi concentration camp. We detoured. None of us had ever before visited such a camp.

The first thing that struck us was the sheer beauty of the setting. It was totally disorienting. How could such indescribable horror have taken place amid such natural splendor? We entered the camp and within minutes, each of us absorbed in his own thoughts, we became separated from each other. I found myself in a building, and before I knew it, I was in the gas chamber, alone. Seized by panic, I rushed for the door, but it was closed. I began trembling. I looked again at the door and realized it had been open all along; it was only my imagination playing tricks on me. I ran out of the gas chamber, only to find myself face to face with the crematoria. I kept running, shaking, sobbing, until I stumbled into Giulietta and Wade. They hadn't yet seen the gas chamber and crematoria, but I insisted we leave as quickly as possible.

Later, as I thought about the visit, if I had had even a shred of doubt about my decision to continue in Jewish communal work, that traumatic visit to Mauthausen sealed my fate. I knew I had to do my part to help ensure that nothing like this ever happened again, whether to Jews or, for that matter, any other vulnerable and targeted minority.

In January, I showed up at AJC headquarters and Ira offered me a job. In the meantime, I had done some homework and learned that AJC was regarded by many Jewish professionals as the classiest and most admired organization of its kind, the "Harvard of Jewish agencies," as one communal veteran aptly put it.

I joined AJC in March 1979, after my wife and I moved our belongings from Vienna to New York. I would be disingenuous if I said I never looked back. My four and a half years in Europe had been extraordinarily enriching personally (including meeting my future wife) and professionally, and my time "in the trenches" of Rome and Vienna made me realize how temperamentally well suited I was for frontline work. But AJC gave me other opportunities I might otherwise never have had, especially the chance to help shape public policy, both domestic and international, by dint of the agency's mission, influence, reach, and scale of operation.

Which brings me to the present volume. Over the years at AJC, I have had the opportunity to write frequently and to give more than my share of speeches. This book contains selections from both the writings and the speeches. It is quite heavily weighted toward those topics I have been most involved in and with which I have had the greatest experience—Israel and the Middle East, the communist world, the Holocaust, endangered Jewry, and the role of AJC as an American Jewish institution.

A last word: The longer I have been associated with the American Jewish Committee, the more I have come to admire it, indeed the more I am in awe of it. To be sure, I am not a disinterested party. That said, it truly is an extraordinary institution that blends the best of American ideals and Jewish values to create a powerful advocate for Jewish well-being and security, and for the advancement of democratic institutions, the protection of human rights, and the strengthening of mutual understanding. This fundamental appreciation of the inextricable link between the Jewish condition and the human condition is at the heart of AJC's ethos, and central to my own.

The agency is made up of exceptional people, both lay and staff, who are, I firmly believe, the best, the brightest, and the most dedicated to be found anywhere in Jewish life. Among those exceptional people is AJC's current president, Bruce Ramer, who has been my partner, mentor, and friend. It was he who gave vision and form to this book, and it is to him especially that I owe a heartfelt debt of gratitude.

I would also like to express my deepest appreciation to several wonderfully gifted AJC colleagues: Dr. Larry Grossman, who, through his well-honed organizing and editing skills, ably supervised this project in its early stages; Dr. Steven Bayme, who read this opening essay and, as always, offered several invaluable suggestions; Bob Rosenbaum, whose breathtakingly vast knowledge of the English language and all its mind-bogglingly complex rules and peculiarities saved me from embarrassment more than once; Rebecca Neuwirth, who with characteristic patience and perseverance read and reread the manuscript for content, organization, and style; Aleida Rodriguez, who ably and devotedly undertook the arduous task of inputting the original material; Alina Viera, who, with consummate grace and professionalism, adjusted, revised, shifted, added, and deleted text during a months-long process; Linda Krieg, whose graphic design skills are second to none; and Dr. Stephen Steinlight, who helped bring this project to fruition by initiating discussions with the publisher. Moreover, the staff at Ktav Publishing House were unfailingly helpful, efficient, and courteous, with a special word of appreciation for Bernie Scharfstein, who has been a joy to work with.

And last but by no means least, the writing of every article and the drafting and delivery of every speech were inevitably time taken away from the four people in my life who make it all worthwhile and special—my wife, Giulietta, and our three wonderful sons, Danny, Mishy, and Josh.

New York, June 2000

1. SOVIET JEWRY

Report on the 1981 Moscow Book Fair

The participation of the Association of American Jewish Book Publishers ("Association") in the biennial Moscow Book Fair can only be described as a success. Together with the Israelis, our booth was the most sought after and best attended of all the booths in the Western pavilion. Each day, long lines of people waited, more or less patiently, for a glimpse of our exhibit, and some of the visitors had traveled long distances especially for the occasion.

The Book Fair represents an unparalleled opportunity to make contact with large numbers of Soviet Jews, put a finger on their pulse and sense their mood, display and ultimately distribute a large number of books (as well as souvenirs), and make a statement, by our presence, both to Soviet authorities and Soviet Jewry.

The only negative, though in no way surprising, note is our continued inability to sign any contracts with Mezhkniga, the Soviet international book authority, for the sale and translation into Russian of English-language books on Jewish themes. After all, this is our ostensible reason for being at the Moscow Book Fair in the first place.

Accommodations

The Hotel Cosmos was a comfortable, convenient hotel. It turned out there was no need to bring along the infamous bathtub stoppers or soft towels—the hotel provided decent versions of both—and my room came equipped not only with a color television and radio but also, surprise of surprises, a working refrigerator. Dining facilities were adequate, a far cry from my previous experience in other Soviet hotels where just getting seated was a feat in itself, much less finding an interested waiter or a decent choice of foods.

(As an aside, in my very first dinner experience in a Soviet hotel, in 1974, it took me over an hour to get seated in a half-empty restaurant. Eventually, after repeated requests, I even got a menu. While I read it, the waiter stood there with what can only be described as a condescending smile. "What's the matter?" I asked. His reply: "You can look at the menu all you want, but we've only got roast chicken, so why bother?")

The Metro station is located across from the hotel. There are public telephones near the entrance; most of these phones accept American dimes—presumably by coincidence, not design, though you can never be sure with the Soviets. Rather than using monitored hotel phones to call Soviet Jewish activists, we relied on these public phones.

A word of caution: Taxis should never be taken from the hotel entrance. The drivers are likely to be in touch with the security services whenever an obvious foreigner is involved, especially if the destination is a residence. Far better to hail a taxi in front of the Metro station.

Book Fair Registration

Our association group assembled at noon on the day prior to the formal opening of the fair and walked over to the exhibition area together to survey it. The exhibition consists of four buildings: two large pavilions used for display, one housing primarily Western publishers and the other Soviet and East European publishers; and two smaller buildings, one for the general directorate and the other for officials dealing with cargo.

The next step was to locate our stand. Unfortunately but predictably, it turned out to be rather cramped and remote, adjacent to the booth of a Western communist publisher. Next came a check of the furnishings and freight provided against what had been ordered and sent.

Customs officials arrived and began to look through the books we had shipped from the States. The team consisted of one uniformed customs official, four or five nonuniformed women, all fluent in English, and a Mr. Rakhelis, who appeared to be conversant in both Hebrew and Yiddish.

The examination of the books was brief and perfunctory; however, to guard against particular problems that might arise, we had earlier called several members of the American press corps and asked them to observe the process. In the end, two unexpected titles were confiscated—*American Jewish Year Book, 1981* and Abba Eban's children's adaptation of *The History of the Jews*. Initially, we weren't given an explanation, but later we were told by Ramaz Mchedlivze, one of the Book Fair's top officials, that the books would not be returned to us until closing day because their treatment of Soviet policy toward the Jews and Israel was "at variance" with Soviet "perceptions" of that policy.

All souvenir items were approved, including a specially prepared record with Jewish and Hebrew songs. However, as the button with the Star of David and the record had not been okayed beforehand, we were asked, strictly as a formality, to compose a letter to the head of the Customs Department requesting permission to distribute these items. As it turned out, the customs officials and the Book Fair officials apparently had not coordinated policy on the record.

While customs was telling us that the record was okay, we were advised by Mr. Mchedlivze to the contrary. It was a decision made in our interests, we were told, as we would be presented with enormous physical problems of distribution. We noted that we, too, had considered this possibility and developed a system for distribution while providing for crowd control. Rebuffed, Mr. Mchedlivze went back to his office, only to return shortly thereafter to advise us that the record could not be distributed because of its commercial value, which was at variance with the rules governing the fair. We responded that a similar record had been distributed at the 1979 fair. The answer was still "*Nyet*," so we sought the advice of an American publishing veteran, Bob Baensch, who suggested that together we visit the director-general of the Book Fair, Mr. I. Kozansky.

The next day we had what we thought was a constructive meeting that would lead to a compromise solution. It was a surprise, therefore, to be advised later that their decision stood; the record could not be distributed because it was deemed of commercial value. We were told, misleadingly of course, that the record's contents were not at issue; it was strictly a matter of its potential resale value. As a small concession, however, the record could be displayed on the shelves of our booth.

Later, we were told by a Soviet journalist of a rumor circulating that an Arab delegate had gotten hold of the record and protested to officials about inclusion of the song *Yerushalayim Shel Zahav*, "Jerusalem of Gold."

Fortunately, if oddly, the 8,500 souvenir records were never actually confiscated, so we were able, during the course of the fair, to distribute quietly some 2,500–3,000 of them.

Commercial Contacts

If success were measured in terms of commercial contacts alone, the fair was an abysmal failure for the association. Still, it does represent an important, perhaps unique, contact point with Soviet book officials.

Other than the obligatory visits by various Soviet book officials, we were approached by a Bulgarian offering translation rights to a book on that country's role in saving its Jewish population during the Second World War, a Briton offering us rights to a book on the Yiddish language, a Spaniard offering Ladino music, and a Soviet who wanted to know of our interest in the recently published book, *Heavy Sand*. That was the sum total of the commercial interest shown us.

General Public

An estimated 5,000–6,000 people visited our stand in the course of several days. It was simply impossible for us to accommodate all the visitors; our assigned space was just too small. Lines formed, snaking down the corridor and blocking the entrance to as many as four or five neighboring publishers. While it's in the nature of Soviets to reflexively join just about any line because they assume there is something worthwhile and in limited quantity being offered at the end of it, most of our visitors knew exactly what they were waiting to see.

We also had to worry about distribution of our souvenirs. All the items were eminently successful, and many people, not wanting to wait in line to see the books, rushed our desk from all sides to receive a button, bookmark, or catalog. Some were simply collectors; Soviets love buttons and pins of all kinds. Most, though, appeared to be Jews seeking a "Jewish souvenir." As this congestion not only caused us serious staffing problems but also created difficulties for our coexhibitors in the immediate area, we decided the souvenir items would only be given to those people who actually visited the stand.

In all, we were able to exhibit about 250 books at any given time. We divided the books by subject area—children's literature, Israel, Judaism and Jewish customs, Yiddish literature. Clearly, the most successful books were the coffee-table books on Jews and Israel, elementary Hebrew textbooks, children's books, and books that served as a source of Jewish pride. In the last category were books dealing with Jewish resistance during the Holocaust, the Six-Day War, the achievements of Israel, and notable Jews in history.

We had visits from a number of well-known refuseniks, including Irina Brailovskaya, Alexander Lerner, Pavel Abramovich, Ilya Essas, Yuli Kosharovsky, and Naum Meiman. We made every effort to see that the books they wanted, particularly for the Hebrew teachers and religious and cultural instructors, reached them sometime during the fair, though it was illegal to distribute any books; they were for display purposes only, Soviet officials insisted.

We had music playing constantly, but the selection was limited, given the regrettably few tapes we had. Even so, the music, too, must be judged a success, however many times we heard the same tunes. Soviet Jews, culturally starved, are eager for any contact whatsoever with *yiddishkeit*.

Security

It soon became clear to us that our effort to limit the Soviet security presence was a lost cause. The militia director advised us that his people would be posted there from start to finish. Quite frankly, there were times when the crowds became so overwhelming, not to mention aggressive, that an accident could easily have occurred had there not been uniformed security people to help us regain order.

There were, in fact, two types of security personnel. The first were the militiamen assigned to help us with crowd control; they were generally friendly and not unsympathetic. The second were the nonuniformed types, there to keep an eye on our visitors (and us) and on those trying to secretly take books from our booth. In addition, paranoia aside, it is likely that the interpreters assigned to the nearby stands had the additional task of monitoring our activities.

All Soviet visitors had their bags searched on leaving the hall. Each morning, a batch of books would be returned to us by the pavilion director with the cheery note that we ranked first in the number of books confiscated by security officials at the exit. In those very few cases where we felt comfortable advising people on smuggling books out, we suggested hiding them under clothing before exiting.

Every evening, each of us carried out at least one bag of books, usually fulfilling requests from a known refusenik. Our free time was largely devoted to distributing those books. In this respect, the Israelis proved more physically fit than we, as they made several trips a day between the exhibition hall and the Metro station transporting books. None of the official delegates, including us, had their bags searched leaving the exhibition hall, but one delegate was warned by Soviet officials that he was under surveillance for having distributed several hundred copies of his books, which turned out to be on Scientology.

I should mention the support of the representative of the Times-Mirror Company of London. When we were finally turned down on the record, he offered to start up a petition on our behalf, but discovered that only two minor publishers of a dozen polled would agree to sign. Tellingly, several American Jews representing U.S. publishing houses reacted negatively. We were stirring the waters, they said. Principle is principle, but business is business.

Book Distribution

While we were able to distribute clandestinely several hundred books during the exhibition's six days, we were still left with many books at the fair's end. To their everlasting credit, Bob Gillette of the *Los Angeles Times* and Walter Wismiewski of UPI helped us transport the remaining books out of the pavilion, ostensibly on their way to the library of the Anglo-American School in Moscow. To our delight, we were able to get all our books out, and some of the Israeli books as well.

Press

The American correspondents were generally sympathetic to our situation. Several dropped by three or four times during the course of the fair to inquire about developments.

All three networks did interviews and film clips of our stand, but only the ABC spot was aired.

We were also contacted by the Soviet press, and I did an interview with Vadim Fotin of Radio Moscow World Service, which was broadcast September 4, and Maya Gordeeva of *Soviet Life*. In both cases I requested a taped transcript of the interview. The radio interview was broadcast virtually in its entirety, and I was advised of the proposed cuts before they were made. The interview with Mrs. Gordeeva turned into a battle of wits. She tried to get me to admit that a viable Jewish cultural and religious life existed in the Soviet Union simply because I could have her assurance on that score. I seriously doubt that any part of the interview will be used for publication, as I was careful not to give her even a single usable clause that might be taken out of context.

Books and Politics

The Moscow Book Fair represents a unique and absolutely critical opportunity for the Soviet Jewish community, and we American Jews, therefore, must do all we can to ensure our continued representation at future book fairs.

By stressing our commercial interest, we will serve to further legitimize our presence at the fair. The problematic question is what should be the role of the National Conference on Soviet Jewry. The NCSJ should continue to play a central part in planning, but excessive mixing of "books and politics" may lead to a reconsideration of our legitimacy by Soviet authorities.

Thus the majority of the delegation should not get involved in "politics" while representing the association at the fair, and their contacts with activists and refuseniks ought to be severely limited. The covert distribution of books and more extensive contact with refuseniks should be left to "tourists" who are conveniently in Moscow at the time of the Book Fair. In this respect, Alan and Ann Bernstein of New Jersey did a simply heroic job of distributing books and making contact with activists, while not maintaining any official status with the association.

As a final note, suggesting a model for future delegations, each person in our group had a unique role to play: Israel and Helen Kugler with the Yiddish speakers, David Hill with the religious and cultural activists, Lee Hill as tireless courier of books, Janet Scharfstein with the Hebrew-speaking young people, and Sol Scharfstein as our publishing *maven* and ingenious improviser. If our participation at this year's Book Fair was a success, it is in very large part due to the extraordinary and indefatigable efforts of these wonderfully dedicated people.

Testimony Submitted to the
United States Congress
House of Representatives
Subcommittee on Human Rights
and International Organizations
February 10, 1982

Mr. Chairman:

I am pleased to have the opportunity to submit testimony on behalf of Yuli Kosharovsky, a central figure in the historic Jewish emigration and cultural movement in the Soviet Union.

Yuli Kosharovsky first applied to emigrate from the Soviet Union in April 1971. His application was refused a month later on the grounds of the "secret" nature of his previous work as an engineer. In May 1980, Kosharovsky was advised that his period of "secrecy" had expired, but that he would not be permitted to emigrate for a new reason—the absence of close relatives in Israel.

During the more than ten years that Kosharovsky has been compelled to live as an internal refugee in the Soviet Union, he has been the target of unrelenting harassment and intimidation. Not being able to work in his profession because he is seeking to emigrate, he has been threatened with arrest on the unique Soviet charge of "parasitism." He was placed under house arrest during President Nixon's visit to the Soviet Union, and he has been imprisoned for fifteen-day periods on charges of "hooliganism" and "disturbing the public order," even to the extent of being led away from his home in chains on one occasion. Most recently, on October 15, 1981, the KGB carried out a search of his home and confiscated sacks of books on Jewish themes.

Why has Kosharovsky been treated this way? Because he is committed to the study and teaching of the Hebrew language, because he is regarded with great respect by other Jewish activists and is looked to as a leader, and because he has not feared to assert even those limited rights provided to Soviet citizens under Soviet and international covenants, including the right to study one's culture and language. Kosharovsky has recently been warned that he will face more serious charges if he persists in his efforts to teach the Hebrew language.

I met Kosharovsky most recently in September 1981 (in connection with the Moscow International Book Fair). He is a gifted teacher, a learned man, a devoted father to his children, and a modest, self-effacing individual. His wife, Inna, has never been permitted to work in her field of mathematics because of her desire to live in Israel and his stepson, Mikhail, has been the target of physical and verbal abuse in school.

Kosharovsky's long-standing dream has been to live in Israel and to rejoice in the traditions of the Jewish people. For this "crime," he and his family have endured ten years of suffering and hardship at the hands of the Soviet government. They are part of a large and growing number of Jews across the USSR who have come to realize that there is no future for them as Jews in their native country and who seek to establish new lives in Israel.

Thank you, Mr. Chairman, for this opportunity to address the Sub-Committee and for your own interest and support.

More on Refuseniks' Views
Moment
October 1984

I read with interest Ira Silverman's moving account of his visit to the USSR ("Routes and Roots: To Moscow," *Moment*, June 1984) and Arden Shenker's response in the "Letters" column (September 1984).

As Arden Shenker correctly implies, in the absence of polling it is impossible to determine scientifically the views of Jews in the USSR, forcing us to rely to a great extent on the reports of travelers. I have met scores of American travelers to the USSR and Soviet émigrés in Israel and the United States in recent years, and have personally visited the USSR three times, including a three-month stint as an exchange teacher. Given this background, I was struck by some of Shenker's findings, which are completely at variance with Ira Silverman's impressions and, indeed, with my own experiences and those of people with whom I have spoken, to wit:

1. Refuseniks believe in a strong American foreign policy vis-à-vis the USSR, albeit one that does permit negotiation, and in the continued use of such instruments of leverage as the Jackson-Vanik Amendment.

2. Refuseniks may have an understanding of the dropout phenomenon (Jews leaving the USSR with Israeli visas but instead seeking entry to the United States, Canada, etc.), but they have little sympathy with it, believing that it undermines the Jewish national movement that emerged in the USSR in the late '60s and may be in part responsible for the decline in emigration since 1979.

3. Refuseniks have enormous respect for Andrei Sakharov and certain other figures in the political dissident movement, but firmly believe that the emigration and dissident movements must be kept separate to preserve the uniqueness of the repatriation struggle [to Israel] and to avoid the potentially calamitous complications that could issue from an overt alliance.

4. Most refuseniks, especially those active in the emigration struggle or in religious activities, are absolutely certain their phones are bugged by the KGB, their contact with foreign visitors mon-

itored, their overseas correspondence tampered with, and their neighbors or concierges charged with reporting unusual activity.

5. When Rabbi Adolf Shayevich, rabbi of Moscow's Choral Synagogue, visited New York in May 1984, he indicated that there were but a handful of bar mitzvah celebrations during the last year in his synagogue, the principal synagogue serving the largest Jewish community in the USSR. Knowing the source, it is fair to say Rabbi Shayevich was not underestimating the number. Therefore, while it may be true that some bar mitzvahs do take place, they are exceptionally few in number, not to speak of the virtual nonexistence of opportunities for the observance of other Jewish rituals and practices.

Review of Robert O. Freedman (ed.),
Soviet Jewry in the Decisive Decade, 1971–1980
(Duke University Press, 1984)
Soviet Jewish Affairs
vol. 14, no. 3, 1984

Since 1970 almost 275,000 Soviet Jews have established new lives in Israel and the West. An understanding of this emigration phenomenon is especially important now inasmuch as the exodus has been virtually halted and the repression of Jewish activism in the USSR has increased. Western Jewry faces two vital challenges in relation to Soviet Jews: to formulate effective new strategies and tactics to reverse the current situation, and to confront the pressing problem of absorption, not simply into the larger host community but especially into the Jewish community.

In the United States, for example, most of the Soviet Jews arrived in the last half dozen years. Having naturally preoccupied themselves in these first years with such pressing issues as language, housing, employment, education, and understanding the American way of life, they are increasingly addressing the more existential questions of ethnic and religious identification and spiritual needs. There is already evidence of a tendency on the part of the Soviet Jews to distance themselves from the Jewish community when self-sufficiency in the new setting has been achieved; there have even been reports of conversions to Russian Orthodoxy.

The search for a response to these challenges is facilitated by the book under review. Dr. Freedman, a specialist on Soviet foreign policy, particularly as it relates to the Middle East, and on the issue of Soviet Jewry, has compiled a volume comprising nine papers, each by an academic or communal figure eminently qualified to discuss the subject. The papers were prepared for a conference on Soviet Jewry hosted by the Baltimore Hebrew College in 1981.

The book is divided essentially into two sections. The first, which consists of a historical overview of the emigration movement and analyses of the conditions facing Jews in the USSR and the politics of emigration, includes excellent articles by Professor Jerome Gilison of Baltimore Hebrew College, Mr. Jerry Goodman of the National Conference on Soviet Jewry, Dr. William Korey of the B'nai B'rith International Council, and Professor Freedman himself.

In the second section, which focuses on immigration and resettlement, Professor Theodore Friedgut of the Hebrew University analyzes the absorption process in Israel, a process that has handled 160,000 Soviet Jews since 1970. Fabian Kolker, a Soviet Jewry activist and Baltimore attorney, puts forward a new plan to address the long-standing controversy over the country of destination of Soviet Jewish emigrants. Professor Zvi Gitelman of the University of Michigan examines several of the core resettlement questions facing Soviet Jews in the United States and finds that employment is the most vexing. Professor Stephen Fainstein of the University of Wisconsin studies the attitudes of American Jews in St. Paul, Minnesota, to the influx of Soviet Jews into the community, and presents conclusions relevant to resettlement everywhere. Finally, Ilya Levkov, a Soviet Jewish emigrant now living in New York, reports the findings of a comprehensive questionnaire completed by 130 randomly selected Soviet Jewish respondents living in the United States for periods ranging from under one year to nine years. The findings include data on the decision to emigrate, language study, finances, perceptions of Americans, and attitudes toward Judaism and organized Jewish life in the United States.

Professor Freedman's major study of the Soviet Jewish issue in the context of Soviet-American relations until 1980, with further consideration of the issue until 1982 in a separate epilogue, merits particular attention. Seeking to explain the fluctuations in the emigration rate by analyzing relations between the superpowers, Professor Freedman isolates three factors—SALT negotiations, trade and commerce, and Soviet fear of a Sino-American alliance—as the crucial variables in the Soviet-American relationship in the 1970s. At this critical juncture, as Western Jewry searches for new approaches and an American presidential election has just taken place, the importance of a full understanding of the impact on Soviet Jewry of Soviet-American relations is abundantly clear.

While Professor Freedman appears at times to have stretched historical interpretation to explain the fluctuations in emigration, he has nonetheless commmendably sought to unravel a crucial element in understanding the process. What is missing from his study, however, is reference to internal developments in the USSR that may also have played a role. These include: (1) the explosion in the numbers of those seeking to leave that occurred, for example, in 1978 and 1979, numbers surely well beyond the projections of any Kremlin estimate; (2) the reported opposition to Jewish emigration of important elements of the Soviet authorities, including the KGB; (3) the fear of contagion to other Soviet nationalities who may be susceptible to "emigration fever"; (4) the impact of emigration on Soviet science, medicine, and industry; and (5) the uncertainties in Soviet leadership that began in Brezhnev's declining years and continue through 1984.

Fabian Kolker's plan, referred to above, would result, it is suggested, in an increased rate of repatriation to Israel without, at the same time, denying Soviet Jews the right to choose their final destination. Mr. Kolker proposes that, with the exception of those emigrants with immediate relations elsewhere, all exiting Soviet Jews be transferred to Israel where they would have an opportunity to experience life there firsthand. If within a year they wished to go elsewhere and had chosen the status of "temporary residents" upon arrival, they would have the same opportunity to enter the United States as is presently the case when transiting in Rome. Mr. Kolker hopes that more Soviet Jews will decide to remain in Israel as a result of the year-long stay, and his plan takes into account the extensive resettlement opportunities for Soviet Jews in Israel and the importance Israel attaches to increased emigration from the USSR.

Mr. Kolker makes no mention, however, of what might be the reaction of the U.S. and Austrian governments and other interested parties to such a plan. Might, for example, the plan conflict with the concept of "firmly resettled" in another country, now a part of U.S. immigration law? What would be the reaction of the Austrians, who have always insisted on freedom of choice for Soviet Jews transiting in Vienna, if some Soviet Jews refused to proceed to Israel? (I personally recall instances in the late 1970s when arriving Soviet Jews refused to relinquish their visas to Austrian officials for fear of being "compelled" to proceed to Israel.) Would not Rav Tov (an arm of the anti-Zionist Satmar Hasidim) or another, even non-Jewish, organization rush to fill the vacuum in Vienna, as happened before, if, as Mr. Kolker suggests, the Hebrew Immigrant Aid Society curtailed its operation? And, given that the first year of resettlement is usually the most difficult in *any* new country, might more, rather than fewer, Soviet Jews seek to leave Israel at the end of one year, attributing—mistakenly or otherwise—their adjustment difficulties specifically to Israeli conditions? More discussion of these and other questions is needed to evaluate Mr. Kolker's plan fully.

In further considering this book, it should be noted that there is an excessive amount of overlap and repetition of material from one chapter to the next. There are also several omissions and factual errors. For instance, reference is made to the Leningrad hijacking trial in 1970 and to the nine Jewish defendants, but no mention is made of the two non-Jewish defendants, Yury Fedorov and Aleksey Murzhenko, who were from the time of their arrest adopted by the Jewish community as "prisoners of conscience." . . . In several cases, there is a confusion between the terms *refusenik* and *dissident*, which ought not to have occurred in a volume of this type. . . . And, finally, there is a troublesome comparison: "Like the Jews, they [Soviet Germans] have suffered a considerable amount of discrimination in the Soviet Union . . ." While it is certainly true that the Germans and Jews have several points in common—size, repatriation, discrimination in *some* respects—Soviet Germans have been faced to a lesser extent with the particularly ominous problems confronting Jews, namely, the threat of obliteration of culture, including national language, and the vicious anti-Semitism on which Dr. Korey elaborates in his excellent chapter on this subject.

These minor criticisms aside, the reviewed book is a valuable addition to the relatively scant analytical literature on a compelling issue for world Jewry, and merits the widest possible attention.

Crisis in Soviet Jewry
Midstream
March 1986

Emigration from the Soviet Union has all but ceased. Harassment and imprisonment of Jewish religious and, especially, Hebrew-language activists have increased in the last year. Media attacks on Jews, Judaism, and Zionism continue. And the net effect is that we in the West are today witnesses to a deliberate Soviet policy to bring about the gradual disappearance of 15 percent of world Jewry, or some 2 million Jews. Yet our response has not been commensurate to the catastrophic dimension of the problem. How could this be in a post-Holocaust period in which we explore, analyze, and study the lessons of that tragedy on an almost daily basis, agonize over our own inability to influence the course of events, and pledge "never again" to let history repeat itself?

When Soviet Jewry emerged on the world scene as an issue in the late 1960s and early 1970s, it captured the imagination and galvanized a substantial segment of the American Jewish community. A genuine miracle had occurred and we were privileged witnesses to it. Fifty years after the establishment of Soviet power, cut off from the rest of world Jewry, deprived of the means to learn, transmit, and develop a religion and culture, subjected to inordinate pressure to deny their identity, the voices of Soviet Jews could be heard. Some whispered, others shouted, but the message was clear: "We are Jews and we want to live as Jews in our historic homeland, Israel. Help us, for we cannot do it alone." And an extraordinary chapter in history unfolded.

A small group of modern-day Maccabees, employing nothing more than the age-old strength of their beliefs and the knowledge that theirs was a just cause, yet adhering to the letter of Soviet law, challenged the most powerful totalitarian state on earth. And we in the West demonstrated, petitioned, fasted, adopted Soviet Jewish families, contacted our public officials, and involved academic, religious, labor, scientific, and civil rights colleagues. The results were there for all to see. Large-scale emigration began in 1971 and thousands of Soviet Jews seized the opportunity. And despite the tragedy of the prisoner and refusenik cases and unrelenting Soviet anti-Semitism, we felt we had become successful historical protagonists; to some extent at least, it was within our power to help shape Jewish destiny.

Today, however, our mood seems different. Less than 1,150 people emigrated in 1984, compared to 51,000 just six years ago, yet where is the flood of appeals to our public officials, where are the massive public demonstrations, where are the letters and phone calls and holiday messages to an increasingly isolated and fearful Soviet Jewish community? At the time of the November [Reagan-Gorbachev] summit, there was a limited flurry of activity, but in many parts of our community the bad news is met with apathy and indifference. Why? What has happened over the years to explain the decline in our enthusiasm and involvement? I would suggest a number of possible explanations:

1. Soviet Jewry has been a major agenda item for fifteen years and promises to continue so for years to come. Remarkably, an extraordinary group of American Jewish communal activists have persisted in the struggle, some since the founding of the American Conference on Soviet Jewry in 1964 and even before. Yet, for many, the issue is one-dimensional, requiring an almost obsessive single-mindedness of purpose. How else does one grapple with the inherent frustration of the issue? And even among the best-intentioned, "compassion fatigue" may set in.

2. The issue is regarded by some today as beyond the influence of the Jewish community. Whereas in the early 1970s the conventional wisdom was that the Soviet Union was mindful of its public image and thus sensitive to world opinion, the prevailing view now is that the Soviet Union is more often than not indifferent to the pleas of the West

on human rights questions, or at least to the public at large if not to governments. What purpose is thus served in writing to Soviet officials and demonstrating in front of Soviet embassies and consulates? Further, there are many who view the issue as inextricably linked to the ebb and flow of Soviet-American relations, a pawn in a cynical and ruthless Soviet geopolitical strategy, beyond, therefore, the reach of the individual in our community. The only alternative, in this view, is to seek to influence American foreign policy in the belief that a return to détente, or at least a movement in the direction of improved relations, is in the interests of Soviet Jewry. But to do so is to risk positioning the American Jewish community in an unwise domestic political situation: to appear to put the interests of Soviet Jewry ahead of our country's is a potentially dangerous strategy. Thus, the irreducible conclusion for many is to leave the issue to our government in the belief that only at that level can any success be achieved.

3. Our community has become anesthetized to descriptions of the Soviet Jewry condition as "critical," "the worst in years," "facing impending disaster," etc. With each arrest, each decline in emigration, each appearance of an anti-Semitic book or article, the call for immediate action has gone out, to the point, perhaps, where people are no longer able to distinguish a minor from a major crisis, a drop in emigration from a precipitous decline, or the appearance of an anti-Semitic article from a new wave of anti-Semitism.

4. Whereas the issue seized the hearts and minds of national agencies, community leadership, and the rabbinate in the early days of the struggle, the response recently has been more sporadic. Of course, there are many individual exceptions, but, to some degree at least, these principal players in our community have been dealing with Soviet Jewry in fits and starts, not in a sustained manner as a high-priority item, nor with appropriate programming, over the years.

5. The dropout issue has seriously and negatively affected attitudes toward Soviet Jews among many American Jews, who regard the increasing rate of non-Israel-bound emigration, reaching as high as 80 percent in recent years, as having undermined a fundamental premise of this movement, namely, repatriation to the historic Jewish homeland.

6. Many American Jews are disappointed with the Soviet Jews they have met in this country. Expecting refugees thirsty for Jewish life (even in an American Diaspora), like those who came from Russia at the turn of the century, American Jews were unprepared and surprised at the profile and behavior of arriving Soviet Jews. Many newcomers did not act like refugees fleeing a clear and present danger, did not immediately seek to establish Jewish roots here, and did not, in most cases, fit the image of the courageous and beleaguered Jewish activists who, it seems, are the only ones portrayed at our Soviet Jewry rallies. The gap created by false expectations on both sides (Soviet Jews, too, have mistaken views of the United States and the Jewish community) has had an adverse impact on attempts to motivate American Jewry in the struggle on behalf of Soviet Jewry. And the problems associated with absorption, resettlement, and integration have created further negative feeling in some circles.

7. The almost total absence of Soviet Jewish participation in the advocacy movement in the United States has also created an impression among some that "if Soviet Jews don't care about those left behind, why should we?" Of course, many Soviet Jews still fear participating in public demonstrations and worry about the possible repercussions for family in the USSR. Also, in many American communities, no active effort has been made to invite Soviet Jewish participation, either because of the divisiveness of the dropout question or to avoid the appearance of creating émigré organizations that might not be as effective in the public arena (or toward the Soviet Union) as an American Jewish movement.

8. Our movement relied for too long on a number of loyal and active non-Jewish friends. The many years of this struggle have taken their toll on some of them, and their numbers have not been easily replaced, much less augmented.

I have worked over the last ten years on virtually every phase of Soviet Jewry—in Rome, Vienna, Washington, and New York. I believe in the Soviet Jewish movement as fervently as I did when I first became involved, indeed more so, despite the difficulties we have experienced. The positive experiences have been so many and so rich that they dominate my memory, and my meetings with refuseniks in the USSR were among the most significant experiences of my life. I believe we are not just witnesses to, but participants in history, in one of the most extraordinary chapters in modern times.

Emil Fackenheim, a Judaic scholar from Toronto who now lives in Jerusalem, drafted a 614th commandment: "After Auschwitz, thou shalt not give Hitler posthumous victory." It is, unquestionably, our sacred duty to remember the Holocaust and to memorialize its victims, and to transmit the painful lessons of that tragedy to our children, but our responsibilities go much further. We must respond to Jews wherever they may be threatened. And today they are threatened as never before in the Soviet Union.

Survivors of the Holocaust recall two enduring fears during the dark years: first, that the world was unaware of what was happening to them, and second—a far greater fear—that the world *was* aware of what was happening to them but was not sufficiently moved to react. Soviet Jews know that many care—indeed, that is a lifeline that sustains them—but, they ask, are we doing all we can? What will our children and children's children one day ask about our response to the current situation? Will there be any among us who even dare suggest that we did not know the extent of the problem or understand its significance in light of Jewish history?

Shcharansky, Begun, Nudel, Lerner, and countless other Jewish heroes have sought to establish new lives in Israel. These people, who have fought tenaciously in behalf of us all for their right to live as Jews, deserve our steadfast support. Are all Soviet Jews like the activists? No, of course not, but every Soviet Jew who seeks to remain a Jew in the USSR has taken a courageous step and cannot survive alone.

When I visited the homes of refuseniks in Moscow and Leningrad, I listened to the parents but looked at the children. In the eyes of Soviet Jewish children, I saw no choices—neither as free human beings nor as Jews. Even if the parents managed a good education and found work, perhaps not at the level they merit but still in a professionally challenging atmosphere, what future is there in a country where anti-Semitic taunts begin in kindergarten and continue for a lifetime; where higher educational opportunities are increasingly limited; where professional advancement for young Jews entering the job market is ever more restricted; where opportunities to study one's culture and religion are virtually nonexistent; and where Zionists are portrayed as collaborators with the Nazis?

What should our response be? Are the Soviets testing our staying power, hoping that, if we encounter no success in our advocacy efforts, the press of other issues will draw our attention away from Soviet Jewry? If so, we must continue to show that they have seriously misread our resolve.

Our demonstrations; letters to Soviet officials; meetings with the administration and Congress; contact with refusenik families; bar and bat mitzvah twinnings; travel to the USSR; letters to the editor and op-ed pieces; outreach to other groups and to the press; education of our youth; and the myriad other efforts undertaken in our community must be continued, broadened, and intensified, just as we must enlist enthusiastic newcomers to interact with experienced activists in reviewing existing programming and proposing new ideas. The goals of these efforts should continue to be: (1) increased contact with individual Soviet Jews, (2) vigorous protest to Soviet officials, (3) requests for stepped-up action from our political leaders (as well as frequent acknowledgment of their effort and support), and (4) heightened public awareness in the United States of the condition of the Soviet Jewish community.

Does our involvement make any difference? I believe it does. It often cannot be measured in easily quantifiable ways, but the Soviet Union is not totally insensitive to world opinion, particularly if it is thunderous and reflects the views of both Jews and non-Jews in this country and abroad. And if it strengthens the resolve of Soviet Jews to remain Jews, keeps people like Shcharansky alive, reduces the term of a prison sentence or keeps others out of prison, or results in an exit visa, then it has had a significant impact.

As difficult as the situation is today, it could only have been more difficult in 1964 when but a few visionaries believed, against all the odds, in a possible reawakening of Soviet Jewry. The subsequent emigration of 265,000 Jews was tangible proof of the importance of the efforts of the world Jewish community. Without our voices, who in the West would have spoken for 2 million Soviet Jews? Who would have lobbied the administration and Congress? Who would have approached other Western governments? Who would have enlisted the interest of academic, religious, and other key communities? Who would have offered hope to otherwise isolated Soviet Jews? Indeed, without our support, one can only speculate whether there would have been *any* emigration and what further tragedies might have befallen Soviet Jews.

We must forge greater unity in the advocacy effort. We must put aside differences over such issues as the dropout question, especially when virtually no one is even arriving in Vienna. If Soviet Jews are sometimes difficult to resettle, it is worth reviewing the resettlement experience of East European Jews at the turn of the century. It was not an easy process then either. And if many Soviet Jews are cut off from Judaism, let us try to understand whence they come; and let us remember that in twenty years Jews in the USRR will be still more cut off from their roots.

Ours is a race against the clock. We have no moral right to apply any kind of "Jewish standard" to other Jews as a determinant for whether or not we become advocates for them. And let us not forget that more than 160,000 Soviet Jews have resettled in Israel where they have had a beneficial impact on every aspect of Israeli life.

After Shcharansky: What's Next for Soviet Jewry?[*]
Washington Jewish Week
February 13, 1986

Together with millions of other people around the world, I spent several days holding my breath, praying silently and passing each hour with one ear glued to my radio. Could this latest report, unlike so many previous others, of the imminent release of Anatoly Shcharansky be accurate? Would he, a moral giant of the Jewish people and a name synonymous with the struggle for repatriation to Israel, finally be released almost nine years after his arrest?

---

[*]Inserted in the *Congressional Record* by Congressman Dante B. Fascell, March 4, 1986.

Would the unimaginable suffering and agony he endured in Soviet prisons and labor camps be over? Would he finally be permitted to join his wife, Avital, whose unstinting devotion to her husband's cause has inspired people everywhere, after eleven and a half years of separation? Would his elderly mother's courage and perseverance in support of her beleaguered son no longer be necessary? Would the unstinting efforts of President Ronald Reagan and Secretary of State George Shultz, members of Congress, foreign leaders and private citizens everywhere at last yield results?

Would Shcharansky's profound faith, stated so eloquently during his trial in Moscow in July 1978, finally be redeemed? At that time, he said: "For more than 2,000 years the Jewish people, my people, have been dispersed. But wherever they are, wherever Jews are found, they have repeated, 'Next year in Jerusalem.' Now, when I am further than ever from my people, from Avital, facing many years of imprisonment, I say, turning to my people, my Avital: Next year in Jerusalem." Would it be this year in Jerusalem?

We rejoice in the news of his release and reunification with Avital. We are humbled by his courage, and inspired by his faith. Yet, at the same time, it is difficult to overlook the fact that his release, as welcome and important as it truly is, is not necessarily the result of an altruistic, humanitarian gesture on the Soviets' part. Rather, it serves four very concrete purposes for the Kremlin: (1) It is part of an exchange involving spies, hence permitting Moscow to maintain its original contention that Shcharansky was in the employ of the CIA—even though Shcharansky always denied the espionage charge despite the fact that, had he yielded to extreme Soviet pressure to admit to the accusation, he might well have been released years ago. (2) It generates favorable media attention for the Soviets at a time when the battle for Western public opinion is being waged fiercely by the Kremlin. (3) It serves to rid Moscow of one of the two preeminent human rights symbols (the other is Andrei Sakharov) within its borders. (4) It returns several key East bloc agents.

Is Shcharansky's release, nevertheless, a genuine signal by the Kremlin?

As much as one would like to believe so, the prevailing condition of Soviet Jewry gives serious pause. Consider:

The emigration rate, which was inching upward from a mere 29 in August 1985 to 128 in November, the month of the summit, has now reversed direction; 92 people left in December and only 79 in January.

On January 8, Vladimir Lifshits, a Leningrad refusenik, was arrested on a charge of anti-Soviet propaganda and now faces trial.

On Jananuary 17, seven young Jews in the Leningrad area participated in an Oneg Shabbat celebration. The party was disrupted by the local police, who accompanied the group to the local police station, beating a few along the way and threatening them with expulsion from university and with military conscription. They were interrogated about their Jewish activities and study of Torah, and accused of holding a private religious ceremony.

Inna Meiman, the wife of mathematician Naum Meiman, has been suffering from a growing tumor on the back of her neck, near her spinal column, for more than two years. The only apparent remaining hope for treatment, after four painful and ultimately unsuccessful operations in Moscow, is at one of a few oncological centers in the West that have the sophisticated equipment to treat the cancerous growth. Despite countless appeals, the Kremlin has adamantly refused the Meimans permission to travel to the West for medical care, citing Professor Meiman's classified work—work that was performed thirty years ago! . . .

How, then, does one interpret current Kremlin policy?

It is to remain tough at home as a signal that no loosening of the reins is in the offing. On the other hand, for Western consumption, it pursues a two-pronged strategy. First, the staggered release of a few prominent figures, such as long-term refuseniks Mark Nashpitz, Yakov Mesh, Eliyahu Essas, and Yakov Gorodetsky, succeeds in generating positive publicity for the Soviets at relatively little cost and serves equally to deflect attention from the stark reality facing the Soviet Jewish community. Second, the traditional Soviet campaign of disinformation abroad continues apace. In this regard, events of the last year are revealing:

(1) In January 1985, Soviet State Bank chairman Alkhimov told U.S. undersecretary of commerce Olmer that if good relations with the U.S. were restored, 50,000 Jewish emigrants annually would be "no problem." After a flurry of Western press attention and U.S. interest in studying the apparent opening, the Soviets subsequently denied the story.

(2) Three months later, optimism was again generated when the *New York Times* carried a front-page story from Moscow that as many as 1,000 Jews, including long-term refuseniks, were reportedly being summoned to OVIR (the visa and passport office) and being issued exit visas, but nothing resulted.

(3) In July, at a meeting with the Israeli envoy in Paris, Soviet ambassador Vorontsov indicated his country's preparedness to move forward on diplomatic relations in exchange for Soviet participation in the Middle East peace process and Israeli flexibility on the Golan Heights issue. Much media attention was given to the story, but no real progress has occurred.

(4) Reports, originating in Moscow, of an imminent release of 15–20,000 Soviet Jews and their transfer to Israel via Warsaw have appeared in many Anglo-Jewish papers this fall. To date, though, nothing has happened.

(5) During his visit to France in October, Soviet leader Gorbachev addressed the emigration question by noting that the Soviet Union "solves" the problem of family reunification, refusing permission "only where state secrets are involved." In such cases, added Gorbachev, applicants can leave after waiting between five and ten years. Despite these well-publicized assertions, the several thousand long-term refuseniks with close relatives in Israel and elsewhere, whose first applications were submitted as long ago as 1970, offer ample proof of the inaccuracy of the claim. And, a shrewd and sophisticated communicator, Gorbachev also used the occasion to speak of Soviet Jews as a "privileged nationality," yet another element of the Soviet disinformation campaign.

(6) Finally, there was the *New York Times* front-page story on December 26, headlined "Russian Said to Predict Israeli Ties and Increased Jewish Emigration," referring to a Soviet embassy official in

Washington. TASS, the Soviet news agency, later denied the story.

If Moscow genuinely seeks to send an unambiguously positive message, it should follow the advice of Anthony Lewis (*New York Times*, March 14, 1985): "What is needed as a signal is evident: not words, but convincing actions by the Soviet Union."

What would be convincing action? In my view, it would mean significant progress toward an orderly process of repatriation to Israel and reunification of families with a definite time limit on those cases involving previous security clearance, a resolution of the prisoner of conscience and long-term refusenik cases, an end to harassment of Jewish activists and arrests on trumped-up charges, and a guarantee of the religious and cultural rights for Jews (including the right to study Hebrew) given to other Soviet citizens.

If movement can be achieved in these areas, it will doubtless be welcomed in this country and contribute to further progress in other dimensions of the bilateral relationship, not to speak of a more general improvement in the "atmospherics" that can play such an important role in shaping the direction of superpower relations.

In the meantime, welcome Anatoly. We pledge that our efforts will not cease until all in whose name you struggle so valiantly will be able to join you and Avital in Israel.

A Change in the Wind Concerning Soviet Jews?
The World & I
April 1986

A few hours after Natan (Anatoly) Shcharansky's arrival in the West, a journalist called me to ask if the struggle for Soviet Jewry was over. After all, he said, the main symbol of the movement now was liberated and a principal demand of the Western world—Shcharansky's freedom—was met. What more needed to be done? I responded by telling him an anecdote recounted by Jews in Moscow:

Shortly after publication of the Soviet census in 1979, General Secretary Brezhnev asked Premier Kosygin the official Soviet Jewish population figure. "The total is 1.8 million," replied Kosygin. "I have an idea," said the Soviet leader. "What if we permit the troublemakers among the Jews to emigrate. Won't that win us some favorable publicity overseas and, at the same time, defuse tensions here?" "A fine idea," exclaimed Kosygin. "How many do you think would leave, Kosygin?" "No less than 5 million," he responded.

The point is, of course, that the struggle in behalf of the Jews in the Soviet Union, whose actual numbers may well be between 2 and 2.5 million (given serious inadequacies in the Soviet census method), is far from over. And many other Soviet citizens also seek to leave for a variety of political, religious, and family reasons. This in no way diminishes the importance of Shcharansky's liberation. Shcharansky's name long ago entered the lexicon of human rights and became, together with those of still-exiled Nobel laureate Andrei Sakharov and imprisoned South African antiapartheid activist Nelson Mandela, among the best known of prisoners of conscience in the world. His unyielding struggle, including a 109-day hunger strike, to maintain his innocence and identity as a Jew and a Zionist during nearly nine years of the most unimaginable prison conditions, is an extraordinary example of courage.

Conjugal Advocacy

Avital Shcharansky's relentless advocacy in her husband's behalf, including countless meetings with Western leaders, demonstrations, and petitions, symbolizes the indomitable will of a loving and devoted spouse. As Anthony Lewis wrote in the *New York Times* in June 1983: "Moving the Soviet leadership on an individual human rights case often seems a hopeless business. But if you meet Avital Shcharansky . . . you will know there is no alternative to trying." In addition, Shcharansky's elderly mother's unstinting efforts from Moscow to secure her son's release, and her arduous trips to remote regions to seek even a brief glimpse of him, have touched many of us. I will never forget meeting this remarkable woman in Moscow in 1981. At the time, she said tearfully:

> I have not received a single card or letter from my son in months. I traveled to the Perm labor camp in May, but they would not let me in. I

begged the camp commander to simply show me my son, even from a distance, to assure me that he was still alive, but he wouldn't even do it. Can you imagine, I don't even know whether my son is living!

Shcharansky's arrival in Israel—the realization of a decades-long dream—is a triumph of the human spirit, the power of faith, and the yearning to live in freedom. It is, too, a tribute to the efforts of the U.S. government, joined by other Western governments, parliamentarians, Jews, and Christians who never let his name be forgotten and never yielded to the temptation of indifference.

But for tens of thousands of other Soviet Jews the situation remains unchanged:

Emigration, which peaked at more than 50,000 in 1979 and totals 270,000 since 1970, has declined precipitously in recent years. In 1985, fewer than 100 Jews per month were issued exit visas, a drop of more than 95 percent from the 1979 figure. Some Soviet leaders have sought to explain this decline by suggesting that few Jews now seek to leave. "Family reunification has essentially been completed and, for this reason, emigration has diminished," said Samuel Zivs, first deputy chairman of the official Soviet Anti-Zionist Committee, at a press conference in June 1983. "Very few people indeed have any desire to leave their [Soviet] country," added Avtandil Rukhadze, a Soviet journalist writing in the English-language *Soviet Weekly* in 1984. Despite Soviet assertions, the Israeli government has the names and addresses of more than 375,000 Soviet Jews who have requested a *vyzov* (affidavit) from Jerusalem as the first step in the emigration process but have not yet left. No doubt, others are reluctant even to request affidavits because they accurately perceive that their chances of leaving the Soviet Union today are virtually nil.

Fourteen thousands refuseniks—that is, individuals whose exit applications have been denied, some for ten years or more—live as "internal refugees." Beniamin Bogomolny, for example, enjoys the dubious honor of being listed in the *Guiness Book of World Records* as the world's longest standing refusenik, having made his first request twenty years ago. If a reason for refusal is given, it may be the absence of parental permission (regardless of one's own age) or "state security," even if a person has left (or lost) his job years ago in connection with an exit application. Unable to comprehend such arbitrariness, Soviet Jews often use humor to face these anomalous situations.

> Rabinovich was summoned to OVIR (the visa and passport office) and told that he had been refused an exit visa due to possession of a state secret from his work. "What possible state secret could I know," protested Rabinovich, "when the technology we employ at our plant is at least twenty years behind the Americans?" "That, my dear Rabinovich, is the state secret!" replied the official.

Other prisoners of conscience remain in Soviet labor camps and prisons, including Iosif Begun, a victim of "triple jeopardy." Begun is now serving a third sentence—twelve years—for the "crime" of teaching Hebrew. Vladimir Lifshits, a Leningrad refusenik, was arrested after the November Geneva summit meeting for the "crime" of writing about the Russian Jewish condition, as a signal to Jewish activists and people in the West that domestic conditions in the Soviet Union have not eased. In early February, Lifshits was badly beaten by criminal inmates and suffered a brain concussion.

The Kremlin has always sought to portray itself as anti-Zionist but not anti-Semitic; the reality of the officially orchestrated campaign over the years has been to attack Zionism, Israel, Jews, and Judaism. For example, in Vladmir Begun's *The Creeping Counter-Revolution*, published in two editions totaling 200,000 copies, the author writes: "If we view the Torah (Five Books of Moses) from the standpoint of modern civilization and progressive Communist morality, it proves to be an unsurpassed textbook of bloodthirstiness and hypocrisy, treachery, perfidy, and licentiousness—of every vile human quality." And in a frequently echoed theme in the Soviet press, V. V. Bolshakov, author of *Zionism in the Service of Anti-Comminism*, alleged that "in many cases the Zionists served as Hitler's 'fifth column,' and their international network was used to establish Nazi German domination of the world."

At the same time that these libels are being featured in the Soviet media, Jews also endure another ominous form of anti-Semitism, namely, increasing restrictions on employment and enrollment in institutions of higher education. The London-based Institute on Jewish Affairs noted that the Jewish student population in the Soviet Union had declined from 112,000 in 1968–1969 to 50–55,000 in 1980, a decrease of more than 50 percent. During the same period, the total Soviet Jewish population dropped only 16 percent.

The virtual absence of any serious religious and cultural opportunities for Soviet Jews is another major problem. Twenty years ago, this situation was denounced by the Reverend Martin Luther King Jr.:

> While Jews in Russia may not be physically murdered as they were in Nazi Germany, they are facing every day a kind of spiritual and cultural genocide . . . the absence of opportunity to associate as Jews in the enjoyment of Jewish culture and religious experience becomes a severe limitation upon the individual. These deprivations are part of a person's emotional and intellectual life. They determine whether he is fulfilled as a human being.

Keeping the Flame Alive

In the same year, the noted author Elie Wiesel wrote an account of his visit to the Soviet Union entitled *The Jews of Silence*. Had Soviet Jews, he asked, been destined for oblivion through a deliberate Kremlin effort to assimilate them forcibly? However, fifteen years later a delegate of the Association of American Jewish Book Publishers to the Moscow International Book Fair recounted his amazement at the sight of thousands of Soviet Jews lining up to view the hundreds of books on Jewish themes brought by the delegation. He recounted the story of a young woman with four children. On each of the first four days of the fair, she brought one of her children. They would sit together in a corner of the exhibit, as she translated from English stories of Jewish religion and history. Somehow, she was seeking in that hour or two to instill in the child a sense of Jewish identity and pride.

An elderly man also visited the exhibit. At one point, he was standing in the middle of the exhibit, away from the books. The line to enter was so long, in fact blocking access to the adjoining Western Communist Party publishing booths, that an American approached the man and asked him to move on. "Young man," replied the Russian, "you don't understand. Unfortunately, I am unable to read your books in English, Hebrew, and Yiddish. But don't deny me this opportunity, if only once in my lifetime, to breathe your Jewish air!"

Notwithstanding such a bleak picture, the question that persists, in light of Shcharansky's release, is whether this act augurs a fundamental policy shift or is simply a singular event. While it is still too early to discern any major change in Soviet policy, it is clear that the Kremlin long ago recognized the utility of at least symbolic gestures in the human rights sphere, at opportune moments, as a tool for seeking to improve its image in the West. Hence, in addition to Shcharansky's inclusion in the spy exchange, there was an attempt to defuse the case of Sakharov, the other renowned Soviet human rights symbol, by issuing a temporary visa to Elena Bonner, his wife, to permit her medical care and a visit with her family in the Boston area. Of course, she will shortly rejoin her husband—although one would hope for the reverse—in the prisonlike conditions to which they have been sentenced in remote Gorky.

The Soviets also resolved several of the divided international marriage cases in connection with the Geneva meeting. In reuniting ten cases, however, they leave another twenty unaddressed. With three summit meetings scheduled, perhaps the Kremlin has decided to release one-third of the group for each meeting and thus seek to exploit fully these calculated gestures in the continuing battle for Western public opinion.

Cracking the Door

Finally, the Soviets have begun to issue exit visas to a handful of the long-term refuseniks. Mark Nashpitz, Yakov Mesh, Yakov Gorodetsky, and Ilya Essas are among the few well-known activists whose exits are occurring in a carefully staggered fashion. Yet as welcome as the resolution of these long-standing cases may be, the obstacle to unbridled Western enthusiasm remains the overall low emigration numbers and the continuing repression of Jewish activists.

There is reason today for guarded hope of change if one is mindful of the risk of succumbing to a Soviet strategy that may be little more than a smoke screen to deflect attention from continuing human rights abuses within its borders.

There is no question that the fate of Soviet Jewry has been linked to the ebb and flow of superpower relations and made hostage to a ruthless Kremlin geopolitical strategy. When superpower relations sour, the fortunes of Soviet Jews decline accordingly. Conversely, if the Kremlin desires to soften the atmosphere and gain reciprocal advantage in other areas of the bilateral relationship, it may choose to turn on the emigration spigot. This was well illustrated both in the early 1970s during the era of détente and again in 1978–79 when a Soviet desire for Senate ratification of SALT II and improved economic ties led to a record year of emigration. Subsequently, as relations declined in 1979 and beyond, emigration took a nosedive.

The current reestablishment of a modicum of dialogue between Moscow and Washington, the expansion of contacts in the diplomatic, economic, cultural, and other spheres, and the increased, if still remote, chance for progress on arms control issues, all help set the stage for possible progress on Soviet Jewry. On the other hand, there is also a serious risk that just as Soviet Jews could benefit if bilateral ties improve, they might lose if ties worsened. The Kremlin will be watching very carefully to ascertain how much flexibility they will have to demonstrate in this area to secure desired agreements in other sectors. If their conclusion is that a few carefully timed gestures such as the release of Shcharansky or the resolution of a handful of binational marriage cases succeeds in muting the outcry over human rights violations, why, from their own viewpoint, should they do more? Thus, it becomes critical that the administration, Congress, and public opinion remain united in insisting on significant progress toward an orderly emigration process and an end to harassment and imprisonment at home as a sine qua non of progress in other nonsecurity areas.

Renewed Interest

A second area that bears watching is the Kremlin's policy vis-à-vis Israel. Moscow broke ties with the Jewish state in 1967 after maintaining relations, except for one brief interruption, since Israel's founding in 1948. Indeed, the Soviet Union and the United States were the first two countries to accord diplomatic recognition to Israel. In 1947, speaking at the United Nations in support of the plan to partition Palestine, Andrei Gromyko stated: "During the last war, the Jewish people underwent exceptional sorrow and suffering . . . It may well be asked if the UN, in view of the difficult situation of hundreds of thousands of the surviving Jewish population, can fail to show an interest in the situation of these people." Regrettably, despite these words of support, it did not prevent the Soviet Union from embarking on an unprecedented anti-Jewish campaign at home that continued until Stalin's death in 1953 and came to be known as the "black years of Soviet Jewry," nor did it then encourage the Kremlin to permit Jewish emigration to Israel.

Still, some Soviet sources have privately suggested that the Kremlin has belatedly recognized its mistake in severing ties in 1967. Having been excluded as a principal player in the Middle East while the United States succeeded in strengthening its own position, the Kremlin may seek to reenter the scene. One way would be to restore relations with Israel. Is there a realistic chance today? The evidence is still scanty but noteworthy:

Poland recently reestablished low-level diplomatic ties with Israel, nineteen years after it broke relations. It became the first Warsaw Pact nation to do so (with the exception of Romania, which has always maintained ties with Israel). Obviously, Warsaw could not have taken this step without the approval of Moscow.

Hungary, while not having diplomatic ties with Israel, has expanded commercial, cultural, and tourist contacts with the Jewish state. The volume of annual trade exceeds $15 million and thousands of tourists are traveling back and forth. Will Hungary follow Poland's lead and set the stage for further diplomatic breakthroughs between Israel and the Warsaw Pact nations?

A publicized spate of diplomatic contacts between Soviet and Israeli officials at the United Nations, in Paris, and elsewhere last year has led to speculation of warming ties. If, indeed, a thaw is in the offing, and this is far from clear, it may be accelerated by the Kremlin's belief that it can strike a better deal with Prime Minister Peres than with Foreign Minister Shamir, who is slated to become the Israeli leader in October under the agreement worked out by the Labor and Likud parties in the fall of 1984. But Israeli leaders have made clear they would be more amenable to the reestablishment of diplomatic ties or Soviet involvement in an international conference on the Middle East if the Kremlin acts on the Soviet Jewish emigration question.

A third area of potential importance to the fate of Soviet Jewry lies in recent Soviet leadership changes. With Gorbachev's accession to power, his growing consolidation of control, including the purging of both the Politburo and Central Committee, and his desire to instill vigor into the beleaguered Soviet economy, there will be major implications in all segments of Soviet life, including Soviet Jewry. For the moment, though, it would be premature to draw precise conclusions, at least vis-à-vis Soviet Jewry.

Interesting, but Unchanged

The Chinese have an old curse: "May you live in interesting times!" The reality of the Soviet Jewish situation remains unchanged—low emigration numbers, divided families, harassed activists, prisoners of conscience, a ban on the teaching of Hebrew, monitored telephones, disrupted mail, lost jobs, no rabbinic seminaries and only one rabbi for every 300,000 Jews, and frequent anti-Zionist/anti-Semitic books, articles, and television programs. Soviet Jews are fearful of attaching too much hope to the prospects for improvement, but these are admittedly interesting times.

Soviet Jews have been disappointed before. Nevertheless, there just might be something in the air, the hint of a possible change. This is the first opportunity in six years for the two superpowers to engage in serious discussions on the four principal agenda items: arms control and security matters, regional conflicts (Central America, Middle East, Afghanistan, Southeast Asia), bilateral issues (trade, culture, etc.), and human rights. On the last item, a Leningrad Jewish activist recently told an American visitor: "Don't be misled. Our situation is as grim as it has ever been. Still, even in spite of our best instincts, we are holding our breath and walking on pins and needles in the hope that change may be in the offing."

It can only be through continued, indeed intensified, efforts in the West at this critical moment in both East-West relations and Soviet history that the current bleak situation may be reversed and the gates reopened. As a refusenik friend from "atheist" Moscow once said in response to frustration I expressed about the lack of progress, quoting *Ethics of the Fathers*: "The day is short, the work is great . . . It is not thy duty to complete the work but neither art thou free to desist from it."

Soviet Jews: *Nyet* Again?
Moment
October 1986

In 1979, more than 4,000 Soviet Jews were permitted to leave the USSR each month; in 1986, that number has dwindled to fewer than 100. Natan Shcharansky is free, but arrests of Hebrew teachers and other activists have continued, and harassment of those engaged in religious and cultural study has intensified. How are we to understand what is happening? And what can we do about it?

Recent visitors, Western diplomats stationed in the USSR, and refuseniks themselves are agreed that the situation of Soviet Jews has deteriorated since Mikhail Gorbachev's accession to power in March 1985. Indeed, some refuseniks now talk of a modern version of Konstantin Pobedonostsev's solution to the Jewish question at the turn of this century. Pobedonostsev, the influential procurator of the Holy Synod, formulated the infamous "third-third-third" strategy: one-third will emigrate, one-third will be assimilated, and the last third, rejecting either option, will die.

Today, the Kremlin's approach remains three-pronged, though with somewhat different content and proportions. First, Moscow technically retains the emigration option. Although it keeps the exit door only slightly ajar, it claims that its policy conforms to the applicable international agreements to which it is a signatory. When challenged on the low emigration rate, it explains that few now leave because "the process of family reunification has almost been completed." Moscow concedes that it sometimes delays emigration for family reunification from five to ten years. It has also alleged it restricts emigration because so many Soviet Jews have gone to the United States rather than to Israel despite their Israeli visas, according to, among others, former foreign minister

Gromyko; former Soviet envoy to Canada Yakovlev, who is now a key party secretary; and Victor Louis, the Soviet journalist.

By carefully manipulating emigration, the Kremlin seeks to enhance its image overseas. The staggered and well-publicized releases of even a few well-known refuseniks, former prisoners of conscience, and other compelling humanitarian cases bring Western media attention. The Kremlin hopes this will deflect attention from the country's true human rights picture. And by issuing exit visas to some refuseniks, the Kremlin is attempting to reinforce Gorbachev's assertion that long-standing cases are resolved against a backdrop of rapidly declining demand.

Second, Moscow is also eager to accelerate the process of assimila-tion. By reducing emigration to a trickle, the Kremlin seeks to drive home a point to those who would apply for exit visas, a point made explicit in the offices of OVIR, where such applications are reviewed: "You have no chance to leave, so why not resume 'normal' lives as Soviet citizens? There are jobs and educational opportunities available to you. Housing, pensions, medical care, and safety are at much high-er levels here than in the West. Just look at the experiences of those for-mer Soviet citizens who were duped into leaving their motherland only to suffer the consequences of living as unwanted, unemployed, unhap-py strangers in a decadent, dangerous, and often anti-Semitic New World. Here, nationalities live happily together and we value [as Gorbachev himself said in October 1985] the contributions of the tal-ented Jewish minority." The message is strikingly clear: The time of high emigration is over, and there is no realistic alternative to reinte-gration.

Third, terror continues to be employed against those who refuse assimilation. No one today speaks of the annihilation proposed by Pobedonostsev, or of the mass deportation of Jews to Siberia that Stalin had been planning on the eve of his death. The current approach is nei-ther that of Stalin's mass terror of the 1930s nor the massacre of Jewish cultural figures of the early 1950s. Rather, it is a policy of selective ter-ror. The weapons are isolation, harassment, harsh sentences, remote camps, rigorous prison conditions, and physical assault from common criminals placed in the same cells.

There is no need to arrest every Jewish troublemaker, the authorities reason. Arrest a few key figures and shock waves will spread throughout the emigration movement. To make life unpredictable for those contemplating the teaching or study of such "subversive" subjects as Hebrew language, Judaism, or Jewish history—and unpredictability is key—all that is required is to arrest some who do not even seem deserving of the KGB's attention. That will deter the rest.

When Gorbachev came to power, there were those who thought Soviet policy toward the Jews might be liberalized. After all, here was a "modern" leader, one concerned with image and sensitive to public opinion both at home and abroad. Plainly, such hopes have been disappointed. Yet it is precisely with such a Soviet leader—firmly in control, open to change, and likely to be around for years to come—that the chance of striking some kind of deal is enhanced. The prospect of significant change in Soviet policy continues to depend, as it has all these years past, on superpower relations. U.S.-USSR relations chilled in 1979 and remained frigid until the spring of 1983, when a partial thaw set in.

A five-year grain agreement was signed, a cultural pact was in the offing, and the United States lifted some restrictions on the export of oil and gas equipment. The thaw, however, was interrupted by the shooting down of the Korean airliner in September 1983. It was not until 1985 that superpower dialogue began in earnest, providing the first serious opportunity since 1979 for consideration of, among other issues, the vexing question of Soviet Jewry. Although bilateral relations remain rocky, there has been a significant change in both substance and tone in the last year. A structure is now in place for more frequent official contacts and further summits. President Reagan appears to have come a long way from the days of his "evil empire" speech. Now, we are told, he seeks to assure his place in history as a peacemaker.

And Gorbachev, faced with the monumental task of energizing the perennially anemic Soviet economy, which is plagued by declining foreign currency earnings due to lower oil prices, burdened by the high cost of the Chernobyl cleanup, and reportedly preoccupied with the staggering challenge posed by America's Strategic Defense Initiative

("Star Wars"), just might be open to further dialogue with Washington, leading to improved ties. If so, then it is possible—just possible—that the next two years will prove an especially important period in Soviet-American relations. Obviously, the thaw is only partial, and could quickly be interrupted by any number of developments, including unplanned events quite distant from the borders—and far removed from the current intentions—of both powers. Or, perhaps, Reagan's own firmly rooted views or pressure from his right might deter him from moving "too far." Or Gorbachev, who will be closely watching the 1986 and 1988 U.S. elections, might decide that he can get a better deal by waiting until January 1989.

Still, the next two years may offer uncommon possibility for Soviet Jewry and for its advocates abroad.

A number of national and community-based agencies led by a group of devoted individuals have succeeded in maintaining the visibility of the Soviet Jewry issue and its priority on the Western agenda. And now, energized no doubt by the release of Natan Shcharansky in February 1986, the plight of Soviet Jewry is gaining increased attention. Almost single-handedly, Shcharansky has galvanized public opinion, recharged the advocacy movement, and unified often disparate groups. The extraordinary reception accorded him in Washington in May, the electricity he generated in the record crowd at New York's Solidarity Sunday demonstration, and the lavish press attention he has received have all served to restore hope, and even optimism, within the movement, and to restore interest in the issue of Soviet Jewry among government leaders and the general public.

It is also worth noting the growing commitment of the major Jewish philanthropic, religious, and community-relations agencies to the advocacy movement. As awareness of the stark reality facing Soviet Jews takes root and all hope of a sudden reversal is dashed, a new level of response has emerged: heightened interagency cooperation; increased travel to meet with refuseniks; more appeals to the administration and Congress; greater participation in local and national demonstrations, vigils, and petition campaigns; and increased efforts to educate and mobilize constituencies.

The success of the Soviet Jewry movement—and it should be noted that this nonviolent movement has been among the most successful in modern history—has always been dependent on four interconnected factors.

The first is the struggle that Soviet Jews themselves undertook in the mid-1960s to assert their Jewish identity, refuse assimilation, and demand—consistent with international covenants and the concept of repatriation as the Soviet government itself defines the term—to be permitted to depart for Israel. Their willingness to risk retribution by writing appeals to Soviet and Western officials, demonstrating, petitioning, fasting, meeting with Western diplomats and correspondents, and engaging in study groups captured the world's imagination and sparked Western efforts on their behalf.

The second is the vital role Israel has played. Not only would there be no legal basis for this emigration if Israel did not exist as a sovereign state (Soviet Jews formally apply for an exit visa based on an affidavit notarized by the Israeli government for family reunification with relatives resident in Israel), but Israel also provides invaluable information and support for the advocacy movement.

The third factor is the actions of Western governments, led by the United States. One can only wonder if any Soviet Jews would have been granted exit visas had the U.S. administration and Congress not shown such concern for their fate. Other countries, too, have played important, if less publicized, roles. The Netherlands has been quietly representing Israeli diplomatic interests in Moscow since 1967. Belgium was the first country at the Madrid Review Conference of the Helsinki Final Act publicly to express concern over Soviet anti-Semitism. Australia, Canada, and Great Britain have sent their Moscow-based diplomats to monitor the trials of some Jewish activists. France's President Mitterrand was the first Western leader to include a Jewish communal leader, Theo Klein, as an official member of his delegation during a 1984 state visit to the USSR. West Germany helped secure Shcharansky's release. And Austria has maintained open borders to emigrating Soviet Jews, providing transit to hundreds of thousands of Soviet Jews and other East European refugees for decades.

Finally, the role of voluntary organizations and public opinion has been an important factor. American agencies such as the National Conference on Soviet Jewry, Coalition to Free Soviet Jews, Student Struggle for Soviet Jewry, Committee of Concerned Scientists, and their counterparts in other Western countries have stimulated public attention, lobbied governments, and helped draw Christians and Jews, blacks and whites, scientists and artists, public officials and private citizens into the advocacy ranks.

What more needs to be, and can be, done, especially in light of the current gloomy situation?

A key concern is to avoid a situation wherein, notwithstanding the current commitment of the U.S. government to Soviet Jewry's rescue, Soviet Jews become the victims and not the beneficiaries of improving Soviet-American relations. In the last year alone, several bilateral agreements have been signed; Moscow has succeeded in raising more than $600 million in credits from American banks; the National Academy of Sciences, reversing its earlier decision to curtail exchanges because of the Soviet treatment of Orlov, Sakharov, and other dissident scientists, has resumed ties with the Soviet Academy of Sciences; American cities such as Chicago, Philadelphia, San Francisco, and Washington are considering sister-city ties with Soviet cities; American travel to the USSR was expected to rise considerably, had it not been for the Chernobyl disaster; the United States, in contrast to the Olympic boycott in 1980, did participate in the 1986 Moscow Goodwill Games; ballet and opera companies, orchestras, and art exhibitions are beginning to travel back and forth; and some U.S. corporations are exploring business opportunities in the USSR. Yet all of this has occurred against a backdrop of unrelenting repression of Soviet Jews and, for that matter, of religious, peace, labor, Helsinki, and other dissident Soviet groups, of the continued exile of Nobel laureate Andrei Sakharov, of the brutal occupation of Afghanistan, and of the crushing of Solidarity in Poland.

During this period, what positive behavior—or even gestures—have the Soviets displayed? A handful of divided family cases resolved, a few refuseniks released (Shcharansky's prominence should not blind us to the fact that he is but one—and one who was "traded," not freed—and the rest of his family, scheduled for freedom at August's end, only five more); a six-month visit to the West for Elena Bonner, Sakharov's wife; and very little else. From Moscow's viewpoint, things have not been going badly. If it can achieve most of its desired aims in other sectors of the bilateral relationship while paying only a minimal price in the areas of Soviet Jewry and human rights, what incentive could it have for increasing emigration?

The Kremlin is seeking to focus attention on arms control, security, and trade, as well as on areas that confer international respectability, such as tourism, culture, sports, and science. Through a combination of disinformation, counterpropaganda, and tiny concessions, Moscow is seeking to mute criticism of its emigration and human rights policies and push forward in other sectors of the bilateral link.

Moscow has sought as well, albeit unsuccessfully so far, to persuade American Jewish organizations to take a leading role against "Star Wars" and in favor of a return to détente. The bait here has come in the form of vague hints of increased emigration. From its inception, the Soviet Jewry movement has always tried to make clear that its agenda was pro-Soviet Jewry, not anti-Soviet, and that the difference was more than academic. It has also sought, persuasively, to portray its goals as attainable, not as mere fanciful thinking. And it has always under- scored the full compatibility between its goals and the objectives of American foreign policy. In recent years, for example, the movement did not seek to block the long-term grain agreement or the new bilat- eral accords, and has stated that it will not enter into the debate over arms control, even though issues of credibility and trust of the Soviet word do appropriately arise. (If the Soviets cannot be trusted to abide by the Helsinki Accords, how can they be trusted to abide by other agreements, including arms control accords?)

But what if there is no progress on emigration? What if the internal situation facing Soviet Jews remains as it is, or even worsens? It then becomes impossible to defer debate over very difficult questions. Are larger demonstrations alone a sufficient response? Are more nonbind- ing congressional condemnations and appeals going to have an impact? Or must the advocacy movement consider proposing to the administration and Congress—and the American people—shifts in one direction or the other in American policy toward the Soviet Union? Should the movement press for additional nonstrategic carrots or should it propose punitive measures? And would the government even be responsive to such proposals, especially if they were punitive in nature, at a time when bilateral ties are otherwise improving?

The focus on strategy becomes more immediate because of the current opportunities and challenges, including, of course, a second summit meeting. Every major Soviet Jewry organization and the World Jewish Congress endorsed in May a statement on the Jackson-Vanik Amendment, the 1974 act that links the granting of most-favored-nation trade status for communist countries to emigration performance.

Written in part for Congress and as a response to business groups' demands for repeal of the act, the statement asserts: "We vigorously reiterate our support for the principles and the policies represented by the Jackson-Vanik Amendment and affirm that we would strongly oppose any legislative effort to repeal or modify it. The Soviet Union must be shown that unless and until it has complied with the terms of the Amendment, U.S. policy will remain as it is. There is no room for unilateral gestures until the Soviets show that they are willing to abide by the rule protecting these human rights to which they gave their pledge at Helsinki. . . ."

The support of the World Jewish Congress, an organization that the Soviets have been in contact with for several years, is especially important. In July 1983, Edgar Bronfman, WJC chairman, wrote an op-ed in the *New York Times* calling for the repeal of the Jackson-Vanik Amendment "as a sign of good will that challenges the Russians to respond in kind." That position was publicly questioned by, among others, Morris Abram, chairman of the National Conference on Soviet Jewry, and Leon Dulzin, chairman of the Jewish Agency and head of the International Council of the World Conference on Soviet Jewry. The significance of the WJC's participation in the 1986 statement, therefore, could not have been lost on the Kremlin.

Some others have taken different positions with regard to Jackson-Vanik specifically and détente more generally. On the one hand, for example, we have the advertisement of an organization called the International League for the Repatriation of Russian Jews. The ILRRJ placed a quarter-page ad in the *New York Times* in March calling for waiver of the Jackson-Vanik Amendment, thus permitting the USSR to benefit from reduced tariffs on exports to the United States; repeal of the Stevenson Amendment, which limits the extension of government credits to the USSR to $300 million in a four-year period; and increased nonstrategic trade.

The May statement of the Soviet Jewry movement effectively makes clear that the ILRRJ ad does not represent the views of the organized Jewish community. At the same time, by recognizing the president's ability to waive the most-favored-nation restriction in response to increased emigration, the statement implicitly repudiates the position of *The New Republic*, as expressed in a lead editorial in April 1985.

A month earlier, four major American Jewish organizations had placed an ad in the *Washington Post*, timed to coincide with the visit to the United States of a Soviet delegation led by Ukrainian party chief and Politburo member Shcherbitsky, which stated: "We believe many people in this country would be responsive to positive changes, especially in your emigration policy. Why should emigration continue to be a barrier to improved trade and investment relations, and to expanded cultural and scientific exchange?"

The New Republic attacked this approach in a vehement argument: "Well, maybe that is good for the Jews of Russia, though maybe not. But what about the Soviet citizens whose rescue is not a part of the proposed transaction? What about those left in Russia for whom no one speaks? . . . And just because no one cares for the dozens of endangered ethnic and national groups submerged under Soviet rule—truly captive nations, these, with no diaspora to invoke their destiny in world capitals—this doesn't justify a human rights transaction made exclusively for Jews. What would an expanded cultural exchange look like if it were to be accompanied by a stream of departing Russian Jews and a torrent of Russian bombs over Afghanistan?"

The editorial went on to charge the Jewish organizations with moral and political obtuseness, haughtiness, naïveté, and single-mindedness. In effect, *The New Republic* editorial proposed that until every admittedly despicable feature of Soviet life was corrected, all of us should stand still.

The Jackson-Vanik Amendment, to which the *Washington Post* ad had made implicit reference, was not passed by Congress in 1974 to procure the release of every dissatisfied Soviet citizen or to foment revolutionary democratic change, much as its sponsors may have privately shared these goals. Rather, it was prompted by the imposition in 1972 of an onerous education tax on Soviet Jews seeking to leave, and its primary focus, as its legislative history clearly indicates, was directed at the particular plight of Soviet Jews. The amendment's sponsors also believed that Soviet Jewish emigration was a realistic goal, not fundamentally threatening to the Soviet system.

In sharp contrast to that kind of realism, *The New Republic* editorial did not offer a single constructive word on how to deal with the current impasse facing Soviet Jews—or Pentecostalists, Jehovah's Witnesses, etc. (And, as it turned out, a cultural agreement was signed despite "a torrent of Russian bombs over Afghanistan" and with no "stream of departing Russian Jews"—or anyone else, for that matter.)

Thus the May statement articulating a centrist position is welcome because it artfully navigates between the extremes of unilateral repeal of Jackon-Vanik—a repeal that would almost surely leave Soviet emigration at its current near-zero level—and retention of Jackson-Vanik no matter the Soviet effort to satisfy its terms, an equally unproductive stance.

Indeed, the statement conveys to the Kremlin the now widespread recognition that in 1979, at the peak of emigration, the American Jewish community was slow to acknowledge the outflow, that it might well have recommended implementation of Jackson-Vanik's waiver provision (notwithstanding disturbing internal repression of Jewish activists), and that its position today is more flexible. This is a very important signal, since the Kremlin almost certainly concluded that its effort to soften U.S. public opinion by permitting record-level emigration had failed to achieve its primary goals in 1979—Senate ratification of the SALT II treaty and granting of most-favored-nation status. It is reasonable to conclude that Moscow's decision to curtail emigration followed from its perception of this failure.

But is such a statement, however broad the agreement it reflects and however significant its wording, enough? Obviously not. After all, much as the Soviets may desire a waiver of Jackson-Vanik, whether for purposes of trade advantage or prestige, they have in the meantime learned to live with its restrictions. And though their current economic situation might be improved by reduced tariffs and easier access to U.S. government credits, they are managing without either. Moreover, if private credit with which to finance purchases abroad is made available to them, as seems quite likely, their need for U.S. government credits will diminish.

It would be wise, therefore, for the American Jewish community to avoid single-minded preoccupation with Jackson-Vanik, and to focus as well on the broad range of nonstrategic bilateral ties. What is needed is the formulation of a calibrated set of positive and negative responses to changing Soviet conditions vis-à-vis emigration, which is the principal, though not the only, yardstick used in assessing the Soviet Jewry picture. And the time may yet come when the Soviet Jewry constituency in this country will again have to consider challenging other interest groups concerning their respective agendas with the USSR, just as happened with the business community in the early 1970s.

At the same time, greater effort should be directed at enlisting broader support from both Western European governments and leading political, intellectual, religious, scientific, human rights, and peace figures. Since Moscow has been engaged in a long-term, although thus far rather unsuccessful, effort to wean America's NATO allies from Washington and to capture the high ground in the battle for Western public opinion, such an approach becomes especially important. The thirty-five-nation Vienna Review Conference of the Helsinki Final Act—the successor to the Belgrade and Madrid review conferences— provides a useful immediate target for Western European initiatives.

And it is equally true that the U.S. advocacy movement, which has for years relied on the stalwart support of individuals like Sister Ann Gillen and Bayard Rustin, desperately needs an infusion of new participants drawn from key segments of American society.

Finally, the wild card in any discussion of the future of Soviet Jewry is the state of Israel's relations with the USSR. Admittedly, when Moscow and Tel Aviv maintained diplomatic ties from 1948 to 1967 (with a brief interruption in the early 1950s), there was virtually no Soviet Jewish emigration. Still, were any diplomatic deal between the two to be struck today, it would almost certainly have to contain some provision for emigration. Otherwise, the Israeli government would have great difficulty in selling the arrangement.

In the second half of 1985, a flurry of speculation suggested the possible resumption of ties between Jerusalem and Moscow. There was a meeting between the Israeli and Soviet envoys in Paris in July. This was followed by Prime Minister Peres's publicly expressed desire to establish contact, voiced in the fall at the UN General Assembly session, and a statement by Soviet justice minister Soukharev, in a Geneva press conference in November, that the USSR which "helped in the creation of the Jewish state, was interested in establishing diplomatic relations."

Word began circulating of possible flights from Moscow, via Warsaw or another East European point, to transport Soviet Jewish emigrants directly to Israel. Then there was a report of a meeting between a representative of the Simon Wiesenthal Center and an unnamed Soviet diplomat attached to the Soviet embassy in Washington, during which the latter reportedly spoke of the prospect of full diplomatic relations between Israel and the USRR in February 1986 and large-scale emigration (*New York Times*, Dec. 26, 1985). Further, talks between Israeli and Polish officials in the fall, leading to the reestablishment of low-level diplomatic ties, the first Israeli diplomatic breakthrough in Eastern Europe since 1967, fueled rumors that Hungary and Bulgaria were likely to follow Warsaw's lead. Since none of this would have happened without Moscow's assent, could ties with the USSR be far behind?

Indeed, the announcement on August 4 that the USSR and Israel would hold talks on the establishment of consular ties signals a potentially important new dimension in the bilateral relationship. Though both sides have sought to play down the significance, and progress may be slow, the very fact that formal discussions will be held after nineteen years without diplomatic links, and given the complex web of Soviet-Arab relations, Soviet domestic policy, and East-West ties generally, introduces an intriguing element into the Soviet Jewry picture.

Twenty years ago, only a few visionaries might have foreseen the redemption of the world's third-largest Jewish community; most people had reluctantly written off the possibility of any Jewish future for a community consigned to forced assimilation.

Today, believers can speak proudly of 270,000 Jews enjoying new lives outside the Soviet Union, of the remarkable emergence in the USSR of self-taught Hebrew teachers, of a growing number of mostly young observant Jews, of a spreading national consciousness—all this nearly four generations after the Bolshevik Revolution. Apparently, miracles still can and do happen, aided and abetted by faith, commitment, endurance, and very hard work.

There are times when, wrapped up in our own work on behalf of Soviet Jewry, we lose the capacity to assess the significance of the issue to others. In that connection, it is worth noting Lawrence Elliot's article "Buried Alive: The Plight of Soviet Jews" in the June 1986 issue of *Reader's Digest*. Elliot writes that "Anatoly Shcharansky's walk across Berlin's Glienicke Bridge to freedom on a stinging cold morning last February exhilarated the non-communist world . . . Millions rejoiced; some even hailed his release as proof that freedom was an irrepressible idea. If so, it was an idea whose time had not yet come for the rest of Soviet Jews—and Shcharansky was the first to say so . . . Can we in the West help? . . . Do we have the will? Let your voice be heard. Public opinion can be a vital force—even against the USSR. To make your feelings known about the persecution of Soviet Jews, write to the Soviet Ambassador to the U.S." The full text of the article appeared in a full-page ad in the *New York Times* in June, paid for by *Reader's Digest*, under the banner headline: "Soviet Jews are damned if they do and damned if they don't. You can make a difference."

The circulation of *Reader's Digest* is 50 million.

Andrei Sakharov: A Righteous Gentile
Israel Today
October 10, 1986

Soviet physicist Andrei Sakharov is one of the moral giants of our age. Scientist, Nobel laureate, human-rights crusader, and, since 1980, an internal exile in his own country, Sakharov epitomizes the grandeur and indomitability of the human spirit. The next few months of intensified superpower diplomacy may determine his fate.

Once among the most privileged of Soviet citizens, Sakharov enjoyed all the perquisites accorded the scientific elite. His material well-being and security were assured, his status unquestioned. Yet he abandoned it all to pursue higher goals: world peace, human rights, an end to internal repression. And he has paid a heavy price.

In 1974, while an exchange teacher in the USSR, I had a revealing conversation with a Soviet colleague.

"Sakharov is crazy and should be forcibly placed in a psychiatric hospital," my colleague asserted.

"But why?" I protested. "He is a responsible and decent man."

"Listen," he retorted, "of course he's crazy. After all, he must have known that to challenge the state would land him in lots of trouble, probably force his dismissal from work and place him in prison. Therefore, you see, he's crazy because anyone who would knowingly embark on such a course couldn't possibly be sane."

In 1977 Sakharov's stepdaughter and her family emigrated to the United States. His wife, Elena Bonner, was able to accompany them as far as Rome. Ms. Bonner's devotion to her husband and their joint work in behalf of human rights and world peace impelled her to leave her daughter, son-in-law, grandchildren, and mother in Italy and to return to an unimaginably difficult life in the Soviet Union. Those of us then in Rome working on migration were tremendously moved by Ms. Bonner's seemingly limitless courage and strength.

Since 1980, Sakharov and Elena Bonner have been forced to live in exile in Gorky, a city closed to foreigners. There, cut off from family, friends, and colleagues, under constant surveillance, denied even necessary medical attention, they are prisoners in everything but name.

This year Elena Bonner was permitted to travel to the West for medical care and a family reunion. In May she attended the massive Solidarity Sunday for Soviet Jewry in New York, where Anatoly Shcharansky was welcomed to freedom. Seated alone far from the speaker's platform, she listened intently to Shcharansky's powerful words. What a poignant scene! Shcharansky, the former prisoner of conscience, still savoring the first breaths of freedom; Bonner savoring her last. Shortly after the rally, Elena Bonner said good-bye to her family and to freedom and returned to her husband in Gorky.

Jews owe Andrei Sakharov a special debt of gratitude. Not only has he fought indefatigably for peace and human rights, but also he has been outspoken on behalf of Soviet Jewish emigration, Jewish prisoners of conscience, and a safe and secure Israel.

As early as 1970, Sakharov monitored the trial of the nine Jews and two non-Jews who had sought to divert a plane from Leningrad to Sweden, an incident that sparked world interest and dramatized the plight of those seeking to leave the USSR. The next year, together with the other two members of the Committee on Human Rights, he called on the Kremlin leadership "to end the persecution of repatriates [Soviet Jews seeking to leave for Israel] and to stop violating the right to leave the country."

In September 1973, Sakharov sent a letter to the U.S. Congress supporting the withholding of most-favored-nation trade status until Soviet citizens were given the right to emigrate. "In our country there are tens of thousands of citizens . . . who wish to emigrate and who, with endless difficulties and humiliations, for years and years on end have been struggling to obtain this right." The next year both houses of Congress overwhelmingly passed the historic Jackson-Vanik Amendment linking U.S. trade policy with communist countries' policy on emigration.

In October 1973, two terrorists seized Soviet Jewish hostages in Austria and demanded the closing of the Schoenau camp, the transit site for Soviet Jews proceeding to Israel. Chancellor Kreisky acceded to the demand, provoking outrage from Andrei Sakharov. "It is extremely painful for us to hear that two terrorists could blackmail whole nations on whom we placed our hope," Sakharov wrote. "That is a dreadful thing not only for our Jewish emigrants, but for all men who oppose bondage and terror."

Shortly thereafter, the Yom Kippur War broke out. Reuters reported that, on October 21, two guerrillas claiming to belong to Black September entered Sakharov's Moscow flat, cut his telephone wires and threatened him with reprisals if he did not remain "silent on the Arab-Israeli war and cease active support for Israel."

In 1975, while the UN was considering the infamous "Zionism is racism" resolution, Sakharov warned the world body against sanctioning anti-Semitism. "If this resolution is adopted," he stated, "it can only contribute to anti-Semitic tendencies in many countries, by giving them the appearance of international legality. No less important is that this resolution indirectly denies the lawfulness of the existence of the state of Israel and thereby contradicts the spirit and letter of the most important UN decisions on this question."

Through the years, Sakharov has continued to speak out for the right of emigration and Jewish culture and against the persecution of Jewish activists, including his friend Anatoly Shcharansky. Indeed, in an interview with the *Jerusalem Post* shortly after arriving in Israel, Shcharansky referred to Sakharov as "the conscience of the Soviet Union." And the Knesset, the Weizmann Institute, and other leading Israeli institutions have honored Sakharov.

As the United States and the Soviet Union enter a new round of high-level bilateral diplomacy, the Jewish community and its friends are vigorously mobilizing to press demands for increased Jewish emigration and an end to repression of Jews. Never in recent memory has the situation of Soviet Jews been worse. At the same time, there is an unparalleled opportunity to demonstrate support for Andrei Sakharov and Elena Bonner.

Some have argued that to extend overt Jewish support to the beleaguered couple might only complicate their situation. After all, Sakharov is not Jewish and his wife is half-Jewish, half-Armenian. Could not Jewish support hurt them in the Kremlin's eyes? Frankly, it is hard to imagine their situation being any more difficult than it already is. But more appeals to public officials and international bodies can only strengthen the worldwide campaign on the Sakharovs' behalf.

Still others contend that it would be inappropriate to "mix" the Sakharov case with that of Soviet Jewry. According to this view, Soviet Jewry is a unique issue that must not be confused with human-rights questions. Soviet Jews are not seeking the liberalization of the Soviet state, only their right to repatriation and family reunification. To mix their cause with dissident concerns might damage chances for further emigration. But the Sakharov case is so unique and embodies such overriding moral issues that we must find every appropriate channel to press for an end to their exile.

Could our conscience permit us to do any less?

Notes on the Reagan-Gorbachev Summit
Reykjavik, Iceland
October 11–13, 1986

I have just returned to New York from a truly remarkable three-day visit to Iceland, together with other Jewish activists, to press the Soviet Jewry issue in the context of the Reagan-Gorbachev summit meeting.

Having originally encountered Soviet officials in 1974 as an exchange teacher in Moscow, I was struck by the transformation in appearance and manner of Soviet representatives at the Reykjavik talks. As a group, they were clearly more polished, engaging, and accessible than ever before. This was evidenced by the publicized ways in which they dealt with individual approaches by former Soviet Jews in behalf of their relatives in the USSR, the adroit handling of potentially embarrassing moments at press conferences, and the unprecedented availability of these officials to chat in the lobby and meeting rooms of the Saga Hotel, their base of operations.

If the Soviets are indeed so preoccupied with their public image, and there is considerable evidence to support this claim not only from Reykjavik but from other recent meetings as well, then it surely provides an opportunity for the Soviet Jewry advocacy movement. In fact, one of the major successes of the Reykjavik meetings was the omnipresence of Jewish activists from the United States, Israel, Great Britain, and other Western countries. Although there were advocates for a number of causes, including Hare Krishna, Greenpeace, International Physicians for Prevention of Nuclear War, Peace Bird, and an independent Cyprus, no other group was nearly as well represented nor as effective in generating attention and media coverage as the Soviet Jewry activists. Though not always working in coordinated fashion—what else is new?—these several dozen individuals mounted a largely successful campaign to ensure attention to both the larger questions affecting Soviet Jewry and compelling individual cases.

At the press conference held on October 10 at the International Media Center, American Jewish leaders made an effective case for the Soviet Jewry issue.* Three aspects of the conference, two planned and the third unanticipated, generated particular attention: (a) the presence of members of divided families lent credibility to the event and provided a focus for the journalists to personalize the coverage; (b) the warm words for Iceland and the presentation of a specially selected gift for the Icelandic government offered an important angle for the local press; and (c) the unexpected presentation to [National Conference on Soviet Jewry chairman] Morris Abram of a bouquet of flowers by an Anglican priest from Great Britain, who was dressed in white collar and black suit, aroused the interest of the electronic media.

Unquestionably, these are lessons we need to constantly bear in mind in planning events, for each—the personal angle, the local connection, and the non-Jewish participation—should, when possible, be utilized. In addition, the fact that the Soviets chose to call their own press conference on human rights at the Hotel Saga, at the very same time as ours, underscored yet again their concern over negative publicity regarding the treatment of Jews.

Reassuringly, a number of the American officials present in Reykjavik were well versed in the human rights and Soviet Jewry issues. They included, in addition to the president and secretary of state, Rozanne Ridgway, assistant secretary of state for European and Canadian affairs, who led the working group discussions on bilateral,

*It should be noted that no other private group was given access to the center for a press event.

humanitarian, and regional issues; Thomas W. Simons Jr., deputy assistant secretary of state for European affairs; Mark Parris, director, Office of Soviet Union Affairs; Arthur Hartman, U.S. ambassador to the Soviet Union; Jack Matlock, senior adviser on Soviet affairs at the National Security Council; and Max Kampelman, the chief U.S. arms control negotiator.

President Reagan did present General Secretary Gorbachev with documentation on Soviet Jews and other victims of Soviet human rights abuse and made clear to the Soviet leader that the desire to focus exclusively on arms control issues—to the exclusion of other matters of great importance to the United States—would not succeed. Fuller discussion of the issues was pursued in the working group led by Secretary Ridgway, including reference to a list of 11,000 Soviet Jews barred from emigrating and a proposal for a joint working group on the issue.

The Soviets gave no hint of a willingness to reverse their current restrictive policies. Indeed, it again became clear that they were seeking to define the issue in terms of individual cases rather than broad categories. In so doing, their aim has been to persuade the West that "family reunification has essentially been completed," as Soviet spokesmen have repeatedly and disingenuously asserted, and what remains are a handful of cases that, for security or other reasons, have hitherto not been resolved. It is those cases that, in a carefully orchestrated fashion, are now being given attention.

On a related note, notwithstanding the expressed hope of the Icelandic prime minister that activists would stay away from Reykjavik during the summit, and the attempts by some journalists to convert negotiations by American Jews with the Icelandic government into a major squabble, Iceland proved a genial and hospitable host. Finding itself in a very difficult position at very short notice, it truly fulfilled its responsibilities with grace and efficiency. There is no confrontation between Jews and Iceland.

Indeed, Iceland's history is one of friendship with Israel, world Jewry, and human rights groups. And Icelandic customs officials and police, had they wished, could have created many more difficulties for arriving activists; instead, they chose to permit those who sought entry to do so with an absolute minimum of difficulty, subject only to proof of housing in the country. Also, as the press widely reported, an outdoor prayer service and demonstration in behalf of Soviet Jewry was permitted on October 11. Joining with Iosif Mendelvich and other Jewish activists were approximately sixty Icelandic Christians waving Israeli flags and holding signs supporting the refuseniks. Strong winds, nearly horizontal rain (a must-see Icelandic meteorological phenomenon), and bitter cold did not deter them from the vigil.

I might add that ten of us from the United States were housed by an Icelandic family I had come to know years earlier through the AFS international exchange program. Without their generosity and support, we would not have been admitted, as hotels were solidly booked and entry was forbidden without a prearranged place to stay.

My original positive impression of Iceland, formed during a week-long stay in 1973, was reconfirmed and then some; indeed, it is quite a special country. With a population of only 240,000, it manages to support a thriving economy, extensive cultural life, and all the trappings of a thoroughly modern and cosmopolitan society. Although there is a NATO base at Keflavik, thirty miles from Reykjavik, Iceland itself has no standing army and an unarmed police force (except for an elite fifteen-man Viking squad). Indeed, one of the oft-heard concerns of Icelanders during the superpower summit was that too many armed agents and bodyguards had desecrated the country's nonviolent daily life. Cars, bicycles, and even homes are generally left unlocked, and even young children feel comfortable and safe on the streets alone. The air is unpolluted, thanks in large part to the remarkably extensive geothermal energy sources available within the country. Except for the need to import oil, primarily for motor vehicles (some of which, apropos this report, are purchased from the USSR), the country is energy self-sufficient.

People are friendly, conversant in English, and very polite. Other than a handful of Indochinese refugees and a few Westerners who married Icelanders (e.g., Vladimir Ashkenazy, the pianist, was one who for many years maintained a residence in Reykjavik but now lives in London), the country is made up entirely of an indigenous people fiercely proud of their Viking heritage and rich literary tradition. While many Icelanders have lived and studied overseas, mostly in the United States or Scandinavia, without fail they almost all return to Iceland and remain there.

With an extremely high literacy rate, a pleasant lifestyle that contributes to the longest life expectancy rate for women (and second for men) in the world, a rough but very scenic landscape, no television on Thursdays, and blessed isolation from some of modern society's ills (with the exception of alcoholism, a serious problem), it is easy to understand why Icelanders are so tied to their country.

The Joke(s) of Oppression:
How Soviet Jews Relieve the Pain
Moment
January–February 1987

The secret source of Humor itself is not joy but sorrow. There is no humor in heaven.

—*Mark Twain*

Few Americans realize how vital a role political humor plays as a commentary on society and as an emotional outlet for people behind the Iron Curtain. Deprived of opportunities for self-expression through the ballot box, the press, assembly, or cultural forms, political humor becomes a treasured, if private, means of conveying anger, frustration, or criticism in an often hostile environment.

Soviet Jews, finding themselves unable to live as Jews or to leave the country in substantial numbers, long ago turned to humor to deflate the extraordinary pressures and tensions in their daily lives. In doing so, they have drawn on two long-standing traditions: the anecdotes, vignettes, and stories of Jews in Russia since time immemorial, and the poignant black humor that is so much a feature of life in every communist country.

Shortly after Abram left Kiev for a business trip to Eastern Europe, his friend back home received a telegram from Poland: Greetings from free Warsaw, Abram. A few days later a second telegram, this one from Czechoslovakia, arrived: Greetings from free Prague, Abram. Several more days passed before a third telegram, from Hungary, came: Greetings from free Budapest, Abram. Then followed a long period of silence before the friend in Kiev received a telegram from Israel: Greetings from Jerusalem, free Abram.

Three prison inmates began talking.

"What are you here for?" asked one inmate of another.

"They put me in for beating up some old Jew named Khaimovich."

"And why are you here?" asked the second of the first.

"For having defended some old Jew named Khaimovich in a fight."

"And what were you arrested for?" the third inmate was asked.

"For being Khaimovich."

A class at the Soviet War College.

"Professor, I have a question. How can we, 260 million people, ever rebuff an attack by almost 1 billion Chinese?"

"Easy. Just look at how the 3 million Jews in Israel have handled 100 million Arabs."

"Yes, you're absolutely right. But where are we going to find 3 million Jews to fight the Chinese for us?"

There was a knock at the door of Shapiro's apartment at 3 a.m. He put his head under the pillow and tried to ignore it, but the knocking persisted. Reluctantly, he put on his slippers and robe and went to the front door.

"Who is it?" he asked.

"The postman."

Shapiro opened the door and was promptly set on by five hulking KGB agents.

"Tell us, Shapiro, what is the greatest country in the world?"

"Our homeland, of course."

"And what is the best political system yet invented?"

"Communism."

"And in what country do the workers enjoy real freedom?"

"The Soviet Union."

"Then tell us, Shapiro, why have you applied to emigrate to Israel?"

"Because at least there the postman doesn't wake you up at 3 a.m."

Question: Why are there no Jewish cosmonauts?

Answer: The Soviet authorities are afraid that they would never return.

Khaimovich was called to the OVIR office.

"Khaimovich, I want to know why you have decided to leave the country," said the OVIR official.

"No, no, you've got it all wrong. I don't want to leave; my wife does."

"So divorce and let her emigrate by herself."

"Yes, but . . . it's not quite that simple. It's not only my wife who wants to leave but also her mother."

"What's the problem? Let those bloody Zionists go. We don't need them here, do we Khaimovich?"

"Yes, well . . . but then there is also my wife's brother's family and then there are my wife's in-laws and their other children."

"So, they'll go, and you and I will remain to build communism."

"But there's a problem."

"What?"

"They can't leave without me. I'm the only Jew among them."

"Shapiro, we know you have a brother abroad," said the KGB official.

"I do not."

"Don't lie to us, Shapiro. We even have these letters from him addressed to you and postmarked Jerusalem."

"Ah, but you see, it's not he who is abroad, it is I!"

To show the world the true equalitarian spirit of the Soviet Union, an orchestra of representatives of various nationalities was organized. Each member was then introduced to the foreign press corps in Moscow by the conductor, Ivanov.

"This is Fyodorov the Russian," he began. "And this is Murzhenko the Ukrainian, Saroyan the Armenian, and Chikvili the Georgian. And here is Rabinovich the violinist."

Glasnost and the Jews
The Washington Report
March 16, 1987

Each day brings new surprises under Mikhail Gorbachev's glasnost campaign: the return of Sakharov to Moscow; the release of political prisoners; criticism of the KGB; shakeups in the economy; and most recently, the turnaround on medium-range missiles in Europe. These efforts should not be dismissed simply as cosmetic changes aimed at exploiting Western gullibility. But neither do they necessarily herald the outbreak of Western-style democracy.

Until now, the new Soviet thrust has only minimally affected the country's long-suffering Jews. During the first two years of Gorbachev's regime, emigration averaged fewer than 100 per month; and nearly half of all the Jewish prisoners of conscience were sentenced after his accession to power. But the release of a few Jewish prisoners and recurring reports that 11,000 long-term refusenik cases are under review have raised hopes for an upturn in emigration as well.

In January, Samuil Zivs, the Soviet Anti-Zionist Committee spokesman, told talk-show host Phil Donahue that 500 exit visas had been issued to Soviet Jews that month. Gennady Gerasimov, the Foreign Ministry spokesman, used the same figure in talks with reporters in Moscow; and *U.S. News and World Report* (Mar. 2) has predicted the departure of several thousand Soviet Jews in connection with an upcoming visit to Moscow by some Western Jewish leaders. Many believe that with the Geneva arms talks at a critical stage, Moscow cannot afford to renege on public statements by authoritative officials.

Normally, those granted exit visas in January would begin to come out by late February. Indeed, the February emigration figure of 246 represents an increase over January's 98. Whether this presages a trend remains to be seen. Even if emigration increases in the coming months, it is feared that the total allowed out will be sharply limited. The new, narrow definition of family reunification may reduce to only 30–40,000 those Jews considered eligible to leave for Israel or other countries. Nor is there any sign that a time limit will be set on refusals for security grounds. Thus, tens of thousands of Soviet Jews who do not have spouses, siblings, parents, or children abroad must wait at least a few more months to see how the new decree affects their chances of leaving.

A major reason for the emigration cuts in the 1980s, many believe, was Soviet disappointment at the U.S. failure to grant the Kremlin most-favored-nation (MFN) trade status—as a waiver permitted by the Jackson-Vanik amendment—despite the record number allowed out in 1979. Now the American Jewish community is searching for responses that would acknowledge improvements and provide incentives for further advances without overreacting to short-lived or cosmetic steps—or moving forward too hastily under pressure from U.S. business and trade groups.

A wild card in any discussion of Soviet Jewry is the relationship between the Soviet Union and Israel. Diplomatic relations between the two countries were broken off by the Kremlin after the Six-Day War— a move that Soviet officials privately acknowledge was a mistake, because it relegated Moscow to the sidelines for twenty years while the United States enhanced its position as the key player in the Middle East. Jerusalem is eager to renew those ties, both in the hope that this would lead to increased Soviet Jewish emigration and also because it might make possible direct flights of Soviet emigrants to Israel and reduce the large number (80 percent in some months) who opt to go to other Western countries.

With so many forces at play, it is hard to quarrel with Samuel Goldwyn's wise counsel: "Never prophesy, especially about the future." But many experts on East-West relations feel that possibly— *just possibly*—there are enough winds of change blowing for Soviet Jews to feel a beneficial breeze.

Soviet Jewry at the Crossroads
Washington Jewish Week
September 10, 1987

The Soviet Jewry issue is entering its most critical phase since the heated discussion in 1979 over the proper response to record emigration levels that year. Indeed, the coming months are filled with potentially significant opportunities to achieve progress. At the same time, there are serious dangers and high risk. The unfolding of this complex situation could determine Soviet Jewry's fate for years to come.

At first glance, the Soviet Jewry news is quite encouraging. The expected departure of former prisoners of conscience Josef Begun and Viktor Brailovsky and some other high-profile cases is most welcome, though the length and harshness of their detention will not be easily forgotten. The only known remaining Jewish prisoner, Alexei Magarik, is expected to be released from labor camp this month. Moreover, after years of decline and stagnation in the emigration numbers, there has been a marked increase in recent months. A few visible gestures in the religious and cultural fields have been made; others have been promised. And Soviet officials certainly seem more approachable by Westerners to discuss the Soviet Jewry question than in the past.

Yet, at the same time and with much less attention, the exit numbers have stabilized at about 800 per month. Of the lucky ones, approximately 80 percent or more are refuseniks. Now only those with first-degree relatives abroad—just a fraction of those who seek to leave—are able even to submit new applications, much less be assured of success. The fear among Soviet Jewry observers is that the recent increase in the exit rate is not really a harbinger of better times, but rather a belated Kremlin effort to rid the country of the hard-core refuseniks, simultaneously removing a long-standing public relations stigma and stripping the national Jewish movement of its leadership. Once these refuseniks are out, the thinking goes, the gates may slam shut to all but those with first-degree relatives abroad. The aim is to extinguish the hopes of those seeking to join more distant relatives in the West or those who assert their basic right to return to the historic homeland of the Jewish people, Israel. After all, if these Soviet Jews cannot even apply to leave, perhaps they will eventually opt to "reintegrate" (i.e., assimilate) into Soviet society.

Many refuseniks, including such well-known figures as Ida Nudel, Alexander Lerner, Yuli Kosharovsky, and Naum Meiman, continue to wait. At best, like Begun and Brailovsky, their release will be linked to creating a more favorable climate around high-level superpower talks. Countless others, less well known but nonetheless victims of the same repressive and arbitrary system, continue to be faced with repeated denials of their visa applications.

Concern increases about the growing and whimsical use of secrecy as a justification for rejecting exit requests. And on another ominous note, the emergence in the USSR of unchecked chauvinistic, anti-Semitic Russian groups like Pamyat (Memory) arouses anxiety.

Gradually, with fits and starts, the three key factors that can, at least in theory, directly benefit Soviet Jewry are moving in the right direction. First, a strong ruler with consolidated power, unafraid of making bold decisions, has emerged in the Kremlin. Second, Soviet-American relations are warming and bilateral contact points in virtually every official and private field are burgeoning. Third, Gorbachev, in acting decisively to reestablish Moscow as a key actor in the Middle East, has begun to reciprocate Israel's long-standing desire for improved ties, though the future of Soviet-Israeli ties remains particularly fraught with uncertainty. (A Peres-Shevardnadze meeting is expected in connection with the UN General Assembly's opening later this month.)

The next several months of high-level superpower talks and summitry provide the United States with an unprecedented opportunity to press yet again the importance of Soviet Jewry on the bilateral agenda.

Now is the time for the Soviet Jewry movement and its many friends around the world to be heard from. Planned demonstrations, petitions, vigils, and letter-writing campaigns require large-scale participation. The message should be clear. Of course, supporters of Soviet Jewry welcome those steps that reduce global tension and increase mutual understanding. At the same time, Soviet Jews in large numbers must be included among the beneficiaries of improving East-West relations. Moscow's recent steps, designed to defuse the Soviet Jewry issue and mute criticism of its practices in key Western sectors, remain inadequate, though it would be foolish to dismiss them entirely.

What is needed is a *regularized* procedure in the USSR leading to *substantial* and *sustained* emigration. In response to such a Soviet move, the mainstream Soviet Jewry movement has already made abundantly clear its readiness to advocate appropriate reciprocity.

But, regrettably, no one ought to take for granted that Soviet Jews will, willy-nilly, benefit in large numbers from the current improved climate or future superpower deals. Moreover, Gorbachev's shrewdness and ability to impact on Western public opinion cannot be overlooked. Consequently, the challenge becomes increasingly daunting to interpret Soviet Jewry's pressing needs to a West ever more dazzled by the admittedly profound changes occurring in the USSR and understandably anxious for improved superpower ties, and to pursue a political strategy that gives the Kremlin a genuine stake in improving its record on Soviet Jewry.

The next several months are likely to place demands on friends of Soviet Jewry as almost never before; in the balance lies the fate of many Jews. The time to act is now.

Peace, Human Rights Cannot Be Separated
USA Today
November 2, 1987

The December 7 [Reagan-Gorbachev] summit may prove to be an historic step in reducing global tensions and promoting high-level dialogue between the superpowers. The anticipated signing of the first-ever nuclear arms reduction agreement has understandably been hailed as an important step toward nuclear containment.

It is important to point out, however, as the Soviet-U.S. announcement indicated, that the meeting will also address other compelling matters, including "human rights and humanitarian issues."

Why human rights? Because our government has rightfully insisted that human rights is not simply an internal matter, as the Kremlin contends, but a legitimate subject of international discussion. Civil and political liberties are enshrined in international agreements to which Moscow is signatory.

Moreover, our own country's uniqueness is rooted in its dedication to democracy, freedom, and the rights of the individual. As President Carter said in his farewell address to the nation in 1981: "America did not invent human rights. . . . Human rights invented America."

If the Kremlin truly seeks fundamental improvement in its relations with the United States and an increase in mutual trust between the two countries, it can well demonstrate its sincerity by permitting Jews and others who seek to emigrate from the USSR to do so, and by according those who stay genuine religious and cultural freedom.

Until now, Gorbachev's strategy toward the 2 million Soviet Jews, despite a number of well-publicized gestures largely benefiting individuals, has involved no basic changes, even within the limited liberalization provided by glasnost.

Yes, there has been an increase in emigration to about 800 per month, but this must be compared to the 1979 figure of more than 4,000 per month. A number of well-known prisoners of conscience and refuseniks have been released, shrewdly staggered to maximize favorable publicity for the Kremlin. Such minimal steps, while surely welcome, must not deflect our attention from the tens of thousands of other Soviet Jews who continue to be prevented from leaving by unreasonable restrictions and an arbitrary and capricious bureaucracy.

These Jews seek to exercise a fundamental freedom that we take for granted—the right to choose our place of residence and to be masters of our own destiny. On December 6, a day before the summit, a mass mobilization will take place in Washington. Jews and Christians, Democrats and Republicans, blacks and whites, public officials and private citizens will gather in the capital to remind the Soviet leader that, for Americans, peace and human rights are indivisible.

A Significant Moment in History
Washington Jewish Week
November 26, 1987

There come moments when, as Jews, it's time for each of us to stand up and be counted, when we must seek to take our history into our own hands. Such a moment will take place in the nation's capital on Sunday, December 6. On the eve of General Secretary Mikhail Gorbachev's first visit to the United States, thousands of Jews, joined by many non-Jewish friends, will mass together in Washington to express solidarity with Jews in the USSR.

Looking back, the rally for European Jewry at Madison Square Garden in December 1940 was one of those moments. So, too, were May 1948—the birth of Israel; June 1967—the Six-Day War; October 1973—the Yom Kippur War; and November 1984—Operation Moses. Each was a unique moment in Jewish history. Each demanded our attention. Each challenged us to make a snap decision—to become a participant or remain a bystander. Each, in hindsight, perhaps caused us to judge ourselves. Did we recognize the significance of the event at the time? Did we respond immediately? Did we do all that we could to mobilize interest and support from those around us?

By our presence in Washington on December 6, we will have an unparalleled opportunity to demonstrate for Soviet Jewry, for the world's third largest Jewish community, for the fate of 15 percent of our collective selves.

The world will be watching. Thousands of journalists from around the globe will descend on Washington for the summit. Much of their attention will doubtless be directed at our mobilization, and the stories they file will be transmitted to dozens of nations. But nowhere will the reports be more closely monitored than in the Soviet Union. If the Kremlin had its choice, there would be no demonstration in Washington. It's no secret that Soviet leaders are deeply worried about the prospect of a rally for Soviet Jewry, just as they were concerned about planned demonstrations in France at the time of Gorbachev's visit there in October 1985. The Kremlin wishes our movement would fizzle and die. On the other hand, Soviet Jews will be eagerly awaiting reports of the rally, for they rightly believe that such public manifestations represent their lifeline. Were it not for Western support, their cause would, in all likelihood, have been suppressed long ago.

The Soviet Jewry advocacy movement has been one of the most successful nonviolent, human rights movements in modern history. As a result, nearly 300,000 Soviet Jews today live in freedom and dignity in Israel and other countries. But many others wait.

Our efforts over two decades have truly had an impact. And they can continue to make a difference if only we believe in our own ability to affect the course of events.

Join us on December 6. Join Vice President George Bush. Join Ida Nudel, Natan Shcharansky, Vladimir Slepak, Yuli Edelshtein, and other courageous former prisoners of conscience and refuseniks coming from Israel. Join thousands of Jews traveling by regularly scheduled and charter planes, buses and trains from across the country. Join Catholic and Protestant clergy, labor leaders, and black and Hispanic friends. Join the leaders of Congress and state and local officials. Join hundreds of Canadians, including as many as thirty members of parliament. Join Nobel laureate Elie Wiesel. Join us for the largest demonstration in behalf of a Jewish cause in Washington's history. And bring your children and grandchildren. We may not be able to promise good weather, but we do guarantee you a moment in history.

Sending a Message
Washington Times
December 3, 1987

As President Ronald Reagan and General Secretary Mikhail Gorbachev approach their third summit meeting, the Soviet leader has been forced to realize that his country's insistence that the human rights of Soviet Jews and others are an internal issue only simply cannot be sustained.

Unyielding U.S. emphasis on balanced progress in all the key sectors of the superpower relationship, including arms control and human rights, has prevailed. The joint October 30 communiqué announcing the upcoming summit and its agenda confirms this striking development.

There should be no misunderstanding. Support for human rights in the USSR need not in any way suggest opposition to an arms reduction accord. An intermediate-range nuclear forces agreement that serves America's security interests and contributes to a more peaceful world will benefit Americans and Russians alike. But there remains the lingering question of whether Moscow can be trusted to keep its word on this or any other agreement. Improved technology and agreement on short-notice inspections may largely address the verification problem, but the human factor remains.

The Kremlin can do a great deal to enhance its credibility by fulfilling other international obligations to which it has committed itself. Among the most important of those are the Helsinki Accords, which provide for a broad range of human rights, including the right of family reunification. Another is Article XIII of the Universal Declaration of Human Rights, which affirms that "everyone has the right to leave any country, including his own." Past Soviet compliance in these areas has been uneven at best, to say the least, undermining American's trust in the value of the Soviet word.

One of the most pressing human rights questions today remains the fate of 2 million Soviet Jews. Admittedly, there has been progress on permission to emigrate for the long-standing refusenik cases, as well as a few notable steps in the religious and cultural spheres in recent months. Such progress is welcome. Still, deep-rooted problems remain. It is vital that these problems be brought to public attention at this time.

On December 6, one day prior to the summit meeting, concerned citizens from around the country will gather in Washington for a mass mobilization to register support for the rights of Soviet Jews to emigrate if they so wish, or to continue to live in the USSR in dignity and with their group identity intact. Jewish and non-Jewish demonstrators will raise several questions:

- Why has one-sixth of the world's Jewish population been subjected over decades to a policy of spiritual extinction?
- Why is Jewish emigration, which numbered more than 4,000 a month in 1979, fewer than 1,000 a month this year?
- Why is the teaching and study of Hebrew virtually impossible?
- Why is there not a single rabbinic seminary to serve the world's third-largest Jewish community?
- And why do Soviet Jews face endless hurdles, including narrow restrictions on the definition of family reunification and capricious use of secrecy as grounds for refusal, when they seek to establish new lives in Israel and other countries?

We Americans take great pride in what our government's ongoing effort on behalf of Soviet Jews and other victims of human-rights abuse has achieved—nearly 300,000 Soviet Jews now live in Israel and the United States. Many Soviet Armenians have also been reunited with family members in this country. And courageous Soviet dissidents have long found American support to be their oxygen supply.

The message to Kremlin leaders of the mass mobilization in Washington is that Soviet treatment of its own citizens will be an important measure of its sincerity in the entire bilateral arena. It is a message we trust Mr. Reagan will once again stress in his discussions with Mr. Gorbachev the next day.

The Nation Has Spoken
Washington Jewish Week
December 10, 1987

For weeks prior to the historic Freedom Sunday rally, calls had been coming from the press. One question was a constant: How many people are you expecting? Frankly, because none of the organizers could be certain, we coyly asserted only that it would be the largest ever organized by the Jewish community in Washington. For normally inquisitive reporters, it was surprising how few asked what the previous record was. Had they inquired, they would have been shocked to learn that the figure was a small one. Only 12–14,000 demonstrators greeted Leonid Brezhnev in 1973. Based on reports from around the country of scheduled and chartered planes and buses, by the last week of November we could more boldly respond that "tens of thousands" were likely to attend.

Why were we so cautious? Obviously, we did not want to overestimate numbers, then be proved wrong. But we also wondered how much could be accomplished with only thirty-seven days' notice. And the uncertainty of December weather concerned us. Moreover, lurking in the back of everyone's mind was the hovering jinx of past poorly attended Jewish demonstrations in the nation's capital. Finally, there was the question of whether, in these politically complex times, people would understand both the opportunity of the moment and the urgency of the situation. Might we be perceived as spoilers of the summit? Could we successfully walk the tightrope between arms control and human rights?

The answer is in. The response was beyond our wildest expectations—250,000 participants. There are several reasons, I believe, why people came in such large numbers.

- First and foremost, the post-Holocaust legacy played a central role. People again and again indicated that they wanted to demonstrate their understanding of the lessons of history. They wanted to be counted among those who acted, not among those who stood by. And they wanted their children to be present, able to say in ten or twenty years that they had been at the Washington rally.
- Many felt a special kinship with Jews from that great wellspring of American Jewish life, Russia.
- Virtually every Jewish institution and leader sent out a clear and constant call. Freedom Sunday was *the* Jewish obligation of the year, perhaps of the decade. Countless rabbis, Jewish agencies, and Anglo-Jewish newspapers (most notably the *Washington Jewish Week*) reinforced this unmistakable message.
- People also participated because they felt that there truly might be a chance to affect events in this period of improving Soviet-American relations, notwithstanding the bilateral twists and turns, given a bold Soviet leader in charge in Moscow. Today was no longer the icy period of the early 1980s.
- The Washington area Jewish community, the key to a successful event, responded magnificently to the mobilization, forever putting to rest the notion that ours is an impossible community to move.

Freedom Sunday—December 6, 1987—will enter the history books as a remarkable demonstration of our collective concern for our brothers and sisters, and of the extraordinary support that leaders of every key sector of American life, many of whom graced the stage, have given to this effort.

Will our voices be heard? In Soviet Jewish homes they already have, thanks to live broadcasting of the demonstration by the Voice of

America Russian Service. In Washington, the rally significantly strengthens our country's position in human rights discussions with the Soviets. And in the Kremlin? We will have to wait and see, but one thing is certain. Silence has never proved a cure for a people in need.

"Did You Hear . . .?"
Washington Talk
The New York Times
May 24, 1988

David A. Harris, Washington representative of the American Jewish Committee, is doing his part to humor those traveling with President Reagan to the Moscow summit. He has sent copies of his book, *The Jokes of Oppression: The Humor of Soviet Jews*, to President Reagan, Secretary of State George Shultz, and the principal correspondents who will be accompanying the president.

The jokes were collected over a ten-year period by Mr. Harris and his coauthor, Izrail Rabinovich, a Soviet émigré now with the Defense Language Institute in Monterey, California, from Soviet Jews living in the Soviet Union, Israel, the United States, and Western Europe.

President Reagan is known to collect jokes but he may not find these suited to his meetings with Mikhail S. Gorbachev. Mr. Harris expressed the hope that, if nothing else, the book will provide "some appropriate light reading for a long plane ride."

Recent Soviet Jewish Émigrés: Unpredictable Soviet Behavior
Restrains Others from Leaving
Washington Jewish Week
May 26, 1988

Earlier this month, I spent five days in Rome conducting individual interviews with dozens of recently emigrated Soviet Jews en route to new countries of resettlement. The information gathered was submitted to the State Department, whose assistant secretary of state for human rights had suggested the fact-finding visit. The interviewees came from Leningrad and Lvov, Riga and Ryazan, Moscow and Minsk, and a half dozen other cities. Half had been refuseniks, the other half first-time applicants.

The purpose of these meetings was to gain a better understanding both of the nationwide emigration picture and the current state of internal Jewish life under Gorbachev in the era of glasnost and perestroika.

Clearly, the Soviet Jewish community increasingly is mindful of recent steps to liberalize the emigration process, but uncertain whether the changes are temporary or long-term. Many of those with whom I spoke, fearful that the easing up would prove short-lived, had rushed to submit their exit applications. But they reported that many friends, relatives, and colleagues had hesitated to file an application for fear that the Soviets suddenly would change the rules, thereby thrusting them into the unsought role of refuseniks.

As they explained to me, this group is still traumatized by the 1979 experience. A record number of people emigrated that year, 51,000. But less well known, a large number of refuseniks also emerged during that period, only a small percentage of whom became activists. People who applied late in the year became victims of bureaucratic measures introduced to stem the tide of Jewish emigrants. This generation of refuseniks, turned down for such ambiguous yet catch-all reasons as "no reason for you to leave," "absence of family reasons for departure," and "state interests," was to be consigned to nearly a decade of refusenik existence.

More recently, the Kremlin again turned the tables on would-be emigrants. In the fall of 1987, OVIR, the Soviet agency handling exit applications, finally began to interpret liberally the definition of family reunification, thereby including not only those with parents, children, siblings, and spouses abroad but also other relatives. However, in January, they suddenly narrowed the definition, thus preventing many from submitting applications. Yet, in February, OVIR once again relaxed the definition of family reunification.

Time and again, my interviewees referred to this inconsistent and unpredictable Soviet behavior as a force that restrained Soviet Jews from trying to leave.

People cited two other principal barriers to emigration: the continued denial of visas based on alleged possession of state secrets, and the requirement that all applicants, regardless of age, receive formal permission from their parents, including verification of the absence of outstanding financial obligations between them. The latter sometimes is used by parents, irrespective of financial realities, to prevent their children's emigration.

With these important exceptions, the news on the emigration front was moderately encouraging. In a seemingly remarkable transformation, officials of OVIR, known to hundreds of thousands of Soviet Jews over the years for unmatched surliness and short tempers, now have become correct, at times even cordial, in their dealings with Jewish applicants. And *vyzovs*, the affidavits from Israel essential to initiate the application process, are being delivered to Jewish homes with greater frequency, a far cry from previous Soviet practice. Most Soviet Jews also report that the very application procedure, hitherto replete with endless documentation, is being simplified.

To be sure, the interviewees noted, Soviet practices continue to vary from city to city. In Odessa, some families with draft-age sons have encountered particular difficulties. In Tashkent, *vyzovs* reportedly were being delivered irregularly and the processing time for applications was three months or more. In Vilnius, on the other hand, applications now take four to six weeks to be reviewed.

On the domestic front, virtually all the interviewees agreed on several points:

(1) While glasnost and perestroika have brought an easing of restraints on intellectual life, they have not led to any essential change in official attitudes toward Jews. Jews continue to complain about discrimination in employment, promotion practices, and admittance to universities.

(2) Some superficial changes have occurred in the sphere of Jewish cultural life—a play here, a musical ensemble there—but no fundamental shift has been noted in attitudes toward religion, culture, and Hebrew language.

(3) Nearly universal concern was expressed about the emergence of Pamyat, a highly nationalist, xenophobic, and anti-Semitic organiza-

tion that has surfaced in the liberalized era of glasnost. Soviet Jews likened Pamyat to the anti-Semitic Black Hundreds in czarist times, and voiced fear about its potential for scapegoating and violence. Moreover, Soviet Jews were skeptical of Kremlin claims that it is a private organization, that is, simply an outgrowth of democratization. In fact, the interviewees claimed that Pamyat could not function effectively in Soviet society without an official wink and a nod.

(4) No one with whom I spoke was betting on Gorbachev's long-term future. They cited too much resistance in the bureaucracy and too much trampling on vested interests, and, as a result, argued that today's window of opportunity for Jews and others to emigrate should be pursued with the utmost vigor.

Just before I left Rome, one young Jew from Moscow wearing a button from the [December 6] Freedom Sunday for Soviet Jewry rally approached me. "Were you at the demonstration [in Washington]?" he asked, pointing to the button. "Yes," I replied. "I was with all of you in spirit that day," he beamed, "and next time there's a march I'll be with you in person."

A particularly nice thought on which to end my visit.

The "Dropout" Controversy: More Questions Than Answers
Forward
August 19, 1988

There are few more highly contentious—or more complex—issues in Israel-Diaspora life than what has been termed the Soviet Jewry dropout question. Over the years, this issue has aroused passionate debate, rivaled only by the "Who is a Jew" issue. Recently, the debate has intensified. Faced with a dropout rate of nearly 90 percent, the Israeli government has developed a preliminary plan, not the first since this problem initially erupted in the mid-1970s, to try and increase Soviet Jewish aliyah. Israeli commentators, former refuseniks, American Jewish spokesmen, U.S. columnists, and editorial boards from Seattle to Philadelphia already have joined the debate.

Rumors concerning the plan and the future abound, but there are many more questions than answers, and it is not yet certain whether any significant changes will, in the end, result. What is clear is that in June the Israeli cabinet endorsed a "direct flight" option that would seek to bypass Vienna and channel Soviet Jews to Israel through Romania, the only East European country with full diplomatic ties with Jerusalem. Such a plan would deny Soviet Jews the chance to fly to Vienna and then "dropout."

Soviet cooperation is needed if the Israeli plan of bringing more Soviet Jews to Israel is to work. The support of the U.S., Dutch, Austrian, and Romanian governments, and assent from the American Jewish community, are also required, not to speak of agreement from Soviet Jews themselves who, after all, are the objects of these efforts.

It's worth looking briefly at each of these important players.

(1) *Soviet Union:* Will the Soviets go along with the Israeli move? For the Israeli plan truly to succeed—and that means both an end to the "abuse" of Israeli visas used as no more than exit documents, as well as, much more importantly, an increase in immigration to Israel—Moscow must cooperate in ensuring that Soviet Jews with Israeli documents fly either directly to Israel, which is currently impossible, or via East Europe, where it presumably would be impossible to dropout. As long as Moscow permits Soviet Jews to exit to a Western transit point—i.e., Vienna—the dropout phenomenon will continue. But is it in Moscow's interests to accede to the Israeli desire? The Kremlin knows both that the United States supports freedom of choice and that Arab nations are hostile to greater Soviet Jewish migration to Israel. Some Soviet Jews have speculated that the Kremlin might agree to the Israeli plan only if it determined that the end result would be fewer Soviet Jews seeking to leave than under the current system.

Moscow's cooperation also is needed in another area: An Israeli diplomatic team shortly will obtain entry visas and travel to Moscow, thereby mirroring the presence since 1987 of a Soviet diplomatic contingent in Israel. What will the Israelis' role be in Moscow? Will they be permitted to replace the Dutch—Israel's representative in the USSR since 1967—and issue visas? Soviet officials have stated that the Israelis would not be allowed to do so. In that case, an arrangement between Jerusalem and The Hague is needed. Such an agreement is possible but not certain.

(2) *United States:* The United States has traditionally supported freedom of choice for Soviet Jews and therefore has opposed any Israeli move to compromise that principle. But U.S. cooperation is essential for the Israeli plan to work. For example, Israel's position would be undermined if the United States broadly interpreted a proposed change in regulations on asylum, drafted in April by the Immigration and Naturalization Service. This change could have the practical effect of redefining Soviet Jews arriving in Israel as eligible for priority admittance to the United States as refugees. Such a step of defining these Jews in the Jewish state as refugees would raise profound moral and political questions. However, Secretary of State Shultz has not yet indicated his views on such a regulations change. To some degree, Shultz is likely to be guided on this and related issues by the views of the American Jewish community.

The United States has still another option that would undermine the Israeli position: The United States could press the Kremlin to permit Soviet Jews to depart for Western transit points even if their documents indicated Bucharest as the first destination point, and provide assurances to, say, Austria that Soviet immigrants arriving in Vienna would be offered resettlement in the United States.

Finally, the United States also could press the Kremlin for a genuine two-track policy. Those who want to go to Israel would leave via Bucharest; those seeking U.S. resettlement would apply for a visa at the American embassy in Moscow. Indeed, the two-track concept is often cited in the ongoing debate as a workable compromise, and well it might be. But, if the Soviets were to relax further their emigration policy and permit even those Jews without immediate family in the United States to apply for an American visa, no increase in aliyah would result.

(3) *Netherlands:* As noted earlier, unless the Israeli team in Moscow is permitted to issue visas, the Dutch will continue to play a central role. They have supported freedom of choice and have indicated some displeasure with the Israeli plan to reroute emigrants through Bucharest. If there is to be a shared diplomatic arrangement in Moscow, will the Dutch fully cooperate to help implement the Israeli plan? The issue was on the agenda for the bilateral talks that took place

during the Dutch prime minister's recent visit to Israel, but nothing is yet known of the outcome.

(4) *Austria:* From the Israeli viewpoint, Austria could play a spoiler's role. If the Kremlin should prove indifferent to transit points, thereby permitting Soviet Jews to purchase tickets for Vienna, the way station for the past twenty years, the Israeli goal would be sabotaged once again. Austria has adamantly resisted past Israeli efforts to bring more Soviet Jews to Israel via Vienna while denying them resettlement opportunities elsewhere.

(5) *Romania:* Bucharest is the least of Israel's concerns. The iconoclastic Warsaw Pact nation presumably would stand to benefit (financially) from the Israeli plan. And with an Israeli embassy in Bucharest and direct air links between Bucharest and Tel Aviv, logistics would be quite easy.

(6) *American Jewry:* The vast majority of American Jews have supported Soviet Jewish immigration to Israel as essential to the well-being of the Jewish state, but most American Jews also have endorsed the principle of freedom of choice. On June 8, eleven major national Jewish agencies expressed support for the direct flights concept. However, several, including the American Jewish Committee, based this support on the existence of a genuine two-track policy that offers Soviet Jews freedom of choice in Moscow. It is uncertain at this point whether such a two-track policy is already in effect, even with the recently announced resumption of the issuance of some U.S. entry visas in Moscow. (The entry visas had been suspended due to a shortage of funds.) Unlike the Armenians who have been leaving the Soviet Union directly for the United States in large numbers, Jews who apply for a U.S. visa are subjected to a strict interpretation of Soviet emigration policy concerning family reunification. Would American Jews support the Israeli plan if Soviet Jews had only limited opportunity to leave the USSR for the United States?

(7) *Soviet Jews:* Here lies the biggest question mark of all. No one can accurately predict how Soviet Jews would react to an Israeli plan to bring more of them to Israel. And if more do not land at Ben-Gurion Airport with the intention of permanently resettling in Israel, then what has been the point of the whole exercise? If it all only proves an effort

to restore the dignity of the Israeli visa by ending its abuse, it certainly will have come at a high price—tensions between Jerusalem, Washington, and other governments; between Israel and segments of American Jewry; and between Israel and those Soviet Jews who will feel that Israel sought to deny them their freedom of choice. But, if the net result is a significant boost in immigration, Israeli officials understandably will deem the effort a success.

The jury is still out on whether the plan will ever effectively be implemented and, if so, if it actually will shift the emigration flow toward Israel. What is not in doubt is that the future direction of Soviet Jewish emigration is one of the most discussed and intriguing questions in Jewish life today.

Challenges Facing the Soviet Jewry Movement
Washington Jewish Week
October 20, 1988

While there's finally some good news for a change on the Soviet Jewry front, including increased emigration numbers, significant challenges remain for activists.

Advocacy: Long-term refuseniks remain; a second generation of refuseniks has emerged; thorny bureaucratic rules too often persist; restrictions on Hebrew continue; and the specter of anti-Semitism, generated particularly by nationalist groups such as Pamyat, has risen. While most of the best known refuseniks and those prisoners whose plight came to symbolize the larger movement have exited, tens of thousands of Soviet Jews, perhaps many more, are seriously considering emigration today.

Unless we continue to make our voices heard, there is no guarantee the gates will remain open. The Kremlin's decision to permit greater emigration was a carefully calculated acknowledgment of the priority the issue is accorded in the West's dealings with Moscow. Our challenge will be to maintain Soviet Jewry as a priority matter on the West's conscience and, more practically, on its political agenda.

Neshira: The controversy over the "dropout" phenomenon persists.

The stakes for Israel have grown much higher as the emigration rate increases and the ratio of Soviet Jews who resettle in countries other than Israel reaches 85–90 percent. A workable compromise must be found or else, to the amusement of the Kremlin, American Jews and Israel will be at each other's throats. The best answer to date is to press for a two-track solution: Those Soviet Jews who want to travel to Israel would do so on Israeli visas, while those who seek resettlement in the United States would exit on U.S., not Israeli, visas. The United States has pressed the Soviets in the most recent Shultz-Shevardnadze talks to ease restrictions on direct emigration to the United States. Such a plan would end the "abuse" of Israeli visas. Still, it would not in and of itself increase aliyah. Consequently, American Jews must consider what further steps they can take to assist Israel in the areas of *hasbarah* (information) in the USSR and *klitah* (absorption) in Israel that would help make it a more appealing destination.

Numbers and Dollars: The United States establishes annual overall and regional ceilings for refugee admissions. If the current emigration trend continues, there simply will not be sufficient slots available for the Soviet and East European region in this fiscal year (Oct. 1, 1988–Sept. 30, 1989) to permit the entry of those Soviet Jews who seek to resettle in this country. To overcome this, the American Jewish community will probably have to urge the government to allocate additional emergency slots. That's cumbersome, though not necessarily an impossible task. What will be still more complicated is finding additional federal dollars to assist in processing and resettling those additional Soviet Jews not currently provided for in the budget. Given the federal budgetary crunch, that may not be easy.

In response, the government might seek to shift an increasing share of the cost of the refugee movement onto the private sector. However, the heightened numbers of arriving Soviet Jews will present a significant financial challenge for the Jewish federations in the United States as it is.

Integration: One hundred thousand Soviet Jews already have resettled in the United States, with more on the way. Federations and their partners have worked magnificently to ensure a speedy adjustment. As an American immigration story, Soviet Jews have been a resounding success; however, as a Jewish immigration story, the results have been decidedly mixed. The reasons are complex, rooted largely in the lingering impact of the decades-long separation of the vast majority of Soviet Jews in the USSR from any vestige of Jewish culture or religion. The American Jewish community must consider additional outreach efforts, especially to those Soviet Jews who have now been here for several years and who, having solved most of their basic problems of language, education, jobs, housing, and cultural adaptation, might be more open to Jewish communal involvement.

How many of us count Soviet Jews among our friends? How many Soviet Jews are on the membership lists of the Jewish organizations to which we belong? The challenge of integration does not belong to any one agency alone; it is our collective responsibility. What a sad irony it would be if history recorded that the American Jewish community expended such extraordinary efforts to help secure the release of hundreds of thousands of Soviet Jews, only to see too many quickly disappear into the American melting pot.

Serious Error
Baltimore Jewish Times
December 30, 1988

Micah Naftalin discussed the disturbing denial by the Immigration and Naturalization Service of refugee status for some Soviet Jews on the grounds that INS did not consider that they had proved a well-founded fear of persecution (Dec. 2).

Compelling as this issue is, Naftalin makes a serious error in comparing the situation, if only by implication, with the U.S. response to Jews fleeing Nazi Germany. Indeed, he invokes images of the ill-fated ship *St. Louis* and the 1943 Bermuda Conference. There are, however, at least three significant differences today:

(1) The issue now is not whether to let Soviet Jews enter the United States. That already has been decided favorably by the U.S. government. Rather the question is how they will be admitted—i.e., as refugees, parolees, etc.—in light of the surge in emigration of Soviet

Jews, Armenians, and Pentecostalists. True, there are financial and other implications attached to each status, but the possibility to enter this country currently is not in dispute.

(2) Disturbingly, nowhere does Naftalin mention Israel. How can he even think of drawing parallels between the Nazi era, when so many Jews were denied a safe haven precisely because there was no Jewish homeland, and today when a sovereign Israel exists to welcome and resettle Jews in distress? I happen to believe in freedom of choice for Soviet Jews, but also recognize that, thankfully, Israel remains a true country of refuge.

(3) Unlike the period between 1933 and 1945, the U.S. administration and Congress today share our goals. Indeed, if Soviet Jews are emigrating in increasing numbers, it is in no small measure due to official efforts. Yes, the work is far from over. But a word of acknowledgement for our government's dramatic change in attitude, as compared to forty-five years ago, to the plight of Jews in distress would have been appropriate, even while highlighting the current serious problems in the U.S. processing of Soviet migrants.

Soviet Jews and the West Bank
The Washington Post
February 20, 1989

In discussing Israel's effort to attract a higher percentage of Soviet Jews leaving the USSR for resettlement in the West, columnists Rowland Evans and Robert Novak make an outrageous claim ["Swap Soviet Jews for U.S. Trade?" Jan. 23].

They allege that "Israel needs more Jews to populate its U.S.-opposed West Bank settlement and offset the high Palestinian birthrate. The only source for this ingathering of the Jews is the Soviet Union."

What an absurd rationale! It completely ignores the very essence of Zionism, the national liberation movement of the Jewish people, and Israel's forty-year-old raison d'être. Israel's 1948 Declaration of Independence stated: "After being forcibly exiled from their land, the people kept the faith with it throughout their dispersion and never ceased to pray and hope for their return to it and for the restoration in it of their political freedom. . . . The State of Israel will be open for Jewish immigration and for the ingathering of the exiles."

In other words, Israel desires immigration, particularly from the USSR, which represents the world's third-largest Jewish community and the one in greatest flux, to underscore the continued viability of Israel as the Jewish homeland. Moreover, if Israel seeks to increase its Jewish population, it is because through numbers a more stable, secure, permanent, and flourishing Israel may be attained. Given the disparity in population figures between Israel and its neighbors, such a goal is especially understandable.

Finally, Mr. Evans and Mr. Novak err in maliciously suggesting that Soviet Jewish newcomers are used to populate the West Bank as a bulwark against the Palestinians. Soviet Jews, like other Israelis, are free to choose their place of residence. Israel's advocacy in behalf of Soviet Jewish immigration began long before the acquisition of the territories in the 1967 Six-Day War and surely in no way is linked to the future disposition of the territories.

AJC and Soviet Jews
Washington Jewish Week
May 18, 1989

Apropos Prof. David Korn's letter on the Jewish identity of recent Soviet Jewish arrivals to the United States (*WJW*, May 11), his research results appear both confusing and contradictory. For instance, we are told that "only 18 percent of Soviet Jews who came to the U.S. in the last two years regard themselves as Jews," but then we learn that "45 percent [of the total sample] do not regard themselves as Jews from a religious, cultural or ethnic point of view . . ." Which is it, an alienation rate of 82 percent or 45 percent?

Then we learn that "fully 35 percent consider themselves to be atheists or would attend church if allowed." Apart from the fact that, to the best of my knowledge, no one is stopping anyone from church attendance, this also suggests that 65 percent are neither atheists nor candidates for proselytization. Who, then, are they?

Professor Korn voices surprise "that so much time, effort and money are being spent in bringing Soviet Jews to the U.S." He offers no alternative solution, though I suspect that he would like to see more Soviet Jews choose Israel. I would, too, although the difficulties of achieving that elusive goal are many. But I also accept that, regardless of whether direct flights from Moscow to Tel Aviv are inaugurated, or the United States applies more strictly the refugee standard for admission, or the resettlement agencies cut back on their services to make the United States less inviting, the reality is that many Jews will continue to come here if Soviet doors remain open. Accordingly, the American Jewish community has an ongoing obligation, mindful of the particular history and psychology of Soviet Jews, to seek ways to foster their Jewish acculturation within our midst.

At a recent national consultation on the Jewish identity of Sovet Jews in the United States, sponsored by the American Jewish Committee, it was clear that, despite the many problems, successful local models already exist, including initiatives taken by some federations, other agencies, synagogues, and Soviet Jews themselves. We need to learn from them these, create others, and apply them nationally as a matter of high priority.

Take My Comrade . . . Please!*
The Washington Post
September 17, 1989

When Boris Yeltsin addressed a packed house in Baltimore last week, he pleased the crowd most when he poked fun at communism. "Bearing in mind that communism is just an idea, just pie in the sky," he quipped, "we shouldn't try to implement it here on Earth."

Surprising as it may be to hear a Soviet leader say such things, the Soviet people have been delivering similar lines for years. The breeding ground for Soviet political humor has always been adversity; the

---

*This article was also published in the *International Herald Tribune* and dozens of other newspapers.

worse things have been, the better the jokes. And it used to be a sure bet that the Soviet landscape—marked by repression, religious persecution, and corruption—would yield ever new jokes, while preserving the validity of stories decades old. But all this is now threatened by reform.

Take the issue of elections. For years Soviet citizens have been telling the following joke: An American and a Russian were debating the question of whose country had the better intelligence service. "The KGB is tops," boasted the Soviet. "They've managed to steal all the designs of the major American weapons systems for the last ten years."

"That's nothing," the American retorted. "The CIA has stolen from the Kremlin's safe the results of all the Soviet elections for the next ten years!"

With the recent elections, including the victories of Andrei Sakharov and Yeltsin, this joke may be out. And if the liberalizing trend continues, it won't be long before another stalwart will be consigned to history: What is meant by an exchange of opinions in the Communist Party of the Soviet Union? It's when I come to a party meeting with my own opinion, and I leave with the party's.

Of course, many problems persist, along with the jokes about them. Take the Soviet economy. Please.

Ivan walked into a shop. "Do you have any meat?" he asked the clerk. "No, here we don't have any fish. Next door, at the butcher's they don't have any meat."

What do the United States and USSR have in common? The ruble isn't worth anything in either country.

Ivanov had finally saved enough money to purchase a car. He went to the appropriate office and paid the money. "Your car will be delivered exactly ten years from today," the clerk advised Ivanov.

"Morning or afternoon?" Ivanov asked.

"Why is it so important for you to know that now?" the clerk asked.

"Because the plumber is coming that morning."

Soviet Jews, who have been both the source and object of so much Soviet political humor because of their particular plight, continue to have their difficulties. Many of the jokes dealing with them remain as current today as when they were conceived years ago.

With the recent emergence of xenophobic, ultranationalistic groups like Pamyat, some old jokes gain an even truer ring.

Rabinovich was called to the visa office to discuss his application to emigrate. "Isn't everything good for you here, Rabinovich? Don't you have all that you need?" asked the official.

"Well," began Rabinovich, "the fact is I have two reasons for wanting to leave. The first is because of my neighbor. Every night he comes home stone-drunk and starts cursing the Jews. He's always saying that as soon as the communists are overthrown, he and his nationalist Russian friends will go out and hang all the Jews."

"But Rabinovich, you know that we communists will never be overthrown," said the official smugly.

"That," said Rabinovich, "is my second reason."

Despite increased legal emigration, defections are still occurring. What's the definition of a Soviet string quartet? A Soviet symphony orchestra just returned from a tour of the West.

The Gorbachev era has spawned several new jokes, largely focused on the impact of political changes, the antialcoholism campaign, and the deteriorating economic situation. Some examples:

Question: What's the difference between Catholicism and Gorbachev's communism? Answer: In Catholicism there's life after death. In Gorbachev's communism, there's posthumous rehabilitation.

As Gorbachev's antialcoholism campaign intensified, it became increasingly difficult to purchase once-ubiquitous vodka. So it was that two Russians, forced to wait in a long line in a store, began to complain about Gorbachev's restrictions on the sale of vodka. "You know," said one, "the problem with our leader is that he must be a teetotaler."

"Maybe so," replied the other, "but look at the bright side. He could have been celibate."

Shortly after Gorbachev's antialcoholism campaign got into full swing, the Soviet leader returned to his apartment from his Kremlin office and knocked on the door of his wife's bedroom.

"Hurry up and get out of here," Raisa whispered to Foreign Minister Shevardnadze, who was with her in bed. "But why?" protested Shevardnadze. "We're not drinking."

Ivanov was standing in a very long line for vodka. "We have General Secretary Gorbachev to thank for such a long line," one of Ivanov's neighbors in line muttered. "He's making the stuff very scarce."

"I can't endure this any more," Ivanov said, walking away. "I'm going to get my rifle and kill Gorbachev."

Two hours later Ivanov returned. "What happened?" the others asked.

"I decided to get back in this line. It's shorter than the line to kill Gorbachev."

An international polling agency decided to conduct a comparative opinion survey. They sought out an American, a Pole, and a Soviet.

"Excuse me, we're conducting a poll on the shortage of meat in your country," the pollster informed each of the three.

"What's a 'shortage'?" the American asked. "What's 'meat'?" the Pole asked. "What's a 'poll'?" the Soviet asked.

Soviet Succession
U.S. News & World Report
July 2, 1990

Having recently returned from a visit to Moscow, I too was struck by the entrepreneurs selling the politicized version of the "matrushka" doll ["Inside Gorbachev," Whispers, June 4], with the 10-inch Gorbachev, the 8-inch Brezhnev, the 6-inch Khrushchev, etc. In fact, I was about to buy one when I noticed an even better variation, symbolizing the decline of communism. Lenin is the largest, followed by the progressively smaller Stalin, Khrushchev, Brezhnev, Andropov, Chernenko, Gorbachev, and, last but by no means least, all 1 inch of him, Boris Yeltsin.

Presentation of AJC's American Liberties Medallion
to Yevgeny Yevtushenko
New York
May 2, 1991

The day was September 28, 1941. Two thousand notices were posted throughout Kiev by the Nazis, the occupying power. They read: *"All
Jews of the City of Kiev and its environs must appear on the corner of
Melnikov and Docturov Streets at 8 a.m. tomorrow, September 29,
1941. They must bring their documents, their money, their valuables,
and their warm clothing. Jews who fail to obey this order and are
found elsewhere will be shot."*

As the late chronicler of the Holocaust, Lucy Dawidowicz, wrote:
"Thousands upon thousands of Jews jammed into the assembly area in
Kiev. They thought they were going to the railway siding but there
were no trains at their next stopping point. Then the Germans began
shoving the Jews into narrower and narrower lines. They moved very
slowly. After a long walk they came to a passageway formed by
German soldiers with truncheons and police dogs. The Jews were
whipped through, bruised and bloodied. Numbed by the incomprehen-
sibility of their fate, the Jews emerged onto a grassy ravine. They had
arrived at Babi Yar. Ahead of them lay the ravine itself. The Germans
led small groups away from the clearing toward a narrow ledge along
the ravine. At a sand quarry behind the ledge, hidden from the view of
the Jews, the Germans had mounted machine guns. When the ledge
contained as many Jews as it could hold, the Germans gunned them
down. The bodies toppled into the ravine, piling up, layer upon layer.
Where once a clear stream flowed now blood ran. Thirty-three thousands Jews were killed in less than two days, setting a record in the
annals of mass murder. Even Auschwitz-Birkenau couldn't match it."

After the war, and after the cold-blooded murder of more than a
hundred thousand people at that site, a silence prevailed. The extermination of the Jews in Kiev became a nonsubject in Soviet history, subsumed entirely within the larger and tragic losses incurred by the
Soviet Union during the war. So subsumed in fact that when the
American Jewish Committee undertook a national survey late last year

of attitudes toward Jews in the Soviet Union, we found that less than 2 percent of Soviet citizens were able to identify correctly the number of Jews killed by the Nazis during the war. Ninety-eight percent didn't come close to the 6 million figure.

Soviet engineers tried to fill in the ravine and build a sports stadium in its place. In the process they built a dam. Over the years the waters behind the dam rose higher and higher until finally they overflowed. Dozens of people in the neighborhood were killed and eerily, in that horrible scene, bones surfaced as well. Local Ukrainian people said the Jews had had their revenge. But it was in that year as well, 1961, that a young Soviet poet went to Babi Yar.

Listen to his words and seek to imagine the extraordinary courage that it must have taken to defy Soviet history. He wrote: "I have long wanted to write a poem on anti-Semitism. But only after I have been to Kiev and seen Babi Yar with my own eyes did the poetic form come to me. I wrote a poem in only a few hours after my return to Moscow. That evening I gave a talk. After the talk I read Babi Yar for the very first time. Ordinarily, I recite my poems by heart, but this time I was so agitated that I had to have the text in front of me. When I finished there was dead silence. I stood fidgeting with the paper. Afraid to look up, when I did I saw that the entire audience had risen to their feet. Then applause exploded and went on for a good ten minutes. People leaped onto the stage and embraced me. My eyes were full of tears." So wrote Yevgeny Yevtushenko.

His poem, subsequently published in *Literaturnaya Gazeta*, one of the nation's leading cultural papers, took the country by storm. Yevgeny Yevtushenko became an even more venerated poet in the USSR. Remember, the Soviet Union is a country that honors its artists and poets. It's a country capable of filling a soccer stadium for a poetry reading. By contrast, we live in a country that can hardly fill a soccer stadium with soccer fans, much less with fans of poetry. The excitement generated by Yevgeney Yevtushenko and his unprecedented poem led to huge crowds and rapt audiences.

One Western literary specialist, after returning from the Soviet Union at the time, wrote: "After nearly all of his recitations of poetry the audience began clamoring again, 'Babi Yar, Babi Yar,' pounding on the floor with a deafening roar with their feet. And he, Yevtushenko read it again and again and they clamored for it still more. Toward the end of the evening when this happened once more, Yevtushenko shouted for silence and said, 'Comrades, you and I have been in this hall for five hours and I have read this poem four times already. I should think that you'd be as tired of hearing it as I am of reciting it.' But again they pounded and again he complied."

And later, in a Moscow meeting of several hundred intellectuals on December 17, 1962, the poem became a central issue. When he recited the last two lines of his poem to the audience, Nikita Khrushchev himself interjected. "Comrade Yevtushenko," said the Soviet leader, "this poem has no place here." But Yevgeny Yevtushenko stood up, faced the leader of the Soviet Union and said: "Anti-Semitism is a problem. Nikita Sergeyevich Khrushchev, it is a problem. It cannot be denied and it cannot be suppressed. It is necessary to come to grips with anti-Semitism in this country. Time and again, I myself was witness to anti-Semitism in this country. And moreover, it came from people who occupied official positions. We cannot go forward to communism with such a heavy load of Judeo-phobia."

Yevgeny Yevtushenko, though he may not speak Hebrew, has understood the meaning of the word *zachor*, remember. For him history has meaning, history has power, history has identity. Yevgeny Yevtushenko became a conscience for his nation.

And displaying further courage, in 1974, he stood up when Aleksander Solzhenitsyn was under fire and wrote an open letter defending the noted writer. And in it, again, he came to the question of the absence of history in the Soviet Union. Here's what Yevtushenko wrote: "Last year, around a campfire in Siberia, one good young girl, a student about eighteen years old, raised a toast to Stalin. I was shaken. Why, I asked. Because everyone believed in Stalin and with this belief they were victorious, she replied. And do you know how many people were arrested during the years of Stalin's rule, I asked her. Yeah, twenty or thirty, she replied. Other students sat around the fire and they were about her age. I started asking them the same question, too. Two hundred, said one child. Maybe two thousand, said another girl. Only one student among the twenty even ventured a guess of ten thousand.

When I told them that the figure was reckoned not in thousands but in millions, they didn't believe me. Did you read my poem the *Errors of Stalin*, I asked. Did you really have such a poem, the girl replied. When was it published? Where? In *Pravda* in 1963, I answered. But I was only eight years old at the time, said the girl. And then I suddenly understood as never before that the younger generation really does not have any sources nowadays for learning the tragic truth about that time. Because they don't read about it! They can't read about it in books or in textbooks."

Today Yevgeny Yevtushenko is not only a poet and an essayist but a film writer as well. He is also a politician. He's a people's deputy of the Soviet Union and a strong supporter of the dissident and democracy movements. He, together with Andrei Sakharov, was one of the founders of Memorial, an organization committed to the memory of the victims of Stalinism.

And so it is with enormous pleasure and pride that the American Jewish Committee pays tribute to this individual whose life truly exemplifies the inscription of our American Liberties Medallion:

"Yevgeny Yevtushenko, Courageous Champion of Freedom. For Exceptional Advancement of the Principles of Human Liberty."

And, I might add, for the preservation of memory. The memory of the innocent. The memory of the silenced.

The Role of the American Jewish Committee in Helping Reconstitute Jewish Life in the Former Soviet Union
Davis Center for Russian Studies
Harvard University
February 15, 1999

Introduction

In reviewing the American Jewish Committee's activities and initiatives since the collapse of the USSR in 1991, one is inevitably reminded that the AJC was founded ninety-three years ago in response to attacks against Jews in Russia, especially the 1903 and 1905 pogroms in Kishinev, and elsewhere in Eastern Europe.

Interestingly, one of the very first steps taken by the new organization was the creation of a press bureau. The rationale, which could as easily have been written in the mid-1960s when the Soviet Jewry campaign first began in earnest, was set forth in a resolution adopted by AJC's Executive Committee on January 27, 1907:

> For the prevention of massacres of Jews in Russia, no means can be considered so effective as the enlightenment of the people of the western world concerning real conditions in Russia, which have hitherto been systematically concealed or distorted by the power of the Russian Government; that to this end a Press Bureau should be established to gather and disseminate correct news of affairs in Russia.

Let me offer several highlights of AJC's efforts respecting Russia and later the USSR since the agency's founding:

Notwithstanding the provisions of the Treaty of Commerce and Navigation, signed in 1832 by Russia and the United States, that "the inhabitants of their respective States shall mutually have liberty to enter the ports, places and rivers of the territories of each party, wherever foreign commerce is permitted," American Jews were routinely denied entry visas by Russian consular officials, beginning by the 1890s.

According to Professor Naomi Cohen, AJC leaders became still more outraged when the U.S. State Department, in 1907, announced that it would refuse to issue passports ". . . to Jews who intend on going to Russian territory, unless it has the assurance that the Russian Government will consent to their admission." This position appeared to sanction the objectionable Russian policy. Although the State Department subsequently reversed itself, AJC leaders became convinced that the appropriate response to the Russian policy of discrimination against some Americans was to press for outright abrogation of the 1832 treaty rather than for diplomatic exchanges that had hitherto proved ineffective.

It took five years for the AJC leadership, collaborating with key congressional leaders while facing resistance from the White House and State Department, to achieve the treaty's abrogation.

What is particularly noteworthy in reviewing the history of this campaign is the strikingly similar script to the campaign for the Jackson-Vanik Amendment sixty-five years later.

First, there was precisely the same division between American Jewish communal leadership and a majority of the U.S. Congress on the one hand and the executive branch on the other, each invoking arguments that were again to be used, in only slightly updated form, in the battle over Jackson-Vanik.

Second, no European country followed the U.S. example in applying a "stick" to protest Russia's discriminatory policy, thus weakening the American effort. The same European resistance occurred in the wake of the adoption of Jackson-Vanik.

And third, once the treaty was in fact abrogated, each side sought vindication for its position. The White House argued that not only were American businesses negatively affected but the position of Jews in Russia experienced further decline because of such a confrontational American approach. On the other hand, the proponents of abrogation hailed the move as a victory for high-minded principle in American foreign policy. Again, this split was a forerunner of the conflicting and self-justifying views expressed by the two contending sides in the months and years following Jackson-Vanik's enactment. Jacob Schiff most dramatically stated the case of the winning side in the battle over the 1832 treaty:

> We have just passed through an episode which, in my opinion, is of greater importance than anything that has happened since civil rights were granted Jews under the first Napoleon, or since English Jews were admitted to parliament...For the first time, Russia, that great Colossus, has received a slap in the face from a great nation, which act, I cannot help thinking, must be of the greatest consequence in the history of civilization.[*]

*Quoted in Naomi Cohen, "The Abrogation of the Russo-American Treaty of 1832," *Jewish Social Studies*, 25 (January 1963): 40.

Consistent with its traditional emphasis on research and analysis, AJC sponsored the first book-length studies on the effect of Soviet aggression on the life of Jewish communities under Communist rule.

In 1951, *The Jews in the Soviet Union*, by Solomon M. Schwarz, was published by Syracuse University Press. Three years later, the companion volume, *The Jews in the Soviet Satellites*, by Peter Meyer, was issued by the same publishing house. Other AJC pamphlets on Soviet Jewry were published throughout the 1950s, as well as articles in *Commentary* and the *American Jewish Year Book*, both sponsored by AJC. And in 1954, then AJC president Irving Engel was called to testify before the House Select Committee on Communist Aggression against the Jews in the Soviet Union and Eastern Europe, which resulted in a special congressional report entitled *Treatment of Jews Under Communism*.

On January 15, 1959, an AJC delegation met with Soviet first deputy premier Anastas Mikoyan during his U.S. visit to discuss the condition of Soviet Jewry. This was the first high-level meeting between a Soviet official and American Jewish leaders in over forty years.

Among the concerns expressed by the AJC delegation were: the absence of Hebrew or Yiddish language schools in Birobidjan, the so-called Jewish Autonomous District in the Far East, or, for that matter, anywhere else in the USSR; the paucity of rabbis, numbering no more than sixty, to serve nearly 3 million Jews; the mounting barriers to Jewish advancement in Soviet life; and the failure to build a single synagogue since the Second World War, leaving hundreds of Jewish communities with sizable populations without any house of worship at all in the wake of the destruction wrought by the Nazis (and, of course, Soviet policy itself toward synagogues). Following the meeting, AJC sent Mikoyan a lengthy letter further documenting instances of cultural, religious, and other discrimination against Soviet Jews.

The *Christian Science Monitor* reported, on February 24, 1959, that the Soviets, in response to the harsh attack Mikoyan had encountered in his U.S. visit, would permit the publication of some books in Yiddish, including selected works of Sholom Aleichem.

International attention was focused on Soviet anti-Semitism when Morris Abram, AJC's president, held a special press conference in New

York in 1964 to denounce *Judaism Without Embellishment*, an anti-Semitic polemic containing Nazi-like caricatures, written by T. K. Kichko and published by the Ukrainian Academy of Sciences. The resulting international furor, including, it should be noted, several Western Communist parties, led to official Kremlin disavowal of the book and its author, though this was by no means the last such book to appear.

In 1964 AJC was one of the four original sponsors—together with the Synagogue Council of America, the Conference of Presidents of Major American Jewish Organizations, and the National Jewish Community Relations Advisory Council (NJCRAC)—of the American Conference on Soviet Jewry. Seven years later, AJC became a founding member of the successor organization, the National Conference on Soviet Jewry (NCSJ). Indeed, the first president of the NCSJ, Richard Maass, and the first executive director, Jerry Goodman, came from the lay and professional ranks, respectively, of the American Jewish Committee.

In late 1971, AJC, utilizing its extensive contacts in the American faith-based communities, spurred the establishment of the National Interreligious Task Force on Soviet Jewry, whose first honorary chair was R. Sargent Shriver, and quietly provided the new entity with financial support. Drawing on the leadership of the Protestant, Roman Catholic, Orthodox, and Jewish communities the task force was to add an important, broadly based ecumenical voice to the Soviet Jewry campaign over the next two decades.

During the height of the Soviet Jewry campaign, from 1971 to 1991, AJC was deeply involved in all phases of the effort, both individually and in collaboration with other interested agencies: in the political and diplomatic efforts in Washington and capitals throughout Europe; as public members—or as lobbyists—to several of the CSCE conferences in Europe and at U.S.-Soviet summits; as delegates to the biennial Moscow International Book Fair representing American Jewish book publishers; as visitors to refusenik homes and synagogues in major Soviet cities; as sponsors of Russian-language materials on Jewish themes clandestinely sent to the USSR; as supporters of expanded Voice of America broadcasts aimed at Soviet Jews; and in other ways too numerous to recount in this summary report.

A distinguishing feature of AJC's approach was to support the Soviet human rights movement. Most other Jewish organizations refused, fearing that this could only further complicate advocacy efforts on behalf of Soviet Jewry by persuading the Kremlin—which undoubtedly needed little convincing—that the larger Jewish aim was not simply "repatriation to the Jewish homeland," as the Soviet Jewry movement insisted, but, in fact, the overthrow of communism.

Never breaking with the consensus of the Soviet Jewry movement, AJC nonetheless demonstrated solidarity with Soviet dissidents through our semiautonomous Jacob Blaustein Institute for the Advancement of Human Rights. The institute regularly published material on and by Soviet human rights activists, sponsored seminars and symposia, and awarded grants to nongovernmental organizations addressing Soviet human rights issues, including, it should be noted, cases related to the right to practice one's religion and to speak one's language—i.e., Hebrew.

In addressing the contributions of the Jacob Blaustein Institute, Elena Bonner said in 1997:

> In the early 1970's, the Jacob Blaustein Institute was one of the very few, if not the only one, among Jewish organizations concerned with the general state of human rights in the Soviet Union. The Institute did not limit itself to issues of Jewish emigration, understanding that an injustice anywhere on the face of this earth is a threat to justice everywhere.

Incidentally, it was this same Institute that, in 1972, convened, together with the International Institute of Human Rights and the Faculty of Law at Uppsala University (Sweden), the landmark Uppsala Conference, as it came to be called, on the right to leave and to return. These fundamental rights were enshrined in Article 13 of the Universal Declaration of Human Rights, which was adopted without dissent by the member states of the United Nations in 1948.

The conference, attended by legal scholars from a number of Western countries, focused on the application of the Universal Declaration to, among others, those Soviet Jews demanding the right to emigrate. The practical consequence of the gathering was to give an important international legal imprimatur to the still fledgling Soviet Jewry movement.

The proceedings of the conference were published by the American Jewish Committee in 1976 under the title *The Right to Leave and to Return.*

One other highlight of AJC's efforts should be noted. In October 1987, when Chairman Mikhail Gorbachev scheduled his first visit to Washington for meetings with President Ronald Reagan, the organized American Jewish community, led by the National Conference on Soviet Jewry and the Council of Jewish Federations, asked the director of the American Jewish Committee's Washington office to coordinate the organization of a mass demonstration.

In the ensuing thirty-seven days, American Jewry mobilized as never before, leading to the largest single gathering of American Jews in Washington history. Two hundred and fifty thousand people, including a sizable number of non-Jews, came to the nation's Mall on December 6, 1987, to express support for the right of Soviet Jews to emigrate, to call particular attention to the plight of the prisoners of conscience and the long-term refuseniks, and to demand an end to restrictions on the study of Hebrew and the practice of Judaism. Vice President George Bush and the recently released Natan Shcharansky were among the many prominent speakers at the day-long event, which took place literally on the eve of Gorbachev's first meeting with Reagan in the White House.

1991 to the Present

With the collapse of communism, first in the Soviet satellite states of Eastern Europe and, within two years, in the USSR itself, AJC saw an unprecedented opportunity for the United States, Israel, world Jewry, and, not least, the people of the region. A four-pronged agenda emerged that remains to this day the general blueprint for AJC programming:

Assist local Jewish communities to achieve full protection under the law and equal status with other citizens, thus allowing these communities—shadows of what they once were before Nazi occupation and communist domination—to rebuild themselves.

Respecting a division of labor, AJC enthusiastically applauded but did not seek to duplicate the estimable efforts of the Jewish Agency for Israel, the American Jewish Joint Distribution Committee, the Memorial Foundation for Jewish Culture, and the Ronald S. Lauder Foundation. These organizations were involved in strengthening Jewish life through the rebuilding of synagogues, founding of Jewish day schools and summer camps, provision of essential social services, sponsorship of communal leadership training programs, introduction of Israeli cultural and Hebrew-language programs, and publication of books and periodicals on a multitude of Jewish themes. Instead, as mentioned, AJC focused on seeking to help ensure the place of Jews and Jewish communities in the emerging postcommunist societies.

It pursued the "unfinished business" of the Holocaust regarding Central and Eastern Europe, including pensions for survivors; identification, preservation, and protection of sites of tragedy; restitution of communal property; acceptance, where appropriate, of historical and moral accountability; and introduction of nationally tailored curricula on Holocaust education and local Jewish history.

It encouraged the broadening and deepening of bilateral relations between Israel and the nations of Eastern Europe and the successor states of the USSR. It was clear early on that Israel could become one of the principal beneficiaries of communism's collapse, as the new governments sought to reorient their foreign policies. Traditional East European support for anti-Zionism, anti-Israel terrorist groups, and the most hard-line Arab states gave way to pro-Western policies that included favorable attitudes toward Israel. The reasons ranged from desire for Israeli technology, to the view that close ties with the Jewish state could advance their standing in the United States, to a more generalized belief, however exaggerated, in international Jewish political and economic power.

Moreover, and of special note, many of the postcommunist societies came to believe that their attitudes toward Jews were regarded in the West (and often by democrats within the societies themselves) as the best possible litmus test of the sincerity and effectiveness with which they pursued their new reformist policies. Thus, the opportunities available to Jewish agencies such as AJC throughout the region were quite without limit.

This entirely new geopolitical situation, and the enhanced influence accorded world Jewry, also permitted AJC to assist Israel not only by encouraging closer bilateral ties but also by pressing the successor states (and the countries of Eastern Europe) to end their supply of weapons, know-how, and personnel to nations in the Middle East posing a threat to Israel, including Iran, Iraq, Libya, and Syria.

Consistent with AJC's philosophy dating back to its founding, the agency recognized the importance of participating in the building of democratic institutions, the rule of law, civil society, human and civil rights protections, and tolerance-building programs for ethnically diverse, sometimes stratified, societies. In the final analysis, we have come to understand, the best protection for minority communities in majority cultures, be they Jews or others, is safeguarding the rights of all by fostering respect for democracy and pluralism. And in this case, it was not simply a matter of trying to better protect Jewish communities, important though this obviously was, but actually helping extend the reach of freedom and ending for once and for all the East-West conflict.

Against the backdrop of this four-pronged agenda, let me cite some of the initiatives we have launched in the Former Soviet Union (FSU). Again, mindful of time and space limitations, the list will be illustrative rather than exhaustive.

(1) *Pensions for Holocaust Survivors:* In the early 1990s, shortly after the breakup of the Soviet bloc, AJC began developing close working ties with the emerging leaders of the remnant Jewish communities in the region. Understandably, these communities' first priorities were to reconstitute themselves, begin to identify fellow Jews, organize basic communal services, deepen links with world Jewry, and ensure their rightful place in the newly independent societies.

As they assessed their needs, they quickly recognized the importance of providing some modicum of support for the rapidly aging and often indigent Holocaust survivors in their midst. Unlike survivors in Western countries, these survivors, despite identical wartime experiences, were denied pensions from the German government. Bonn's reasoning was that, even if it could reach agreement with the communist countries, itself doubtful, those regimes could not be trusted to live up to such accords. Hence these Jews became known as the "double victims," in the words of U.S. under secretary of state Stuart Eizenstat.

Once communism collapsed, Bonn offered other rationales for refusing to provide monthly payments—it feared a flood of new claimants from Russia, Belarus, Ukraine, and elsewhere well beyond the limited number of Jews still alive; its economy was battered, its budget already stretched, its unemployment rolls growing; it preferred to consider not pensions but modest one-time payments made through national foundations provided with German funds.

(A billion deutsche marks were transferred to Moscow for precisely this purpose just before the USSR imploded. The funds were then distributed among rather poorly administered and inadequately audited foundations established in Russia, Ukraine, and Belarus—400 million, 400 million, and 200 million, respectively. In Ukraine, for example, well over 90 percent of the recipients have been non-Jews and the average one-time payment for Jewish and non-Jewish survivors of Nazi persecution has been a paltry 600 DM, or about $350.)

In 1996, we discovered that while Holocaust survivors in, for instance, Latvia were deemed ineligible for German pensions, disabled veterans of the Third Reich were eligible. Consequently, a Latvian Waffen SS veteran injured during the war received a monthly check from Bonn, while a Latvian Jewish survivor received nothing.

To summarize the long and complex, if fascinating, story that unfolded, our talks with the German government—first in private, but later, after achieving no progress, coupled with the public pressure we were able to generate from the White House, Senate, and media—resulted in a German decision, announced on January 12, 1998, to allocate 200 million DM (approximately $120 million). The funds were intended specifically for pensions for the estimated 20,000 Jewish Holocaust survivors who had spent at least six months in a Nazi concentration camp or eighteen months in a ghetto or hiding. Two days later, on January 14, a *Washington Post* editorial commented as follows:

Germany overall has set a positive model for the world, one that few other nations have matched, in facing up to the evils of its history and paying about $60 billion in reparations for admittedly unrightable wrongs. But in the case of the Eastern Europeans, it stalled for nearly half a decade, offering varying untenable excuses. Only when the American Jewish Committee went public with its tenacious campaign, beginning last spring, did it begin to make progress. Recent State Department pressure and a Senate resolution endorsed by 82 Senators may also have helped. [The Senate Resolution, introduced by Senators Dodd (D-CT) and Hutchison (R-TX), was drafted in close cooperation with the American Jewish Committee.]

(2) *Research and Publications:* AJC, known for its frequent polling of attitudes toward Jews, has conducted two significant surveys in the former Soviet Union.

(In the fall of 1990, the Soviet Center for Public Opinion and Market Research, at the request of AJC, carried out the first—and the last— survey to be conducted in the Soviet Union, which systematically examined on a national level attitudes toward Jews, Israel, and a broad range of Jewish concerns. The complete findings are reported on in Lev Gudkov and Alex Levinson, *Attitudes Toward Jews in the Soviet Union: Public Opinion in Ten Republics* [American Jewish Committee, 1992].)

In the first post-Soviet survey, undertaken in 1992 by the Moscow-based Russian Center for Public Opinion and Market Research on AJC's behalf, 3,965 respondents were interviewed face to face in their homes in ten of the fifteen successor states (Russia, Ukraine, Belarus, Moldova, Azerbaijan, Kazakhstan, Uzbekistan, Estonia, Latvia, and Lithuania). The 144 questions dealt with a wide range of topics, including views of Jews, political and economic perspectives, civic values, and perceptions of a broad array of nationalities.

Among the key findings were the wide variation in attitudes toward Jews from one state to another; the overall unfavorable trend in the view of Jews when compared with the 1990 study; and the importance of placing attitudes toward Jews in the context of attitudes toward other groups, many of which are viewed even more negatively than Jews.

The full results and interpretive data are to be found in Lev Gudkov and Alex Levinson, *Attitudes Towards Jews in the Commonwealth of Independent States* (American Jewish Committee, 1994).

The second survey, conducted in 1996 by ROMIR, a public-opinion and market-research company in Moscow, was narrower in focus. Geographically, it was limited to the Russian Federation. Only twenty-six questions were asked, eight of which focused on the Holocaust. Nonetheless, the survey used a number of the questions regarding attitudes toward Jews that had been asked previously, allowing a degree of longitudinal analysis. Moreover, the questions related to the Holocaust were identical to those asked by AJC in eight other countries at more or less the same time (United States, England, France, Germany, Austria, Poland, Slovakia, and Australia), permitting a comparative analysis.

In this study, some of the striking findings included a decidedly pessimistic view about the overall situation in Russia, especially among older and less well-educated respondents; a plurality of support for the Communist Party; relatively low hostility toward Jews but, given the large percentage of "don't know" responses to a number of questions dealing with Jews, the potential for an increase in such hostility; greater negative attitudes toward some other groups, among them Chechens, Azerbaijanis, Armenians, and Gypsies; and the absence of basic factual knowledge about the Holocaust, but even so a recognition of the importance of keeping the memory of the Holocaust alive.

The complete data can be found in *Current Russian Attitudes Towards Jews and the Holocaust: A Public-Opinion Survey* (American Jewish Committee, 1996).

Mention should also be made of an important three-day conference—"Jews of the Former Soviet Union: Yesterday, Today and Tomorrow"—held in St. Petersburg in June 1996.

Sponsored by AJC, together with our London-based partner, the Institute for Jewish Policy Research, and cosponsored by the Moses Mendelssohn Zentrum of Potsdam University (Germany), the European Council of Jewish Communities, the National Conference on Soviet Jewry and Petersburg Jewish University, 150 Jewish leaders from across the FSU, Europe, Israel, and the United States gathered. On the agenda were the political, cultural, religious, and educational challenges facing Jews in the FSU and appropriate strategies for responding to them. It should be noted that one of the speakers was Galina Staravoitova, the outspokenly courageous democracy and human rights activist who was fatally shot in St. Petersburg in 1998.

Regrettably, I was unable to attend the conference. I was denied a Russian entry visa on the grounds of my "past political history" with the country. State Department and congressional efforts to reverse the unexpected Russian decision proved unsuccessful. (I was subsequently issued an entry visa one year later to participate in an AJC delegation visit to Moscow for meetings with political officials and leaders of the Jewish community.)

(3) *Curriculum Project:* Earlier in this century, AJC undertook two important curricular projects, one a systematic examination of the contents of German school textbooks regarding Jewish themes, the other of the textbooks of Catholic and Protestant schools in the United States.

Utilizing these models, AJC launched a similar program in 1997 to review the textbooks in the national primary and secondary school systems of postcommunist societies. The aim was to commission qualified local scholars to evaluate the treatment of Jews, especially Jews of the particular country under study, Judaism, the Holocaust, and Israel in these textbooks, and to issue the conclusions, in both English and the native language, with the hope of encouraging revisions where needed.

In 1998, two national studies were completed—in Poland and the Czech Republic—and in 1999 another three are expected to be released, those examining textbooks in Slovakia, Hungary, and Ukraine. Studies of Russia and Lithuania have been commissioned and are likely to be published in 2000.

(4) *Archival Project:* With Western scholars gaining access to Soviet-era archives, AJC decided to begin its own archival project in Eastern Europe and the FSU to shed light on important chapters in post-World War II Jewish history in the region.

Among the research topics currently under study are the role of the synagogue in Soviet life, the 1968 anti-Semitic campaign in Poland, Romania's "sale" of Jews to Israel, and East Germany and Bulgaria's support for international terrorism directed against Israel. The Polish study is slated for publication in 1999 and the Soviet study no later than 2000. The other studies are in more embryonic stages, largely due to the slow pace of release of relevant archival data. It is not yet clear therefore when these studies will be issued.

(5) *Political Contacts:* Traditionally known as the "American Jewish State Department," AJC sought to establish links with high-level political officials in the FSU in pursuit of the four-pronged agenda enumerated above, tailored of course to the individual country.

AJC delegations have traveled frequently to Russia, Ukraine, Belarus, Estonia, Latvia, and Lithuania for meetings with government officials and representatives of the Jewish communities, and visits to the Central Asian nations are being planned. Moreover, AJC meets with the foreign ministers of most of the FSU countries each fall when they come to address the opening of the UN General Assembly session.

In 1998, for example, AJC held separate, private meetings with the presidents of Lithuania and Moldova and the foreign ministers of Ukraine, Armenia, Azerbaijan, Georgia, Kazakhstan, Kyrgyzstan, and Turkmenistan. On other occasions, we have also met with leaders of Belarus, Estonia, Latvia, the Russian Federation, and Uzbekistan.

It is obviously difficult to evaluate the results of such meetings, for there is seldom direct causality between a single meeting and a policy decision. At the same time, it is clear from the fact that these ministers carve out substantial blocks of time from very busy schedules to meet with AJC delegations—and do so year after year—that they understand the importance of the American Jewish community on the American scene, especially in terms of international affairs.

Many of these countries, lacking a diaspora community in the United States, believe they can entice American Jewry to play that role or, in the case of Ukraine, supplement the effort undertaken by Ukrainian Americans. In the process, they also have come to understand the AJC agenda as well.

Our FSU interlocutors know that we seek for our fellow Jews an atmosphere of equality free of anti-Semitism, certainly from mainstream sources; that the state of their bilateral relations with the United States and Israel is vitally important to us; that concern for Iran's quest to acquire weapons of mass destruction, especially with assistance from Russia, ranks very high among our priorities; and that we care deeply about the health of democracy and respect for human rights. Moreover, with the encouragement of local Jewish communities, we often raise matters of particular concern, such as communal property restitution, return of Jewish libraries and ritual objects, or cemetery desecrations and other egregious instances of anti-Semitism.

(6) *Training Jewish Leadership in Meeting External Challenges:* As I indicated earlier, other Jewish agencies have established as a priority the training of Jewish leaders in the FSU for communal service. Our aim has been to identify those Jewish leaders who interact with the general community and to help them develop skills in working in the political arena, in fostering interreligious and interethnic dialogue, in strengthening understanding of pluralism and tolerance, in countering hate groups, and in developing research programs.

(7) *Project Ukraine:* Lastly, largely as a result of AJC's long-standing connections with an important segment of the Ukrainian American community, as well as a generous grant from an AJC benefactor, AJC in 1993 launched Project Ukraine. An additional element was the belief, not without foundation, that the bulk of attention in the post-Soviet world would be directed to Russia and therefore, given Ukraine's considerable size and large Jewish community, we would be well served devoting resources to the second most populous FSU state.

The aims of the project are twofold: to assist Ukraine to successfully navigate the transition to a multiethnic democratic nation by strengthening selected institutions of civil society that could act as watchdogs for the well-being of democracy and pluralism; and to work directly with Ukrainian Jewish leadership in enhancing their civic, political, and legal defense skills, so that they themselves could help ensure the protection of their own rights.

Conclusion

These past seven years have provided previously unimaginable opportunities to reestablish open links with Jewish communities in the FSU and to launch a number of important programming initiatives. Even so, given the seemingly infinite avenues of possible activity that have bearing on FSU Jewry, and in light of the limited staff and budgetary resources of an agency like AJC, there is an admitted frustration at not being able to do still more.

Moreover, with growing concern among American Jews that the already tenuous situation in the Russian Federation is further unraveling, more of American Jewry's attention and resources may once again be devoted to defense, as was the case in 1906 when the American Jewish Committee was founded and throughout the height of the Soviet Jewry campaign in the 1960s, 1970s, and 1980s.

The next two years are likely to be key in shaping Russia's future political direction, largely because of looming elections. As I recently mentioned to a German diplomat concerned about Russia's direction, watch carefully Russia's Jews. They have always been the most accurate barometer of the country's climate. If, heaven forbid, attacks against Jews, whether verbal or physical, mount, it will bespeak volumes about the health (or, more accurately, ill health) of Russian society, all the more so if political and legal mechanisms available to counteract these trends are not employed by the competent authorities.

Similarly, if Russia's Jews in urban centers like Moscow and St. Petersburg start to talk seriously about emigration and begin packing their bags, take note. These are after all the Jews who, having had essentially every opportunity to leave in the past decade, chose to stay, whether for family, economic, or other reasons.

Thus, the American Jewish Committee will continue its multifaceted programs outlined in this paper, and, at the same time, cast a still closer eye on developments in the Russian Federation, the home of the largest Jewish population in the FSU. History has certainly taught us that, when dealing with this part of the world, erring on the side of caution is always the wisest course.

Anti-Semitism in Russia:
Testimony Before the
Committee on Foreign Relations
Subcommittee on European Affairs
United States Senate
February 24, 1999

Mr. Chairman, I wish to express my deepest appreciation to you and
your distinguished colleagues for the opportunity to appear here today
on the pressing topic of the state of anti-Semitism in Russia.

I have the privilege of representing the American Jewish
Committee, with which I have been associated since 1979. Much of
that time, given my own background in Soviet affairs and knowledge
of the Russian language, has been devoted to matters affecting the
USSR and the post-Soviet successor states.

The American Jewish Committee, our nation's oldest human relations agency, was founded in 1906, and today comprises more than
75,000 members and supporters across the United States. We have thirty-two offices in major American cities and eight overseas posts.

We are in close contact with Jews throughout the former Soviet
Union, travel regularly to Russia, commission research and polling on
conditions affecting Russian Jews, and meet frequently with high-level
Russian officials to discuss issues of concern to the Russian Jewish
community, as well as Russia's relations with the United States and the
countries of the Middle East.

Indeed, our organization was founded in response to the pogroms of
Jews in czarist Russia at the beginning of this century. On January 8,
1906, five leading American Jews sent out a letter to fifty-seven of their
colleagues inviting them to a meeting in New York. The letter read in
part:

"The horrors attending the recent Russian massacres and the necessity of extending to our brethren a helping hand in a manner most con-
ducive to the accomplishment of a permanent improvement of their
unfortunate condition, have, with remarkable spontaneity, induced
thoughtful Jews in all parts of the United States, to suggest the advis-
ability of the formation of a General Committee, to deal with the acute

problems thus presented, which are likely to recur, even in their acute phases, so long as the objects of our solicitude are subjected to disabilities and persecution owing to their religious belief."

Later that year, the American Jewish Committee was founded. Its mission statement read: "The purpose of this Committee is to prevent infringement of the civil and religious rights of Jews, and to alleviate the consequences of persecution."

Two months later, in establishing a press bureau, the AJC leaders declared with prescience: "For the prevention of massacres of Jews in Russia, no means can be considered so effective as the enlightenment of the people of the Western world concerning real conditions in Russia."

These AJC leaders were right on target at the time; their approach is equally valid today. Human rights danger zones require outside monitoring and exposure, lest potential perpetrators believe they can act with impunity and benefit from the world's indifference.

Senators, I wish to commend you. You are carrying on a remarkable congressional tradition, dating back to the last century, of examining Russian attitudes toward, and treatment of, Jews.

In the earliest known case, on June 11, 1879, Congress passed a joint resolution that cited laws of the Russian Government that "no Hebrew can hold real estate" and condemned Russia because a naturalized American Jewish citizen was prohibited from gaining title to land in Russia he had purchased and paid for.

As another illustration, in 1890 the House of Representatives passed a resolution requesting President Benjamin Harrison "To communicate to the House of Representatives . . . any information in his possession concerning the enforcement of prescriptive edicts against the Jews in Russia, recently ordered, as reported in the press."

And on December 13, 1911, the Senate Committee on Foreign Relations held a hearing on S.J. Res. 60, "a joint resolution providing for the termination of the treaty of commerce and navigation between the United States of America and Russia concluded at St. Petersburg December 18, 1832."

I mention this particular 1911 Senate hearing for three reasons.

First, it illustrates the direct and long-standing involvement of this

Committee on Foreign Relations in matters affecting the treatment of Jews in Russia.

Second, the outcome of the hearing was that the Foreign Relations Committee voted unanimously to adopt the resolution because of the Russian government's refusal to issue entry visas to American citizens of the Jewish faith, in contravention of the 1832 bilateral commercial treaty. Within days, the measure had been approved overwhelmingly by both Houses of Congress and, on President Taft's instructions, the U.S. ambassador to Moscow, Curtis Gould Jr., was instructed to advise Russia of the termination of the 1832 treaty.

This marked the first—though not the last—time Congress would establish a direct linkage between Russia's human rights record and America's economic policy toward that country. The landmark Jackson-Vanik Amendment, passed over sixty years later by Congress, linked the extension of American most-favored-nation (MFN) trade status with the emigration policy of communist countries.

And third, that 1911 hearing was addressed principally by the leadership of the American Jewish Committee, including Judge Mayer Sulzberger, president of AJC at the time, and Louis Marshall, Esq., one of the nation's most eminent jurists. While honored to follow in their footsteps, I am dismayed that the issues that preoccupied them in the early years of this century remain with us, in one form or another, as the century closes.

One hundred and twenty years after Congress first acted regarding Russia's mistreatment of Jews—and eighty-eight years after the American Jewish Committee first appeared before this very Committee on the same subject—we gather here once again to examine the condition of hundreds of thousands of Jews residing in Russia who are living in an uncertain environment.

In the brief time allotted to me, let me emphasize just a few central points, some of them implicit in my introductory comments.

To begin with, anti-Semitism in Russia has a tragically long history. Mistreatment of Jews in Russia can be documented for hundreds of years.

There was the intolerance and hostility of the Russian Orthodox Church toward Jews and Judaism over the centuries, as well as the government decree in 1727 that "all Jews found to be residing in the Ukraine and in other Russian towns shall be forthwith expelled beyond the frontier and not permitted under any circumstance to reenter Russia."

There was the restricted residency of Jews in the so-called Pale of Settlement beginning in the late eighteenth century, as well as the wave of pogroms spurred by the accession to the throne in 1881 of the antireformist, militantly nationalistic Czar Alexander III, after the assassination of his father, Alexander II. This situation continued for twenty-five years through the reign of the equally reactionary Nicholas II.

There were the anti-Semitic attacks by both communist and anticommunist forces during the post-1917 Soviet civil war, Stalin's ruthless purges, and the determined communist campaign to extinguish all vestiges of Judaism as a religion while restricting the vertical mobility of Soviet Jews.

For hundreds of years, then, waves of violence, blood libels, restrictive or punitive decrees involving education, employment, residency, and military service, and other forms of repression have been all too familiar features of the Russian landscape. As a result, countless Jews were killed and millions emigrated, especially to the United States. Still, many remained. Russia was, after all, their place of birth, their home, and all that was familiar to them.

Precisely because of the centuries-old pattern of persecution— punctuated, it must be noted, by occasional periods of hope and relative calm, depending largely, if not entirely, on the ruler of the day— there is a need to take very seriously manifestations of anti-Semitism in Russia at any time, not least today. Put most starkly, we ignore the lessons of history at our peril.

The situation today for Jews in the Russian Federation is extraordinarily complex.

On the one hand, Jewish life in the postcommunist era is miraculously reemerging, notwithstanding the relentless, seventy-year-long effort of the communist apparatus to uproot and destroy it. Synagogues, schools, community centers, and a myriad other Jewish institutions are developing, and contacts between Russian Jews and Jews beyond Russia's borders are frequent and unrestricted. The presence here on our panel of Rabbi Goldschmidt of Moscow is but one testament to this remarkable development.

Yet, at the very same time, the intractability of the country's economic and political travails should be a cautionary note for us, as should its fragile democratic system.

Given the widespread impoverishment and the glaring income gap between the wealthy few and the rest of the population, persistent unemployment and underemployment, widespread pessimism about the future, endemic corruption, and mounting criminal violence, Russia's democratic experiment is not assured of permanence—especially against the backdrop of Russian history, which lacks any sustained encounter with democracy, the rule of law, and civil society.

Instead, the fear persists that this embryonic democratic effort could yield—perhaps even in the upcoming elections—to a more nationalistic, authoritarian, or communist regime, whose rallying cry might well include the alleged responsibility of the Jews or, in only slightly more veiled terms, the "non-Russians," for Russia's economic stagnation, loss of empire, or domestic turmoil. In a word, scapegoating.

It has worked before in Russian history; it could well occur again. The recent disturbing anti-Semitic incidents, whether by spokesmen of the extreme right or by the left in the Communist-dominated Duma (parliament) or, for that matter, outside Moscow—most notably in provinces like Krasnodar, whose governor, Nikolai Kondratenko, elected in 1996, is an unabashed anti-Semite—should give us serious pause. The National Conference on Soviet Jewry, represented here today by its executive director, Mark Levin, and of which the American Jewish Committee is a founding member, has closely monitored these and other incidents.

Again, history has shown the enduring appeal of anti-Semitism as a political weapon in this part of the world, especially during periods of transition, when a country like Russia is convulsed by dramatic and unsettling change.

This is one such period. Should political, economic, and social conditions in Russia improve, Jewish vulnerability could ebb. If, however, conditions either continue to stagnate or decline, the Jews might well be blamed, as they have in the past, for Russia's daunting difficulties—

accused of profiting at Russia's expense or attacked as outsiders disloyal to "Mother Russia."

Second, the best antidote to anti-Semitism in such a situation would be clear, consistent, and unambiguous statements from Russia's leading political figures and by spokesmen for the country's key institutions, coupled with appropriate action to relegate anti-Semitism to society's margins.

Anti-Semitism may not be entirely extinguishable, but the aim must be to deny it acceptability in mainstream society. In other words, there can be no compromise with anti-Semitism or anti-Semites in the legitimate political discourse and debate of the country. Anything less, history again has taught us, sends the dangerous message that anti-Semitism is in fact a negotiable political issue.

Come elections, will there be Russian politicians with the courage to denounce unequivocally those who openly or in coded language "play the anti-Semitic card" as part of their campaign platform, and instead appeal to the higher instincts of the Russian people? One can only hope so.

Will there be a critical mass of the Russian people prepared to reject any such crude charges against the Jews? Again, one can only hope so.

But we are entering an election period when there will be a temptation to sound the nationalist theme, that is, to pander to a disaffected electorate looking for simplistic explanations for the country's deeply rooted difficulties, or to conjure up "enemies"—internal or external— who allegedly undermine the country's well-being. This may prove dangerous.

Some key Russian institutions, especially the Russian Orthodox Church, could, if they choose, play a constructive role in this regard. Until now, the church's role has been at best equivocal. The Russian Orthodox Church, which occupies a privileged place in the religious life of Russia, has never undergone the kind of soul searching and moral and historical reckoning regarding its relations with the Jews that the Catholic Church and many Protestant churches, to their credit, have initiated in the second half of this century. Such an undertaking is overdue.

The Russian educational system surely could do much more to promote concepts of tolerance and understanding among the country's many and diverse nationalities and religious groups, including the Jews.

During the communist era, when I had an opportunity to spend several months in the USSR teaching in elementary and secondary schools in Moscow and Leningrad, an essential element of the prevailing ideology, however factually untrue, was the so-called brotherhood of Soviet nationalities. Since it was a given, there was no need to teach it, or so the conventional communist wisdom went.

Russia today desperately needs to teach its young people the importance, especially for a democracy society, of the genuine equality of all its citizens, be they of Jewish, Chechen, Gypsy, Armenian, or other origin, and of the consequent need to appreciate and respect the culture and contribution of each group.

The American Jewish Committee has launched a curriculum review project to examine what is taught about Jews, Judaism, and the Holocaust in postcommunist societies. The studies on Poland, the Czech Republic, and Slovakia have already been issued. A study on the Russian educational system is currently under way (as are studies in Ukraine and Lithuania). I would be pleased to submit the Russian study to this Subcommittee when it is completed.

Are new laws needed in Russia to deal with anti-Semitism and other forms of hate? It is a difficult question to answer, in part because our American Bill of Rights enshrines freedom of speech, however repugnant that speech may sometimes be, as an essential tenet of democracy. At the same time, there are already several laws on the Russian books respecting incitement and empowering the government to prosecute publishers of extremist publications, including those deemed to be anti-Semitic. To date, however, even these laws have seldom been invoked, which may be interpreted benignly as just another manifestation of the country's current inefficiency, or more darkly as a calculated unwillingness to confront the country's hatemongers.

Mr. Chairman, I conclude as I began. In 1907, the American Jewish Committee understood that "For the prevention of massacres against Jews in Russia, no means can be considered so effective as the enlightenment of the people of the Western world concerning real conditions in Russia."

I would add that today, unlike 1907, we in fact have the possibility of pursuing two parallel strategies to ensure the well-being of Jews in Russia.

The first is the recognition that democracy and democratic institutions are the best assurance that Jews—indeed, all who live in Russia—will be governed by the rule of law, not the rule of whim. We have an extraordinary opportunity, previously unimagined or unimaginable, to help transform Russia into a full-fledged member of the family of democratic nations. Needless to say, we cannot as a nation do it alone, nor, as our experience since 1991 has demonstrated, are we yet assured of success. But to shrink from the challenge at this stage would be historically irresponsible.

And second, we as a nation must continue to make clear to Russia and its leaders that, as they look to Washington for assistance, support, and recognition of their international standing, unstinting respect for democracy, human rights, and the rule of law is central to our bilateral agenda with Moscow, never a footnote or an afterthought. And history has in fact taught us that the political and social condition of Jews in a country such as Russia is just about the most accurate barometric reading of the overall state of democracy, human rights, and the rule of law.

As the leaders of the Moscow Anti-Fascist Centre wrote in an open letter in 1996: "We are deeply convinced that anti-Semitism in Russian threatens not only Jews. . . . The growth of anti-Semitism threatens the foundations of Russian democracy, the rights and freedom of the Russian people itself and other people of Russia." In other words, for Russia to make the full transition to genuine democracy, as we pray it will, means, among other things, exorcising the demon of anti-Semitism from its midst.

In this regard, the Congress and this Subcommittee in particular have a vitally important role to play in addressing the condition of Jews in Russia. Judging from the impressive historical record stretching back 120 years, and exemplified by hearings such as this one today, I am confident that the Congress will do so with characteristic distinction, unswerving principle, and relentless commitment.

Thank you, Mr. Chairman.

(An adapted version of this testimony appeared in the *Boston Globe* as an op-ed on March 4, 1999.)

2. ISRAEL AND THE MIDDLE EAST

UN Perfidy
The Jewish Week
January 24, 1986

The *Jewish Week* should be commended for drawing attention in a December 27 editorial to the most recent and regrettable anti-Israel resolutions passed in the UN General Assembly. It is important, I believe, that friends of Israel be made aware not only of the nature of such efforts but also of the voting records of particular UN member countries.

On December 11, the assembly considered three separate resolutions critical of Israel. Each was sponsored by a rather predictable cast of Arab and other Muslim nations, plus India and Yugoslavia. Two of the measures, by virtue of their substance and tone, deserve particular attention.

The first, which advocates the "immediate, unconditional and total withdrawal of Israel from all the Palestinian and other occupied Arab territories" and support for the PLO as "the representative of the Palestinian people," calls "once more upon all states to put an end to the flow to Israel of any . . . aid, as well as of human resources, aimed at encouraging it to pursue its aggressive policies against the Arab countries and the Palestinian people."

In addition, the resolution criticizes the 1981 Strategic Cooperation Agreement and the Free Trade Area between the United States and Israel. The final vote on this measure was 98 in favor, 19 opposed (Australia, Canada, Costa Rica, El Salvador, New Zealand, the United States, and most West European countries), and 31 abstentions (Austria, Colombia, Finland, Ivory Coast, Japan, Liberia, Panama, Paraguay, Spain, Sweden, Uruguay, and Zaire, among others). Noteworthy among those voting in favor of this resolution condemning

Israel were Argentina, Brazil, Ecuador, Egypt, Greece, Mexico, Peru, and Turkey.

The second resolution was especially reprehensible. Asserting "that Israel's record, policies and actions confirm that it is not a peace-loving member state," it calls on all member states to "sever diplomatic, trade and cultural relations with Israel." It also reiterates its call to all members "to cease forthwith, individually and collectively, all dealings with Israel in order to totally isolate it in all fields." In this case, the vote was 86 for and 23 against, with 37 abstentions.

Especially disturbing in light of previous statements to American Jewish leaders were the votes of Argentina and Mexico. In the case of Argentina, Foreign Minister Caputo, meeting with an AJCommittee delegation in April 1984 to discuss another anti-Israel vote by Argentina, this time at the UN Human Rights Commission, assured the group that the vote was an "error" and that "official rectification" had been made. He explained the error as due to the "cumbersome administrative machinery" inherited by the then-new Alfonsín government.

Greece and Turkey also supported the resolution. Among abstainers were Austria, Brazil, and the other South American countries (with the exception of Argentina), and Spain. All except Spain have diplomatic ties with Israel. Those opposed to this pernicious measure included Australia, Canada, Costa Rica, Haiti, Japan, New Zealand, the United States, and the rest of Western Europe.

It would be important for readers of the *Jewish Week* who are disturbed about this voting pattern to convey their concerns to the political leaders of those countries as well as to the U.S. administration and members of Congress. American public officials should be asked to raise the matter in bilateral contacts with relevant countries.

Although we may rightfully assume the attitude that no country need be thanked for acknowledging—nearly thirty-eight years after its establishment and thirty-seven years after its admission to the United Nations—Israel's fundamental right to exist as a full member of the community of nations, we must bear in mind those states that voted with Israel. In so doing, they rejected political expediency and capitulation to the Soviet-Arab axis.

Israel and Black Africa:
A Step Closer[*]
September 2, 1986

The recent announcement of the restoration of diplomatic relations between Israel and Cameroon, the California-sized West African country, signals another important step forward in Israel's efforts to renew the close ties that characterized its links with the African continent in the 1950s and '60s.

Beginning in 1967—when Israel captured the Sinai Peninsula from Egypt, a member of the Organization of African Unity—and culminating in 1973—when Israel crossed the Suez Canal and entered North Africa in pursuit of the Egyptian army—all but four black African states severed relations with Israel either as genuine expressions of "Afro-Arab solidarity" or, in many cases, as the result of irresistible Arab economic pressure. (Mauritius followed suit in 1976.)

Today, seven black African countries maintain diplomatic links with the Jewish state. Lesotho, Malawi, and Swaziland, located in southern Africa, were the only three nations that did not sever relations with Israel in the 1970s. Zaire reestablished ties in 1982, followed by Liberia in 1983 and the Ivory Coast earlier this year. In addition, Gabon, Ghana, Kenya, and Togo are among those countries that maintain relations through diplomatic interests sections. In all, some two dozen black African countries maintain commercial contacts with Israel. Many also benefit from Israeli technical assistance. Indeed, between 1974 and 1985, 3,000 black Africans received Israeli technical training either at home or in Israel.

Israel's record of development assistance in black Africa is legendary. Especially during the decades when Israel maintained diplomatic relations with all but two black African countries—Mauritania and Somalia, members of the Arab League, were the exceptions—Israeli specialists in agriculture, nutrition, low-cost housing, education, and a dozen other fields compiled a remarkable record of practical achievements, as well as forging strong bonds of friendship. And black

*Coauthored with Harry Milkman and published in several Anglo-Jewish newspapers.

African countries could identify with Israel as a fledgling state with a strong, developing economy and commitment to democracy.

A recent American visitor to Marxist Ethiopia was struck by the undisguised nostalgia shown by several local officials for the Israeli assistance of an earlier era. Faced with the overwhelming problems of famine and drought, of desertification and deforestation, of inefficient land management and antiquated farming methods, Ethiopia could benefit tremendously from Israeli advances in desert agriculture, drip irrigation, water resources engineering, arid zone medicine, solar energy, and hydrobiology. Such pioneering centers as Ben-Gurion University's Jacob Blaustein Institute for Desert Research have made enormous strides in these areas. But Ethiopia has cut virtually all ties with Israel.

A former State Department official who served in the early '70s at the U.S. embassy in Yaounde, Cameroon's capital, in welcoming the news of the renewal of diplomatic relations between Israel and Cameroon, recalled the "genuine mutual affection" that characterized pre-1973 ties. He described the "significant impact" of Israeli technical aid on the West African nation, and noted the "profound sorrow" with which Cameroon and many other black African states, succumbing to the simultaneous fear of oil blackmail and lure of extravagant promises of Arab assistance, broke relations with Israel. The exuberant welcome that greeted Prime Minister Peres on his recent visit underscored the depth of Cameroonian goodwill toward Israel, which could only be futher enhanced by the prompt Israeli response to the freakish tragedy that took 1,500 lives when toxic gas was released from a lake inside a volcanic crater. An Israeli medical team accompanied Peres to Cameroon and remained to treat hundreds of victims and study the long-term effects of poisoning.

The lavish aid promised by the Arabs to black Africa was only partially forthcoming and could not begin to offset the devastating impact on fragile economies of OPEC's quadrupling of oil prices and the concomitant effect on the prices of such petrochemical products as fertilizers and insecticides.

But dropping oil prices and disarray in the Arab world have weakened the Arab position in black Africa. As the Jordanian daily *Al-*

Dustur (August 26) noted in commenting on the reestablishment of Israeli-Cameroonian relations, "the resumption of diplomatic ties between Israel and black African countries is not only a significant development for Israel, but a severe defeat for Arab policy in Africa." The paper added that "this development is a bitter result of the split in the Arab world."

In recent years there has been a gradual but marked shift in the level of political support for Israel among black African countries at the UN and other international bodies. The most recent effort by the Arab and Soviet blocs to deny Israel's UN credentials, in October 1985, garnered the support of only six black African members, four of which— Djibouti, Mali, Mauritania, and Somalia—have overwhelmingly Muslim populations. And Western diplomats attending UN specialized agency meetings report growing complaints from African and other third world diplomats angered by Arab efforts to "hijack" these gatherings away from their mandated technical functions, of such potential value to underdeveloped countries, by unrelenting preoccupation with Middle East political issues.

Similarly, an American delegate to last year's End-of-the-Decade-for-Women Conference in Nairobi, Kenya, cited numerous complaints by black African women furious with Arab efforts to politicize the world's women.

With declining, though still considerable, economic leverage, the Arab countries have also sought to dissuade black Africans from establishing close ties with Israel by exploiting the perception of a "special relationship" between Israel and South Africa. Surely, this perception has created difficulties for Jerusalem, notwithstanding repeated Israeli denunications of apartheid and assurances of compliance with the 1977 UN arms embargo on South Africa. Some observers note that Arab countries' trade with South Africa, though impossible to quantify precisely because of official silence on both sides, is far more substantial than the very limited Israeli-South African trade. The authoritative Shipping Research Bureau in Holland, which monitors worldwide oil deliveries, reported "the Arab proportion of oil exports to South Africa increased from 38 percent in 1981 to 79 percent in 1985" and estimates its total value at "about $2.5 billion a year." (By comparison, Israel's exports to South Africa in 1985 totaled $54 million, according to the International Monetary Fund.) Such revelations have helped undermine Arab credibility in black Africa.

Additional diplomatic opportunities for Israel do exist in black Africa. Among the key factors determining the pace of Israeli progress will be: (1) the price of oil; (2) Israel's ability to offer tangible assistance to African countries, including trade, investments, development aid, and military cooperation; (3) the role of the United States and other Western countries, especially France, whose ties to Francophone Africa remain strong, in encouraging a further diplomatic rapprochment; (4) the state of relations between Israel and Arab countries (both Israel's relations with Egypt and the recent talks in Morocco with King Hassan having contributed to a greater African willingness to consider normalization of relations with Israel); and (5) the growing strength of Islam in some black African countries and the links it creates between Arabs and Africans.

A final cautionary note: When first Zaire and then Liberia resumed ties, Israeli officials hoped for a snowballing effect, but progess has proved slower. The geopolitcal complexities of African-Arab links, in particular, militate against quick solutions. PLO, Arab League, and other Arab representatives continue to actively court black African countries. Nevertheless, the prospects for further Israeli gains in black Africa remain bright.

The First Step Toward an Israeli-Soviet Rapprochement
The World & I
November 1986

On August 18, 1986, some nineteen years after the Soviet Union broke diplomatic relations with Israel, representatives of the two countries met in Helsinki to discuss the reestablishment of consular ties. Although unexpectedly brief, the meeting, which ended with no agreement on further talks, signaled a significant change in Soviet policy. Sharp differences over the issue of Soviet Jewry, in particular, underscore the gap separating the two sides and the difficulty of further negotiations. Still, the very fact of the meeting and the likelihood of additional contacts, whether direct or by proxies, are important developments in a complex and often stormy relationship that spans four decades.

In the fall of 1947, Soviet deputy foreign minister Andrei Gromyko offered the Kremlin's support for the United Nations' plan to partition British-held Palestine. "The representatives of the Arab states," he told the world body, "claim that the partition of Palestine would be an historic injustice. But this view of the case is unacceptable, if only because, after all, the Jewish people have been closely linked with Palestine for a considerable period of history." Indeed, the Soviet Union was the third nation, after the United States and Guatemala, to recognize the fledgling Jewish state and the first to extend full de jure recognition. With Soviet assistance, Czechoslovak arms were sent to the Jews in Palestine even before the establishment of the state in May 1948. In 1949, the Soviet Union joined thirty-six other UN members in supporting Israel's admission (twelve were opposed, including nine predominantly Muslim states, and there were nine abstentions).

At the same time, the Kremlin hardened its stance toward the Soviet Jewish population. The welcome extended by Soviet Jews to Golda Meir when she arrived in Moscow in the fall of 1948 as Israel's first ambassador to the Soviet Union alarmed the Kremlin. After all, Soviet Jews were supposed to have been either assimilated or cowed into silence, but they thronged to meet Meir when she visited the Choral Synagogue in Moscow's center. The years 1948 to 1953, known as the "black years" of Soviet Jewry, were marked by the execution of leading Jewish cultural figures, the infamous "Doctors' Plot," and Stalin's plan to deport the entire Jewish population to Siberia—a plan unrealized due to his death in 1953.

On the international level, the Soviet Union's support of Israel as a counterweight to British influence and a potential socialist bulwark in the Middle East quickly gave way to a courting of the Arab nations. Diplomatic ties, however, were maintained until 1967, although they were interrupted for several months in 1953 after a bomb was set off at the Soviet embassy in Tel Aviv and despite a growing anti-Israel campaign in the Soviet Union. As a result of the 1967 Six-Day War, the

Kremlin and its East-bloc allies (except Romania) severed diplomatic ties.

Periodic Contacts

Since 1967, there have been periodic contacts between Soviet and Israeli officials in a number of capitals around the world. And delegations organized by Rakah, the pro-Moscow Israeli Communist Party, have regularly visited the Soviet Union. Participants in these groups have included many noncommunist Israelis. Other Israelis have traveled to the Soviet Union for academic and cultural purposes. Soviet citizens, including Russian Orthodox clerics, delegates to Rakah congresses, and observers at ceremonies commemorating the end of World War II, have visited Israel. From time to time, rumors of an impending resumption of formal ties have surfaced in the press, and Israeli officials have on several occasions publicly expressed a desire to renew links—asserting, however, that diplomatic protocol requires Moscow, which broke the ties, to take the first step. The pace of the contacts has notably quickened in the last fifteen months.

In May 1985, the Soviet Union's two leading newspapers, *Pravda* and *Izvestia*, unexpectedly and prominently displayed messages from Israel, including one from President Chaim Herzog, marking the fortieth anniversary of Nazi Germany's defeat.

In July 1985, the Israeli and Soviet ambassadors to France met secretly in Paris, but news of the session was leaked to Israel Radio. The report, if accurate, was sensational: The Soviet ambassador offered a deal that included resumption of diplomatic ties and Soviet Jewish emigration in exchange for Israeli withdrawal from the Golan Heights, assurances of an end to the "dropout" phenomenon (whereby many Soviet Jews leaving the Soviet Union with Israeli visas settle in the United States), and Israeli cooperation in toning down anti-Soviet propaganda in the West. The Kremlin, clearly disturbed by the leak, promptly denied any such offer, although it never denied that a meeting had taken place.

Viktor Louis, the Moscow-based journalist often used by the Kremlin to pass messages to the West, emphasized, in an interview with Israel Radio, that "there are no grounds for expecting this to herald an immediate restoration of diplomatic relations," though he added that "most likely, it will lead to occasional consultations on Middle East problems in general."

At the same time, other Soviet spokesmen, wary of Arab reaction, rushed to downplay the news. A week after the Paris meeting, Jiddah Domestic Radio Service (Saudi Arabia) reported that "an official Soviet spokesman announced today in Kuwait that the reports about the resumption of relations between the Soviet Union and Israel have been fabricated by Western sources for media sensationalism."

The next month, conflicting reports on the Soviet position surfaced. A Soviet Middle East specialist, Robert Davydkov, suggested on August 7, 1985, on the *New York Times* op-ed page, that the Soviet Union "has never questioned whether or not the state of Israel should exist" and "has sought to use its political weight and prestige in the Arab world to convince those circles that their attitude toward Israel is unrealistic and illegitimate." But, he added, "the Israeli occupation of considerable Arab and Palestinian territory is the main cause of tension in the Middle East. It is also the reason that the Soviet Union decided, in June 1967, to sever diplomatic relations with Israel." He artfully skirted the question of restoring ties.

On August 10, 1985, the Israeli daily *Yediot Ahronot* carried a report that a "high-ranking Soviet diplomat has told West German chancellor Helmut Kohl that the new Soviet leadership intends to take steps toward improving relations with Israel." Three days later, however, Leonid Zamyatin wrote in the weekly *Moscow News*: "While reasons which led to the severance of Soviet-Israeli diplomatic relations in 1967 exist, it is unrealistic to expect changes in the Soviet approach."

Heightened Anticipation

In the autumn of 1985, a whirlwind of diplomatic activity heightened speculation that progress might be at hand. Israeli prime minister Shimon Peres sent a letter to Soviet leader Mikhail Gorbachev, via World Jewish Congress chairman Edgar Bronfman, urging improved ties. Ovadia Sofer, Israel's ambassador to France, who had met with Soviet ambassador Vorontsov in July, was invited to a reception in Paris given by French president François Mitterrand in honor of the visiting Soviet leader and had occasion to talk with several Gorbachev aides. The Israeli weekly *Koteret Rashit* reported that Peres had secretly flown to Paris to meet with Gorbachev, a claim quickly denied by Israeli officials.

Attention then turned to the UN, where world leaders had assembled to mark the opening of the General Assembly and the UN's fortieth anniversary. Israeli foreign minister Yitzhak Shamir held meetings with counterparts from Bulgaria, Hungary, and Poland, the last resulting in an agreement to expand bilateral ties, including, significantly, an accord to establish low-level diplomatic links, the first such reestablishment of ties with a Warsaw Pact country since 1967. Because such a step could not possibly have been taken without the Kremlin's assent, further speculation on a possible Soviet-Israeli rapprochement was fueled. Still, the continued trickle of Jewish emigration from the Soviet Union—an average of fewer than 100 per month compared with a monthly rate of more than 4,000 in 1979—and an intensified campaign against Soviet Jewish activists raised concern in some quarters that Moscow's diplomatic initiatives were simply a shrewd public relations ploy, timed to coincide with the November Reagan-Gorbachev summit.

Peres, addressing the UN in October, declared his willingness to place Middle East peace talks under international auspices, a longstanding Soviet demand, if Moscow would agree to resume diplomatic ties. At the same time, he reiterated profound concern for the fate of Soviet Jewry. In Washington, Peres urged President Reagan to raise the issues of diplomatic ties and emigration with Gorbachev in Geneva.

Rumors of a large-scale airlift of Soviet Jews to Israel via Warsaw began to circulate, particularly after Bronfman's visit to Moscow at the end of September, his subsequent meetings with Polish officials in Warsaw, and Mitterrand's talks with Polish leaders. On October 30, 1985, Agence France Presse reported that a delegation from El Al, Israel's national airline, had visited Moscow and discussed the logistics of such an airlift. The report speculated about a possible route via Bucharest (which had been a transit point for some Soviet Jews in 1972–73), although other reports spoke of Warsaw.

Two weeks later, another Israeli paper, *Hadashot*, reported: "The Soviet Union will soon decide whether to resume its diplomatic relations with Israel. The final decision depends on the success of the summit meeting between Reagan and Gorbachev. . . . This message was delivered to Israel by a senior Soviet diplomat who conferred with a senior Israeli diplomat in New York last week."

Reports from the November summit indicate that Reagan did, indeed, raise the issue of Jewish emigration in his private meetings with the Soviet leader and that the Middle East, not unexpectedly, figured prominently in their discussion of pressing regional issues.

Despite this flurry of rumors, Peres apparently concluded by mid-December, as he stated at a press conference in Geneva, that no fundamental change in Soviet policy toward either Israel or Soviet Jewry could be discerned. Then, unexpectedly, in late December, the *New York Times* reported in a front-page story that a meeting was held in New York between a Soviet embassy official and an American Jewish representative in which the latter was allegedly told of the prospect of diplomatic ties by February 1986, perhaps in connection with the Twenty-seventh Soviet Communist Party Congress.

Calming the Fears

In a further effort to allay the fears of some Arab countries (significantly, neither Egypt nor Jordan protested reports of a possible resumption of Soviet-Israeli diplomatic ties, largely because they believed it might spur progress toward their goal, shared by Moscow, of an international conference on Middle East peace), Moscow International Service broadcast in Arabic, on December 27, a message to the Arab world: "They [the Western media] have begun to propagate rumors about preparations to restore diplomatic relations between the Soviet Union and Israel and, as is the case now, about Soviet Jews leaving the country on a larger scale to the promised land of Zionism. The aim of such a campaign is to spread feelings of mistrust and doubt in the friendly Arab countries toward their friend, the Soviet Union, and to convince Arabs that the Soviet Union has agreed, behind their backs, to something that can only arouse their concern. . . . The fabrications of the Western media are just baseless."

Undaunted, Israeli officials continued to hope that changing East-West conditions and a new Kremlin foreign-policy team, which included former Soviet ambassador to the United States Anatoly Dobrynin, might lead to changes in the Soviet posture. In March 1986, during a visit to Israel, the Finnish foreign minister agreed to convey to Moscow Israel's ongoing concern about both diplomatic ties and emigration. (Finland has represented Soviet diplomatic interests in Israel since 1967, while the Netherlands has represented Israel in the Soviet Union.)

The announcement of the Helsinki talks on consular ties in August suggested that the Kremlin, after considerable hesitation, had finally decided to test the waters—and to do so prior to the scheduled October transfer of power in Israel from Peres to Shamir. In an attempt to minimize the talks' political significance, Soviet spokesmen attributed them to concerns of the Russian Orthodox Church, which has important real estate and other interests in the Holy Land that would undoubtedly be served by the resumption of low-level diplomatic ties. But this is surely not an adequate explanation for the resumption of diplomatic talks after nineteen years. The complex web of Soviet-Arab ties and problems of Soviet-American relations, together with internal factors including the policy toward Jews, strongly suggest that the Soviet Union may have broader objectives.

What's to Be Gained?

What could the Kremlin hope to achieve by embarking on a process that might lead to restored diplomatic ties with Israel?

(1) In diplomacy there is seldom a substitute for the role played by diplomats in situ, charged with representing a country's interests and monitoring local developments. The absence in Israel creates a serious vacuum for the Kremlin—one that cannot be adequately filled by iconoclastic Romania, the only Soviet ally that currently maintains an embassy in the Jewish state. In fact, the Soviet Union has only infrequently used diplomatic rupture as a weapon, probably upon the realization that it can, at times, prove counterproductive. (A number of State Department figures contend that the United States learned the same lesson when, in reaction to the Soviet invasion of Afghanistan,

Washington canceled a consular exchange agreement with the Soviet Union that would have permitted the opening of an American consulate in Kiev. In fact, several knowledgeable Soviet officials have privately noted to Westerners that the Kremlin seriously erred in breaking off ties with Israel in 1967 rather than expressing its ire at the time by, say, merely recalling its ambassador.)

(2) Moscow is anxious to position itself at the center of Middle East affairs. For too long it has ceded primacy in the region to Washington, in part because even Moscow's Arab friends have recognized that only the United States is in a position to talk to both sides in the Arab-Israel equation, leaving Moscow to play a marginal (and usually disruptive) role only. Success in brokering a resolution of the Golan Heights issue would demonstrate to Arab states not only the Kremlin's value as a patron (in this case of Syria) but also its ability to influence events in the region.

(3) The Kremlin believes it might well enhance its image in the West, particularly in the United States, if it reestablishes ties with Israel. Were the Helsinki talks timed to soften U.S. public opinion on the eve of a new round of superpower diplomacy? Indeed, when plans for expansion of Polish-Israeli ties were first revealed last year, speculation on the motives focused, in part, on Poland's desire to improve its badly tarnished image in Washington and to strengthen economic ties with the United States.

For Israel, there would be several advantages to the reestablishment of diplomatic ties:

(1) Any agreement on the resumption of diplomatic ties would likely include a provision for increased Soviet Jewish emigration. Such a provision is indispensable to Israel. But former prisoner of conscience Anatoly Shcharansky has forcefully urged Jerusalem not to move on the diplomatic front at all until the Kremlin first permits large-scale Jewish emigration.

(2) It might enable the Jewish state to achieve its desire of direct flights from Moscow to Israel, thereby preventing the emigrants from "dropping out." Until now, Vienna has been the transit point for exiting Soviet Jews, and the Austrian government has always insisted on their right to choose their final destination.

(3) It would give Israel the chance to reestablish a physical presence in the Soviet Union. During the nineteen years when the two states maintained diplomatic ties, the presence of an Israeli embassy in Moscow held significant symbolic value for the 2 million isolated Soviet Jews.

(4) Resumption of ties with Moscow would reduce the diplomatic isolation imposed on Israel in 1967 by the Warsaw Pact countries. Indeed, it could augur a renewal of links with other countries, in both the East bloc and the Third World, that severed ties between 1967 and 1973. Since Israel's creation, one of its primary foreign policy goals has been universal diplomatic acceptance.

Of course, resumption of diplomatic ties would entail serious risks for both sides. For the Kremlin, it could strain relations with such Arab states as Syria, Libya, and Algeria, unless Moscow could induce Israeli withdrawal from the administered territories and action on the Palestinians. Also, the Kremlin worries about the potential impact on the Soviet Jewish population of an Israeli embassy and a cadre of Israeli diplomats in the Soviet Union. From Jerusalem's viewpoint, acceptance of a Soviet role in the

Arab-Israeli peace process could complicate chances for settlement. It might also lead to differences with Washington. Finally, if the Israeli government fails to achieve substantial progress on the emigration question, the government would face a serious domestic backlash.

Observers will be closely watching the progress of the diplomatic contacts, as well as the rate of Soviet Jewish emigration, and watching, too, the development of ties between Israel and Eastern Europe—especially with Hungary, which is likely to be the next country to restore formal relations—to determine whether a new chapter in Soviet-Israeli relations is truly unfolding.

Once Upon a Time in Libya*
Moment
May 1987

The year 1987 marks the twentieth anniversary of two distinct but intimately related events, one that has been the focus of considerable attention, the other virtually ignored. As the world followed the June 1967 war raging between Israel and her Arab neighbors, an ancient Jewish community was on the verge of disappearing. It was then that Libya's remaining 4,000 Jews—who had survived colonial occupiers from the Phoenicians and the Greeks to the Italians and the British, as well as sixteen years of Libyan national independence—were forced to leave their country in the wake of a vicious pogrom, the third since 1945.

"American Jews often ask me the same questions when they hear where I am from," said Giulia. (She, like the other Libyan Jews interviewed, asked that her real name not be used.) In 1967, at the age of sixteen, she fled her native Libya. "'Do you mean Lebanon? Oh, Libya! Was there really a Jewish community in Libya? Do you speak Yiddish? And how was it to live under Qaddhafi?' In other words, most American Jews have absolutely no idea that we ever existed, much less that we were once a thriving Jewish community. . . . We were expelled from Libya before Qaddhafi seized power in 1969. Yes, there was a pre-Qaddhafi Libya! It was a sometimes wonderful and beautiful country that, notwithstanding the complexities of being Jews in an Arab country, my family and I considered home. And it was a special place where we enjoyed the influence of Italian, British, French, American, and local cultures, together with an unshakable identity as Jews. But we were forced to leave, and the experience has scarred us for life."

According to the first-century Jewish historian Josephus, Jews were first settled in Cyrene and other parts of present-day eastern Libya by the Egyptian ruler Ptolemy Lagos (323–282 B.C.E.). With their numbers likely bolstered by Berbers who had converted to Judaism, later supplemented by Jews fleeing the Spanish and Portuguese Inquisitions

*Variations of this article appeared as op-eds in the *International Herald Tribune* and the *Jerusalem Post.*

and, from the seventeenth century, by Jews from Leghorn and other Italian cities, Jews lived continuously in Libya for well over two millennia, predating the Muslim conquest in 642 C.E. by centuries.

In 1911, 350 years of Ottoman rule ended and the Italian colonial period began. At the time, Libya's Jewish population numbered 20,000. The next quarter century was to prove a golden age for Libya's Jews. They enjoyed equal rights with the country's other residents and benefited from increased employment and educational opportunities. By 1931, nearly 25,000 Jews lived in Libya, of whom all but 4,000 lived in Tripoli and a dozen towns and villages in Tripolitania province, the westernmost of the three provinces that make up modern Libya. The remainder were centered in Cyrenaica province, to the east, largely in the coastal city of Benghazi. No Jews lived in the interior province of Fezzan.

The introduction of anti-Jewish legislation in Fascist Italy was extended to Libya in 1936. Under its provisions, on Shabbat Jewish shops had to remain open and Jewish schoolchildren were required to attend school. Identity cards stamped "Race: Jewish" were issued to all Libyan Jews. By 1940, Libya became the scene of heavy fighting between the Axis and British armies. On orders from the German military commander, the Axis forces, in 1942, plundered Jewish shops and deported 2,600 Benghazi Jews to Giado, a remote military outpost overlooking the Sahara Desert.

More than 200 Libyan Jews of British nationality were among those deported to Italy in 1942 by the Fascists. Rita, now a U.S. resident, was eleven years old at the time. She remembers:

"The Fascists sent us to a camp in Abruzzi, the mountainous region east of Rome," she recalled. "We were well treated, even permitted kosher food and a synagoguge. Italian Jews sent us matzoh for Passover and books. You must understand that the Italians were very different from the Germans. After nearly two and a half years in Abruzzi, we were deported by the Nazis to Bergen-Belsen. In our group was a three-month-old boy who had been born in the Italian camp. He was circumcised in secret in Bergen-Belsen. You see, we never gave up our beliefs. We never forgot who we were, even there. Fortunately, through a combination of luck, our British passports, and

Red Cross interest in the camps in Germany, we were transferred to a civilian prisoner-of-war camp after six months. In September 1945, I returned to Tripoli and, as far as I know, virtually all the others deported from Libya survived as well."

By contrast, nearly 2,000 able-bodied Tripoli Jews were conscripted into forced labor. In January 1943, two weeks before these conscriptees were to be sent to Tunisia, the British army liberated Libya. Louis Rabinowitz, a senior Jewish chaplain with the victorious forces, recorded his impressions:

"Under Axis order, the conscripted Jews of Tripoli toiled from daybreak to nightfall throughout the long summer days, with one meal a day. . . . But they only worked six days a week. Even the Axis knew that nothing would induce these pious . . . Jews to work on the Sabbath." And, referring to Giado, the camp for Benghazi Jews, Rabinowitz noted that "no one was exempt from this cruel edict. . . . Were it not for the weekly loads of food which were sent to them by the Tripoli Jewish community, they would surely have starved to death. . . . As it was, 215 of the internees were laid to rest. They had died from undernourishment and typhus."[*]

Jewish soldiers of the British Eighth Army, recruited in Palestine, were the first to enter Tripoli in 1943. Under their influence, Zionist activity among Libyan Jews, which had gained strength in the 1920s and '30s but was curtailed by the Axis powers, was revived. The Joint Distribution Committee (JDC) provided cash relief to indigent Jews; the Jewish soldiers assisted in reestablishing the Jewish schools that had been closed by the Axis occupiers.

Pan-Islamic and anti-Jewish propaganda fueled by the Arab League, coupled with the rise of Libyan nationalism, led to Muslim rioting in 1945 in Tripolitania province. Not until the third day did the British even attempt to end the rioting. (Many Libyan Jews are persuaded that the British were, in fact, at least partially responsible for the pogrom, citing the otherwise inexplicable British delay in responding to the violence. According to this view, the British were disturbed by Jewish calls for an independent Jewish state in Palestine. Also, they were reportedly anxious to hold on to their colonies and manipulated Arab-

*"Chronicles: Liberation in North Africa," *Menorah Journal* 33 (April-June 1945).

Jewish relations in Libya to prove that the country was not ready for independence.) In the end, the death toll was 130, with 450 injured and 4,000 left homeless; nine synagogues were destroyed and countless Jewish-owned shops damaged.

Three years later, provoked by Libyan nationalists and Tunisian volunteers passing through Libya to the Palestine front, mobs again attacked the Jewish quarters. But this time a quicker British response, as well as the efforts of the Jews themselves, in the form of a self-defense organization created in the wake of the 1945 pogrom, limited the damage. Even so, fifteen Jews were killed and hundreds of families were left homeless.

As a result of the two pogroms, decades of reasonably cordial relations with Muslims came to an end. Driven by fear for their safety and well-being, and drawn by the creation of the Jewish state, the vast majority of Libya's 39,000 Jews began to consider aliyah, emigration to Palestine. In 1948, because of British restrictions, emigration to the fledgling Jewish state was carried out clandestinely via Tunisia, France, and Italy. Twenty-five hundred Libyan Jews—mainly young people eager to aid Israel's struggle for independence—had succeeded in reaching Israel by April 1949, when it became possible for the Jewish Agency openly to organize monthly trips by ship from Tripoli to Haifa. By 1952, the first year of Libyan independence, 33,000 Libyan Jews had emigrated to Israel. Abe Loskove, who was director of the JDC's Libyan operation during those tumultuous years of mass aliyah, recalled the period in a recent interview:

"There was a veritable clamor to get out of the country as a result of the 1948 pogrom and the excitement of the new Jewish state. Everyone was shouting 'aliyah.' We had to work fast, as the handwriting was on the wall. Once Libya achieved independence, we knew aliyah would stop. But as much as people wanted to leave and Israel wanted them to come, we were presented with a formidable challenge. Many of the Libyan Jews, especially from the *hara* (ghetto) in Tripoli and the interior, suffered from trachoma, tinea, tuberculosis, and malnutrition. Our primary goal was to address these urgent medical needs before people left. . . . Jews departed in such large numbers that the ships were often carrying twice as many passengers as they were built for. In all, this aliyah was very successful. Libyan Jews integrated quickly and beautifully in Israel."

In December 1951, Libya became an independent state ruled by King Idris I, who had been the leader of Cyrenaica province. The 6,000 Jews who remained did so for a variety of reasons: ties to the land and culture, age, infirmity, nontransferable business interests, quality of life, indecision, missed opportunities, faith in the country's leadership. The 1945 and '48 pogroms had certainly left their mark, but they were still seen as aberrations from the true Libyan character of tolerance. After all, Arab-Jewish relations in Libya had been good. In the 1943–44 *American Jewish Year Book*, for instance, it was reported that the Libyan Jewish condition under Axis occupation "would have been far worse, had it not been for the friendly attitude of the Muslim population." Relations would undoubtedly remain cordial, the Jews felt, under the leadership of the king, who had been admired for his benevolent rule in Cyrenaica. And the Libyan constitution, drafted under the supervision of a special UN commission and adopted in 1951, contained important protection clauses. Jews and the other minorities (Italians, Maltese, and Greeks) were accorded full rights. In fact, the document was regarded as a model for other Muslim countries with Jewish populations destined for decolonialization.

Abraham Karlikow, then assistant director of the American Jewish Committee's Paris office and later the AJC's director of foreign affairs, worked closely with Libyan Jewish leaders to achieve these guarantees. He described the community in a 1951 report, less than a year before Libyan independence: "The Jewish community of Tripoli is extremely Orthodox, and this applies to the Westernized, better-off Jews as much as to the poor Jews of the *hara*, where half of Libya's remaining Jews continue to live. On the Sabbath the leading business street in Tripoli, the Corso Vittorio Emanuele, is virtually shut down. . . . The community had thirty synagogues before the war; now there are seven. The interests of the men center around their business.... There is hardly a Jewish professional in the country. [A study of more than 6,000 Libyan heads of household who arrived in Israel between 1948 and 1951 found that, among the respondents, 47 percent were artisans, 15 percent merchants, 7.5 percent clerks and administrators, 7 percent construction and transport workers, 6 percent farmers, and 3 percent in the liberal professions.]

"The community was sharply divided on economic grounds. The financially better-off Jews in Tripoli adopted Western dress and manners . . . and could double for middle-class businessmen in New York without any particular difficulty. The poor Jews lived much like the Arabs around them. On the surface, in dress, language, and manner, they could hardly be distinguished from their Arab neighbors. Their living conditions were frightful. . . . The leadership of the community is centered in the Jewish Community Board, whose major responsibilities include the provision of relief to the disadvantaged, synagogue and cemetery upkeep, Jewish educational assistance (together with JDC and the Alliance Israelité Universelle), and contact with the authorities. . . . Whereas eleven rabbinical academies existed in Tripoli in 1880, by 1950 there were none, and a Hebrew teachers' seminary that opened in 1947 was shut down a few years later because of the large-scale emigration."

Notwithstanding constitutional guarantees, restrictions on the Jewish community were gradually imposed. As early as 1952, Jews were forbidden to return home if they visited Israel, and access to Libyan passports became virtually impossible. Few Libyan Jews were granted citizenship in the newly independent Libyan state, though most families had lived in the country for generations. The next year, Libya joined the Arab League and increasingly echoed its anti-Israel rhetoric. All contact with Israel was proscribed. In 1958, the Tripolitania Jewish Community Board was forcibly dissolved and the authorities appointed a Muslim to administer the affairs of the community. Two years later, the Alliance Israelité Universelle school, which had functioned since 1870, was closed. In 1961, a law was promulgated permitting the seizure of all property belonging to Jews who emigrated to Israel.

Ten years after independence, Jews could not vote, hold public office, serve in the army, obtain Libyan passports, purchase new property, acquire majority ownership in any new business, or supervise their own communal affairs. Yet the Jews remained. Their daily lives were, to a substantial degree, largely unaffected by these prohibitions:

Access to the synagogues was unimpeded; businesses often prospered; for many, their British, French, Italian, or Tunisian citizenship inspired a degree of confidence and security; and faith in King Idris's basic friendship to the Jewish minority continued. An elderly Tripoli Jew whom I met in Israel in 1984 tried to explain his decision to stay in Libya through the '50s and early '60s:

"It's quite natural to wonder why we remained in a country increasingly inhospitable to Jews and implacably opposed to Israel and Zionism. How could we live tranquilly when we constantly feared the uncovering of our contact with relatives who had left for Israel in 1948 and 1949? I guess the answer is really rather simple: Our roots in Libya were deep, our attachment to the country strong, and our daily lives as Jews, believe it or not, unhindered. We came to resign ourselves, almost to take for granted our political powerlessness and physical vulnerability. Without specific provocation, it would have been difficult to just get up and leave for an uncertain future."

As late as January 1967, Tripoli's Jews felt sufficiently confident of their position to plan the construction of a new synagogue in the city center. But in the ensuing months, growing tension throughout the Middle East and North Africa was fueled by Egyptian president Gamal Abdel Nasser's provocative actions against the Jewish state and fiery anti-Israeli rhetoric. Libya's Jews hoped they would somehow remain untouched by events beyond their country's borders, but the outbreak of war in the Middle East in June of that year dispelled any such hopes. A Libyan Jew who served as a correspondent in Tripoli for an international Jewish organization recalled the impact of the Six-Day War on the Jewish community:

"At ten o'clock in the morning of June 5, the news that hostilities had started between Israel and the Arab states spread throughout the city like lightning. 'The Week for Palestine' (inspired by Nasser's pan-Arab pronouncements), which had begun a few days earlier with controlled and pacific demonstrations, . . . exploded into fanatic and destructive demonstrations against the peaceful Jewish population. . . . The mob, drunk with fanaticism and constantly excited by false news (from the battlefront), hurled itself ferociously and violently upon Jewish stores and homes, provoking fire, destruction, and massacre.

The sections most heavily attacked included the *hara*. . . . The government had to proclaim a state of emergency and ordered a curfew from 7 p.m. until 6 a.m. For the safety of the Jews of the *hara* and the distant sections, they were taken to a barrack at Gurgi, about four kilometers from the city center, but those Jews living in other sections were asked not to leave their homes since the police were unable to give them adequate protection. . . . Several Arabs and Italians who tried to buy bread for their Jewish friends were blackmailed and threatened with serious measures if they did it again."

Corriere della Sera, a leading Italian newspaper, carried an interview on June 13 with a fourteen-year-old boy, one of six Jewish refugees who managed to flee Libya at the time. "From the day the war began, I did not go out of my house," he recalled. "For a while we used the food we had; then we began fasting. Once in a while, threatening phone calls came for us. We decided to escape from Tripoli when the eleventh call came and a man's voice said, 'Dirty Jew, we shall chop you into a thousand pieces.'"

Giulia, who was then a sixteen-year-old pupil in an Italian school in Tripoli, still remembers those traumatic events with obvious pain:

"Tensions were building in the weeks prior to the outbreak of the war. Then the war began, and we huddled at home—my parents and eight children, ranging in age from seventeen to three. The mob came. It seemed there were a thousand wild-eyed, chanting men. Some had jars of gasoline which they began to empty on our house. One was about to strike a match when another Arab, whom we had known for years, called on the crowd to withdraw. He said that we were a decent family who had never harmed anyone. Amazingly, everyone complied. That act took unspeakable courage."

Beda, Giulia's mother, had had warm relations with Muslims all her life. During the 1950s, her family had been the only Jews in a town midway between Tripoli and Benghazi, where they remained observant. The children attended a Catholic school (the alternative being an Arab/Muslim school), but were excused from prayers. The family does not recall any anti-Semitic incidents either in that coastal town or later in Tripoli, where they moved in the early '60s. Thus, the ferocity of the

Muslim outburst in June 1967 not only surprised them but also caused great anguish and soul-searching.

"Many Jews were murdered during the riots," Beda recalled. "I had known several of the victims well, and it causes me untold grief to this day to recall their fate. And the wanton destruction of the Jewish buildings, homes, and stores, and our forced expulsion rip at my soul. The graves of all my relatives are there. The most difficult thing of all is that I have not been able to return to the grave sites of my family. And were I allowed to travel in Libya today, I would find that the Jewish cemeteries have been destroyed to make way for roads and hotels.

"Qaddhafi ignored our appeals to exhume and transfer the bodies before construction began. And our synagogues have been desecrated, turned into mosques or cultural centers. Still, despite everything that happened in 1967, Libya was my country. Yes, many local Arabs came to kill us, and did viciously kill the others. But I cannot overlook the fact that other Arabs saved us at great personal risk. After the mob left our home that first day, we were afraid to stay there. Muslim friends broke the curfew to shepherd our family to the safety of their own home and kept us there for ten days until things quieted down. We owe them our lives."

By the time calm was restored, eighteen Jews in Tripoli were dead. Two families were killed by a Libyan official who said he was escorting them to shelter. An old woman and a young boy were murdered as they ventured out of their homes in search of food. A girl tried to get to the *souk* (market) dressed in a *barracan* (Arab dress) and with covered face, but was recognized and killed on the spot. And an elderly Maltese was mistaken for a Jew and fatally stabbed. Property damage was in the millions of dollars.

The 230 Jews in Benghazi fared somewhat better. Though shops were destroyed, the police controlled the situation much sooner than in Tripoli and transported the Jews to a camp near the city for their own protection.

The death toll might have been even higher had it not been for the courageous intervention of Cesare Pasquinelli, Italy's ambassador to Libya, who personally extended protection to several Jews in danger and ordered all Italian diplomatic missions in the country to help in any way they could. Pasquinelli, who had acted similarly during World War II to rescue French Jews, died shortly afterward. Libyan Jews in Israel honored him posthumously for his heroism.

Finally, faced with a complete breakdown of law and order, the Libyan government urged the Jews to leave the country temporarily. Whereas, in the past, Jews had had considerable difficulty obtaining travel documents, Libyan officials were now visiting Jewish homes and issuing such documents on the spot. Escorts were provided to the airports. But departing Jews were permitted only one suitcase and the equivalent of $50.

In June and July, some 4,000 Jews traveled to Italy, where they were assisted by the Jewish Agency, JDC, the Hebrew Immigrant Aid Society, the ad hoc Emergency Committee of Jews from Libya, and the Italian Jewish community. About 1,300 of these refugees continued on to Israel, where they joined 33,000 Libyan Jews who had emigrated in the 1940s and early '50s and were by then well established in such locales as Netanya and Bat Yam. Twenty-two hundred remained in Italy, primarily in Rome and Milan. Already fluent in Italian and heavily influenced by the dominant Italian culture in Libya, they adapted with comparative ease. A few hundred eventually resettled in the United States. Today, only six elderly Jews remain in Tripoli.

The Association of Jews from Libya, whose current president is Raffaelo Fellah, was founded in 1970. Based in Rome, it has sought to pressure the Libyan government to provide compensation for seized Jewish communal and personal assets. The association also collaborates with the Cultural Center of the Jews of Libya in Israel and Beth Hatefutsoth, the Tel Aviv-based Museum of the Jewish Diaspora, to help preserve the legacy of the community. A photographic exhibit was featured at the museum, and several booklets on Libyan Jewish history have been published.

Predictably, the so-called temporary exodus in 1967 became permanent. A few score of Jews remained in Libya, while others managed, in the two years prior to Qaddhafi's coup d'état in September 1969, to return briefly in an attempt to regain their possessions. While a few succeeded, others, who became trapped in Libya after Qaddhafi's accession to power, had great difficulty in getting out, and some were forcibly detained for years.

In 1970, the Libyan government announced a series of laws to con-fiscate the assets of Libya's Jews, issuing bonds providing for fair com-pensation payable within fifteen years. But 1985 came and went with no compensation ever paid, despite the efforts of the Association of Libyan Jews and others to gain the help of Western governments and international organizations. Qaddhafi has excused his defaulting on the bonds by asserting that "the alignment of the Jews with Israel, the Arab nations' enemy, has forfeited their right to compensation."

And so, with only a few scattered international protests and scant press attention, another once-thriving Jewish community came to an end.

Indeed, within two decades of Israel's founding, nearly 1 million Jews from Muslim countries emigrated or were forced to leave. Ancient communities in Egypt, Iraq, Yemen, and other countries dis-appeared. Still, as Yusef, a fifty-five-year-old Rishon le-Zion resident who arrived in Israel in the 1950s, explained: "After more than 2,000 years, it has all come to an end for us. Or maybe not. Maybe it was all by way of preparation for the next 2,000 years, for our lives in the Jewish homeland. We are strong believers in God, you know, and in the fulfillment of His will."

Israel's Door Is Mostly Open
St. Louis Post-Dispatch
August 1, 1987

The recent reports of alleged Israeli harassment of some black and Arab-American passport-holders leave an unfair impression of Israel's entry policy for foreigners. Western visitors to Israel are not required to apply beforehand for a visa. Instead, they are processed, usually per-functorily, at their point of disembarkation on Israeli soil. While it is regrettable that a handful of travelers have gone to the length of arriv-ing in Israel only to find their admittance blocked—and this policy needs to be periodically reviewed to avoid unnecessary complications—every sovereign state claims the right to deny entry to individuals who, it believes, may create problems. Ask any foreigner about procuring a U.S. visitor's visa. The process can be cumbersome; some do not succeed. Indeed, in light of legitimate Israeli security concerns, it's laudable that Jerusalem seeks to keep its doors open.

Forty American citizens of Palestinian origin were reportedly denied entry this summer. Still, 400,000 visitors a year—Christians, Jews, and Moslems—go to Israel from the United States; and tens of thousands of visitors are expected to cross into Israel from Jordan this summer alone, many of them bearers of passports from countries technically at war with Israel. In contrast, Israelis are flatly denied the chance to visit these neighboring countries. Moreover, virtually all Jews, regardless of nationality, find it impossible to enter some Arab lands. Perhaps we expect more of Israel as a democracy, yet where is the condemnation of such blatantly discriminatory practices? Has the State Department protest been sent to, say, Saudi Arabia?

Finally, some reports have focused on the harassment by Israeli immigration officers of a few black Americans because of the fear that they may be Black Hebrews, a group that has entered Israel from the United States illegally and refuses to leave. No country would knowingly admit persons who come under the guise of tourists but plan to stay indefinitely. This is much less so, in the case of Israel, with a controversial sect whose leader associated himself with the Jew-hating Louis Farrakhan in 1984, and whose members were deported by Liberia in 1969 after two years there because, according to a Monrovia news account, they were "undesirable aliens." To deduce, as some readers might, that this implies racism is unfair. The 15,000 Ethiopian Jews who were dramatically rescued from the throes of widespread famine and persecution and welcomed to Israel, and the thousands of black Africans and Americans who have come to Israel to tour or study are more than ample proof that racism is not the issue.

A "Shrill Account" of the Arab-Israeli Conflict
The Washington Post
January 2, 1988

Mary McGrory's shrill account of a complex and deeply troubling situation [Outlook, Dec. 27] does little to advance the cause of reasoned discussion about the Arab-Israeli conflict.

I too am pained by the loss of life and the accusations of excessive lethal force leveled against Israel. If Israel did indeed use unnecessary force, as McGrory states, it is saddening, and I trust there will be a thorough investigation and review of procedures once calm is restored. The experience of the Kahan Commission, which engaged in an exhaustive and no-holds-barred review of the Sabra and Shatilla tragedy in Lebanon, should reassure us of Jerusalem's commitment to rule by law and official accountability. If Israel's army and police are inadequately equipped and trained to deal with riot control, as the U.S. administration asserts, immediate steps must be taken to reverse the situation. And if individual soldiers engaged in acts of brutality, Israel's generals in charge of the troops in both the Gaza and West Bank regions must follow through and, if warranted, prosecute, as Israel has publicly said it would.

But the blindly scathing criticism McGrory directs at Israel without more than a passing nod at its unenviable predicament is deeply troubling. Especially repugnant was her preposterous moral equation: "The Jews have never accepted the Arabs as human beings any more than the Arabs have accepted the existence of a Jewish state." It is precisely the Arabs' unwillingness over decades to accept a Jewish state in their midst that has been at the root of the Arab-Israeli conflict for four decades, not the offensive and undocumented notion that Jews have "never accepted the Arabs as human beings."

And what occurred when one courageous Arab, Anwar Sadat, came forward in 1977? Israel responded and, with U.S. assistance, concluded the historic Camp David Accords. The result: Israel yielded a huge tract of land containing air bases and precious oil fields, not to speak of the vital strategic depth the land represented, for written promises of peace, nothing more. Still, Israel has correctly never regretted this risky exchange. And the Arab leader? Assassinated for having pursued peace. That fear of the gunman's bullet has prevented many other Arab heads of state and Palestinian leaders from issuing similar calls for face-to-face negotiations.

In no way can we deny the poignancy of the Palestinian problem, for which a just solution must be found. But let us not fool ourselves. The Arab world has skillfully manipulated the Palestinian problem as a weapon in the struggle against Israel by permitting the Palestinians to live for as long as forty years in squalid camps. Where else in the world can one point to such a phenomenon? Moreover, when the West Bank and Gaza were under Jordanian and Egyptian control respectively until 1967, what did these countries do for Palestinian aspirations? Suppress them.

It's also worth remembering a few basic facts about the current situation that McGrory completely ignores:

- Israel, in accordance with its international obligations under the Geneva Convention, has the responsibility to restore law and order in Gaza and the West Bank.
- Israel faced a violent uprising, not an American campus protest. The protesters' use of firebombs was intended to maim and kill, not simply to make a debating point. In fact, in interviews with Western journalists, some of the demonstrators explicitly cited their aim of expelling Jews from Israel proper, arousing the worst visceral fears among Israelis.
- If we have knowledge or visual images of events in the troubled areas, it is largely because Israel is committed to a free press. Where were the media, for example, when 20,000 Syrians were slaughtered in Hama from 1979 to 1982 or, for that matter, during the [Argentine-British] war in the Falkland Islands?
- If soldiers overreacted to civil unrest, ought it to be so entirely strange to the world? Is the record of the United States and other countries in coping with unrest perfect?
- McGrory's assertion that "inside Israel, there is silence" is directly contradicted by photographs and an accompanying report that appeared in various U.S. papers the same day as McGrory's col-

umn of a sizable protest demonstration in Jerusalem, the third organized by Peace Now since the unrest began.

• McGrory's claim that "Palestinian youth . . . were living under apartheid" is especially pernicious. No conceivable ultimate settlement in the Arab-Israel conflict could codify the separation and inequality central to South Africa's institutionalized racism.

The challenge for those committed to peace—in Israel, the United States, Jordan, and among Palestinians prepared to repudiate senseless armed struggle and recognize Israel's right to exist—will be how to accelerate the process. As McGrory states, "negotiation is clearly the answer." I agree. The alternative to peace talks is indeed unthinkable.

For Jews in Arab Countries, Morocco Is the Exception
The Washington Post
February 20, 1988

Mostafa Albulghaith Albalghiti's letter [Free for All, Feb. 6] concerning Jews from Arab countries must not go unchallenged.

Albalghiti asserts that "the Jews' departure from North Africa, after centuries of peaceful . . . coexistence with Arabs, was caused by Zionist European Jews who mounted propaganda campaigns of lies and distortions in the 1950s to scare them into emigrating to the newly established Jewish state. . . ."

Not quite. For example, take Libya. Jews had lived there since the Phoenician period. In 1945, three years before Israel's creation, rioters launched a pogrom against the 39,000-member Jewish community, with drastic consequences: 130 Jewish dead, 450 injured, 4,000 homeless, and synagogues and Jewish-owned shops destroyed. Three years later, provoked by Tunisian volunteers passing through Libya to the Palestine war front, mobs again attacked the Jewish quarters. Better Jewish security (and a quicker British response) limited this pogrom's damage to 15 dead. Add the fear of Arab nationalism from the granting of Libyan independence in late 1951 and joy over Israel's establishment to help understand why, by 1952, all but 6,000 of Libya's Jews had departed for Israel.

Those Jews remaining in Libya believed in the goodwill of King Idris I and trusted the 1951 constitution, drafted under UN supervision, which accorded full rights to minorities. Yet ten years later, Jews could not vote or hold public office, obtain Libyan passports or supervise their own communal affairs. And during the 1967 Six-Day War, 18 Libyan Jews were killed in mob violence. The Jews who still remained in the country, including my wife, then a teen-ager, and her family, were encouraged to leave by a government that could not guarantee their safety. Each departing Jew was permitted to take one suitcase and the equivalent of $50.

This pattern—pogroms, second-class citizenship, uncertainty about the future—has been repeated in Iraq, Syria, Egypt, and several other Muslim countries, compelling Jews to leave in large numbers. This is the other side of the Palestinian refugee problem. Any final resolution of the Arab-Israeli conflict, including indemnification for Palestinian refugees who lost property because of Israel's creation, also must take into account the property claims of hundreds of thousands of Jewish refugees from Muslim lands. UN Security Council Resolution 242 buttresses this claim by asserting "the necessity for achieving a just settlement of the refugee problem."

Albalghiti's Morocco is the exception, not the rule. Yes, Muslim-Jewish relations are much better than in almost any other Islamic country. Moreover, King Hassan's moderate stance on the Arab-Israeli conflict, including his promotion of early Israeli-Egyptian contacts in the 1970s and reception of Prime Minister Shimon Peres in 1986, provides a welcome alternative to Arab rejectionism. But there have been problems.

Jewish apprehension first manifested itself prior to Moroccan independence from the French in 1956. Tens of thousands of Jews, uncertain about their future under local rule, departed. Emigration was then restricted. When restrictions were lifted, more than 100,000 Jews left between 1961 and 1964.

Albalghiti writes that "after the 1967 war, some Jews in Morocco were reported to have celebrated the Arabs' defeat. These reports caused tensions, broke countless friendships and caused many but not all of the remaining Jews to emigrate in the following few years. . . ."

In fact, history records other events. According to a UPI report (June 12, 1967), two Jewish youths were murdered, their throats slit by a Meknes mob as they were leaving a café. Another Jew was critically wounded in Rabat, and yet another was assaulted in Casablanca. While King Hassan quickly denounced these anti-Jewish acts and fired the Meknes police commissioner, Jews understandably were anxious, all the more so given the dissemination of virulent anti-Semitic and anti-Zionist propaganda by the anti-regime Istiqlal Party.

Even in such relatively moderate countries as Morocco and Tunisia, without the stability ensured by democratic process, and with the apprehension generated by growing radicalization and fundamentalism in much of the Muslim world, it is not surprising that many Jews might seek refuge in such countries as Israel and France, which have offered much greater long-term prospects for Jewish normalcy and security.

Israel's in Trouble: What Can We Do?[*]
Heritage
April 22, 1988

Israel is in trouble. Even were the issues not enumerated daily for us in both the print and electronic media, our *kishkes* tell us as much. But what is not as obvious is what we can do from this end to help.

Many American Jews have anguished and agonized over the past four months. Difficult questions without apparent answers have been brought into sharp focus. Confusion and uncertainty have gripped parts of the community. But in too many cases a paralysis has resulted. People aren't certain what to do, so, as often as not, they do nothing.

Whether an individual agrees with, say, the current Labor or Likud viewpoint, there is a strong underlying case to be made for Israel, and we need to make it. Israel is faced with painful choices that go to the heart of its security concerns. No other sovereign state in the region must confront such core survival issues.

If the American Jewish community does not fulfill its task to interpret Israel sympathetically in this country—and this does not neces-

*This article also appeared in numerous other Anglo-Jewish newspapers.

sarily require agreement with every action taken in Jerusalem—American support for the Jewish state could erode.

Five specific activities where friends and supporters of Israel should be concentrating their efforts are:

(1) *Learn the facts.* If we are to be effective in interpreting events, we ourselves need to be on top of the issues. Too many of us are not. The debate is becoming increasingly sophisticated and requires a good understanding of background and context. For many Americans, it seems, the Arab-Israeli conflict began on Dec. 9, 1987, the starting date of the current wave of unrest. Obviously, that's not true. We have to be able to explain that more than four decades of significant history have brought us to this point. For example, the current picture might be very different had the Arabs, including the Palestinians, been at all forthcoming since 1947.

(2) *Contact members of Congress.* Perhaps uncertain of what to say, too few friends of Israel have written to their congressmen and senators. It is vital to write these officials and urge their continued support and understanding for Israel's unenviable predicament. Send an informative article or sympathetic editorial that you found in the press and urge the legislator to place it in the *Congressional Record.* Seek meetings with your members of Congress; be sure to acknowledge it if they publicly say something favorable about Israel.

(3) *Don't be afraid of the media.* Lots of people complain about the media's reporting, but mostly they do it to themselves and their friends. If you think the media has mishandled a story, shown a lack of objectivity, ignored the context, used a misleading headline, presented an unbalanced editorial, etc., say something. The assumption is incorrect that nothing can change the media's mind, so why even try. Indeed, if people do nothing to show displeasure, then what will ever change? Write directly to the editor or the ombudsman, especially if you can thoughtfully document a pattern of unbalanced coverage. Submit letters to the editor and opinion pieces. Place phone calls or write letters to the networks, particularly when an especially offensive segment is shown, such as the by-now notorious ABC piece on Israel and South Africa.

Experts note that the media seldom will openly acknowledge error or imbalance, but well-reasoned protests by viewers or readers may nonetheless have a beneficial impact. One example: A colleague met with the editorial board of a leading newspaper that had published several editorials chiding Shamir for his alleged intransigence on the "land for peace" question. "I don't deny your right to make such statements," said my colleague, "but I assume you are also writing about the Arab failure to be forthcoming." The editors shamefacedly admitted they had not but would now consider doing so.

(4) *Travel to Israel.* This is not a time for us to hold back on visiting Israel. To the contrary, it is an opportunity to underscore our close links with Israel, to share impressions with Israelis, to learn more about the current situation, and to assure Israelis that they are not being abandoned. Recent travelers report that life is continuing normally and peacefully in most parts of the country.

(5) *Talk about Israel with non-Jews.* America's support for Israel has always been drawn from a broad spectrum of this country's population who have understood the fundamental moral, strategic, and historical ties that have bound the United States and Israel for four decades. It is vital that we find opportunities to meet with representatives of Christian, civil rights, ethnic, labor, and other civic groups to explain our perspectives and hear theirs, and to answer their questions. But again, to do so effectively requires a good grasp of the issues.

If we don't undertake these tasks, who will?

Israel Has Never Sought Military Domination
The Washington Post
May 28, 1988

I searched in vain for even a single reference in Colman McCarthy's tirade against Israel [Style, May 15] for some recognition of Israel's extraordinary forty-year-long security predicament. Alas, not a word. Instead, we are treated to an unfettered and reckless attack on Israel's "soulless militarism," its "terrorists," and its policies as a "rabid arms peddler" and "mindless retaliator."

Forty years ago, at the time of Israel's creation, the nation's declaration of independence stated: "We extend our hand to all neighboring states and their peoples in an offer of peace and good neighborliness, and appeal to them to establish bonds of cooperation and mutual help with the sovereign Jewish people settled in its own land. The State of Israel is prepared to do its share in a common effort for the advancement of the entire Middle East." The Arab response? Attack by the armies of five countries against the fledgling country of 600,000 Jews.

Put simply, Israel has never sought military domination over another people, nor have Israelis aspired to the highest tax rate in the world to support their country's defense, nor have Israeli men desired to continue their active military reserve duty until the age of fifty-five, nor have Israeli parents wanted to raise their children to know how and when to use bomb shelters. Those are the realities, Mr. McCarthy.

Israel's survival is due, first and foremost, to the courage of its people and the strength of its armed forces. Would that it were otherwise, but in a world where, according to the 1987 report of the U.S. Arms Control and Disarmament Agency, eight of the ten top countries in terms of military expenditures as a percentage of GNP are Arab (Israel ranks twelfth), and where six of the world's ten leading arms importers are Arab/Muslim (Israel ranks twelfth), does McCarthy naively expect Jerusalem to pursue its policies with plowshares alone?

Israel needs a domestic arms industry to ensure sufficient weaponry and to prevent what has happened in the past when, for example, Britain and France cut off supplies in times of emergency. Yes, Israel does what, for varying political and economic motives, including economies of scale, thirty-eight other nations in the world do—namely, export weapons. It's a nasty, ugly business, but one that seventeen other countries, including the USSR, the United States, France, Brazil, and Sweden, do much more than Israel, according to the Arms Control and Disarmament Agency.

No nation yearns more for peace and normality than Israel, but the sad reality, though McCarthy inexplicably dismisses it, is that peace can only be achieved through strength. That was the lesson of the Israeli-Egyptian peace treaty. Only when President Anwar Sadat recognized that he could not wipe Israel off the map and that future wars

would only lead to more victims on all sides, did he take his courageous and historic step, one to which Israel responded generously.

That desire for peace was forcefully articulated by Israeli ambassador Moshe Arad in the same interview in the *Washington Jewish
Week* (April 21) for which McCarthy criticizes Arad for lack of intro-
spection and for harping on Israel's military prowess. Indeed, Arad
stated: "Those who doubt the sincerity and the willingness of Israel to
make sacrifices . . . to achieve peace should put Israel to the test. . . .
Did this government or any other government ever get put to the test
and then not live up to its responsibility?"

The Metro Ad: Moral Inversion[*]
Washington Jewish Week
August 18, 1988

The outrageous ad now appearing in the Washington, D.C., Metro
system turns reality upside down. The slogan "Israel, Soviet Union,
South Africa—One Yardstick for Human Rights," sponsored by the
American Arab Anti-Discrimination Committee (ADC), is the latest
example of moral inversion in the Arab-Israeli conflict.

Absurdly, the ad suggests equivalence among Israel, the Soviet
Union, and South Africa. The differences among these three countries
are so profound and obvious with respect to democracy, political
process, freedom of speech and assembly, media access, capital punishment, and other basic human rights tenets, that to rebut the ADC
canard in detail is to accord it excessive dignity.

However, if the ADC is truly looking for flagrant human rights
abusers to condemn, perhaps it might focus its attention on a region
where it may even wield some influence, namely, the rest of the Middle
East. There, it might well find appropriate company for the Soviet
Union and South Africa. Let the ADC examine the human rights
records of Syria, Saudi Arabia, Iraq, Iran, South Yemen, Libya, and
other countries, and then compare these countries' records on human
rights with that of Israel.

*This article also appeared in numerous other Ango-Jewish newspapers.

Is Israel a perfect society? Has it handled the *intifada* exemplarily? Supporters of Israel are unafraid to acknowledge that forty-year-young Israel has its flaws, that genuine resolution of the Palestinian issue presents a major challenge to Israel (and her neighbors), and that no country, not even the long-standing democracies, has found an easy method of coping with violent unrest. But Israel clings tenaciously to a democratic system that permits political parties ranging from the Moscow-oriented Rakah Communist Party to Meir Kahane's Kach Party on the right. Israel has never resorted to capital punishment (except in the case of Adolf Eichmann). If we are aware of events in the West Bank and Gaza, it is because Israel not only has permitted foreign press, but has a higher ratio of overseas journalists to its population than any other country in the world. And Israel's army, despite provocations, threats and, yes, some regrettable excesses, has sought to exercise maximum restraint—or else there would have been many more casualties.

Let the ADC give some thought to human rights in Saudi Arabia. The State Department's annual country reports and other respected human rights surveys indicate that forty-five public executions occurred in Saudi Arabia in the first nine months of 1987. Moreover, these reports indicate that adultery is punished by capital punishment; trials are generally closed and normally held without counsel; no provision is made for bail or habeas corpus; criticism of Islam and the royal family is forbidden; labor unions and strikes are prohibited; political demonstrations are illegal; all Saudis must be Muslim and the practice of Christianity is against the law; conversion to another religion is a crime punishable by death; and women may not drive cars or travel alone without the permission of their nearest male relative. And the Saudi response to unrest? Last year in Mecca, 401 people were killed in a single clash between Iranian Shiites and Saudi security forces.

Let the ADC publicize human rights violations in Syria where, according to the same sources, thousands of political prisoners have been detained without charge; reports of torture and executions surface regularly; public criticism of the ruling Ba'ath Party and other official institutions is not permitted; the government strictly controls the dissemination of information; and public meetings can be held only with official permission. In addition, President Assad wields virtually absolute power. Palestinians—a presumed object of the ADC's concerns—may not acquire Syrian citizenship or vote in Syrian elections, and in a 1987 report on Syrian torture, there was evidence of systematic abuses inflicted on detainees, including about 3,000 Palestinians held in Syrian prisons. And the Syrian response to unrest? As many as 20,000 killed by security forces in 1982 in the city of Hama, with no media allowed to cover, of course.

And maybe the ADC will have some time left over to deal with Iraq, where, without even the benefit of legal proceedings, hundreds of executions take place each year. Further, murder has been the government's preferred method of dealing with political opponents; the death penalty was introduced for the crime of insulting the country's officials; arbitrary arrest and detention without trial are commonplace; Christians are not permitted to proselytize or hold meetings outside of church premises; the government owns the press, radio, and television and forbids the expression of dissenting views; and, most ominously, the military has used chemical warfare against neighboring Iran. And the Iraqi response to unrest? Chemical warfare against its own Kurdish citizens earlier this year resulted in the deaths of as many as 5,000 civilians. Also, in 1987, some 500 Kurdish villages were deliberately destroyed by the Iraqi army, dislocating several hundred thousand residents.

Too much of the world continues to demonstrate utter moral hypocrisy and applies double standards when it comes to Israel as opposed to the rest of this rough, tough region. The current ADC ad is only the latest sorry example. For First Amendment reasons, we may not be able to prevent its display, but we can ill afford to leave the baseless charges unanswered.

Arad-Jackson Meeting Important
Washington Jewish Week
August 25, 1988

Larry Cohler's excellent report on the meeting between Israeli ambassador Moshe Arad and Rev. Jesse Jackson (*WJW*, Aug. 11) indicated that some American Jewish leaders had criticized the ambassador's decision to engage in discussion with Jackson. They were particularly critical of the Israeli envoy because he may have overstepped his mandate by discussing the domestic issue of black-Jewish relations. This criticism is mistaken.

First, it was important for Arad and Jackson to meet. If Jesse Jackson, who presents himself as a friend of Israel, is going to seek to continue to be involved in the Middle East, he must hear Israel's case. He must understand Israel's rejection of a Palestinian state, Israel's deep yearning for peace, and Israel's vision of the future. Moreover, he must come to understand why the pernicious 1975 UN resolution equating Zionism with racism is so offensive to every Israeli, indeed every Jew. He must be told that there simply is no role in the Arab-Israeli conflict for private negotiators. He must comprehend Israel's policies on the Black Hebrews cult. He must grasp that Israel condemns apartheid and is reducing its bilateral ties with South Africa.

As I understand the meeting, Arad made all of these points forcefully and constructively. That can only be to the good.

Second, the ambassador doubtless understands the boundaries between Israel's and American Jewry's agendas in the United States. I somehow suspect he has a sufficiently full plate dealing with issues affecting the Middle East without seeking to involve himself in American domestic issues. And if Jackson was attempting an end run around the organized American Jewish community, I doubt he received satisfaction. According to several participants at the meeting, while understandably expressing his concern about manifestations of anti-Semitism in the United States (and why, as a Jew, shouldn't he?), the ambassador made it clear—during the meeting and in the press statement issued by the Israeli embassy—that the address for black-Jewish dialogue on domestic topics is the organized community.

Arad's step took foresight and courage. It may or may not contribute to an easing of the thorny Jackson issue, but it was worth the risk.

Jackson and Israeli Spoke of Black Hebrews
The New York Times
August 30, 1988

Your report on the meeting between Moshe Arad, Israel's ambassador to the United States, and the Rev. Jesse Jackson (news story, Aug. 8) noted that, among other issues, the two men discussed "the plight of black Israelis." That's not quite true. Jews from Ethiopia and other black Jews were not the focus of discussion. Why should they be?

Israel has welcomed more than 15,000 Ethiopian Jews, who in recent years have realized a 2,000-year-old dream to return to Zion. In doing so, as Marvin Arrington, president of the Atlanta City Council and a black, wrote in 1985, "The people of Israel have demonstrated that we are our brothers' keepers, and that kinship transcends race."

The issue raised by Mr. Jackson dealt specifically with a sect known as the Black Hebrews, a group of about 2,000 former Americans who claim to be the true descendants of the original Israelite nation. The first thirty-nine Black Hebrews entered Israel in 1969 after having been expelled from Liberia. Over the years, their numbers were augmented by others who entered Israel as tourists or pilgrims but continued their residence illegally. The group, which has not been recognized by the Israeli rabbinate as Jews, has shown all the trappings of a cult. Until now, Israel has generally sought to avoid deportation despite the group's illegal status, searching instead for a humane solution.

In 1981, a delegation of American civil rights leaders visited Israel to study the Black Hebrews' situation. They concluded: "From all the evidence we have heard, including that from the Black Hebrew community, we conclude that official racism plays no part in this sensitive problem."

It was this specific issue of the Black Hebrews that was the subject of talks between Ambassador Arad and Mr. Jackson, not a larger racial question.

Watch Your Language
Newsday
December 6, 1988

Your article on Egypt's recognition of the Palestine Liberation Organization's declaration of an independent Palestinian state contained one significant error ["Egypt Chooses Sides," Nov. 21]. In referring to United Nations Resolution 242, which would be the basis of any peace negotiations to settle the Arab-Israeli conflict, the article noted that the resolution calls for an Israeli withdrawal from "the territories" it captured in the 1967 Six-Day War. This formulation necessarily implies complete withdrawal.

In fact, the actual wording of the resolution is deliberately more vague: "withdrawal of Israel armed forces from territories occupied in the recent conflict." Note that it says territories, not *the* territories. In this case, one word can make a lot of difference. The drafters of the UN resolution felt it important not to predetermine the final boundary lines of any peace settlement. That must be up to the parties themselves.

Jewish Exodus from Arab Lands
The Wall Street Journal
January 12, 1989

A Palestinian named Rafiq, mentioned in your December 19 International-page article "Giddy Mood of PLO Leaders Is Tinged With Apprehension and Anger at U.S.," is quoted as saying, "It is because of Israel that I am here, not there.... I don't think Americans understand the price we have paid."

Rafiq's claim may be one side of the equation. There is, however, another less-well-known side. Unlike the Palestinian issue, this other side never has been the topic of discussion at the United Nations, much less special sessions. Never has it been a matter of debate at the national political convention of a major American political party, nor the stuff of many editorials, columns, or news reports. It is the mass exodus of Jews from Arab countries since Israel's creation in 1948, an exodus that numerically rivaled the number of Palestinians who departed from Israel.

My wife was among those Jews compelled to leave. Born in Libya, she was part of a community that had lived uninterruptedly in that country since the time of the Phoenicians. The vast majority of Libya's 40,000 Jews left between 1948 and 1951, following pogroms in 1945 and 1948. Despite constitutional guarantees granted in 1951, the Jews who remained were denied the right to vote, hold public office, obtain Libyan passports, supervise their own communal affairs, or purchase new property. After a third pogrom in 1967, Libya's remaining four thousand Jews fled, permitted to leave with only one suitcase and the equivalent of $50. In 1970, the Libyan government announced a series of laws to confiscate the assets of Libya's departed Jews and issued bonds providing for fair compensatioin payable within fifteen years. But 1985 came and went, with no compensation ever being paid.

If one hears so little about the hundreds of thousands of Jewish refugees from the Arab world, it is because they were quietly resettled, primarily in Israel. This resettlement stands in stark contrast to the situation of the Palestinians, who often were kept in camps and cruelly used by their own leaders and Arab countries as part of a calculated campaign to keep alive hatred against Israel.

This brief review does not solve the compelling problem of finding a humane solution to the Palestinian issue without, at the same time, endangering Israel. But it does suggest that Rafiq, the Palestinian quoted, regrettably has ignored, or is unaware of, the other group of refugees rendered homeless by the forty-year-long Arab-Israeli conflict.

Moral Hypocrisy
Baltimore Jewish Times
February 3, 1989

Re your report on the latest UN condemnation, by a vote of 130 in favor, 2 opposed (Israel and the United States), and 16 abstentions, of Israel's policies in the territories:

If anyone still has doubts about the moral hypocrisy and political double standards of the world body, they should consider that, on the same day this one-sided resolution was passed, the General Assembly also approved a resolution on Afghanistan. In this case, however, though the General Assembly called for the immediate withdrawal of foreign forces from Afghanistan, there was no reference by name to the source of those foreign forces, namely, the Soviet Union.

One can only wonder what magnitude of tragedy is necessary before the General Assembly would directly criticize a country like the Soviet Union.

No Clear-Cut Formulas for Mideast
The Christian Science Monitor
March 9, 1989

The opinion-page column "The Best Kept Secret in the Middle East," February 2, boldly asserts that a Palestinian state "will almost certainly have far better, far closer relations with Israel than with the surrounding Arab countries. Why? In a word, 'self-interest.'" Later, the column asserts that "the state which Palestinians intend to create will be governed democratically."

The history of the Middle East suggests there seldom are such clear-cut, neat formulas. When has there been a truly democratic country in the Arab world? Is there a guarantee of a stable Palestinian state? The feuding between various Palestinian factions has temporarily subsided—though certainly not ended—due to the attempt to maximize gains from the current uprising. Would internecine fighting quickly erupt in a new state?

If such a state looked to Israel, it could be, as this column predicts, as an economic partner, but it could also be to continue the irredentist struggle to seize Israel proper. Given Palestinian history and rhetoric, is this fear so far-fetched?

Would that Middle Eastern politics were as simple to forecast—and unnuanced—as this column presents. Experience, however, has abundantly shown how difficult a business it is.

Hypocrisy at the UN
The Jewish Week
November 3, 1989

Your editorial on blatant moral hypocrisy at the United Nations (October 13) raises another interesting question: How would the world respond if the Baltic states—Estonia, Latvia, and Lithuania—pressed forward with their current nationalist movements and asserted their right of self-determination, demanded secession from the USSR, and appealed to other nations for support?

When the Palestine Liberation Organization unilaterally declared the creation of the "State of Palestine" last year, dozens of nations, mostly from the communist bloc and third world, rushed to extend diplomatic recognition. The UN General Assembly accommodated the PLO by convening a special session in Geneva when the United States refused to issue Yasir Arafat a visa to address the world body in New York, only the latest example of the UN's numerous efforts on behalf of the PLO.

It would be fascinating to watch the world's reaction to possible demands for self-determination from the Baltic republics. If the Palestinian statehood issue was so easy for many countries, this one should be a piece of cake. After all, Estonia, Latvia, and Lithuania were once independent nations, unlike the "State of Palestine." Their borders are not in dispute. They pose no threat to their immediate neighbors, have no larger territorial designs, and have not engaged in nationalist violence either within their borders or beyond. Their occupation by the USSR was entirely illegal, as the 1939 Nazi-Soviet protocols reveal; no one today seriously suggests otherwise.

Let's see how those same countries that recognized the Palestinian claim for self-determination would react if faced with a similar call from the Baltic republics. Would these countries, allegedly committed to the principle of self-determination for all peoples, risk the certain displeasure of Moscow? Would the PLO?

And let's see how the UN would handle it. Would there be the same special sessions and lopsided votes as regularly occur on the Palestinian issues?

Any bets?

Quayle
Washington Jewish Week
January 4, 1990

I was startled to read reporter Jon Greene's treatment of Vice President Dan Quayle's recent speech at Yeshiva University calling on the United Nations to reverse the infamous "Zionism is racism" resolution (*WJW*, Dec. 21). Rather than praise the vice president for a timely statement on an issue that touches us all so deeply, he chose instead to offer gratuitous insults and rather flippant comments quite extraneous to the heart of the matter. Who cares whether the vice president should or should not have quoted Albert Einstein's definition of education? What explains such a snide remark as "send him [Quayle] back to finishing school" in an article prompted by Quayle's welcome step on the "Zionism is racism" question? Who cares what impact the speech had in Iran or Kuwait? The fact is that Quayle, to the credit of this administration, has raised an important issue and signaled to the world this country's determination to seek repeal of a UN resolution whose main purpose was to delegitimize Israel's right to exist.

Instead of chiding Quayle, we ought to be encouraging him and the other members of the administration to press forward in this worthy effort with the full backing of the Jewish community.

Israel Isn't the Only Haven for Soviet Jews
The New York Times
March 26, 1990

"Again, Palestinians Suffer" by Edward Said (op-ed, March 6) is replete with misinformation. Unchallenged, his argument will add even more confusion to the discussion on Soviet Jewish emigration to Israel.

Why, he asks, "did the U.S. and Israel agree in 1989 that Soviet Jews, who once enjoyed the right to go anywhere after receiving visas, would be given the option of emigrating only to Israel?" There is no such agreement. And Soviet Jews never "enjoyed the right to go any-where"; only Israel, the United States, and, to a lesser extent, Australia and Canada have accepted emigrating Soviet Jews.

Mr. Said suggests that now Soviet Jews can emigrate only to Israel. Not true. The United States continues to accept Soviet Jews and other Soviet citizens seeking admission. (So do Australia and Canada.)

Indeed, 50,000 of the 125,000 refugees to be admitted to the United States in this fiscal year are expected from the Soviet Union. In addi-tion, as many as 20,000 others from the Soviet Union may be admitted as parolees and several thousand more Soviet citizens as immigrants. The vast majority of these new arrivals to the United States will be Jews. More Soviet Jews are expected to enter this country in this fiscal year than in any previous year since the onset of Soviet Jewish emi-gration in 1971. While these slots may not be sufficient to meet the demands of all who seek entry, the situation is still a very far cry from closing the United States' gates, as Mr. Said asserts.

Mr. Said states that "many Soviet Jews have made no secret of their 'mission to settle' in the occupied territories." That is preposterous. Most Soviet Jews arriving in Israel are driven not by ideological fervor but by fear of the future in the Soviet Union. Moreover, according to the decennial Soviet census, Soviet Jews are the most highly urbanized nationality group in the country. Their overwhelming desire is to reset-tle in urban areas in Israel.

As your Jerusalem correspondent noted in a March 7 article, "So far, only about 300 of the roughly 20,000 Soviet Jews who have moved here"—to Israel—"in the last year have chosen to live in the West Bank." That's 1.5 percent of the total, hardly the mass effort to replace the Palestinians that Mr. Said states.

Isn't Mr. Said using the statistically insignificant resettlement of Soviet Jews in the West Bank as a smoke screen for a larger purpose, consistent with the Arab world's long-standing aim of seeking to pre-vent mass Jewish immigration to Israel?

After all, Jewish immigration strengthens Israel's permanence in the region, a permanence that too few in the Arab world have openly accepted.

Quotation of the Day
The New York Times
July 4, 1990

"We created a mythical image for Israel that neither Israel, despite all of its remarkable achievements, nor any other nation could ever live up to."

The Real Meaning of Israel
Jewish Telegraphic Agency
August 10, 1990

To better understand Israel's raison d'être, it's worth a visit today to a gray, three-story building on a tree-lined street named Bolshaya Ordynka. If the location does not sound readily familiar even to frequent Israel-goers, it's because the building is located 2,000 miles to the north, in Moscow. There, at the Israeli embassy site, six accredited Israeli consular officials—the maximum number allowed by the Soviets—work under extremely difficult conditions to facilitate the unprecedented flow of Soviet Jews to Israel.

On any given day, hundreds of Jews assemble to request or receive a visa, to exchange the latest information and rumors about Soviet bureaucratic obstacles, to discuss the best available transit routes, to assess the absorption process in Israel.

These are the Jews who were not meant to be, the Jews who, according to Soviet plans, should have disappeared, but who instead persist in asserting their Jewish identity.

Jews are on the move—no one knows quite how many may be caught up in this mass exodus. The 1989 Soviet census states that there are 1.45 million Soviet Jews, but the actual number—and thus potential pool of emigrants—may be much higher, perhaps even double that amount, some experts assert.

This image of Soviet Jews on the move made me think back to a period fifty years earlier—a period I had not witnessed personally, but had tried to visualize in my mind so many times.

As I stood outside the Israeli building on Bolshaya Ordynka, I imagined an eighteen-year-old Jewish girl and her parents in France in 1941, frantically seeking an entry visa to a distant country, a ticket to safety.

How that girl must have trembled when she was told, after waiting outside the U.S. consulate, to return in three months because the application forms had not been properly filled out! Here were the Germans establishing control over Europe and rounding up the Jews, and the girl was told: Sorry, try us again in three months.

In the end, fortune was on her side. She and her parents managed to cross the Spanish border and eventually arrived in the United States. That girl became my mother. But how many other European Jews tried in vain to obtain visas to safe countries?

There was no Jewish state in those years. Persecuted European Jews were dependent on others. A tiny few responded; most did not.

Not to compare the Soviet Union of today with the Europe of the Nazi era; the two situations are quite different. But Soviet Jews similarly feel themselves a population at risk. Many have become amateur meteorologists, looking toward the horizon, trying to guess tomorrow's weather. Clearly, there are some dark clouds out there, but are they moving in our direction? How quickly? Is a storm inevitable, or might it pass us by?

And they worry, in particular, about their children's future. What awaits the youngsters? Will Soviet society become a genuine democracy with safeguards for minorities and commitment to the rule of law? Or will power be seized by the sinister forces—the anti-Semites, the xenophobes, the extreme nationalists—lurking in the wings? Will there one day be civil war, social upheaval, anarchy in the streets? Few Jews, and not many non-Jews either, are willing to bet on the future.

Increasingly, each Soviet Jew has a particular fear: that Pamyat's threats of pogroms will one day materialize; that Jews will be scapegoated for the country's deteriorating economic situation; that Jews will be blamed for the end of the Romanov dynasty and the onset of communism; or that, in a country whose various nationalities increasingly are asserting their territorial autonomy, there really is no place for Jews.

For many, of course, the fears are overlapping. But there is one common denominator: the fear that the exit doors, currently open to all but a few, may one day close, notwithstanding the declared Soviet intention to adopt a liberalized exit-and-entry law.

The doors are now open, the thinking goes, but they never remained permanently open in the country's history. Take 1979, for example, when 51,000 Jews emigrated. Yes, there were refuseniks and obstacles to emigration, but some Soviet Jews were lulled into a false sense that, for those with no connection to state secrets, the odds on leaving were pretty good.

So instead of rushing out, they deliberated. That was a tragic mistake, since, by 1982, the total annual number of Jews permitted to leave was only 2,688. Now, in some Soviet cities and towns, Jews say that, if current emigration trends continue, there will not be many Jews left within a few years.

And that's what makes Israel so important. These Soviet Jews feel apprehensive. Whether the objective circumstances in the USSR warrant this apprehension may be a subject of debate among Soviet observers, but it almost seems irrelevant. Those well-honed Jewish instincts are telling Soviet Jews it's time to go. But where to were there no Israel?

The United States now allots 40 percent of its annual refugee intake to the Soviet Union (approximately 50,000 slots), but is not willing to expand its numbers infinitely to absorb ever larger numbers of Soviet, or other, refugees. Australia and Canada accept only a handful of Soviet Jews, New Zealand and Western European countries even fewer.

Some, even many, Soviet Jews might have preferred resettlement in the United States, but they are not hesitating to emigrate to Israel. No doubt, they are mindful of Israel's myriad problems, including the staggering challenge of absorption of such large numbers of newcomers, high unemployment, insufficient housing, security issues, religious-secular tension, political divisions and so on.

(If 150,000 Soviet Jews arrive in Israel in 1990, it represents, in proportional terms, the equivalent of more than 9 million refugees settling in the U.S. in one year!)

But 10,000 to 15,000 Soviet Jews per month are boarding planes and trains to transit points in Europe and then proceeding to Israel. That ought to tell us something both about the conditions that prompt Jews to leave the Soviet Union and the role played by Israel as a sanctuary and home. And that ought to move us sufficiently to respond to the moment.

One immediate way is to contribute to the United Jewish Appeal's Operation Exodus campaign to raise the huge sums necessary to absorb Soviet Jews in Israel and, in doing so, to be an active part in the nation-building now going on in Israel. This campaign is absolutely vital to ensuring the success of the aliyah; a successful aliyah, in turn, will have an incalculable effect on Israel's future well-being.

Israel, Unlike Iraq, Fought to Protect Itself
Chicago Sun Times
August 27, 1990

In his Aug. 18 Forum ["Inconsistent foreign policy threatens U.S. security"], Fadi Zanayed compares Iraq's recent occupation of Kuwait to Israel's defensive war against Egypt, Jordan, and Syria in 1967.

A brief look back shows how absurd the comparison is.

On May 16, 1967, Cairo Radio blared forth: "The existence of Israel has continued too long. The battle has come in which we shall destroy Israel."

That same day the Egyptian government called for withdrawal of the United Nations peacekeeping forces that had been in place for ten years.

Just a week later, Egyptian president Gamal Abdel Nasser, the Saddam Hussein of his day, annmounced he would bar Israeli ships from the Straits of Tiran, an act that Israeli prime minister Levi Eshkol said would be considered "an act of aggression." A few days later Nasser repeated that "our basic objective will be the destruction of Israel."

King Hussein of Jordan ignored Israel's pleas that he stay out, and he placed his forces under Egyptian control on May 30. Troops from Egypt, Iraq, and Saudi Arabia were sent immediately to Jordan. A few days later, Iraq's president said, "We are resolved, determined, and united to achieve our clear aim of wiping Israel off the map."

With Arab leaders poised against a backdrop of such threats, Israel had little alternative but to make a preemptive strike, which came June 5. In six days the war was over, with Israel capturing territory from Egypt, Jordan, and Syria, and thus preventing the destruction sought by the Arab nations. Ironically, had King Hussein heeded Israeli pleas and stayed out, the West Bank would have remained within his jurisdiction.

When Mr. Zanayed compares Iraq's actions today to Israel's twenty-three years ago, he either forgets the facts of history or conveniently omits them from his analysis to take gratuitous potshots at the Jewish state.

There's No Comparison
Newsday
August 29, 1990

Shame on Mohamed Mehdi, president of the American Arab Relations Committee, for making the false comparison between Iraq's illegal and unprovoked occupation of Kuwait and Israel's 1967 defensive war against the combined forces of Egypt, Jordan, and Syria that resulted in the Israeli capture of the West Bank (and other territory) ["Arab-American Fear Backlash From Invasion," Aug. 8].

Why must Mehdi resort to Israel-bashing to help explain the current intra-Arab conflict? How can he question the difference in U.S. reaction to two entirely dissimilar events?

Did Kuwaiti leaders explicitly and repeatedly threaten in public statements to eliminate Iraq in the weeks prior to Iraq's invasion? Did Kuwait mobilize its troops to match deed to chilling rhetoric? Did Kuwait move to close off Iraq's vital shipping lanes?

Kuwait didn't do any of these things; but in 1967, Israel's neighbors on three sides did, which led to the Six-Day War.

On the eve of that war, Israel's leaders sought in vain to persuade Jordan's King Hussein to stay out. The king, however, couldn't resist the temptation to join with Egypt and Syria to strike a blow against Israel. Had wiser heads prevailed in Amman, the Jordanian-controlled West Bank would not have become a battlefield and fallen into Israeli hands.

Israeli Ambassador Arad
Washington Jewish Week
October 4, 1990

As Israel prepares to send its new ambassador, Zalman Shoval, to Washington (News, Aug. 16), it is well worth noting the important contributions of the current envoy, Moshe Arad, who will be returning home in mid-September.

Arad came to Washington as Israel's ambassador three years ago. To say the least, it has not been a quiet period. The *intifada*, Israel's handling of the Palestinian uprising, the U.S. dialogue with the PLO, a new U.S. administration, the peace process, the Israeli unity government's collapse and an ensuing period of paralysis, and the Gulf crisis are just some of the issues that took place during Ambassador Arad's tenure here.

Through it all, Moshe Arad, working under very difficult circumstances, particularly when representing a Labor-Likud coalition government that often seemed to be at cross-purposes, effectively presented Israel's message. He dedicated himself to maintaining and advancing the vital U.S.-Israeli bilateral link and strengthening ties between Israel and American Jewry.

He deserves considerable credit for the work he has accomplished. And no matter what the circumstances, he always managed to conduct himself with consummate graciousness and aplomb.

Those of us who have had the pleasure of working with Ambassador Arad will long remember his considerable skill and talent as Israel's ambassador during these past three years.

Let's Not Condemn Israeli Misfortune
USA Today
October 12, 1990

As thousands of Jews gathered Oct. 8 at Judaism's holiest site, the Western Wall in Jerusalem, to mark the holiday of Sukkot, they were pelted with hefty rocks thrown by Palestinians. Simultaneously, in another well-planned assault, thousands of Palestinians attacked forty-five Israeli policemen at the Temple Mount. Miraculously, only a few worshipers were injured. But the police, faced with a raging mob urged on by Muslim clergy and others, were unable to protect themselves with the use of tear gas or rubber bullets. In the end, they resorted to live ammunition. More than twenty Palestinians were killed, over one hundred injured.

The loss of life was regrettable, but it could have been avoided. The pretext for the Palestinian gathering was the knowingly false claim that a fringe group of Jews was planning to lay the cornerstone for a "Third Temple" on the Temple Mount. No such group appeared. Indeed, the Israeli Supreme Court had specifically barred the group from the area, and that decision had been conveyed to the Muslim leadership.

Since Jerusalem was unified in 1967, Israel has made every effort to maintain the delicate balance of the three religious faiths that consider the city a holy site (in contrast to Jordan's rule of the eastern part of the city from 1948 to 1967). Mayor Teddy Kollek has been a shining example of Israel's commitment to respect the "complexity of life" in the city, as he refers to it.

Moreover, in the past year Israel has strenuously sought to avoid violent clashes with Palestinians. This helps explain the few Palestinian casualties at Israeli hands that have recently occurred. Indeed, until the Jerusalem incident, more Palestinians had been killed this year by fellow Palestinians than by Israelis.

But somehow all of this was lost in the world reaction. No one cared to examine the facts or weigh the Israeli explanation, much less await the results of the independent commission of inquiry. Predictably, the UN Security Council was brought into the picture immediately. (When was the last time the Security Council was convened to discuss the deaths of Jews, victims of Palestinian terrorist attacks in Rome, Vienna, Istanbul, Antwerp, Munich, Ma'alot, and dozens of other places? The answer: never)

What was surprising and troubling was the U.S. willingness to participate in the Security Council effort. Clearly driven by a desire to hold the current coalition of forces in the Gulf together, the United States appears willing to lay the lion's share of blame for the incident at Israel's doorstep. This ignores the deliberate provocation of the Palestinians and their obvious desire to recapture world attention, which had withered due to the Iraqi attack on Kuwait and the Palestinians' rush to embrace Saddam Hussein.

Instead, the United States should make clear its unwillingness to participate in any one-sided resolution that skews the facts. It is one thing to seek to maintain a diverse coalition to oppose Saddam. That's a worthy and understandable goal, even if it includes such unsavory thugs as Syria's Assad. But it's quite another to victimize a proven friend and ally over an incident that Israel, least of all, desired.

U.S. Will Stand by Israel
The Orange County Register
January 3, 1991

Saddam Hussein's latest threat to attack Israel as Iraq's first target if war breaks out in the region needs to be taken seriously. All along, Israel has been trying to warn the world of the growing Iraqi threat, in the spheres of both conventional and nonconventional weapons, but, rather than heed those warnings, too many countries and private companies devoted their energies to helping create a muscular Iraq. . . . Thankfully, Israel destroyed the French-provided Osirak nuclear facility in 1981, or else the current U.S.-led coalition would have had to factor into its strategic planning the possibility of a nuclear-armed Iraq.

All of this underscores the extreme dangers and volatility of the region in which Israel exists. And it reinforces the point made by the Israeli government in its 1989 peace initiative, namely, that as compelling as the Israeli-Palestinian issue is, there can be no true peace in the region without parallel progress on the conflicts between Israel and the Arab states.

The United States has already made clear it will stand by Israel in the event of an attack by Iraqi forces. This is an important statement of U.S. principle and policy. American support and assistance to Israel will be vital should a conflict begin. At the same time, in the final analysis, Israel is America's one truly stable, dependable, and democratic ally in the Middle East.

Rx for the Mideast: Democracy
USA Today
January 17, 1991

It is useful to look beyond the seemingly endless cycle of violence, strife, and bloodshed in the Middle East. In this respect, the example of Europe is instructive:

For forty years, East and West faced a tense, potentially explosive standoff. But now Germany is a united, democratic republic, Czechoslovakia, Hungary, and Poland have thrown off communism, and Bulgaria and Romania have taken significant, if still tentative steps in that direction. Likewise the USSR, though given Soviet actions in the Baltics, its commitment to democracy is in serious question.

Still, there has been a quick shift away from military confrontation. Sure, conflicts arise, but democracies are able to resolve differences through negotiation. Talks have now replaced tanks in Europe. Indeed, when was the last time one democracy sent its armies against another?

It is precisely any semblance of democracy that is missing from the Middle East, with the exception of Israel. Whatever its imperfections—and, like all democracies, Israel has them—it has remained fundamentally committed to free and fair elections, the peaceful transfer of power, an independent judiciary, basic civil liberties, a free press, and respect for religious, racial, ethnic, and other minorities within its borders.

The West has pursued, with considerable success, a democratic revolution in Europe, Latin America, and parts of Africa. But the West largely turns its back on the tragic consequences of undemocratic rule in the Arab world—the vulnerability of minorities, including Christians; the inferior status of women; and the absence generally of the rule of law.

Arab societies have been shaped by powerful religious and historical forces. It will not be easy to encourage fundamental reforms that retain cultural distinctiveness but permit the creation of stable, tolerant, and free societies. Still, such a shift could transform the region's landscape, encouraging mutual confidence among nations, serious arms control possibilities, and multilateral efforts to address such urgent issues as the scarcity of water. Most important, it might bring peace to the area—genuine and lasting peace.

Israel Under Siege
Baltimore Jewish Times
February 22, 1991

The Tel Aviv-bound El Al plane [on January 18] was full. That came as a pleasant surprise, given the media's preoccupation with conditions at the other end—people reportedly besieging airline counters at Ben-Gurion Airport, rushing to leave Israel as war appeared imminent.

The flight carried Israelis hurrying home to their families; reservists who, though they had not been called up, wanted to be close by; television camera crews assigned to cover unfolding events in Israel; and a sprinkling of American Jews, including the comedian Jackie Mason, eager to show, somehow, by their presence in Israel a physical identification with the Jewish state as the first Iraqi missiles hit civilian population centers.

As we disembarked at Ben-Gurion Airport, a fellow passenger pointed to another group of travelers filing into the customs hall. One hundred twenty Soviet Jews had just arrived on a flight from Bucharest. Astonishingly, even while the country was under attack, new immigrants continued to stream in. One can only imagine the absorption worker's words: Welcome to Israel, Mr. and Mrs. Rabinovich. Here are your identity cards, pocket money for initial expenses and, oh yes, your gas masks for yourselves and your children. Keep them with you at all times.

Surely, their arrival at this time speaks volumes both about the immigrants' perception of the situation in the USSR and their determination to settle in Israel. Equally remarkably, Israel has not for a moment reduced its absorption effort, although other immediate life-and-death needs compete for the nation's attention.

Within an hour of our registration at a Jerusalem hotel, the sirens went off, signaling another possible missile attack. From launching to impact is a matter of minutes, yet the hotel residents quietly made their way up the stairs to the designated ninth-floor rooms. Ten people to a room, we were told, then close the door, seal its edges with tape, place a wet towel along the bottom, put on the gas mask and filter, make sure it fits snugly, turn on the radio for further instructions—and remain calm.

The recommendation of sealed rooms on high floors was a calculated gamble by Israeli authorities. Uncertain whether Iraq's military had the know-how to mount chemical warheads on their missiles, the government made a difficult choice. If chemical warheads were deliverable, sealed rooms—the higher, the better—would be safer and, in any case, easier to reach than underground shelters. On the other hand, if the missiles carried only conventional warheads, underground bomb shelters would be the more secure refuge.

The historic irony of the situation facing Israel was not lost on our group—an Israeli army colonel; an American student studying in Jerusalem; her father who had come to be with her when she refused to go home in the crisis; and other Americans, all of us looking like Steven Spielberg creations in our surrealisitic gas masks. Here were Jews, forty-six years after the Holocaust, once again facing the very real prospect of poison gas. Only recently, Saddam Hussein had threatened to turn Israel into a "crematorium." What's more, the Iraqis had acquired their chemical weapons with the help of West German companies.

When the all-clear signal sounded, life immediately returned to normal—to the extent that toting a gas mask everywhere (a plastic tent for small children) and not knowing when the siren would sound again, can be called even remotely normal.

Dinner service was resumed, Mozart's *Eine Kleine Nachtmusik* was heard in the background, and children played in the hotel lobby. But beneath the surface, a sense of anxiety prevailed. Had this last alert been a false alarm? Did the Patriot antimissile missiles work? Had the Iraqi missiles self-destructed in midair, or had they overshot their mark and landed in the Mediterranean?

The answer was not long in coming. A missile had hit a residential area near Tel Aviv. The toll was heavy—three dead from heart attacks, dozens injured, some still trapped in the rubble, many buildings severly damaged.

The Patriot, it seemed, had not worked. Once again, people in Israel felt an unaccustomed sense of vulnerability. If not with the Patriots, how could the country defend itself against incoming missiles? Had the United States tied Israel's hands, preventing it from retaliating against Iraq? Could the U.S. Air Force find the remaining mobile missile launchers in Iraq's western desert?

The next day was filled with discussions about what Israel should do: continue its policy of restraint or rely on its ingenuity and daring to retaliate. That evening, the sirens went off again. This time we shared a sealed room with eight Soviet Jews, four veterans of the first immigration wave in the early 1970s and four who had arrived in Israel only two days before. Amazingly, the mood was light-hearted, the parents and children disarmingly relaxed. As one newcomer commented: "God did not bring the Jews back to their homeland after 1900 years to see them destroyed. I am unafraid."

The news that night was exhilirating. The Patriot missiles had apparently hit their targets! Moreover, although the previous night's attack had ended in tragedy, a Patriot had in fact engaged the Scud, unfortunately hitting its engine rather than the warhead. There was a surge of renewed confidence, of admiration and gratitude for the U.S.-supplied miracle weapon. Moreover, there was certainty among Israelis that, sooner or later, the Israel Defense Force would not let the missile attacks go unpunished.

On our final day, we visited the sites of the first two missile attacks. Among the heavily damaged buildings was a school. Thankfully, the authorities had ordered all children to remain home, so no one was hurt there. But a walk through the site was a sobering reminder of the potential for destruction of this frightening weapon. Iraq's arsenal, Israelis constantly noted, had been provided all too willingly by the world's leading industrialized countries—France, Germany, Italy, the Soviet Union, Belgium, England, the United States, and others.

Before we left, Israelis asked whether more Diaspora Jews would visit and express their solidarity by their physical presence rather than their rhetoric. Israelis were aghast that so few had come, that many had in fact canceled visits, or had rushed to leave the country before January 15. If anything, the anguish of isolation only added to the Israelis' fierce pride in their self-reliance.

Israelis also asked us whether the world would learn any lessons from this war—lessons about the true nature of this highly volatile area, about the consequences of seemingly limitless arms sales and technology transfers to ruthless despots, about the PLO's love affair with Saddam Hussein, about the fatuity of seeking simplistic solutions to complex regional issues. One can only hope. Yes, one can only hope.

Lessons from the Mideast
Kansas City Star
March 10, 1991

Editor: Mr. Harris, what are three lessons the United States should learn from the invasion of Kuwait and the Persian Gulf war?

1. The Middle East truly is a dangerous, unstable, and unpredictable region in which the absence of democracy and the rule of law in all the countries except Israel helps ensure continued cycles of violence and conflict.

2. It's time for the United States to bite the energy bullet. In addition to searching for new sources of oil, we need to address much more seriously the question of energy conservation and alternative energy

sources. Our nation's excessive reliance on unstable sources of foreign oil makes us too vulnerable to the whims of a Saddam Hussein.

3. It's long overdue for the Arab states in the region to recognize—as Egypt has—once and for all Israel's permanence and legitimacy. That surely would lead to a new climate for peaceful resolution of differences and a more likely solution of the vexing Palestinian question. This crisis has again demonstrated the greatest danger facing Israelis—the hostility of Arab states. The United States, through its enhanced influence in parts of the Arab world, now has an historic opportunity to help reverse that.

After 43 Years of Arab-Israeli Conflict, a Chance to "Seize the Day"
USA Today
March 12, 1991

Carpe diem, seize the day, Robin Williams implored his students in the film *Dead Poets Society*. As Secretary of State Jim Baker visits the Middle East in the wake of the resounding U.S.-led victory in the Gulf war, hopes run high that the United States will be able to seize the moment to breathe new life into the Arab-Israeli peace process.

Indeed, the United States is now uniquely positioned to help resolve the Arab world's forty-three-year-long state of belligerency with Israel. But to do so will require extraordinary patience, perseverance, and commitment. Any expectation of a quick and comprehensive solution to this long-standing and deeply rooted conflict is misplaced.

It's vital for policy makers to keep one lesson of the recent Gulf war in mind. For years, the claim has been made—by Arabs and some Westerners—that satisfaction of Palestinian grievances against Israel holds the key to peace. At times, Saddam Hussein used this notion in his propaganda, disingenuously trying to convince the world he had swallowed Kuwait to help resolve the plight of the Palestinians.

Reality proved otherwise. Saddam used the Palestinian issue only to deflect attention from his true crimes, and the Palestine Liberation Organization, which claims to speak for the Palestinians, discredited itself yet again, this time through its fawning allegiance to Iraq, sworn enemy of the United States and Israel. The PLO's willingness to negotiate peacefully with Israel was revealed as a sham when its leaders praised Iraq's terror attacks and called for use of chemical weapons to destroy Israel.

If there is ever to be Arab-Israeli peace, the first step will have to include the state-to-state dimension. It is states such as Iraq (and Syria) that have posed the greatest threat to Israel's security. It took the United States and its allies nearly six months of military buildup and economic sanctions to prepare to fight Iraq. Yet prior to August 2, 1990, Israel was expected to face its sworn enemy, plus any combination of other Arab forces, alone.

Clearly, as long as the Arab world, save Egypt, remains in a state of belligerency with Israel, even the most far-reaching efforts to accommodate Palestinian interests will not ensure lasting peace. Resolution of the Palestinian issue can come only in the context of Arab-Israeli reconciliation.

The United States is now in a unique position to facilitate that reconciliation. First, the United States and other advanced countries must stem the flow of sophisticated weaponry and nonconventional weapons technology to unstable, nondemocratic countries in the region. Ending the arms race in the region will have a stabilizing effect. Second, the United States must make clear that the PLO has no role to play in the peace process. Palestinians committed to peaceful negotiation with Israel do. Third, the United States should use its unprecedented influence with its current Arab allies to insist on a new approach to Israel.

This process will have to be step by step, building a new climate of trust and cooperation. But the long-term aims should be nothing less than full diplomatic relations, an end to the state of war and the Arab economic boycott against Israel, and regional cooperation in security, economic development, and environmental cooperation.

The United States played this crucial role in securing the historic peace between Egypt and Israel. It may be able to do it again. Some of the same ingredients will be necessary—direct, face-to-face talks between the parties involved, a facilitator's role for the United States, and flexibility on all sides.

This in no way ought to ignore the Palestinian question. Efforts to ease the tension and improve the situation in the West Bank and Gaza should not await other developments. Israel can encourage elections to identify indigenous leaders with whom to talk, unless the PLO sabotages the process. Autonomy arrangements, as provided for in the Camp David Accords, ought to be seriously explored. In turn, an end to Palestinian violence in the territories should be demanded. Violence will achieve nothing.

Such an end to the threat of war and violence surely would create a new atmosphere in the region, both politically and psychologically, making solutions to hitherto intractable problems, including the Palestinian issue, far more likely.

There's an old saying in Israel: The only realistic thing in this part of the world is to believe in miracles. The United States now has an unprecedented chance—with its prestige high, Iraq severely weakened, and Kuwait, Saudi Arabia, and Syria closer to us—to help build a more peaceful and stable Middle East. Secretary Baker can begin that process by pressing our Arab allies to "seize the day" and reconsider their decades-long hostility toward Israel.

Distrust of UN
The New York Times
June 20, 1991

Is it any wonder that Israel continues to have grave reservations about permitting the United Nations a role in an Arab-Israeli peace process?

The Security Council voted unanimously to condemn Israel for deporting four convicted terrorists. There may be disagreement over the wisdom of using deportation as a punishment, though whether it constitutes a human rights violation is debatable. But the continuing and flagrant United Nations double standard reveals the hypocrisy of its actions.

Whether it was the Chinese crackdown in Tiananmen Square or Tibet, the Iraqi use of poison gas against the Kurds, or Syria's domination of Lebanon, the United Nations has not uttered a word.

And when it comes to deportations by countries other than Israel, the United Nations can be strangely silent, as it was shortly after the Iraqi invasion of Kuwait last year, when Saudi Arabia began deporting [hundreds of thousands of] Yemeni residents to express anger over Yemen's friendly stance toward Iraq. Yet when democratic Israel deports four convicted terrorists after a lengthy judicial review, the UN rushes into action.

During the Persian Gulf crisis, the United Nations clearly demonstrated by its actions against Iraq that it could assume the role its founders had envisioned for the world body, namely, to seek to safeguard peace and resist acts of aggression by one member state against another.

The United Nations must decide whether to be the impressive United Nations of the Gulf crisis or the United Nations of double standards and moral hypocrisy.

Loan Guarantees for Israel
International Herald Tribune
July 19, 1991

Those concerned with Israel and its well-being should know that its forthcoming request for $10 billion in loan guarantees from the United States may well be the most important Israel-related legislative issue on the horizon. The extension of these guarantees is absolutely critical to Israel's ability to absorb the million immigrants it expects over the next four to five years.

There is no question that Israelis are doing their share, meeting the challenge of absorbing Soviet and Ethiopian newcomers to the utmost of their capabilities. Israel is a country of only 4 million people. It has allocated $6 billion this fiscal year—more than its expenditures on defense—to absorb the immigrants. Israelis, already one of the most heavily taxed populations in the world, recently accepted an additional 5 percent across-the-board tax increase for the same goal.

Israel is not seeking additional aid from the United States, nor even loans, but rather guarantees, which will cost American taxpayers nothing. With the U.S. government as guarantor, Israel can borrow money from commercial banks and other nations at reasonable rates with reasonable repayment schedules.

Only in the unprecedented eventuality that Israel defaulted in its payments would an expense to the American people be incurred. Israel's credit history is impeccable—the country has never defaulted or been late in external debt payment in its forty-three-year existence—and, according to Bank of America's Country Risk Monitor, is one of the most secure financial opportunities in the world.

U.S. Loan Guarantees and Israeli Immigrants
The Christian Science Monitor
August 1, 1991

You batted zero-for-three in the front-page photo caption with the July 18 article "With Syrian Consent to U.S. Plan for Peace, Baker Heads to Israel." The caption read: "Israel wants a $10 million loan from the U.S. to house Jewish immigrants in the occupied territories."

First, Israel is not seeking a loan but a loan guarantee, which requires no actual disbursement of U.S. funds. And with Israel's exemplary record of debt repayment, the risk of Israeli default is virtually nil.

Second, the loan guarantees, which would permit Israel to borrow on the private market, are sought to settle immigrants not in the disputed territories but rather within Israel proper. This reflects an agreement between Israel and Washington. Moreover, Israel does not mandate where new arrivals should live, as the caption implies, but allows them freedom of choice.

And finally, the requested loan guarantees will be for $10 billion over a five-year period. This is but a part of the cost Israel is expected to incur in the coming years as it seeks to absorb hundreds of thousands of Jews fleeing uncertain conditions in Ethiopia, the USSR, and other countries in flux. In doing so, Israel is fulfilling its raison d'étre as a haven for all Jews, but the burden is immense. Israel is trying its best to cope, but needs help. Loan guarantees are one important way to do so.

Visions of Peace
Boston Globe
August 12, 1991

Is that elusive day of true peace and normalcy, for which Israel has yearned since the state's creation in 1948, finally near? Will Secretary of State James Baker's potent diplomatic mix of persistence, perseverance, and patience yield a breakthrough in the seemingly intractable Arab-Israeli conflict?

Watching the dramatic events unfold, I confess to a mix of hope and anxiety. The reason for the hope is obvious. Israel has lived in an abnormal situation since its founding. For forty-three years Israelis have faced endless war, terrorism, boycotts, and undisguised hatred from their neighbors, with the notable exception of Egypt since the Camp David process.

Men serve in the active military reserves until they are into their fifties. Too many parents have buried their sons. . . . The economy has suffered the consequences of the defense burden.

Hence the hope that a peace process, should it get off the ground, will provide an alternative vision for Israelis—and their friends—long fearful that unrelenting Arab rejectionism could never provide the eventual possibility of peaceful borders, human contact, flourishing commerce, and the ultimate transformation of swords into plowshares.

Even if the peace process is complex, protracted, and unpredictable, as it surely must be, it still ignites a hope that, once begun, the parties would have crossed a threshold. It invites Israelis—the ultimate realists—to dream, if only for a moment, of a new era.

At the same time, I confess to a gnawing sense of anxiety as well. After all, as the Iraqi invasion of Kuwait, the missile strikes against Israel, and the subsequent revelations of Baghdad's nuclear program remind us yet again, Israel lives in a particularly dangerous, arms-laden region. Nor does Syria's continued military buildup, intensified in recent months by a generous infusion of Saudi money, give much room for comfort.

Indeed, it is a rough neighborhood, made more dangerous and unstable by the absence of democracy and the consequent political instability it brings among Israel's neighbors.

And another question persists. Has the Arab, including Palestinian, attitude toward Israel fundamentally changed? Has the Arab world come to accept Israel's right to exist, or is the current posturing nothing more than a short-term gambit to gain back, as a first step, land Israel took in a legitimate, defensive war in 1967, and then, over time, to resume the age-old aim of Israel's destruction? Can the Arab and Islamic worlds fully accept a sovereign non-Arab, non-Muslim presence in their midst? In trying to answer these questions, hopes and anxieties once again clash.

Finally, while proud of the remarkable U.S. diplomatic achievement to date in seeking to launch an Arab-Israeli peace process, it is fair to ask if our country's linear, Cartesian approach to issues is too naïve, too shortsighted for the murky politics of the Middle East.

Are we too quick, for example, to embrace Syria's president as a man we can deal with, just as we did Iraq's Saddam Hussein? Does Washington sometimes forget, in its occasional impatience with Jerusalem, that the real risks in any peace process will be asked of Israel and that Israel, as a democratic country, must achieve a sufficient domestic consensus if is to move forward? After all, neither Syria's nor Saudi Arabia's survival is in question; Israel's is.

Jews have waited for nearly 2,000 years for the creation of a sovereign Jewish state. Thankfully, that state now exists. Whatever its warts and imperfections, its ability to survive, provide safe haven to millions of newcomers, and establish an admirable commitment to democratic values represents a remarkable achievement.

But what's been missing is peace. That's why I believe Israel will move forward in the search for a true and lasting peace it so desperately needs, but understandably with its back very close to the wall. The stakes are too high, the risks too great for any other approach.

American Jews Grow More Hawkish on Israel
The New York Times
December 9, 1991

Seldom have I read in the *Times* as misleading an article as your Nov. 21 report that Prime Minister Yitzhak Shamir of Israel would, on his visit to the United States, find American Jews dovish. I question the facile conclusions to which you jump from a telephone survey of 205 leaders of the Council of Jewish Federations.

The American Jewish Committee has for years sponsored national studies of a representative sample of American Jews on issues affecting Israel. The principal researcher has been Prof. Steven Cohen, one of the scholars who conducted the survey you discuss. Surprisingly, you make no reference to the findings of our 1991 study, released last month.

Our data show a far more complex picture of American Jewish attitudes toward Israel. While American Jews can be characterized in our latest study, as in previous studies, as more liberal than the Likud-led government of Israel, the discussion cannot end here. Our 1991 study, conducted during the summer, showed that, since the Persian Gulf war, American Jews have hardened their views on the Arab-Israeli conflict, to become more, rather than less, hawkish.

Your article states that the survey of 205 individuals is "consistent with recent surveys." Which surveys? Not our 1991 study, the only broad-based survey of American Jews undertaken lately. In any case, every survey, whether narrowly targeted, like that of the Council of Jewish Federations, or wider focused, such as those we commission, depicts a temporary, partial picture. One must be careful in drawing sweeping lessons.

For example, why did you not refer to such findings in the council survey as the continuing preoccupation with Israel's security (72 percent of the Jewish federation leaders believe the U.S. administration does not adequately appreciate Israel's security problems), the virtual consensus (97 percent) that it is "the refusal of most Arab states to accept Israel's legitimacy which represents the major obstacle to peace," or the even split on whether American Jews should publicly criticize Israeli government policies?

Over many years you have reported on the multiplicity of American Jewish organizations, voices, and viewpoints on Israel. Yet this article suggests that the latest survey results will bring American Jewish doves out of the closet. I never knew they were in the closet or that the American Israel Public Affairs Committee (AIPAC) has somehow denied American Jews alternatives for expression. To imply, therefore, that mainstream American Jewish leaders are candidates to bolt en masse to alternative groups is highly unrealistic, if experience is any guide.

Settlements Not Only Obstacle to Peace in Mideast
USA Today
March 27, 1992

We need to get back to some basic realities when thinking about the Middle East. To read the press, one would think that the Israeli settlements policy is the sole issue preventing peace. That's wrong.

Since Israel's creation in 1948, the Arab world has categorically rejected Israel's right to exist and its legitimacy in the region. That central fact of rejection led to war, terrorism, boycotts, and diplomatic isolation against Israel.

Even some Israeli settlement building in the period after 1967 did not stop the late Anwar Sadat from negotiating a peace treaty with Israel that has endured.

In fact, Israelis instinctively understood that Sadat was sincere in his search for peace, which led Israel to take the unprecedented step of returning the Sinai, with its strategic depth, oil fields, air bases, and, yes, settlements, to Egypt in exchange for a promise of peace.

Signals from the Arab countries and the Palestinians are murky, ambiguous, and contradictory, making Israelis understandably hesitant to risk their fragile national security in haste.

That's why peace, if it is to be lasting and genuine, can only come about slowly, painstakingly. Israel must be allowed to feel that its right to exist and its genuine security interests are recognized.

The Arab world has hardly begun to create that atmosphere. When it does, it will find Israel an eager partner to end the decades of conflict that Israelis have had to face from their neighbors.

Buchanan's Gratuitous Advice to Prime Minister Rabin
New York Post
December 30, 1993

Pat Buchanan has once again donned his ill-fitting Middle East strategist's uniform to offer gratuitous advice to Israeli prime minister Rabin, suggesting this time that the entire onus for the success of the peace process rests on Rabin's shoulders.

There's no question about Rabin's proven commitment to take risks to advance the prospect of peace, or the Israeli public's earnest desire for peace after more than four decades of war, terrorism, and economic and political isolation from its neighbors (except Egypt since 1979). But, regrettably, the intentions of some other Middle East players, including the PLO, are, to date at least, less clear—and their performance, frankly, disappointing.

Buchanan's prescription for Middle East peace hasn't changed since his outrageous reference to a so-called Jewish "amen corner" backing President Bush's tough line against Iraq, and his campaign to stir public opposition to that war against an expansionist tyrant by hyping predictions of massive American losses.

In Buchanan's view, Israel—a country that hasn't been allowed a minute of true peace since its founding forty-five years ago—must unilaterally give, and keep on giving, to resolve the conflict with its neighbors. This isn't the way the Middle East peace process, or any negotiation, works. Progress can be achieved only if all the parties, and not just Israel, demonstrate the necessary commitment, courage, and flexibility to chart a new course for the Middle East.

An Exchange of Letters with President Ezer Weizman of Israel Regarding American Jewry
March 1994

Dear President Weizman,

I had the privilege of attending your presentation last week before the annual meeting of the American Jewish Committee's Institute on American Jewish–Israeli Relations. It was a great honor to have you join us for discussion of a most timely and topical subject.

Mr. President, I hope you will permit me to share with you some thoughts prompted by your presentation. As one who devotes considerable effort to seeking to enhance the links between Israelis and American Jews, I believe certain things should be borne in mind.

First, I strongly subscribe to the view that these two largest Jewish communities in the world are inextricably linked and must remain so for the well-being of Jews in both countries, indeed throughout the world. To sustain this requires constant sensitivity and cultivation on both sides of the Atlantic; otherwise, I fear, the two communities will increasingly drift apart.

The common bonds that held us together these past nearly fifty years—the impact of the Holocaust, Israel's birth and security needs, the waves of aliyah, our shared roots in the towns and villages of Eastern Europe—no longer hold the same immediacy for younger generations of Israelis and American Jews.

Young Israelis are shaped by their own unique national experience and an indigenous culture that has sprung up from Israeli soil; American Jews have an entirely different national experience and sadly, with few exceptions, are far removed from Israeli culture, including the Hebrew language. What, then, are the ties that will bind us together in the years to come, especially if, as we all pray, Israel is able to move toward an era of peaceful relations with its immediate neighbors?

The vast majority of American Jews, at least for the foreseeable future, are not prepared to make aliyah. American Jews have had a love affair with the United States and regard it as a unique Diaspora experience in which Jews have been able to achieve success in society at large and, simultaneously, when they choose, sustain their Jewish identities. I can well understand that, from a Zionist perspective, such thinking may seem unconvincing, but this is nevertheless the prevalent viewpoint among American Jews.

If American Jews are not prepared to make aliyah, and only a minority are studying Hebrew, what to do? Do we dismiss the majority as inevitable candidates for assimilation? Or do we recognize that many do want to affirm their Jewishness, however they may define it, and that we must therefore, all of us, strive to emphasize the oneness of the Jewish people and acknowledge diverse expressions of that identity? I subscribe to the latter approach, believing that Israel, over the long run, will gain more adherents, indeed more candidates for aliyah, via an admittedly drawn-out and incremental approach.

Second, I was concerned from your presentation that the historical role of American Jews vis-à-vis Israel, since 1948 and indeed even before, may not have been fully appreciated. American Jews over the past forty-six years have made remarkably successful efforts to affect the climate of public opinion in the United States toward Israel. In doing so, there is no doubt that they have helped shape the attitudes of successive administrations and congresses. This, in turn, has redounded again and again to Israel's benefit in the diplomatic, political, strategic, and economic spheres.

Moreover, while Americans regrettably have not heretofore invested significantly in the Israeli economy, the degree of philanthropic generosity has been considerable, and has made a difference, as you know so well, in the areas of social services, immigrant absorption, health care, education, and culture. American Jews are proud of their contributions to these efforts.

In sum, I welcome the current focus on relations between Israel and American Jewry, believing that it warrants the best thinking of concerned people in both communities. We will long need one another as fellow Jews to contribute to each other's well-being, in both good times and bad. This, then, becomes our most compelling challenge—to find ways to widen and deepen our ties even as the terms of reference, or at least some of them, change in light of the march of time.

I earnestly hope that you will have an opportunity, as president of Israel, to visit the United States and spend time with the Jewish community. Such contact is vitally important for American Jews. Concurrently, it would afford you the possibility to take the current pulse of the community, to see both the vast reservoirs of committed Jews engaged in a range of religious, cultural, and political pursuits, as well as the dark clouds of assimilation, indifference, and ignorance that afflict a not insignificant portion of our population.

I know that you are planning a dialogue with world Jewry on June 22nd and 23rd. Among the invitees will be a considerable number of American Jews. I applaud your decision to host such a discussion, and hope, Mr. President, that you will find the thoughts expressed in this letter helpful in anticipation of that gathering.

Dear Mr. Harris,

Thank you for your kind and thoughtful letter of March 21st. I appreciate the frank spirit of your letter and the ideas and thoughts you raise, which have not come to me as a surprise as I have heard so much of your activities and contribution to Jewish affairs in the United States and of your involvement in Israel. Your efforts in strengthening the relationship between the United States and Israel and between the American Jewish community and Israelis are to be commended.

As you know, I was born and raised in Israel. My whole life has been dedicated to the realization of the Jewish dream, building a homeland for the Jewish people. It has always been agonizing for me, as well as for others, to see the majority of the Jewish people choosing to live somewhere else, not in Israel. As I said in my meeting with AJC's Institute on American Jewish–Israeli Relations, it is my understanding that if more Jews had chosen to immigrate to Palestine some seventy years ago, perhaps, just perhaps, our modern history would have been different.

Having so said, it should not be regarded as disrespect for Jewish life elsewhere. It will always be our expectation and hope to have as many Jews as possible living in Israel, but at the same time we know it depends on their free will. Jewish life throughout our history has been centered both in Israel and in the Diaspora. More than two thousand years ago it was Jerusalem and Alexandria. For too many centuries it was only in the Diaspora, while Jerusalem was in our dreams. The end of the nineteenth century and the beginning of the twentieth century saw the changed course of our people with political Zionism and the acquisition of our Land. Israel and national Jewish life became a reality and today Israel is stronger than ever before, both in defense and economy. This should direct us toward a new partnership, a partnership of cooperation, whereby we do not only receive but also give. I share your view that Israel and the American Jewish community, the two largest Jewish communities, as well as other communities in the world, are inextricably linked and must remain so for the well-being of Jews in Israel and throughout the world and for the fulfillment of the Zionist idea.

I concur with your inference that the achievement of this goal requires constant sensitivity and cultivation on both sides of the Atlantic. New awareness should be fostered and this is why I decided to convene leaders from the Jewish world and Israel for a frank and open dialogue. I believe that a future of peace in the Middle East creates new challenges for Israel and new responsibilities.

It is time for us in our partnership with world Jewry to contribute more. I regard the dialogue to be convened in Jerusalem on June 22nd and 23rd as the launching pad of continual discussions and efforts to strengthen the relations between Israeli and American Jews as well as Jews throughout the world, and in this way to face the threat of assimilation and the potential loss of another major part of our people in this century. New bridges are needed. Through education, youth exchanges, courses in Israel, Hebrew lessons, summers in Israel, investments, having homes in Israel, we will be able to bring about a change and prevent ourselves from drifting apart.

In conclusion, let me add that I do not doubt nor do I have disrespect for the role the American Jewish community has been playing toward Israel since 1948. It is my understanding that the American Jewish community has contributed immensely to the close relations between our two countries. The bonds and ties that strengthen American-Israel relations are based on common values and interests and, at the same time, the role American Jewry has played in bringing Israel's word and message to every corner of the United States.

I fully appreciate American Jewry's identification and involvement in Israel in good as well as in bad times. At the same time, I still hope that more Jews will choose to live in Israel. My constant call for aliyah does not mean the dismissal of those who choose not to live here. We must make every effort to strengthen the oneness and togetherness of the Jewish people.

I once again thank you for sharing your thoughts with me and look forward to having you participate in the dialogue.

A Basis, Still, for Peace
International Herald Tribune
April 1, 1994

Regarding "The Chance for Middle East Peace Is Collapsing," by Flora Lewis:

Notwithstanding my considerable respect for Ms. Lewis's views on international affairs, I found myself in disagreement with her particularly gloomy prognosis for the Arab-Israeli peace process following the tragic Hebron massacre.

While the peace process has clearly suffered a setback, Israeli and Palestinian leaders recognize that a way must be found to move forward, lest the talks collapse and any hope to move beyond a century of conflict be eradicated.

This recognition that a unique moment exists, and that a basis for progress has been established, first in Madrid, later in Oslo, will, I believe, prove more powerful in spurring the talks forward than the forces, however considerable and unpredicatable, seeking to destroy the process.

We Asked Some Leading Experts in the Field:
Is the West Too Complacent About the Middle East?
The International Economy
September/October 1994

David Harris: The Middle East is in a race against itself. On one side is an historic Arab-Israeli peace process that holds the prospect not only of defusing a major regional conflict, but also replacing it with an architecture of peace built on widening diplomatic, economic, and cultural ties.

Set against it are two ominous forces: regional predators—Iran, Iraq, Libya, and Syria—whose ambitions to develop weapons of mass destruction are no secret; and the relentless pursuit by extremists who, in the name of their vision of Islam, seek to exploit the weaknesses of inefficient or corrupt regimes and wide disparities in wealth to achieve power. Already successful in Afghanistan, Iran, and Sudan, they press forward in Algeria and look to gains elsewhere, including Egypt.

The stakes for the West in these conflicting trends should be apparent. A Middle East dominated by nuclear-armed, anti-Western regimes controlling the crossroads of three continents and awash in oil and petrodollars surely is a formula for a major confrontation.

Accordingly, what must the West (including Russia) do?

1. Devote the necessary long-term diplomatic and financial resources to help ensure the success of the Arab-Israeli peace process. In this regard, Syrian-Israeli progress is vital, requiring a decision by President Assad that, in a postcommunist world with no Soviet patron available, he has no real alternative but to pursue serious peace with Israel.

2. Sustain the collective will to maintain the current UN embargo on Iraq, despite efforts by some nations to weaken it.

3. Confront Iran's weapons ambitions and desire for regional domination by tougher economic policies, however tempting the Iranian market is to Western countries.

4. Urge the introduction of democratic principles—rule of law, free and fair elections, economic reform, etc.—in the Arab world.

5. Ensure that nothing the West does weakens Israel's military edge or strategic advantage, as Israel remains the West's strongest and most reliable ally in the region.

6. Return to major energy policy questions, however unrealistic it may be at a time when cheap oil is readily available. The United States, in particular, has once again been deluded into believing oil a permanent and permanently inexpensive commodity, and our growing dependence on imported oil exposes both our vulnerability and short-lived memory.

Clinton's Record on Israel
The Jerusalem Post
June 3, 1995

I read with considerable surprise the following statement in Moshe Zak's column on the proposed transfer of the U.S. embassy to Jerusalem: "The president [Clinton] makes frequent declarations of friendship toward Israel. Let's see how he decides principal questions relating to the Jewish state. . . ."

Well, let's see. Within the last few weeks alone, the Clinton administration concluded a difficult, but ultimately successful, international campaign to block Egypt's move against Israel linked to the indefinite extension of the Nuclear Non-Proliferation Treaty.

Further, the United States exercised its first veto in years at the UN Security Council to block a resolution condemning Israel over the Jerusalem issue, thereby incurring the wrath of Arab and other Muslim states.

Finally, the Clinton administration, whether on the peace process, foreign aid, strategic cooperation, or the antiboycott campaign, has demonstrated an acute understanding of Israel's needs.

And more generally in the region, the United States has shown, via its "dual containment" policy toward Iran and Iraq, political courage that surely serves American interests in this vital area and, at the same time, Israel's as well.

Thus, whatever the current passions on the U.S. embassy location, to suggest that the outcome of this issue, and this issue alone, will demonstrate Clinton's *real* attitude toward Israel is strikingly unfair to the consistently strong record of the president regarding Israel.

I say this, by the way, as a nonpartisan whose agency is prevented by law from endorsing or opposing any candidate for political office, but who believes the factual record needs a public airing in light of Zak's regrettable phraseology.

Ink Dripping with Venom
San Antonio Express News
June 10, 1995

Most shocking of all about Alan Parker's May 28 "Your Turn" piece was not the vehemence of his twisted and unrecognizable history of Israel, or his outrageous attempt to draw a parallel between Israelis and Nazis, or his historical inversion that turns Jews from victims to perpetrators, or even his barely disguised sympathy for the Nazi genocide against the Jews.

Sad to say, we've seen that kind of raw, maniacal hatred all too often before, although, thankfully, it is today usually relegated to the extreme fringes of civilized societies such as our own.

No, what is most shocking about the piece was your decision to print it. The First Amendment allows Parker to write what he chooses, however vile, but there is no similar obligation of a responsible newspaper to publish such trash, for you confer a mantle of legitimacy, however unintentionally, by considering it fit to print.

Responsible debate on Israeli policies is a regular feature of the American media, as it should be and as is the case with a wide range of complex international issues of particular concern to the United States.

But this was not Parker's aim at all. Rather, he used "Your Turn" as an opportunity to spew forth his venom and, regrettably, you played right into his hands. Shame on you.

Why Israel Is Denied Security Council Seat
The New York Times
September 11, 1995

In discussing Italy's plan to expand the United Nations Security Council, you note that 79 of the world body's 185 members have never served on the Council, "including Iceland, Israel and most Caribbean and smaller African nations."

This description neglects one important difference between Israel and the other countries mentioned. The latter, at least theoretically, are able to aspire to one of the ten nonpermanent seats on the Security Council, whereas Israel is denied even this hope.

To gain a nonpermanent seat requires membership in a regional group, for it is these groups that select the one or more countries that will represent them on the Security Council for the rotating terms.

Iceland, as a member of the West European and Others Group, could at least in theory be selected. The Caribbean nations, being members of the Latin American and Caribbean Group, and the African nations, as members of the African Group, have the same opportunity.

Israel has been rejected, for overt political reasons, by the Asian Group, its natural geographic home. And its efforts to gain temporary membership in the West European and Others Group (WEOG) have been unsuccessful to date.

A majority of United Nations member states have begun to rectify the pattern of unfair treatment of Israel, especially in annulling the infamous "Zionism is racism" resolution.

Solving Israel's situation as the only member nation denied any regional group membership would be another important step forward in normalizing Israel's status at the United Nations.

Perspectives on the Middle East Peace Process:
Testimony before the
Committee on International Relations,
United States House of Representatives
September 20, 1995

Mr. Chairman, thank you for affording the American Jewish Committee this opportunity to present perspectives on the Middle East peace process at this critical stage in its evolution, as well as to outline the findings of our most recent survey of American Jewish attitudes about Israel and the peace process.

Before proceeding with my testimony, Mr. Chairman, I also wish to thank you on behalf of the American Jewish Committee for the keen understanding you have always demonstrated of the importance of the mutually beneficial relationship between the United States and Israel, and for your leadership in support of Israel as it seeks to open a new era of peaceful, cooperative relations between Arabs and Jews across the Middle East.

Indeed, Mr. Chairman, it is the belief of the members and officers of the American Jewish Committee that Israel and its Arab neighbors arc moving toward a new era in the Middle East. The Arab-Israeli peace negotiations—which began in Madrid in October 1991, passed a significant milestone with the signing of the Israel-PLO Declaration of Principles (DOP) in Septembers 1993, and achieved dramatic success in the Israel-Jordan peace treaty signed last October—hold the promise of thoroughly and constructively remaking relations between Israel and the Arab world.

Our perspective is the result of four years of intensive experience with the peace process and some forty-seven years of close involvement with Israel. The American Jewish Committee, dedicated to the protection of Jewish communities in Israel and around the world and the first American Jewish organization to establish a permanent office in Israel, has monitored the peace process from its inception and sought to advance its cause here and in other capitals. AJC attended the Madrid conference and the January 1992 Moscow opening of the multilateral peace talks as an observer, and we have engaged in regular and detailed discussions on the process with senior officials of the U.S. and Israeli governments, and with the governments of Arab states across the Middle East and North Africa. Further, our confidence in this process has led us to change the scope of our Jerusalem office from Israel alone to Israel and the entire Middle East.

Our analyses and our discussions with the principals engaged in the process here and in the region lead us to one conclusion: For all its difficulties, the peace process set in motion four years ago represents Israel's best chance to depart from the troubled course of its modern history and achieve peace with its neighbors.

The difficulties that have marked the road to peace cannot be minimized; the tragedies—the repeated terror attacks by those bent on destroying the peace process—cannot be forgotten. Our support for the peace process, and our trust in the judgment of the duly elected government of Israel on matters of Israel's security, are given in full awareness of the dangers Israelis face, indeed have always faced in a region and among people largely hostile to their existence. It is not the intention of the framers of, and participants in, the peace process to simply dismiss the dangers and redefine the hostility of Israel's foes; it is to fundamentally alter the nature of relations between Israel and its neighbors in order to strengthen Israel's present and future security. Future generations of both Jews and Arabs deserve nothing less.

In just two years since the signing of the DOP, those relations have already changed, to Israel's benefit. Not only has Israel made peace with Jordan, but it has engaged in diplomatic and commercial contacts from North Africa to the Persian Gulf, eroding the Arab League's economic boycott of Israel and laying the groundwork for future political and economic cooperation throughout the region. Further, Israel's withdrawal from Gaza more than one year ago was not an essential element in establishing a new relationship with the Palestinians, but it was and remains highly popular within Israel itself. And in Gaza, as anyone can attest who visited there before the transfer of authority and has been back in recent months, there are significant indications of economic, political, and even social progress, achieved with the help of U.S. and European aid; indeed, with the Palestinian Authority increasingly succeeding there against the Hamas extremists for control and popular allegiance, Gaza may be the only place in the Muslim world that has actually moved farther away from fundamentalism in the last year.

The Israeli government's vision since Madrid has been bold but clear-eyed, and we stand behind it in its pursuit of peace with security. Similarly, Mr. Chairman, we commend and support the continued role of the United States—this Congress and this very supportive administration—as it seeks to assure Israel's security on the perilous but promising road to peace. In the American Jewish Committee's support for the government of Israel as it pursues peace with security, and for our own government as it seeks to advance the peace process for the benefit of Israel and its neighbors, I know that a sister organization, the American Jewish Congress, wishes to associate itself with my remarks today.

Progress in the talks between Israel and its negotiating partners has not been easy; in fact, on two of the bilateral tracks, with Syria and Lebanon, there has been little progress at all. On the Palestinian track, we are cautiously hopeful that the intensive negotiations in Taba this week will shortly yield a long-sought second-phase agreement on the redeployment of Israeli forces, the transfer of broad authority to Palestinians in the West Bank, and elections to a new governing council. We hope and expect that, when concluded, this critical next step in Arab-Israeli reconciliation will increase the Palestinians' stake in forging a new and mutually beneficial coexistence with Israel. It will strengthen Israel's long-term security while offering maximum protection to Jewish communities on the West Bank.

On the Syrian track, we are disappointed by President Assad's continued failure to fully engage Israel in direct high-level talks—even after giving assurances to do so in meetings with senior American officials in recent months. Nevertheless, we are hopeful that, with continued American involvement, Jerusalem's willingness to take concrete steps to achieve a new relationship with Syria will be met with an appropriate response from Damascus.

To strengthen the prospect of satisfactory conclusions to these negotiations, and the achievement of true and lasting peace in the region, the American Jewish Committee believes that the critical role played by the United States as facilitator, supporter, and honest broker for peace must be extended. We call upon the Congress, Mr. Chairman, to continue to provide the president with the resources and the authority he requests—in the Middle East Peace Facilitation Act and other measures that may come before this and the other body—so that the United States may press forward in this noble endeavor for peace. We believe that these efforts by the United States will be further enhanced by the critically important efforts of America's friends and allies in Europe, Asia, and the Middle East.

In expressing our hope and our support for the Middle East peace process and for continued U.S. engagement in that process, Mr. Chairman, the American Jewish Committee articulates the view of the overwhelming majority of American Jews. In an attitude survey that we published just last week, copies of which have been made available to the Committee, we found that 68 percent of American Jews—more than four in five who expressed a view—support the Israeli government in its current handling of peace negotiations; 87 percent endorse a continuing American role in the peace process. I should note that there are those who are choosing to read selected data from our survey, and employing those data to justify their own views on the peace process, without examining the survey in its complex and compelling totality.

I'd like to take a moment to outline some of the key findings of our poll—our third annual survey of American Jewish attitudes toward Israel and the peace process—and I will then ask that the full survey report be printed in the hearing record.

First, I think it is important to address American Jewish concerns and fears for Israel's security. In the two years since the signing of the Oslo Accords—two years of difficult and frustrating negotiations, and repeated terrorist acts intended to destroy the peace process— American Jewish support for the Israeli government's handling of the negotiations has declined; the level of support was 84 percent two years ago in the euphoria surrounding the White House signing ceremony, 77 percent one year ago, and 68 percent in our most recent poll. Further, there is widespread, persistent skepticism about the Arabs' intentions toward Israel.

Asked if they believed "the goal of the Arabs is not the return of occupied territories but rather the destruction of Israel," 56 percent responded in the affirmative, while 37 percent disagreed—reflecting deepening doubts since 1993, when a similar question found 42 percent in agreement, and 50 percent in disagreement. Asked if they believed the PLO is "doing enough to control terrorist activity against Israel by Hamas and other Palestinian extremist groups," 91 percent answered "no," 5 percent "yes." Asked if they believed "the Palestinians are interested, or are not interested, in a true and lasting peace with Israel," 51 percent answered "not interested," while 37 percent responded "interested." Asked a companion question about Syrian intentions, 45 percent responded "not interested," 38 percent "interested." By contrast, 74 percent of American Jews believe Jordanians are "interested in a true and lasting peace with Israel," while 17 percent do not.

The message in these numbers, I believe, is twofold: First, American Jews, like their Israeli counterparts, need far greater assurance of Arab—and particularly Palestinian—intentions of peaceful coexistence with Israel. The rhetoric from Arab leaders has begun to change; it must change more, and quickly. And the action by the Palestinian Authority to control terrorism and punish its perpetrators must continue to be intensified. The United States, this Congress, must continue to convey that message to Palestinian leadership and to the Arab world generally. The second message in this regard from our poll is that there is a clear differentiation by American Jews between those neighbors of Israel—in this case Jordan and Egypt—that have signed a peace treaty and made conciliatory gestures and those that have not.

I see no contradiction, Mr. Chairman, between American Jews' overwhelming support for the peace process and their profound wariness about the intentions of Israel's neighbors. Indeed, I share those two feelings. Similarly, I am not surprised by the response to another question we posed—whether the United States should "provide economic aid to the Palestinians"; 63 percent said "no," 30 percent "yes." I find that result consistent not only with American Jews' skepticism about Palestinian leadership, but consistent with general American attitudes about foreign aid to any country. Further, based on the results of other questions we posed, when we asked respondents to weigh their own inclinations and concerns about elements of the peace process with their judgment about the overall merits of the process and the need to press forward in accord with the decisions of the elected government of Israel, we believe that if we had asked a similarly linked question on Palestinian aid we would have recorded a substantially different response.

But on the critical questions about the validity and the potential of the Arab-Israeli peace process—and about the Israeli government's responsibility to manage that process in a manner that assures its nation's security—American Jews express support for the policies pursued jointly by Jerusalem and Washington.

Asked, for instance, if they felt the last two years of negotiations "increase the likelihood of another war, or increase the likelihood of peace with the Arabs," 66 percent said they viewed the process as leading to peace, 18 percent to war—a ratio of more than three to one. By three to one—66 percent versus 22 percent—American Jews support the Israeli government's "current handling of the peace negotiations with the Palestinians." And although American Jews do not strongly support "the establishment of a Palestinian state," with 46 percent in favor and 39 percent opposed, a significant margin—62 percent versus 32 percent, or two to one—would support such a move if that should be a "decision made by the duly elected Israeli government."

In the final analysis, regardless of their own justified fears and concerns, American Jews are willing to set aside those concerns in deference to the decision made by the democratically elected government of Israel. Our survey confirms the confidence our community feels in that government—and its confidence, as well, in America's partnership with Israel in pursuit of peace in the Middle East. We look to the committee to maintain that partnership, and we call on it to continue its critical support of the government of Israel as it seeks—and takes risks for—a new era of peace with its neighbors.

On the Assassination of Yitzhak Rabin, Prime Minister of the State of Israel
New York
November 6, 1995

What does one say on such an occasion, especially after hearing the eulogies at today's funeral service in Jerusalem—and particularly the moving, poetic, and loving comments of Noa, the prime minister's granddaughter?

What does one say that hasn't already been said during the past forty-eight hours?

What does one say that each of us hasn't already thought about in our own reflections during these past two days?

Words yet again seem so hopelessly inadequate to describe our welter of emotions—from utter dismay to profound sadness, from seething anger to the persistent but ultimately unanswerable questions.

There's simply no haven to shelter us from these feelings, or from the gnawing questions. How could such a tragedy have happened? For two years, since the signing ceremony on the White House lawn on September 13, 1993, we have asked what if Chairman Arafat were felled by the bullets of Palestinian extremists. What, then, for the peace process?

But never, not once, did any of us stop to ask what if the Israeli prime minister were the target, and, even more beyond our realm of imagination, at the hands of a fellow Jew. Never did such a thought even cross our minds. Israel, we devoutly believed, was somehow different. With all its domestic tensions and fissures, surely there were still certain lines no one would cross. But now we have to confront the question not only of how an Israeli could commit such a heinous crime but also actually exult in it, only expressing regret that he was unable to slay the foreign minister as well.

How could a student of law, exposed to two noble legal traditions—halakhah and Anglo-Saxon jurisprudence—have rejected the essence of both those traditions, which teach respect for the sanctity of life and the concept of justice, and not celebration of cold-blooded murder?

How could someone truly claiming love of God have invoked the name of the Divine Being in justifying his evil deed?

Is this to be the opening salvo in a fratricidal war among Israelis divided over their fundamental vision of the Land of Israel—those who advocate a Greater Israel above all, even if it means abandoning democracy and the chances for peaceful coexistence, and those willing to make territorial sacrifices in the interests of a more pragmatic and democratic Zionism, even if it means forfeiting part of the biblical Land of Israel?

I for one have no answers to these questions. I do, however, cling to some hope, even in the darkness of the hour, hope that I trust is not born of naïveté.

I hope that this tragedy will serve as a wake-up call, reminding Israelis of all political stripes that what unites them far outweighs what divides them, even as they legitimately pursue their political differences. I hope Israelis will recall that democracy is a fragile instrument that requires constant care, protection, and nurturing. It cannot be left unattended to.

I hope that God will not become a political weapon for Jews and that God's name will not be sullied by those who would invoke it for a particular cause or grievance. We know all too well what can happen when extremists cite their God—or their interpretation of "God's will"—to justify their nefarious deeds. Extremist Muslims kill Jews and strike at the World Trade Center in the name of God and the Prophet Mohammed. Extremist Hindus kill Muslims and burn down mosques in the name of their gods. And extremist Christians kill doctors who perform abortions, again in the name of God.

Such gods are false gods. Such gods are not your God, nor mine.

Into this vortex must now step Shimon Peres. His challenges are, to say the least, daunting. He must:

(1) Guide a nation through a period of mourning and profound self-examination, of *heshbon nefesh*—moral reckoning.

(2) Encourage, together with political leaders of all the main political parties, a toning down of the public rhetoric. We have seen the escalation of that rhetoric in Israel, leading to the devaluation of lan-

guage's true meaning. Words such as *enemy, murderer, traitor,* and *Nazi* are now all too frequently bandied about. Such words should best be left for their originally intended purposes. Otherwise, yes, they do contribute to a climate where acts by a Yigal Amir become more, not less, likely. After all, if someone is labeled a "Nazi" or a "traitor," does this not lower the threshhold and potentially encourage violence? Why should a "Nazi" or "traitor" be allowed to continue to live in our midst?

(3) Overcome the doubts among many in the Israeli public about his ability to lead a divided nation. Don't underestimate Shimon Peres, though. He is a man of great intellect, vision, eloquence, and political savvy. While he may not have the same military record as Yitzhak Rabin, and few do, he contributed singularly to helping build Israel's defense and deterrence capacity. And by all accounts, he was a very effective prime minister during his two-year stint in the '80s as part of the National Unity government.

(4) And press forward on the difficult, but still promising, peace front, to which he has made such an important conceptual and diplomatic contribution. At the same time, he must assure the Israeli public that he will be no less vigilant than Prime Minister Rabin in maintaining the nation's security against all would-be foes, be they such rejectionist states as Iran or Iraq, extremist Palestinian groups, or, we now sadly have to admit, radical Jews within Israel prepared to use violence to achieve their aims.

To Acting Prime Minister Peres, whom we have known and admired for decades, we pledge that we shall do our utmost to help him meet these Herculean challenges. He can count on our full support.

And as we inevitably must look ahead, for history does not stand still for long, we shall long remember not only the tragic details of Yitzhak Rabin's death two days ago, but, even more importantly, the telling circumstances of his life. For his life was the life of Israel. His history was the history of Israel.

Other than his beloved family and the weekly game of tennis, he simply had no other focus in his lifetime but a full-time determination to protect Israel, to ensure its security and prosperity, and to achieve, if possible, a degree of peace, if not for his generation then for his children's; if not for them, then for the generation of Noa, his granddaughter.

In a sense, the Yitzhak Rabin I had the privilege of meeting over the past ten years was a study in apparent, though not real, contradictions.

A shy man, he nonetheless was able to exude leadership and enjoy the confidence of so many Israelis because of who he was and what he represented. So shy was he that few could believe he would actually sing at Saturday's rally in Tel Aviv in front of 100,000 supporters, but he did—off-key, of course, as Eitan Haber, his long-time aide, noted in his eulogy today. The translated words from that song, which was entitled in Hebrew *Shiru Shir Lashalom*, or "Sing a Song for Peace," bear repeating here:

"Let the sun penetrate through the flowers. Don't look backward. Leave those who have departed. Lift your eyes with hope not through the rifle sights. Sing a song for love and not for wars. Don't say the day will come; bring the day, because it is not a dream. And within all the cities' squares, cheer for peace."

A reluctant student of war, he became a *rodeph sholom*, a pursuer of peace.

An innately cautious man, he took bold risks as prime minister.

A gruff, dour man in public, he had a soft, gentle side that his family and his soldiers frequently experienced and that was so poignantly described in his granddaughter's remarks today at the funeral service. The weeping face of his beloved wife and former comrade-in-arms, Leah, said it all.

A not-so-young man in not-so-good health, he was indefatigable, working his staff and himself to the bone.

A national and international political leader, he shunned many of the trappings of office that others revel in, disliked intensely pomp and circumstance, and pooh-poohed hype and luxury. Blunt to a fault and notoriously impatient, traits not necessarily suited to international statesmanship, he nonetheless became one of the most respected and revered world figures. The extraordinary array of international personalities at today's funeral bore ample testimony to the enormously high esteem in which he was held.

An archfoe of Shimon Peres, with whom he vied for Labor Party leadership again and again, Yitzhak Rabin was sufficiently visionary and pragmatic to recognize that there was no more experienced colleague in his cabinet than Foreign Minister Peres, and, to the surprise of many observers, together they worked to develop and advance the peace process.

Few among us, politicians included, are able to say that our lives have truly made an historic difference. Few among us have the necessary ingredients of leadership, vision, courage, integrity, and tenacity to create an indelible imprint on the course of events and the lives of people around us in the pursuit of a better world.

Yitzhak Rabin was one of those rare people. Soldier and statesman, he was, to borrow from the title of Mikhail Lermontov's novel, *A Hero of Our Time*. A hero in war, a hero in peace. His was a life devoted to a secure Israel, an Israel at peace. Our best gift to Yitzhak Rabin's blessed memory will be to help carry on that quest—for a secure Israel, an Israel at peace.

Frontal Assault
The Jewish Week
December 1995

In the wake of the tragic assassination of Yitzhak Rabin, it is time for all of us to take stock, to step back from the edge, to lower the rhetorical temperature, and to recognize the existential dangers to the Jewish people posed by the deep divides that have been exposed among us, whether in Israel or here.

Against that backdrop, Henry Siegman's article ("Radical Fringe Is Now Orthodox Norm," Nov. 17), which can only be described as a frontal assault on the entire Orthodox community, is not helpful; in fact, it's downright harmful. Are there elements of truth in his accusations? Yes, no doubt there are. But a broad-brush stroke against an entire community? No, that's irresponsible and inaccurate.

Those who helped create the environment in which Yigal Amir increasingly felt religiously justifed in his heinous deed deserve exposure, condemnation, and marginalization, and they include rabbis, yeshivot, and their followers. But they do not add up to an entire Orthodox community; far from it.

Where I do agree with Mr. Siegman is that the Modern Orthodox, those who have been silent or passive too long, need to stand up and assert that they will not permit others—who falsely invoke God's name, undermine democracy, and commit acts of violence—to speak or act on their behalf. That is truly a compelling challenge of the day.

Arafat Must Support Israel
USA Today
March 7, 1996

Let's be crystal clear. Hamas and its allies seek Israel's destruction ("Israel: Hamas can't hide," news).

Whatever they may say for gullible Western consumption, whatever gloss they may place on themselves by other activities, the goal of these terrorists is Israel's disappearance, pure and simple, in accordance with their religious and political views.

That's why Israeli prime minister Shimon Peres has declared war on Hamas. And that's why we steadfastly support a resolute and determined Israel in taking whatever steps it deems necessary to protect its citizens and root out this evil.

Moreover, Palestinian Authority chairman Yasser Arafat must decide, once and for all, to engage in the same enterprise. After all, Hamas ultimately threatens the prospects for Palestinian progress and dignity no less—indeed, much more—than it threatens Israel.

Thus Arafat can no longer have it both ways—seeking a promising peace with Israel while coddling the extremist elements in Palestinian society.

Placing Blame for Terror
Newsday
March 8, 1996

My grief over the terrorist acts in Israel turned to dismay when I read the comment of Ghazi Khankan of the National Council on Islamic Affairs, who said: "It is easy to condemn an act of violence and we should condemn both sides of violence, but more important is to condemn the cause of the Hamas violence." Predictably, he places blame squarely on Israel for creating the conditions leading to the Hamas violence [Feb. 26].

Israel has embarked on an extraordinarily courageous—and risky—peace process in which it is trading something tangible, land, for something intangible, peace. The Palestinian Authority has been Israel's partner. Both sides have agreed that negotiation and compromise are necessary to overcome decades of mutual suspicion and hatred. Both sides have also agreed that violence has no place in the process.

For Khankan, in the midst of this peace process, to seek to justify the grievances of Hamas and thus, by implication, its horrific acts, is an outrage. As he surely knows, the Hamas aim is the elimination of the State of Israel; therefore, nothing short of Israel's disappearance would satisfy these extremists or, I fear, Khankan.

Letter on Ethiopian Jews
Newsweek
March 11, 1996

Was Israel wrong in its handling of the Ethiopian blood issue? Yes, and it is to Prime Minister Shimon Peres's credit that he publicly acknowledged this. But did this admittedly serious error warrant your frontal assault on Israel's handling of waves of refugees since its founding in 1948? Hardly. Israel's entry policy for Jews everywhere, regardless of age, number, health, or family condition, is unparalleled. And the country has never faltered in its obligations to new arrivals—not during lean economic times, not during war, not even while Iraqi

Scud missiles were falling in '91. It's a shame that such balance was missing from your report.

We Stand With Israel:
Memorial Service for the Victims of Terrorism
New York
March 4, 1996

We gather today in a state of shock—angry, grief-stricken, shaken by recent events. Last Sunday in Jerusalem and Ashkelon, yesterday again in Jerusalem, today in Tel Aviv. And reports that dozens more suicide bombers are in place in Israel and ready to blow themselves up as soon as they are given notice to do so are ever present in our minds.

The bombers, led to believe by religious charlatans that this is a ticket to martyrdom and boundless heavenly rewards, have reminded us yet again that, for the blind haters, we are all Jews. So focused has the Jewish community been since November 4, the date of the horrific assassination of Yitzhak Rabin, on the rifts among us, that these bombers have recalled for us that in their book we are all the same.

And so the latest victims have included the young and old, observant and secular, hawk and dove, native-born and newcomer, Ashkenazi and Sephardi, military and civilian, male and female, resident and tourist. Indeed, it has included non-Jews as well, both Arabs and Europeans.

Not for the first time in our history, all Jews are the intended victims. But let the extremists remember: Today there is an Israel, proud, strong, resolute. Today there is a Jewish community worldwide that will speak out and stand shoulder to shoulder with fellow Jews in danger. And today there are governments and individuals of goodwill, particularly in this land, but also abroad, who will not, at moments like this, look the other way or bury their heads in the sand.

For people of goodwill recognize that the terrorists' assault threatens us all—it threatens democratic societies, it threatens our common sense of values, decency, and principles. Therefore, we cannot, we will not, be paralyzed by fear, nor rendered mute by apprehension.

We stand with Israel and its people as one in solidarity and shared destiny, and our will shall not be broken by terrorist thugs any more than it was broken by a succession of demagogues over the span of thousands of years who wished us harm or sought our disappearance. Indeed, the advent of Purim this evening is another compelling reminder that we have been under siege before, and have vanquished our foes.

And that's why Israeli prime minister Shimon Peres said that Israel is now at war with Hamas, for its aim is Israel's elimination. And we at the American Jewish Committee steadfastly support Israel in doing whatever it considers necessary to root out and eliminate this cancer in its midst.

Moreover, we call on the Palestinian Authority and its chairman, Yassir Arafat, to pursue the same objective. Hamas threatens the current peace process and the promise it holds for Palestinian progress and dignity, no less than it poses a danger to Israel's security.

A young Israel, barely a month old, faced squarely the challenge of dissident Jews who defied the authority of the new government by destroying a ship, the *Altalena*, carrying weapons to the dissidents. Some of the crew were killed, but the point was made: henceforth, only a single government authority existed.

Chairman Arafat must do no less than David Ben-Gurion did at the time.

And Western countries must step up their efforts to combat the scourge of international terrorism embodied by Hamas and about which we have been talking for years. Hamas has friends, support groups, and funding sources abroad, including here in the United States. In this regard, we applaud President Clinton's strong statement of support for Israel made earlier today and his denunciation of terrorism. But let me emphasize: The support for Hamas must be rooted out in this country, whether in Virginia or Illinois or Texas, as it must abroad. And significantly, if not surprisingly, nowhere does it operate more openly than in Syria.

The European countries and Japan must reexamine their ties with nations in the region that support, fund, and train terrorists, including, especially, Iran. Western countries can no longer sell us a bill of goods that their strong economic ties moderate extremist forces in the region; they do not. And it's high time they face up to this stark reality and send a clear message that countries that support terrorism have no place in the international community. Period. Moreover, influence ought to be exerted on Russia and China to follow suit because ultimately it is in their interests as well; after all, Islamic extremists also have aspirations in southern Russia and western China.

So we gather here this afternoon, in sadness and mourning, yes, but also to stand firm and resolute, to express once again our solidarity with Israel, to reach out to the families of the victims both in Israel and here in the United States, and to reaffirm our prayer for an end to the violence and the dawning of a new day.

Israeli Democracy Faces Defining Election
The Gannett Reporter Dispatch
May 28, 1996

Perhaps the most important, and certainly the most innovative, aspect of the current Israeli election is the introduction of direct election for the office of prime minister. For the first time, Israelis will be casting two ballots: one for a Knesset list—choosing among more than twenty parties—and a second for either Shimon Peres or Benjamin Netanyahu as prime minister. This reform, promulgated some five years ago by the Knesset, the Israeli parliament, was designed to ensure more stable government; it sought to subordinate coalition politics to a strong executive who enjoys a direct mandate from the people.

No one is certain exactly how successful this innovation will prove. Currently, Peres is slightly ahead in most opinion polls, but Labor and Likud are virtually tied in polls for the Knesset, with a variety of small parties splitting the remainder of the vote. This means that a newly elected prime minister seeking to form a government could find himself subject to considerable pressure from minor Knesset factions that hold the balance of power. Consequently, the new government might prove as unstable as some of its predecessors, with their narrow majorities, or even be faced with an opposition majority.

This raises another ramification of the new system. As in many countries that have direct elections for the executive, this election is focusing primarily on personalities and buzzwords, and only secondarily on carefully defined issues. The two main parties are competing largely for the allegiance of some 5 percent to 10 percent of the electorate who are defined by the pollsters as the floating vote, located in the political center and likely to remain undecided between Labor and Likud, Peres and Netanyahu, right up to election day.

The candidates' pollsters and assorted spinmasters also tell them that the majority of the electorate, including the floating vote, has firmly bought into two concepts: the need to maintain the peace process and the need to provide security. Hence, essentially, Peres and Netanyahu are each vying to persuade the voter that he can provide the better "mix" of peace and security.

Peres ostensibly has the initiative, but is also more vulnerable. As the incumbent, he can speak to the voters with actions rather than words. He can take steps that he believes advance either peace or security, such as imposing closure upon the Palestinians, extracting from the PLO its recent annulment of anti-Israel and anti-Jewish clauses in its covenant, or initiating Operation Grapes of Wrath against Hezbollah in Lebanon.

But, by the same token, if he is seen to fail—if Hamas and Hezbollah attacks appear to portray his policies as ineffective—he may pay a higher electoral price. Hence the widespread "common wisdom" that holds that a serious terrorist atrocity carried out just before tomorrow's election could perhaps damage the chances of Peres and his Labor Party.

In order to balance his image of peacemaker with that of "Mr. Security," Peres has taken tough steps against terrorism. He has also adopted the strategy of "separation" (clearly delineated borders and barriers between Israel and Palestinians), even though it negates the concept of integration implicit in his "New Middle East" philosophy.

Netanyahu and the Likud, on the other hand, entered the electoral campaign with a reputation for toughness on security issues but lack of initiative on peace issues. Accordingly, Netanyahu has been moving toward the center from the opposite direction: acknowledging, however reluctantly, the Oslo process; expressing a readiness to negotiate with Arafat and the PLO, and generally claiming a capacity to make peace more effectively by holding out for Arab concessions that Peres allegedly forgoes in the interest of haste; and standing up better for Israel's security needs. Netanyahu constantly criticizes Peres's peace and security accomplishments as being too little, too late.

When all is said and done, this is an important, even defining, election for Israel. Two parties, two candidates that have a fundamental disagreement about the future direction, pace, and nature of the peace process and its impact on Israel's security are vying for power. But whatever the differences, the one thing that shouldn't be overlooked is the health of Israel's robust democratic process, still a rarity in that turbulent part of the world.

Iranians Pose a Real Threat to Mideast Security
The New York Times
July 2, 1996

Michael Field (Op-Ed, June 28) misses the mark when he dismissively refers to United States and Israeli "paranoia" regarding Iran. To the contrary, the United States and Israel are doing the civilized world an enormous favor by focusing attention on the threat posed by Iran.

The State Department's latest "Patterns of Global Terrorism" report points to Iranian arms, financing, and training for Hezbollah, Islamic Jihad, the Popular Front for the Liberation of Palestine, and Hamas "to resist Israel and the peace process through violence and terrorism," and names Iran "the premier state sponsor of international terrorism."

Let's not forget, too, that when Secretary of State Warren Christopher was trying to reach an agreement to end hostilities in Lebanon, Iran was delivering, through Damascus, Katyusha rockets to Hezbollah to fire at Israeli towns and villages. Paranoia? No, reality.

For years Iran has been intent on developing the ability to manufacture weapons of mass destruction and the means to deliver them. Its Persian Gulf neighbors are worried, as are the United States and Israel.

In an American Jewish Committee study last year, Patrick Clawson of the National Defense University wrote that despite Western restrictions on selling weapons and dual-use items to Iran, that country "is still able to import a great many dangerous items" from Europe and Asia. An Arab foreign minister told me of his fear that Russian arms merchants were seeking to sell nuclear components to Iran.

To deny the dangers Iran poses to regional and global stability is shortsighted.

Israel and the UN
*International Herald Tribune**
August 20, 1997

In response to the editorial "Bigger Security Council?" (Aug. 16), it is worth noting that just one of the 185 member countries of the United Nations is ineligible to sit, in any capacity, on the Security Council. All seven countries on the U.S. terrorism list are eligible. So, too, are tiny Andorra and the Seychelles Islands.

Only democratic Israel, a UN member for nearly five decades, is denied that possibility because, for practical purposes, nonpermanent members are always selected by one of five regional blocs—Africa, Asia, Eastern Europe, Latin America, and "West European and Others."

By geography, Israel should be in the Asian Group, but Iraq, Saudi Arabia, and other states have denied Israel membership. As a temporary measure, Israel has sought inclusion in the West European and Others group, but a few European Union countries, on one pretext or another, have blocked Israel from joining.

If UN reform is on the agenda, then remedying Israel's anomalous situation, which denies it participation not only in the Security Council but also in the Economic and Social Council, the International Court of Justice, and other key UN organs, ought to be at the top of the list for those who care about the credibility and effectiveness of the United Nations.

*A letter on the same theme was published in the *New York Times* on August 18, 1997.

The Middle East: Emerging Challenges
AJC Milwaukee Tribute Dinner
November 13, 1997

In a speech at Amherst College four weeks before his death, President John Kennedy said: "A nation reveals itself not only by the men it produces but also by the men it honors."

So, too, an organization, I believe. We reveal ourselves by the men (and women) we honor. And in honoring Stan Bluestone this evening, the American Jewish Committee has selected an outstanding individual. Stan, you honor us by allowing us to honor you. And I'm delighted to see his wife Judy as well—a member of our national Board of Governors and former staff colleague.

Some time ago, I was invited to speak at a parlor meeting on the world scene. After serving the guests drinks and hors d'oeuvres, the hostess approached me and said: "David, shall we let the guests continue to enjoy themselves, or would you like to begin speaking?"

Ladies and gentlemen, guess what I was asked to speak about this evening? Yes, the world scene, so perhaps I should apologize in advance. Seriously, though, there is much to say.

On August 1, 1990, a three-person American Jewish Committee delegation, myself included, traveled to Washington, D.C., for meetings with senior officials in the State Department and National Security Council.

Our primary aim was to discuss, once again, our concerns regarding Iraq and our inability to understand the Bush administration's opposition to sanctions legislation against Iraq that was then being considered in the United States Congress.

The response we heard was troubling. We were told that, in the administration's view, Iraq could be a positive factor in the region, perhaps one day joining with Egypt, Jordan, and Saudi Arabia in a pro-Western coalition opposing extremist and fundamentalist forces. To state the painfully obvious, we at AJC were unsuccessful in our mission.

Incidentally, this naïve view of Iraq was not limited to the administration at the time. There were at least some influential senators, of both major parties, who shared it, especially a small group who had recently visited Iraq and been impressed by what they heard. One prominent senator—still in office, I might add—even said in my presence that Iraq was ready to make a gesture toward Israel, just you wait and see.

On August 2, 1990, exactly one day after our meetings in the State Department and National Security Council, Iraq invaded and occupied Kuwait, precipitating, as we all know, a major international crisis that led to war. And, oh yes, it did lead to a gesture toward Israel, but not the one the senator had in mind—thirty-nine Scud missiles aimed at targets in Israel's heartland.

I needn't rehearse the entire history of that period; it's still fresh in the minds of many of us. But certain points are important to recall now, here, as we witness a new crisis looming with Iraq.

First, let's not again underestimate Saddam Hussein.

Many believed he'd blink when President Bush and the coalition forces gave him a deadline to leave Kuwait. He didn't.

Many believed he'd buckle under the awesome military, especially air, power unleashed by the coalition forces. He hasn't.

To the contrary, ironic though it seems, both President Bush and Prime Minister Thatcher, the two prime movers of the Western response, lost their jobs shortly after the Gulf war. Saddam Hussein still has his.

Second, Saddam Hussein will exploit any perceived weakness, any crack in the wall, that he sees in the forces arrayed against him. Just as that well-known conversation in 1990 with the then-American ambassador in Baghdad led him to conclude that he wouldn't encounter opposition were he to occupy Kuwait, so, too, now, observing the growing impatience of France, Russia, China, and Egypt with the sanctions—and believing that the United States and Britain are becoming isolated—Saddam Hussein deliberately precipitated the current crisis.

Third, leaders like Saddam Hussein are absolutely ruthless and there's no taming them. Let's be clear. He was prepared to sacrifice millions of his countrymen in the eight-year war with Iran, from 1980 to 1988, and the same in the Gulf war.

He was building an arsenal of weapons of mass destruction. Thank

God, in 1981, Israel, acting alone, destroyed Iraq's Orsirak nuclear reactor, which had been a gift, so to speak, of the French. Just imagine that, in addition to his stockpile of chemical and biological weapons, he had had access to nuclear weapons when he occupied Kuwait, and then challenged the world to dislodge him. The entire strategic equation would have been totally different.

As it was, he had already used chemical weapons against his own Kurdish population, and, as our valiant troops who served in the Gulf now know all too well, he was stockpiling chemical weapons, to which our forces may have been exposed in March 1991.

I was in Israel when Scud missiles landed in the Tel Aviv area. Like everyone else, I carried with me my gas mask and spent time in the sealed rooms during each missile attack. Israelis, I must say, carried on stoically and admirably. Moreover, Israel, acting as a true friend of the United States, resisted the very understandable impulse to go after the mobile missile launchers in western Iraq that were used to fire the missiles, only because President Bush said that to do so would risk splintering the American-led coalition of forces.

And that's a fourth lesson. Genuine friends are tested under fire. Israel once again demonstrated its true friendship and dependability as our ally. While some other so-called friendly nations try to have it both ways, Israel has always been there. And, let's be clear, it's not a one-way street. Israel's proven strategic value to the United States, not to speak of its shared commitment to our democratic values, makes it a highly valued ally of the United States.

The United States has no choice whatsoever but to stand strong and resolute in the current face-off with Baghdad. Anything less will prove disastrous. And we have to demand of our friends the same firmness. It is unthinkable that such nations as Egypt, France, and Russia can straddle the fence or, worse, undermine our position in dealing with Saddam Hussein.

Iraq is determined to acquire weapons of mass destruction—and if it succeeds, there's every reason to believe it will use them. We are the only nation in a position, and with the will, to deter Baghdad. That's why the American Jewish Committee has expressed our full support to President Clinton.

What are our interests in deterring distant Iraq, skeptics ask. Our interests are really quite simple. We need to send the strongest possible message to rogue states—Iraq, Iran, Libya, and others—that they will not succeed in their efforts to bully, blackmail, menace, or attack neighboring or, for that matter, distant states.

Yes, we have more specific diplomatic, economic, energy, and other interests in the region. These can't be underestimated either. But there's a larger issue here as there was earlier in this century. In 1938, Hitler seized Czechoslovakia and the world sat still hoping the Nazi leader would be appeased, only to discover that not only was he not, but, to the contrary, he was actually emboldened to go further by his perception of the world's weakness and indifference.

The American Jewish Committee has sought to understand such lessons of history and apply them in today's world. That's why we care so deeply about the outcome in Iraq.

And that's why, for nearly a decade, we've been trying to alert the world to similar dangers emerging in neighboring Iran, which, after the protracted conflict with Iraq, set out aggressively to acquire its own weapons of mass destruction. Frightful though it is to consider, they've made a lot of headway.

Indeed, with active Russian help, Iran today is on the threshold of a major breakthrough in missile technology that will give Teheran the capacity to fire medium-range missiles a distance of 800 miles, and they're already hard at work on the next stage, a long-distance missile with a range of 2,000 miles. Look at the map and you'll realize that, from Iran's borders, those distances allow them to reach a dismayingly large and strategically significant part of the world.

True, Iran has a new president and he seems to want a less suffocating social order, but, as the experts all know, despite his title he doesn't hold the reins of real power in his hands. Those reins are held by unabashedly anti-American, anti-Western religious leaders who openly call for the destruction of the "great Satan," the United States—and, not incidentally, the "Zionist entity." The Iranians, you see, don't even utter the world "Israel" since they deny its right to exist.

Just as Saddam Hussein signaled his intentions regarding Kuwait, so the Iranians signal theirs—to spread their radicalized form of Islam and to attack their enemies, for now at least, principally through assassination, terrorism, and such proxy groups as Hezbollah in Lebanon.

Remember: History teaches us that these demagogic leaders usually *do* mean what they say, however preposterous their rantings and ravings may at first sound. It was Adolf Hitler, for example, who said in September 1942: "At one time the Jews of Germany laughed about my prophecies. I do not know whether they are still laughing or whether they have already lost all desire to laugh. But right now I can only repeat: they will stop laughing everywhere, and I shall be right also in that prophecy."

And yet despite the obvious threats, the United States finds itself swimming upstream, trying to muster support, especially in Europe and Russia, both of which would be within target range of these missiles. Not for the first time, though, these countries have chosen to place their own short-term commercial interests ahead of their long-term strategic interests, while arguing, unpersuasively, that their approach of engagement is more likely to change rogue states' behavior.

The role of the United States is crucial. There are those here who long for an American retreat from the world scene, as if such were even possible in a world where it's harder and harder to sort out international and domestic issues, so interconnected have they become. The stock market in Southeast Asia collapses and Wall Street trembles. That's our world today.

These neoisolationists are simply wrong. History has amply shown that. Whenever America turns inward, dictators feel empowered and step into the breach. Then America must return to the world scene and pay a still higher price to restore a measure of needed security and stability.

The late Eleanor Roosevelt, speaking at Brandeis University in 1954, put it well. "We are the strongest nation in the world," she said. "We, whether we like it or not, are the leaders. And we lead not only in military and economic strength, but we lead in knowing what are our values, what are the things we believe in, and being willing to live up to them, and being willing to accept the fact that living up to them here, we help ourselves, but we also help the world."

America's leadership responsibility, though, in the final analysis, is not principally a burden, even if it does not come costfree. No, rather it's an extraordinary opportunity.

Despite all the problems, there hasn't been a more promising era in modern history than the one in which we live right now, and we'd be tragically shortsighted to underestimate the possibilities.

More people live in freedom than ever before. The bulk of the communist world has been shattered, the legacy of apartheid destroyed, the reach of democracy extended throughout most of Latin America. Old enemies, including France and Germany, Romania and Hungary, the United States and Russia, live in peace with one another. And international human rights standards and monitoring have some meaning, where previously they had precious little.

I certainly don't mean to downplay the difficulties we still face, from weapons proliferation, about which I spoke, to the spread of international terrorism; from only partially resolved conflicts, such as the Arab-Israeli dispute, to gruesome mass murders in the former Yugoslavia and Central Africa.

Yet, even with all the challenges, I confess to a certain overall optimism about the world. Okay, so it's true that in the Soviet Union they used to define an optimist as someone "insufficiently pessimistic," but listen to the words of the great American poet Robert Frost:

Take human nature altogether since time began ...
And it must be a little more in favor of man,
Say a fraction of one per cent at the very least ...
Our hold on the planet wouldn't have so increased.

America's global role was brought home to me yet again this fall when I participated in an unprecedented diplomatic marathon of the American Jewish Committee—forty-six private meetings, in a three-week span, with the world's presidents, prime ministers, and foreign ministers in New York for the opening of the new UN session.

These meetings are part of our extensive, in fact unparalleled, international programming focused on some of the issues I've mentioned here tonight, and also on one I'd like to close my remarks with, namely Israel and its place in the world. But before doing that, let me simply say that I could take you through each of those forty-six meetings—don't worry, I have no intention of doing so—and show you key U.S. interests, key U.S. opportunities, and key U.S. challenges.

It's an especially timely moment to note that fifty years ago this month, in November 1947, the United Nations, by a vote of 33 to 13 with 10 abstentions, approved the creation of a Jewish state in Palestine. This came nearly 1,900 years after the destruction of the last Jewish commonwealth, exactly fifty years after the first Zionist Congress met in Basel, Switzerland, and just two years after the end of the Second World War and the Holocaust. The right of Jewish political sovereignty was affirmed by the international community.

And of course this is an especially appropriate city in which to note the momentous significance of the birth of the modern state of Israel. We should pay homage to Israel's heroes and heroines, the many whose names, regrettably, are no longer easily recalled, and the few whose accomplishments cannot be forgotten—including, of course, Golda Meir, whose ties to Milwaukee are well known to you all.

These determined individuals ignored the dire predictions of Secretary of State George Marshall and others that tiny, underarmed Israel could not possibly survive militarily. Not only did 600,000 Jews living then in the new Jewish state ensure the sheer physical survival of the state against all the odds, but they also laid the groundwork for a dynamic, democratic country governed by the rule of law—a country that has never faltered, not even when Scud missiles landed, in fulfilling its role as a Jewish sanctuary; a country with no natural resources to speak of whose GNP now surpasses the combined gross national products of all its immediate neighbors; a country that has become a valued and trusted ally of the United States; and a country that never yielded to a garrison mentality but rather has created a lively and fertile ground for universities, scientific research, and culture and the arts.

As Israel celebrates its fiftieth anniversary, we friends of Israel around the world, Jews and non-Jews alike, take pride in its accomplishments, even as we recognize that Israel, like the United States and other countries, is always going to be, in significant ways, a work in progress.

Moreover, AJC takes pride in the steadfastness of our commitment to Israel since its founding in 1948. Abba Eban, the distinguished diplomat and author, said of the AJC's link to Israel: "You were able to play an indispensable role. . . . You stood in vigilant brotherhood at the cradle of our emergent statehood; you helped us lay the foundations of our international status and of our crucial friendship with the Government and people of the American Republic."

And yes, we recognize that in following the complex events affecting Israel from day to day through television and the papers, one can too easily lose sight of the big picture, and the big picture in this case is an IMAX screen—a remarkable multidimensional saga of the nearly 4,000-year-old connection between a people, a faith, a vision, and a land. It is an epic saga of dispersion and return.

Ladies and gentlemen, as we gather here this evening to confer honor on a truly worthy recipient, Stan Bluestone, I am pleased to use this occasion to reaffirm the American Jewish Committee's commitment to the values and principles of a democratic world; a world respectful of human rights; a world in which Israel is able to achieve, once and for all, the security, normalcy, and peace it has yearned for since its founding; a world in which Jews and other minority communities fully participate in the societies in which they live; and a world in which peoples of different faiths and nationalities no longer feel threatened by differences in skin color, in faith, in language, in otherness.

Forgive my institutional immodesty—if not me, who, and if not here, when—but I daresay that the world at large, and this country in particular, are far better places for AJC's ninety-one-year-long unstinting commitment to these ideals. Tonight I reaffirm them before you, on behalf of this dynamic Milwaukee chapter and the 70,000 members and supporters of AJC across the country.

As Rabbi Tarphon taught in the first century: "It is not thy duty to complete the work. But neither art thou free to desist from it."

With your continued support, I assure you that we shall not desist in seeking to fulfill the prophetic vision of a world at peace, a world in harmony.

Not the Time to Go Easy on Saddam
New York Post
December 26, 1997

Sadly true to form, Rowland Evans and Robert Novak have it backward, praising the French leadership for "diplomacy" and sharply criticizing President Clinton for his principled policy of containment of Iraq (Op-Ed, Dec. 22).

Rather than support sustained pressure on Baghdad, Evans and Novak propose instead that President Clinton back off and cash in on a craven policy that the French and Russians seem to favor. To Evans and Novak, French president Chirac's reported proposal for "a nonproliferation pact on weapons of mass destruction for the entire region, with international inspection" makes great sense. "That would require negotiations with Saddam," they write.

The columnists (and the French president, if his proposal was accurately reported) appear to have forgotten that Saddam Hussein lost a war he initiated, and submitted to UN-mandated international inspections to find prohibited weapons. What makes Evans and Novak think Saddam would allow a new regime of international inspections when he has successfully hidden weapons of mass destruction and stonewalled the international community until today?

If America's allies stood firmly together against Iraq, Saddam Hussein would not get away with the dangerous games he plays and the ridiculous notions he floats. Sadly, even some world leaders—and columnists—who should know better naively fall for his ominous tricks.

A New Low in Hope for Peace
New York Post
March 18, 1998

A new poll commissioned by the American Jewish Committee confirms the sad truth: Since 1993, when American Jews, in the wake of the now-famous Rabin-Arafat handshake on the White House lawn, peaked in their hope for bringing to an end the long-standing Arab-Israeli conflict, there has been a steady, year-to-year decline in that hopefulness. Now, it has reached a new low.

Today, American Jews are less optimistic about the chance for a lasting peace, more skeptical about Arafat's commitment to a nonviolent solution, more reluctant to see the creation of a Palestinian state, more convinced that the Palestinian Authority is not controlling terrorist activity, and more fearful that the true goal of the Arabs is Israel's destruction than at any time in the past five years.

Some people use surveys the way drunks use lampposts—for support rather than illumination. Indeed, two recent studies of American Jewish public opinion have presented diametrically opposing pictures of the community's views on Arab-Israeli issues. But the American Jewish Committee has been conducting annual surveys since 1981, and with no ideological ax to grind. We seek data that will illuminate, not simply support a particular viewpoint.

Here are some questions from the survey and the results:

- "The goal of the Arabs is not the return of occupied territories but rather the destruction of Israel." Sixty-eight percent of the survey respondents agree, 24 percent disagree. Five years ago, only 42 percent agreed.
- "Given the current situation, do you favor or oppose the creation of a Palestinian state?" In the survey, 42 percent favor a Palestinian state, 49 percent oppose. Five years ago, 57 percent were in favor and only 30 percent were against.
- "To what extent does PLO chairman Yasir Arafat support or oppose peace with Israel?" Of the respondents, 40 percent said he supports peace. On the other hand, 55 percent replied that the Palestinian leader opposes peace. Just one year ago, a majority—62 percent—said he supported peace and only 31 percent felt otherwise.

There's a lot to chew over in this poll. For instance:

- Prime Minister Netanyahu is viewed favorably by two-thirds of the respondents, whereas 30 percent regard him unfavorably. Though a decisive margin, there has been erosion from just a year ago, when the numbers were 75–18.

- Similarly, a majority—56 percent—support his "current handling of the peace negotiations with the Arabs," but 34 percent oppose. Again, there has been some slippage in the level of support from last year; the margin then was 61–24.
- On the issue of American "pressure," the diplomatic buzzword *du jour*, 69 percent of the survey respondents believe the United States should apply pressure on Arafat "to advance the peace process, even if this creates a strain in U.S.-Palestinian relations." When asked an identical question about putting pressure on Netanhayu, 52 percent said no, 45 percent said yes.

What's going on?

For one thing, American Jews have become increasingly antsy about Palestinian words and actions, particularly regarding the fundamental question of Israeli security. At such times, American Jews tend to rally around Israel, especially when they feel it is becoming increasingly isolated or beleaguered.

American Jewry has long been divided into three groups. There are those on the left and right who, depending on the political party in power in Jerusalem, will almost reflexively support or oppose policies. Then there is the mainstream, a far larger body of opinion that tends to identify with the democratically elected government in office.

The AJC survey results make it clear that American Jews are increasingly pessimistic about the chances for a lasting peace. Reading the data, Washington should realize that any U.S. initiative in the peace process that was perceived as heavy-handed toward Israel would probably not go down well with most American Jews, though clearly there would be some division in Jewish ranks.

Prime Minister Netanyahu will find comfort in the current support levels for the government, as well as satisfaction that his oft-repeated accusation of Palestinian noncompliance seems to be getting through to many here. Still, he cannot ignore the erosion in support that he's experienced in the past year.

The Palestinians, who view American Jewry as a key player in U.S. policy formulation and therefore an important target audience, will have to take into account their own failure to persuade American Jews of their commitment to peaceful coexistence with Israel.

The famous telegram read: "Start worrying, letter follows." These survey results paint a portrait of a largely worried American Jewish community that's not waiting for the letter; they get their daily news from the Middle East and it has put them in an anxious and uncertain mood.

The American Jewish Committee poll of 1,001 self-identified adult Jewish respondents, interviewed by telephone between February 19 and March 8, was conducted by Market Facts and has a margin of error of +/- 3 percentage points.

Remarks on American Jewry
to Chiefs of Missions Conference
Department of State
April 7, 1998

Ambassador Gabriel [U.S. ambassador to Morocco], I appreciate your gracious introduction.

I would like to thank the department, and in particular Assistant Secretary Indyk, for the invitation to appear here before this distinguished group of American ambassadors and diplomats from the Bureau of Near Eastern Affairs. It is indeed an honor and a privilege. . . .

It is my understanding that my role here today is to share with you a sense of the Jewish landscape in the United States, as it pertains to American foreign policy and the Middle East. It is also my understanding that I must do this within ten minutes. The Jewish landscape is so complex, so multifaceted, that it is simply impossible to offer more than a few opening thoughts.

Recall, if you will, the purported conversation between President Truman and Israel's first president, Chaim Weizmann. The two leaders got into an argument about who had the more difficult task.

Truman said: "With all due respect, President Weizmann, I am the president of 140 million American citizens." "Yes, Mr. President," replied the Israeli leader, "but I am the president of 1 million Israeli presidents."

Put another way, for those of you who have dealt with American Jewish groups—and a number of you have—let me ask whether you have ever met a Jewish "follower." Every American Jew who travels to Washington or meets with a public figure is, it seems, by definition a Jewish "leader." I can't wait to meet the first American Jew who identifies himself as a follower. Hence the difficulties of my task.

To summarize the relevant data from our annual American Jewish Committee surveys of American Jews: Approximately two-thirds to three-fourths of American Jews feel a connection to Israel, some more intensely, some less so. Ideologically, American Jews fall into three broad categories: (a) those who identify with the left, in Israeli terms; (b) those who identify with the right, again in Israeli terms; and (c) those in the middle who, whatever their personal convictions, defer to the democratically elected government of the day in Israel. Quantifying these three groups is not easy, but I would say those in the first group represent about 25–30 percent of the Jewish community, the second about 15–20 percent, and the third 50–60 percent.

What also emerges from this and our previous polls is a kind of schizophrenia among American Jews. While the yearning for peace is absolutely clear, as is the recognition that to achieve peace Israel will have to make further territorial concessions, the fear that the Arabs, and the Palestinians in particular, may not be trustworthy partners for Israel is clearly growing.

Which brings me to the larger forces motivating American Jews. I'm going to set aside for now the daily spats, such as the one reported in today's *New York Times* regarding the appropriate U.S. role in the peace process, not because they are unimportant—they are very important—but because I trust we will address them in the discussion period. Rather, especially in light of the fact that this is Israel's fiftieth anniversary, I would like to step back and ask why it is that Israel has occupied such a central place in the hearts and minds of most American Jews. Even at the risk of stating the obvious, let me make three points.

First, the emergence of a sovereign Jewish state, after 1,900 years of dispersion, represents an event of extraordinary proportions for world Jewry. Specifically, the actualization of the biblical vision, when God said to Abraham, *Lekh, lekha*, go forth—the return to Zion, the very same land viewed by Moses from Mount Nebo, and the realization of *this* year in Jerusalem, not next—is the driving force in an identity that melds a land, a people, a faith, and a vision, and has done so for over 3,500 years.

Second, the state was created in the wake of the Holocaust. If ever there was a powerful reminder of the need for a Jewish state, it emerged from 1933 to 1945. American Jews understand this. They chastise themselves to this day for their inability to do more—to rescue more Jews, to slow down the Nazi Final Solution, to find more havens and sanctuaries for those seeking refuge.

Israel has become that haven, that sanctuary. Israel has become the Jewish people's answer to centuries of the teaching of contempt and blood libels, of exiles and pogroms, of ghettos and pales of settlement, of forced conversions and inquisitions, and of the entirely new vocabulary of destruction introduced by the Holocaust. Israel is seen as the means to overcome, once and for all, our historical victimization and vulnerability and replace it with the normalization and security of the Jewish people.

But American Jews have chosen to pursue their lives in the United States. We do so because we believe profoundly in the American democratic, pluralistic experiment; we subscribe fully to this country's basic premise that all Americans are entitled to equal shareholder status in America. This notion of full equality distinguishes the United States from the countries so many immigrants and refugees, Jews included, left behind.

At the same time, American Jews recognize the indispensability of our own role in ensuring Israel's safety and prosperity, most especially through our support of the special bilateral relationship between the United States and Israel.

American Jews learned all too painfully during the Holocaust the effects of powerlessness. As a consequence, in the postwar years we have sought to gain access and influence on the U.S. political scene, with some notable degree of success regarding American policy toward Israel and the rescue of endangered Jewry.

And lastly, in terms of American Jewish psychology, Israel has been viewed for much of its life as beleaguered, even as its military grew stronger. It has been seen as the object of efforts to destroy it, whether through diplomatic isolation and economic boycotts or war and terrorism. American Jews have watched in dismay as too many countries, in international forums like the United Nations, join the enemies of Israel out of political and economic expediency.

Other Jewish communities scattered throughout the Diaspora are numerically much weaker than American Jewry and often live in societies that do not invite their citizens to petition the government. Also, most other Jewish communities are located in countries with decidedly less clout on the world scene. That places a special responsibility on the shoulders of American Jews to foster the closest possible U.S.-Israel relationship, which serves the highest values and most important national interests of both countries and, of course, is vital to Israel's well-being.

All this said, though, it does not hide the fact that there are deep fissures in the Jewish community, but then again, what's new? Even a cursory reading of Jewish history reveals that there have always been such chasms. Indeed, we are told that the very destruction of the Second Temple, in Jerusalem in 70 C.E., was precisely the result of such internal strife.

These divisions continue to this very day, so no doubt we will continue to see the war of the ads, the polls, and the competing congressional letters, while Israelis of different political stripes appeal to their respective American Jewish supporters to raise funds or press Congress on this or that issue.

But please keep in mind that, with all of this frenzied activity, what motivates American Jews, whether of the left, the right, or the center, is the deeply held sense of responsibility that Israel has been established on our watch. We American Jews wish to be engaged in ensuring not only its survival but in helping define the soul of this sovereign work in progress. Moreover, given that we are at a very delicate point in the peace process when core issues shaping Israel's—and the Palestinians'—very future are in the balance, it is inevitable that the political temperature rises; the stakes are incalculably high. But in the final analysis, whatever our political or, for that matter, denominational orientation within the Jewish community, we yearn above all for the fulfillment, in our lifetimes, of the prophetic vision of an era of lasting peace for Israel and the entire region.

Much to Celebrate
in *Israel at 50: 1948-1998*[*]
American Jewish Committee
May 1998

As I sit down to write this piece, I am surrounded by reports of gloom regarding Israel's golden anniversary.

Israelis aren't in the mood to celebrate, the newspapers note. Even if they were, we are told, the organizing committee is underfunded, behind schedule, and inept. And, observers suggest, American Jews are too preoccupied with the fierce debates over pluralism, conversion, and legitimacy, not to speak of the political divide regarding the Netanyahu government, to step back, see the lush forest that represents Israel's first fifty years, and joyfully mark the anniversary.

If true, these reports are profoundly disturbing. Whatever the difficulties and controversies, this nonetheless is an epochal occasion for Israel and its friends to celebrate with unrestrained enthusiasm and pride. What a shame if the opportunity were lost.

Let me put my cards on the table. I am not dispassionate when it comes to Israel.

I believe that the very establishment of the State of Israel in 1948; the fulfillment of its envisioned role as home and haven for Jews from around the world; the embrace of democracy and the rule of law, including an admirable independent judiciary, free and fair elections, and smooth transfers of power; and the impressive scientific, cultural, social, and, not least, economic achievements are accomplishments beyond our wildest imagination. I am grateful beyond words to be able to witness this most extraordinary period in Jewish history.

And when one adds the key element, namely, that all this was accomplished not in Scandinavia but in the Middle East, that Israel's

[*]An abridged version of this essay appeared in the *New York Post*, April 30, 1998.

neighbors were determined from day one to destroy it and were prepared to use any means available to them—from full-scale wars to
wars of attrition; from diplomatic isolation to attempts at international
delegitimation; from primary to secondary to even tertiary economic
boycotts; from terrorism in the skies to terrorism in crowded market-
places, packed buses, and even elementary schools; from spreading the
poison of anti-Semitism, often thinly veiled as anti-Zionism, to Arab
populations through schoolbooks, Friday sermons, and government-
controlled newspapers to the sometimes all-too-receptive precincts of
the United Nations—the story of Israel's first fifty years becomes all
the more remarkable.

No other country, certainly no other democratic country, has been
subjected to such a constant challenge to its existence, to its very legitimacy, though the age-old biblical, spiritual, historic, and physical connection between the Jewish people and the Land of Israel is quite
unique. Indeed, it is of a totally different character, one must say, from
the basis on which the United States, Australia, Canada, New Zealand
or the bulk of Latin American countries were established, i.e., by
Europeans with no legitimate claim whatsoever to these lands deci-
mating indigenous populations and proclaiming authority.

No other country has faced such overwhelming odds against its survival or experienced the same degree of international vilification by an
automatic majority of nations that has reflexively followed the will of
the energy-rich and more numerous Arab world.

Yet throughout, Israelis never succumbled to a garrison mentality,
never abandoned their yearning for peace or willingness to take
unprecedented risks to achieve peace, and never flinched from their
determination to build a thriving state.

In fact, I believe this story of nation-building to be entirely without
historical precedent.

Here was a people brought to the brink of utter destruction by the
genocidal policies of Nazi Germany and its allies. Here was a people
that had lost one-third of its total number, including 1.5 million children. Here was a people shown to be entirely powerless to influence
the world to stop this unprecedented and unparalleled carnage. And
here was a people numbering but 600,000 living cheek by jowl with

often hostile Arabs, under unsympathetic British occupation, on a harsh soil with no significant natural resources in then Palestine. That the blue-and-white flag of an independent Israel could be planted on this land, to which we had been linked since the covenant between God and Abraham, just three years after the Second World War's end is truly astounding.

To understand the essence of Israel's meaning it is enough to ask how the history of the Jewish people might have been different had there been a Jewish state in 1933, in 1938, even in 1941. If Israel had controlled its borders and the right of entry instead of Britain, if Israel had had embassies and consulates throughout Europe, how many more Jews might have escaped and found sanctuary?

Alas, such was not to be the case. Instead, Jews had to rely on the goodwill of embassies and consulates of other countries and, with woefully few exceptions, they found neither the "good" nor the "will" to assist.

I have witnessed firsthand the meaning of Israeli embassies and consulates in recent years to Jews drawn to Israel by the pull of Zion or the push of hatred. I have stood in the courtyard of the Israeli embassy in Moscow and seen thousands of Jews seeking a quick exit from a Soviet Union that showed signs of cataclysmic change but who weren't sure if the change was in the direction of democracy or renewed chauvinism and anti-Semitism.

I have seen Israel do what no other Western country had ever done before—bring out Africans, in this case Ethiopian Jews, not in chains for exploitation but in dignity for freedom.

Awestruck, I have watched Israel never falter, not for a moment, in bringing Jews, principally from the USSR, to the Jewish homeland, while Scud missiles from Iraq traumatized the nation. It says a lot about the conditions they were leaving behind that Soviet Jews continued to board planes for Tel Aviv even as these missiles were exploding in Israeli population centers. And equally, it says a lot about Israel that, amid all the pressing security concerns at such a moment, it managed without missing a beat to continue to welcome the new immigrants.

And how can I ever forget the surge of pride, Jewish pride, that completely enveloped me twenty-two years ago on hearing the extraordinary news of Israel's daring rescue of the 106 Jewish hostages held by Arab and German terrorists at the airport in Entenbbe, Uganda, 2,000 miles from Israel's border?

To be sure, nation-building is an infinitely complex process. In Israel's case, the nation-building took place against a backdrop of intercommunal tensions with a local Arab population that also laid claim to the very same land; as the Arab world sought to isolate, demoralize, and ultimately destroy the state; as Israel's population literally doubled in the first years of existence, putting an unimaginable strain on severely limited resources; as the country was forced to devote a vast portion of its budget to defense despite the compelling socioeconomic needs of its citizens, especially the new arrivals; and as the country groped with the unprecedented issues of forging a national identity, a common culture, and a social consensus with a population that could not have been more geographically, linguistically, socially, and culturally heterogeneous.

Here we come to a complicated and perhaps underappreciated issue—the potential clash between the messy realities of statehood and, in this case, the tenets of a faith or a people. It is one thing to be a people living as a minority in often inhospitable majority cultures; it is quite another to exercise sovereignty, as the majority population. Inevitably, there will be clashes between a people's faith or ideals and the exigencies of statecraft. And there will be clashes as well between our ideals of human nature and the quotidian realities of individuals in decision-making positions wielding power and balancing a variety of often-competing interests.

The results are at times bound to disappoint, as, for example, the often patronizing manner of the Ashkenazi elite toward North African immigrants in the first decades, the excessively close ties with South Africa during the era of apartheid, or, until today, far too many instances of political shenanigans that ill befit the state.

Still, can we raise the bar so high as to practically ensure that Israel, forced to function in the often gritty, morally ambiguous world of international relations and domestic politics, will always fall short?

On the other hand, the notion that Israel would ever become morally or ethically indistinguishable from any other country, always hiding behind the convenient justification of realpolitik to explain its behavior, is equally unacceptable.

Israelis, with only fifty years of statehood, are among the newer practitioners of statecraft. Look at where the United States was fifty years, or even 150 years, after independence, and of course in the U.S. case we speak of a vast country blessed with abundant natural resources, oceans on two-and-a-half sides, a gentle neighbor to the north, and a weaker neighbor to the south.

Though guided by the lustrous principles of democracy and human dignity, the United States has experienced the ignominy of slavery, segregation in the armed forces until after World War II and in the southern states until well into the 1960s, legalized inequality between the genders, blatant discrimination against Asians in our immigration policy and the stain of Japanese-Americans forced to live in internment camps during the Second World War, impediments against Jews in most sectors of American life until well into this century, several disastrous foreign policy adventures, and, to this day, striking disparities within the American population. For instance, the infant mortality rate among whites (6.3 per 1000 births in 1995) is considerably less than half that of blacks (15.1) and the per-capita income of Hispanics ($9,300 in 1995) is one-half that of whites ($18,304).

Why do I refer to America? To place the Israeli situation—and the remarkable record of these past fifty years—in some context, even against the standard of the world's leading democratic nation.

Of course, the Israeli record is imperfect, yet Israel remains an astonishingly impressive work in progress. In fifty years, Israel has built a thriving democracy; an economy whose per capita GNP exceeds the combined total of its four contiguous neighbors—Lebanon, Syria, Jordan and Egypt; seven universities that contribute to advancing the world's frontiers of knowledge; a life expectancy that places it among the healthiest nations; a thriving culture utilizing an ancient language rendered contemporary; and an agricultural sector that has shown the world how to conquer an arid land.

In the final analysis, even more than any of these truly significant milestones, the story of Israel these past fifty years, above all, is the wondrous realization of a 3,500-year link between a land, a faith, a language, a people, and a vision. It is an inspiring story of tenacity and determination, of courage and renewal, of the ascendancy of hope over despair.

That said, what are the major challenges before Israel? Let me leave aside the most obvious and compelling—the quest for a lasting and secure peace—if only because it is beyond the scope of this symposium. While Israel has gained remarkable peace treaties with Egypt and Jordan, as well as some advances with the Palestinians, the neighborhood remains, to state the painfully obvious, exceedingly menacing.

The absence of the rule of law and civil society as we know it among Israel's Arab neighbors means that transfers of power are inevitably achieved by nondemocratic means, with all the attendant uncertainties. In the larger scheme, the emerging mix in the region of rogue states, terrorist groups, and weapons of mass destruction and the means to deliver them suggest that Israel will not be able to rest easy, certainly not for the foreseeable future, regardless of what happens in the short term on the Palestinian front.

Within Israel, the major challenge will be to ensure that the ties that bind Israelis—i.e., the centripetal forces—remain far stronger than the centrifugal forces threatening to pull the country apart. The most ominous of these centrifugal forces—and the most difficult to find a solution for—is the religious/secular divide.

Surely, the religious camp is not monolithic, nor, for that matter, is the secular camp. Still, it is fair to say that a deep rift has existed among Jews for centuries, especially since the Enlightenment, and among Israelis for the past half century, along these essential lines.

Not only has this divide not been narrowed in Israel, where regrettably, unlike the United States, no middle ground of non-Orthodox forms of religious practice has yet taken root, but, in fact, it threatens to grow ever wider. Israel increasingly encompasses two centers, two worldviews, essentially embodied by Jerusalem, the religious, and Tel Aviv (and Haifa), the secular.

How to manage this divide remains a daunting challenge for Israel (and extends beyond Israel's borders as well). It is coterminous with the underlying challenge of defining the very nature of the Jewish state, still incomplete after fifty years. What exactly is, or ought to be, the Jewish character of the Jewish state? How Jewish must it be? Whose definition of Jewish should prevail? How are the notions of religion and state to be reconciled? And since Israel is a Jewish state that includes a non-Jewish minority numbering close to 20 percent of its citizens, is there not a permanent tension, as evidenced, for example, regarding army service (Israeli Arab citizens do not serve) or, for that matter, the very words of *Hatikva*, the national anthem, which speak of Jewish yearning?

These questions have bedeviled Israel from the very beginning, though the compelling security situation, as well as a more or less sustainable domestic status quo, often relegated them to the back burner.

With the ultra-Orthodox population growing quickly and the emergence of a surprisingly popular religious-based political party, Shas, attracting mostly Sephardi voters, these issues begin once again to take on greater urgency. And if Israel should achieve accommodation with the Palestinians and Syria—itself a big if, of course—domestic attention almost certainly will turn more toward the essential character of the state and away from the immediate existential threats (though, as I have noted, regional threats, including Iraq, Iran, and better armed terrorist groups, are still likely to loom large).

Other domestic issues will also perforce claim Israel's attention, and rightly so. Just as many observers came to believe that the ethnic divide—i.e., the Ashkenazi/Sephardi split—was rapidly receding, parties like Shas and politicians like the Moroccan-born David Levy remind us of the continuing power of the resentment experienced by Sephardim in Israel.

The economic divide as well cannot be ignored. A not insignificant segment of Israel is prospering. This well-to-do crowd spends winter vacations in St. Moritz and Davos, is plugged into the new technologies, and is virtually indistinguishable from its counterparts in New York, London, or Tokyo. But hundreds of thousands of residents of development towns and neglected urban neighborhoods have been left behind, creating a wide income gap, not to speak of a disparity in both opportunities and services.

Much more can be said about other major challenges facing Israel in the next fifty years, including the need to:

- inculcate a greater sense of civility in civil society and the concomitant need to foster an enhanced understanding of the concept of compromise as an essential element of democratic society;
- encourage a greater sense of respect and tolerance for the viewpoints of others within Israeli society;
- serve at all times as a catalytic agent for strengthening the unity of the Jewish people in Israel and beyond, not its fragmentation;
- overcome a lingering gender gap that is much in evidence in both public and private leadership ranks, notwithstanding the familiar image of Golda Meir as prime minister and Israeli women as soldiers in the Israel Defense Forces;
- pay far more attention to Israel's fragile physical environment. This last point will, I believe, increasingly be discussed, as Israel witnesses a growing population crammed into limited space and the attendant strains placed on the land and its scarce resources.

Finally, as an American Jew, there is another gap I worry about, that emerging between Israel and the Diaspora. In some respects, perhaps, this is unavoidable. With the passage of time, we grow more distant from one another. If our grandparents were siblings, then we are now, at best, second cousins.

Here in the United States we have developed our own dynamic forms of Jewish culture wherein Israel figures only marginally. How many Israeli authors, playwrights, poets, artists, filmmakers, philosophers or, for that matter, theologians, are known here, much less have become integral parts of our American Jewish culture?

Notwithstanding this growing cultural divide—the countervailing ties that increasingly "bind," such as the internationalization of American pop and consumer culture, which many Israelis have embraced, from the NBA to McDonald's, are hardly likely to cement the Jewish people—American Jews have consistently sought to mobilize support for Israel in the United States, some adopting the secular religion of "Israelism," expressing their Jewish identity principally through political advocacy.

Inexplicably, there have been a few prominent Israelis dismissive of this support's value. They could not be more wrong.

American Jewish support has been crucial in building the foundation of the U.S.-Israel relationship. Without it, I fear—from long years in these very trenches—U.S. foreign policy would far more likely resemble Europe's essentially evenhanded attitude toward Israel.

But maintaining this political support among American Jews depends on an undiminished sense of kinship, of identification with Israel. The force of inertia alone surely will not sustain it.

American Jews increasingly will be tempted to turn their full attention to the daunting challenge of Jewish life in this country, from strengthening Jewish education to providing adequate social services for an aging population. Other groups in the United States, with very different goals for American foreign policy in the Middle East, will seek to step into the breach, as they have already, though hitherto with minimal effect because of the unstinting efforts of the pro-Israel community.

Briefly put, without constant attention to this important dimension between Israel and American Jews, the support could over time begin to fizzle, with potentially disastrous long-term consequences for the U.S.-Israel relationship.

Yet how many Israelis have any real understanding of the makeup and significance of American Jewry? Of the vitality of Jewish life in America? Of the key role Israel plays in our identity and consciousness? Of the sophisticated, complex, and multiple forms of Jewish expression in this country? Far too few, I fear.

Does it matter? To those of us who believe that close ties between Israel and the Diaspora, and especially the American Jewish community, are essential underpinnings of Jewish peoplehood and security, it matters tremendously.

In sum, the agenda is still a long one, but even as we consider it, how could we lose sight, even for a single moment, of the extraordinary accomplishments of these past fifty years?

With this in mind, I suggest that we—Israel and its friends around the world—pause from the twists and turns of the daily information overload and consider the sweep of the last half century. In doing so, we might more readily appreciate the light-years we have traveled since the darkness of the Shoah, and marvel at the miracle of a decimated people returning to a tiny sliver of land—the land of our ancestors, the land of Zion and Jerusalem—and successfully building a modern, vibrant state, against all the odds, on that ancient foundation.

It is indeed cause for celebration, and celebrate we should.

Presentation of AJC's
Distinguished Public Service Award
to Ambassador Rolf Ekeus
Washington, D.C.
May 14, 1998

On August 1, 1990, a small delegation of American Jewish Committee leaders traveled to this city to press once again for a tougher stance toward Iraq. Once again, we were told that we fundamentally misread Iraq, which could, in the thinking of these officials, one day become an anchor of a Western-oriented, moderate Arab alliance in the region.

The next day, of course, Iraq invaded Kuwait, launching a set of events that everyone in this grand ballroom remembers all too well, including subsequent Scud missile attacks against Israel and Saudi Arabia.

Enormous credit must be given to the members of the coalition forces who ousted Iraq from Kuwait with extraordinary courage, determination, and unity of purpose.

But even with this signal victory, the threat posed by Iraq did not end, far from it. Thus, a new effort was launched by the United Nations.

The Swedish playwright, novelist, and poet, August Strindberg, once defined drama as "Seeking out the points where great battles take place."

Perhaps it was with this sense of drama in mind that the UN, not for the first time, looked to Strindberg's native country for leadership, specifically to a trained lawyer and diplomat, a member of his country's foreign service since 1962, and an acknowledged specialist on disarmament—Rolf Ekeus.

Ambassador Ekeus accepted, apparently thinking that it would be a six-month assignment. It turned into six years.

From 1991 to 1997, Ambassador Ekeus, as executive chairman of the United Nations Special Commission, or UNSCOM, led his team of scientists, technicians, and diplomats in seeking, locating, and destroying weapons of mass destruction in Iraq, and trying to prevent Iraq from rearming.

In doing so, he not only contended with Iraq's nefarious aims but also with the effects of an earlier willingness, even eagerness, of too many industrialized countries to help in those efforts, knowingly or simply by turning a blind eye.

Ambassador Ekeus fought an unimaginably complex daily battle against Iraqi resistance that might have sapped the energy and will of many, but most definitely not of our honoree this evening.

The Iraqis came to understand that their nemesis, Ambassador Ekeus, was about as tough as they come—a man of deep religious faith, unshakable conviction, and principle; a man of consummate diplomatic skill who helped sustain an international consensus; a man of extraordinary knowledge concerning weapons of mass destruction—how one builds them, how one hides them; a man of indefatigable work habits.

I can now reveal to the ambassador that some of his staff—all of whom, I must say, could not have been more admiring of him—told me they hesitated to sit near him on the eighteen-hour flights to Baghdad because they knew they'd get no sleep, instead working throughout and then in Baghdad hitting the ground running.

The world owes this self-effacing man its profound gratitude for his six-year-long effort to defang Saddam Hussein's Iraq.

Ambassador Ekeus, you and your team determined the scope of Iraq's program to build weapons of mass destruction, revealing that it was far beyond anything we might have feared.

Ambassador Ekeus, you and your team destroyed more weapons and facilities related to the biological, chemical, nuclear, and missile fields than the Gulf war did.

Ambassador Ekeus, you and your team set a new standard in the field of disarmament by creating a monitoring system to assure that Iraq would not be able to acquire weapons of mass destruction, *as long as* the international community sustained its will to keep this monitoring system in place.

Today, I might add, Ambassador Ekeus is Sweden's envoy to Washington. In September 1997, he presented his credentials. In accepting his letters on September 8, President Clinton noted: "We are very grateful for your efforts over the past six years in dealing with Iraqi President Saddam Hussein. . . . With that experience behind you, you should be prepared to meet any challenge Washington has to offer." Ambassador, I trust that President Clinton was right.

Ambassador Ekeus, for all that you accomplished at UNSCOM, for your pursuit of a safer Middle East and a more secure world, it is my honor, on behalf of the American Jewish Committee, to present you with our Distinguished Public Service Award.

Presentation to Israeli Foreign Ministry, Embassy, and Consular Staff
Washington, D.C.
September 7, 1998

I was delighted when Ambassador Zalman Shoval called and asked if I'd offer the American Jewish perspective at your conference. In fact, I was so delighted that I accepted without even asking the date. Little did I know that Israel, of all countries, would give new meaning to Labor Day—an American holiday dating back to 1882 and, may I point out, intended for parades and picnics, neither of which, I understand, has been placed on today's agenda by my otherwise esteemed friend, Avi Granot.

As I look around this room, and as I think back to the countless times I've been in this embassy building and the consulates represented here today and the venerable Foreign Ministry itself, I feel a special kinship with many of you. We've collaborated on so much, we've agonized over so many challenging issues, and we've even celebrated some happy moments together. That really explains why I jumped at the chance offered by Ambassador Shoval.

Let me get right to my main concern, which is maintaining the strongest possible link between Israel and the American Jewish community, and discuss it from an American perspective.

I believe this link is vital to both sides of the ocean. I also believe it cannot be taken for granted for reasons I will discuss. To jump ahead, though, any diminution in the link would be catastrophic for both of us and, more broadly, for the Jewish people.

Israel is, I believe, absolutely indispensable to the Jewish identity of American Jews. Israel makes American Jews stand taller. Its rebirth and its manifold achievements are a source of immense pride.

Jewish identity, whether in the Diaspora or Israel, stands on three interconnected legs—the land, the people, and the book. Removing the land from the equation because it might no longer seem relevant to American Jewry—or even diminishing its centrality—would be nothing less than disastrous and only accelerate the deeply worrisome assimilation of American Jews.

Moreover, American Jews are indispensable to a pro-Israel stance by this or, for that matter, any U.S. government.

Israel can neither go it alone nor assume, as some Israeli politicians have contended, that Washington's favorable posture toward Jerusalem can be sustained over the long haul without American Jewish involvement. That is a foolish, indeed dangerous, notion.

In the final analysis, Israel's most stalwart and dependable ally—with all due respect to Costa Rica and Micronesia—is world Jewry, led by the largest and most influential Diaspora community, the United States, where over 40 percent of world Jewry resides.

Given the overall infinitesimal Jewish numbers—though, judging from our decibel level, I wonder whether we've perhaps skipped a zero or two in computing our worldwide population figures—we pay an incalculably high price for alienation or division in our ranks.

Yet that is precisely the long-term prospect we face—alienation from one another, not immediately but over time, and not necessarily affecting everyone but a sufficient critical mass to weaken the strength of the whole; and division, division along various fault lines—within Israel, between Israel and American Jewry, and within American Jewry.

In thinking about the internal dangers we face, I'm reminded of the legendary Yogi Berra, the oft-quoted former baseball star. Berra unintentionally made a second illustrious career out of his misstatements. He once said of an automobile trip: "We're lost, but we're making good time."

Well, we're not yet lost, but we're in danger of beginning to lose our way. Since we've been making such good time—that is, since many of the Israel-Diaspora vital signs seem at first glance to be reasonably healthy—we have become just a bit too smug about the relationship. We have begun taking each other for granted and assuming, I fear, that what is the case today will perforce be the case tomorrow.

Or put another way, there's the story of the construction of the Chunnel. Under British law, the Chunnel authorities were obligated to consider the lowest bidder, which came from a previously unknown London firm called Shapiro and Goldberg. The authorities paid a visit to company headquarters, located, as it turned out, in a dilapidated building.

A wizened old man introduced himself as Shapiro.

"How can you possibly build the Chunnel so cheaply?" an official asked him.

"Simple," said Shapiro. "I stand in Dover and face Calais. My partner Goldberg goes to Calais and stands on the water's edge facing Dover. I wave my shovel at him and he waves back, then we each start digging toward the other. Within a short time, *voilà*, you have your Chunnel connecting England and France."

"But what if you don't meet in the middle?" asked a stunned official.

"No problem," responded Shapiro. "Then you get two tunnels for the price of one!"

Are we using shovels to build the connective tissue between our two communities? Are we in danger of failing to meet in the middle? Do we run the risk of facing a day without a tunnel at all, or, perhaps, with a tunnel, or even two, but insufficient two-way traffic?

These are the things we ought to be concerned about. Why? Again, I'm looking at it from an American Jewish perspective only.

(a) American Jews in increasing numbers, especially younger people, do not share the same historical memory or familial ties with Israel that their parents or grandparents do (or did).

(b) American Jews, unlike other Diaspora communities, have viewed Israel with immense pride, yes, but often as a distant land. That may help explain why just one-third of American Jews have ever even visited Israel. American Jews believe that their permanent future is right here, that America truly is an exception to the historical Diaspora experience—and Zionist belief—and therefore, with only few exceptions, do not tend to look to Israel as a potential home or haven.

Relevant to our discussion this evening, one of the principal reasons for this deeply held feeling about America is the inviolability of the constitutional principle of church-state separation, which most American Jews not only consider a sacred notion but also indispensable to understanding America's "exceptionalism."

(c) Thus, when Israel sends a message that is understood by many American Jews to question their authenticity, or at least equality, as Jews, we're obviously headed for major problems.

First, because the message itself is profoundly offensive. How ill befitting the office of chief rabbi to hear Reform Jews referred to as "terrorists" who should be "vomited" out of the Jewish state! How ill-befitting the state to see issues of religious legitimacy, authority, and conversion become again and again political footballs within and between the executive and parliamentary branches of government!

Second, because 90 percent of American Jewry is directly affected. Less than 10 percent of American Jewry defines itself as Orthodox, though, given high birthrates and much lower rates of intermarriage, that number will surely grow. Thirty-five percent consider themselves Reform, roughly an equal number Conservative, and the rest "just Jewish."

And third, because, a significant number of American Jews might conclude, however reluctantly, that Israel is not central to their identity, yet still believe they can sustain themselves in this large and unique Diaspora experience called America.

Now some of you might interject to say that this is not Israel's message at all, or that the message is far more complicated than this simplistic notion, or that it only reflects a minority Israeli view and should not be ascribed to the entire country, or that it may in fact be the message but the only realistic way to change it is by mass aliyah of non-Orthodox Jews prepared to wage the spiritual and political battles in Israel itself.

The problem is that, whatever the complexities, whatever the nuances, the message that many American Jews have been receiving is reduced to one simple proposition: Reform or Conservative identity is seen, at best, as a second-class status in Israel, the *Jewish* state. The response?

It might go something like this: "No one, not the Knesset, not the Chief Rabbinate, not Shas, not even the prime minister, can call into doubt my authenticity as a Reform or Conservative or Reconstructionist Jew. That's beyond the pale and, if it persists, then Israel becomes largely irrelevant to me, my sense of self, my politics, and my philanthropy.

"This only underscores the dangerous entanglement in Israel between a narrow interpretation of religion and state—corrupting both religion and state in the process. And the worst culprits are the Israeli politicians of the major parties who, though they have the power to alter the system while still retaining the special Jewish character of the state, have played along in an ultimately shortsighted and cynical game of political expediency."

The British writer George Bernard Shaw once said: "England and America are two countries divided by a common language." Will it one day be said that American Jewry and Israel are two communities divided by a common heritage?

Of relevance to our discussion, in the American Jewish Committee's 1998 Annual Survey of American Jewish Opinion, the following question was asked:

"Do you agree or disagree with the following statement? 'Conversions performed in Israel by Reform and Conservative rabbis should be recognized as much as Orthodox conversions.'"

The response: agree, 89 percent; disagree, 9 percent

So, we have here a situation where, to begin with, the inevitable passage of time takes its toll on the Israel consciousness of new generations of American Jews, where sheer distance and a certain sense of American Jewish self-sufficiency threaten to weaken ties to Israel, and where, in addition, a sense of religious disfranchisement has been at work.

Moreover, the rough and tumble aspects of Israeli life are often disillusioning to many American Jews, who have sought to cling to an idealized, perhaps mythical, and certainly unrealistic view of Israel, which inevitably clashes with the daily realities of the exercise of power and the foibles of human nature in Israel, as elsewhere.

Coming back to our 1998 AJC survey, the following question was asked:

"Please rate the importance of each of the following to your Jewish identity, indicating whether it is extremely important, very important, somewhat important, or not important."

Remembrance of the Holocaust: 76 percent (replied extremely or very important)

Celebration of Jewish holidays: 67 percent

Jewish study: 39 percent

Participation in synagogue services: 33 percent

Jewish organizational activity: 15 percent

Travel to Israel: 22 percent

In other words, travel to Israel ranked fifth of the six possibilities offered and far behind the front-runners—Holocaust remembrance, which year after year tops the list, and holiday obervance.

We also asked a related question:

"Which one of the following qualities do you consider most important to your Jewish identity?" Respondents could select only one of the following:

Being part of the Jewish people: 46 percent

Religious observance: 18 percent

A commitment to social justice: 15 percent

Support for Israel: 5 percent

Something else (unspecified): 14 percent

At the same time, when asked the question: *"Do you agree or disagree with the following statement? 'Caring about Israel is a very important part of my being a Jew,'"* the response was 74 percent in agreement and 23 percent in disagreement. The highest level of support came from Orthodox Jews, who perhaps not surprisingly show the most consistent level of identification with Israel generally, and the lowest from Reform.

Five years ago, in 1993, we asked the same question. At the time, 79 percent agreed and 19 percent disagreed, so there has been slippage of about five points. We've seen the same modest slippage over time in the responses to other questions in our annual surveys regarding Israel-related feelings.

Let me be absolutely clear. I'm not here to suggest that the sky is falling, because it is not. I'm not here to suggest that all the news on the Israel-American Jewry front is bad, because it, too, is not.

All of us in our daily professional and personal lives see countless examples of American Jewry's resilience and the unshakable commitment of the community's core to its relationship with Israel.

And all of us are aware of the ambitious plans now under consideration to inject new energy into the link, especially among young people—from Project Birthright to exploitation of the revolution in information technology and communications, to Israel's growing and welcome awareness of its responsibility to strengthen Jewish communities in the Diaspora.

Strikingly, the profound dangers of assimilation here have created a new awakening. To our collective dismay, the 1990 National Jewish Population Study revealed that 1.1 million Jews said they were born Jews but have no religious identity; 210,000 people said they were born and raised Jewish but converted out; 415,000 adults said their parents were Jewish but they practice another religion; and 700,000 children in households with at least one Jewish parent are being raised in another religion. In short, we are facing an unprecedented crisis.

These shocking statistics—and the inescapable conclusion that over time American Jews run the risk of being added to the list of "endangered species"—have prompted more and more Jewishly committed families to intensify their Jewish way of life, *however defined*. This includes a much deeper understanding of the Israel connection as an essential component of that three-legged identity—land, book, and people. In this effort, they are finding growing, if belated, support from Jewish institutions.

I see this phenomenon at work all around me and it provides us with new opportunities: more family experiences in Israel, more teen trips to Israel, more high-school and college study programs in Israel, as parents seek more actively to instill Jewish content into the lives of their families and thereby combat apathy or alienation.

If this bifurcated picture is accurate, it means a slow but steady decline in the numbers of those closely connected to Israel, with all the manifold political, philanthropic, and human consequences, while, at the same time, the countervailing force of a further intensification of those links that bind the community's (shrinking?) core to Israel.

What can be done? Let me respectfully offer some modest recommendations for you as Israeli diplomats.

First, I have long believed that Israel's diplomatic representatives need to expand their reach in the Jewish community. It can become tempting, indeed comfortable, to focus on the major Jewish organizations alone. Obviously, there's good reason to do so since the bulk of support comes from this sector. But much more attention needs to be devoted to other sectors, for example, Jews in the professions, who could benefit from contact with their Israeli counterparts (and vice versa).

Second, many Israeli visitors travel to your cities. Use them with Jewish audiences and not always with the same "organizational suspects." There is no substitute for this kind of personal contact.

Third, more attention must be paid to the synagogues, especially the Reform and Conservative congregations. They need to hear from you, especially when they feel under assault from some political and religious figures in Israel. And if I may say so, you also need to hear from them, so find opportunities for smaller group discussions in addition to lectures.

An example: My synagogue asked me to spend a Sunday morning facilitating a discussion on Jewish priorities. When I asked each of the twenty participants to identify the two or three major issues likely to face Jews in the coming years, only one mentioned Israel. When I pointed this out, they seemed embarrassed and offered apologies. They do in fact care about Israel, they added, but it's simply not near the top of their daily priority lists. Other than through the filter of the media, many simply don't have regular contact with Israel or Israelis. You can help change that.

Fourth, recognize that there are few American Jewish families untouched by intermarriage, even in leadership circles. This makes conversion that much more salient a matter for us, since it allows the possibility, or at least the hope—if not today, then tomorrow—of a fully Jewish home.

American Jewish and Israeli leadership must show greater sensitivity to converts, of whom there are an estimated 185,000 in the United States (with no readily available breakdown by denomination), and those open to conversion.

The Ne'eman Commission took a major step forward in proposing a joint conversion institute encompassing faculty from each of the major denominations, thus conferring a measure of legitimacy on the non-Orthodox movements, and a uniform conversion procedure to enter the Jewish covenant. As you know, however, the Israeli Chief Rabbinate was predictably quick to throw cold water on the proposal.

Let me readily confess to a liberal view on the subject of conversion. I believe those who show a sincere willingness to identify themselves with the Jewish destiny, especially in the wake of the Shoah, ought to be welcomed enthusiastically.

Let me speak anecdotally for a moment. I have close friends. He is Jewish, she is a convert to Judaism, via the Conservative movement, from Greek Orthodoxy. They have three sons, all in Hebrew school. A few months ago, the oldest boy, then twelve, was publicly ridiculed at another child's bar mitzvah as a half Jew. The parents were outraged. I wrote the mother a note decrying the incident. She wrote back and I quote:

"When my husband and I discussed the religious upbringing of our future children twenty-two years ago, I reasoned that the world could survive with a few less Christians, but modern Jewry could not withstand such a loss. . . . My family in Greece were Righteous Gentiles and my mother had narrowly escaped two Nazi firing squads in Sparta. Thus, against this backdrop, I made my children's religious choice calmly and without hesitation.

"Although it subjected me to rejection from my family, friends, and the Greek community, I naïvely expected acceptance and respect from the Jewish community. Unfortunately, my experience has been just the opposite. I have withstood anti-Gentile remarks from my husband's family, friends . . . and various Jewish people we have met over the years. No one, Gentile or Jew, has recognized the difficulty of my decision to convert nor appreciates the complexity of the consequences it presented."

To me, this story—and others like it—movingly underscores the need for far greater sensitivity on everyone's part, including, not least, Israel's.

Fifth, use the media much more than you do in reaching the American Jewish community to explain today's Israel. The free space is there and, by virtue of your position, you have access to it. From my experience, it is not nearly utilized often enough. Where, for example, is the steady flow of op-eds and letters to the editor?

And sixth, we need a more vocal lobbying group within Israeli officialdom and society at large for the importance of Israel-Diaspora relations, just as we, American Jewish leadership, have a reciprocal obligation to explain Israel's indispensability to American Jewry and the role we must continue to play in its support.

If not you who have served in the Diaspora, who have lived in the United States, then who? There can be no more knowledgeable group in Israel on this subject. Help those influentials in Israel who should but, regrettably, do not always recognize the importance of these ties, who by acts of rhetorical commission or omission reveal their ignorance or indifference.

Help Israelis to appreciate that the totality of American Jewry goes well beyond the busloads of camera-toting tourists posing for pictures with Israeli soldiers, or deep-pocketed donors who don't for a moment let anyone forget how much they've done for Israel. Help Israelis see another side—a well-organized and politically sophisticated American Jewish community involved at every level and in every major sector of American society.

Help Israelis understand that the times ahead require a strong American Jewish community, which in turn, as I've already said, will be vital to maintaining America's special relationship with Israel, a task likely to grow only more difficult in the years ahead.

In addition to battling creeping alienation and apathy that could eventually erode our numbers, unity, and ultimately, I fear, clout, we will be facing an increasingly assertive Arab and Muslim community here whose numbers are growing, whose aims are nothing less than to reorient American objectives and priorities in the Middle East, and whose tactics, surprise of surprises, are largely copied from us.

To close, let me once again turn to the irrepressible Yogi Berra, the American folk hero I quoted earlier. On another occasion, he said: "You've got to be careful if you don't know where you're going because you might not get there."

Let's hope that this discussion, and others like it, will help us all better understand not only where we need to go but also the best ways of getting there.

Enough Is Enough[*]
Ha'aretz
January 21, 1999

I can no longer remain silent. For years, in the interests of Jewish unity, I would not join in the all-too-frequent public choruses of criticism directed at Israeli policies. But American Jews and Israel are moving away from one another, and the consequences over time could be disastrous for both sides. The current election season in Israel may well accelerate the process. It's time, therefore, to speak out, as one who has devoted many years to strengthening the partnership among the United States, American Jews, and Israel.

The link between Israel and American Jewry is vital to both sides. This link, however, cannot simply be taken for granted. If it begins to fray, the consequences could be catastrophic. With Jewish religious issues once again before Israeli lawmakers and likely to be the curren-

---

*The article appeared in both the Hebrew and English daily editions. It was subsequently reprinted in the *Los Angeles Times* and *Chicago Sun-Times*, and excerpted in the *International Herald Tribune*.

cy of aggressive deal-making for politicians seeking election in May, the risks are real.

Israel is absolutely indispensable to the Jewish identity of American Jews. Israel makes American Jews stand taller. Israel's miraculous rebirth, sheer survival, and remarkable development should be sources of immense pride to Jews everywhere.

Moreover, in a very practical sense, American Jewry is indispensable to America's pro-Israel stance. Put most starkly, if the American Jewish component is gradually removed from the equation, it will not be too long before we witness a more "evenhanded" American approach. There are other forces in the United States, whose foremost goal is the neutralization of American Jewish influence in Washington.

Maintaining American Jewry's sophisticated political involvement— an involvement insufficiently understood by the vast majority of Israelis—depends heavily on a strong sense of identification with Israel.

All the survey data indicate that American Jewish ties with Israel are closely linked with age. The younger generations, while wishing Israel well, increasingly feel less kinship with Israel than their parents. Thus, even under the best of circumstances, those of us profoundly committed to American Jewish–Israeli bridge-building have our work cut out for us.

But other troubling factors are also at work, foremost among them a growing religious disfranchisement, felt most strongly among younger American Jews—overwhelmingly non-Orthodox—who are not as prepared as their elders to "excuse" Israeli behavior in this arena.

It would be absurd to seek to export the United States' strict notion of church-state separation, which has worked so well in our country, to Israel. Israel is, after all and thankfully, a Jewish state, however elusive the definition may still be. Yet the entanglement of religion and state in the Israeli political arena—and never more so than in an election year—is profoundly dismaying for most American Jews. Images of rabbis wheeling and dealing in the insatiable pursuit of secular political power to buttress their religious agenda cannot be reconciled with our traditional views on Judaism. Such an unbridled meshing of religion and government is bad for the state; it's still worse for religion. Its effects are perforce corrosive and corrupting.

However desirable, the Israeli religious parties will not have a sudden "epiphany" and disband in favor of study and teaching. Consequently, the Israeli majority—and it is still a majority—needs to finally find the courage to say "enough already" to religious coercion. This still relatively silent majority must overcome its own petty divisions to define an alternative vision for Israel that maintains democratic values and ensures an enlightened Jewish character of the state.

The religious minority's imposition of its will is doing real damage. For American Jews, it may mean less willingness to engage politically on Israel's behalf. For Israelis, it is reflected in the growing Jerusalem-Tel Aviv cultural divide and the sense that the country they worked so hard to build is slipping away from them.

When is enough enough? When will people of goodwill, Orthodox and non-Orthodox, who understand the dangers to religion and state of the current situation, plan a new vision and a strategy to achieve it?

In the final analysis, we are one people and a small one at that. We can ill afford further splintering, yet that's precisely what is at stake with Knesset backroom maneuvering now going on, sending the message to 90 percent of American Jews—and many other Diaspora and Israeli Jews as well—that their deeply felt Judaism is inauthentic or, at best, second-class.

This is not simply a debate about what's good for American Jews, though, with 40 percent of the world's Jewish population and U.S. political support for Israel heavily dependent on the active involvement of American Jewry, the stakes are certainly high.

No, it's every bit as much about what's good for Israel. It is in fact a long overdue debate over Israel's soul. David Ben-Gurion took the path of least resistance in the founding days. But the real debate can't be postponed forever. The recent admirable courage of the Israeli courts has moved us forward toward legitimizing Jewish religious pluralism, but unless the Israeli political establishment stiffens its spine, we risk regression, with its resultant alienation and division.

I pray—yes, non-Orthodox Jews also pray—that finally we will see the same courage Israel has so frequently demonstrated in diplomacy, rescue, and defense applied to preventing religious dogmatists from hijacking the state.

Israel's Symbol Deserves Recognition by the Red Cross
International Herald Tribune
March 13–14, 1999

When one thinks of the Red Cross, what comes to mind? Most of us see dedicated individuals, renowned for their courage and compassion, helping people desperately in need of assistance. The international movement's bright red emblems are synonymous with hope and relief around the world.

Discrimination, exclusion, and rejection are not words usually associated with the International Red Cross. But in at least one instance, they should be.

For more than fifty years, Magen David Adom, Israel's national counterpart to the American Red Cross, has been denied full and equal membership in the International Federation of Red Cross and Red Crescent Societies, comprising over 150 national groups. Magen David Adom has been excluded solely because its emblem is a red Star of David, not the cross of Christianity or the crescent of Islam.

Since its founding, Magen David Adom has unquestionably upheld the most exemplary traditions and values of the federation both within Israel and abroad. Recently, it was part of the highly trained Israeli rescue and medical teams sent into the wreckage of the U.S. embassy in Nairobi. Arriving just hours after the terrorist bombings, the Israeli rescue workers, bearing the red Star of David, were credited for their professionalism and life-saving efforts.

So why is Israel the only country in the world whose humanitarian emblem has ever been formally rejected?

The founders of the International Red Cross actually never intended for any religious symbol to become its emblem. In 1864, they chose as its universal symbol the inverted flag of Switzerland, paying homage to the Swiss origin of this vitally important initiative.

In 1929, however, Turkey said that in Muslim countries the red cross was viewed as a Christian symbol. As a result, the red crescent, a symbol derived from Islam, was recognized as a second emblem.

The image of a juxtaposed red cross and red crescent decidedly became a religion-based symbol.

Israel's national relief society understandably refused to operate under the banner of the cross or the crescent, choosing instead the ancient symbol of the Jewish people. But the International Federation of Red Cross and Red Crescent Societies refused to recognize the red Star of David.

Despite the fact that Magen David Adom meets all the other criteria and conditions for full membership, the Israeli group to this day holds only limited "observer" status in the federation. This denial of membership translates into reduced cooperation and coordination for its efforts, less financial support, and the inability to vote on key issues pertaining to the federation's activities and policies.

Such blatant discrimination is unacceptable and must be changed. The next meeting of the federation, scheduled for October, offers the perfect opportunity to remedy, once and for all, this outrage.

Fortunately, Magen David Adom has an ally in the American Red Cross, which has accepted, de facto, the Star of David as a symbol of humanitarian relief and has encouraged other national societies to do the same.

Securing international recognition of Israel's symbol—or, alternatively, creating a truly universal symbol for the Red Cross that is devoid of religious significance and is acceptable to all parties—is by no means unattainable.

Ultimately, the International Federation of Red Cross and Red Crescent Societies needs to be reminded of its own founding principles of universality, morality, and civility. Politics has no place in the international humanitarian arena.

High Time for Western Europe to Put Israel in Its UN Group
International Herald Tribune
October 12, 1999

Total United Nations membership increased to 188 countries last month when Kiribati, Nauru, and Tonga were admitted before the opening of the fifty-fourth session of the General Assembly. Each of these three nations was subsequently invited to join the Asia and

Pacific Group, one of the world body's five regional groups, which in turn makes them eligible to serve on the Security Council and in other UN bodies.

The opportunity to vie for one of the ten coveted rotating seats on the key deliberative body of the United Nations comes with regional membership. But, contrary to the UN Charter, not all member states are treated equally.

More than five decades after the founding of the United Nations, there still is one nation—in fact, one of the world body's earliest members—that is not eligible to serve on the Security Council because it is has been deliberately prevented from joining a regional group. That country is Israel.

All of the other 187 members, including countries cited by the U.S. State Department as sponsors of terrorism, are eligible to serve on the Security Council. Iran and Iraq are eligible. So are Syria, Sudan, North Korea, Libya, and Cuba.

Geographically, Israel, a UN member since 1949, should be part of the Asian bloc, but Iraq, Iran, Saudi Arabia, and others have blocked its entry for decades. Secretary-General Kofi Annan has called for an end to this injustice and for "normalization of Israel's status within the United Nations."

As a temporary measure, Israel has sought acceptance in the West European and Others Group, which includes not only the democracies of Western Europe but also Australia, Canada, New Zealand, and the United States. The United States, Australia, Canada, and Norway have supported Israel's admission to the group, but the fifteen-member European Union refuses to act.

This posture has been maintained by nations that are not themselves hostile to Israel. European Union member states maintain extensive bilateral diplomatic, political, economic, and other ties with Israel.

Two basic concerns appear to underlie the Europeans' unwillingness to admit Israel to their United Nations group.

First, with each new member of any regional group the pool of potential candidates vying for the nonpermanent Security Council seats grows, thus increasing the competition and extending the waiting period, since fairness dictates that each member eventually have a turn on the Security Council.

True, adding Israel could extend the waiting period just a bit. Yet this argument has certainly not stopped other regional groups from adding countries to their rosters. In each case, equity has appropriately outweighed convenience.

Second, whenever discussion among the group's members about Israel's inclusion comes up, politics becomes the focal point. Is this the right time in the Middle East? What message is being sent?

In effect, membership in the group has been turned into an issue of reward and punishment. If Israel "behaves" itself in the peace process, then there is a chance for membership—although no decisive action was taken after the historic 1993 Oslo Accords that launched the current Israeli-Palestinian talks, or, for that matter, after the 1979 Israeli-Egyptian peace treaty.

Now, against the backdrop of a new climate in the peace process, and of growing international acknowledgment of the injustice at the United Nations, there may be a realistic chance for a shift in the EU stance.

Officials of the American Jewish Committee met during the last two weeks of September with the presidents, prime ministers, or foreign ministers of fifty-two countries, including many EU members, who were visiting New York to attend the opening debate of the General Assembly. We were encouraged by what we heard.

We sensed a more receptive attitude among some European government leaders toward fairer treatment of Israel in international organizations. At least one senior EU official admitted that the EU had adopted a pro-Palestinian outlook that undermined trust in Israel, and pledged to improve ties.

Meanwhile, Secretary of State Madeleine Albright has pressed the issue in her meetings with European foreign ministers, making clear the determination of the United States to end this injustice.

In the end, it is up to the fifteen-member European Union to act. No one else can do it.

Several member countries are ready to move, but a consensus is necessary. The time to end the anomaly of Israel's exclusion from the West European group is now.

3. EUROPE

The Freedom to Leave Romania
News and Views from the American Jewish Committee
March–April 1980

Winston Churchill once described Soviet policy as "a riddle wrapped in a mystery inside an enigma." He might well have been speaking of Romania too.

On the one hand, Romania is an authoritarian communist country with a centrally planned economy. Its president, Nicolae Ceauşescu, rules with an iron hand and does not tolerate dissent of the sort found in neighboring Hungary or Poland. Yet Romania has steered an independent course in foreign policy, going so far as to condemn the Soviet invasion of Czechoslovakia in 1968, maintain strong ties with China despite the freeze in Sino-Soviet relations, and continue its diplomatic, economic, and cultural ties with Israel—the only communist country to do so in the wake of the 1967 Six-Day War in the Middle East.

And while most Western Jewish attention has been focused on the Soviet Union and its emigration policy, for the Jews of Romania the vicissitudes of government policy have meant wide swings in official attitudes toward emigration to Israel.

Whereas in 1948 there were more than 400,000 Jews and 600 rabbis in Romania, the community today numbers just 35,000 and three rabbis. Most Romanian Jews who applied for emigration were permitted to leave for Israel in two large waves, in the late '40s and the early '60s. But in later years the emigration figures diminished markedly: 3,700 in 1974, 2,400 in 1975, 2,200 in 1976, 1,500 in 1977, and 1,100 in 1978. American Jewish organizations contended that significantly larger numbers were seeking to emigrate but that official obstacles prevented them from doing so. The Romanian government responded that the shrunken demographic base and the advanced age of the remaining Romanian Jews, rather than any official opposition to emigration, accounted for the decline to the present rate. Indeed, more than two-thirds of Romanian Jews are more than fifty years old and only 7 percent are under twenty-one.

Ever since his visit to Romania in 1976 as part of an AJC delegation, AJC vice president Alfred Moses has been working vigorously and effectively on behalf of freer emigration for Romanian Jews. Moses, a respected Washington lawyer, was not satisfied with the official Romanian explanation that the decline in emigration was due solely or even primarily to demography; and during the last four years he has met frequently with leading Romanian and American officials to press the case for unrestricted Jewish emigration.

In 1978 President Ceauşescu was invited to Washington for a state visit. At the behest of Moses, the issue of Jewish emigration was raised in the talks between the two presidents. Later, Moses headed a delegation of American Jewish leaders that met with the Romanian president in New York. During the meeting President Ceauşescu assured the delegation that Jews wishing to emigrate to Israel would be free to do so. At the same time, he candidly admitted that it was his government's general policy to discourage emigration.

As a result of the continuing decline in the rate of emigration, the Conference of Presidents of Major Jewish Organizations considered adding its voice to those émigré, dissident, and human rights groups planning to submit testimony to Congress in July 1979 in opposition to renewal of most-favored-nation trade status for Romania. Under the Jackson-Vanik Amendment to the Trade Reform Act of 1974, free emigration is a condition for the renewal of MFN status and the president must determine annually whether Romania, as a communist country, is acting in compliance.

Fearing nonrenewal, Romania sent Corneliu Bogdan, director of the Western Hemisphere Directorate of its Ministry of Foreign Affairs, to Washington to try to rescue the situation. Theodore Mann, president of the Conference of Presidents, asked Moses to head the negotiations on emigration on behalf of the Conference with Bogdan. After extended talks an agreement was reached: Rabbi Moses Rosen, the chief rabbi of Romania, would be authorized to announce publicly to the Romanian Jewish community that Jews wishing to emigrate to Israel were free to do so; and periodically, the Romanian government would furnish the Conference of Presidents with accountings of the number of passport applications pending and the date each application was filed.

The State Department was kept fully informed on the progress of the negotiating team, and at the conclusion of the talks Moses and Bogdan met with State Department officials to report on the accord. Based on the agreement, the Conference of Presidents endorsed the renewal of MFN trade status for Romania for yet another year.

As a follow-up, Mann asked Moses and Jack Spitzer, president of B'nai B'rith, to represent the Conference in a visit to Bucharest at the same time as the Congressional Subcommittee on Trade, headed by Congressman Vanik of Ohio, was in Romania, to report on steps taken by the Romanian authorities to facilitate emigration to Israel.

In January 1980, Moses and Spitzer traveled to Romania for a four-day visit and a private meeting with President Ceauşescu at his mountain villa. They also met with several ministers and other leading government officials, the American and Israeli ambassadors, Chief Rabbi Rosen, officers of the Romanian Jewish Federation, and numerous members of the Romanian Jewish community. They visited the new building of the Jewish Old Age Home, attended Sabbath services, and participated in a special commemorative service for victims of the 1941 fascist Iron Guard pogrom. Describing this special service Moses said: "If I had to choose the event in Romania that stood out above all others, it would clearly be this, a Jewish service, in an ancient synagogue deep in Eastern Europe, commemorating the victims of a pogrom, a service performed by Romanian children, many of whom will someday live in Israel."

There seems to have been nothing of the Potemkin village in what greeted Moses and Spitzer in Romania. The two American Jewish leaders were given a warm reception and learned that, since July 1979, there had in fact been substantial increases both in the number of Jews applying for passports and in the number of passports issued. And there is now available to the Conference of Presidents a complete and regularly updated list of pending applications, including the applicant's name, biographical data, the date the application was filed, and the status of the request for emigration.

Prior to July, persons in "sensitive" occupations, including radio and television broadcasting and the press, were routinely removed from their jobs when their intention to emigrate became known. Students and young men seeking to leave were often expelled from the university or suddenly inducted into the army. Now these forms of harassment have been stopped.

Moses reports that the Romanian government, with very few exceptions, is living up to the letter of the July agreement. "It is clear," says Moses, "that the [Romanian] government has determined not to give the Jewish community in the United States cause to oppose the renewal of MFN on emigration grounds."

It is equally clear that Al Moses might well have unwrapped some of the mystery that surrounds Romanian policy-making and, in doing so, given hope to the many Romanian Jews seeking to establish new lives in Israel.

Jacques Chirac, France and the Middle East[*]
Heritage
April 18, 1986

Jacques Chirac, the newly named French prime minister, returns to the key position he first held from 1974 to 1976 under President Giscard d'Estaing. Leader of the Rally for the Republic (RPR), the neo-Gaullist party he has led for a decade, and two-term mayor of Paris, Chirac's accession to power portends a possible shift in France's pro-Israel posture under President Mitterrand. Although Mitterrand's term continues until 1988, the French political structure provides for a distribution of power between the top two posts, thus permitting Chirac to have a major impact on the direction of French domestic and foreign policy.

As mayor of France's largest city, Chirac has enjoyed good relations with its 300,000-member Jewish community. Jewish leaders praise his openness, accessibility, and energy. In December, Chirac addressed a

*This article appeared in numerous Anglo-Jewish newspapers.

mostly Jewish gathering at the naming of René Cassin Square, even quoting from the Talmud in honoring the late French Jewish Nobel Peace Prize winner and human rights activist. Early this year, after lengthy and complex discussions between the Paris City Hall, Ministry of Culture, and Jewish community, agreement was reached to create a museum of Jewish art. Chirac's support for this project was crucial to its successful outcome. Indeed, the municipality has offered a building gratis.

In August 1982, a kosher restaurant in Paris was attacked, leaving six dead and twenty-two wounded. Mayor Chirac returned from vacation to attend a memorial ceremony and condemned the "horrible" and "racist character" of the tragedy. At the time of the bomb blast at the Rue Copernic synagogue, which left four persons dead, Chirac immediately dispatched an aide to the scene and himself came to the site the next day. Yet when a mass demonstration to protest this anti-Semitic attack was organized, the RPR hesitated to participate because of the heavy involvement of the Socialist and Communist parties in the manifestation. Finally, however, the RPR decided to join to "express its solidarity with the national élan against racism," according to Chirac.

Chirac was interviewed at length in 1982 in the French Jewish monthly *L'Arche*. Of the French Jewish community and its ties with Israel, he said, "History shows that Jews have resided in what is today France for more than 2,000 years, and that, despite the persecutions and expulsions, they always lived in at least one part of the country, from Marseilles to Alsace. . . . I do not forget that during the Middle Ages the French rabbis were celebrated and one of the first to use the French language was the famous Rashi. . . . It is normal that in the hearts of the Jews there is a place for Israel, the object of twenty centuries of hope and prayers, the biblical Promised Land, and the place where Holocaust survivors live."

French Jews, nevertheless, are concerned about the possible impact of Chirac and his RPR party on French foreign policy in the Middle East. France is a significant military and economic power with substantial global interests, not least in the Middle East and North Africa. One of five permanent members of the UN Security Council and a founding member of the twelve-nation European Economic

Community, France is further centrally placed to address Middle East issues.

The election of Mitterrand in 1981 ushered in the most unabashedly pro-Israel French leader in years and strengthened Franco-Israeli bilateral ties, a move that Chirac has criticized as excessive, according to a 1982 study on France by the London-based Institute of Jewish Affairs. Does the Socialist reversal in the recent election and the ascendancy of the RPR, under Chirac's leadership, therefore augur a change in this generally favorable French policy to Israel? Chirac's previous foreign policy record, notwithstanding his good ties with French Jews, suggests this possibility.

As prime minister, Chirac negotiated the French nuclear cooperation agreement with Iraq. He claimed that the construction of a reactor near the Iraqi capital posed no risk to Israel and was adequately safeguarded by French restrictions on its operation. Israel, of course, did not share Chirac's sanguine view. It found it necessary to conduct a successful preemptive strike against the facility in June 1981.

According to a *New York Times* account, Chirac flew to Libya in 1976 for an official two-day visit, the first by the head of a Western government since Qaddafi came to power in 1969. At the time Chirac spoke of the "close and long-standing" ties between France and Libya, and added, "I think we shall be discussing political problems as well as French-Libyan cooperation, which should be extended and well balanced." At the end of the visit, Chirac and Libyan officials signed agreements for France to build a nuclear power plant in Libya (but not research facilities or the means to produce heavy water), and several technical and cultural accords. Three months later, France agreed to build ten naval ships for Libya armed with sea-to-sea missiles and anti-aircraft guns.

Also during Chirac's tenure as prime minister, France permitted the PLO, which had hitherto been part of the Arab League representation, to open its own information and liaison office in Paris. He claims, again in the *L'Arche* interview, that "Everyone knows—for reasons about which I will not now comment—that I learned about this decision from the radio." Other observers, however, argue that Chirac had certainly never opposed the move in government decision-making circles, though it is true that the final decision was, in any case, President Giscard d'Estaing's.

In the *L'Arche* interview, Chirac dwelled at considerable length on his Middle East views: "France has never equivocated about Israel's right to exist and live in peace. I recall the discussions I had as prime minister, especially in Tripoli and Baghdad, where I emphasized this point as a fundamental tenet of French policy. . . . If there are differences between France and Israel—and this is the case—it is due to the different ways in which we approach the search for peace in the region. These concern method but not the substance [of Israel's right to exist]."

On the Palestinian question, Chirac told *L'Arche*, "It is indisputable that there is a Palestinian problem and that any return to peace in the region requires, in one way or another, a Palestinian entity—a land for this people—and, therefore, negotiations to determine its modalities. . . . I well know that Israel asserts that the PLO is not representative. This was, at one time, France's position on the Algerian FLN [independence movement]. I am not certain such an approach is the best way to achieve peace."

In response to a question concerning the RPR's unenthusiastic reaction to the Camp David Accords, Chirac replied, "If I had reservations about the Accords, it was because I do not believe in the adage 'divide and conquer.' Cutting the Arab world in half, as a result of the Accords, resulted, it seems to me, in further alienating certain Arab states from the peace process." In addition, explained Chirac, France did not participate in the multinational Sinai peacekeeping force because "this initiative was an outgrowth of Camp David . . . about which we had our reservations. I wish to add that it is my belief that what France can best do for Israel is not to align itself systematically with every Israeli position. In such a case, France would lose its credibility as a mediator. . . . I am terribly upset by the Middle East situation and wish, above all, that there could be a conciliation of feelings which could lead to peace."

In 1984, in a meeting with an American Jewish Committee delegation, Mayor Chirac, while acknowledging his strong and long-standing ties with Iraq and its leaders, said, "If Israel is attacked, the Europeans should immediately be on Israel's side. We have first to support Israel, but also to support peace. Nobody contests Israel's right to exist, but the problem is that Israel wants territory and settlements. The political costs, however, are too great." He added that Iraq and Israel actually had common interests in their opposition to Syria, the real Middle East menace. One day, he speculated, Baghdad and Jerusalem might actually reach an understanding and draw Amman in as well.

Later in the year, Chirac made his first trip to Israel and, by all accounts, it was a successful mission. He met with a wide range of senior government officials and toured the country. After meeting with Prime Minister Peres, Chirac stated in a January 1985 interview in *L'Arche*, "I was very impressed by my conversation. He is a profound, forward-looking, honest man, and I was taken by this approach."

The mayor also visited Yad Vashem, the memorial to the Holocaust victims. He said in the same interview, "My emotion became a physical reaction, pressing on my soul and heart and constricting my throat. The exceptional quality of the monument and especially the intensity of the exhibitions, particularly the photographs, are such that one truly discovers a new dimension of the Holocaust tragedy." And as is the case with so many first-time visitors to Israel, Chirac was struck by the country's small size. "It is true that if one does not know Israel first-hand, it is difficult to appreciate the exigencies that geography places on the life of the people, especially because of the shortness of distances and what this means for the country's security," he explained.

Will Chirac's pro-Arab tilt of the '70s once again prevail as he assumes office? To what degree will the unprecedented leadership configuration of a Socialist president and neo-Gaullist prime minister result in changes in French external policy until the 1988 presidential elections? Has Chirac's position been softened by his warm ties with the Paris Jewish community and visits to Israel? Will the new foreign minister, Jean-Bernard Raimond, the current French envoy in Moscow and a career diplomat, reflect the traditional Arabist thinking prevalent in the Foreign Ministry, or counsel a more independent line? And how will the unprecedented success of the extreme right-wing National Front Party, gaining nearly 10 percent of the vote and thirty-three seats in the National Assembly, affect the political process?

While it would be premature to answer these questions, there is an apprehension in segments of the French Jewish community that the advent of Chirac and the RPR may bring an effort to strengthen further France's position in the Arab world, even at the expense of its ties with Israel, and that the heady days of Franco-Israeli relations of the last five years may perforce be numbered.

An American Jewish Perspective on Greek Foreign Policy: Submitted to the Office of Andreas Papandreou, Prime Minister of Greece December 12, 1986

A Jewish perspective on Greek foreign policy must begin by noting recent steps taken by the Greek government to improve bilateral relations with Israel and expand the dialogue with world Jewry. In the last year, the director general of the Israeli Foreign Ministry visited Athens; a three-year agreement on scientific and cultural cooperation was signed; a joint campaign on tourism was launched; and Dr. Karolos Papoulias, the Greek foreign minister, indicated his intention to visit Israel, which would represent the first such visit by a Greek foreign minister since Israel's founding in 1948.

In addition, the Greek government has sought to establish improved communication with world Jewish figures. Earlier this year, for example, Prime Minister Papandreou met in Athens with World Jewish Congress president Edgar Bronfman and former Israeli ambassador to the United States Ephraim Evron. This month, Foreign Minister Papoulias held a ninety-minute meeting in New York with leaders of the American Jewish Committee. The message of Greek officials is both clear and welcome: Greece seeks a continued improvement in its bilateral relations with the State of Israel, and neither the Greek government nor the Greek people harbors any enmity to the Jewish people, either toward the remaining 5,000 Jews in Greece or elsewhere in the world.

Still, notwithstanding these encouraging signs, a full review of the state of relations, first, between Greece and Israel, and, second, between Greece and world Jewry must take into account a number of troublesome issues. These include:

(1) With the establishment of full diplomatic relations between Spain and Israel at the beginning of 1986, Greece became the only Western democratic nation that does not maintain full ambassadorial ties with Israel. Compounding the difficulties, in 1981, as one of the first foreign policy acts of the new (Papandreou) government, de facto recognition was accorded to the Palestine Liberation Organization (PLO), a terrorist organization whose charter calls for the destruction of the Jewish state. In 1984, Greece became the first European Economic Community member nation to extend full diplomatic recognition to the PLO. Thus, the Greek government has placed Israel and the PLO on equal diplomatic footing.

(2) When Great Britain uncovered compelling evidence of Syrian government complicity in the attempt, last April, to blow up an El Al plane departing from London, the Greek government stood alone among Britain's eleven European Community partners in refusing to hold Syria accountable for the terrorist attempt. It declined to support a ban on new arms sales to Syria and other limited measures, though Greece would not have had to break ranks with the rest of the Community because in point of fact it sold no arms to Syria and planned no high-level visits. Most recently, the *New York Times* (December 10, 1986) reported that, at a meeting in London, "the interior ministers of the European Community, except Greece, agreed on which countries backed terrorism."

Moreover, in 1981, there was Yasir Arafat's visit to Athens, the very first by a major foreign figure after the October elections in Greece, at which time Prime Minister Papandreou was quoted as declaring: "You, brother Yasir Arafat, are the epitome of popular struggles for freedom and independence." The prime minister also reportedly commented to Faruk Qaddumi, the PLO's "foreign minister": "What the Nazis did to them [the Jews], the Israelis are doing to you," referring to Israel's Lebanon incursion in 1982.

There is a strong perception among Jews that, because of Greece's historical, political, and economic ties with the Arab world, it has lent itself not only to rhetorical excesses but also to a fundamental misreading—and perhaps, even, unwitting encouragement—of terrorism in the Middle East.

(3) United Nations voting patterns shed light on government attitudes, although many governments are quick to add that they may feel compelled to act in a particular manner in such public forums, whereas, in reality, their policies are more nuanced. In fact, though, UN votes do send a message to the world community. Thus, on the one hand, we note with pleasure that Greece has voted consistently in favor of Israel's UN credentials when they come under annual attack by a coalition of Arab and Soviet bloc member states. Yet, on the other hand, as recently as December 1985, Greece voted in favor of UN resolution A/40/L.44, which called on member states "to sever diplomatic, trade and cultural relations with Israel." In a 1985 tabulation of key UN votes concerning Israel among twenty-three Western nations, the average nonnegative vote was 73 percent (the U.S. figure was 96 percent), but Greece's was only 33 percent. This figure, however, was better than 1984 and augurs, we would hope, continued improvement.

(4) An area of great concern to world Jewry is the fate of 2 million Soviet Jews, who are, by and large, denied both the right to leave the USSR or to live as Jews in the country. Among the most important international venues for discussion of these fundamental human rights questions are the conferences and experts' meetings of the thirty-five-nation Helsinki process, created by the adoption of the Helsinki Final Act, in 1975, by all the countries of Europe, East and West (with the exception of Albania), and the United States and Canada.

Many Americans, including American Jews, while having few illusions about the ability of this Helsinki process to effect fundamental change in domestic behavior, nevertheless regard the structure as providing a unique opportunity to review the compliance records of member nations. According to U.S. delegates who have participated in all the relevant meetings since 1975, as well as to outside observers, the Greek delegations have seldom, if ever, raised their voices about human rights abuses behind the Iron Curtain.

We recognize and respect the Greek government's understandable preoccupation with the continuing plight in Cyprus, after twelve long years, of 200,000 refugees and 1,400 missing persons, as well as the situation of the Ecumenical Patriarchate in Istanbul. We also fully recognize the concern in Athens for the condition of those tens of thousands of Greeks who live in the USSR, some of whom seek to emigrate to Greece but encounter serious obstacles.

At the same time, we would hope that the Greek government, through such significant international vehicles as the ongoing Vienna Review Conference of the Helsinki Final Act, as well as appropriate bilateral channels, might lend its support to the consensus of Western nations that seeks to forestall a deliberate Soviet policy of spiritual genocide of 15 percent of world Jewry and an officially sponsored anti-Semitic campaign.

We are clearly mindful of the need and right of every nation to pursue its national interests and to attempt to balance its relations between often adversarial nations or blocs. We recognize, in this regard, that Greek foreign policy is a function, first and foremost, of its membership in the family of Western democratic nations, including participation in the European Community and NATO and the bilateral relationship with Washington. We also understand that relations with Turkey and the key question of Cyprus are other central determinants of its foreign policy. And we entirely appreciate that Greece's geographical location as a Mediterranean nation and its links with the Near East and North Africa are significant factors in the formulation of its foreign policy. Lastly, we note that Greece seeks to maintain cordial relations and open lines of communication with Eastern bloc nations.

In our view, there need not be incompatibility between the strengthening of bilateral relations with Israel and the preservation of existing ties with the Arab world. Other countries, including Italy and Spain, have similarly deep connections, yet are able to maintain full diplomatic relations with Israel and, particularly in the case of Italy, a strong network of economic, cultural, and other links as well.

The case of Spain is particularly instructive. When Madrid first considered the establishment of diplomatic relations with Israel, Arab League nations threatened numerous reprisals against the government of Prime Minister Gonzales. Unwilling to yield to such blatant pressure, he moved forward to establish ties, while assuring Spain's Arab friends that Madrid desired continued close links but would not succumb to what amounted to blackmail. In the end, relations were established, ambassadors were exchanged, and the threats of Arab nations fizzled.

In sum, we look forward to the continued improvement of Greek-Israeli relations. We believe this to be in the best interests of both nations.

We hope that Foreign Minister Papoulias will indeed visit Israel in 1987. Such a visit would, we might note, have important symbolic and substantive meaning for world Jewry.

We hope the Greek government will reconsider its position on the PLO, which remains committed to armed struggle and has never formally acknowledged Israel's right to exist within secure and recognized borders, as well as Greece's lone position in the European Community on the equally compelling issue of state-sponsored terrorism.

We trust that the Greek government will continue to review its posture on issues affecting the Middle East at the United Nations and other international forums.

And finally, we respectfully request that the Greek government use its good offices in behalf of the Jewish community in the USSR to permit them to exercise their rights under the Universal Declaration of Human Rights, the International Covenant of Civil and Political Rights, and the Helsinki Final Act.

The respective heritages of Greeks and Jews form the cornerstones of the Western democratic tradition. Indisputably, Greeks and Jews have much upon which to build ever greater mutual understanding and closer cooperation and friendship.

Poland and Israel, 1967–1987
Forward
June 5, 1987

Twenty years ago, following the Kremlin's lead, Poland severed diplomatic ties with Israel during the Six-Day War. Like the other Warsaw Pact nations, with the exception of iconoclastic Romania, Poland maintained no diplomatic links with the Jewish state until last year, when it became the first Soviet-bloc country to restore low-level relations. Today, fledgling political and economic ties are emerging, while cultural and tourist connections develop. Although progress is slow, the significance of these bilateral steps should not be minimized.

Poland supported the establishment of Israel and maintained diplomatic ties until Israel's 1967 victory over its Arab enemies. The few remaining nondiplomatic links—commercial and cultural—that survived the break ended the following year when the Gomulka regime, faced with pressing economic problems and domestic unrest, sought a convenient scapegoat—the country's remaining 20,000 Jews—and embarked on a vicious anti-Zionist, anti-Semitic campaign. Polish leaders charged "Zionist centers in the West" with an anti-Polish conspiracy and accused Israel of "using Nazi methods against the Arabs." Jews were purged from key positions in the political, economic, cultural, and academic spheres, and encouraged to emigrate. Many did. Some 12,000 left in 1968 and 1969, resettling primarily in Western Europe—especially Denmark and Sweden, North America and Israel.

With no political or commercial ties left, the principal links between the two countries were Holocaust-related activities: Yad Vashem, which continued its research on the Holocaust and the naming of Righteous Gentiles (as of December 1986, the Israel-based institution had honored 2,074 Polish citizens, the second largest national group after the Dutch); the International Janusz Korczak Society, named after the valiant Warsaw Jewish doctor who sought to protect Jewish children during the Holocaust and who has been honored both by Poland and Israel; and annual ceremonies marking the anniversary of the 1943 Warsaw ghetto uprising.

Another link has been the Polska Kasa Opieki (PKO) Bank in Tel Aviv. Founded in Poland in 1929, the PKO opened a branch in Tel Aviv in 1933—one of only three overseas branches, the others being in Paris and Buenos Aires—to attract business from the growing number of Polish immigrants in Palestine, later Israel. A Polish-owned bank, it remained open even after the diplomatic break in 1967, offering the full range of banking services and facilitating the transfer of money to Poles who hid Jews during World War II.

Other than an hour-long meeting between the Israeli and Polish foreign ministers in New York in 1981, no significant diplomatic contact occurred until the fall of 1985. Then, against the backdrop of the new

Kremlin leadership, Yitzhak Shamir, Israel's foreign minister, met in New York with the Polish foreign minister (and, separately, with the Bulgarian and Hungarian foreign ministers). To bolster the view that something potentially important was afoot, Poland, for the first time in 1985 and again in 1986, distanced itself from the USSR and was recorded as absent from the annual Arab/Soviet effort at the UN General Assembly to deny Israel its credentials.

Following the New York meeting, Israeli and Polish officials continued to meet, reaching an agreement to restore limited diplomatic ties and to renew cultural, tourism, and other links. By the fall of 1986, Mordechai Bar-Zur, who had served as Israel's ambassador to the Dominican Republic, was named to head Israel's interests section in the old Israeli embassy building vacated nineteen years earlier. The Polish team moved into the PKO Bank on Allenby Street in Tel Aviv. Technically, the top representatives were accorded "second secretary" diplomatic status.

At the same time, a surge in cultural exchanges was taking place. In 1985 and 1986, Israeli and Polish ballet, opera, and theater companies exchanged visits. With a resurgence of interest in Jewish topics, and the legacy of a once-flourishing prewar Jewish community that at its peak numbered well over 3 million, there has been growing interest in Poland in contacts with Israel and world Jewry. In Israel, the presence of a sizable population that traces its roots to Poland has stirred interest in both cultural and tourism opportunities. Still, for Polish-born Israelis, memories of their former homeland are understandably complex, dominated by the almost complete devastation of Polish Jewry during the Nazi period (and widespread prewar anti-Semitism).

Why the sudden change in Polish political attitudes in 1985 and 1986? Clearly, the accession to power of Mikhail Gorbachev in Moscow greatly influenced events. Cognizant of the Kremlin's mistake in 1967 in severing ties with Israel and thereby relinquishing primacy in the Middle East to the United States, the only superpower able to speak to all sides in the Arab-Israeli conflict, the new Soviet team moved quickly to test the waters for a more activist diplomacy in the area. What better way to send a signal than by use of a proxy, Poland, that clearly stood to benefit from the move?

After all, Poland suffered from a serious image problem in the West arising from the imposition of martial law in 1981, brutal suppression of the Solidarity movement, and widespread imprisonment of political and Catholic Church activists. It also suffered from severe economic difficulties, made worse by the imposition of U.S. economic sanctions, in 1981 and 1982, that denied Poland most-favored-nation trade status and access to official U.S. credits and credit guarantees. Renewing ties with Israel (and American Jews, whose friendship Poland has also sought) would help generate support for Poland's efforts to improve its international position, especially in Washington. (The sanctions, in fact, were lifted by President Reagan in February 1987 in response to a Polish political amnesty last September and other liberalizing steps.) And it was a low-cost move. With only a few thousand aging Jews left in the country, Poland, unlike the USSR, has little to fear from a nationalist revival inspired by the flying of the Israeli flag in the capital. And it calculated that the interest of Israeli and Diaspora Jewry in searching out roots, restoring dilapidated synagogues and neglected cemeteries, as well as preserving the memory of the Holocaust, could provide an influx of tourists and the possibility of joint projects.

Israel has made no secret of its desire since 1967 to restore ties with the Eastern-bloc countries. It saw Warsaw's move as a possible harbinger of similar steps by other Warsaw Pact countries, including, ultimately, the USSR. It also believed that Warsaw's move might encourage third world countries that broke ties in the early 1970s to follow the Polish example. Finally, in 1985, Israel believed that Poland might become the long-sought East European transit point where emigrating Soviet Jews could transfer directly to Israel, avoiding Vienna and the prospect of migration to countries other than Israel. Indeed, in the fall of 1985, there was a flurry of press reports, later proved untrue, that Polish leader General Jaruzelski, after meeting with French president Mitterrand in Paris and World Jewish Congress president Edgar Bronfman in Warsaw, had agreed, with Soviet backing, to permit the Polish capital to serve as a transit point for Soviet Jews. Recent reports, however, indicate that the Kremlin, as part of its current minuet with Israel, has decided to send Soviet Jews to Israel via Romania, a country that maintains full diplomatic ties with Israel and has existing air links.

The prospect is for continued advances between Israel and Poland in the area of human contacts, the establishment of limited economic ties, and maintenance of a low-key political relationship until such time as the Kremlin might decide to gamble for higher stakes in the Middle East. But considering where the relationship was just after June 1967, the progress is indisputable and welcome.

Will the Anti-Semitic Right Hold the Swing Votes in France?
Moment
April 1988

On April 24, France will hold its septennial presidential election. It is an election that holds special interest for Jews because of the possibility that a far-right candidate who enjoys only 10 percent of the electorate could end up controlling the swing votes that will determine the winner. Jean-Marie Le Pen, the candidate of the National Front, not only occupies a slot on the far right of France's political spectrum, he has also exhibited some frightening signs of racism and anti-Semitism.

The principal election battle will be among France's three mainstream political parties—President Mitterrand's left-of-center Socialist Party, the right-of-center Union of French Democracy (Union pour la Democracie Française, or UDF), and Prime Minister Jacques Chirac's neo-Gaullist Rally for the Republic (Rassemblement Pour la Republique, or RPR). If none of them receive a clear majority in the election, then a runoff between the two top vote-getters will be held two weeks later. If a runoff is required—or even if a runoff looks likely—Le Pen could seek a broker's role and may be crucial in determining the winner.

The real questions are whether any of the three mainstream parties will be willing to deal with Le Pen and, if so, what price they will be prepared to pay.

Though the January polls indicate that Le Pen will get only 10 percent of the vote, his influence should not be underestimated. His National Front Party is Europe's strongest far-right political movement. As its presidential candidate, Le Pen purveys a highly nationalistic and xenophobic message that seeks to exploit the country's economic malaise (which includes double-digit unemployment) and appeals to the basest instincts of voters who fear that alien hordes are taking control of the country's destiny and culture. Le Pen has attracted a constituency that includes *pieds nors* (French former residents of Algeria), as well as disgruntled ex-supporters of the Communist Party who are unhappy with the party's inability to respond effectively to pressing economic questions, and urban dwellers—often middle-class and well educated—who increasingly are concerned about the changing character of cities such as Marseilles and Toulon that have become, in their view, overrun with Arabs. Support for the National Front also comes from such neofascist, racist, and anti-Semitic publications as *Militant* and *Present*.

Le Pen himself is a devilishly dynamic and articulate leader, clever and politically astute. First elected to France's National Assembly in 1956 on the short-lived Poujade party list (a movement of the petite bourgeoisie to protest the impact of modernization and industrialization), he left the parliament for an army tour of duty in conflict-ridden Algeria. He returned a year later amid whispers of his complicity in torture by French troops. Le Pen then founded the National Front for a French Algeria and, until 1962, continued as a parliamentary deputy. Simultaneously, he became active in the presidential campaign of Jean-Louis Tixter-Vignanciourt, the extreme right's leader during the 1950s and 1960s and a lawyer close to the circles of former World War II French collaborators.

In 1972, Le Pen founded the National Front Party. He ran for president two years later and received less than 1 percent of the popular vote. He fared even worse in the 1981 presidential elections. However, in 1984 his party's political fortunes enjoyed a spectacular turnaround: In that year the National Front won more than 10 percent of the vote in municipal elections and 11 percent in elections for deputies to the European Parliament. His campaign touched a responsive chord in voters increasingly concerned about crime, unemployment, and immigration. In 1986, the National Front surpassed the once-powerful French Communist Party's performance, gaining 10 percent of the vote in the parliament elections and thirty-three of the 577 seats in the National Assembly.

Le Pen denies accusations of racism, fascism, and anti-Semitism. He portrays himself instead as a defender of freedom and of France's honor. "France for the French" is one of his favorite slogans. The principal target of Le Pen's attacks has been the growing immigrant community, which, according to the National Office of Immigration, currently numbers 4.3 million. Immigrants from the Maghreb—Algeria, Tunisia, and Morocco—have borne the brunt of Le Pen's attacks. He asserts they are "unassimilable," "alien," and "dangerous," and, in his view, should be returned to their native countries. He further argues that they cost the hard-pressed French economy more than $15 billion per year in social services, a figure government officials deny. But Le Pen has succeeded in taking the offensive, pushing the mainstream parties to compete with the National Front on such issues as immigrants, illegal aliens, and law and order.

Despite his party's avowed support for Israel (seen as a bulwark against the Arabs), Le Pen has made several deeply troubling statements about Jews. Here are two recent examples:

• In a September radio interview, Le Pen provoked a national storm and, according to subsequent surveys, even lost some support among his more moderate followers, by describing Hitler's gas chambers as "a point of detail in the history of the Second World War." When the reporter questioned this characterization, Le Pen added: "Do you want to tell me that it is revealed truth that everybody must believe? That it is a moral obligation? I say there are historians who debate these questions."

• Eighteen months earlier, at a National Front annual meeting, Le Pen was greeted by thunderous applause from the party faithful. He responded with these words, which, as explained below, carry a clear message: "I dedicate your welcome to Messrs. Jean François Kahn, Jean Daniel, Ivan Levai, Jean Pierre Elkabach [four Jewish journalists]. I dedicate this welcome to all the liars in the country, to television journalists who dare to film empty chairs. These people are the shame of their profession. Monsignor Lustiger [archbishop of Paris, a Jewish convert to Christianity] will forgive me this moment of anger, it happened even to Jesus . . ."

Had Le Pen simply wanted to identify well-known media figures opposed to him, he could easily have found many non-Jewish journalists. Yet he chose four Jewish journalists. And the mention of Lustiger's name was hardly sheer coincidence. Le Pen is too clever and knows too well what arouses his audiences to have made such statements accidentally. The International League against Racism and Anti-Semitism (Ligue Internationale Contre le Racisme Anti-Semitique, or LICRA) took Le Pen to court for these remarks, accusing him of racial incitement. In March 1986, he was found guilty and ordered to pay the symbolic one franc that LICRA had demanded.

French Jewish groups, joining with Arab and other like-minded community organizations, have formed an organization called SOS Racisme to combat the National Front's thinly disguised racism. Despite the Jewish community's understandable concern about Le Pen's high visibility, it is seeking to avoid overreacting, hoping that the National Front's popularity will prove short-lived. In the April 1985 issue of *L'Arche*, the French Jewish monthly, Roger Ascot summed up this view: "Such slogans as 'France for the French' can only offer division, violence, xenophobia, racism. It should be repeated, therefore, the danger is there. However, let us not exaggerate the real peril. Nine of ten Frenchmen are opposed to the denial of others' rights. It is important that these 90 percent remain united, that no other elected official yield to the worst possible temptation (by pursuing the racist vote), even if their short-term political interests might be served."

Jews and other concerned French citizens are waiting to see whether, faced with a runoff in the forthcoming presidential election, any mainstream political leaders, virtually all of whom have already condemned Le Pen, will retreat in their quest for votes. They are particularly concerned about some local and regional agreements that have been forged in recent years between the National Front and the conservative political parties (UDF and RPR) that form Prime Minister Chirac's coalition. A September 1987 poll, commissioned by a prominent French weekly, *Le Nouvel Observateur*, found that while fifteen big-city mayors belonging to the coalition parties foreclosed any dealing with the National Front, nine others hedged.

What might happen in the likely event of a presidential runoff? No one knows for sure. One hopes that France's front-running politicians will listen to Michel Noir, the minister of foreign trade, who took a strong stand against any cooperation with Le Pen. A politician's responsibility, Noir asserted, "is not only to win elections," but "to ensure that societies do not forget the values on which they are built."

Le Pen is far outside the mainstream of French politics. He seeks to undermine the very values of democracy and tolerance upon which French civilization is built. Consequently, there should be no deals, no compromise with Le Pen. To do or say anything else would prove a sad day for France.

Greece's Shame
Washington Jewish Week
December 29, 1988

The *Washington Jewish Week*'s only treatment of the shocking story of Greece's release of Abdel Osama al-Zomar, a Palestinian terrorist sought by Italy in the 1982 assault on the Rome synagogue, was surprisingly buried in the December 15 issue. In that attack, a two-year-old boy was killed and thirty-seven worshipers injured. The Greek government's explanation for its decision? Zomar's action was not criminal, but motivated by the desire for a Palestinian homeland. According to this peculiar logic, he could not be extradited to another country to stand trial. Instead, he was permitted to leave for Libya.

This is not the first instance of Athens adopting a troubling stance toward terrorism. In 1986, for example, Great Britain uncovered compelling evidence of Syrian complicity in the attempted bombing of an El Al plane departing from London with 340 people aboard. Alone among the twelve members of the European Community, Greece refused to hold Syria accountable for the terrorist attempt and resisted Britain's appeal for punitive measures against Damascus.

Moreover, it should be noted that Greece remains the lone holdout in Western Europe that does not maintain full de jure diplomatic ties with Israel. Indeed, in 1984 Greece was the first European Community member to extend full diplomatic recognition to the PLO, essentially putting the PLO and Israel on equal footing.

But what is most troubling at the moment is Athens's attitude in the Zomar case. How can Greece conclude that a tragic terrorist assault on an Italian synagogue, in this case by a suspected member of the nihilistic Abu Nidal group, be construed as a legitimate act on the part of Palestinians? Are Jews of any age, in any part of the world, fair game for terrorists? This decision suggests they may be, at least in the Greek government's view. Shame!

Oh, No!
Washington Jewish Week
January 25, 1990

What a difference a single letter (of the alphabet) can make! In fact, it even has the potential to create a diplomatic incident.

The January 18 issue contained a very welcome article on our recent luncheon honoring Italy's role in assisting Soviet Jewish refugees to transit there en route to countries of permanent resettlement. The piece quoted me as saying to Italy's ambassador, Rinaldo Petrignani, our guest of honor that day, *grazie tonto*. That literally means "thank you, stupid." Perish the thought. What I said was *grazie tanto*, which translates as "thank you so much."

After German Unification, Will Jewish Concerns Be Addressed?
Jewish Telegraphic Agency
October 5, 1990

There can be few more complex or sensitive issues for Jews to address than the question of German unification. It is an issue fraught with searing emotion for a people who lost 6 million lives as a consequence of the Nazi pursuit of the Final Solution—the attempted extermination of the Jewish people.

The question for those interested in German unification is not whether or not it is a good idea. That has been decided by the people of the two Germanys. Rather, the relevant question is what are the particular interests of those who have suffered at the hands of a once-united Germany, and who want to be certain that their voices are heard, their concerns addressed, their fears lessened.

To be sure, the events in the German Democratic Republic that precipitated the rush to unification caught the imagination of people everywhere. But at the same time, it is fair to wonder aloud where events are headed. Will the end of Germany's division also augur the end of historical memory about the Nazi era and the incalculable tragedy and destruction it wrought?

Will November 9, the anniversary date of *Kristallnacht*, now be wholly replaced in the German consciousness by November 9, the anniversary date of the Berlin Wall's first holes? Will a united Germany ever again flex its muscles and attack its neighbors as it has done twice in this century alone?

It simply is impossible to answer these questions today with any degree of certainty. Still, there is a basis for hope. The striking record over the past four decades of West Germany's transformation into a fully democratic country governed by the rule of law, firmly rooted in the North Atlantic Treaty Organization, committed to the European Community, and active in the Conference on Security and Cooperation in Europe surely provides grounds for optimism.

Moreover, West Germany's willingness to accept historical responsibility as the successor state to the Third Reich; its payment of substantial restitution and indemnification to individual Jewish victims, Jewish organizations, and Israel; and the close links the West German government has maintained with Israel have underscored Bonn's determination to forge a new chapter in relations with the Jewish people. The teaching of Holocaust education in the West German school system also provides some basis for reassurance.

There may be a welcome opportunity to extend these achievements to the German Democratic Republic. Previously, the GDR had rejected any historical responsibility for the crimes of the Nazi era.

Indeed, the GDR had become a principal benefactor and sponsor of numerous anti-Israel terrorist groups operating in the Middle East. It had no diplomatic relations with Israel and actively supported the "Zionism is racism" canard.

In other words, there were no links to speak of between 16 million East Germans and the Jewish people, and East Germany's foreign policy was inimical to Israel's interests.

Unification provides important opportunities to undo this dismal record of East Germany. An important first step was taken in April, on the very first day of the new Volkskammer, or People's Chamber, when this freely elected legislative body asked forgiveness from the world's Jews for the horrific crimes of the Nazis and, by doing so, accepted historical responsibility for the Nazi era.

Moreover, the parliamentarians indicated a desire to move ahead on the questions of claims and compensation, and to establish diplomatic relations with Israel at the earliest possible moment. These first steps by a new and democratic East Germany do portend well for the future.

Thus, it is fair to say that apprehension is mixed with hope. Time and ongoing deeds will determine which prevails.

Thank You, Holland
Jewish Telegraphic Agency
January 18, 1991

On December 24, an important step in the rebuilding of Soviet-Israeli relations occurred in Moscow. Bilateral ties were raised to the level of consul general, upgrading the diplomatic exchange from the low-level links that were established in 1987, but still short of full ambassadorial relations—i.e., normal ties. If recent reports from Jerusalem, Moscow, and Washington are to be believed, those full relations will be achieved within a matter of months.

While much attention understandably has been focused on these developing Soviet-Israeli contacts, one important by-product of the enhanced relationship has been largely overlooked. As of December 24, the Netherlands, after twenty-three years, no longer represents Israel's diplomatic interests in the Soviet Union. Accordingly, it is only fitting at this time to acknowledge Holland's assistance.

When the Soviet Union, which had maintained diplomatic ties with Israel from 1948 to the 1967 Six-Day War, with only a brief interruption, broke those links, Israel approached a third party, as is customary in diplomatic practice, to represent its diplomatic interests in Moscow.

That country was Holland, and the Dutch readily agreed. Unbeknownst to anyone at the time, over the next twenty-three years the Dutch were to play a vital, if little known, role in one of the most important chapters in modern Jewish history.

Not only did the Dutch government fulfill its task as an intermediary with extraordinary discretion, but also every Soviet Jewish family leaving with an exit visa for Israel—and hundreds of thousands have emigrated in this manner since 1967—actually passed through the Dutch embassy in Moscow for a variety of formalities before departing.

Anyone who has spent time with Jews in the Soviet Union just prior to their exit knows that they are understandably apprehensive. Will some last-minute snag occur? Will their visas be revoked? What awaits them on the other side now that years of waiting, of imagining, of romanticizing are seemingly at an end? Will they accomplish the myriad bureaucratic and personal tasks needed to close the books on one life before starting another?

It was in this frame of mind that, during the past twenty-three years, Soviet Jews entered the Dutch embassy—from Moscow and Minsk, from Leningrad and Lvov, from Berdichev and Baku, from Tbilisi and Tashkent. It wasn't easy for anyone, and nerves were easily frayed, but, by all accounts, the staff of the Dutch embassy fulfilled this lifesaving work with considerable efficiency and sensitivity.

Frankly, it ought not to come as a surprise. The Netherlands has long occupied a very special place in the minds and hearts of Jews the world over. Yes, there have been some differences with Israel in recent years over the best route to a political settlement in the Arab-Israeli conflict, and Holland also disagreed with Israel on the ticklish question of "freedom of choice" for emigrating Soviet Jews, with the Dutch insisting on that right, much to the consternation of Jerusalem.

At the same time, however, the Dutch have consistently advocated for Arab recognition of Israel and secure borders for the Jewish state, and denounced terrorism against Israel. Indeed, Holland's UN voting record on issues of concern to Israel has, after the United States', been among the best in NATO.

In addition, when Jews are asked to freely associate about Holland, they may think of a country characterized by religious freedom or a destination for Spanish and Portuguese Jews fleeing the Inquisition.

They may recall the efforts of some courageous Dutch to save Jews during the Holocaust. Indeed, more Dutch have been named Righteous Gentiles by Yad Vashem than citizens of any other country.[*]

They may also recall deep and abiding friendship for Israel; lone Dutch (and American) support for Israel during the 1973 Yom Kippur War, resulting in an Arab oil embargo targeted against the two countries; or the presence of a Dutch embassy in Jerusalem—the only European embassy in Israel's capital city—until 1980, when The Hague reluctantly heeded a UN resolution calling for the withdrawal of member countries' embassies from Jerusalem and, in doing so, succumbed to long-standing Arab pressure.

The list goes on. It includes lesser-known efforts, such as Dutch representation of Israel in Poland from 1967 to 1986, when Warsaw became the first Eastern bloc nation (excluding Romania, which never severed links) to reestablish ties with the Jewish state; opposition to the Arab economic boycott of firms doing business with Israel; and representation of Israel in Moscow in 1953 during a brief rupture in Soviet-Israeli diplomatic ties.

The degree of Dutch-Jewish solidarity can best be illustrated with a story. In 1982, world Jewry decided to launch an international petition campaign on behalf of Soviet Jews to obtain a million signatures on a letter to then-Soviet leader Leonid Brezhnev.

The Dutch Jewish community, misunderstanding the instructions, believed that their goal was to garner a million signatures in Holland alone. Apparently undaunted by this task in the small nation of 14 million, they were able to gain the support of most major institutions—educational, church, and other—and came close to their target.

In the United States, an equivalent goal proportionately would have meant some 16 million signatures, an absolutely unheard of figure for any petition in this country.

---

[*]By 1991 Holland was in second place, having been surpassed by Poland.

As we now welcome a new era in Soviet-Israeli diplomatic relations, world Jewry will always owe a very special debt of gratitude to the Netherlands for its central role in the historic exodus of Jews from the Soviet Union.

Remarks to German High School Students
Hamburg, Germany
January 1995

Let me right off tell you a secret which, in any case, would become obvious to you before long: my German is quite poor, but I nonetheless thought it best to try to speak to you in German—at least I hope it sounds like German—for a bit before switching to English. I hope you will understand my English. Otherwise, we'll rely on translation.

I'd like to explain why I'm here. First, that requires a few words about myself. I am forty-five, live in New York with my wife and children, and work for an organization called the American Jewish Committee, which was founded in 1906 by German Jews who had come to the United States.

The American Jewish Committee works along two tracks. First, it seeks to help ensure the security and well-being of the nearly 6 million Jews in the United States, as well as the State of Israel and Jews in other countries. Second, it works for a better world in which democracy, pluralism, human rights, and the rights of all minorities, including but not limited to Jews, are strengthened.

My father, Eric, lived in Berlin from the year of his birth, 1920, until Adolf Hitler came to power in 1933. Then Eric's parents, my grandfather, Michael, a journalist for a Berlin daily, and my grandmother, Rela, a housewife, sent him away to what they thought was a safe place, Vienna. Immediately after the *Anschluss* in 1938, he left for Paris—surely *that* was a safe place, he thought—while his mother went to Poland and ended up a cook with the Russian army, and his father eventually found himself in Asia and then America.

Seven years later, by the war's end in 1945, my father, the onetime schoolboy in Berlin with a love of math and science, had fought in three armies—the French, British, and American, endured three years of special regime prison camp as a Jew, and spent the last part of the war in espionage behind Nazi lines.

My mother, born in Moscow in 1923, and her family were lucky enough to be able to leave the Soviet Union in 1929 because of Stalin's anti-Semitic and antidemocratic policies and settled in Paris. Their peace was shattered in 1940 with the Nazi invasion, and they fled south, eventually escaping across the border to Spain, later entering the United States.

Without going into a still longer story, and it is much longer, my larger family experienced virtually every aspect of the Second World War—concentration camps, resistance movements, local collaborators, combat, fear, hunger, family separation, death, human indifference, and only seldom, too seldom, human kindness.

It was into this milieu that I was born in 1949. I used to think all my family members were especially smart because each spoke four, five, even six languages, until I realized why. They had been forced to move from country to country, and to survive they had to learn the local language.

I used to think that it was normal for families to be spread across countries and even continents. My family, for example, was spread over four countries—the United States, France, Russia, and Israel. I couldn't believe anyone could have all his relatives in one country, much less one city.

It probably will not surprise you that Germany was not my family's favorite country. In fact, some, though not all, of my relatives refused to have any contact with Germany, would not buy German products, and hoped Germany would remain weak and divided forever.

Incidentally, they did not feel much better about Austria—the Nazi partner, or what they deemed to be viscerally anti-Semitic Russia and Poland, or, for that matter, even France, where collaboration was very high. In their worldview, only the United States and a few other countries offered any real hope to Jews outside, of course, of Israel, though the United States certainly could not have been proud of its own immigration policies during the war.

So if this is the family I came from, and it is a family that profoundly affected me, including my eventual career decision to work in the Jewish community rather than the UN or U.S. government, my other ideas as a university graduate, why am I here?

Beginning twenty years ago, I had contact with Germans, especially young Germans, who came as exchange students to the United States. I met new generations who not only could not be held responsible for the crimes of the past, but who showed in so many cases a remarkably positive outlook, both toward Jews and Israel and against racism, xenophobia, and excessive nationalism.

I have come to see Germany's evolution as a peaceful, democratic state closely allied to Europe and the United States, and deeply engaged with Israel. Germany's role in NATO, the European Union, the Commission on Security and Cooperation in Europe (CSCE), and the United Nations system have all impressed me as both forward looking and constructive.

I have chosen to work for an organization, the American Jewish Committee, that believes it is ultimately better to light a candle than eternally to curse the darkness. Just as we must remember and understand the past—and we must, however painful, however difficult—so must we, at the same time, seek to write new chapters of history together, better chapters, more hopeful chapters.

The American Jewish Committee, through forty years of relations with Germany—its governments, political foundations, Catholic and Protestant religious leaders, intellectuals and media—has tried to help write these new chapters. Indeed, we are the only Jewish organization in the United States to have supported German unification and Germany's quest for a permanent seat on the UN Security Council, and to sponsor for fifteen years now regular exchanges for younger Germans and American Jews.

Germans and Jews, you and I, are in some way locked together for eternity since the Holocaust. Isn't it therefore best that we come to know each other, humanize each other, establish contact with each other, talk with one another—about the past, about the present, and about the future?

And that's why I've come this week.

In the last few years I have been traveling to Germany two or three times a year, always shuttling between Bonn and Berlin and always meeting with government and other officials. Such meetings, I believe, are very important. As trust builds, we can talk more openly about a growing array of issues—the place of memory in German history and education, anti-Semitism, Germany's relations with Israel, the Arab-Israeli peace process, developments in Central and Eastern Europe, violence against foreigners in Germany, Germany's citizenship laws, German-U.S. ties, and much more. Many are the issues that unite us; some still divide us. But we talk as friends today, and there is much progress to report in many areas.

I have long felt that one dimension was missing for me in my recent travels—talking to young Germans, to Germans at schools, universities, in the military. To state the obvious, you are Germany's future.

I wanted, in this the fiftieth anniversary year of the war's end, to go beyond the commemorative events, many of which I will of course attend, and to meet you, talk with you, and hear what's on your mind. In doing so, I want to contribute, however modestly, to strengthening relations between Germans and Jews for the generations to come. Thus, I am spending eight days visiting six German cities and towns, and meeting from morning till night with high school and university students, church youth groups, and military personnel.

With my German exhausted but my curiosity about you very much alive, I now look forward to our discussion. Share with me your thoughts on the subject of Germans and Jews and ask any questions on your mind. But first, I have some questions for you. Let me begin with one. There's a game called association. I say a word and you tell me the first thing that comes to you. Okay? Let's start. "Germany." "America." "Poland." "France." "Israel." "Catholic." "Protestant." "Muslim." "Jew." "Judaism."

Trends in Polish-Jewish Relations
United States Holocaust Memorial Museum
Washington, D.C.
October 1996

Walking into the museum this afternoon for a meeting that was held here prior to this evening's event, I noticed a food vendor standing just outside the Fourteenth Street entrance. He advertised Polish sausage and kosher beef hot dogs. I wondered if it was something staged by Miles Lerman (chairman of the U.S. Holocaust Memorial Museum) to create a harmonious spirit for this evening, or whether, as was more likely, it was just another enterprising entrepreneur who knew a good thing when he saw it.

On a more serious note, I'm deeply honored to have been asked by you, Miles, and your colleagues to participate on this distinguished panel. I'm especially moved when I look at the remarkable wisdom, experience, courage, and integrity represented here by my fellow panelists. We all agree, I'm sure, that this is an important, if exceptionally difficult, discussion, and I'm pleased the museum took the initiative.

I bring to the table some experience working with Poland and Polish-Jewish issues, Catholic-Jewish issues as they affect Poland, and Polish-Jewish relations as they play out here in the United States. I also confess that I bring more personal dimensions as well, like many of you, I'm sure. I am a child of the so-called second generation, part of an extended family all of whose members had lived in Europe and of whom I was the first to be born in this country.

Some in my family ask me: Why are you at this, trying to build new relations? I would say new bridges, but I think by now it's a well-worn metaphor in this election year. New relations with the Poles or, for that matter, with the Germans. Why? Isn't it a wasted, misguided effort, perhaps even a hopeless undertaking? And anyway, these countries represent our past, not our future, so why bother?

Indeed, if we look at recent years and simply want to remind ourselves of the difficulties in Polish-Jewish relations, many examples come to mind, some referred to by the previous speakers. As they were speaking, I simply jotted down a few:

- The planned construction of a shopping mall in Auschwitz;
- The religious symbols on the grounds of the camps at Auschwitz and Birkenau;
- The Carmelite Convent, again, connected to Auschwitz;
- The speech of Elie Weisel on the fiftieth anniversary of the pogroms in Kielce;
- The comments of Israeli prime minister Shamir that were referred to by you, Jan Novak, namely, that Poles suck the milk of anti-Semitism from their mothers' breasts;
- The film *Shtetl*;
- The film *Shoah*, by Claude Lanzmann;
- The anti-Semitic comments of Father Jankowski in Gdansk in the presence of the Polish president, Lech Walesa;
- The comments of a prominent American Jew that Poland would be "attacked and humiliated" if the vexing questions of restitution were not satisfactorily resolved;
- The subtle presence of anti-Semitic motifs in the first Polish democratic, postcommunist presidential election, to which Professor [Yisrael] Gutman made appropriate reference;
- The controversy surrounding the comments of Cardinal Glemp, troubling to many Jews;
- The controversy surrounding the comments of Professor Yaffa Eliach, troubling to many Poles;
- The Polish handling, or mishandling, of the fiftieth anniversary commemoration of the liberation of Auschwitz.

And that's only the beginning of the list as seen by Jews, as seen by Poles. Many of you, I'm sure, could add to the list and would quickly want to jump into the fray on one side or the other. But again, it reminds me of the question I'm sometimes asked: Why get involved in the first place?

True, at best, it's like the children's game of giant steps—one step forward, two steps back or three steps to the side. There certainly isn't the kind of linear progress one might hope for. Still, my answer to those who ask is really twofold. First, I'm in this business because of Professor Bartoszewski, because of Jan Novak, because of Jan Karski.

I owe it to them, and others like them, however many, however few.

I owe it to them, to what they stood for during the war and what they stand for to this day, to do my best to see if we can in fact create a new beginning in this thousand-year relationship.

And second, I'm in this business because, consistent with my Jewish values, I believe fervently in the possibility of a better future. This century gave Jews and Poles opportunities to develop a relationship in the years before the Holocaust, which did not materialize, as Professor Gutman correctly noted, because anti-Semitism in Poland was just too rife.

The Nazi era might have brought Jews and Poles together. After all, were we not the common enemy of the Germans? But it didn't, and to this day, as we see, it still divides us.

And the onset of communism in postwar Poland, too, might have begun to bring Jews and Poles closer together, since, in the final analysis, it was our common enemy, and yet, once again, we were divided.

Now, we have our last and, I believe, best chance to give it one more try. It derives from the advent of democracy in Poland. I believe this provides at least some room for optimism. Yes, in the communist era, an optimist was described as someone "without all the facts." And I'm certainly not here simply to wax optimistic; I'm ever mindful of Professor Gutman's admonitions. But as a Jew assessing this relationship, and especially looking at Poland as the heart of the link, there are for me four criteria by which I measure the health of our ties and on some fronts, at least, they offer encouragement.

First is the well-being of democratic institutions, the rule of law, and respect for human rights in the new Poland. There is much to applaud here. And Poland's ultimately successful integration into the Western value system, every bit as much as into Western regional institutions, will be key. This becomes our challenge, too.

Second, as has been mentioned by several previous speakers, is the vitality of Poland's bilateral relationship with Israel and, conversely, Poland's attitude toward Israel's enemies. And we have seen the welcome inversion in those two relationships taking place in recent years, that is, increasingly close Polish-Israeli ties and more strained links with many of Israel's foes, a far cry from the situation just a few years ago.

Third is the status of Poland's small but still viable Jewish community. Not long ago, I met a Polish-Jewish contemporary of mine who commented that growing up in Warsaw in the late '50s, she was told there were only a few thousand elderly Polish Jews and the community would shortly die. "And here it is in 1996, forty years later," she said, "and I look around me in Warsaw, and there are still a few thousand elderly Polish Jews. Lo and behold, though, we're not yet dead!"

The Jewish community is only a glimmer of what it once was; it will remain only a glimmer—it won't be anything more—but the status of Polish Jews as equal citizens and participants in the new Poland means something far beyond sheer numbers. They become a litmus test of Polish tolerance and values. And these Jews must be able to live in a society free of official or mainstream anti-Semitism or any vestige of discrimination. This should mean something to all those of us who seek a truly democratic Poland. And this brings me to my fourth point.

That is the one which Professor Gutman particularly emphasized. If we are finally to move this relationship forward, we must seek a common understanding on the place of Jews in Polish history, the treatment of Jews in that history, the response of Poland to anti-Semitism when it erupted, and the "unfinished" issues—i.e., communal and personal property restitution—arising from the Second World War.

I believe, as I said earlier, that notable progress has been made in the past several years, particularly with respect to the climate of democracy, the bilateral relationship with Israel, and the emergence of some semblance of Jewish life among those few thousand Jews who remain.

And while I would like to believe that anti-Semitism has been completely marginalized, as some in Poland would allege, I have taken careful note of the surveys of the American Jewish Committee and others and see not just significant pockets of anti-Semitism, but also a more general sense among the majority of Poles—in our 1995 study, for example—that anti-Semitism *does* remain a serious problem in Poland.

You can't simply deny it or wish it away, as some Poles would. Anti-Semitism needs to be addressed, seriously and systematically, first and foremost by Polish institutions, including political parties, the media, the church, and other key sectors of Polish society. In the final analysis, ironic though it may sound, anti-Semitism today is more of a potential threat to Poland than to Jews. Jews are few in number and aging, but for Poland any resurgence of anti-Semitism would mean a giant step back in time, and serious damage to its new Western orientation.

In closing, I believe, as Jan Novak said, that there are Jews of good-will as there are Poles of goodwill. We owe it to ourselves; we owe it to each other; we owe it to a thousand years of history to see whether, in fact, this moment in time—a transitory, not a permanent, moment—is one we can seize to move our relationship forward, even as we tackle, honestly and forthrightly, those issues that still divide us.

Having just met with a group of younger Polish leaders the American Jewish Committee had the privilege of bringing to the United States this past week to launch our new exchange program, there is hope, I believe. In fact, in a case of bad timing, they left for Warsaw today. I wish they could have been here tonight, so that I might have introduced them to this audience. Among such young Poles there is a desire to create a new beginning in this infinitely complex relationship. I saw it with my own eyes and heard it with my own ears—and I'd like to believe the same desire exists among a critical mass of young Jews as well.

Chirac Removes France as Honest Peace Broker
The New York Times
October 27, 1996

President Jacques Chirac of France accomplished quite a lot in a short visit to Israel (news articles, Oct. 23 and 24). Looking for a way to insert France into Arab-Israeli peacemaking, he renewed French-Arab solidarity, irritated most Israelis (even those who do not support Prime Minister Benjamin Netanyahu's policies), poked his finger in the eyes of American negotiators, and surely hurt the peace cause.

By publicly articulating how he believes the final Israeli-Palestinian and Israeli-Syrian settlements should look, Mr. Chirac has taken himself and his country out of the running for honest broker. For him, compromise is required on only one side: Once Israel accepts the maximum Arab position, peace will suddenly break out in the Middle East.

Can we attribute Mr. Chirac's current Middle East tour and his outspoken pro-Arab positions to a sudden change in French policy? Let's remember Mr. Chirac's important regional accomplishment as prime minister in the 1970s. He negotiated French nuclear cooperation with Iraq (the same Iraq that invaded Kuwait in 1990, almost had in its hands a nuclear device, and still pursues a nonconventional weapons capacity).

Now, joined by Russia, Mr. Chirac would like to weaken international sanctions against this dangerous regime, but those efforts have been temporarily put on hold by the inconvenient United Nations disclosures of continuing Iraqi biological weapons plans.

And just before this visit to Israel, Mr. Chirac paid a call on President Hafez al-Assad of Syria. We heard much of French-Syrian friendship, but not a word about Syria's gross human rights violations or its hosting of terrorist organizations and their training camps. But of course we'll be told that such issues were raised privately by the French leader.

Let us also recall the French determination to maintain (together with Germany) an utterly bankrupt European "critical dialogue" with Iran, the leading sponsor of terrorism in the world today. What has that policy achieved beyond an Iranian "promise" not to have the British writer Salman Rushdie assassinated on European soil? Nothing!

"It Is Better to Talk within the Family"
Interview with David Harris
Gazeta Wyborcza (Poland)
April 14, 1997

We are not naïve. We know that there is dormant anti-Semitism in many circles of the Polish society. But we also know that many Poles want to work toward new, normal relations with the Jews. It is with them that we want to cooperate, says the director of the American Jewish Committee, David Harris, interviewed by Edward Krzemien.

Edward Krzemien: The Washington Post *published recently a letter proclaiming that the admission of Poland in NATO should be withheld because fire was set to the Warsaw synagogue. It was signed by a British-American Information Security Council.*

David Harris: The reaction of the Polish authorities to the arson convinced many Americans that Poland treats such cases in a serious way. I do not think that one letter can change this opinion, a letter signed, incidentally, by a group I have never heard of.

In the USA there is no shortage of statements against Polish membership in NATO.

The doubts that are expressed differ from the point of the aforementioned letter. They refer rather to the fears concerning Russia's reaction to NATO's expansion. Incidents similar to that in Warsaw regrettably happen everywhere. Also in the USA, in recent years, hundreds of churches were arsoned and synagogues were damaged. Nobody concluded that our standards of human rights are insufficient.

In Poland fears are expressed that the Jewish Diaspora in the USA is not in favor of our entrance into NATO.

Most American Jewish organizations keep silent on the matter. They believe that expressing a position would not be in their interests as it would mean choosing between Central European states and Russia. One of the two sides would feel offended.

I have been expressing for some time my personal opinion concerning the expansion of NATO. I believe that Russian fears have to be taken into account but by no means can it mean a right of veto for Moscow. Inclusion of Poland, the Czech Republic, and Hungary is good for NATO and good for these three countries. Moreover, it can only strengthen respect for human rights, among other things. I know that anti-Semitism is present in some segments of Polish society. It is, however, better to face such problems within the family of Western nations than outside it. Excluding the Central European countries from the Western circle can only make the problems more acute.

The Polish parliament has recently passed legislation on the relationship of the state to Jewish communities. It includes procedures for the restitution of former Jewish communal property. Jewish circles in the world have sharply criticized the law. Can this influence the debate in the U.S. Congress on the ratification of the agreement between NATO and Poland?

I can't exclude the possibility that politicians will pay attention to Polish treatment of such issues, including Jewish property claims. It would be better to have this problem resolved before the meeting of NATO leadership in July.

What do you think about that legislation?

I am not an expert. I understand that it [the legislation] helps solve some issues. Two problems remain. First, the number of properties that should be returned to Jewish communities. The number mentioned by the World Jewish Restitution Organization is higher than the one presented by the Polish government. Second, the private property restitution issue. I know that in the Polish situation this is a much more sensitive and difficult subject.

How do you see Polish–Jewish relations?

They have never been easy. In the American Jewish Committee we believe that in this century there have been several chances for Polish-Jewish cooperation. Two resulted from the fact that we had a common enemy—first Nazis, then communists. Those opportunities were both missed.

Today we have another opportunity. This time it is not a common enemy but a common friend—democracy. The question is: Will there be on both sides enough determined people who want to write a new chapter in Polish–Jewish relations? If not, we will be condemned to a permanent conflict. I want to believe that we can launch a new start.

How many Jews want to do so?

There are some. How many? I don't know. To many American Jews, Poland belongs entirely to the past, not the future. Contemporary Poland interests them less than it should, perhaps not at all. In their vision Polish history is totally dominated by anti-Semitism. And they don't want to reconsider their opinions. They don't want to devote time and effort to look at present-day Poland, to notice the changes there.

The changes are easier seen from Israel than the United States. Why? Because Israel has two levels of relations with Poland. One, the relations of two independent states, and two, relations between the two peoples. The interstate relations introduce a completely new dimen-

sion: diplomatic ties, cultural exchanges, economic and military cooperation. Much is happening between Poland and Israel nowadays. This
is lacking in the case of the 6 million American Jews.

That is one of the reasons why so many Jews in the United States
live in "suspended time" in relation to Poland. Their attitudes have not
changed since the tragic 1946 Kielce pogrom or the forced emigration
of 1968. They glance from time to time at news from Poland when
newspapers report that Lech Walesa introduced anti-Semitic overtones
in his presidential bid of 1990, or Cardinal Glemp made a statement
hurtful to Jews, or Father Jankowski said repulsive things in the presence of President Walesa, or the Warsaw synagogue was set on fire.
And they say: You see, nothing has changed.

*What provokes some American Jews to make statements such as that
of Israel Singer? We recall that the Secretary General of the World
Jewish Congress threatened us with "public attacks and humiliation"
when he was referring to the impatience of his organization with the
slow action of the Polish authorities concerning the restitution of
Jewish property. Such anti-Polish statements from Jewish organizations are not isolated cases. This language of aggression and oversim-
plifications is similar to that of anti-Semites.*

When voices attacking and humiliating Poland appear, we clearly
and strongly condemn them. These voices only reinforce those in
Poland who say: Look at the Jews, whatever we do they will never be
satisfied. Jews are genetically anti-Polish, so why bother? Why go to
the table and negotiate the return of property? Why negotiate the
Auschwitz Program?

Still, we are not naïve. We know from Demoscop polls that there
remains a deeply ingrained anti-Semitism in important circles of Polish
society. But we also know that many Poles want to work toward new,
normal relations with the Jewish people. It is with them that we wish
to cooperate.

Who is the AJC's partner in Poland?

Other Jewish organizations are involved in important educational
and religious missions in Poland, and also provide social assistance for
the Jewish community. Our mission is different. We try to shape the
tone and tenor of Jewish–Polish relations. We find partners in Poland,

among those in the present government as well as in the previous ones, in some circles of the Catholic Church, among the intelligentsia.

We are assisted by our Polish representative, Stanislaw Krajewski, who is well known and active among Polish Jews. Mr. Krajewski chairs the Jewish Forum, co-chairs the Polish Council of Christians and Jews, and is the organizer of the Jewish confidential phone line.

Last year we started an exchange of young political and civic leaders. We got help from Professor Wladyslaw Bartoszewski and Ambassador Krzysztof Sliwinski. In the fall we hosted the first group of young Poles. They visited New York, Washington, and Chicago. A group of American Jews will visit Poland shortly. We'd like to see groups on both sides become interested in each other; we'd like to see American Jews begin to understand contemporary Poland beyond the sensational headlines.

Four years ago, we began an historic cooperation with the episcopate of the Polish Catholic Church. Each year an American university professor in Jewish theology lectures in Catholic universities in Poland. Important aspects of Judaism are presented to future priests. And each year the Polish church selects a theologian who lectures on Catholicism and Polish-Jewish themes in Jewish educational institutions in the United States. Our aim is the fostering—through churches and synagogues—of groups that will engage in Polish Catholic–Jewish dialogue. This requires investing much time and effort, but we see no other way. Of course we can maintain a dialogue with just one or another politician. This is important but not sufficiently widespread.

We try to extend our reach in Polish–Jewish relations through individuals whom we call multipliers. For instance, a Catholic priest will communicate with thousands in his pastoral mission. Or take the young people who come to the States under our auspices. They, too,will act as multipliers, as they work in the media, politics, etc.

Each time, though, that we hear the regrettable statements of a Father Jankowski, our efforts become still more complicated. We are determined, however, to go on.

Your exchange program deals mostly with teaching about Judaism and Catholicism. This is surely important. The problem in Poland, however, is caused not by anti-Judaism but by xenophobic anti-Semitism.

Our experience shows that we are dealing with deep ignorance concerning Jews and Judaism. In a sense, this is sadly understandable today. In a country where there are only several thousand Jews, most people have had no contact with Jews or Judaism. The Jews we send who visit Christian seminaries do more than teach; they create personal links. We see it as a demystification of the image of Jews.

Polish anti-Semitism is not directed against Jews as such but against Poles who allegedly hide their Jewish origins. This is a magical anti-Semitism. In the world, anti-Semites say: Kowalski [=Smith] is a Jew, so he is a villain. And in Poland: Kowalski is a villain, so he must be Jewish. Father Jankowski says: "I love Jews, but let Jews be Jews. I don't accept the fact that there are people who hide their Jewish origins, pretend to be Poles and act against our national interests."

We are talking about one of the oldest pathologies when we speak of anti-Semitism. Perhaps we can't stop it entirely. But Polish anti-Semitism is not so much a problem for the Jews as it is for the Poles. In the West, to which Poland aspires, anti-Semitism today is not encouraged in mainstream social life. How was this achieved? By a very clear, consistent, and unambiguous message from the elite, major political parties, the church, the intelligentsia.

What is the message that Polish society gets when the Polish president sits in a church during Father Jankowski's outrageous sermon, and then keeps silent for ten days? We met with President Lech Walesa in 1995, at the commemoration of the fiftieth anniversary of the UN. An AJC delegation flew specially to San Francisco to see him. Our whole meeting was devoted to Father Jankowski's sermon. Sadly, we talked past each other. President Walesa kept saying that had he reacted in public he would have made the sermon significant. And we kept saying that precisely because he did not react he made the sermon significant.

The issue is not simple. Walesa for sure is not an anti-Semite. He thinks anti-Semitism is a stupidity. Only sometimes he used that leverage to get the votes of anti-Semites. But let me go back to your previ-

ous remarks. It follows from them that there is not much hope for a change of anti-Polish attitudes among most American Jews.

We need time. This can't be replaced. And we also need determined effort on the part of those who want to change Jewish attitudes. I am not so optimistic as to believe that the passage of time alone will effect the change.

There is another issue. In Poland, foreigners perceive an attitude that denies Jews full citizens' rights. Even the phrase that you (and we) use—Poles and Jews—suggests that if you are a Jew you are not a Pole. This alone hints at a pattern of social exclusion.

At the same time, I must express my appreciation to President Kwasniewski. We had an opportunity to meet him recently in the United States. He said in public that one of the aims of his presidency is to change Polish–Jewish relations. This is an important message, not just a symbolic gesture but a real push forward.

Now if Poland is engaged in solving the problem of the restitution of Jewish property, if it has good relations with Israel, if it sells no arms to Israel's enemies, if exchange programs are implemented, this means progress. When the Catholic Church reads in its parishes the pastoral letter about Jews, when Pope John Paul II takes a clear stand about the dialogue, this all suggests progress. But let me stress that these things do not happen by themselves. Just the contrary, they require great effort from both sides. And they require thick skin—preparedness for attacks and criticism.

The American Jewish Committee has been advocating the reconciliation of Jews and Poles for more than twenty years. Last year, though, with great pain, we cut our ties with the Polish American Congress. This came after PAC president Edward Moskal wrote a profoundly disturbing anti-Semitic letter to President Kwasniewski.

We cut our ties with the PAC but we have not abandoned our efforts to reach an understanding with American Polonia. We have created a new Council of American Poles and Jews. We work there with such persons as Jan Nowak-Jezioranski, Father John Pawlikowski, Jan Karski, and other tested friends. True, occasionally we differ in our opinions. So what? The best of friends can have differences of opinions.

Testimony on NATO Expansion
Senate Committee on Foreign Relations
Washington, D.C.
November 5, 1997

Mr. Chairman, it is an honor to appear before the Committee to discuss with you why the American Jewish Committee supports the expansion of NATO.

The American Jewish Committee, Mr. Chairman, was founded in 1906 in response to a series of brutal pogroms carried out by czarist officials against Jews in Russia and Eastern Europe. In the ninety-one years since our founding, we have seen the horrible consequences produced by instability in Central and Eastern Europe. It is precisely because we carry with us the memory of those horrors, and because we believe that America is best served by an active and vigorous foreign policy, that the American Jewish Committee became the first Jewish organization in the United States to publicly speak out in favor of NATO enlargement.

We are convinced that opportunity is temporary, not permanent. Either it is seized or it is lost. The opportunity presented by an expanded NATO is one that should not, must not, be lost. An expanded NATO means greater stability for Central Europe, a region that was the cockpit for the two world wars that brought such horror to this century.

Mr. Chairman, I have spent my professional and academic life involved with affairs in Russia and the surrounding region. I lived and worked in the Soviet Union. I am convinced that to leave Europe divided at its cold war boundaries, to ignore the lands to the east, to have NATO members turn their collective backs on Central Europe, would be to deny the dangers to European—and Western—security that lurk there. From the Balkans to the Caucasus, more Europeans have died violently in this region in the past five years than in the previous forty-five. As Vaclav Havel, the distinguished president of the Czech Republic, said: "Just as it is impossible for one half a room to be forever warm and the other half cold, it is equally unthinkable that two different Europes should forever exist next to each other without detriment to both."

In addition, retaining the North Atlantic alliance in its cold war configuration would have meant continuing an historic injustice—the abandonment by the democratic West of the small nations of Central Europe. Let me remind us all that it happened in 1938 at Munich and 1945 at Yalta, and the West watched from the sidelines as Soviet power squashed fledgling and promising democratic movements in Hungary in 1956, Czechoslovakia in 1968, and Poland in 1981.

An expanded NATO not only strengthens democracy in those nations embraced by the alliance at Madrid but encourages the other countries in the region to accelerate their own democratic and economic reforms, as well as resolve long-simmering disputes. The 1994 Poland-Lithuania agreement on good neighborly relations and military cooperation and the 1996 Hungary-Romania bilateral friendship treaty are just two examples. Moreover, integration in the Western alliance offers a real safeguard for the rights of Jews and other minority communities, historically the target of national, religious, or ethnic hatreds in too many places.

NATO throughout its fifty-year history has been a collective defense pact only. Russian reaction to NATO's decision to extend membership to three former Soviet bloc states has been far more restrained than many had suggested. Indeed, just as was the case prior to the introduction of NATO forces in the former Yugoslavia, opponents of NATO expansion have invoked supposed Russian opposition to any display of Western power largely to boost their own case against using it. The Founding Act signed by Russia and NATO in May does gives Russia a voice in alliance affairs immediately, while the countries currently being invited now will not have a seat at the table for at least two years.

Mr. Chairman, I would like to add a word about Senator Kerry's probing questions. It would be premature to become too specific today about the scope of a second, or a third, tranche of NATO expansion, but it is important to keep very much alive NATO's openness—as demonstrated in Madrid—to further waves of expansion. To do otherwise is to dash the hopes of tens of millions of Europeans, from the Baltic region to the Balkans, that their future might include membership in NATO, and to imply a recreation of European spheres of influence, a profoundly destabilizing step that could have unintended, even unforeseen, consequences.

At the same time, the United States and NATO must make the Founding Act with Russia work—in letter and in spirit—to ease Russia's historical fear of encirclement. This requires ongoing and careful attention to Russia-NATO and Russia-U.S. ties, and a constant focus on those many areas of cooperation, both current and potential, while periodically reminding Moscow that the new NATO of today is not an alliance directed against it.

Lastly, we should not look at NATO expansion as a zero-sum game, where expansion means jeopardizing our ties with Russia. That's simply wrongheaded. This is not the intent of the United States and it is not the intent of NATO. And it certainly is not in the interest of Russia, from its point of view, as it moves toward institutionalizing its democratic and market reforms.

With the implosion of the Warsaw Pact and the Soviet Union, Europe is poised at one of those infrequent moments of historical definition, when choices are clear and alternatives stark. We respectfully urge the United States Senate to grasp the significance of this moment, the chance to solidify the democratic ideal and to enhance European—and Western—security, and support the proposed enlargement of NATO.

The history of our century teaches, or ought to teach, that American leadership is indispensable in building an undivided, democratic, and peaceful Europe. That leadership, embodied today in the drive to NATO expansion, continues a proud tradition. The American Jewish Committee believes that, while the cost of NATO expansion will not be negligible, the cost of failure to assure European stability and security would be far higher. We therefore urge the committee to support the administration in its steady, incremental broadening of the Western alliance.

Remarks on the Occasion of
the Unveiling of a Memorial to the
50,000 Jews of Thessaloniki Murdered in the Holocaust
Thessaloniki (Salonika), Greece
November 23, 1997

Your Excellency President Stephanopoulos, Foreign Minister Pangalos, Alternate Foreign Minister Papandreou, distinguished members of the Greek cabinet, honorable members of the United States Congress (Senator Sarbanes, Congressmen Gilman, Filner, and Waxman), ambassadors (of Germany, Israel, Luxembourg, and Poland), ladies and gentlemen.

Ine timi moo na vriskome etho simera. It is a privilege for me to be here today.

The magnificent monument unveiled in the center of Thessaloniki this morning serves as a powerful symbol that the tens of thousands from this city who perished for one reason and one reason only—because they were Jews—will not be forgotten. This monument hallows and sanctifies their memory.

Such a monument, though, also poses a permanent challenge. After all, in the final analysis, a monument is an inanimate object; it must be given life. It must be woven into the often complex tapestry of a nation's memory, together with the expression and interpretation of that memory through the educational system, the arts, and the national life of a country. Otherwise, over time, a monument will inevitably reveal itself as essentially lifeless, as an increasingly indistinguishable and meaningless feature of the national, and in this case urban, landscape.

This is our collective challenge. I believe that, together, we can rise to it.

We cannot bring back the fallen. We cannot recreate life in this breathtakingly beautiful seaside city as it was until the blackness first descended in April 1941, with the deportations to the death camps two years later.

But we can recall what once was and honor that past—an extraordinary Jewish community that was for so much of recorded history a unique center of Jewish life, energy, scholarship, and creativity; a community described in the year 1537 as the "metropolis of Israel, city of justice, mother of Israel, like Jerusalem."

And we can reaffirm our determination—here, now—to stand against the forces of evil wherever, whenever they rear their ugly heads. In doing so, we are able to draw inspiration and courage from those all-too-rare individuals, here in Greece and elsewhere in Europe, who, even at the risk of their own lives, bore witness to the greatness men and women can achieve through their physical and moral fortitude in seeking to save the lives of others.

Let us always remember these heroes and heroines as a flicker of light and hope in the darkness that enveloped this vast continent earlier this century.

Ladies and gentlemen, our first encounter as Greeks and Jews dates back nearly 2,300 years. Since that time our histories have been intertwined in ways too numerous even to attempt to recount here.

Suffice it to say, though, that we are both ancient peoples fiercely proud of our respective traditions and contributions to history, not least the very underpinnings of Western civilization—democracy and monotheism.

We are both peoples relatively small in number, it is true, but not in the length of our reach, the indomitability of our spirit, or the scope of our vision.

We are both peoples of the homeland and the Diaspora.

We are both peoples of the Mediterranean and the world.

We are both peoples linked to ancient languages that have been given modern form.

And we are both peoples who have faced more than our share of adversity, endured and resisted it, and ultimately, at great sacrifice, conquered it.

Ladies and gentlemen, the American Jewish Committee, which I am privileged to represent, and whose honorary president, Maynard Wishner, is here as well, has stood with the deeply scarred but remarkably resilient Greek Jewish community since its reorganization in 1946.

It is a community determined to carry on the remarkable legacy of more than two millennia to which it is the proud heir.

It is a community, though, that lives with its enduring pain and sense of irretrievable loss. Like other such highly traumatized Jewish communities, it understandably remains deeply sensitive to any threats to its well-being, security, and full and equal participation in society at large.

During these past fifty years, we at the American Jewish Committee have been committed to creating close ties between Greeks and Jews.

• We have sought to deepen our links with Greece and encourage its ever closer cooperation with the State of Israel, the fulfillment of our prayers and hopes during the Jewish people's 1,900-year-long dispersion.

We should be perfectly clear. There is a powerful connection between the monument unveiled here in Thessaloniki this morning and the significance of the modern State of Israel as the sovereign home and haven of the Jewish people. I cannot state this emphatically enough. Those who might wish to disconnect the two have failed, I fear, to understand the lessons of history.

A prominent American entertainer once said: "I've been poor in my life and I've been rich. I can tell you it's a lot better being rich." I can recall a Greece whose relations with Israel over the first four decades of the Jewish state's existence were, to say the least, cool, and a Greece that in recent years has begun to widen and deepen the bilateral link. Though it won't come as a surprise to you, I can tell you that the latter is far preferable. I urge this trend to continue, for there is still considerable potential to be realized.

• We have sought to create a model of intergroup cooperation through our close ties with the Greek American community, led so ably by our beloved friend Andy Athens, and to support one another on numerous issues.

• And we have sought to advance relations between two great faith traditions—the Greek Orthodox and the Judaic. In this regard, a promising start was made in 1972 when the American Jewish Committee convened a landmark event in the interreligious sphere— the first National Colloquium on Greek Orthodox–Jewish Relations. On that occasion we were privileged to have as our partner the Greek Orthodox Archdiocese of North and South America.

The legendary Archbishop Iakavos said at the time: "Both traditions [referring to the Orthodox and Judaic] teach us that repentance leads us to renewal; renewal to the true faith; true faith to freedom; and freedom to salvation, which comes from God only."

He could not have stated our potential commonality any better.

Ladies and gentlemen, the profoundly moving events here today in Thessaloniki remind us of all that was—and of all that was lost. But, even in our sorrow and our tears, they also remind us of our age-old yearning for the fulfillment of the prophetic vision—*Lo yisa goy el goy herev, lo yilmadu od milkhama*. And nation shall not lift up sword against nation, nor shall they learn war anymore.

Let all of us gathered here, Jew and non-Jew, Greek and non-Greek, drawn closer to one another by this extraordinary day, recommit ourselves to that worthy vision. With persistence and determination, we can prevail.

Efharisto poli. Thank you very much.

Jews and Germany
International Herald Tribune
January 20, 1998

In a meeting with an American Jewish delegation three years ago, German president Roman Herzog asked an intriguing question: Why is it that German–Israeli relations are light years ahead of Germany's links with the American Jewish community?

He was absolutely right in his premise. All German–Jewish ties, even fifty-three years after the end of the Second World War, understandably remain fraught with searing emotion and multiple layers of complexity. That said, however, there is nonetheless a dynamism in the German–Israeli connection that is largely missing from Germany's relationship with America's 6 million Jews, whose image of Germany, to a very considerable degree, remains focused on the years 1933 to 1945 and their aftermath.

Why the dichotomy between the world's two largest Jewish communities? The answer, in a word, is sovereignty. Israelis deal with

Bonn on two levels—as a state and as a people; American Jews deal only on one, as a people.

As a state, particularly one that from its very birth endured diplomatic isolation, economic boycotts, attempts at delegitimization, costly arms races, war and terrorism, Israel had, as a practical matter of survival, to find support internationally. Germany presented one such opportunity. Precisely because Germany appeared determined both to come to grips with its past and to establish itself in the family of Western, democratic nations, the moral dilemmas for Israel's statesmen were rendered just a bit easier, far from simple though they were.

Even before the establishment of diplomatic ties in 1965, under various restitution agreements Bonn provided Israel with financial and other assistance crucial to the fledgling state's existence. From 1965 onward, after an impassioned Israeli debate, bilateral links were formalized. Over the years, the bonds widened and deepened to the point where today Germany is Israel's second leading trading partner and its closest ally on the European continent. Indeed, in 1997 Germany took the unusual step of breaking with the other fourteen members of the European Union in their support of anti-Israel measures at the United Nations General Assembly.

The German record regarding Israel has not been perfect. While far from alone, German companies' enthusiastic pursuit in the 1980s of exports, including dual-use technology, to Iraq and Libya was particularly disturbing. So, too, was Bonn's shortsighted policy on Iran, a state implacably hostile to Israel, to craft a so-called critical dialogue, which seemed much longer on dialogue than criticism.

Nevertheless, the German record is impressive and certainly better than that of the other major European countries—Britain, France, or Italy. Israelis know it and see its fruits; most American Jews, on the other hand, are largely unaware. Hence President Herzog's frustration with the discrepancy.

As the nineteenth-century German philosopher Hegel noted, reality is a dynamic, not a static, process. Time—and history—do not stand still, nor, for that matter, do the forces of international or human relations.

That's why, shortly after the establishment of the Federal Republic

of Germany in 1949, the American Jewish Committee (AJC), at first
tentatively after much anguished soul-searching, later with increasing
gusto, began to search out in the new Germany those elements—governmental and nongovernmental—genuinely committeed to writing a
new chapter in German-Jewish relations.

Germany was simply too important to walk away from, however
much our emotions might understandably tell us otherwise. This was a
far from universally held view, however. AJC was roundly criticized by
many in the Jewish community who wanted nothing whatsoever to do
with the bloodstained country, but the AJC decision, with the added
benefit today of hindsight, proved visionary.

Over the course of four decades, we developed unusually extensive
ties with German leaders to bolster German-Jewish understanding. As
a result, we have been able to pursue issues of critical importance,
including, as a recent example, the neglected needs of East European
Holocaust survivors who had never received any German compensation for their suffering, unlike their counterparts in the West. (An
agreement to provide monthly pensions for as many as 20,000 East
European survivors was announced in Bonn earlier this month.)

In the process of building relations between Germany and the
Jewish people, we sought to enhance still further the reach in Germany
of remembrance, democratic institutions, and tolerance. After all, in
Germany attitudes toward Jews and the Holocaust become a litmus test
for broader attitudes toward democracy, history, and human rights.

We saw first-hand a new Germany emerging. To be sure, this was-
n't an entirely linear process; it had its significant setbacks, including
the Bitburg scandal and the paroxysm of violence against foreigners
shortly after German unification. Still, no fair-minded observer could
fail to note the extraordinary progress achieved by the Federal
Republic since 1949.

With Germany's future the key to Europe's, and with Germany
today astonishingly the home of the fastest-growing Jewish community in the world, there is every reason to be present on the ground—as
advocates for closer German–American Jewish ties, as friends of the
soon-to-be 100,000-strong Jewish community, and, not least of course,
as supporters of those who insist on holding Germany to the very high-

est democratic standards that its own postwar leaders have set for it.

That's why when the opportunity arose to establish a presence in Berlin, indeed on a site in the city center that was the prewar home of the Mosse family, prominent German Jews, we jumped at it. The American Jewish Committee office will open on February 9.

An office is not quite an embassy. (For one thing, it comes without diplomatic parking privileges!) But it does reflect the maturing of the American Jewish community and a narrowing of the gap, however belatedly, that President Herzog rightly identified to us three years ago.

Remarks on the Occasion of the Opening of the AJC Berlin Office
Berlin, Germany
February 8, 1998

Foreign Minister Kinkel, distinguished guests, ladies and gentlemen. This is a happy moment, a very happy moment indeed.

It culminates for us nearly four years of planning and anticipation of an American Jewish Committee presence here in Berlin.

Indeed, it was in March 1994 that a member of our national Board of Governors, David Squire of Boston, first called and asked, to my surprise, whether we would be interested in establishing an office in Berlin. Our spontaneous reaction was an enthusiastic yes. And here a story begins.

Prior to the war a distinguished Jewish family, the Mosse family, worked in the publishing business in Berlin. Their lovely home, the Mosse Palais, which was subsequently destroyed, was located on Leipziger Platz.

When property restitution became possible just a few years ago, the surviving members of the Mosse family, and their descendants, regained the piece of land on which their home had stood and subsequently sold it to the well-known German developer, Hans Roëder.

The Mosse family was represented by Professor George Mosse, a native of Berlin, who arrived in the United States in 1939 at the age of twenty-one and later became a world-famous historian, associated principally with the University of Wisconsin and the Hebrew University of Jerusalem. Regrettably, Professor Mosse could not be here this evening.

In April 1994, at a meeting in New York, Mr. Roëder told us that he was interested in building an office tower on the site, to carry the Mosse name. The Mosse family and he also agreed that it would be wonderfully appropriate and meaningful not just to restore the name to the site, but also to make possible a living Jewish presence there as well.

To complete the picture, Professor Mosse's nephew, Hans Strauch, just happened to be an architect, and a very good one at that, whose firm is based in Boston.

Hans Strauch's office had been in touch with our own David Squire to explore the interest of the American Jewish Committee in becoming that living Jewish presence in the Mosse Palais.

We were interested, to say the least. And we consulted with the Zentralrat, so ably led by our friend Ignatz Bubis, and they too shared our enthusiasm.

Four years later, a striking building, designed by Hans Strauch, the nephew of George Mosse, has been erected on a newly reemerging Leipziger Platz, and the American Jewish Committee has become the very first tenant of the Mosse Palais. Speaking of symbolism!

Now having an office is one thing, and a very important thing at that, but an office requires something more; it needs the gift of life. Again, we were fortunate.

Two of the most dedicated leaders of AJC, Lawrence and Lee Ramer of Los Angeles, supporters of many Jewish cultural and educational undertakings, stepped forward. Through their generosity and, I might add, vision, they made possible the creation of the Lawrence and Lee Ramer Center for the Advancement of German–Jewish Relations, headquartered right here in Berlin.

Goethe wrote in 1832, the year of his death: *Die Tat ist alles, nicht der Ruhm* ("The deed is all, and not the glory").

I would like to introduce to all of you this lovely couple, for whom *die Tat*, the deed, of helping in the writing of a new and brighter era in

German-Jewish relations is indeed *alles*, all. Larry and Lee, would you please stand up.

And then came another remarkable AJC leader, with deep roots in this country, who wanted to participate in the revitalization of Jewish life here and who especially wanted to return Jewish books and learning to Germany.

As many of you know, Heinrich Heine once said: *Dort, wo man Bucher verbrennt, verbrennt man am Ende auch Menschen* ("Wherever books are burned, men also, in the end, are burned"). We are of course reminded of these words by the stark and poignant monument to book burning just a few blocks from this hotel, in Bebel Platz.

Dottie Bennett, of Falls Church, Virginia, believes, and we entirely agree, that where there is a reverence for books and for learning, there is at least a chance to assure the victory of civilization in the best sense of the word, though the history of this century painfully reminds us that there can be no guarantee.

Through her generosity, we have established the Dr. Hans Adler Library and Conference Center in our new offices. The library and conference center are named in memory of Dottie's beloved father and as a living memorial to her faith, our faith, in the power of learning, that is, the library, and the power of dialogue, that is, the conference center. Dottie, would you please stand up.

And one other leader of the American Jewish Committee has also come forward to strengthen our presence here by naming an executive office in memory of his late and dear mother, Mitzi Spiegel.

Daniel Spiegel, of Minneapolis, Minnesota, participated in an AJC mission to Germany jointly sponsored with the Konrad-Adenauer-Stiftung, our longest-term partner in Germany. So inspired was he by what he saw during that trip that he wanted to help our efforts as well. Dan, would you please stand up.

This evening, then, is the culmination of four years' commitment.

But it is even more. It is also the culmination of nearly fifty years' commitment.

It was shortly after the establishment of the Federal Republic in 1949 that the American Jewish Committee made a courageous and lonely decision to explore, against the backdrop of the unprecedented and unparalleled crimes of the Third Reich, the possibilities for reengaging Germany by participating in the building of democracy and the rule of law here, and, over time, by initiating an often immensely difficult and painful conversation between Germans and Jews.

With each passing year, this contact has widened and deepened. As such, it has allowed us to understand better the remarkable changes at hand here in these past fifty years and the overriding importance of strengthening the ties that have, in a strange and unexpected historical twist of irony, now joined Germans and Jews at the hip for all time.

And if this evening is the culmination of four years' work, and even of fifty years' work, it is something still more for some of us.

Sixty-five years ago, a thirteen-year-old boy named Eric and his parents, Michael and Rela, lived in the Wilmersdorf district of Berlin. Eric attended the Fichte Gymnasium and, in his spare time, loved to build radios and had a passion for *lakritzen*, black licorice to the Americans. His father was the editor in chief of *Der Lokal Anzeiger*, a Berlin newspaper. The family's world was shattered in 1933 when Hitler came to power.

Thereafter began a harrowing twelve-year odyssey that took each of them, on separate paths, across many countries, indeed several continents. It was only a few years after the war's end that they again found one another and established a family life in the United States.

Eric is my father. His parents of course were my grandparents. Just before coming to Berlin, I called him at his home north of San Francisco. I asked him what he thought of our opening an office in Berlin.

To my surprise, this child refugee, first from Berlin, later from Vienna; this three-year inmate of a Vichy camp in southern Algeria; this veteran of the French Foreign Legion, the British army, and OSS, the American wartime espionage unit, said, and I quote: "Opening such an office is a step in the right direction because we are now, increasingly, living in one world. It's time to remove barriers."

Ladies and gentlemen, it is written in Ecclesiastes, "To every thing there is a season, and a time to every purpose under heaven. A time to plant, and a time to pluck up that which is planted."

Beginning sixty-five years ago, that which was planted here in this soil, right here in this city and throughout Germany—a vibrant and pulsating Jewish community—was cruelly plucked up and destroyed, as was so much more.

Yet in the years after the war, however unexpected, however controversial, we began to see the first tentative signs of a reemerging Jewish presence in Germany. Astonishingly, this presence has picked up steam to the point today where Germany now has the fastest growing Jewish community outside our beloved Israel.

Today, then, is the season for the son of that thirteen-year-old Berlin schoolboy from Wilmersdorf to join in the planting in this soil. By doing so, we are seeking to participate, no longer from a distance, in the dynamic development of Jewish life and German–Jewish relations in a democratic Germany.

Yes, there is a time to every purpose, and for us in the case of Germany that time is now.

Thank you.

From here on in, our chief planter, so to speak, will be the managing director of our Berlin office, a cherished friend and respected colleague who has been a senior professional at the American Jewish Committee for three decades and a true pioneer in our German–Jewish programming. Many of you, I believe, already know him well.

It is my great pleasure to introduce to you Herr Eugene DuBow. He likes the inclusion of *Herr*, he says, because it reminds him of the time when he had a full head of hair!

One Step Forward, One Step Back
Gazeta Wyborcza (Poland)
May 15, 1998

As we walked toward the entrance to Auschwitz to participate in this year's March of the Living, we passed a group of teenagers sitting on a step in front of an apartment building. Several of the building's windows had Catholic religious pictures facing out, identical to others we saw in some Oswiecim windows, presumably for the benefit of the

March participants. One youth pointed at us, muttered something to his buddies and they broke out in derisive laughter.

For a moment, I thought of going over to the group. I even had the delusional idea that I could persuade them on the spot how grossly insensitive they were. Perhaps then they'd drop the laughter and miraculously start waving to other marchers in friendly greeting. But would I successfully communicate absent workable Polish? Would I instead invite violence? Would I distract our own group from the solemnity of this day?

In the end, we walked on without saying a word, shaken by the incident, especially the sixteen-year-olds in our group who simply couldn't understand such behavior.

As we neared the entrance to the State Museum, a busload of March participants passed by, heading for the same destination. Another group of local teens was on the sidewalk, when one made an obscene gesture at the bus.

Again, our shock; again, though, our silence. The same reasons, I suppose.

The next day, we were visiting the beautiful center of Cracow, awestruck by the magnificence of the city. Seeing a kielbasa stand, we approached, wanting to see how this national dish was prepared and served. No sooner did we get close than one young man standing in line looked in our direction, turned to his friends and, just loud enough for us to hear, contemptuously referred to the Jews who were seemingly invading the city. Knowing Russian helped me understand what he said. The Polish man and his friends quickly moved away from us without another word.

Altogether, we were in Poland four days. These unpleasant incidents may well have been the first three of their kind in the lives of our youngsters.

It's sad, really. We had come to Poland in friendship. In preparing the youngsters in our American Jewish Committee group for the visit, we went to considerable lengths to explain both Polish history and contemporary reality. We described Poland's glorious moments, its cultural achievements, the welcome accorded Jews in Poland hundreds of years ago, and the country's cruel treatment at the hands of larger and more aggressive neighbors. We also explained the opportunity today to begin a promising new period in Polish–Jewish relations, thanks to the overthrow of communism and the advent of democracy.

I even shared with our youngsters my testimony before the U. S. Senate endorsing NATO expansion, explaining why it was so important to understand the opportunities presented by the accession to NATO of Poland, Hungary, and the Czech Republic.

They embraced it all. They arrived in Poland open-minded and thirsty for additional information. And despite the incidents, they left Poland captivated by much of what they saw and eager to learn more.

But youngsters are youngsters. They are impressionable. In their short and often sheltered lives, even a small event takes on great significance, however untypical it may be. Now we'll need to work still harder to help them understand that these three moments were the sad product of ignorance, intolerance, and sheer stupidity, but do not necessarily represent a nation.

Even now as I sit in my office in New York, our children's questions still ring in my ears: Why would those Polish teens laugh at us? Why would they make obscene gestures? What did we do to them? Have they learned nothing of the meaning of Auschwitz and Birkenau, despite the camps' proximity? Could they not understand the simple desire to mourn our exterminated brethren and to affirm our own determination to live? And why the religious pictures in the windows? Is there some kind of holy war going on? Why not welcome signs in the windows instead?

Good questions all, without easy answers. But we'll be back next year. My eighteen-year-old was jealous of his younger brother who went, and asked if I would take him. Of course, I said, along with another group.

This year ahead will give me a chance to consider answers to questions that may or may not be raised next April. But maybe, by then, the parents of those young people whom we encountered in Oswiecim and Cracow will give some thought to what their own children are learning. And with any luck, our respective children will one day meet, not through an obscene gesture but rather, perhaps, because of a smile.

Jews in Poland
International Herald Tribune
August 13, 1998

Regarding "Poland Still Has a Way to Go in Ending Anti-Semitism" (Opinion, Aug. 8) by Abraham Brumberg:

Mr. Brumberg's article refers, inter alia, to the problem of Polish textbooks.

The American Jewish Committee launched a major study this year to examine the treatment of Jewish themes in the textbooks of post-communist societies. Our study on Poland, which looked at more than forty history textbooks used in the national school system, was just released in both Polish and English.

The principal findings include:

- Despite the significant role played by Jews in Polish history—they constituted 10 percent of the country's population until 1939 and more than a third in such major cities as Warsaw—the Jewish experience is given scant attention. Indeed, the multiethnic and multicultural history of Polish society is largely ignored.

- While World War II appropriately is a focal point in the textbooks, the Holocaust is usually discussed as a step in the Nazi extermination of the Polish people and not as a separate phenomenon. Moreover, the centrality of anti-Semitism in Nazi ideology is sometimes missing in the textbooks.

- Virtually without exception, the textbooks fail to address the postwar fate of Jews in Poland.

American Jews and U.S. Foreign Policy[*]
Lectures in Berlin, Bonn, and Trier, Germany
January 1999

It is a great pleasure and privilege for me to be here this evening representing the American Jewish Committee before such a distinguished audience.

*Reprinted in *American Jews Today*, a book, in German and English, jointly published by the Emil Frank Institute of the University of Trier (Germany) and the American Jewish Committee Berlin Office, 1999.

Permit me at the very outset to acknowledge the presence of my colleague, Eugene DuBow, the American Jewish Committee's director of our Berlin office. It is he who conceptualized this lecture program and invited me as the third and final speaker in our initial series this year.

Humor, I realize from many years of cross-cultural experience, can be a difficult element to export, especially with the need for translation. Still, let me try two stories because it's an American habit, I suppose, to begin a speech with a joke or two, and, more importantly, because they have implications for my talk this evening.

The first story. A university professor was eager to do a comparative experiment on how individuals of different nationalities would handle a year of complete solitude on a desert island. A Frenchman and a Jew were selected. The year passed and the professor went to the two islands to see how each individual had coped. On the island with the Frenchman, he found three new buildings. "What are these?" he asked. The Frenchman explained: "One is my home, the second will be for my wife when she joins me, and the third will be for my mistress." Then the professor went to the island with the Jew. Again, he found three buildings. "What are these?" The Jew replied: "The first is my home, the second is the synagogue where I pray, and the third is the synagogue where I refuse to enter."

The second story. The United Nations declared the "year of the elephant" and encouraged member countries to sponsor research on some aspect of the elephant. The Danes did a study entitled "100 Ways to Use the Elephant in the Making of Open-faced Sandwiches." The Italians focused on whether elephants could be trained to sing arias from Verdi's operas. And Israel's research was on the topic of "Elephants and the Jewish Question."

Why do I recount these stories? In the first instance because it illustrates how difficult it can be to generalize about Jews. You know—one Jew, two synagogues; two Jews, three opinions; three Jews, four organizations. And in the second instance, because Jews, for understandable historical reasons, have always searched for the Jewish angle, the Jewish stake, the Jewish implication in any issue that arises. "Is it good for the Jews?" is the quintessential, age-old Jewish question. Even, it seems, when it comes to elephants.

And that represents, perhaps, as appropriate an introduction as any to the topic of our session this evening—American Jews and U.S. foreign policy.

The American Jewish community numbers nearly 6 million. Among the many defining characteristics of American Jews, when compared with other American ethnic and religious groups, is a disproportionate interest in foreign policy matters, support for international institutions, and extensive overseas travel. This interest certainly carries over to American Jewish organizations, which have been very deeply involved in international affairs. I'd like to explain why.

The American Jewish Committee—my organization—was founded in the year 1906 as a response to pogroms that had been taking place in czarist Russia. A prominent group of American Jews—largely of German origin, I might add, with such surnames as Adler, Friedenwald, Rosenwald, Schiff, Straus, and Sulzberger—came together to help defend vulnerable Jewish communities in places like Kishinev, where Jews lived without even a modicum of protection and entirely at the whim of the authorities. If it served the interests of local or national officials or, for that matter, the church, Jews became the convenient target—of violence, pillage, murder—as had been the case for centuries.

These American Jewish leaders hoped to influence the U.S. government, as well as international public opinion, to send a new message—that countries like Russia could no longer simply declare open hunting season on their Jews, and do so with impunity.

Over the ninety-three years of our existence, we have came to understand that to assist Jewish communities, whether in Kishinev, Kiev, or Kaunas, we must be prepared to speak out unhesitatingly and to act accordingly. After all, if not us, who? And in doing so, we have gradually discarded the fears that often prevented our acting sooner—the fear of unleashing still more anti-Semitism, the fear of further isolating ourselves, the fear of drawing too much attention to ourselves when some Jews would prefer a low, or even invisible, profile.

But we've also come to understand that we simultaneously need to be working for something still larger than our immediate security. Ultimately, the best guarantee for Jews—and for all groups—is the creation of societies in which the fundamental principles of democracy, the rule of law, civil rights, and human dignity are respected for everyone.

Only in such societies can Jews and other minorities not only survive or be tolerated—necessary but insufficient conditions—but achieve something far more precious—equal participation, equal status in the common enterprise.

For the past nine decades, then, we have been working along these two parallel tracks.

On the one hand, we have tirelessly addressed specific Jewish concerns around the world, especially regarding Jews at risk and, since its establishment in 1948, Israel's unrelenting quest for peace, security, and a rightful place in the family of nations.

On the other hand, we were deeply involved in the successful effort to include human rights protections in the UN Charter. Indeed, historians have documented the indispensable role played by AJC leaders at the founding conference in San Francisco to achieve these worthy aims. So, too, with our role in the adoption of the Universal Declaration of Human Rights, whose fiftieth anniversary we marked last year, and the Genocide Convention. And we remain active to this day in the sphere of human rights; in fact, at AJC we have a unique institute dedicated entirely to the subject and most of its highly praised work focuses on the extension of broad human rights guarantees and on human rights education for all.

Moving ahead, there's often been discussion in the European media of the "Jewish lobby" in Washington. Please remember that the United States Constitution invites its citizens to "petition the government." As a result, in our country citizens are deeply involved in discussions on public policy, including foreign affairs. This is by no means limited to American Jews.

Look at the role played by Greek Americans on matters related to Greece, Cyprus, and Turkey. Want to measure their influence? Just ask Turkish officials in Ankara. They will tell you that this lobby is far more potent on the American scene than they might wish.

Or Polish Americans on all matters related to Poland, including, most recently, NATO expansion.

Or Irish Americans, overwhelmingly Catholic, and their impact over the years on American policy toward Northern Ireland.

Or Armenian Americans regarding foreign aid for Armenia and legislative restrictions on U.S. assistance to Azerbaijan, with which Armenia is locked in conflict over Nagorno-Karabakh.

Or Cuban Americans, who have quite a say on U.S. policy toward Cuba, a matter of particular consternation to the European Union, as evidenced by the recent contretemps over the Helms-Burton bill.

Or, increasingly, African Americans who have sought to focus greater U.S. attention on often neglected black Africa and have also pressed for liberalized U.S. entry rules for Haitians fleeing the endemic poverty of that nation.

This is quite different from most European models with which I am familiar. In Europe, foreign policy decisions have traditionally been driven almost exclusively by the top political and economic echelons, whereas in the United States it is frequently, though certainly not always, more heavily influenced by ethnic, religious, and other interest groups and other so-called lobbies, including of course, as in Europe, the corporate sector.

May I be permitted an additional note here? It would not surprise me if European countries, becoming ever more heterogeneous, moved in the direction of the American model. With sizable Turkish and Kurdish minorities in Germany, for instance, the years ahead may witness their increasingly organized attempts to shape German foreign policy on those issues of particular concern to them.

For us American Jews, though, our energetic involvement in U.S. foreign policy formulation is not simply explained by American cultural norms or even our general internationalist orientation. Rather, it derives to a considerable degree from the ongoing impact of the Holocaust—and its harsh historical lessons—on American Jewish consciousness.

On November 9 and 10, 1938, as you know so well, *Kristallnacht*—"the night of broken glass"—erupted throughout Germany. Hitler had only been waiting to unleash the violence. The pretext, if one were needed, came on November 7 when a German diplomat in Paris was shot by a young Hanover-born Jew, Herschel Grynszpan, who was profoundly upset by the harsh treatment his parents had received at the hands of the Nazis. The diplomat died two days later and the pogroms began at once.

As the *New York Times* reporter on the scene wrote in the paper's November 11 edition: "A wave of destruction, looting and incendiarism unparalleled in German history since the Thirty Years War, and in Europe generally since the Bolshevist revolution, swept over Great Germany today. . . . Beginning systematically in the early morning hours in almost every town and city in the country, the wrecking, looting and burning continued all day. Huge but mostly silent crowds looked on and the police confined themselves to regulating traffic and making wholesale arrests of Jews 'for their own protection.'"

Scores of Jews were killed, thousands were arrested, hundreds of Jewish-owned-businesses were destroyed and thousands looted, and dozens of synagogues were torched.

I do not need to tell this audience what subsequently took place. During the years of unprecedented genocide that ensued, though, the American Jewish community found itself entirely powerless to affect the course of events.

Consequently, to this day within the Jewish community, almost fifty-four years after the war's end, we continue to be haunted by the nightmarish events of the Holocaust. At the same time, we agonize over whether there was something more we might have done to influence our government to bomb even one rail line—just one rail line on the way to Auschwitz-Birkenau, one rail line on the way to Buchenwald or Treblinka, one rail line on the way to Dachau or Sobibor—to stop, or at least delay, even one transport of Jews to the camps. Alas, as is now well known, Allied bombers targeted Nazi synthetic oil factories within just a few kilometers of the Auschwitz extermination complex—yes, just a few kilometers—but never once the rail lines transporting Europe's Jews to their tragic fate.

How could this be so? What was going on in those camps was known to Allied authorities quite early on. The evidence for this is overwhelming and amply documented in a number of books, including

Arthur Morse's *While Six Million Died: A Chronicle of American Apathy* and David Wyman's *The Abandonment of the Jews: America and the Holocaust, 1941–1945.*

Why did the United States not act? Why could America's Jews—or others of good conscience—not prevail on our government? To what degree was it a function of the hostility toward Jews of top-level officials like Secretary of State Cordell Hull—whose place in history was established on April 3, 1933, when he said in *Time* magazine (just ten days after the Reichstag granted Hitler unlimited power): "Mistreatment of Jews in Germany may be considered virtually eliminated."

To be sure, President Roosevelt at the time argued forcefully that the Allied forces should not deviate, not for a single moment, from their central mission of destroying the Nazi military machine and thus bringing the war to the earliest possible end. That was the Allies' overriding aim and it was, he asserted, in the best interests of the Jews as well.

Yet, despite our profound admiration and esteem for President Roosevelt, we cannot help but wonder whether something more might have been done to prevent at least some deaths.

Thus, to understand the American Jewish community in the past half century, this one key point is central—during the Second World War we felt ourselves utterly ineffective as a political factor in the United States in the face of the worst catastrophe ever to befall the Jewish people.

Whatever our educational attainments, whatever our socioeconomic status, we were completely marginalized in our ability to influence policy formulation and decision-making. In the years that followed, we set about trying to ensure that we would never again find ourselves in such a position. We've come a long way.

The sobering lessons of this period also help explain our unstinting commitment to the well-being of the State of Israel.

Israel has been in our prayers, our hopes, our dreams for nineteen hundred years, since the destruction of the Second Temple in 70 C.E. But in the wake of the Shoah (Holocaust), it became strikingly clear that a Jewish sovereign state was vital to Jewish survival in the most literal sense. The UN agreed when it voted, in November 1947, in favor of Resolution 181, the partition of Palestine into two states—one Jewish, the other Arab.

The Zionist movement, dominated by pragmatists, accepted the partition plan despite disappointment with the territorial division; the Arabs flatly rejected the plan. The rest, as they say, is history, though I cannot help but note that a number of Palestinians today nostalgically cite Resolution 181 as the legal basis for a permanent solution of the Arab-Israeli conflict, as if they could conveniently ignore their earlier repudiation of it and now claim this resolution as their own.

To us, American and world Jewry, the establishment of the Jewish state in our lifetimes has meant many things. First and foremost, though, it has meant, finally, a sovereign home and haven for Jews from around the world.

And I cannot help but ask myself, what if? What if, in the 1930s, there had been Israeli embassies and consulates in Europe? How many Jews might have been saved by Israeli legations prepared to open their doors wide to anxious Jews, to hunted Jews, to trapped Jews, while other legations slammed their doors shut or, at best, kept them only slightly ajar? How many Jews might have received precious travel papers when it was still possible to emigrate or to flee?

According to Under Secretary of State Stuart Eizenstat, under whose direction two important historical studies on the war have recently been issued, the United States only admitted some 21,000 Jewish refugees during this period. And Arthur Morse, the author of one of the books I mentioned a moment ago, wrote that "official statistics reveal that between 1933 and 1943 there were more than four hundred thousand unfilled places within the U.S. immigration quotas of countries under Nazi domination." Again, what if Israel had already existed in those years?

Israel for us, then, represents the best possible answer to centuries of inquisitions, blood libels, ghettos, pogroms, forced conversions, expulsions, immigration restrictions, pales of settlement, yellow stars, and, ultimately, the Nazi Final Solution.

We, as a community of nearly 6 million American Jews, are determined, through our active political involvement, to do our utmost to help ensure Israel's security and well-being. Fortunately, we are not alone. Support for Israel runs deep in the United States, as recent national surveys have strikingly revealed. This point is often overlooked in Europe, where there is a widespread belief that American support for Israel is solely a function of American Jewish activity and influence.

In point of fact, whether for reasons of identification with the Holy Land, support for Israel's status as the only—I repeat, only—democracy in the region, appreciation of Israel's reliability as an American strategic ally, or respect and admiration for tiny Israel's sheer determination to survive against all the odds in a rough-and-tumble neighborhood, we have been able to count on many friends—Republicans and Democrats, Catholics and Protestants, blacks and whites—who share our view of the importance of the U.S.-Israel partnership.

In a similar vein, recognizing, as we are taught in our tradition, that "all Jews are responsible one for the other," we continue to focus on the well-being of Jewish communities around the world, especially at moments like this when hundreds of thousands of Jews in Russia are again, sad to say, facing a resurgence of anti-Semitism, of scapegoating for the country's widespread and intractable political and economic travails.

As the French so aptly say: *Plus ça change, plus ça reste le même.* Ninety-three years ago, we were founded to assist imperiled Jewish communities in czarist Russia; ninety-three years later, we are still deeply concerned about vulnerable Jewish communities in the very same part of the world.

Moreover, as I suggested at the outset, we have come to understand the necessity of our involvement in broader issues of international affairs and foreign policy.

In a country where neoisolationist instincts periodically surface, the American Jewish community recognizes the importance of America's engagement with the world, and we do not hesitate to speak out and otherwise act on our beliefs.

We shudder at the notion that a substantial percentage of recently elected members of Congress reportedly have never owned a U.S. passport, reflecting a troubling parochialism. We worry that many of these same members of Congress speak no foreign language, have no experience with America's international security concerns, and may not appreciate the stark lessons of the seminal events of this bloodstained century.

We Jews are battle-scarred veterans of virtually every form of government known to man—not by choice, I assure you. That's precisely why democracy is so precious to us.

We are, by dint of our experience, students of history living in an era with precious little appreciation for the subject and, sometimes, an all-too-short and superficial attention span. We fully understand, to quote the philosopher Santayana, that those who fail to learn the lessons of history are condemned to repeat them.

Our experiences over the centuries have made us students of human nature in a world too often sidetracked by the glittery and salacious elements of a celebrity-driven culture. We understand all too well man's capacity for evil and the consequent need to face that evil, when it surfaces, with strength and resolve, not with denial or equivocation.

Yes, we have some grasp of the world's complexity, some understanding of the dangers lurking out there.

That's precisely why, in our view, America's international leadership role, in concert with our allies whenever possible, is absolutely vital. When America neglects or spurns its leadership role, as it did after the First World War, a truly dangerous vacuum is created.

If not for America, who would lead the struggle to check the aggressive instincts of the world's rogue states bent on acquiring weapons of mass destruction and the means to deliver them?

Who would have the power and the credibility to press for solutions to long-simmering conflicts, whether in the Middle East, Northern Ireland, or the Balkans?

Who would be prepared to act not only with high-minded declarations but, more importantly, with a commitment of resources and national will to match policy with principle?

The lessons of the last fifty years, indeed even of the last five or ten years, remind us of America's special role—here in Germany as elsewhere.

The American Jewish community has been a driving force in encouraging an internationally involved America—an America that works with our allies, Germany among them, to strengthen and solidify the precious family of democratic nations—an America that stands up to the likes of nuclear-aspiring North Korea, Iran, and Iraq and is engaged foursquare in attempting to thwart international terrorists from achieving their nefarious aims, while, regrettably, some other leading nations would more readily acquiesce to these nations and terrorist groups in the name of commercial interests or shortsighted appeasement.

One last word about America and American Jews. True, as I said, many American Jews were deeply disappointed by the U.S. response to European Jewry's tragic fate, and also recognized that the virus of anti-Semitism—to be sure, far less virulent than the European strain—was alive in our country until well into this century. The fact remains, however, that American Jews talk about our country with a sense of awe. This awe doesn't translate into blind faith or the suspension of critical judgment, but it does bespeak an American Jewish love affair, if you will, with our country.

America has been good to the Jews, very good, especially as the last barriers to full Jewish participation in American life were removed in the 1960s and early 1970s.

America has given Jews opportunities unmatched in the two thousand years of our Diaspora experience. The American democratic, pluralistic experiment has allowed Jews to believe with good reason that our country belongs to us every bit as much as to our fellow Americans. In theory at least, and increasingly in practice, there is no inherent hierarchy among America's citizens.

I must hasten to add that the Jews have also been good to—and for—America. Jews have demonstrated our reverential feelings for America by a remarkably full and creative participation in virtually every aspect of civic life and public affairs, in every profession imaginable, in every conceivable philanthropic and charitable endeavor.

We have enthusiastically embraced America, American democracy, American concepts of pluralism, America's founding documents, and the American invitation, enshrined on the Statue of Liberty, to "breathe free."

Permit me a personal word. My wife was born in an Arab country, Libya, which forced its last Jews to leave in the days just after the 1967 Six-Day War, at least those who weren't killed in the pogroms. Parenthetically, the drama of the exodus of hundreds of thousands of Jewish refugees from Arab countries has inexplicably never captured the attention, much less the conscience, of the UN, human rights groups, or even the leading democratic nations, in stark contrast to the Palestinian experience.

From Libya, my wife, her seven siblings, and their parents fled to a European country where Jews have lived for some 2000 years. They were allowed to stay, though it took more than twenty years to acquire citizenship. And yet to this day the members of that European Jewish community—and not just the relative newcomers like my wife's family—continue to feel more like tolerated outsiders than full and equal members of society. That's a very far cry from the American model.

Indeed, I can still recall my wife's initial surprise when she first came to the United States, in 1979, and saw how openly and proudly American Jews affirm the duality of our identities—as Americans and Jews—in fact seeing no contradiction, no tension, between the two. To the contrary, many American Jews, myself included, firmly believe that these two essential elements of our being are mutually nourishing, mutually reinforcing. Being a Jew, I am convinced, has made me a better American; being an American has made me a better Jew.

I cannot end this speech, here in Germany, without at least a few words about German–Jewish relations, though I am mindful of the admonition that "a speech to be immortal need not be eternal."

The American Jewish Committee, unlike other international Jewish organizations, understood early on the importance of engaging the new Federal Republic of Germany shortly after its establishment fifty years ago. It wasn't an easy decision, believe me.

Most Jews understandably wanted nothing to do with Germany, new or old, except for the talks, themselves not without controversy, on restitution and indemnification—what you call *Wiedergutmachung*—culminating in the Luxembourg Reparations Agreement signed in September 1952.

But AJC's leadership, itself deeply involved in those talks, also understood correctly that history can't be frozen in time or place. Germany would move forward with us or without us, and the country was simply too consequential, as history had amply shown, to be ignored. We therefore wanted to be involved in seeking to shape its future orientation.

And so we decided to probe the new Germany, looking for opportunities to participate in the epochal effort to transform Germany through democracy and political education. Over time, we began seeking partners on the German–Jewish theme, hoping to launch the process of writing a new chapter in German–Jewish relations against the backdrop of the painful past. Again, it wasn't easy, and initially there weren't too many eager German partners either, it must be said.

Since that time, however, we've come a long way. We have created valued relationships in the national and state governments, the political foundations, the Catholic and Evangelical churches, the intelligentsia, the Bundeswehr, and the media.

This growing familiarization with and gradually increasing confidence in the Federal Republic led to our decision—unique among international Jewish organizations—to support German unification in 1990; and, most recently, it prompted our opening an office in the new Mosse Palais, housing our pioneering Lawrence and Lee Ramer Center on German–Jewish Relations and the Hans Adler Library, on the soon-to-be-restored Leipziger Platz.

We at the American Jewish Committee recognize the remarkable strides Germany has achieved in these past fifty years in creating a stable, democratic society. And over these past five decades, Germany as a nation, to its credit, has largely sought to come to grips with its past.

This stands in sharp contrast, for example, to Austria, which essentially hid behind the description of "victim" state—a status first incorporated into the Moscow Declaration of the Allied Powers in November 1943—until Chancellor Franz Vranitsky finally acknowledged Austria's extensive role in the Holocaust in two important speeches—in 1991 to the Austrian parliament and, two years later, at Jerusalem's Hebrew University.

Germany has become a responsible international citizen, whose close ties with the United States, active participation in NATO, support for European integration, and growing role in peacekeeping and humanitarian operations underscore its outlook. It is particularly worth noting Germany's special ties with Israel, which have made it Israel's closest friend in Europe—a fact widely recognized in Israel but, unfortunately, much less so among American Jews.

Yet we know that, this record notwithstanding, it is nonetheless impossible to close the chapter on the Holocaust—the single worst crime in recorded history—as those here who plaintively say "enough already" might wish, or who go still further and coin such offensive phrases as "the instrumentalization of Auschwitz," suggesting that Auschwitz has now become a Jewish "moral bludgeon" to be used against Germans for all time.

This chapter cannot be closed. Its shadow remains too long, its wounds too deep, its trauma too great, its legacy—6 million exterminated Jews, including 1.5 million children, and the virtual destruction of European Jewish civilization—even today too overpowering, too shattering, too incomprehensible. The Holocaust will undoubtedly remain a central element in the conscience and identity of Jews; it will, I trust, remain a central element in the conscience and identity of Germans and Germany.

Ironically, perhaps, in a strange twist of history, we—Germans and Jews—have been joined at the hip, perhaps permanently, by the Shoah. Together we become *the* repositories for the world's knowledge of this horrific twelve-year period. It is your youth and ours who will continue to learn the history in schools and homes, and it is precisely we who will continue to be haunted by the implications of the truly unimaginable.

But we will be joined at the hip not only by the horrors of the crimes perpetrated against the Jewish people during the Third Reich but also, I would like to believe, increasingly by a common vision of the future.

Precisely because we both know so well the haunting vocabulary and topography of inhumanity—and the slippery slope that can lead even so-called civilized societies there—can we not together serve as an early warning radar system for a world too easily distracted, too self-preoccupied, too forgetful? Can we not together act to prevent future atrocities, wherever they might threaten to occur? Can we not together stand tall for the values of democracy, human rights, and mutual understanding, and against the demonic forces of hate? Imagine, if you will, the potential impact, substantive and symbolic, of such German–Jewish collaboration!

And you here in Germany will have your own work cut out for you as well in the years and decades ahead, I believe. Let me cite just three challenges, if I may, and with that I shall close.

With the survivors, the liberators, and the Righteous Gentiles rapidly disappearing from our midst, these eyewitnesses tragically will soon be gone. Instead, we will be left with the films; the books; some preserved camp sites; the diaries; the videotaped accounts; the stories that have been passed on from one generation to another; and the museums and monuments—including, I would hope one day soon, a combination monument and museum in the center of Berlin.

Will Germany continue to incorporate this twelve-year period in its history into the national consciousness in ways that are powerful and meaningful, or will notions of responsibility—not guilt, responsibility—and remembrance grow increasingly stale and stilted with the passage of time, more formulaic perhaps than authentic?

Will Germany remain steadfast in its special relationship with Israel, especially as the process of European integration moves forward and includes ever greater coordination of foreign and security policy, thus potentially creating more frequent situations where Germany may have to choose between its links with Israel and its ties to its EU partners?

Will Germany be able to manage successfully its encounter with a growing Jewish community in its midst—the fastest growing Jewish community in the world, I might add? Idealizing exterminated Jews, or bemoaning the disappearance of German Jewry as it once was, is one thing, but living with an ever larger number of Jews—overwhelmingly from the ex-Soviet Union—who now call Germany their home may be another. This raises the twin challenges both of Germany's relations to Jews and also of an increasingly multicultural Germany.

Ladies and gentlemen, I very much appreciate this opportunity to speak with you and now look forward to the question-and-answer period. From my many years of experience in meeting with German audiences, I know this can be the most interesting and provocative part of any such gathering. I'm sure this occasion will prove no exception.

Introduction of Dr. Bronislaw Geremek,
Foreign Minister of Poland
AJC 93rd Annual Meeting, Washington, D.C.
May 6, 1999

There is a famous Polish saying: *W mondroschi sila.* There is power in wisdom.

It is my privilege this evening to introduce an honored guest—and a friend—who is living testimony to these apt words. Bronislaw Geremek is the foreign minister of Poland, and I am delighted that he is with us for this gala dinner.

The American Jewish Committee has had many occasions to work with Minister Geremek over the years, both when he has served in public office and also during times when, quite frankly, he couldn't possibly have ever imagined getting near any public office, at least as an officeholder.

In fact, even today, ten years after the fall of communism, I still pinch myself, as I am sure he most certainly does, when realizing that members of that extraordinary community of protest in Eastern Europe—remarkably determined individuals like Vaclav Havel, Natan Shcharansky, and Bronislaw Geremek—are now among the leaders of their native or, in Shcharansky's case, adopted countries.

Ladies and gentlemen, Bronislaw Geremek was born into a Jewish family in Warsaw in 1932. His father was murdered in Auschwitz. He and his mother managed to escape Nazi terror through the help of a man who later became his stepfather, one of the Righteous Gentiles.

Incidentally, it is perhaps a little known fact that Yad Vashem, Israel's venerable Holocaust museum and memorial center, has honored more Poles than members of any other nationality as *hasidai umot ha'olam*, the Righteous of the Nations of the World.

And I am pleased to tell you that two of the leading figures of the valiant Polish resistance to the brutal Nazi occupation of that country—and to the implementation of the Nazi Final Solution in Poland, which took the lives of 3 million Polish Jews—were to be with us tonight. Our revered friend, Jan Karski, is here, but, sadly, Jan Nowak's wife, herself a leading figure in the wartime resistance movement, just passed away so he could not join us.

After the war, Minister Geremek resumed his studies leading to a doctorate in history. In 1968, a particularly anguished period in Polish postwar history, Minister Geremek became active in the Polish democratic opposition.

Later, he worked closely with Lech Walesa in the Solidarity Movement. Some have referred to Minister Geremek as the intellectual backbone of that courageous response to communist oppression.

He continued his work even after the group was outlawed, and was imprisoned as a result. If the aim, though, was to temper his brave struggle for political and social change, it failed abysmally. Minister Geremek continued his dissident activities after being released and right up to the dissolution of the Iron Curtain in 1989.

While we surely live in a world of unremitting hyperbole, it is no exaggeration, far from it, to call Minister Geremek one of the genuine heroes of the Polish democratic revolution.

Post-1989, Minister Geremek dedicated himself in earnest to the building of a new society, serving as a senator in the first parliament, later heading up the Democratic Union Party, and now serving as his country's foreign minister.

Minister Geremek, we at the American Jewish Committee and you have known each other for a very long time. We have collaborated on many joint initiatives, and we share so many of the same goals.

You and we welcome the return of a robust Polish democracy and a thriving free-market economy.

You and we welcome Poland's full integration into Western regional and multilateral structures, including, most recently, Poland's accession to NATO, a step we enthusiastically endorsed in our testimony before the U.S. Senate.

You and we support an outward looking Poland enjoying the closest possible bilateral ties with its European neighbors, the United States, and Israel.

And you and we support the full and unhindered participation of the Jewish community, as well as other ethnic and religious minorities, in the life of Poland.

In this spirit, you have forcefully spoken out more than once against any reversion to a narrow nationalism in Central and Eastern Europe, to the danger of a resurgent anti-Semitism, and to the potential risk in the region of reigniting ancient national hatreds, such as we now again see in the Balkans.

Minister Geremek, you know you are among friends.

You know that the American Jewish Committee launched a pioneering Polish–Jewish dialogue in this country two decades ago. Indeed, our honoree earlier today, George Szabad, has long been one of the most dedicated leaders of that effort, as has our honorary president, Maynard Wishner.

True, the dialogue hasn't always been easy, but it has created a genuinely promising framework for expanded Polish–Jewish cooperation.

You know of our long-standing efforts, led by Rabbi Jim Rudin, to foster closer ties between the Polish Catholic Church, a major force in Polish society, and the Jewish people through frequent meetings, conferences, and exchange programs.

And you know of our decision several years ago to establish an office in Warsaw, ably directed since its opening by Dr. Stanislaw Krajewski, to enhance still further Polish–Jewish ties.

In sum, you know of our desire to make a positive contribution to the state of Polish–Jewish relations.

Certainly, it is no secret that Polish–Jewish relations have been, and in some ways, continue to be complex.

The current controversy over the regrettable placement of Christian religious symbols at Auschwitz reminds us yet again of the sensitivity and potential volatility of certain issues, but here, too, there is room for optimism.

There are those in the Polish and Jewish communities determined to resolve this matter utilizing the growing mutual trust and friendship that has developed in recent years.

Among them are Miles Lerman and Ralph Grunewald of the U.S. Holocaust Memorial Museum and Jerzy Kozminski, Poland's ambassador to the United States, all here with us this evening.

Minister Geremek truly is a powerful force of goodwill in Poland—a man of dignity and distinction, of principle and perseverance, of statesmanship and scholarship.

Yes, that Polish saying just might have been coined with him in mind. *W mondroschi sila*. There is power in wisdom. With Dr. Geremek today serving as foreign minister, we can rest assured not only that wisdom is power, but also that the power of Poland is wise.

Minister Geremek, *serdecznie witamy*! Heartfelt greetings! We eagerly look forward to your remarks.

Introduction of Mario Tagarinski, Minister of Public Administration, Bulgaria AJC 93rd Annual Meeting, Washington, D.C. May 6, 1999

The original invitation for this dinner indicated the participation of Nadezhda Mihailova, Bulgaria's distinguished and widely admired foreign minister. Regrettably, Minister Mihailova had to cancel because of a crucial vote in the Bulgarian parliament, but we are delighted that her country is so ably represented here by the minister of public administration, Mario Tagarinski.

Permit me a few words about Minister Tagarinski.

An engineer by training, he has devoted himself tirelessly during the last decade to the welcome democratic revolution in Bulgaria, rising steadily through the ranks of the Union of Democratic Forces political alliance and applying his considerable technical expertise to improving the efficiency of the civil service and of management and information technologies. In 1997, following the UDF's victory in national elections, he was appointed to his current cabinet post.

Today is the first time that I have had the pleasure of meeting Minister Tagarinski, but your reputation precedes you, Minister. I welcome you, therefore, as a friend—a friend of the United States and of the Jewish people, and I want you to know that you are among friends.

Ladies and gentlemen, Bulgarian Jews are an old and proud community, most of whose members descend from Jews forced to leave Spain during the Inquisition and welcomed to what was then the Ottoman Empire. Incidentally, the legendary Nobel laureate Elias Canetti was born into this community.

When Nazi Germany pressured Bulgaria to deport the country's Jews to Nazi death camps in 1943, it found resistance. Forty-three members of the Bulgarian parliament drafted a petition against the deportations, and voices of protest could be heard in the church and in professional associations.

When another deportation was attempted during the last year and a half of the war, the Jewish community again found friends, friends who were willing to demonstrate in the streets to prevent the deportations of their Jewish neighbors—and who did this in spite of the country's military alliance with Nazi Germany. Strikingly, anti-Semitism has seldom found fertile ground in Bulgaria.

Bulgaria consistently refused to hand over its Jews to the German slaughter. In fact, of the 50,000 Jewish citizens living in the current borders of Bulgaria in 1943, few, if any, perished in the Nazi death camps.

At the same time, it must be said, Bulgaria's otherwise laudable record was blemished by the direct involvement of Bulgarian forces in the roundup and deportation of the Jews of Thrace, Macedonia, and eastern Serbia; and more recently, by bureaucratic delay in implementing the Bulgarian court's decision to restitute communal property dating from the wartime period—an issue that we hope will soon be successfully addressed.

After the war, many of Bulgaria's Jews, in fact almost 90 percent, emigrated to the newly created Jewish state, where they have played an important, if often unsung, role in the building of the new nation, while harboring strong sentimental attachments to the country of their birth. This close link is perhaps best embodied by Shulamit Shamir, the wife of the former Israeli prime minister and a Bulgarian native.

Bulgaria, today an anchor of regional stability in the otherwise unstable Balkans, is proving its friendship again. As you say in Bulgarian, *Priátel v nujda se poznáva.* "A friend in need is a friend indeed."

This time, it is the friendship with the United States and the NATO mission in Kosovo that is center stage. In spite of the terrible accident last week, not the first, when an errant NATO missile hit a house near the nation's capital, Sofia, Bulgaria has made its steadfast friendship clear.

Just two days ago, on Tuesday, the Bulgarian parliament voted to offer Bulgarian airspace for NATO operations against the murderous Serbian aggression in Kosovo. This is a clear demonstration of Bulgaria's strategic orientation toward NATO.

As Americans and as Jews, we look forward to growing ties between Bulgaria and the United States, between Bulgaria and Euro-Atlantic institutions, between Bulgaria and Israel, and not least, among the American Jewish Committee, Bulgaria, and its small but dynamic Jewish community of 5,000.

Speaking of the community, I would like to acknowledge the presence here this evening of five leading members of the Jewish community—Dr. Solomon Passy, Victor and Victoria Melamed, Solomon Bali, and Stefan Oscar.

I would also like to welcome my good friend Philip Dimitrov, Bulgaria's ambassador to the United States, and his wife Elena.

Minister Tagarinski, we are delighted that you traveled specially from Sofia to be with us this evening. The podium is yours.

4. THE HOLOCAUST

Due: Urgent Delivery from Damascus
International Herald Tribune
January 15, 1992

Fifty years ago, Alois Brunner was a rising star in the Nazi firmament. He was Adolf Eichmann's right-hand man, an expert on the deportation of Jews to concentration camps.

Today, Brunner is one of the world's most wanted criminals. Syria has harbored him for years. The Syrian government refused to host Foreign Minister Roland Dumas of France last month because he was coming with a joint French-German request for Brunner's extradition.

The Nazi-hunter Beate Klarsfeld, who has tracked Brunner for years, recently returned from Syria after a fruitless attempt to persuade authorities to hand him over. But the Syrians—who deny knowing anything about Brunner—have suddenly moved him out of 7, rue George Haddad, his long-time residence. Mrs. Klarsfeld believes Syria will never give Brunner up because he has learned too much in his role as adviser to the Syrian secret police.

After World War II, the UN War Crimes Commission indicted Brunner for crimes against humanity. Britain and France sentenced him to death. But though he was in custody, the Allies mixed him up with a man named Anton Brunner. Alois Brunner was able to flee, first to Egypt, then to Syria. A German magazine has reported that with the aid of the German embassy in Damascus, Brunner found work in Syria, under an assumed name, as an agent for a Dortmund brewery and a Bielefeld manufacturer.

When his identity became known, President Assad granted him personal bodyguards and a monthly stipend. In return, Brunner went to work for the Syrian secret service.

In this capacity, Brunner helped the Syrians plan an unsuccessful bomb attack on a Vienna session of the World Jewish Congress and an attempt, also unsuccessful, to rescue Eichmann from his Israeli captors, according to Mrs. Klarsfeld.

Brunner, an Austrian who joined the Nazi Party at age nineteen, was recruited by Eichmann in 1938 to work at the Central Office for Jewish Emigration in Vienna. Displaying a remarkable talent for organizing deportations, by 1941 he had shipped 50,000 Viennese Jews to concentration camps.

He was then charged with the liquidation of the Jewish communities of Thrace, Macedonia, and Salonika, Greece—for 450 years the center of Sephardic Jewish culture in Europe. He organized the transports to Auschwitz with ruthless efficiency: From March to July 1943, all but a handful of Salonika's 56,000 Jews disappeared.

In Salonika, Brunner demonstrated a particular streak of sadism. The mansion he lived in had a torture chamber in the basement, according to people who saw it. One witness tells how he "flogged his victims with a horsewhip made of thin leather thongs threaded with iron wire."

He was obsessed with deporting children and women of childbearing age. "Vermin," Brunner called them, adding, "they deserve to die."

Through promises, threats, and lies, Brunner lulled the Salonikan Jews into thinking they would not be harmed. "When I give my word to a dog," he told the German magazine *Bunte*, "I keep it—but not to a Jew."

In 1943, Brunner was made commander of the Drancy concentration camp, near Paris. From there, he sent 24,000 Jews to Auschwitz.

Even as it became clear, in late 1944 and early 1945, that Germany would lose the war, Brunner, since reassigned to Slovakia, continued fanatically to round up Jews and deport them to their deaths. He focused more and more on schools and orphanages so that no Jewish children might escape.

Brunner has remained unrepentant. In 1985, he told *Bunte*: "It was my job to get the Jews out. I have no remorse for getting rid of that rubbish."

Finally, the world may be closing in on him. Austria issued a warrant for his arrest six years ago. Germany sought his extradition last year. The German prosecutor has 500 eyewitness accounts of Brunner's crimes.

In July, Syrian authorities received a French warrant for Brunner's arrest. Most recently, France and Germany agreed to cooperate in securing extradition. Resolutions have been introduced in both houses of the U.S. Congress calling on President George Bush to persuade the Syrians to withdraw their protection, and the pending foreign aid bill conditions American aid to Syria partly on progress in the extradition of Brunner.

Syria denies there is any such person in the country. But Damascus has been seeking better relations with the West. Brunner could yet be brought to justice, but it must be done quickly. He is seventy-nine years old and reportedly ill. An unrelenting diplomatic effort by the United States and the European countries is needed—now.

We Must Not Give Aid to Holocaust Distorters
Newsday
June 15, 1992

A French appeals court in April decided that Paul Touvier, a French collaborator with the Nazis who was accused of executing Jews, could not be tried for crimes against humanity.

The decision was both surprising and disappointing; surprising because to many observers the facts appeared indisputable, disappointing because it underscored yet again France's inability to face squarely the role of the World War II Vichy regime in the deportation of 75,000 French Jews, only 3,000 of whom survived.

To date, the French judiciary has been reluctant to convict any Frenchman for wartime crimes against Jews. Thus, the Touvier decision can only please those who would deny or rewrite history.

As the war recedes in our memories, and as the veterans, survivors, and other witnesses to the horrors perpetrated by the Nazis and their helpers grow old and pass away, the task of understanding and learning its lessons becomes all the more compelling.

Why? Not simply so that those who fought and who perished did not do so in vain, but also because memory is the most effective safeguard against any possible recurrence, whether directed at Jews or at other vulnerable minorities.

In France today—and France is not unique in this respect—there are two deeply troubling, and mutually nourishing, phenomena at work. First, there is the disturbing resilience of the extreme right-wing National Front Party, led by its founder, Jean Marie Le Pen. Second is the persistence of a small but active group of pseudoscholars (in other countries as well) whose aim is to deny that the Holocaust ever took place.

Le Pen, whose party garnered 14 percent of the nationwide vote in municipal elections earlier this year and well over 20 percent in some localities (compared to 10 percent in similar elections in 1984), purveys a highly nationalistic, xenophobic, and racist message. He appeals to the basest instincts of voters who fear that alien hordes are taking control of France's culture and destiny.

Submerged within this simplistic and dangerous worldview is a barely concealed anti-Semitism that seeks to minimize the Holocaust. In September 1987, for example, Le Pen provoked a national storm by describing Hitler's gas chambers as "a point of detail in the history of the Second World War."

When a reporter questioned this characterization, Le Pen added: "Do you want to tell me that it is revealed truth that everybody must believe? That it is a moral obligation? I say there are historians who debate those questions."

Who exactly are these "historians"? No doubt, Le Pen had in mind people like Robert Faurisson, the author of *The Rumor of Auschwitz*, who declared on French radio in 1980: "Hitler's alleged gas chambers and the alleged genocide against the Jews are part of one and the same historical lie" (for which he was subsequently found guilty in a French court of racial defamation).

Or Bernard Notin, an instructor at Lyon University, who placed an article denying the existence of Nazi gas chambers in a magazine sponsored by the influential French National Scientific Research Center. And, regrettably, these two are not alone.

The extreme right wing, whether in France or elsewhere, is still anathema to many voters who might otherwise be sympathetic to its current message, if it were not associated with the horrors perpetrated in the name of fascism earlier in this century. Accordingly, any inroads by Faurisson, Notin, and other Holocaust revisionists who downplay or deny these horrors can only help the extreme rightists.

After all, if the gas chambers did not exist and Jews were not exterminated, then perhaps the fascists really were not that bad, seeking "only" ethnic purity, law and order, and the restoration of national pride—goals that, on the surface, appeal to many in an increasingly turbulent Europe buffeted by recession, unemployment, and a relentless influx of refugees and economic migrants. Obviously, Le Pen and the National Front would hope to broaden their appeal if the Holocaust revisionists and deniers gained legitimacy. And so would their ideological soul mates in other countries—the National Front in Britain, the Republican Party in Germany, the Freedom Party in Austria, and the neofascist movement in Italy.

By dropping the Touvier case, the French courts denied an opportunity to do justice, to examine the Vichy period thoroughly, and to educate the French public. Even worse, the court decision played into the hands of the extremist forces in France, which invoke highly nationalistic themes, and now have more room to maneuver as they seek to shed the albatross of the crimes of the war era perpetrated by their ideological forebears.

This battle over memory and historical integrity is one with incalculably high stakes. It is being played out today with intensity not only in France but also in Austria, Croatia, Germany, the Baltic states, Slovakia, and Romania. In Slovakia, for instance, Father Joseph Tiso, the head of the Nazi-backed puppet regime during the war, has been posthumously rehabilitated. In Romania, the parliament acted similarly with another wartime collaborator, Marshal Antonescu, viewing him as a defender of Romanian nationalism.

Fortunately, there are many voices of courage and decency in these countries. French president François Mitterrand quickly condemned the Touvier decision, just as he has criticized manifestations of anti-Semitism and racism. Austrian chancellor Franz Vranitsky has called on his countrymen to stop burying their heads in the sand and to recognize Austrian complicity in the Nazi era. And Czechoslovak president Vaclav Havel, recently addressing an international conference in Prague on anti-Semitism that was convened by the American Jewish

Committee and the Kafka Center, spoke of the past as prologue: "The other day I heard about an inscription on the door of a pub . . . it says something to the effect that persons of Gypsy origin are not wanted there. . . . It is not only that one should mention the impermissibility of such behavior, which, by the way, strongly resembles anti-Jewish notices during the Nazi rule. What I want to do as well is to remind people of the fertile soil from which grew the Holocaust. I want to turn their attention to those thousands of 'anonymous and nonlethal anti-Semites' who helped to send their fellow citizens to the gas chambers."

A great deal about both the past and the future hangs on the outcome of the ongoing debates over historical accuracy, justice, and memory. The French decision in the Touvier case was a step in the wrong direction.

Croatian Anti-Semitism
The New York Times
January 10, 1993

Your December 18 article about President Franjo Tudjman of Croatia speaks of his efforts to foster nationalism in his people to justify annexation of Bosnian territory. Mr. Tudjman has also expressed blatantly anti-Semitic views and tried to whitewash the Nazi puppet state of Croatia, which participated eagerly in Hitler's policy of killing Jews.

Croatian Jews, Mr. Tudjman wrote in his book *Wastelands: Historical Truth* (1988), used their supposed traits of "selfishness, craftiness, unreliability, miserliness, underhandedness and secrecy" to gain control of the Jasenovac concentration camp (where tens of thousands of Yugoslav Jews and others perished) and victimize others. Jews, he alleged, are commanded to "exterminate others and take their place" because they consider themselves the chosen people. Israeli policy toward the Arabs, according to him, makes them nothing less than "Judeo-Nazis."

President Tudjman asserts that the bloodthirsty Ustashe regime that ruled Croatia and exterminated its Jews a half century ago "reflected the centuries-old aspirations of the Croat people." This does not bode well for a new, enlarged Croatian state.

Presentation of AJC's American Liberties Medallion to Jan Karski
87th Annual Dinner, Washington, D.C.
May 6, 1993

Listen, please listen to their own voices, to their pain, to their anguish.

"A coat of snow shines and twinkles in the light of the matchless, golden Polish fall. That snow is nothing other than the down feathers of Jewish bedding left along with all their goods—chests, trunks, suitcases full of clothing, pots, pans, plates—by the 300,000 Jews deported eastward. Abandoned goods: tablecloths, coats, blankets, sweaters, books, cradles, documents, pictures, all that is lying in disorder in the apartments, in squares, in piles covered by that 'snow' of the period of the German mass murder of Jews.

"The ghastly silence is cut by revolver shots, the rattle of machine guns, the clamor of doors broken in and the shattering of furniture, the hoarse cries *'Alle juden raus'* ('all Jews out'), the macabre march of Jewish victims sentenced to death, under the watch of SS officers. Households dead or dying, streets full of barbed-wire entanglements, and, above all, the complete absence of the throngs who two months ago still crowded the main streets of the ghetto. Complete emptiness. *This* is the picture of the Warsaw ghetto in September 1942.

"A human form sneaking stealthily along the walls, the curb splattered with blood, the sharp odor of burning, *this* is the atmosphere of that city of death where, before the fearful 22nd of July, close to 370,000 Jews 'lived' in the shadow of sixteen kilometers of wall enclosing the ghetto."

Listen, listen to their own voices.

"I have no words with which to picture the life of the ghetto during those days. All of us looked upon ourselves as living corpses, as ghosts who no longer belonged to this world. Our every thought and every word was about death. Death seemed to be the only way to escape from the indescribable hell in which we lived."

Tragically, the story of the Jews of Europe, and especially the Jews of Poland, the largest Jewish community on the continent, was exactly that, a story of death at the hands of the Nazis and their collaborators during the war.

But even amid the killing fields, there were a few, oh so few, rays of sunshine. One of them, the man we honor this evening, was Jan Karski.

It is asked: If a tree falls in the forest and no one hears it, does it make a sound? Similarly, one can ask: If humanity cries out in anguish and no one listens, does the pain go unfelt?

Cry out Polish Jews did. Listen to the words of the great Yiddish poet, Haim Leivick, whose daughter-in-law, Ida, is here this evening:

Unzer folk vert oisgekoilet,
un di velt kukt zich knit um,
tsu dem vay foon unzeren koyless,
di gantseh velt bleibt shtoom.

"Our people are being slaughtered, and the whole world pretends not to know. The whole world remains silent to our cries of woe."

Jan Karski devoted his life, indeed risked his life again and again, so that these cries of woe of Polish Jews during World War II would not go unheard. This courier of courage took to the world community his eyewitness accounts of the systematic extermination of the Jews by the Nazis. Many found his stories of gruesome atrocities hard, even impossible, to believe, but Jan Karski told them and retold them to anyone who would listen.

Jan Karski modestly refers to himself as a "human tape recorder," replaying the messages he was asked to deliver. In actuality, he has been a trumpet; a man who has heralded the harsh tones of human indifference and cruelty so loudly that no one can deny hearing them, while at the same time personifying the softest melodies that make up the indomitable spirit and inherent goodness that mankind can still possess.

Jan Karski, a Catholic, was born in Lodz, Poland, in 1914. In 1939 he was drafted into the Polish army as a second lieutenant. Taken prisoner by the Soviets, he managed to escape and join the Polish underground. In December 1939, he was sent, as one of the first couriers, to France, where he briefed the new Polish government-in-exile about the situation in occupied Poland. A few months later, he returned to Poland only to be sent to France again. But this time his mission failed, and he was arrested by the Gestapo in Slovakia. He was tortured but did not betray any secrets. Rescued in a daring action by the Polish underground, he returned to his vital work. He came into contact with leaders of the Polish Jewish underground. They wanted him to see with his own eyes and thus bear witness to the tragedy befalling the Jews. He agreed. He was secretly able to enter the Warsaw ghetto twice. He was also able to enter the extermination camp at Belzec. His eyes saw it all.

Shortly thereafter, he was charged with a mission to London to report to the Polish government. Part of that report was to be an account of the attempt to exterminate the entire Jewish people.

From England he went to the United States where, in August 1943, he personally reported to President Roosevelt, Cordell Hull, Henry Stimson, Justice Felix Frankfurter, and other senior U.S. officials and leaders of the American Jewish community what he had witnessed.

Many years after the war's end, Karski, who had since become an American citizen and a distinguished professor of international relations at Georgetown University, was asked if his mission to inform the world and seek help for the beleaguered Jews had had any results. He replied:

"As to the Jewish part of my mission, it was an obvious failure. Six million Jews died and no one offered them effective help. Not any nation, not any government, not any church. The help they did receive, heroic help, was provided only by individuals."

Jan Karski was one such individual. As Martin Peretz, writing in the current issue of *The New Republic* of his own participation in the recent fiftieth anniversary commemoration in Warsaw of the ghetto uprising, said:

"When Polish president Lech Walesa spoke and mentioned that Karski was in our midst, the crowd's sudden hush indicated that the people knew they were in the presence of one of those obsessives whose obsessions make him both brave and good."

It is precisely for these obsessions—this remarkable courage, this lifelong commitment to combating evil, this friendship to the Jewish people that was so manifest in our darkest days and continues to the present time in the relentless determination to fight anti-Semitism, to promote understanding between his fellow Poles and Jews, and to bear witness—that the American Jewish Committee is deeply honored to confer its highest award on a true hero of our time, Jan Karski.

Remembrance and Resolve: Fifty Years After the Holocaust
AJC 89th Annual Meeting, Washington, D.C.
May 4, 1995

It's a hauntingly beautiful melody, isn't it?* One that evokes memories of the Passover seder table, of our age-old yearning as a people. Remember the words?

> *Eliyahu Hanavi,*
> *Eliyahu Hatishbi,*
> *Eliyahu, Eliyahu,*
> *Eliyahu Hagiladi,*
> *Bim Heira v'yameinu,*
> *Ya'avo aileynu,*
> *Im Mashiach Ben David,*
> *Im Masiach Ben David.*

> Elijah the prophet,
> Elijah the Tishbite,
> Elijah of Gilead,
> Come speedily to us,
> Hailing the messianic days.

Rabbi Israel Spira, the grand rabbi of Bluzhov, fervently believed in those messianic days, even in the midst of indescribable evil.

---

*These remarks were immediately preceded by a cello solo, composed by Michael Shapiro, based on *Eliyahu Hanavi.*

"It was a dark, cold night in the Janowska road camp [near Lvov in the Ukraine]. Suddenly, a stentorian shout pierced the air: 'You are all to evacuate the barracks immediately and report to the vacant lot. Anyone remaining inside will be shot on the spot!'

"Pandemonium broke out in the barracks. In a panic-stricken stampede, the prisoners ran in the direction of the open field.

"Exhausted, trying to catch their breath, they reached the field. In the middle were two huge pits.

"Suddenly, with their last drop of energy, the inmates realized where they were rushing, on that cursed dark night in Janowska.

"Once more, the cold, healthy voice roared in the night: 'Each of you dogs who values his miserable life and wants to cling to it must jump over one of the pits and land on the other side. Those who miss it will get what they rightfully deserve.'

"Imitating the sound of a machine gun, the voice trailed off into the night followed by a wild, coarse laughter. It was clear to the inmates that they would all end up in the pits. Even at the best of times it would have been impossible to jump over them, all the more so on that cold dark night in Janowska.

"The prisoners standing at the edge of the pits were skeletons, feverish from disease and starvation, exhausted from slave labor and sleepless nights. Though the challenge that had been given them was a matter of life and death, they knew that for the German SS and the Ukrainian guards it was merely another devilish game.

"Among the thousands of Jews on that field in Janowska was the rabbi of Bluzhov, Rabbi Israel Spira. He was standing with a friend, a freethinker from a large Polish town whom the rabbi had met in the camp.

"'Spira, all of our efforts to jump over the pits are in vain. We only entertain the Germans and their collaborators. Let's sit down in the pits and wait for the bullets to end our wretched existence,' said the friend to the rabbi.

"'My friend,' said the rabbi, 'man must obey the will of God. If it was decreed from heaven that pits be dug and we be commanded to jump, pits will be dug and jump we must. And if, God forbid, we fail and fall into the pits, we will reach the World of Truth a second later. So, my friend, we must jump.'

"The rabbi and his friend were nearing the edge of the pits; the pits were rapidly filling up with bodies.

"The rabbi glanced down at his feet, the swollen feet of a fifty-three-year-old Jew ridden with starvation and disease. He looked at his young friend, a skeleton with burning eyes.

"As they reached the pit, he closed his eyes and commanded in a powerful whisper, 'We are jumping!' When they opened their eyes, they found themselves standing on the other side of the pit.

"'Spira, we are here, we are here, we are alive!' the friend repeated over and over again, while warm tears streamed from his eyes. 'Spira, for your sake, I am alive; indeed, there must be a God in heaven. Tell me, Rebbe, how did you do it?'

"'I was holding on to my ancestral chain. I was holding on to the coattails of my father, and my grandfather, and my great-grandfather, of blessed memory,' said the rabbi and his eyes searched the black skies above. 'Tell me, my friend, how did you reach the other side of the pit?'

"'I was holding on to you,' replied the rabbi's friend."*

And now listen to another, the words of seventeen-year-old Sarah Fishkin, from Poland, who kept a diary in 1941:

"It is difficult to believe that the good times are gone, that our moments of joy, the hours of studying and enjoying ourselves are past, that I must give up forever my thoughts of future goals and the fantasies I hoped to see realized. I would never have believed that it would all disappear so soon, be cut down, burned out, orphaned in so short a time. Emptiness and desolation, saddened aching hearts, are our present constant companions. There seems to be no future for the Jewish population.

"For the Jew the light of day is covered with a thick veil: his road is overgrown with tall wild grasses. Every horizon upon which his eye rests is stained with the tears of lost children searching for their mothers in the dense woods. Convulsed with sobbing until their little souls expired, the youngsters are now lifeless, at eternal rest. Only the quivering trees know of their death and will later on bear witness about the

---

*This remarkable story appeared in *Hassidic Tales of the Holocaust* by Yaffa Eliach, New York, 1982.

sacrifice of these little ones. Where is human conscience, to demand the truth, to cry out?. . . .

"We seem now to have reached the end of everything. But one wants to live. One craves more of youth and joy. . . . But one's sole thought is to survive this painful, oppressive time and to see something better before one's eyes. . . . A person's mind becomes impaired, far from beautiful thoughts. One goal is dominant: to maintain life.

"All about is shattered, destroyed and burned. All is obstructed by fresh graves, a virtual cemetery. Dark, menacing clouds cover everything. The entire surroundings are weeping and crying out. . .

"On a lovely morning . . . when all the Jews of the city had been gathered together, when the long graves had been dug and prepared and stood open before the eyes of the mothers, fathers, and little children, they looked at them wide-eyed, not knowing what was about to happen in the ensuing moments. Then we heard pain-filled sobs and farewells to one's children.

"Some sought ways to hide. From the hiding places, too, they were led to the slaughter. The thousands of people who fell are now at rest. The long graves have been closed again, but the earth will not rest. One can see it heave, as if to say: Dig away the covering and let out these people who have just fallen, whose blood will not be still and finds no peace in the earth. Our own end could be the same on any coming day. May the one God preserve us from such harm . . ."*

But alas, Sarah Fishkin, unlike Rabbi Spira and his friend, was not preserved from such harm. She did not survive Camp Dvortz. Of her extended family only an aunt and one brother did, and just recently her brother authorized the publication of the diary, fulfilling a request that Sarah had made in the diary itself: It should only be published when the people of the world were most in danger of denying and forgetting the annihilation of the Jews.

Ladies and gentlemen, we gather here today in this extraordinary institution—the Holocaust Museum—to ensure against Sarah Fishkin's very real fear, the fear of those who would deny or forget the annihilation of the Jews.

*Excerpted from *Children in the Holocaust and World War II: Their Secret Diaries* by Laurel Holiday, New York, 1995.

We gather to recall the once thriving Jewish communities that fell victim to the Nazi German onslaught—Riga and Vilna, Bobruisk and Minsk, Lvov and Czernowitz, Kishinev and Bialystok, Berlin and Vienna, Prague and Brno, Frankfurt and Mannheim, Warsaw and Salonika—and to remember the 6 million from these and other communities who are no more.

We gather here to remember the victims of an entirely unprecedented vocabulary of destruction and death—Nuremberg Laws, *Kristallnacht*, the Wannsee Conference, the Final Solution, extermination, genocide, death marches, transport trains, deportation, slave labor, concentration camps, Zyklon B, gas chambers, crematoria, ravines, pits, ghettos, *Einsatzgruppen*, Aktion 1005—a vocabulary that was put into effect by Nazi Germany and its allies, and carried out in places indelibly imprinted in our minds: Dachau, Mauthausen, Sobibor, Treblinka, Chelmno, Ravensbruck, Belzec, Bergen-Belsen, Majdanek, Jasenovac, Flossenburg, Sachsenhausen, Buchenwald, Auschwitz-Birkenau, Babi Yar, Plaszo, Iasi, Rumbula, Ponary.

We gather here today, fifty years later, as I pray others will be here fifty years from now, to bear witness; to sustain the memory both of that which existed before the flames and that which was irretrievably destroyed in those flames; to link ourselves as an unbroken chain to the 6 million who perished and to those all too precious few who miraculously survived; to pay tribute to the valor of those who resisted by the power of whatever weapons they could find—the ghetto fighters, the partisans, those who rose up in Birkenau, Sobibor, and Treblinka—and to those who, like Rabbi Spira, resisted by the power of faith alone; and to continue to grapple with the unanswerable: how and why?

Not how in the mechanical sense, for that is all too well known to us. Rather, how could human beings, created in the image of God, join together to perpetrate such monstrous evil?

How could human beings so dehumanize fellow human beings so as to willingly participate in the attempted extermination of an entire people whose only "sin" was the sin of being? To wreak such havoc across so many countries, resulting in the deaths of nearly 55 million people, including targeted groups from Gypsies and political foes to homosexuals and the handicapped, not to speak of the displacement of countless tens of millions more?

How could human beings, with such a sense of determination and conviction, round up and deport to concentration camps Helene Berger, age two, from Paris; Miriam Sluizer, five years old, and her brother Abel, age two, from Amsterdam; Joseph Skoulsky, ten, and his sister Augusta, five, from Antwerp; or Frieda Reiss, eleven months old, from Angouleme, France? A million and a half children exterminated—a million and a half children. How, in God's name? Why, in God's name?

How could human beings achieve such a level of depravity, of cold-bloodedness, of hate, of inhumanity to round up a Gittel Mandelevitch, ninety-one years old, from her home in Kishinev and send her to her death in Auschwitz? Or a Fania Krinitchevsky, eighty-six, from Odessa, killed in Auschwitz as well? Or a Eugene Mandel, a thirty-five-year-old cantor from Zagreb, or a Victor Cohen, age fifty-two, born in Tunis, or . . . ?*

Like you, I have read countless books about the Holocaust, listened to many survivors, visited the camps, memorial sites, and museums, and watched every available film and documentary. I have thought and agonized, until I have sometimes felt my mind would burst and my heart explode, yet still I cannot begin to find answers to the central questions, no more, I suspect, than any other rational person can.

How could these things have happened? Why did so many remain silent in the face of events taking place before their eyes? Why did so few nations act to help rescue the Jews?

Why were Denmark and, to a considerable degree, Bulgaria, the French village of Le Chambon-sur-Lignon and the Dutch village of Nieuwlande, and such *hasidai umot ha'olam*, righteous among the nations, as Raoul Wallenberg and Oskar Schindler, Jan Karski and Wladislaw Bartoszewski, Chiune (Sempo) Sugihara and Giorgio Perlasca, Zayneba Hardaga and Aristides de Sousa Mendes, the all-too-rare and precious examples of courage and decency in a seemingly endless landscape of evil and sadism, indifference and fear?

---

*The names cited were taken from *Atlas of the Holocaust* by Martin Gilbert, New York, 1993.

Perhaps it is our fate that we shall never be able to find adequate answers to such questions, but it is equally our fate to continue to ask them.

And it is also incumbent upon us, I believe, to use an occasion such as this for the purpose of reaffirming.

Reaffirming our determination to ensure that those who would seek either to deny, distort, rewrite, or relativize the Holocaust, and its uniqueness in the annals of human history, not be permitted to succeed, not today, not ever.

Reaffirming our faith in the future of the Jewish people, a people that has survived not simply for the purpose of survival but rather because of a profound connection to our ennobling faith and civilization and land, and a belief that we Jews have an important contribution to make in creating a more humane world.

Reaffirming our unshakable link with fellow Jews around the world—a number of whom are here in this audience today and will, I am pleased to say, be with us for the next several days—and our enduring commitment to help ensure the security and well-being of each and every Jewish community, anywhere.

Reaffirming our special bond with Israel and our determination to do all within our ability to assist in its quest for lasting peace and security with its neighbors, to continue to serve its vital role as home and haven, and to become a true *or l'goyim*, a light unto the nations.

Reaffirming our age-old mission, as Nobel laureate and Holocaust survivor Elie Wiesel has reminded us, not to make the world more Jewish but to make it more human. And recent tragic events—both here at home and around the world—have reminded us yet again what a long way to go we have, but also must remind us how necessary and significant the voice of an American Jewish Committee can be.

Ladies and gentlemen, we, the American Jewish Committee, have gathered together here to mark this fiftieth anniversary, as we gathered in Auschwitz and Buchenwald earlier this year, to remember what once was and what was taken away from us; to reaffirm our resolve to preserve memory and its integrity; to recommit ourselves to our work in strengthening understanding between nations and peoples, including especially, in this particular context, our forward-looking program with the postwar Federal Republic of Germany; and to fight single-mindedly for a better future for Jews, for *all* people, a future in which such words as *final solution* and *genocide, concentration camps* and *extermination, death marches* and *dehumanization*, are forever expunged from the world's vocabulary. Forever.

Unnecessary Language
New York Post
May 17, 1995

Given the *Post*'s remarkable record of sensitivity to, and understanding of, the history of the Second World War, I was very surprised to read the photo caption (May 9) referring to "a Gestapo greeting" received by your reporter when she tried to visit New York governor Pataki's home in Garrison.

No doubt she was made to feel unwelcome, perhaps even rudely treated by security officials, but don't we greatly diminish both language and history by using such a term as "Gestapo greeting" for this kind of occasion?

The Gestapo represented an unparalleled evil in the twentieth century, which fortunately has nothing even remotely resembling it in this country. Surely, the English language is rich enough to permit your caption writers more fitting descriptive phrases.

Letter to Texas Congressman DeLay (R-TX)
August 7, 1995

Dear Congressman DeLay:

A National Public Radio report of August 2 cited your comments, reportedly delivered on the House floor, with respect to the Environmental Protection Agency. Specifically, the report quoted you as saying: "The critical promise we made to the American people was to get the government off their backs, and the EPA—the Gestapo of government—pure and simply has been one of the major claw holds that the government has maintained on the backs of our constituents."

Assuming this to be an accurate rendering of your words, I write not to discuss environmental issues; that is not within the province of the American Jewish Committee. Rather, I write to share my concern over your attempt to compare the EPA with the Gestapo. I believe this to be a regrettable and entirely inappropriate inflation of language.

Whatever grievances you or your constituents may have concerning the EPA, to compare this U.S. governmental agency with one of the most lethal and destructive governmental agencies ever created, whose record of torture and death is perhaps without parallel in the annals of human history, is startling, to say the least. In doing so, I fear, you diminish our collective understanding of history and do a disservice as well to the cause for which you advocate. Accordingly, I would respectfully urge you to find other, more calibrated terms of description.

Moral Neutrality
Chicago Tribune
February 13, 1997

Almost daily, we are reading about new and deeply disturbing revelations regarding the financial role played by Switzerland and its banks during World War II.

This reminds us yet again that more than fifty years after the war's end, we are still learning important new facts about that nighmarish period and continuing to face a number of pressing and unresolved issues.

No gesture by any government or bank can ever begin to make up for the incalculable losses endured by the victims of Nazi Germany and its allies. That is beyond question.

What is necessary, though, is the urgent need to demonstrate good faith in helping the remaining Holocaust survivors live out their last years in dignity and with the chance of regaining at least some of their assets. Switzerland has this opportunity today; it should seize it.

At the same time, there is an equally compelling need for moral stocktaking in Switzerland. For decades, the Swiss lived with certain myths about their policy of strict neutrality in World War II. Government, insurance, and banking records now reveal a much more messy reality. Political neutrality, in too many instances, tragically turned into moral neutrality.

This presents the Swiss people with a remarkable opportunity to explore honestly and learn from their wartime experience, and in so doing to emerge stronger as a nation and more aware of what can go wrong without moral accountability.

As the philosopher George Santayana once wrote, "Those who cannot remember the past are condemned to repeat it."

Remarks at the Premiere of the Play
Virtue: Sempo Sugihara
Sylvia and Danny Kaye Playhouse, New York
January 16, 1998

In the Jewish tradition, we are commanded *"zakhor"*, remember, and *"lo tishkach,"* do not forget. The play we are about to see this evening fulfills these commandments.

In doing so, it brings to life a remarkable and hitherto little-known story of a man prepared to put his own career on the line, in defiance of his government, so that others—others far from him in geographical, religious, cultural, and national, but not in fundamental human terms—might live.

In 1985, one year before his death, Sempo Sugihara recalled the dramatic days of August 1940 when, as a Japanese diplomat posted in Kaunas, Lithuania, he was approached by a representative of the Jewish Agency Palestine Office in Lithuania and asked to grant Japanese transit visas to Polish Jewish refugees stranded there. He said: "I really had a hard time, and was unable to sleep for two nights. I thought as follows: 'I can issue transit visas . . . by virtue of my authority as consul. I cannot allow these people to die, people who had come to me for help with death staring them in the eyes. Whatever punishment may be imposed upon me, I know I should follow my conscience.'"

Fortunately, he did follow that conscience. The result? A community of Jews was saved. And in doing so Sempo Sugihara, and the other all-too-rare righteous individuals during the Second World War, remind us of the power of a single person to make a difference.

Their example, each in his or her own way, though, poses an unsettling challenge to us, for it means that in the face of human suffering we cannot just hide behind the claim of powerlessness or irrelevance, nor, for that matter, simply resort to generic exhortations of love of humanity and stop there.

Sempo Sugihara, fifty-eight years ago, was approached by a human being seeking the most basic human right—the right to live. Fortunately, this human being, Dr. Zorah Warhaftig, was met by more than mere vague goodwill. He was met by definite ethical action. As a direct consequence, he and those on whose behalf he spoke lived; otherwise, they surely would have perished.

On Yom Kippur, the most solemn day of the Jewish year, many of us find in our prayer books the following passage:

> And yet even in the inferno, even there
> were those we call *hasidai umot ha'olam,*
> the righteous of the nations.
> Some gave their very lives to keep Jews from harm.
> Who can measure such courage?
> When so many were afraid to act,
> they bore witness to the greatness
> men and women can reach.
> Look and take heart.
> If ever such days return,
> remember them and find courage.
> Consider what can be done, what must be done
> not to banish from our souls the image of God.

I wish to thank the producers of this play for bringing Sempo Sugihara's remarkable story to American audiences and challenging us to look and take heart and, if necessary, to find courage.

Exhibition on Camps
The New York Times
March 13, 1998

Your coverage of the upcoming Japanese-American exhibition at Ellis Island and the debate over use of the term "concentration camps" in its title omitted an important point (news articles, March 8, 10; editorial, March 9). There was consistent Jewish support for the Japanese-American quest for an official U.S. government apology and redress.

Indeed, Senator Daniel K. Inouye, speaking to the two groups earlier this week in our office, said that when the Executive Order was issued in 1942 to intern 120,000 Japanese-Americans, the first lonely voice of protest came from the Jewish community. In 1983, the American Jewish Committee was identified by the Japanese American Citizens League as "the first national organization to support our efforts to rectify the injustices of the World War II internment of Japanese Americans."

We have not claimed Jewish exclusivity for the term "concentration camps." There were, of course, non-Jewish inmates in German camps, but Hitler's Final Solution was aimed at Jews.

No Monopoly on Suffering
Newsday
March 25, 1998

Columnist Sheryl McCarthy writes of the upcoming Ellis Island exhibit on the shameful treatment of Japanese Americans during World War II, and reports that the American Jewish Committee objected to the term "concentration camp" in the title. She then chides the Jewish community for its apparent unwillingness to acknowledge the suffering of others ["Suffering Isn't One Group's Exclusive Privilege," Viewpoints, March 16].

We did not initiate any protest of the exhibit title—neither with the National Park Service nor the Interior Department. When asked by the press, we explained that the term "concentration camp" had taken on a new level of meaning under the Nazis and therefore, without some explanation, exhibit viewers could be left confused. Fortunately, that explanation has now been added.

Moreover, we also said, though unreported by the press, that it was the Jewish community that first protested the Japanese American internment during World War II. Furthermore, though Hitler's Final Solution was aimed at the Jews, there were many non-Jewish inmates in the Nazi concentration camps, and there were other horrific camps set up in this century, for example, in Stalin's Gulag and, more recently, in Serb-controlled areas. We were among those who loudly (and consistently) raised our voice in protest.

Remarks on the Opening of the
Japanese American National Museum Exhibit
Ellis Island
April 2, 1998

Ladies and gentlemen, it is a privilege for me, on behalf of the American Jewish Committee, to join with all of you in welcoming the opening of this important exhibit arranged by our friends at the Japanese American National Museum.

In schools, traditionally, we have been taught the three *r*s—reading, 'riting, and 'rithmetic.

When viewing such an exhibit, we should bear in mind three other *r*s—remembrance, reflection, and resolve.

We need, first, to remember, or, for many of us, to learn the facts of history. The facts recorded in this exhibit are not pretty; they do not reflect well on our beloved nation. They tell a story that the American Civil Liberties Union called "the worst single wholesale violation of civil rights of American citizens in our history." They illustrate, in short, a breach of America's contract with its people that occurred fifty-six years ago.

America was understandably seized with concern as it moved to a war footing after the ruthless attack on Pearl Harbor. Nonetheless, there can be no adequate justification for Executive Order 9066, no convincing explanation why such an order was signed by the president, all the more so when nobody here ever dreamed of interning the millions of American citizens of German and Italian descent, with whose countries we were also at war.

The singular treatment of Japanese Americans could never have occurred without the long history of pervasive racial prejudice and formal discrimination by law against them, as the American Jewish Committee testified before the U.S. Congress, in 1986, in support of the findings of the Commission on Wartime Relocation and the Internment of Civilians.

We need, second, to reflect. What is the larger meaning of this sad chapter—for us as individuals, as part of American civil society, as a nation? For one thing, it reminds us of human frailty and vulnerability. For another, it suggests the human capacity to err, even when otherwise great people and great institutions are involved. For a third, it begs the questions: Where were the moral watchdogs? Where were the guardians of the Constitution? Where were the voices of courageous decency?

To this country's credit, however belatedly, we have sought to address some of the pain and anguish experienced by the 120,000 internees. This nation has formally apologized and provided at least a modicum of redress to those whose trust it betrayed. This is not to be taken lightly. Nations, we know all too well, do not easily acknowledge painful truths; indeed, too few have.

Lastly, this exhibit should prompt us to make a resolution. What happened in 1942 was not on the watch of most of us at this gathering. We cannot undo the events; we cannot even chastise ourselves for our own inaction.

What we can do, though, with the benefit of remembrance and reflection, is resolve that on our watch, whether here at home or abroad, whether affecting Japanese Americans or other groups, we will stand together as a community of conscience, as a voice of decency, as a moral beacon.

As the late Adlai Stevenson once noted, the Jewish people contributed to world civilization the revolutionary concept of moral choice. We have the gift, but with it the responsibility, to distinguish between good and evil.

In this regard, Dante wrote: "The hottest fires in hell are reserved for those who in times of great moral crisis maintain their neutrality."

Let us never be neutral in times of great moral crisis. Let us leave this gathering, this exhibit, this fitting venue, further inspired to exercise our moral choices.

Let us demonstrate that we have managed to learn from the tragic events of history, and let us do our utmost, on our watch, to prevent their repetition.

Presentation of AJC's Distinguished Leadership Award to Under Secretary of State Stuart E. Eizenstat
New York
June 4, 1998

In 1975, I was working in Rome on the migration of Soviet and East European Jewish refugees westward. As their number grew, so did the need for additional staff. I recall one day the office director, Evi Eller, called me in and said: "David, you're an American; I'm not. Explain something to me. Here I have several résumés from young Americans. How can it be that they are all in their early twenties and yet their résumés list no shortage of accomplishments?"

She was absolutely right. Their résumés suffered from what could only be described as the kind of "experiential inflation" that too many in our society continue to practice. In their résumés, one year's study of French became "fluency" in the language, one winter break spent as a congressional intern became a "political consultancy," and one summer as a camp counselor became "significant management experience."

In the case of our honoree and speaker this evening, however, quite the opposite pertains. No résumé, no entry in *Who's Who*, no introduction could begin to do justice to the landmark achievements and professional milestones of this truly extraordinary individual.

Perhaps I should simply quote the writer who, in the January 24th issue of the *Economist*, described Stu Eizenstat as a "national treasure" and leave it at that. Such brevity might make me a popular speaker, but please indulge me for just a few more minutes.

Lawyer . . . domestic policy adviser to President Carter . . . ambassador to the European Union . . . under secretary of commerce . . . under secretary of state . . . international troubleshooter . . . author . . . lecturer at Harvard's John F. Kennedy School . . . award winner . . . civic leader, including key positions, I am proud to say, at the American Jewish Committee, such as honorary vice president and founding chair of our pioneering Institute on American Jewish–Israeli Relations. The list goes on.

And those who know Ambassador Eizenstat realize that to each and every one of his manifold commitments, he brings exceptional wisdom, judgment, depth, dedication, and, not least, indefatigability. He reads voraciously, writes prolifically, and speaks knowledgeably.

That's why no fewer than three U.S. presidents—Carter, Bush, and Clinton—have turned to him to deal with some of our nation's most complex and daunting policy challenges.

We have tension with our European allies on the Helms-Burton legislation regarding Cuba, turn it over to Stu Eizenstat. We have to sort out our country's broader approach to the controversial issue of sanctions, turn it over to Stu Eizenstat. We have to defend a tough position at the world climate conference in Kyoto, turn it over to Stu Eizenstat.

And we as a nation seek a long overdue international reckoning with history's most horrific crime—the Nazi Final Solution—and, no surprise, our government turns once again to Ambassador Eizenstat to lead the effort, an effort that requires tenacity, courage, commitment, and well-honed political instincts. This may be a sacred undertaking, and I know that for Stu it is nothing less, but, truth be told, it is at the same time a veritable minefield, requiring a diplomat *extraordinaire*.

Tonight the American Jewish Committee and its National Leadership Council and New York Chapter have the privilege of conferring our Distinguished Service Award on an exceptionally deserving public servant.

We honor Stuart Eizenstat for adhering to the mandate in Deuteronomy, *Tsedek, tsedek, tirdof*—Justice, justice shall thou pursue.

We honor him for seeking to restore to the survivors of the Shoah some measure of dignity in the waning years of their lives and a recognition that their immeasurable suffering was not entirely in vain.

We honor him for pressing for the return of communal properties to Jewish communities in Central and Eastern Europe that can help give them form and shape and, yes, life.

We honor him for doggedly pursuing those governments and other institutions that callously profited from the tragedy of European Jewry, and telling them that they can no longer hide behind their often meticulously constructed webs of myths, half-truths, and denials.

We honor him, and with him our country, for the courage to probe our own past, to acknowledge our own wartime and postwar failings, and to hold us all to the highest standards of ethical behavior.

We honor him for the inestimable pride he has stirred in us by his distinguished record of public service, his unimpeachable integrity, and his relentless quest for the truth about the most painful issues of our time.

Ladies and gentlemen, every day on my way to work, I pass one of those electronics stores that seem to have "gullible tourists" written all over their display windows. You know the kind I mean. This one's on Lexington Avenue, and until recently it was called Avi's, named for the Israeli owner. One day, a painter came along and eliminated the apostrophe in the store's name. Now if you pass the store, it's called Avis, not Avi's. Same owner, but it's now Avis, not Avi's. With the removal of one little apostrophe, a whole new Americanized image has been created.

Why do I tell this vignette? Simply because Stuart Eizenstat, to his everlasting credit, has always been true to himself. He has never sought to erase any part of his makeup; to the contrary, he has always been entirely comfortable living the two integral parts that make him whole—his American and his Jewish identities. And not only has he never regarded these identities as being in conflict, but he has always seen them as mutually reinforcing, mutually nourishing.

In short, Stuart Eizenstat is a serious American and an equally serious Jew. He is a unique individual who cares deeply about the destiny of our country and the destiny of the Jewish people, and he has devoted his life to leaving his indelible imprint on both.

It is, therefore, my honor, on behalf of the American Jewish Committee's National Leadership Council and our New York Chapter, to present to Ambassador Stuart Eizenstat, under secretary of state of the United States, our Distinguished Leadership Award.

Statement on Behalf of the
American Jewish Committee Delegation
Washington Conference on Holocaust-Era Assets
Department of State
November 30–December 3, 1998

To the Delegates to the Washington Conference on Holocaust-Era Assets:

As one of the (thirteen) nongovernmental organizations privileged to be accredited to the conference, we join in expressing our hope that this historic gathering will fulfill the ambitious and worthy goals set for it.

. The effort to identify the compelling and complex issues of looted assets from the Second World War, and to consult on the most appropriate and expeditious means of addressing and resolving these issues, offers a beacon of light at the end of a very long and dark tunnel for Holocaust survivors, for the descendants of those who perished in the flames, for the vibrant Jewish communities that were destroyed, and for all who fell victim to the savagery and rapacity of those horrific times.

We are pleased as well that, in addition to discussion of these enormously important topics, the conference will also take up the matter of Holocaust education, for, in the end, this can be our permanent legacy to future generations.

We hope that the conference will reach a consensus on the need for enhanced international consultation, with the aim of encouraging more widespread teaching of the Holocaust in national school systems. Moreover, we commend those nations that have already taken impressive steps in this regard.

Not only can teaching of the Holocaust provide young people with a better insight into the darkest chapter in this century's history, but, ultimately, it can serve to strengthen their commitment to fundamental principles of human decency, mutual understanding, and tolerance—all of which are so necessary if we are to have any chance of creating a brighter future.

When we speak of education, we must recognize that it cannot be limited to the classroom or the textbook, necessary though both are.

One element regarding both historical memory and education that deserves, in our view, greater attention from the international community is the identification, preservation, and protection of sites of destruction and extermination connected to the Holocaust. Experience has taught us that visits to sites have a profound impact, not least on young people.

In some countries, considerable attention has been devoted to this matter; in others, regrettably, this has not been the case.

In some countries, great care has been taken to designate such sites, provide demarcation, ensure adequate security, and introduce pedagogical elements; in other countries, sites go unmarked, threatened by commercial or other development, and therefore destined for disappearance.

In some countries, comprehensive national legislation exists; in others, either there is no relevant legislation or responsibility lies with local rather than national governments, leading, sad to say, to an inconsistent and unreliable approach.

In some countries, ample funds have been earmarked to maintain the sites; in others, few, if any, resources have been committed.

In addition to our concern for strengthening Holocaust education, we raise this issue because it also serves other vital goals—commemorating what has been lost, and paying our respects to those who perished in the Final Solution and to the vibrant civilization that was destroyed.

Many questions can surely be raised about specific aspects of our proposal—for example, issues of definition and jurisdiction. Our aim is precisely to raise these questions, leading, we would earnestly hope, to greater international consultation and coordination on guidelines and approaches among the distinguished nations and nongovernmental organizations represented at this Conference.

Be assured that the American Jewish Committee stands ready to assist in this effort in the months and years ahead.

Introduction
to *Austria and the Legacy of the Holocaust**
The American Jewish Committee
1999

The idea for this study began at the Austrian Permanent Mission to the United Nations. That is where, last year, I met with the Austrian ambassador and his deputy to seek their support in opposing yet another of the innumerable resolutions criticizing Israel to come before the world body.

In the course of an amiable conversation, I noted that the UN continued its excessive—and unbalanced—preoccupation with Israel at the expense of other compelling issues, and I sought to illustrate the point. No sooner had I finished than the ambassador's deputy forcefully intervened to defend the UN's record on Israel, even justifying the fact that the Geneva-based UN Human Rights Commission year after year dedicated a specific agenda item to Israel's record, the only country in the world accorded such a dubious status.

I responded immediately based on the facts, but, truth be told, my mind was focused less on the facts and much more on a sense of outrage. How dare an *Austrian* diplomat speak this way about Israel? Was there no sense of responsibility whatsoever on Austria's part toward Israel, given Austria's wartime role as enthusiastic participant in the implementation of the Nazi Final Solution? Why was there such a striking contrast between this diplomat's expressed views, seemingly devoid of even an iota of sensitivity for Israel, and those of the many German diplomats with whom I had been meeting for many years?

To be sure, this was not our first encounter with the complexity of Austria's postwar self-image or the ambiguity of its relations with Israel or the Jewish people—far from it. For many years, the American

*This essay preceded a monograph authored by Professor Robert Wistrich and published in English and German editions.

Jewish Committee had sought to engage Austrian governments and political institutions in programming designed to confront the past as a foundation for building constructive ties for the future. Despite widespread access, in the end we always faced the same outcome—a remarkably consistent failure on the Austrian part to follow up on any concrete proposals.

We have also conducted two national surveys of Austrian attitudes toward Jews (1991 and 1995), both of which revealed disturbingly widespread anti-Semitic views. In the 1991 study, for example, 19 percent of the respondents declared that Austria would be better off with no Jews, a figure that is all the more striking given the fact that the Austrian Jewish population is statistically insignificant today. Moreover, as founding members of the Conference on Material Claims Against Germany and Austria, we were well aware of the particularly difficult negotiations on restitution and reparations conducted with Austria.

And then, of course, there was the deeply troubling six-year-long Waldheim saga, sparked in 1986 by revelations that the Austrian presidential candidate (and eventual winner with nearly 54 percent of the vote) and former UN secretary general had failed to disclose his wartime record. Among other things, the episode revealed once again the difficulty many Austrians have in facing squarely their own history, preferring instead to live with ingrained myths, willful denial, and residual hostility toward—in this case—"East Coast Jews," who were seen as spearheading the anti-Waldheim campaign.

At the same time, Austria since the war has compiled an estimable record as a democratic nation committed to the rule of law and peaceful conflict resolution. Though technically neutral during the cold war and often seen as a bridge between East and West, there was never any question where Austria stood. Moreover, Vienna has become an important center for international agencies, including a significant United Nations presence, as well as the headquarters of vitally important bodies such as the International Atomic Energy Agency (IAEA). And of special note, Austria has served as a country of first asylum for millions of refugees fleeing totalitarianism and war, including hundreds of thousands of Soviet Jews, Hungarians, Czechs, and Bosnians, and smaller numbers of Iranian Jews.

In the late 1970s, I had first-hand experience aiding the transit of Soviet Jews when I worked in the Vienna office of the Hebrew Immigrant Aid Society (HIAS). Austria has received insufficient acknowledgment for the role it played in this historic migration. Not only did it provide initial reception when direct migration to Israel and the United States from the USSR was all but impossible, but it also shouldered a very considerable security challenge to protect Soviet Jews on Austrian soil. Terrorist threats were not infrequent, but the Austrians remained undeterred.

In the past decade Austria has finally, if tentatively, come out from under the spell of its collective amnesia and the comforting image first accorded it by the Allied nations in 1943 as the "first victim state" of the Nazi war machine, to engage in a measure of soul-searching and moral and historical reckoning.

Austrian chancellor Vranitzky, to his credit, made two important speeches—in 1991 and 1993—admitting widespread Austrian complicity in the Holocaust. Though forty-six years in coming, Austrian president Klestil, in 1994, became the first Austrian head of state to visit Israel. A Jewish museum was opened in the center of Vienna in 1993 in the presence of a throng of political dignitaries. And Austria has recently established a National Fund to provide modest payments, however late and insufficient, to at least some of those Jews who fled the country in the 1930s, and has been applauded for taking the lead in addressing the thorny international issue of restitution of looted art.

In sum, Austria is, to say the least, an exceptionally complex—and, I should add, understudied—country. Its very name, depending on the context, can evoke images of Theodor Herzl, Sigmund Freud, Ludwig Wittgenstein, Elias Canetti, Stefan Zweig, and Franz Werfel—that is, of a once vibrant Jewish presence that today is but the merest of shadows of the prewar community; or of edelweiss, Sacher torte, the Vienna Boys Choir, the Spanish horses, snow-covered peaks, and Wolfgang Amadeus Mozart—that is, of the fabled Austria of alluring travel guides and legendary *gemütlichkeit;* or of Adolf Hitler, Adolf Eichmann, Odilo Globocnik, Franz Stangl, Alois Brunner, Walter Reder, Mauthausen, and *Kristallnacht*—that is, of a disproportionately active Austrian participation in the Nazi extermination of 6 million Jews and countless others.

Precisely because of Austria's importance to a full understanding of the Second World War and its aftermath, as well as the relative lack of attention Austria has received compared with, say, Germany, the American Jewish Committee commissioned this study as part of our acclaimed International Perspectives series.

We approached one of the most distinguished scholars of our time, Professor Robert Wistrich, a widely published expert on European and Jewish history, to write on how Austria's Second Republic (1945 to date) has dealt with the country's wartime past, and to compare and contrast Austria's approach with that of the Federal Republic of Germany. The result, readers will surely agree, is a remarkably thoughtful, comprehensive, and balanced appraisal of the Austrian record. To ensure maximum readership of this important publication, we are publishing *Austria and the Legacy of the Holocaust* in both English and German.

Open the Files on Raoul Wallenberg[*]
The Washington Post
January 18, 2000

Fifty-five years ago this month Soviet agents operating in Hungary arrested a young Swedish diplomat. Raoul Wallenberg already had become a legend for saving tens of thousands of Hungarian Jews from Nazi death camps in the final months of the war. His disappearance remains one of the greatest unsolved mysteries of the twentieth century.

Wallenberg was only thirty-two years old and without any diplomatic training when dispatched to Nazi-occupied Hungary in July 1944, to take on the mission of saving as many of Budapest's remaining 200,000 Jews as possible. During his six months in Hungary, Wallenberg pursued that mission passionately and with extraordinary ingenuity. He created the *Schutzpass*, a Swedish protective document, which he distributed with the help of a small group of assistants to

---

[*]This article also appeared in the *International Herald Tribune, San Francisco Chronicle, New York Post,* and other general circulation newspapers.

thousands of Jews whom he found on deportation trains or on death marches. And, remarkably, he faced down the notorious Adolf Eichmann and the Nazi occupying forces in Hungary to help prevent a pogrom in Budapest's central ghetto.

Only one week before his arrest, Wallenberg told a colleague: "For me there is no choice. I've taken on this assignment, and I'd never be able to go back to Stockholm without knowing inside myself I'd done all a man could do to save as many Jews as possible."

It is estimated that Wallenberg's heroic efforts saved the lives of 100,000 Jews. He was an angel of mercy—and that is why his mysterious disappearance continues to haunt us.

Why was Wallenberg arrested on Jan. 17, 1945, and what happened to him after he entered the infamous Soviet gulag?

These answers are hidden in Russia—in Soviet-era archives that remain shut and in the minds of aging eyewitnesses who have yet to reveal what they know. Scholars accessing Soviet-era archives in recent years have found them remarkably well maintained. The Wallenberg files most likely were given the same meticulous care. During the Soviet era, inquiries about Wallenberg were met with alternating and contradictory responses. The Kremlin first acknowledged that he was in Soviet hands, then denied any knowledge of him, then claimed he had died of a heart attack, and finally asserted that his death could not be explained. Since the collapse of the Soviet Union in 1991, Moscow has been silent. Rumors abound, but to this day we do not know with certainty whether Wallenberg is alive or dead.

What makes Wallenberg's arrest and disappearance inexplicable is the fact that the Soviet Union was an American ally during the war and suffered enormous losses in its relentless effort to help destroy the Nazi regime. This makes the need to know all the greater.

The United States has a special interest in pressing Moscow to solve this puzzle. While working in the Swedish embassy in Budapest Wallenberg was employed by the U.S. War Refugee Board, belatedly established in 1944 by the Roosevelt administration to try to save European Jews.

In 1981, through an initiative of Rep. Tom Lantos (D.-Calif.), whose wife, Annette, was one of the thousands rescued by Wallenberg,

Congress granted Wallenberg honorary U.S. citizenship. It was only the second time in history that Congress had taken such action. The U.S. Postal Service issued in 1997 a postage stamp in his honor, and his bust stands in the Capitol Rotunda.

But Washington has yet to adequately press Moscow at the highest levels to open the Wallenberg file. As William Korey, a scholar on Soviet affairs, commented recently: "It is now fifty-five years since a U.S. secretary of state expressed, however indirectly, any concern about Wallenberg's disappearance."

Far too much time has passed. Solving the Wallenberg mystery must now become a priority in our bilateral relations with Russia. Acting Russian president Putin can demonstrate his goodwill by opening fully the Soviet-era files in which the answers—and the truth about Wallenberg's fate—can be found.

Hurry Up, the Ex-Slaves Are Old*
International Herald Tribune
January 27, 2000

For Holocaust survivors, Jews and non-Jews alike, last month's agreement establishing a German government and industry fund to compensate Nazi-era slave and forced laborers was a significant milestone. It offers the former laborers who are still alive a small modicum of compensation while acknowledging the gross abuse they experienced at the hands of German industry serving the Nazi war machine.

The exploitation of human labor on an unprecedented scale took place on thousands of sites in Germany with the knowledge of company employees and neighboring residents. Extensive media coverage in recent weeks in Germany has stimulated extraordinary discussions. Significantly, parents now are telling their children for the first time their memories of watching prisoners march to work.

Creating the fund was a laudable initiative of the German government. But reports indicating that it might take the Bundestag many

*This article also appeared in *Die Welt* (Germany), January 28, 2000.

weeks, or even months, to approve the fund and that as many as 60 to 70 percent of eligible survivors could be excluded are not encouraging.

The Bundestag should move expeditiously to legislate the fund and also set up a mechanism for distribution of payments that is as comprehensive as possible. The biological clock continues to tick. I know this all too well from personal experience.

In 1995, Austria created a national fund and invited those Jewish victims who had to leave the country because of the Nazi occupation to apply for a one-time compensation payment of 70,000 schillings—just under $7,000. My father, born in 1920, had lived his first eighteen years almost equally divided between Berlin and Vienna. I thought he might qualify, but he had some qualms.

"It's blood money," he said. And he didn't want them "to think they can close the books at $7,000 a head."

A few weeks later, though, he called me and said he had reconsidered. It was not the money, he emphatically stated. No sum could compensate him for the lost years, the suffering, the brutal dislocation. "But I feel my mortality and I want Austria to acknowledge in some way its complicity in the Nazi crimes. This is the only way, I suppose."

He submitted his application but was turned down because he could prove only eight and a half years' residency in Austria before the war rather than the required ten. He protested, but to no avail. He felt humiliated for even trying.

In November 1998, some eighteen months after Austria rejected my father's application, an official of the Austrian fund told me that the regulations had been eased and my father was now eligible. Too late, I replied. He had passed away, aged seventy-eight, five months earlier. (At my request, the fund approved a grant to the American Jewish Committee in memory of my father for two projects related to Austria and the Holocaust.)

The German fund for slave and forced labor survivors provides for a long overdue moral reckoning by the German government and industry. While some German firms have joined the fund, hundreds continue to hide behind a wall of myth, denial, and legal obfuscation.

The more than 250 firms identified to date by the American Jewish Committee account for just a fraction of all German companies that used slave or forced labor during the Nazi era and are still in operation today, according to Germany's preeminent expert on Nazi-era slave and forced labor, Ulrich Herbert of the University of Freiburg. Every sector of German industry was heavily dependent on such labor during the war.

Publication of our list has spurred a belated but encouraging conversation across Germany, as companies and the communities in which they are based now take a hard look in the mirror.

Time is not our friend. The survivors of Nazi slave and forced labor are almost all in their seventies and eighties. The Bundestag needs to act quickly, and firms which have yet to come forward should do so now.

5. JAPAN

The Elders of Zion in Tokyo:
What Should We Do About Japanese Anti-Semitism?
Moment
October 1987

A startling *New York Times* story last March datelined Tokyo focused on the popularity of two books in Japanese strikingly similar to the infamous, czarist-fabricated *Protocols of the Elders of Zion*.

These mass-circulation Japanese paperbacks by a self-described Christian fundamentalist, Masami Uno, claim that a Jewish network has established hegemony in the United States through its domination of American politics, the media, key professions—law, medicine, and accounting—and the economy, including control of such major corporations as IBM, General Motors, Standard Oil, and Exxon. The next target? Japan. The rising yen, overseas manufacturing by Japanese multinationals, the growing competitive strength of South Korea, and the outflow of Japanese capital to the United States are all part of the Jewish intrigue. Even the Lockheed scandal, which fingered Japanese prime minister Tanaka, and Watergate were, according to this bizarre theory, the work of the Jews, specifically the "Jew" Nelson Rockefeller.

With only the most marginal contact with world Jewry—and this only in the last hundred years—and no more than a few hundred Jews resident in the entire country, what can possibly explain such a preoccupation in Japan with alleged Jewish-inspired plots?

"The problems in Japan cannot be judged by the standards of classical anti-Semitism," observed Isi Leibler, a prominent Australian businessman and president of the Asia-Pacific branch of the World Jewish Congress. "With the exception of a remnant Jewish population of a few thousand in India, there is virtually no Jewish presence anywhere in Asia. In the West and Middle East, we Jews share common roots and have intermingled—sometimes for better, sometimes for worse—with Christians and Muslims. But in Asia, including Japan, we have no common cultural or historical experience."

Yet it is precisely this lack of direct contact, coupled with Japan's island-nation mentality, highly homogeneous people, and relative cultural insularity, that has allowed the creation of false images and stereotypes—not all of them negative, by the way—of Jews and Judaism among a significant element in the population of 121 million, 99 percent of whom have probably never met a Jew. As Bernard Krisher, an American resident in Japan for the past twenty-five years and the former Tokyo correspondent for *Newsweek* and *Fortune*, commented: "To the Japanese, Jews are like dragons and fairies."

A number of experts predict that the current wave of anti-Semitic literature is likely to prove a short-lived fad—as much a derivative of currently strained Japanese-American ties as of any particular feelings about Jews per se. The authors of the current spate of anti-Semitic tracts in Japanese are without any serious reputation. Nobuo Matsunaga, Japan's ambassador to the United States, stated in response to a letter from Senator Arlen Specter (R-PA) and Representative Charles Schumer (D-NY) protesting recent manifestations of Japanese anti-Semitism, that "anti-Semitism has no roots in Japan's cultural history," adding that the views of such authors as Uno can "in no way be interpreted as representative of the views of the Japanese people, much less the view of the Government of Japan."

Yet Uno's books are not alone. Many leading Japanese bookstores have "Jewish corners" where such titles as *The Secret of Jewish Power to Control the World, The Jewish Plan for Conquest of the World, How to Read the Hidden Meaning of the Jewish Protocols,* and *Miracles of the Torah Which Control the World* are displayed. Elsewhere in the same stores, shoppers will find such works as Amos Oz's *In the Land of Israel*, Elie Wiesel's *Night*, Norman Cohn's *Warrant for Genocide*, all in Japanese translation, and serious works on Jewish topics by Japanese scholars. Regrettably, none of these latter authors begin to match the success of Uno and his colleagues, though *The Diary of Anne Frank* has reportedly sold more copies in Japan—4 million—than in any other country outside the United States. Uno's first two books, *If You Understand Judea, You Understand the World* and *If You Understand Judea, You Understand Japan*, have been so successful that last June he brought out a third, *The Day the Dollar Turned into Paper: The Jewish Conspiracy*.

These anti-Semitic books have sold hundreds of thousands of copies each. While it is difficult to assess their impact on opinion-making circles in Japan, *Yomiuri Shimbum*, the country's largest circulation newspaper, reported last January that Uno's works have been cited by some Bank of Japan officials. One of them was quoted as saying that after reading the Uno books, "I suddenly realized why everything is happening," referring to the purported Jewish manipulation of the value of the yen and the dollar.

"The current buildup of anti-Semitism may be more the exception than the rule," said Asher Naim, currently minister of information at the Israeli embassy in Washington and among the first Israeli diplomats to serve in Tokyo in the 1950s. "Let's not forget, however, that exceptions can become the rule. Scapegoating of a mythically omnipotent world Jewry could become possible if political and economic conditions warrant. America is seen by some Japanese as too powerful and too amorphous, so there might be greater receptivity to pointing the finger at a visible, distinct, and vulnerable target, even though no basis in reality exists." If American-Japanese relations continue to deteriorate, Japanese anti-Semitism may grow concomitantly.

Also shaping Japanese views of Jews may be Japan's attitude toward Israel. Japan established diplomatic ties with Israel in 1952. Historically, the Middle East was not an area of much concern to Japan. Oil was plentiful and cheap; otherwise, the Japanese had no major geopolitical interests in the region. But after the 1967 Six-Day War, and particularly after the 1973 Yom Kippur War, all this changed. To some extent, Japanese public opinion, which had earlier been sympathetic to the fledgling Jewish state, came to identify with the Palestinians. Even more significantly, oil-dependent Japan was threatened with Arab blackmail. Reformulate your foreign policy to be supportive of the Arab side, Tokyo was told in no uncertain terms, or lose vital Persian Gulf oil. For Japan, more dependent on imported energy resources (including 99.7 percent of its primary energy staple, petroleum) than any other major industrialized country, the choice was obvious.

Japan hurriedly realigned its foreign policy to curry favor with the Arab states and maintain the vital oil flow. Diplomatic ties with Jerusalem continued, despite Arab pressure to sever them, but they were best characterized as cautious and low-profile. Japanese officials began to speak out in favor of the "legitimate rights" of the Palestinians and an Israeli withdrawal to the pre–Six-Day War borders.

The state of Japanese-Israeli relations is rather dramatically revealed in the following facts:

- No Japanese cabinet-level figure has ever officially visited Israel. High-level Israeli visits have perforce been infrequent: Foreign Minister Abba Eban in 1967, Minister of Transport and Communications Shimon Peres in 1973, Deputy Prime Minister and Foreign Minister Yitzhak Shamir in 1985.

- In 1974, Japan voted to give the Palestine Liberation Organization observer status at the United Nations. Three years later, a PLO office was established in Tokyo. In 1981, Yasir Arafat visited Japan under a convoluted diplomatic arrangement to attempt to mask the official nature of the trip. At the time, Prime Minister Zenko Suzuki became the first head of a major noncommunist country to receive the PLO leader.

- No Japanese economic delegation has ever visited Israel.

- No Japanese company has ever invested in Israel.

- The Japanese External Trade Organization, which maintains offices in dozens of major cities around the world, refuses to establish a presence in Israel.

- El Al, Israel's national airline, has been repeatedly refused landing rights in Tokyo. Japan Air Lines has consistently declined to add Tel Aviv to its air routes.

- Though Israeli ships do make calls in Japanese ports, no Japanese ships reciprocate in Israel.

- Bilateral trade—only around $400 million annually—is far lower than its potential because Japanese companies are reluctant to jeopardize ties with the Arab world. Many major Japanese corporations adhere to the Arab boycott of Israel. Corporations like

Toyota, Nissan, and Hitachi have refused to sign deals with Israeli counterparts. Despite repeated denials of any governmental role, the involvement of such Japanese ministries as the Foreign Ministry and the Ministry of International Trade and Industry in assisting companies' compliance with the boycott has been amply demonstrated, according to experts in the United States and Israel. Subaru cars, however, are widely sold in Israel. Other companies, such as Sony, Sanyo, National, and Sharp, trade with Israel indirectly.

The Japanese are obviously fearful of offending Arab governments and jeopardizing their own Arab markets. Israeli observers regard this as a shameful stance by the world's second economic superpower, the envy of much of the world. With oil now plentiful and relatively cheap, with other leading democratic countries enjoying close political and commercial ties with Jerusalem without sacrificing other interests in the region, with Tokyo's repeated insistence that it favors the principles of free trade, why does Japan continue its hesitant policy vis-à-vis Israel?

Although difficult to assess, these Japanese attitudes toward Israel no doubt have some effect on views toward Jews generally. Historically, a small current of anti-Semitism in Japan can be traced back as far as the 1870s—prior even to the establishment of the first synagogue, built by Russian Jews in Nagasaki in 1894—when fundamentalist Christian missionaries arrived in the Japanese archipelago and introduced the notion of Jews as the anti-Christ. At about the same time, *The Merchant of Venice* became one of the first works of European literature to be translated into Japanese. It enjoyed immediate popularity and eventually was incorporated into the school curriculum, where it remains today.

"The impact of the introduction of the play was indeed very significant," commented Afikumi Ikeda of Tokyo's Institute of Developing Economies in a recent lecture at the Hebrew University. "Before then, nobody cared about differences among the Westerners. They were all alike; they were all *gaijin* [aliens, outsiders], and the only distinction between them was the language they spoke. . . . For the first time, Japanese began to realize that Westerners had their own social outcast group . . . and without a Jewish community at hand, it is impossible to verify the validity of such imported images."

Among the non-Jewish refugees fleeing eastward from the 1917 Russian Revolution were some who spread the false notion that Jews were behind the overthrow of the last czar and the ill-fated Kerensky regime, an unsettling notion in anti-Bolshevik Japan. These refugees brought with them copies of the *Protocols of the Elders of Zion*, which was first translated into Japanese in 1924 by Captain Norihiro Yasue, head of the Imperial Army's Jewish bureau. (Because of the army's growing perception of Jews as a threat to Japan's security, they established an office for the purpose of studying the Jewish people.) Nearly forty different translations of the *Protocols* are available in Japanese; according to Professor Herbert Passin of Columbia University, the book is more easily accessible in Japan today than in any other country in the world.

The Axis alliance between Nazi Germany and Japan also prompted the emergence of anti-Semitic organizations in Japan, as well as the distribution of some anti-Semitic hate literature.

But Japan's attitudes toward Jews were not then and are not now wholly negative. Some Christians, who form a tiny but intellectually significant segment of the Japanese population, embrace the notion that the Jews are God's chosen people, the People of the Book. The Christian Makuya movement, founded in 1948 as the Japanese New Zionist Movement, has several thousand members who learn Hebrew, make regular pilgrimages to Israel, conduct demonstrations on behalf of Israel in Japan, and raise money for philanthropic purposes in the Jewish state.

Other Japanese continue to recall with gratitude, even awe, the vital financial assistance extended by Jacob Schiff, an American Jew and president of the investment banking firm of Kuhn, Loeb and Co., during the Russo-Japanese War of 1904–5, at a time when other international financiers proved unresponsive.

Moreover, the attitude of the Japanese during World War II differed markedly from that of the Germans. In Israel there is a forest named in honor of Sempo Sugihara, the Japanese consul in Kaunas, Lithuania, who risked his career to issue visas to thousands of Jews who succeeded in escaping to Japan or Japanese-occupied Manchuria. Through his effort, the entire Mir Yeshiva in Kaunas—300 students and faculty—was saved.

In all, as many as 18,000 German, Austrian, and Polish Jews were able to find a safe haven in Manchuria, according to David Kranzler, a historian at Queensborough Community College. In part, the Japanese government's generally benign attitude may have been prompted by a desire to assert independence from its Nazi allies. And no doubt the hope to utilize Jewish talent and capital, especially in Manchuria, played a part.

While a ghetto was established for some Jews in Shanghai in 1943 due to Nazi pressure, and the Jews faced serious restrictions, the circumstances can in no way be compared to conditions in Europe. Thus, as Passin noted, "when the war ended, the Germans had to face the enormity of their war crimes against the Jews, but the Japanese did not. Not having experienced active hostility toward the Jews, the Japanese felt no need to purge themselves. And there remained a continuing ambivalence toward Jews: On the one hand, they accepted the notion that Jews were successful and powerful, but they also admired this success and believed that Jews could be helpful to Japan."

This suggests another element in the Japanese attitude toward the Jews: admiration for what some Japanese see as shared traits—a drive for success, respect for education and hard work, a desire to preserve long cultural and historical traditions. Unfortunately, these feelings can get carried away in books that may be intended as flattery but more readily contribute to dangerous stereotyping. Japanese bookstores carry such titles as *Make Money with Stocks Targeted by the Jews, How Jews Negotiate, How Jews Make Money,* and *Jewish Methods on Negotiating in Law.*

What can be done to promote greater understanding between the Japanese and the Jews? Unfortunately, Jewish organizations have devoted too little attention and effort to Japan, despite its growing world importance. There is an urgent need for long-term programming—sensitively tailored to take into account the specific characteristics of Japanese society. The only major conference in Japan on relations between the Japanese and the Jews was held in 1976. It was sponsored by the Lutheran World Federation, the Seibunsha (Lutheran) Publishing House, and the Japan Lutheran Theological College.

According to one participant, Arne Sovik of the Lutheran World Federation, the delegates agreed that "efforts must be made to correct prejudicial treatment of Jews in Japan in three areas: (a) the mass media, which since 1967 has been increasingly anti-Jewish; (b) textbooks, which deal with Jewish history in an oversimplified way; and (c) Christian teaching, which has sometimes encouraged negative attitudes through poorly researched sermons and study materials on the New Testament record."

According to David G. Goodman, an associate professor of Japanese and comparative literature at the University of Illinois, who has been concerned with promoting Japanese–Jewish understanding over the past thirteen years and has written two books in Japanese that deal with both Jewish and Israeli themes, "There is no Jewish organization, no group of people, either in Japan or elsewhere, prepared to actively and systematically work toward the promotion of mutual Japanese–Jewish understanding. The small Jewish community in Japan is simply unable to undertake such a major project. Major Jewish organizations, which are not currently equipped to deal with the complexity of Japanese society, must begin to do so."

Goodman sees the possibility of a larger recrudescence of anti-Semitism in Asia, signaled by the spate of anti-Semitic books in Japanese. Uno's first two books have recently been translated into Korean. "Unfortunately," Goodman notes, "few Japanese intellectuals of stature have stood up to openly condemn these dangerous trends. In the end, the only pressure that will truly work in Japan is not outside pressure, though there is a need for outsiders respected in Japan to speak up, but the pressure of leading Japanese figures who publicly denounce this anti-Semitism."

A number of areas need to be explored by American Jewry, bearing in mind that the first priority must be to gain a better understanding of Japanese society. Otherwise, some well-intentioned efforts may be doomed to failure, lost in the wide cultural abyss that separates our two countries. Future program possibilities include symposia in Japan on Jewish themes, cosponsored by respected Japanese institutions; reciprocal exchanges between leading American Jewish and Japanese figures; interreligious dialogue; and review of treatment of Jewish subjects—Jewish history, Holocaust, Judaism, Israel—in the Japanese educational system and the media.

Former news correspondent Krisher says that "what is needed is some educational program about Jews and Judaism in Japan. Not public relations but something more substantial. There are American, British, French, Italian, and German cultural centers. Why not a Jewish or Hebraic cultural center—attached to the Jewish Community Center in Tokyo and funded by American Jewish organizations, as neither the Jews here nor the Israeli embassy has the funds?"

Others have suggested a chair in Jewish studies at one of the major Japanese universities—a small but significant beginning.

Given the press of other compelling issues in Jewish life and limited resources, the current difficulties (and opportunities) in Japan may not be seen as a top priority, but such a conclusion ignores the rapidly growing significance of Japan, and indeed of all Asia, on the world scene, not to speak of the potential dangers posed by recent anti-Semitic manifestations in Japan. This situation poses a major challenge to world Jewry. It would be a mistake if we did not rise to meet it.

Making a Difference:
The American Jewish Committee and Japan—
A Case Study
Hilda Katz Blaustein Leadership Institute
Aspen, Colorado
June 24, 1994

In 1987 Clyde Haberman wrote in the *New York Times* of Uno Masami, the Japanese author of several anti-Semitic books.

It blindsided us, I admit. The Jewish community was woefully unprepared to deal with Asia. Our attention traditionally focused on the United States, Europe, the Middle East.

How AJC chose to deal with the narrow issue of Uno and the broader question of Asia reveals, I believe, the essence and distinctiveness of the agency.

Other Jewish agencies contented themselves with issuing statements of denunciation and perhaps getting cited in the JTA or a local paper.

Our aims, however, while similar in seeking to eradicate a problem, were governed by an entirely different strategy.

If the ultimate goals were to influence Japanese society, we admitted we didn't have a clue how to go about it.

We spent literally one year seeking the answers—from Japanologists in the United States, from State Department officials, from Japanese themselves.

At the end of the year, we established a Pacific Rim Institute, with Dr. Neil Sandberg as its director, and embarked on the first of fourteen visits to Japan.

We did not rush to judgment; we sought to meet a wide group of people in Japan; we emphasized the positive goal of enhancing relations between Japanese and Jews and, in so doing, filling the void of ignorance which feeds stereotypes and scapegoating.

The strategy began to pay off. With each visit we were upgraded to a higher level of officials until we were able to meet, for example, the foreign minister, the first time in history any Jewish group had ever met the Japanese foreign minister.

We were able to enlist the government's help on the issue of mainstream publishers and booksellers selling anti-Semitic books.

We were able to procure from the government the unusual step of a letter to the Japanese Publishers' Association expressing the embarrassment to Japan at the publication of such books.

We were able to meet with some of the publishers and with editors of newspapers that carried ads for these books.

And, over time, we were able to broaden our discussion to include Japan's role in the Middle East, including its tepid bilateral ties with Israel and its widespread adherence to the Arab boycott.

The results? The Japanese foreign minister chose his meeting with us in December 1992 to announce that formal steps had been taken for the first time to end adherence to the boycott.

And, when asked by journalists why this step had been taken, a Foreign Ministry spokesman said on the record: "Because of the patient, persistent work of the American Jewish Committee which adapted to the Japanese method and dealt with us in that manner."

And, a year earlier, the Japanese deputy foreign minister agreed to our request that Japan not only support but also cosponsor the repeal of the infamous "Zionism is racism" resolution.

At the same time, we made clear that our dialogue with Japan was two-way.

We wrote to President-elect Clinton in December 1992 about the importance of Japan-U.S. relations.

We involved ourselves in the attempted purchase by a Japanese consortium of the Seattle Mariners baseball team, first rejected by the baseball commissioner for what could only be xenophobic reasons, later accepted, in part, due to our efforts.

We talked to Columbia Pictures, together with the Japanese American Citizens League, concerning fears of ethnic stereotyping in the then-forthcoming film, *Rising Sun*.

Emanating from this work as well has been similarly deep involvement with Korea (and the Korean-American community), now China, and, increasingly, certain other Asian countries.

I mention these examples of our work not only because of my pride in what we have accomplished—and the appreciation we have received, particularly from Israel—but because it encapsulates for me what I believe to be the essence of this organization.

Consider:

- A determination to look at long-term trends, in this case the rise of Asia, and to consider the implications for the Jewish community;
- A willingness to study and understand the unique characteristics of an issue, knowing that techniques with one country or institution may not be readily duplicable elsewhere;
- An approach that combines perseverance, persistence, and patience;
- A balance of public and private activities, but never endangering the long-term goal in a desire for public recognition;
- The involvement of lay and staff working as a team, the lay people at times providing entrée into Japan's corporate, cultural, and political worlds, the staff the ongoing work and backup;
- The active participation of chapters through their local coalitions with Japanese-Americans and by establishing relations with

Japanese consulates and the local Japanese business community;
- High-level contacts in the U.S. and Israeli governments. We always meet in Japan, for example, with the U.S. ambassador—now Walter Mondale—to consult and exchange views, as we do with the Israeli ambassador. AJC works hard to develop and maintain such contacts both at home and abroad.
- And, again quite unique, as I mentioned earlier, a recognition that a true relationship cannot be a one-way street. We have to be able to listen as well as talk, to seek to understand—if not always agree—with those with whom we speak, and to work to build an atmosphere of trust.

Time does not permit elaboration today, but the basic elements of our approach in this case study, I believe, could as easily be applied to our decades-long work with the Christian world, especially the Catholic Church, and to the field of intergroup relations in the United States, as well as to other key issues on our agenda.

As a consequence, we have been able to achieve a great deal—much more than is generally known—to advance Jewish well-being both in the United States and abroad, as well as to make a major contribution to the general good with respect to pluralism, social policy, civil rights, and human rights.

The problems now facing us are no less daunting or complex than those we have faced to date, among them:
- the rise of extremist forms of nationalism and group differentiation (e.g., Bosnia, Rwanda, Russia);
- the challenge of achieving durable peace in the Middle East;
- the future of relations between Israel and American Jews;
- intergroup challenges here at home, especially regarding black-Jewish relations but potentially also with Hispanic and Asian communities that we still don't know well enough;
- the prospects for Jewish identity and continuity, perhaps the single most compelling issue we face and the one whose fate we alone will ultimately determine;
- the future of Jewish philanthropy to Jewish causes, the level of commitment of American Jews to the Jewish communal agenda, and the degree of political influence of American Jews in an era when other groups in America are seeking their share.

I don't know that we have all the answers, but I firmly believe that the involvement of a new generation of AJC leaders—yourselves—gives us a fighting chance.

If we step back for a moment and look at the forest, not the trees, in our lifetimes we have witnessed three miracles:

- Israel's survival and development, against all the odds, to the point now where maybe, just maybe, an era of peace with its neighbors awaits it;
- The emergence of a once cowed Soviet Jewish community and the emigration from the USSR to Israel and the United States of approximately 1 million people, while Jewish life in the former Soviet Union strikingly takes root;
- The emergence of a truly unprecedented Diaspora Jewish community in the United States—large, powerful, successful, fully engaged domestically and internationally, organized, vibrant, creative.

Imagine, in the course of less than fifty years, we have transformed Jews from a weak, vulnerable, marginalized, powerless people to a strong, dynamic, influential community, which is sovereign in the Jewish homeland, Israel.

Today, countries want links with Israel. Today, in Bosnia, all sides want a Jewish moral *hechsher*; Russian non-Jews, and Ethiopian non-Jews as well, seek to identify as Jews because they see it as a ticket to freedom and redemption. Today, countries and groups actively seek contact with American Jewry, believing this can be to their benefit.

All this—and you and the existence of organizations like AJC—give me great hope for the future.

Welcoming Remarks at
AJC-Sponsored Concert by Shinonome Choir
Congregation Rodeph Sholom, New York
November 6, 1997

Erev tov. Konbanwa. Good evening.

It is my privilege and pleasure, on behalf of the American Jewish Committee and its New York Chapter, to welcome you all to a very special evening.

I can confidently make three promises about the evening.

First, no politicians—of any political party—will come before you this evening and ask for your vote. That's a relief after a busy and noisy electoral season.

Second, for those of you who are hearing the choir for the first time, you're in for a real musical treat.

And third, even for the most jaded New Yorkers among us who may feel they've seen it all, this performance tonight promises to be something entirely different and likely to leave an imprint on you for a long time to come.

Why is the American Jewish Committee, an organization known for its work in international and domestic policy issues, in interreligious and interethnic relations, and not exactly as a cultural impresario, the sponsor of this event?

There's a good reason. In 1987, the American Jewish community was caught completely off guard by reports of the popularity of anti-Semitic books in Japan.

Japan? Anti-Semitism?

We at the American Jewish Committee embarked on a program, now ten years old, to better understand Japan. Japan was simply too important in world affairs to ignore, all the more so if canards about the Jewish people were circulating in some circles. And the tiny Jewish community in Japan, numbering a few hundred expatriates, was in no position to undertake the task alone on behalf of world Jewry.

Over these past ten years, working principally through our Asia and Pacific Rim Institute, we have pursued several issues, among them:

- On the international front, to encourage closer political and commercial ties between Tokyo and Jerusalem, and to urge an end to Japanese corporate support for the Arab economic boycott against Israel;
- Domestically, to raise the consciousness of major Japanese publishing houses about the damage done by printing such unadulterated anti-Semitism, and of Japanese mainstream booksellers who too often made the books readily available.

We can report success.

Japanese-Israeli relations have improved dramatically in recent years. And not only has the adherence to the Arab boycott ended, but today Japan is one of Israel's three leading trading partners, together with the United States and Germany.

Moreover, the popularity of anti-Semitic books has declined dramatically, not because of censorship but rather because respectable Japanese society came to understand that these weren't serious books; no, they were hate-filled volumes with no redeeming value.

Lastly, during this decade of our work in Japan, we set as a major goal enhancing understanding between two proud and ancient peoples—the Jews and the Japanese—who knew too little about one another because history had only infrequently brought us together. That work has been going on in Japan; it's also been going on in cities like New York, where our AJC chapter has reached out to the large Japanese community living and working here.

And it has been a goal of others as well, including especially Rabbi Marvin Tokayer, here with us this evening, who through his years in Japan and his extensive writings, has helped the Japanese appreciate the beauty and riches of the Jewish tradition.

In the course of our efforts in Japan, we came to know—and respect—an impressive group of people. Inspired by their own religious faith, many studied Hebrew. They traveled to Israel to show their solidarity with the Jewish state. They even established a Holocaust museum and education center in Japan, with which we cooperate and which receives thousands of visitors each year.

And they sing; they sing beautifully. They created this choir, the Shinonome Choir, which you're about to hear, to express their love of Israel and the Jewish people, and they've carried their musical gift around the world.

In just a moment you'll hear that gift. Let me first note the presence in the audience of two distinguished diplomatic guests: Mitugo Saito, counselor of Japan's Mission to the UN, and Oren David, counselor of Israel's Mission to the UN. Also with us is Professor Hillel Levine of Boston University, the author of a highly acclaimed book on Sempo Sugihara, the Japanese consul in wartime Kaunas, who, defying his government's orders, issued lifesaving visas to thousands of Jews fleeing the Nazis. We're delighted they are here.

Moreover, I'd like to express our deep appreciation to Rabbi Robert Levine, a friend, and this magnificent congregation for agreeing to open their doors, and hearts, for this concert.

Thank you very much. *Oregato gezaimusto. Toda raba.*

Never Let Complacency Guide Us Again,
in *Courage to Remember: Interviews on the Holocaust*[*]
by Kinue Tokudome
(Paragon House, 1999)

It was with this question of reflection on the wartime Jewish leaders' stance and the lesson it has taught the postwar generation of Jewish leaders that I met David A. Harris, executive director of the American Jewish Committee.

AJC was founded in 1906 by a small group of influential Jews, including Jacob Schiff, who volunteered to underwrite Japan's war bonds during the Russo-Japanese War to defend the rights of Jews around the world. Together with the World Jewish Congress, it was one of the major Jewish organizations in the United States during the Holocaust. Although its membership was small, AJC "possessed substantial prestige and influence, had entry to some high levels of government and American society, and controlled considerable funds."[†] Yet, its leaders did not think their organization could exert a major influence on rescuing of the European Jews as its wartime executive vice president's remark revealed—"Nothing will stop the Nazis except their destruction."

Today, AJC has 50,000 members. Its stated missions are "ensuring the security of Jews," "safeguarding pluralism," and "enriching American Jewish life." [Its] activities also have expanded worldwide. For example, AJC spearheaded the successful drive in 1993 to establish a UN High Commissioner for Human Rights.

Mr. Harris, together with Dr. Neil Sandberg, director of the Asia and Pacific Rim Institute, which AJC created in 1989, largely in response

[*]The following is an excerpt from the interview that appeared in *Courage to Remember*, which was printed in Japan and the United States.

[†]David S. Wyman, *The Abandonment of the Jews* (New York: Pantheon Books, 1984).

to the rise of anti-Semitic publications in Japan, visited Japan to promote a dialogue between the Japanese people and the Jews. Their
approach to Japan has been in accordance with the AJC's tradition of
low-key diplomacy. Their efforts in Japan seem to have paid off, resulting in Japan's diplomatic warming toward Israel during the late 1980s,
which was due in good measure to Tokyo's blossoming tie with the
American Jewish Committee.*

Mr. Harris was named by *Lifestyles* magazine as one of eighteen
North American Jews who will serve as the leaders in the twenty-first
century. He studied at the University of Pennsylvania, the London
School of Economics, and Oxford University. He has written three
books and numerous articles on East-West relations and the Middle
East.

I interviewed him at AJC's headquarters in New York.

*What is your assessment of the level of knowledge about the history
of the Holocaust held by the general population? What are the lessons
of the Holocaust we should learn?*

People have the opportunity to learn about the Holocaust. Many of
the school systems in this and other countries discuss the Holocaust.
There are any number of books, films, television programs, and now,
of course, we in the United States have a very substantial museum. And
there are also traveling exhibits, like that on Anne Frank. So I think the
possibility for knowledge is there. But the challenge really is how to
continually translate the meaning of the Holocaust as something that
has significance . . . for new generations, so it doesn't simply become
another historical fact that people memorize. It should translate much
more substantially than that. It should not just be a general awareness
of what took place, but the realization that truly civilized people stand
between what took place and what might take place again somewhere
in the world, whether against Jews or perhaps against other groups. So
the real challenge is not just to get information out. The real challenge
is to get information out and translate it in ways that have meaning and
relevance, morally and ethically, for people today and in the future.

*David Goodman and Miyazawa Masanori, *Jews in the Japanese Mind* (New York: The Free
Press, 1995).

What do you think is the best way to achieve that?

I don't think there's any one best way. There have to be many different approaches. Perhaps in different societies and cultures different ways are needed. Lately, a focus on individuals and the difference they made in the history of the Holocaust has become important. In Japan, for example, it is a focus on Sugihara, or on Schindler in Germany, or on Wallenberg in Sweden. I think this is very important because it teaches us all that an individual, you or I, can, if we choose, make a difference. This really destroys the argument that we are powerless in the face of evil. And I think that's a very important moral lesson. So, in that sense, a focus on individuals, both those individuals who try to act and, conversely, those who are complicit—or try to ignore—is important for us to understand.

To ignore means?

To bury their heads in the sand, to look the other way.

And they were the majority?

Yes, they were the majority, but what we learned is that individuals count. They can count positively, they can count negatively. But in a time of moral crisis, people cannot believe they can achieve some level of neutrality. Neutrality, by definition, becomes a kind of subconscious association with the oppressor. So, an emphasis on the difference an individual can make is one important approach.

But there is a danger even in this approach. The danger is that Japanese society, for example, begins to associate its history with Sugihara, or German society with Schindler, when in fact what Sugihara did ran contrary to his own Foreign Ministry, and what Schindler did was certainly the exception in Germany. So there is a danger here and we have to be conscious of it.

But I still think this approach of focusing on the issue of ethics and morals—why certain people acted the way they did, what was in their upbringing, their family, their religion, and their community that gave them the courage and determination to help—is important.

And they did not have to be saints or heroes, did they?

Schindler was not a saint. Anyone who saw the movie realized that from the beginning. I think the most powerful thing about that movie was that he was a very unlikely hero. Here was a flawed individual who could have been anyone, and yet there was something within him, some moral imperative, which led him to do what he did.

Now, that's a part of it. The second moral lesson of the Holocaust which we have to teach is that democracy is the single best form of assurance against tyranny and oppression. When Germany abandoned the democratic Weimar Republic in 1933, the safeguards and protection disappeared. The best form of government to protect human rights, civil rights, and minority rights is a thriving, functioning democracy. It's not a perfect guarantee but still the best we have. But for a democracy to thrive and function, it requires the active involvement and participation of its citizens. And so the second lesson of the Holocaust, a practical lesson, it seems to me, is that good people have a profound stake in the system of government under which they live. It is true, we get the government we deserve; therefore, unless all of us care and act, we run the risk of governments that become anti-democratic, that become oppressive.

You mentioned that people get the government they deserve. It is also said that people get the media they deserve. Of course, you remember the incident last year when one of the major Japanese publishing companies ran an article in their monthly magazine saying that gas chambers did not exist. I understand your organization's approach to that kind of incident has always been educational, low key, and behind the scenes. But it ended in an opposite manner. How do you feel about it?

I don't think there's any quick solution. Japan is a country of 120 million people and there are really no indigenous Japanese Jews. There are only 500 to 1,000 Jews living in Japan, some of them for only a few years. So basically Japanese and Jews have very little contact and, even when they do, it may not be as Japanese and Jews but rather, say, as businessmen or professors. I think we have to understand that the challenge which we set for ourselves at the American Jewish Committee in 1987 in trying to develop relations between Japan and the Jewish people was intended as a long-term process. Those who wish to see immediate results will be frustrated. But there have been some encouraging developments. I have been especially pleased by the warming of relations between Japan and Israel. Israel brings not just political and economic, but also cultural and human, dimensions to the relations, and vice versa.

We are looking for more opportunities to introduce Japan to the Jewish experience. We have talked with some Japanese TV stations about the possibility of television programming. And although there are a number of good books dealing with Jews, none of them is terribly popular in Japan other than the famous one many years ago, *Japanese and Jews*. Maybe your book will be equally successful.

That was written by a Japanese author.

Yes. Again, there haven't been many popular books about Jewish people. Even *The Diary of Anne Frank*, which many Japanese proudly remind us is one of the best-selling books in the history of Japan, is not really seen as a Jewish experience by many Japanese. It is read more as the tragedy of a young girl in a particular historical setting. In Japan it has become a kind of universal metaphor for youth and suffering and dreams rather than a very direct expression of Jewish anguish during the Holocaust.

So there's still a lot of work to be done. I am not one of those who assert that every Japanese is anti-Semitic. I don't believe that. I believe, however, that there is much ignorance in Japan about Jews. There is some ignorance among Jews about Japan. I don't think the two are equivalent. There is much more ignorance in Japan about Jews, and it's very understandable. Jews are a very small percentage of the world's population. If we know more about Japan, it's because Japan has the world's second largest economy and is one of the world's major countries. When you have these anti-Semitic incidents in the Japanese media from time to time, I think it embarrasses many responsible and educated Japanese. They know this is foolish and shameful, yet they also know that with a free press people can write what they want. But they know it stains the image of Japan. And it does, it really does.

What impact did your family's wartime experiences in Europe have on you?

My parents didn't hide things from me. But they didn't teach me every night about the history of the Holocaust, the need to remember, the need to be strong, and so forth. There was a kind of quiet dignity about my family. It was something I absorbed, I suppose, by breathing the family air . . . ; it became very much a part of my own identity. As time passed, I wanted not just to absorb it, but to see whether there was something I could do about it with the blessing of freedom I had been given, having been born in the United States.

I asked myself: Was there something I could do for the Jewish people rather than simply pursuing a career defined by making money or acquiring material goods? And, in the end, there was. I found it in my work in the Jewish community, which again was the direct result of the experiences of my family; all of that together created a foundation for my life. This happened slowly, though, almost unknowingly. And I now realize I was inexorably drawn in that direction and, by the time I was twenty-five, it had became clear to me that this is what I wanted to do. I wanted to work in the Jewish community and on behalf of the Jewish people.

You chose a very old and established organization to do that, didn't you? I understand that the AJC is almost [a] hundred years old and the people at the top must be much older than you. You are young. Why did you choose this organization?

The prime minister of Israel is younger than I, and his country is thousands of years old. Well, this organization, unique among those I know, reflects the balance within me. It embodies both the concern for specifically Jewish issues and broader universal interests. This organization balances quiet diplomacy and public advocacy. In other words, this organization is quite sophisticated in its methodology and in the way it approaches matters. It also is a nonideological organization. By contrast, a lot of organizations, Jewish or non-Jewish, are ideologically driven. They are to the right or left, hawkish or dovish, conservative or liberal.

Your organization is not conservative?

No, we are not, not at all. We are a highly nuanced organization. By the way, that's who I am, too. . . . This organization matches me best. I want to be able to be concerned about manifestations of anti-Semitism in Japan, but I also want to participate in the broader transpacific dialogue about relations between the United States and Asian countries. The American Jewish Committee is the only organization I know that allows me to do both.

It's not an organization driven solely by fear, nor an organization simply protective and defensive. It's an organization that is protective and defensive when it needs to be. But, at the same time, it is also an organization that is forward-looking and believes in the possibility of a better tomorrow, and knows it can make a contribution to improving the world in which we live. Again, the balance between hope and fear.

Many agencies, Jewish or non-Jewish, are driven principally by fear. They believe that they can raise money and attract members by speaking to their fears. What we try to do is both to understand people's fears in the Jewish community and to speak to their aspirations and hopes. That's the balance I am most comfortable with.

But isn't there anything you would like to try that this organization did not do in the past?

This organization is ninety years old. I wasn't alive for the first forty-three years of its history. This organization has enough achievements and accomplishments to fill volumes. And books have indeed been written. It has a proud history of significant contributions to human rights and social justice and principles of fairness for all. I can go on and on.

Are there any moments in this organization's history that I wish could have been different or we could have rewritten? Yes. And the most obvious one is during the Holocaust period. I wish this organization—I wish Jewish organizations generally in the United States—had had the influence, the access, and the ability to change the American policy toward Nazi genocide. And many people here to this day, fifty-one years later, continue to agonize over what might have been done differently. Was there anything in our approach that somehow could have persuaded the American government to bomb the rail lines leading to the concentration camps and thus slow the extermination? And the answer here is that we almost certainly could not have changed the American policy, but we still should have tried even harder. Maybe we were too nervous, too worried about the possibility of unleashing American anti-Semitism as a reaction to our advocacy efforts. We weren't as self-confident in the 1940s, about our place in America as we are fifty years later. Yes, I also inherited this legacy in my current job.

Now being in a leadership position, do you think about that past often?

I do. But I can't undo what has been done. I do not want to second guess because it is too easy to judge others with the benefit of history. I would like to think that I know how I would have acted had I been in this position in 1941. But do I really know? Do I really understand the then-prevailing circumstances, the configuration of power in this country, or the possibilities to influence decisions in this country, whether in the Congress, the White House, the State Department, or the War Department? So, all I can do really is to try to learn the lessons of that history and remain ever mindful of those lessons, and ever vigilant. We have to understand that we must never allow complacency to guide us.

We are supported by the Jewish community because they see us as a kind of radar system. They believe that an organization like ours needs to exist to keep an eye on what is going on; to understand when and how to act or react, how to address what remains the sense of vulnerability among many Jews because of the tragedies of Jewish history, including, but not limited to, the Holocaust. This sense of vulnerability is, by the way, often little understood among non-Jews, who today see Jews as very powerful and successful in America but don't see another side.

So do many Japanese. Some even believe that Jews are so powerful that they would take over the world someday.

Yes. Japanese see Jews as quite powerful. Some books in Japan go to great length to propound foolish conspiracy theories about Jews. Too many Japanese have no framework for understanding the sort of delicate psychology that exists. Of course, any people has a particular psychology, not just Jews. Japanese people are often said to have a superiority-inferiority complex. You have to understand the interrelationship between the superiority and the inferiority when you try to understand the Japanese. Well, among Jews, there's a different kind of psychology that you need to understand. That is the interrelationship between the external success of Jews and our ongoing internal sense of vulnerability.

So you must address the psychology of your people?

Yes. But there are many reactions one can take from the Holocaust.

Some Jews say, for example, that there's no other historical experience identical to the Holocaust. They are right. I believe it was an entirely unique event. But what they draw from that conclusion is that no other events merit their attention quite the same way. The lesson I draw is that the Holocaust requires us Jews to be ever alert and to take threats seriously, and not just against Jews. This means, if you will, a special moral obligation to be sensitive to other human rights situations, whether or not they amount to a Holocaust. For instance, we are very proud that the Japanese American Citizens League honored the American Jewish Committee for our considerable assistance, over many years, in securing reparations for the shameful chapter in American history of incarcerating Japanese Americans after Pearl Harbor.

I think that Jews, because of our Holocaust experience, have a particular moral responsibility, and, I might say, a special credibility, to speak out against other tragedies, such as those in Cambodia, Bosnia, and Rwanda, and we have. We have to talk about man's capacity for inhumanity, but also about the need to bring greater sanity to this world. And it's no surprise that such a disproportionate number of Jews worldwide are involved in just such activities.

So you are optimistic?

I don't want to be pessimistic. At the same time, I want to be realistically optimistic. I wish I could be unconditionally optimistic. But here we are, fifty-one years after the Holocaust, and we have seen brutal communist repression, the Cambodian tragedy, and a horrible war in Bosnia. We see continuous strife and tragedies on the African continent, and we see intractable divisions in places like Kashmir, Cyprus, and Northern Ireland. And anti-Semitism certainly hasn't disappeared, though it has fortunately diminished, for now at least. So it would be absolutely foolish and naïve for me to sit here in 1996 and say that, fifty-one years after the Holocaust, however great the cost, however great the tragedy, people at least woke up and realized that unless they learn to live with each other, more human tragedies will take place, whether against Jews or against whomever. I wish I could say that.

But, at the same time, we today have democracy in more countries in the world than ever before. More countries respect human rights and civil rights now. I see these as very encouraging signs. And I see as well an international constituency made up of some governments, human rights organizations, individuals, and groups like the American Jewish Committee that understand that unless they speak up and act, unless they focus world attention on the problem areas, unless they remain persistent, there could well be regression. Unless they, we, have a moral backbone, the world will begin slipping back. But this constituency, I believe, is strong today.

People living in Latin America, with the exception of Cuba, would be the first to argue that there are indeed chances for improvement. Look at the remarkable democratic revolution on that continent. And people in the former communist bloc would say, "Yes, it is a better world." True, economically they face real problems in making the transition. But there is genuine reason to be hopeful.

And the Jewish experience itself suggests the need to cling to a certain optimism. Jews have survived every conceivable form of hatred, oppression, and tyranny; of organized systems of murder and extermination; of exiles, ghettos, and pogroms. Whole new vocabularies were established to find ways to deal with Jews. And yet 3,500 years later, not 35 years, not 350 years, but 3,500 years later, here we are. Yes, here we are, a thriving people and a thriving State of Israel. And where are our oppressors? They are, in most cases, underground. They are dead and buried, and many of their civilizations, too. From Hitler to Stalin and going all the way back. So the Jewish experience may be a very appropriate and encouraging metaphor for the power of hope.

But it's not hope alone. It's hope coupled with a profound commitment to a set of core values. And the values I am talking about, in addition to the power of faith, of course, are those of democracy, equality, the rule of law and justice—values consonant with Jewish ethical teachings and traditions.

6. LATIN AMERICA

Chile's Uncertain Future Clouds Jews' Fate
The Jewish Week
July 11, 1986

Events worldwide and in Latin America have turned many eyes once again toward General Augusto Pinochet's right-wing regime in Chile. First, the democratic revolution sweeping Latin America has brought the area's surviving authoritarian regimes into sharper focus. Second, the fall of autocrats in the Philippines and Haiti has encouraged those seeking the ouster of Latin American dictators. And third, U.S. policy shifts toward Chile—including U.S. support for a UN Human Rights Commission resolution critical of the Pinochet regime, and a more activist approach by the new U.S. envoy in Santiago—point to increased pressure from Washington for changes in Pinochet's rule.

Chile, with 12 million inhabitants, is the home today of 15,000 to 25,000 Jews, who cannot be counted more exactly because many Jews are unaffiliated with any Jewish organization.

In 1970, when Marxist Salvador Allende Gossens was elected president, several thousand of the 35,000 to 40,000 Jews then living in Chile fled the country, along with thousands of other Chileans. Some returned after Allende was ousted by Pinochet in 1973, while others, who had supported the Allende regime, left.

The community has also felt the familiar effects of intermarriage, assimilation, a falling birthrate, and aging.

Chile's Jewish community dates back to the turn of the century, when Russian and other East European immigrants arrived, largely via Argentina. To these were added Sephardi Jews from the eastern Mediterranean, German, and other Central European Jews fleeing Hitler, and a small group of Hungarian Jews who immigrated after the failed 1956 uprising. Most settled in Santiago, the capital; others went

412

to the resort city of Viña del Mar, the port of Valparaiso, and a dozen other cities and towns.

Chile today has excellent Jewish day schools in Santiago and Viña del Mar and an impressive network of religious, fraternal, and recreational facilities. These, however, reach only about 30 percent of the Jewish population.

For a time, the community was divided by national origin and religious orientation. Jews of German, Hungarian, Russian, and Sephardi background all had their own congregations, and the arrival of Conservative Judaism—centered in the Latin American Rabbinic Seminary founded in Buenos Aires twenty-five years ago—led to further tension.

These issues, however, no longer loom large—as pointedly illustrated by the appointment of Rabbi Angel Kreiman, the former rabbi of the Russian/East European congregation, as the rabbi of the Sephardi synagogue. Indeed, Rabbi Kreiman reports, more than half of his congregants today are of Ashkenazi origin. Further, his appointment as Chile's chief rabbi has meant full acceptance of the Conservative movement.

But now the nation's political upheavals are reflected in the Jewish community. No Jewish representative whom I met in a recent visit expressed unqualified support for a military government or for restrictions on political and civil liberties, but they differed profoundly over how to respond to the current climate.

Several said it would be unwise for the small Jewish community to become publicly identified in politics. They believe this might well provoke anti-Semitic forces on one side or the other. These individuals, whose views probably reflect those of the majority, see Chilean politics as essentially a struggle between right and left. The alternative to Pinochet, they believe, is more likely to be turbulence leading to left-wing rule rather than a democratic, centrist government. The Chilean Communist Party is one of the best organized, most powerful, and most rigidly pro-Soviet in the West, and Chilean Jews tend to doubt that communists and their sympathizers would participate in a democratic consensus.

Moreover, these Jewish figures are reluctant to alienate the Pinochet regime. The current regime, in their view, has permitted freedom of conscience (a long Chilean tradition), kept open lines of communication with the Jewish community (government figures, for example, regularly attend High Holy Day services), and maintained strong diplomatic ties with Israel. Thus, while not comfortable with authoritarian rule, they fear leftist rule even more. Still, they hope that, by 1989, the political and economic scene will be sufficiently stable to permit the national elections Pinochet has promised.

An opposing view, expressed by other Jewish representatives, holds that the community cannot remain indifferent to the country's political situation. They note that Catholic and Methodist leaders, together with Chief Rabbi Kreiman, have joined in the human rights struggle through the Catholic-based Vicaria de la Solidaridad. (They agree, however, that not all Jews support Rabbi Kreiman's participation.) They point out that the government has not quelled signs of neo-Nazism and other forms of anti-Semitism. They cite the recent bombing of the home and car of Amiti Pilowski, a former president of the B'nai B'rith Santiago lodge, who has been involved in interfatih activities with the Catholic Church and has criticized government excesses. Was the bombing directed at Pilowski the Pinochet critic or Pilowski the Jew? Was the government involved in the bombing? The Jewish community does not agree on the answers.

The economy also causes concern. After a period of growth in the late 1970s, Chile's economy nose-dived in the early 1980s. It has recently shown signs of revival, but problems persist, including widespread unemployment, and some Jews have been among those hit. At least three Santiago congregations now have lunch programs, each feeding as many as sixty Jews a day, and as many as a third of the 1,200 students at Santiago's Jewish day school receive full scholarships to enable them to attend. At least 10 percent of the Jewish community is believed to be impoverished, and many estimates run much higher.

In 1984, the Joint Distribution Committee helped establish a social welfare department, under the umbrella Representative Committee of Jewish Institutions, to help destitute Jews.

Needless to say, the community's future depends heavily on the country's political and economic future. If reasonable stability continues, or a democratic alternative takes firm root, most Chilean Jews will probably remain in a country that historically has been relatively free of anti-Semitism. But if violence mounts (Risk International reports that, in 1984, Chile had the world's highest number of terrorist incidents: 649), leading to a possible left-wing takeover, Chilean Jews will doubtless seek to move. Thus, events in Chile bear especially close watching in the coming months.

Catholic-Jewish Relations in Brazil
Washington Jewish Week
October 1, 1987

Permit me to add a significant point omitted in David Twersky's op-ed about Catholic-Jewish relations in Brazil (August 27) and, at the same time, to strike a note of institutional pride.

The historic Pan American Conference on Catholic-Jewish Relations, held in São Paulo in November 1985 to coincide with the twentieth anniversary of Vatican Council II's adoption of *Nostra Aetate*, had two sponsors, not one as the article suggested. In addition to the Brazilian National Conference of Catholic Bishops, the American Jewish Committee was the other principal convenor of the event. Also, the Confederation of Brazilian Jewish Communities played a significant role.

The magnitude of the three-day event can be illustrated by the participation, on the Catholic side, of six cardinals and five bishops, including the Argentine president of the Latin American Conference of Catholic Bishops (CELAM), the cardinals of São Paulo and Rio de Janeiro and the archbishops of Brasilia and Porto Alegre, and the Vatican's secretary of the Commission for Religious Relations with the Jews. According to one Jewish participant, the event marked the first time in the 500-year history of Brazilian Jewry that such a public outpouring of respect, appreciation, and solidarity had come from such a galaxy of Catholic ecclesiastical leaders.

As Mr. Twersky correctly noted, seven resolutions were adopted at the end of the deliberations. The one on Zionism, which was subsequently reprinted in full-page ads in several leading Brazilian newspapers, read: "To acknowledge that Zionism—as an expression of the everlasting yearning of the Jewish people for its liberation and its return to Zion, the land of its origin—does not carry the stain of despotism or racism, but is rather the motivating force behind the survival of the Jewish people." The other six resolutions dealt with such key issues as the further promotion of Catholic-Jewish understanding, support for human rights worldwide, recognition of the historical events and deeper theological implications of the Shoah, the importance of study of the Shoah in educational curricula, and the "sacred principles" of religious freedom.

In sum, the conference was regarded as a breakthrough in Catholic-Jewish relations not only in Brazil but throughout Latin America, and contributed to a new level of interreligious relations in the continent's most important and populous country.

Letter from Costa Rica
Forward
April 4, 1997

For those whose image of Central America comes from Woody Allen's comedy *Bananas*, with its portrayal of a mythical jungle dictatorship racked by insurrection, the situation of Costa Rica may come as a surprise.

Since its first democratic elections in 1899, Costa Rica has established a remarkably stable democracy, marred only by two years of dictatorial rule—from 1917 to 1919. For the past forty-eight years, despite repeated turbulence in the region, the country has maintained no army, only a small police force. As the then-president, Luis Alberto Monge, said in 1983: "We are the only nation in history which has disarmed itself voluntarily and unilaterally."

Further, Costa Rica enjoys a tradition of social democracy. The state has built up an impressive network of schools and health centers, which helps explain why, together with neighboring Panama, it has the highest literacy rate in the region—94 percent—as well as one of the highest average life expectancies in the world (seventy-two years for men, seventy-six years for women).

The place is also gorgeous. Some 25 to 30 percent of the country is protected as national parks and conservancies, including miles of Atlantic and Pacific coastline, dramatic mountains, and verdant tropical and subtropical landscape. Some 10 percent of the world's flora and fauna are to be found within Costa Rica's borders.

True, San José, the capital, is nothing to write home about. Street crime is a growing preoccupation, but for tourists, especially eco-tourists from North America and Europe, this city is little more than a stopover en route to dramatic natural settings. For us, though—I came as part of an American Jewish Committee delegation to the country—it was our principal destination. After all, it is the seat of government and home of the nearly 2,500 Jews who constitute the community.

To the nearly 6 million American Jews who understandably worry about continuity, a community this small surely must be earmarked for disappearance. Hold your bets.

Costa Rica's Jews mostly arrived from Poland between World War I and World War II and are now in their third generation. Well organized and closely knit, facing relatively infrequent manifestations of anti-Semitism, they have established an impressive infrastructure, comprising synagogues, day schools, community centers, and communal organizations, while immersing themselves in the larger society. More than 70 percent of the children attend Jewish day school through high school graduation. Even if they go to university abroad, they come back and establish families—intermarriage rates are very low—and see their future in Costa Rica.

That explains why we didn't encounter much pessimism about the future, although, barring unforeseen immigration, the community is not likely to grow. Some Israelis have settled in Costa Rica, we were told, but keep to themselves. Among the 25,000 to 30,000 Americans who have opted to retire here are a handful of Jews, but they, too, are not part of the community.

If Costa Rica's Jews are proud both of their internal cohesion and their contribution to the country at large—Costa Rica's current vice president, the minister of public health, and two of the fifty-seven members of parliament are Jewish, not to mention well-known businessmen, professionals, and artists—they are equally proud of their country's remarkable record of friendship and support for Israel.

Costa Rica was one of the first nations to recognize Israel. Then-president José Figueres, the founder of the country's post-1948 era of democracy, who was known to all as Don Pepe, identified closely with the fledgling Jewish state. Indeed, his wife was appointed the country's ambassador to Israel. Years later, during the 1973 Yom Kippur War, Mrs. Figueres volunteered to go to Israel, but Prime Minister Golda Meir prevailed upon her to devote her considerable energy to fund-raising efforts for Israel in Costa Rica.

The tone set by Mr. Figueres toward Israel was continued by all his successors except one, President Rodrigo Carazo Odio, who during his term of office, 1978 to 1982, transferred Costa Rica's embassy from Jerusalem to Tel Aviv and pursued a more pro-Arab line. His successor, Luis Alberto Monge, reestablished the embassy in Israel's capital within two days of assuming office and in defiance of the UN Security Council resolution calling on member states to withdraw their embassies from Jerusalem.

In fact, Costa Rica is one of only two countries in the world today with an embassy in Jerusalem; the other is El Salvador. This principled step, however, has not been costfree. The Arab world retaliated by severing diplomatic ties with Costa Rica. During our recent visit, we learned that there are still no Arab diplomats posted in San José. We were also told that the Arab world has not given up its efforts to cajole Costa Rica into changing its policy.

The current president, José Maria Figueres, the son of the legendary Don Pepe, indicated to us his determination to maintain Costa Rica's close political, economic, and cultural ties with Israel, but hinted at growing international pressure on his country to distance itself from Israel now that Costa Rica is serving a two-year term on the UN Security Council and will be called on to vote on Middle East-related matters.

To what does Costa Rica owe its good fortune? Many point to an egalitarian tradition that goes back hundreds of years, explaining that the lack of natural resources made it impossible for colonizers from Spain to create the sharp class distinctions that emerged elsewhere in Latin America. Others point to the absence of an indigenous Indian population—although the reasons for its absence are not entirely clear—that again prevented the temptation to exploit. In more modern times, the emergence of able political leaders, rooted in the democratic tradition and committed to ensuring social welfare and social justice, established admirable norms and values.

That these leaders also identified strongly with Israel and the local Jewish community helps explain why anyone formulating a list of countries special to the Jewish people ought to have Costa Rica at—or very near—the top.

Tribute to the Honorable José Maria Figueres, President of Costa Rica, and to the Honorable Julio Maria Sanguinetti, President of Uruguay
AJC 92nd Annual Meeting, Washington, D.C.
May 14, 1998

Tonight is a particularly auspicious occasion. The film clip we've just seen reminds us why. It's exactly fifty years to this very day that the State of Israel was declared.

Let me read from the Proclamation of the State (May 14, 1948): "The Land of Israel was the birthplace of the Jewish people. Here their spiritual, religious, and national identity was formed. Here they achieved independence and created a culture of national and universal significance. Here they wrote and gave the Bible to the world."

Or to quote from a slightly older text, Psalm 126: "When the Lord returns the exiles to Zion, it will seem like a dream. Then our mouths will fill with laughter, our tongues with joyful song."

Yes, fifty years later, it still seems like a dream. As we said in a statement in Sunday's *New York Times*: "The story of Israel these past fifty years is, above all, the wondrous realization of a 3,500-year-old link between a land, a people, a faith, a language, and a vision. It is an inspiring story of tenacity and determination, of courage and renewal, of the triumph of hope over despair."

In marking such a special anniversary this evening, what could be more appropriate than to have the prime minister of Israel with us? But we also wanted to use this occasion to pay tribute to other countries that have made a difference in Israel's first half century.

This evening we recall the thirty-three UN members who gathered on that historic Saturday afternoon at Flushing Meadows, on November 29, 1947, to endorse the creation of a Jewish state.

This evening we recall the indispensable arms from Czechoslovakia that proved so consequential to the 600,000 Jews during Israel's War of Independence and the crucial role played by French weaponry in the 1967 Six-Day War.

This evening we recall the representation by the Netherlands of Israel's diplomatic interests in Moscow during the crucial decades of Soviet Jewish emigration, as well as its valiant stand against the 1973 Arab oil boycott.

This evening we recall the thirty-five nations—yes, sadly, it was only thirty-five—that voted against the infamous "Zionism is racism" resolution at the UN General Assembly in 1975, and the 110 nations that voted for its repeal sixteen years later.

This evening we recall the courage of the late Egyptian president Anwar Sadat and the leadership of Jordan's King Hussein who forged landmark peace treaties with Israel.

This evening we recall that in 1991, with Israel under attack by Iraqi Scud missiles, it was Germany and the Netherlands, together with the United States, that provided batteries of Patriot missiles for Israel's defense.

This evening we recall that Turkey has withstood unrelenting pressure from many members of the Islamic Conference, and has developed close links with Israel in so many areas.

And of course, this evening—and every evening—we recall the singular role played by the United States, in ways too numerous to even think of enumerating now, as Israel's staunchest ally and friend.

But there are two countries whose enduring friendship with Israel, over five decades, may be less well known to you and who deserve our heartfelt recognition.

We are deeply honored that the leaders of Costa Rica and Uruguay flew specially from their respective capitals to be with us here in Washington.

President Figueres of Costa Rica, a West Point and Harvard graduate, has just completed his four-year term of office. He captures the essence of his country's enduring links with Israel in his own family.

He has been an ally of Israel, a friend to the local Jewish community, and a staunch opponent of anti-Semitism. And his beloved father, José Figueres, known by the nickname Pepe, was president of Costa Rica three times and a confidant of David Ben-Gurion.

As a result of the 1973 Yom Kippur War, our guest's mother, Karen Olsen Figueres, with the encouragement of then-prime minister Golda Meir, devoted her considerable energy to fund-raising for Israel. Later, Mrs. Figueres became her country's ambassador to—guess where?—Israel.

Costa Rica both then and now has had a very special tie with Israel. Indeed, it has even located its embassy in Jerusalem, inviting the wrath of those that have sought to pressure Costa Rica to reverse itself, but, since 1982, this Central American nation hasn't bent.

We salute Costa Rica's fifty-year friendship with Israel. We salute two generations of the Figueres family for the remarkable web of relations with Israel they have woven. And we salute the 2,500-member Costa Rica Jewish community—active in every phase of their country's life—whose president, Julio Kierszenson, is here this evening.

Costa Rica and Israel may be divided by geography, but a profound dedication to democracy, the rule of law, and commitment to social progress surely unite them.

Like Costa Rica, Uruguay was an early supporter of the Jewish state. Indeed, Uruguay was one of eleven countries to serve on the 1947 UN Special Committee on Palestine, or UNSCOP.

The UNSCOP majority report, signed by Uruguay and seven other nations, proposed partition of Palestine into Jewish and Arab states. The rest, as they say, is history.

In other words, Uruguay was one of the midwives for the birth of modern-day Israel. And it became the first Latin American country to recognize Israel and the first to receive an ambassador from the new state.

Lawyer, politician, statesman, journalist, and art critic, President Sanguinetti, now in his second term as Uruguay's leader, has nobly carried on the tradition of close ties with Israel, as well as with Uruguay's 35,000-member Jewish community, whose president, Saul Gilvich, is also here with us tonight.

Speaking at the Holocaust monument in Montevideo last year, President Sanguinetti showed remarkable understanding when he said: "This is the generation of Jews who achieved the dream to recover its own soil in ancient Palestine. . . . This is the historical generation of Jews who will be remembered for eternity . . . ."

The late Dag Hammarskjold, the distinguished Swedish-born diplomat, once described friendship as "a loneliness relieved of the anguish of loneliness."

Costa Rica and Uruguay, true friends, have certainly eased Israel's anguish of loneliness throughout its history.

Ladies and gentlemen, please join me in expressing our deepest appreciation to the governments and people of Costa Rica and Uruguay. President Figueres, may I ask you to speak first, followed, please, by President Sanguinetti.

7. INTERNATIONAL HUMAN RIGHTS

Presentation on Ethiopia
AJC Board of Governors
December 10, 1984

Last week I returned from a ten-day visit to Ethiopia. Perhaps at another time Ethiopia might well be a wonderful country to visit. Its topograpy is magnificent, its people are, indeed, beautiful, and its sunny climate is superb for tourists, but it is racked by a succession of problems that have brought it to its present and well-publicized state.

It suffers from civil wars in Eritrea and Tigre provinces. Its famine now affects between 6 and 8 million of its 42 million citizens. It supports some 500,000 refugees from neighboring Sudan, Somalia, and Djibouti. It has an annual birthrate of more than 3 percent per annum, one of the highest in the world. It is one of the poorest countries on earth, and—breathtaking as is its landscape—it is rugged and difficult to farm. And farming comprises some 90 percent of the economy.

I was there on a mission organized by the National Jewish Community Relations Advisory Council. Our group came from three countries—the United States, Canada, and Israel. Our original purpose was to focus on the remnant Jewish community in Ethiopia that numbers, it is estimated, from 8,000 to 10,000. But, as word of the famine began to spread, several of us urged that this tragedy also become a primary focus of our mission.

The first five days of our visit were spent in Gondar Province, situated in the northwestern part of the country, where most of the Jewish community lives. They're spread out over nearly 500 villages and are surrounded by a primarily Christian and, to some extent, Muslim population. Geographically, Gondar is bordered by the Sudan on the west, and by Eritrea, Tigre, and Wello provinces on the north and east. It is precisely in these three provinces that the famine is at its worst.

We were permitted to see five villages, more than any Jewish group in recent years. Let me attempt to describe what these villages are like. We would be driven to the side of a road from the provincial capital of Gondar and told by our guide that over that mountain or valley we would find three or five or a dozen teepee-style huts, known in Amharic as "tukuls." That would be the Jewish village. The tukuls are made of dung, straw, twigs, and branches—perhaps ten or twelve feet in diameter—and house as many as ten members of an extended family. No electricity, telephone, sewerage, running water, shops, and, in most cases, schools were present; there were no cars or even bicycles, no glass windows, no staircases, practically no furniture, and no roads. But in each case there was a synagogue. Perhaps you will understand the sensation that we experienced after walking, say, two miles over hill and dale to come to a typical African village, see a black face emerge from a tukul, and hear a voice say *"Shalom,"* and then be taken to the synagogue. In one synagogue, as we walked in, we were greeted by the children singing *"Dovid, Melech Yisrael."*

My most enduring visions of those villages were of the children. And I think I spent most of my time trying to remove the flies from their eyes, for it was there that the flies lingered, often producing trachoma and, in some cases, blindness. Scalp infections, goiter, juvenile diabetes, gum problems, and general problems of mental and physical growth affect children and adults in the Jewish villages, just as they affect people throughout Ethiopia; saddest of all, much of the disease could be easily prevented by modern medicine and nutrition.

But we were also privileged to experience something unique to Ethiopian Jewish life—an annual holiday, the Sigd, which derives, it is believed, from the books of Nehemiah and Ezra, that falls on the fiftieth day after Yom Kippur. On this particular day it brought together some 800 Ethiopian Jews to the village of Anbober, some of whom had walked for six hours or more. Together with those 800 Jews we went in a procession to the top of a nearby mountain in a symbolic reenactment of Moses's ascent of Mount Sinai. We stood for five hours, the men and the women separated, as the *cohanim* and elders prayed in Ge'ez, an ancient Semitic language. They read from the Torah, recited the Ten Commandments, and prostrated themselves, asking for mercy from God and forgiveness of sin.

When the service was over, as everyone was preparing to descend, the government officials present insisted on the right to speak to the assemblage. The thrust of their message was, "You are Ethiopians, you have no right to leave this country. You are permitted to practice your rites and rituals here. If you leave, you may die en route since the conditions outside the country are indeed difficult. And if you do make it to Israel, remember that Israel doesn't want you; it is a racist society. Therefore, don't pay attention to these foreign agitators who encourage you to leave."

The Ethiopian officials clearly did not understand that the Jews' desire to leave for Israel is rooted in biblical faith, and that these Jews firmly, indeed literally, believe that Israel is the land of milk and honey.

From 7,000 to 8,000 Ethiopian Jews have already arrived in Israel, and more than 10,000 are currently in refugee camps in neighboring countries where they face malnutrition, disease, and the hostility of other refugees. Israel has embarked on an effort, which unfortunately has received publicity of late that can only jeopardize the operation, to engage in the rescue of those 10,000 Jews over the next three to four months. And congruent with that, the UJA has recently launched a campaign, Operation Moses, to raise $65 million in the United States to resettle them in Israel.

Every Ethiopian Jew with whom we met in the country dreams of Israel, but those who have remained behind are precisely those least able to go on foot the more than 250 kilometers required to reach the nearest refugee camp—on foot in breach of the law, on foot through treacherous terrain which the government does not necessarily control at night, on foot through regions where food is scarce, on foot, in other words, to an uncertain future. And yet they want to go.

Gary Ackerman, the congressman from Queens who accompanied us, addressed this problem with the Ethiopian foreign minister. Here's what the foreign minister said: He felt the West was using the Jewish issue "as a stick to beat over the head of the Menghistu regime, whereas there was silence until 1975," that is, during the reign of Haile Selassie. "Why," asked the foreign minister, "were you silent before 1975? Why has the world Jewish community been silent for 2,000 years on the issue of Ethiopian Jewry and now suddenly focuses its attention and directs its anger at our revolutionary regime?" Fortunately, he ended on a more positive note, suggesting that there might yet be the possibility for reunification of families.

It was precisely the question of family reunification that was among the most poignant for us. We sat one afternoon with a Jewish couple who have four children, the oldest of whom is eleven. The four children are now in a Youth Aliyah village in Israel, while the parents are at present unable to leave Ethiopia. This is but one of the tragic problems we encountered during our visit. In the meantime, the Jews eke out their existence from an inhospitable soil, and from blacksmithing and pottery, which are traditional Jewish professions in Ethiopia regarded with hostility by superstitious non-Jewish Ethiopians. Can Jews practice their religion and learn Hebrew? To a large extent, it depends on whether there are non-Jews in the village in which they live. In one village yes, for there are no non-Jews, but in other villages no.

The famine is beginning to hit the Gondar Province. Of the nearly 3 million people in the province, 375,000 are currently affected. They are primarily located in the areas closest to Tigre and Wello and near the Sudanese border in the west. The famine has not yet directly affected the heavily populated Jewish area in the center. But the price of food has gone up, and in general food is increasingly scarce. If the short rainfalls do not come in February or March, Gondar province may well become another Tigre, Wello, or Eritrea. In the meantime, the Joint Distribution Committee has signed contracts with the Ethiopian government to administer food aid for all the citizens of Gondar, and this, fortunately, assures a Jewish organizational presence in the region, the first since 1981.

On the broader question of famine, we spent five days meeting with relief officials from the Ethiopian government's Relief and Rehabilitation Commission and the international community— Catholic Relief Services, Save the Children, League of Red Cross

Societies, and American Red Cross, and with Western diplomats—largely to express our concern, as both Americans and Jews, about the famine. Hitherto, there had been all too little visible Jewish interest in the devastating famine, a fact that had not gone unnoticed. Indeed, one Catholic relief worker with whom we met exclaimed plaintively: "If the Jewish community can raise $65 million to resettle 10,000 Ethiopian Jews, can it not raise $10 million to save the lives of 8 million Ethiopian citizens?"

The immediate problem, of course, is the absence of rainfall, but the root causes of this famine are much deeper: deforestation over hundreds of years, soil erosion, the encroachment of desert, the death of livestock, a shortage of seed and tools and other implements, and inadequate irrigation and water development. It is feared that as many as 900,000 people will have died by the end of this year, but of course no one can be certain of exact numbers. Those who have seen the horrific scenes on television can perhaps begin to understand what it is like to be in the country, to feel a sense of total impotence at one's inability to rescue the dying.

Moreover, there is the unsettling knowledge that as difficult as the moment is, it will somehow pass for the foreign observer; that our food and clothing and shelter are assured for tonight. And that the cost of our hotel room in Addis Ababa for one night is actually equivalent to the annual per capita income of an Ethiopian citizen.

The international community has indeed begun to respond to the crisis, as has the Ethiopian government. It is fair to say that since October—and, of course, that was very late—the pace of the relief effort has quickened. In September, there was the much publicized—and, given the circumstances, obscene—tenth anniversary commemoration of the Ethiopian revolution, when some $100–150 million was reportedly spent by the government. But since then have come countless Western public officials, journalists (who hitherto had found access to the famine sites restricted), and relief officials who are very carefully watching the off-loading, port handling, and distribution of donated supplies. The consensus among those with whom we spoke was that most of the food—not all, but most of the food—is indeed now reaching the needy.

Is it reaching all the needy? Probably not. Is the government using some of the food as a weapon in its fight against the rebels of Tigre and Eritrea? Probably so. Do government soldiers or civil servants look famished or emaciated? Absolutely not. But the fact remains, and relief officials and Western diplomats have confirmed this, that most of the food is now moving to the people who need it. And the harbors of Assab and Masawa, the two principal ports of Ethiopia, are today virtually empty, for the pace of delivery from abroad is still too slow.

The Soviet bloc's response has been far less adequate. Ethiopia is a satellite of the Soviet Union. Pictures of the troika—Marx, Engels, and Lenin, their faces slightly shaded in a vain effort to present a more third world complexion—dot the country. The East Germans reportedly run the security system, the Cubans advise the military, and the Russians run the propaganda in the universities and government ministries. The Ethiopian government is in debt to the Soviet bloc to the tune of nearly $3 billion in loans for military equipment. And there is considerable hostility aimed at the United States on purely ideological grounds, as well as for past U.S. support of the Selassie regime and of Somalia in its war against Ethiopia over Ogadan. But the fact remains that there is a glint of an opportunity for the West, especially for Western Europe and Canada, to drive a wedge into the Ethiopian link with the Soviet bloc. And if only allowed to do so, Israel could play a vitally important and cost-effective role in the sphere of technical assistance.

Ethiopia is but one of as many as twenty-six sub-Saharan African countries facing current or expected drought and famine. Some of the other countries—Niger, Mali, Chad, Mozambique, and Upper Volta— are concerned that their problems are not drawing the attention they deserve. Indeed, the problems are real and immediate, threatening as many as 150 million Africans.

The United States must respond accordingly. We in the Jewish community must also do more. We must step up our efforts if only because a moral imperative impels us to do so; the catastrophic conditions demand no less a response. I would suggest, therefore, three areas in which we can play a useful role:

The first is in the area of fund-raising. What is really needed more than anything else is money—money for the relief agencies to buy food, livestock, and seed, and to send medical teams now.

The second is on the governmental level. With the advent of the Ninety-ninth Congress in January, there will be a number of bills introduced by Congressmen Mickey Leland, Howard Wolpe, Ted Weiss, and others to spend as much as $1 billion in short-term and developmental assistance to black Africa. We will need to review and adopt positions on these bills, as well as to consider a coalition-based approach to President Reagan, Peter McPherson, the head of the Agency for International Development, and other key officials.

And finally, we can join with the interfaith and black communities to heighten public consciousness and to sustain interest over the long term.

The recurring fear of relief officials in Ethiopia is what happens when the issue is no longer today's headlines, when it is replaced in tomorrow's newspapers by other news events elsewhere in the world, or when "compassion fatigue" sets in.

The problems of African famine and development, I fear, will remain with us for months and years and decades. But will the issue remain a priority item on the American agenda? We can help determine the answer to that challenging question.

Ethiopia
Commentary
December 1985

I read Edward Alexander's article with considerable interest, and would like to offer some comments concerning the unfortunate disclosure of the rescue operation of the Ethiopian Jews that led to its halt in January 1985.

Mr. Alexander writes that Arye Dulzin, chairman of the Jewish Agency, "all but revealed it [Israel's rescue effort] in a statement to the press in early December." In fact, Mr. Dulzin made his disclosure even earlier, on November 21, 1984, in a speech to the American section of the World Zionist Organization, when he said:

> While I am not free to discuss it publicly, I can tell you that the Jewish Agency is preparing for a sudden jump in emigration. . . . One

of the ancient tribes of Israel is due to return to its homeland. . . . We will take pride in what we have already achieved in this most difficult and complex operation.

What had indeed been an open secret in some circles quickly became a matter of public record and press attention—with ultimately devastating effect.

Mr. Alexander then states that ". . . the American and Israeli press had in general showed rare and admirable self-restraint in withholding the story. . . ." Yet if the press showed restraint prior to November 21, it certainly showed much less thereafter.

On November 23, the *Jewish Week* of New York carried a front-page story with the headline: "Reveal Plan for Rescue of Falashas; Israel Prepares for Absorption of Thousands of Ethiopian Jews." On November 28, the Jewish Telegraphic Agency carried a page-three story: "Dulzin: Jewish Agency Is Preparing for a Sudden Jump in Immigration," which clearly referred to the Ethiopian Jews. On December 6, despite the strenuous efforts of Israeli and American Jewish leaders, the *Washington Jewish Week* published a front-page article entitled "An Ancient Tribe Returns Home: The Ethiopian Exodus Has Begun." Then, specifically citing "articles . . . in the Jewish press" and the *Washington Jewish Week* story in particular, the *New York Times*, which had indeed shown restraint by sitting on the story for a considerable time, published a front-page piece headlined "Airlift to Israel Is Reported Taking Thousands of Jews from Ethiopia."

The next day, in a particularly damaging story carried by leading newspapers in Miami, Philadelphia, and other major cities, William Beecher of the *Boston Globe* reported on a "dramatic, secret operation" involving "unmarked planes" and "boats pulling in surreptitiously along the Red Sea coast near Port Sudan" and "sympathetic Sudanese military men providing protection." He cited diplomatic sources reporting on the role of the United States as "intermediary in getting Sudanese officials and Israeli agents together to set up the complex logistics for the humanitarian mission." Beecher went on to say that "American officials also urged news organizations that found out about the operation, including the *Globe*, not to print the story prematurely. . . ." He even went so far as to quote an American official that

"We've got to get them [Ethiopian Jews in the Sudan] out as quickly as possible *before it comes to public attention* and the whole thing collapses" [emphasis added].

Almost beyond belief, this article was written when thousands of Ethiopian Jews were still languishing in camps and other thousands remained behind in their native villages. As a result of these revelations, individuals involved in the rescue operation were perilously exposed, and the already shaky Sudanese government, a moderate regime in the Arab world and a U.S. ally, could only be further exposed to internal and external opposition elements.

Yes, it is undoubtedly true that the original leak came from an Israeli leader and the halt to the operation resulted most immediately from the unfortunate Israeli government confirmation in early January. At the same time, however, I would question whether the American press, and more specifically the Anglo-Jewish press that initiated the coverage, acted with proper restraint, or whether it unwittingly contributed, to some degree at least, to the premature cancellation of what had up to that point been one of the most daring and humanitarian rescue operations in modern history.

Finally, it is well worth noting that while there were predictably vicious interpretations of the rescue operation offered by Soviet and Arab commentators, as well as the West German source cited by Mr. Alexander, there was, happily, recognition in other non-Jewish circles of its importance. Let me cite two examples. Marvin Arrington, president of the Atlanta City Council and a non-Jewish black man, wrote in an op-ed piece in the *Atlanta Journal and Constitution* (January 20, 1985):

As no group of people has ever done, the people of Israel have demonstrated that we are our brothers' keepers and that kinship transcends race. A tiny nation of approximately three million people has shown the world clearly that we can live by our loftiest ideals. As we recall the contribution of Martin Luther King, Jr. on the anniversary of his birth, I am proud to say, "Martin, look how well your dream works."

And, second, in a letter to Secretary of State Shultz (February 21, 1985) urging continued U.S. efforts to secure the emigration of those

Ethiopian Jews who had not yet reached Israel, Julius Chambers, the director-general of the NAACP Legal Defense and Educational Fund, wrote:

> Were the victims of Ethiopian famine white, countless nations might have offered them refuge. But the people dying every day of starvation in Ethiopia and the Sudan are black, and in a world where racism is officially deplored by virtually every organized government, only one non-African nation has opened its doors and its arms. The quiet humanitarian action of the state of Israel, action taken entirely without regard to the color of those being rescued, stands as a condemnation of racism far more telling than mere speeches and resolutions.

Messrs. Arrington and Chambers eloquently remind us, in this the tenth year since the passage of the infamous Zionism-is-racism resolution, of the special significance of the effort undertaken by Israel, and supported by its friends, in seeking to bring home the Ethiopian Jewish community after more than 2,000 years of exile.

A Connected World
The Washington Report
May 11, 1987

Ask most Americans about the foreign-policy concerns of the Jewish community, and most likely they will talk about Israel and Soviet Jewry. They'll be right, of course: both issues are of grave importance to Jews everywhere. But to stop at these priorities is to seriously misunderstand how American Jews view the world and its problems. Our history and traditions, the widely varied circumstances of Jewish life in different lands, and the complex political, social, and economic realities of our time all dictate a nonparochial foreign-policy agenda.

A few examples of how this agenda plays itself out at the American Jewish Committee:

First, of course, there is the ongoing effort to rescue Jews in danger: Virtually forgotten in the ongoing tragedy of Lebanon, for instance, is the plight of several Jewish hostages being held by radical Shi'ites who have claimed responsibility for kidnapping and killing eight Lebanese Jews. The AJC is working against great odds, with the help of Western governments that still have some influence in the region, to win freedom for the remaining hostages and encourage the immediate departure of eighty other Lebanese Jews still in the country.

Then there are the small communities that need help to remain Jewish. Fewer than 1,000 Jews, a small, aging remnant of a much larger prewar Jewish population, today live in East Germany. Since 1982, thanks to informal contacts with the U.S. State Department and East German government and Jewish leaders, the AJC has arranged to supply them with books, religious articles, kosher wine—and, since 1984, a German-speaking American rabbi to conduct High Holy Day services. Recently, East Germany agreed to consider hiring a full-time rabbi to serve the community. A similar AJC program is in operation in Cuba, where the tiny Jewish population is quite unable to sustain itself by itself.

Another way to protect Jews is to overcome age-old stereotypes and build new, enhancing relationships. Two decades ago, the Second Vatican Council's Declaration on the Jews was a major advance along this road, and the AJC, then and since, helped pave the way. In late 1985, in São Paulo, Brazil (the world's most populous Catholic nation), the AJC, together with the National Conference of Brazilian Bishops, sponsored a historic three-day conference—attended by six cardinals and five bishops—to mark the twentieth anniversary of Vatican Council II. And last December, the Bishops' Conference published a manual for Brazilian Catholics on understanding Jewish history and the Holocaust and promoting Catholic-Jewish ties.

Many broader foreign-policy issues, some not expressly "Jewish" at all, occupy the AJC, day in and day out: international terrorism, which—with or without a Jewish component—threatens the very fabric of Western democracy; the impact of energy policy on the freedom of the United States and other Western nations to conduct their own foreign policy; the failed dream of a United Nations deflected from its primary mandate by a malevolent preoccupation with trashing Israel.

Nor can we forget that Jewish security is inextricably bound to the protection of basic human rights around the world. The AJC's Jacob

Blaustein Institute for the Advancement of Human Rights, which has led many battles on this front, recently cosponsored, in Strasbourg, a conference of world-renowned legal experts on the international safeguards that protect an individual's right to leave, and to return to, his or her native land. A declaration underscoring this right, adopted by the experts, has been presented to the thirty-five participating states at the Vienna Review Conference of the Helsinki Final Act, the Organization of American States, and the Council of Europe.

Our historic experience and Jewish teachings impel us to even broader concerns—for Jews have long known what it means to be hungry and frightened and oppressed. Eighteen months before the famine in Ethiopia made the nightly TV news, the AJC appealed to the United States to allocate special funds to help save some of the starving millions. (An AJC drive among its own members brought hundreds of thousands of dollars to relief agencies working in the field.) Now, the Committee has joined the campaign to increase long-term development aid for the sub-Saharan region.

Is it conceivable that Jews could watch the desperation of the Indochinese boat people without responding to their plight? AJC leaders joined fact-finding missions to Southeast Asia; raised money to help establish a school for refugee children in Thailand; pressed our government to open wide for these escapees the doors that were shut to Jews half a century earlier. Finally, is there anyone who would argue that U.S. immigration policy, and this country's continued role as a haven for the needy and oppressed, are not "Jewish issues"? Not at the AJC there isn't. We know we live in a connected world.

To Indochinese Refugees—"We Are All Boat People"*
Forward
April 22, 1988

In a very real sense, we are all boat people. Most of us in this country are ourselves or the descendants of boat people. We are the lucky

*Text of a speech given at a mass rally for Indochinese refugees across from the White House in Lafayette Park earlier that year and inserted in the *Congressional Record* by Congressman Stephen J. Solarz, April 21, 1988.

ones. Whether it was the *Mayflower* more than three centuries ago, or the crammed steamships of the late 1800s and early 1900s that brought millions of Southern and East European immigrants and refugees to these shores, or the makeshift rafts of the Haitians, or the boat flotilla of the Cubans, we are the lucky ones. Those boats somehow proved seaworthy enough to make the perilous voyage, and we were given safe haven and refuge in this country.

As Jews, we understand very well the motivations of refugees. We understand the fear, threats, persecution, and violence based on fanatical and misguided religious, national, ethnic, and political beliefs that force people to flee their homelands in the hope of a more secure life for themselves and their children. Yes, we know these things all too well from the school of personal experience.

When the first reports appeared in the 1970s about people fleeing Vietnam, Laos, and Cambodia, often by boat, it struck a very special and poignant chord in the Jewish community. Images of boats being turned back from safe haven, of people dying at sea, chillingly reminded us of our own tragic experiences just thirty-five years before.

In 1939, a ship carrying 930 Jewish refugees from Germany—the *St. Louis*—was refused permission to disembark all but a few of its passengers in Cuba, its first port of call, even though all held Cuban landing certificates. Subsequently, the United States, Chile, Argentina, Colombia, and Paraguay refused permission for the refugees to enter. Believe it or not, the ship was actually compelled to return to Europe. Finally, four European countries agreed to accept the refugees. In the following years, three of the four were overrun by the Nazis. Many of the original passengers were among the victims of Hitler's death camps.

And one other tragic example. In 1942, the *Struma*, carrying 769 refugees from Romania bound for Palestine, stopped in Turkey for badly needed repairs. Turkey sadly yielded to Arab pressure not to cooperate in facilitating immigration to Palestine and to the British, who refused to issue permits for the refugees to proceed onward to Palestine. The ship sank off the Turkish coast. All but one of the passengers died.

That's why we raised our voices, calling, first, on the Ford and then the Carter administration to respond generously to the crisis in

Indochina with increased admissions numbers. We were pleased they did.

It's why, in 1980, the American Jewish community sponsored a full-page ad in the *New York Times*. It read "Do a Mitzvah—Save a Life." With the money raised we were able to construct a school to serve the needs of children in one of the refugee camps in Thailand.

And it's why we called on synagogues throughout the country to join with Catholic and Protestant churches in aiding those refugees seeking admission who had no other sponsor, and many responded. The Jewish migration agency, HIAS, has helped thousands of refugees from Indochina to come to this country and be resettled. And I am very proud that my wife and I personally sponsored a refugee couple who had fled Saigon, enabling them to enter the United States and start a new life.

And it's why in June 1977 tiny Israel welcomed the entry of sixty-six Vietnamese refugees to that country after they had been rescued off the Vietnamese coast by an Israeli ship, and in January 1979 admitted another 101 Vietnamese refugees.

Its capacity to absorb large numbers is understandably very limited, but Israel wanted to make an important gesture of solidarity, and at the same time, perhaps, challenge those countries more capable of absorbing large numbers but seemingly indifferent to this human tragedy, to do the same.

It's why just two weeks ago our organization's president, Theodore Ellenoff, joined with Mr. Khoa, the distinguished head of the Indochina Resource Action Center, in publishing in the *New York Times* a letter appealing for increased refugee numbers for the current year to accommodate the unexpected exodus of refugees from Indochina and the Soviet Union. In a joint letter sent to both the president of the United States and the secretary of state, we made a similar appeal.

And it's why we have urged Bangkok to take additional steps to insure that Thailand remains a country of first asylum for refugees. But we also understand that the Thai government needs the assurance of the United States and other receiving countries that refugees will be permanently resettled elsewhere.

We note with pride the warm welcome our country has extended to hundreds of thousands of Indochinese refugees in recent years. We believe that such a refugee admissions policy is an act of humanitarianism and generosity, a reaffirmation of the strength and values of our nation, and a recognition that our society respects and welcomes the newcomer. In so doing, it underscores the point that in the final analysis all Americans benefit. We become a better society for our diversity, a richer society.

And let's be clear. Advocates of a generous refugee policy need not be defensive. Every study has shown that refugees give back to their adopted country much more than they ever take. That's why we stand shoulder to shoulder with you and offer our full support to your call for an additional 15,000 refugee slots for the current year.

Finish the Job[*]
Washington Jewish Week
June 16, 1988

In 1986, thirty-seven years after being presented for ratification, the Genocide Convention was overwhelmingly approved by the Senate (83-11). It was a long overdue step. Popular wisdom to the contrary, however, the U.S. is not yet a formal party to the international treaty. Congress must still pass implementing legislation to make genocide a federal crime punishable in our country. Both Houses should act quickly.

The impetus for the Genocide Convention largely stems from the vision of the late Raphael Lemkin, a Polish Jew who miraculously escaped certain death at the hands of the Nazis and who succeeded in resettling in the United States Forty-nine members of the Lemkin family were not as lucky. They were victims of the Final Solution. Lemkin, who coined the term *genocide*, dedicated the remainder of his life to redeeming the memory of the victims. What better way than through the recognition of governments, most of whom had remained silent during the war years, that genocide ought to be regarded by the international community as a horrific crime?

*Inserted in the *Congressional Record* by Senator Carl Levin, June 16, 1988.

Subsequently, in 1948, the United Nations unanimously passed the Genocide Convention. Two days later, the United States signed the treaty, and President Truman forwarded it to the Senate for ratification. There it became stalled, the victim of unfounded fears that adherence to the treaty would undermine U.S. sovereignty. Notwithstanding support from every president from Truman to Reagan, with the one exception of Eisenhower, and favorable Senate Foreign Relations Committee recommendation on a half dozen occasions, parliamentary maneuvering prevented full Senate consideration, "a national shame," as Wisconsin Senator William Proxmire commented.

Indeed, it was Senator Proxmire, frustrated with Senate inaction on this human rights measure, who announced on the Senate floor on January 11, 1967, that "I intend to speak day after day in this body to remind the Senate of our failure to act . . . ." Three thousand speeches later, and after the Soviet bloc had enjoyed a propaganda bonanza because of U.S. unwillingness to ratify a treaty that nearly one hundred other nations had already approved, the Senate finally acted, though adding some weakening language in the approval measure.

Would such a Genocide Convention have prevented Hitler's genocidal acts? Or did it in any way deter the Pol Pot regime from murdering as many as 3 million of its own citizens? Or prevent the victimization of the Hutu in Burundi or the Bahais in Iran? Regrettably, the answer is no. But Nobel laureate Elie Wiesel, testifying at the 1985 Senate Foreign Relations Committee hearings on the treaty, put it well: "I know the Genocide Convention will not bring back the dead. It is too late for the dead. But at least in signing such a convention we could remember the dead without shame. Not to remember them would mean betraying them and betraying ourselves."

It's time for the Congress to act on the treaty implementing legislation contained in H.R. 807, introduced by Representative Peter Rodino (D-NJ), and the companion Senate measure (S. 1851) sponsored by Senators Biden (D-DE), Metzenbaum (D-OH), and Proxmire (D-WI). As Senator Biden explained, "This bill provides protection to members of any national, ethnic, racial, or religious group by creating a new Federal crime of genocide or attempted genocide for any person who attempts to destroy such a group—in whole or in part—through murder, serious bodily injury, mental or physical torture . . ."

Not only is quick congressional passage of the pending legislation the right statement for our country to make in reaffirming its abhorrence of genocide, but also it would be a fitting tribute to mark the upcoming retirement of Senator Proxmire, the driving Senate force in behalf of U.S. ratification during more than two decades.

Statement at the Funeral of Five Turkish Victims of Hate-Inspired Violence Central Mosque, Cologne, Germany June 3, 1993

I have come to this funeral specially from New York in the belief that sometimes words of grief alone in a letter or press release are insufficient. Rather, by our very presence we must make a demonstrable statement of solidarity both with the victims and with those decent, peaceful people who identify with the victims, who reject the violence and hatred that can too easily lead to tragedies such as occurred in Solingen a few days ago.

I am neither a Turk nor a German nor a Muslim, but an American Jew profoundly concerned with the evil of crimes inspired by hatred based on so-called "differentness" or "otherness" wherever they may occur. Tragically, such crimes do occur with ever increasing frequency, it seems, both in my own country and around the world, including here in Germany.

Everywhere, governments, educators, the media, the law, and religious leaders all have a key role to play in rooting out and exposing the hatemongers, while seeking to nurture societies based on age-old principles of respect for one another, tolerance, and understanding. As we are taught in Judaism, we are all—all of us—created in God's image.

Individuals also have a role they cannot, and should not, shirk. That is why I stand with you today, on behalf of the American Jewish Committee, in this period of mourning. My heartfelt sympathies are with the families of the victims, and my pledge is that we shall continue to stand together as one against those who would divide us.

Chemical Weapons Treaty Makes the World a Safer Place
Arizona Republic
April 29, 1997

The vision was stark and unforgettable. On a concert stage in Jerusalem stood Isaac Stern poised with violin—wearing a gas mask. Iraq's threat to use chemical weapons during the Gulf War was real.

Last fall, after years of equivocation, the Pentagon admitted that as many as 20,000 U.S. troops had been exposed to Iraqi chemical weapons during the demolition of a series of bunkers housing tons of nerve and blister agents at Khamisiyah in southern Iraq. Those weapons were intended for Saddam's enemies in the Allied coalition and against enemy number one—Israel.

The horrors that American troops faced on the battlefield and Israeli civilians faced in their homes and schools has been sharply reduced—not eliminated entirely—by U.S. ratification of the Chemical Weapons Convention (CWC), a treaty negotiated by the Reagan and Bush administrations and supported by President Clinton. Signed by 162 countries, the Chemical Weapons Convention enters into force today.

Ratification was endorsed by our most senior military leaders, the current and previous directors of the Central Intelligence Agency, the Chemical Manufacturers Association, and arms-control experts who served both Presidents Bush and Clinton. The conclusion of hardheaded and respected military and foreign policy experts from both administrations is that American participation will enhance our security, advance American commercial interests, and support our policy of preventing the spread of nonnuclear weapons of mass destruction. As Gen. John Shalikashvili, chairman of the Joint Chiefs of Staff, testified, "From a military perspective, the Chemical Weapons Convention is clearly in our national interest."

Opponents who say the treaty imposes unwanted expense on American industry are 180 degrees off the mark. Some of our biggest trading partners—the United Kingdom, France, Germany, Japan—have already ratified it. Countries that haven't ratified the treaty will face trade restrictions by those that have. U.S. failure to ratify would have cost hundreds of millions of dollars annually in lost exports.

The convention requires all members to destroy their chemical weapons stockpiles—as America has pledged to do—and forswear ever developing, producing, or acquiring such weapons. To enforce the ban, the CWC provides for the most extensive verification regime ever negotiated. It also strengthens law enforcement agencies by giving them new and vital tools to investigate a growing terrorism threat—the use of illicit chemical agents against our citizens. Ratification increases the possibility that Americans will never suffer as Japanese civilians did in 1995, when a cult released a chemical nerve agent in the Tokyo subway that killed twelve and injured more than 5,000.

Rogue states—such as Iraq, Iran, Libya, and North Korea—view chemical weapons as an equalizer to offset American and Western conventional military superiority, a perception enhanced when Iraq used them extensively against Iranian troops in the 1980s. The Western community's failure to punish or even censure Iraq weakened international norms against their use. Tough new trade controls will now prohibit anyone from selling chemical weapons ingredients to nonmembers. States outside the CWC thus become international pariahs; adhering to the CWC is one price they must pay to rejoin the community of nations.

By giving its consent to CWC ratification, the U.S. Senate has done its part to prevent future Khamisiyahs. Isaac Stern may keep his gas mask, but hopefully only as a souvenir.

On the Occasion of
the 25th Anniversary of
AJC's Jacob Blaustein Institute
for the Advancement of Human Rights
AJC 91st Annual Meeting, Washington, D.C.
May 7, 1997

In 1974, I was teaching in Moscow when I had an argument with my supervisor, Alexander Bessmertnikh, concerning Andrei Sakharov. I described Sakharov as a hero. He said Sakharov was insane. I asked how he could make such an outrageous claim. Bessmertnikh said that any man who knows that the consequences of his actions will land him in jail or a psychiatric prison must, by definition, be crazy. Sakharov was just such a man.

Sadly, Andrei Sakharov is no longer with us, but his world—the world of human rights activists and supporters—is abundantly represented here tonight by some of the other sanest, and most exceptional, people I know, and I could not be more delighted to be among you. We gather on the occasion of the Jacob Blaustein Institute's silver anniversary—and a truly auspicious occasion it is.

The JBI has been a precious jewel in the AJC crown since its founding twenty-five years ago, reflecting the centrality of human rights concerns to the raison d'être of this agency, as well as the extraordinarily close link between the Blaustein family name and the AJC.

The JBI is based on what should be a self-evident proposition, namely, that the protection of universal human rights and the goal of Jewish security are intimately intertwined. In that spirit, not only is AJC proud of the JBI's uniqueness among Jewish organizations, but also it has allowed us to make human rights an informed subject of conversation in our extensive interaction with world leaders from around the globe.

If the JBI has achieved a hallowed place in the pantheon of international human rights institutions, credit is surely due to many, but allow me to cite two individuals in particular, both here with us this evening—the JBI's first director, Sidney Liskofsky, and its special adviser throughout its history, Selma Hirsh.

Sidney began his association with AJC in 1944, after receiving a strong recommendation from the legendary Professor Salo Baron of Columbia. In 1971 he became the founding director of JBI.

As a lawyer, Sidney was profoundly convinced that norms were the building blocks of a new system of human rights protections for all.

In his own self-effacing way, Sidney had a unique capacity to bring together top scholars and jurists and encourage them, in their role as nongovernmental advisers, to prepare the groundwork for those officially responsible for drafting the legal instruments.

In his remarkable career, this 1935 graduate of Seward Park High School in New York and 1938 graduate of the City College of New York was most instrumental in helping draft the following instruments: the 1963 Declaration on the Elimination of All Forms of Racial Discrimination and the 1965 Convention on the same subject; the draft Declaration on the Elimination of All Form of Intolerance based on Religion and Belief begun in the 1960s but not adopted until 1981; and, not least, the draft Declaration on the Right to Leave.

Sidney profoundly believed—and he was absolutely right—that the strength of the JBI would depend on its capacity to anchor itself in scholarship of the highest order and, at the same time, establish working relationships with like-minded partners dedicated to advancing human rights.

Moreover, and this, too, is essential to understanding Sidney's genius, he recognized the need to create a corps of human rights experts, in this country and abroad, and encouraged the development of educational materials on human rights, as well as training and scholarships for talented young professionals.

Sidney, I know how much you dislike hyperbole, but the fact is your decades of service have genuinely helped change the post-World War II world and institutionalized human rights—both standards and monitoring—on the international agenda. And your decades of modesty have kept your work a big secret from too many. I hope you will forgive me for divulging that secret this evening, though in this room at least it was always a poorly kept secret at best.

And as for Selma Hirsh, she is unquestionably among the most elegant and eloquent, gracious and graceful, wise and worldly people I have ever had the pleasure of working with—and for. I can only say that her insight, her breadth of knowledge, her understanding of the importance of the human rights field, together with her unswerving commitment to AJC—an association, incidentally, that began in 1945 and continues to this very day—have made her indispensable both to the JBI and to AJC in ways far too numerous to enumerate here.

Selma has always been there, throughout the twenty-five-year life of the JBI, just behind the curtain and therefore usually out of sight. But, let's be clear, her imprint is indelibly stamped on the JBI. It is seen every day in the JBI's commitment to the highest professional standards and to the unique collaborative style that brings together our staff, today ably led by Felice Gaer, and the lay members and outside scholars who together form the JBI's Administrative Council.

To Sidney, my friend, my teacher, and my occasional walking partner, and to Selma, my friend, my mentor, and my Westchester neighbor, someone once said: "When all is said and done, usually more is said than done." In both your cases, it has been precisely the opposite. Little has been said; enormous amounts have been done.

I salute you both, as I salute the JBI itself, on this happy anniversary occasion that brings us all together in celebration and reaffirmation of common purpose.

Dedication Ceremony,
American Jewish Committee School
Adapazari, Turkey
October 25, 1999

Prime Minister Ecevit, Prime Minister Barak, distinguished guests, leaders of the Turkish Jewish community, ladies and gentlemen,

Friends are tested in times of need. You have an expression for it in Turkish.

Biz sadece iyi gün dostu degiliz, kara günde de yaninizdayuz. We are not just friends on a nice day, but also on a rainy day.

For centuries, Turkey has been a cherished friend of the Jewish people. And so your tragedy in August became our tragedy, your loss our loss.

We at the American Jewish Committee issued an emergency appeal for support for the earthquake victims, and thousands of Jews across the United States responded generously.

We were determined to help as best we could in the immediate relief effort. But we also wanted to contribute something more lasting, to create a living reminder of our strong ties to your country.

What could be more fitting than a school, an investment in Turkey's future? And what more appropriate site for the school than this remarkable Israeli-built village?

Maimonides, the most revered Jewish scholar of the Middle Ages, once wrote:

"We [humans] have been given free will. No one forces us, no one decides for us . . . ; we ourselves, by our own volition, choose our own way."

Yes, we all have to make choices. And in the case of Turkey, we, the Jewish people, have chosen to stand with you, our friends, in your darkest hours, just as you have chosen to stand with us on more than one difficult occasion in our own history. In other words, we have chosen to be friends, not only on the nice days but on the rainy days as well.

8. INTERNATIONAL TERRORISM

Chilling Talk, Reminiscent of Nazis
The Wall Street Journal
April 28, 1992

The page-one news brief on the Islamic Jihad's statement of responsibility for the car-bomb attack on the Israeli embassy in Buenos Aires told only part of the gruesome story (What's News, March 24). Another chilling part of the statement, as reported by Reuters on March 23: "The war is on until Israel ceases to exist and until the last Jew in the world is eliminated."

This view that Israel and Jews everywhere must be destroyed is consistent with earlier utterances by the Islamic Jihad. For example, in an interview published in the German weekly *Stern* (Feb. 14, 1991), Islamic Jihad leader Sheik Tamimi declared: "No Jew is innocent! All Jews must be killed. . . . And our Holy War, which we are engaging against them and their allies throughout the world, will finally eradicate this race." When the interviewer noted that "you are talking like the Nazis," Tamimi replied that "Hitler always saw us [the Arabs] as honest allies against Zionism."

Lest any reader conclude that Islamic Jihad has been preoccupied only with Israel and the Jewish people, in the same interview Tamimi also called on his followers to support and "attack all enemies of Saddam [Hussein] and of Islam throughout the world—destroy their installations, kill them regardless of where you meet them, even if it means the loss of your life."

This is the kind of blind, ruthless fanaticism that struck against the Israel embassy in Buenos Aires with tragic consequences, that threatens Jews everywhere, and that sees the West as its permanent enemy.

Given the close ties between the Islamic Jihad and Iran, those Western states, including the United States, that are now so actively pursuing better relations with Tehran must insist on an end to support for such international terrorist groups. Eliminating the assistance and sanctuary provided by countries like Iran (and Syria) is one vital element in any campaign to reduce the scourge of international terrorism.

AMIA Bombing in Argentina: One Year Later
AJC Press Conference, New York
July 17, 1995

One year ago tomorrow, the worst single postwar terrorist act against Jews anywhere outside the State of Israel took place when the AMIA building—the building housing many of the key Argentine Jewish institutions—was destroyed in the center of Buenos Aires. Nearly 100 people—Jews and non-Jews alike—were killed; more still were injured.

This was the second bombing of its kind in Buenos Aires, the first having occurred slightly more than two years earlier—in March 1992—when the Israeli embassy was destroyed with 28 killed and 250 injured.

All people of goodwill were shocked by the bombing of the AMIA building. The American Jewish Committee was no exception. Committed to Jewish security throughout the world, and recognizing the threat that international terrorism poses both to Jews and to democratic values, the AJC, for its part, mobilized its resources.

Within a day of the bombing, we had already met with Argentina's minister of the interior who was in New York for UN meetings.

We immediately dispatched a delegation to Buenos Aires, including Jason Isaacson, the director of our Washington office, and Jacob Kovadloff, our consultant on Latin American affairs, to stand in solidarity with the Argentine Jewish community and to meet with government officials, including Foreign Minister di Tella.

We have since had two additional meetings with the foreign minister, one in New York, the other in Washington.

When Argentine president Menem came to the United States, we joined in the session with him in New York and hosted a separate meeting with him in Los Angeles. At each of these meetings, we discussed at considerable length the state of the investigation of the 1994—and still unsolved 1992—bombings.

We commissioned a special report, entitled *Why Argentina*, that was published eleven days after the bombing and is available.

We met with FBI director Louis Freeh and other U.S. officials involved in counterterrorism efforts to urge U.S. cooperation in the investigation.

And several months ago, anticipating this first anniversary, we approached Sergio Kiernan, a distinguished Argentine journalist and editor, to do a comprehensive study on the state of the investigation and the mood of the Argentine Jewish community.

We issue this report today because we believe it important to assess where things stand and to remind the world that none of us will rest until justice is done. And be assured that we will be back here next July 17 with another report if there are no major breakthroughs in the case.

Let me be clear:

- If the perpetrators of this heinous act believe that the passage of time will diminish our resolve and memory, they are wrong.
- If the perpetrators believe that they can attack a Jewish target anywhere with impunity today, they are wrong.
- If the perpetrators believe that they can hide behind safe borders or find protection from nations that give them encouragement and support, they are wrong.

We stand here today in solidarity with our fellow Jews in Argentina and with all those, Jews and non-Jews alike, who know that none of us can rest easy until the perpetrators are found and put behind bars, until those nations that support terrorists are successfully quarantined, until Western democratic nations—the United States, Argentina, and others—succeed in forging sustained international cooperation based on an ironclad domestic will and the most modern and sophisticated methods to combat this scourge.

On the Unsolved Bombings
Noticias (Argentina)
July 24, 1997

The tragedies of the Israeli embassy bombing in 1992 and the AMIA bombing in 1994 remain open wounds for Jews everywhere. Not only do we continue to mourn the loss of life, but we are troubled by the inability of the Argentine authorities to achieve significant progress in the investigations.

We at the American Jewish Committee have frequently met with top Argentine officials to discuss both cases. Each time we have been assured of an unflinching determination to pursue the matter. We want desperately to believe these assurances. We know that investigative stagnation reflects badly on Argentina.

But with the passage of time and little, if any, apparent progress, our sense of frustration and anger only grows.

Why have we seen so few breakthroughs in the cases? Is there an attempt to thwart the investigations within the bureaucracies, and especially the police and security apparatus? Is there a fear the trail will lead to uncomfortable conclusions about domestic and international connections?

Yes, we know that Argentina's capacity to probe such acts of terror may be limited, but that alone cannot explain the paralysis and confusion we have witnessed so far. And yes, we know that Argentina is a country that prides itself on its tolerance and pluralism. But failure to resolve these cases only increases the sense of vulnerability and suspicion of the indigenous Jewish community.

It's high time for Argentina to enhance its counterterrorism capacity lest terrorists conclude they can act with impunity in the country, for, make no mistake, these bombings were an attack not only on Jewish targets but on the very notion of Argentine (and Western) democratic values.

We, those who mourn the victims, will not rest until justice is done. Nor, we trust, will Argentina.

An Admitted Terrorist
Newsday
August 20, 1997

Ellis Henican's interview of Hamas leader Abu Mousa Marzook ["Hamas: Not Our Boys," Aug. 4] needs to be examined from the perspective of what we know and what we do not know.

Briefly, here's what we do know: Marzook is an admitted leader of a notorious Islamic terrorist organization who spent many years in the United States organizing and raising money for an unabashedly anti-Semitic, anti-Israel, anti-Western terrorist group that proudly boasts of the human carnage it is responsible for, most recently the bombing in a Jerusalem market that claimed the lives of fourteen individuals.

Here's what we don't know: Why Henican, or Newsday for that matter, would lend any legitimacy to a recognized international terrorist deported by the United States by giving him an uncritical platform from which to espouse ludicrous views, such as claiming that Israel was involved in the alleged Brooklyn terrorist subway bombing plot?

The jury is not yet in on the accused plotters, and therefore we can't be certain who sent them. But we should be able to distinguish between America's friends and enemies. Marzook and Hamas are our enemies. It's unfortunate that Henican didn't make that sufficiently clear.

Be Wary of Iran's Approach
Newsday
January 13, 1998

I read James A. Bill's article "U.S. Should Pursue Iran Opening" [Viewpoints, Jan. 6] with some dismay. True, the recent election of Mohammad Khatami as president of Iran bears close watching. Clearly, he parts company with the more strident clerics who rule the country. But not yet apparent is the degree to which he, as president, will be in a position to influence matters, especially in foreign policy.

Further, the short shrift given by Bill to Iran's "alleged quest for weapons of mass destruction" is profoundly disturbing. There's nothing alleged about the quest. Major Western intelligence agencies all agree that Iran is in the midst of a major effort to develop medium-range missiles that could reach targets in South and Central Asia, the Persian Gulf, and the Mideast. Such missiles, fitted with biological or chemical warheads, would profoundly change the region's strategic equation and directly affect key American interests.

Lastly, Bill creates a troubling symmetry between Iran and the United States when he writes that "both sides have legitimate grievances." Nonsense. Notwithstanding the kudos given by Bill to Iranian foreign and domestic policy, the truth is that Iran has been the world's leading sponsor of terrorism, not to speak of a menace to a long list of nations, near and far, including the "Great Satan," as Iranian leaders frequently refer to the United States.

Here's hoping that serious change is afoot in Iran; but, despite Bill's unbridled optimism, a more sensible U.S. policy requires clear benchmarks to measure Iranian behavior before any significant change in our country's approach takes place. Anything less could prove as short-sighted as the Bush administration's support of Baghdad until August 2, 1990, when Iraq occupied Kuwait, leading to Operation Desert Storm.

Be Cautious, Don't Ignore Recent History in Reevaluating Relations with Iran
USA Today
January 15, 1998

USA Today's editorial on Iran calls for reevaluation of U.S. policy toward Tehran in light of the more dulcet tones coming from that country's new president, Mohammad Khatami ("Bit of Iranian 'pingpong' might repair the past").

While I fervently hope Khatami offers a new opening, Washington's approach should be governed by caution rooted in the sobering experience of our efforts to deal with Iran over the past two decades. Let's be very careful and open-eyed.

For one thing, it's not at all clear what power Khatami holds, and even if he does wield more than we think, he's not yet established himself as the gleaming white knight. His vituperative words on Israel, for example, echoing the aggressive Iranian line, are but one reminder.

Despite your headline citing the need to "repair the past" in the U.S.-Iranian relationship, the major challenge today is repairing the "present" in Iranian behavior.

Confirmed by U.S. and other Western intelligence agencies, Iran has embarked on a major effort, with Russian assistance, to develop sophisticated, intermediate-range ballistic missiles and weapons of mass destruction to accompany them. Against whom?

Moreover, Iran is the principal state supporter of international terrorism. Egyptian president Hosni Mubarak, PLO chairman Yasser Arafat, and former Israeli prime minister Shimon Peres are among those who have accused Tehran of terrorist activity.

Left to the major European nations, China, and Russia, shortsighted commercial interests and self-serving political maneuvering would dictate international policy toward Iran. What else is new? It is only the United States, to its credit, that has sought to challenge those Iranian policies that threaten peace and stability.

That's why it is incumbent upon Washington to explore any possible changes afoot in Iran, but to ensure that we not rush headlong into a new approach driven by no more than our own wishful thinking or self-delusion, or by pressure from countries whose interests are not necessarily our own. Iranian deeds rather than words are what count. Otherwise, I fear, we ignore the painful lessons of recent history in that part of the world at our peril.

9. MAKING A BETTER AMERICA

Identifying All Participants
Washington Jewish Week
November 3, 1988

Your report and accompanying photo (*WJW*, Oct. 13) on the troubling incident of anti-Semitic vandalism at Temple Rodef Shalom in Falls Church each had one regrettable omission. The article referred by name and title to the Jewish participants at the press conference held to denounce this tragic event, but then inexplicably lumped together the other attendees with the description "local Christian clergymen." Similarly, the photo caption identified by name both the police officer and rabbi pictured but failed to identify the third person in the photo, obviously, from his apparel, a Christian clergyman.

Why weren't these righteous individuals properly identified? *WJW* readers deserve to know who these caring people are.

Anti-Semitism
Washington Jewish Week
March 5, 1992

In your front-page story on the ADL annual audit of anti-Semitic incidents and the lead editorial in the same issue (WJW, Feb. 13), you juxtapose the ADL findings with a recently released study on attitudes toward Jews in the United States conducted by the National Opinion Research Center for the American Jewish Committee and try to reconcile the seemingly contradictory results. On the one hand, ADL reported a significant increase in anti-Semitic acts nationwide, whereas the AJC study found growing acceptance of Jews by non-Jews. In fact, there need not be any contradiction between the two findings.

Both are undoubtedly true. Extremist hatemongers continue to come out of the closet believing, presumably, that the current climate of social and economic dislocation is favorable to them. The perpetrators of anti-Semitic acts, however, are still sufficiently few, thank goodness, that they do not represent a statistically significant number in any national survey. At the same time, it is abundantly clear by virtually any index that American Jews have found a remarkable degree of acceptance in virtually every sphere of society.

To be sure, some barriers, either invisible or even visible, still remain and cannot simply be dismissed. Yet I recall in 1969–70 serving on a board to select the president of the University of Pennsylvania. When a Jewish candidate was proposed, it was noted that no Ivy League university had ever before been led by a Jewish president. As it turned out, Penn did select that Jewish candidate, but by then Dartmouth had also filled a presidential vacancy with a Jew and suddenly the Ivy League had two Jewish university heads. Today, that number is four.

This good news notwithstanding, the author of the AJC study, Tom Smith, cautioned: "Today anti-Semitism in America is neither virulent nor growing. It is not a powerful social or political force. . . . But neither is anti-Semitism a spent force. Jews are recognized as an ethnic and religious out-group and are judged and treated in a distinctive manner accordingly. While at present the negative repercussions of Jewish identity are limited, hostility to Jews because of their material success, ties to Israel, or some other reason could manifest itself in the future."

Smith's right. Constant vigilance is required. Still, we ought not to ignore or diminish the significance of the good news found in the AJC study, which attests to the remarkable success achieved by American Jews in recent decades. Indeed, that success in combating anti-Semitism has, ironically, facilitated Jewish assimilation into American society. As a result, the challenge of perpetuating a distinctive and creative American Jewish ethos and identity is rapidly emerging as the critical priority on the Jewish agenda in the 1990s.

The Old Alliance
The New York Times
May 9, 1992

You assert that "Blacks and Jews, old partners in better times, disagree sharply over affirmative action, racial solutions, and American policy in Israel" in an article on the National Association for the Advancement of Colored People (The Week in Review, March 29). While no one will argue that blacks and Jews have [not] experienced tension in recent years, this is hardly the whole story.

On the legal front, for example, the American Jewish Committee has joined the NAACP Legal Defense and Educational Fund in recent court cases on school segregation, voting rights, minority broadcast licenses, and exclusion of blacks from juries. Jewish organizations actively worked with the NAACP and other groups to support the Civil Rights Act of 1991. Many support affirmative action programs, including goals and timetables (though not quotas), and there are new joint initiatives on social policy and combating poverty.

On foreign policy, our polls conducted over several years indicate general black support for Israel, though at lower levels than other Americans, and strong Jewish opposition to apartheid in South Africa.

Incidentally, this level of cooperation among Jewish and black private agencies is also to be found in Congress, where Jewish and black members often work very closely on these same domestic and overseas issues.

Yes, there have been difficulties on both the policy and neighborhood levels that cannot be easily dismissed, but the facts show that the black-Jewish alliance nevertheless has much to contribute to a fair and just America.

Helping to Build Ties
The Jewish Week
November 6, 1992

In discussing Project Understanding (Inside Washington, Oct. 2–8), a new program that will bring Jewish and African-American high school students from Washington, D.C., to Senegal and Israel for a shared experience, the *Jewish Week* correctly notes that the program is modeled after a similar effort begun eight years ago in Philadelphia.

Mention is appropriately made of the instrumental role of former congressman Bill Gray in launching the Philadelphia program. But missing is any reference to the other founding partner, the Philadelphia chapter of the American Jewish Committee. Together, Congressman Gray and the AJC created Operation Understanding to provide a unique opportunity for Jewish and African-American youth to spend intensive time together exploring one another's roots. Later, the Urban League also became a cosponsor.

The program has been a big success, measured by the reactions of the participants themselves, the amount of media attention, including an hour-long documentary on the CBS affiliate in Philadelphia, and the subsequent desire of other cities, including Washington, to begin similar efforts.

As such, the American Jewish Committee is proud of its role in helping to build relations between future leaders of the Jewish and African-American communities.

Black-Jewish Alliance*
The New York Times
May 1, 1993

The American Jewish Committee welcomes the two op-ed articles by Profs. Henry Louis Gates Jr. and Cornel West (April 14) calling for closer ties between African-Americans and Jews. Indeed, our organization, along with several others in both the black and Jewish communities, has never abandoned the alliance. We have been working together over the past few years on issues as diverse as promoting the Civil Rights Act of 1991, endorsing strong programs to combat poverty and promote self-sufficiency, and countering all forms of racism and anti-Semitism.

*This letter was cosigned with Alfred H. Moses, AJC president.

But we take issue with two points raised by Professor West. First, his analogy between former Israeli prime ministers Menachem Begin and Yitzhak Shamir and the hatemongers Louis Farrakhan and Leonard Jeffries is entirely inappropriate. Messrs. Begin and Shamir were democratically elected to head their government. One can argue with their policies, but there was no hint in either administration of racial hatred against any Arab group, including Palestinians. By contrast, Mr. Farrakhan and Professor Jeffries have engaged in pure anti-Semitic demagoguery, openly promoting falsifications of history to stir hatred against Jews, and mouthing centuries-old anti-Jewish stereotypes. That is why repudiation of them by people like Professor West is so important.

We also question how Professor West can charge Jews with "visible . . . resistance to affirmative action and government spending on social programs. . . ." All polling data indicate that Jews are the most likely white group to support government social programs. And many Jewish agencies, our own included, have long supported public efforts to reduce poverty, promote job training, and rebuild our cities.

What we do oppose, however, are numerical quotas that set aside fixed numbers of professional or student slots for designated group members. We believe that it is both possible and desirable to maintain vigorous programs for minority inclusion in business and academia without compromising on requirements for high qualifications to fill positions.

Voices From the "Swivel Chair"
New York Post
August 13, 1993

Sidney Zion's attack on mainstream Jewish leaders and organizations for allegedly doing nothing to protect the Jews of Crown Heights from the fury of the anti-Semitic mobs because we were "embarrassed" by the Lubavitch Hasidim is scurrilous ("Crown Heights and the failure of Jewish leaders," July 30).

Had Mr. Zion bothered to check with the Jewish leaders he is so quick to bash, he would have found out that Jewish groups did, in fact, mobilize to meet the emergency. Could we have done more? Should we have done more? With the benefit of hindsight, the answer is, of course, yes. Everyone—elected officials, the Police Department, community and religious leaders, and Jewish organizations—could have done more to seek a quicker end to the violence against the Hasidic community of Crown Heights.

At the same time, it should be noted that, soon after the violence began, Jewish leaders were pressing City Hall and other city, state, and federal officials for action. We demanded that the police stop the riots and restore order, and that, if it was unable to do so, the National Guard should be called in. We were told that the police could and would do the job. Jewish groups, including the American Jewish Committee, worked feverishly behind the scenes in order to try to end the violence. And today, we continue to work cooperatively with organizations such as the Crown Heights Coalition, formed by Brooklyn borough president Howard Golden in the aftermath of the crisis. Indeed, the Coalition's work was honored by us in June.

Nation of Islam's Sermons of Hatred
The Wall Street Journal
March 10, 1994

Your article "Blacks' Increasing Vocal Opposition to Violence Is Matched by Strong Opposition to Crime Bill" gives the Nation of Islam undue credit when you say its leadership has "spoken out against crime and for the kind of values that make it unacceptable." The Nation of Islam's leadership, on and off campus, preaches selective violence and the "value" of bigotry.

Last November 29, for instance, Khalid Abdul Muhammad, one of the Nation of Islam's leading spokesmen, gave his "stump" speech at Kean College in New Jersey. The value he ascribed to interreligious respect was clear: "[T]he old, no good pope, you know that cracker, somebody need to raise that dress up and see what's really there."

He preached about killing all white South Africans (babies included) if they do not get out of the country in twenty-four hours. He laughed when he described "political prisoners" in the United States, who became such when they "put the gun to the white judge's head . . . and they blew the judge's head off." He said "the white man is the devil."

According to Muhammad, the lesson of World War II was that "Everybody always talk [*sic*] about Hitler exterminating 6 million Jews. But don't nobody [*sic*] ever ask, 'What did they do to Hitler?'" Minister Louis Farrakhan, leader of the Nation of Islam, has not only refused to repudiate Muhammad's remarks, but has accused Jews and others of using "Khalid's words against us."

When white racist organizations speak out about "crime" and "values," as they do from time to time, we expect the media not to take their words at face value, but to report them in the context of their speakers' hateful agenda. The Nation of Islam's pronouncements are no less selective and bone-chilling.

Special American Jewish Committee Award
to Billings, Montana
AJC 88th Annual Meeting, Washington, D.C.
May 5, 1994

When we first saw the segment we just showed you on ABC television, we quickly decided that we wanted in some way to honor the town of Billings—the thousands of its citizens who expressed their moral decency and courage when some of their fellow citizens were, as you saw so vividly, threatened and attacked.

Last year at this time, we honored one man—Jan Karski—a Polish Catholic who had gone to extraordinary lengths during the Second World War, as a member of the Polish underground, to alert a largely indifferent world to the Nazi extermination of the Jews. As we know so well, there were all too few Jan Karskis at that time.

And there were too few communities that stood together with their fellow Jews in the face of unspeakable evil. The remarkable story of the Danish people, who managed to smuggle to Sweden nearly 7,500 of the country's 8,000 Jews, will forever stand as the quintessential act of communal solidarity and courage. And there were other, often lesser known examples—Bulgaria's protection of its own Jews, Albania's, Finland's, and a few towns and villages. Among these, perhaps, the most poignant was the French town of Le Chambon-sur-Lignon, which took in some 5,000 Jewish children during the war and saved them from deportation and probable death. Imagine, if you will, not one but a dozen, two, three dozen such villages doing the same and what the result might have been, but alas, it was not to be.

Pierre Sauvage, one of the Jewish children rescued in Le Chambon, subsequently wrote:

> If we do not learn how it is possible to act well even under the most trying circumstances, we will increasingly doubt our ability to act well even under less trying ones.
>
> If we remember solely the horror of the Holocaust, it is we who will bear the responsibility for having created the most dangerous alibi of all: that it was beyond man's capacity to know and care.
>
> If the hard and fast evidence of the possibility of good on earth is allowed to slip through our fingers and turn into dust, then future generations will have only dust to build on.

Ladies and gentlemen, the world today is an increasingly complicated place. More and more, we are seemingly presented with two contrasting ways to live—as one human family in which everyone, whatever our race, religion, ethnicity, recognizes that each of us is created in God's image, that each of us is worthy of respect, that this respect for others in no way diminishes our own self-worth or, for that matter, our own distinctiveness.

Or, we can let the haters and hatemongers, the bigots, the anti-Semites, the racists, the ethnic cleansers seek to divide us and replace pluralism with so-called purity. As the late Martin Luther King Jr. said: "We must all learn to live together as brothers, or we will all perish together as fools. That is the challenge of the hour."

The American Jewish Committee has from its inception eighty-eight years ago stood unyieldingly for the principles of pluralism, intergroup harmony, and enhanced understanding among peoples of diverse faiths and racial and ethnic backgrounds. And, to this end, we have sponsored two of the most seminal research works of the postwar era—the landmark five-volume study entitled *Studies in Prejudice*, published after the war, and its converse, if you will, *The Altruistic Personality*, in 1988.

These studies teach us that if we are to build a world based on tolerance and mutual respect, it is not enough that we preach it from the podium. To succeed, as the examples of Denmark and Le Chambon tellingly illustrate, these values must become an integral part of our daily lives, of what parents, educators, clergy, and political leaders demonstrate by example, not by words alone. It must be part of a profound and unshakable belief system of the intrinsic worth of each and every human being.

The response of the people of Billings, Montana, to the unprecedented wave of fear generated by skinheads, whose aim was to attack vulnerable minorities, especially Jews, but also African-Americans, Hispanics, and Native Americans, proved the point. A sense of authentic community existed, and residents truly felt that an attack on one was an assault on the entire community. In other words, they felt that each neighbor was as much part of the fabric and fiber of the community as any other. This story should also serve to remind us yet again why minority groups need to strengthen their links with one another and not cede ground to those who would divide us.

And what is so exceptional about the people of Billings, just like the people of Denmark, the villagers of Le Chambon, or individual rescuers during the Second World War—though the circumstances clearly are different—is that they do not regard their acts of solidarity and identification as anything exceptional or out of the ordinary.

Yes, they have experienced fear in Billings, fear, for instance, that a rock might be thrown through their children's window and cause injury or worse. No doubt, however, they have taken strength from the many who have stood together, from the inspiring example of some community leaders, and from the knowledge that what they are doing is, in fact, the ultimate fulfillment of the words of Leviticus: "Love thy neighbor as thyself."

Among those community leaders are our two special guests this evening, Police Chief Wayne Inman, whom you saw in the film clip, and Wayne Schile, the publisher of the *Billings Gazette* that printed the thousands of copies of the menorah which eventually were placed in the windows of so many homes.

And in this there is a lesson for all of us. If we have the courage and conviction of Police Chief Inman and Mr. Schile to strive toward affirmation of that which is right and good, then our example just might become contagious for those around us. And we—and our worldview—shall prevail. But if we simply mouth pieties, preach but don't practice, legislate but don't lead—or if our attitude reflects only apathy or indifference—then the skinheads, the bigots, the anti-Semites, the racists will step into the breach. And we know only too well from history what that can bring.

And so, on behalf of the American Jewish Committee, it is my profound honor and privilege this evening to present this special award to the town of Billings, Montana, for showing us all how we can practice the principles of decency, goodness, and caring and, in doing so, prevail over the purveyors of raw hate.

America's Christian Crusader
Time
June 5, 1995

We should bear in mind the late Senator Sam Ervin's admonition: "When religion controls government, political liberty dies, and when government controls religion, religious liberty perishes." Notwithstanding persistent disclaimers, [Ralph] Reed and the Christian Coalition continue to raise genuine concerns that the Coalition seeks to tamper with a successful constitutional arrangement between religion and state.

Count Me Out[*]
The New York Times
November 2, 1995

Toward the end of his speech at Monday's ("Million Man") march in Washington, Minister Louis Farrakhan said it's time to start a dialogue—with no preconditions—with the Jewish community. After all, he said, if Israel and the PLO can sit down to talk, why not the Nation of Islam and American Jews?

On its face, it sounds reasonable, doesn't it? After all, what harm could possibly come from a face-to-face meeting with an individual who seemingly seeks such an encounter? When did talk ever hurt anyone?

But I won't join the dialogue, at least for now. Not until a few things happen. Yes, Minister Farrakahn, call them preconditions, if you will.

And I can't accept the Israel-PLO analogy. Israelis and the PLO were at war with one another over land. African Americans and American Jews share the same land and citizenship. American Jews are not, nor have they ever been, at war with any segment of the African American community. To the contrary, the American Jewish record in this country's civil rights struggle is unparalleled.

To this day, American Jews are disproportionately represented in the ongoing pursuit of justice, intergroup harmony, and a fair shake for our nation's poorest and most vulnerable. And it is worth noting that, whether in the U.S. Congress or local voting booths, African Americans and Jews continue to demonstrate remarkably similar voting patterns.

To be sure, the relationship is not problem-free. In recent years it has become more fraught with complication over such thorny issues as individual vs. group rights and, yes, from the Jewish perspective, the vitriolic anti-Semitism peddled by Minister Farrakhan's Nation of Islam as well as by some Afrocentric spokesmen.

Complications notwithstanding, the dialogue and cooperation between many African American and Jewish agencies continue on both the national and local levels. That cooperation should be strengthened

[*]Appeared as an "advertorial."

to counter recent regressive trends—increased racial polarization, growing disenchantment with government's role in addressing societal needs, and declining compassion for the weakest among us. Moreover, the struggle for equal opportunity is far from over.

Why shouldn't we then widen the black-Jewish circle and include Minister Farrakhan? Put simply, there can be no room at the table for an unrepentant anti-Semite and racist. We know from our own experience the danger of equivocating with extremists, whether black or white, left-wing or right-wing. As long as the minister, his aides, and the movement they represent continue to engage in broad-scale attacks against Jews and other groups, both in speeches and publications, there's simply nothing for us to discuss.

In fact, just two days before the Washington march, at a gathering in Chicago, Nation of Islam National Youth Minister Quanell X said: "All you Jews can go straight to hell . . . I say to Jewish Americans: Get ready . . . knuckle up, put your boots on, because we're ready and the war is going down." And Minister Khalid Muhammad added: "This is the time of the black man's rise and the white man's demise." In our book, such raw anti-Semitism and racism are not debatable issues.

Minister Farrakhan cannot have it both ways—one voice that today purports to speak of inclusion and ecumenism, and another that obsessively demonizes Jews and others and consistently distorts history.

Minister Farrakhan, if anti-Semitism and racism continue to be an essential part of the Nation of Islam's credo, kindly drop the disingenuous pretense of seeking dialogue with the Jewish community. On the other hand, if they are no longer to be a part, then clear words and action that repudiate anti-Semitism and racism, however overdue, would be welcomed. And then we'll have something to talk about.

William F. Buckley's "Slippery Slope"
New York Post
February 7, 1996

William F. Buckley Jr.'s column of January 22 ("Religion is political . . .") is a setback to the cause of interreligious harmony in America.

By declaring that "The Christian owes absolutely nothing more to other religions than a respectful tolerance of them," Buckley displays a severe case of Christian triumphalism. Instead of seeking to develop mutual respect and understanding among America's diverse faith communities, Buckley calls instead for an icy Christian tolerance. And, as the world has painfully discovered, tolerance is a necessary, but insufficient, condition for true coexistence.

Buckley also reveals an apparent inability to recognize the lethal dangers of anti-Semitism. To equate Jew-hatred with a New York Yankee fan's anti-Boston Red Sox feeling is to trivialize and minimize. After all, Yankee fans have no historical record of systematically killing Red Sox followers, but anti-Semites have murdered Jews.

One has the sense that discussion of anti-Semitism is a kind of intellectual game for Buckley; a clever theological thrust here, a brilliant parry there, followed by a clever riposte, and then the fencing match is over and it's on to something else. But to state the obvious, anti-Semitism is not a fencing match or, for that matter, a baseball rivalry.

However, the main point of Buckley's article—the need for religious and political leaders to be more assertive in publicly declaring their religious beliefs and affirmations—does deserve serious thought. On its face, it sounds fine, but because America is increasingly multireligious in its population, such a policy, however well-intentioned, could prove seriously divisive.

Just imagine if President Clinton, or any other president, based his policies on his own interpretation of doctrinal beliefs. What kind of message would that send to the millions of Americans who do not share those beliefs? Having a deep personal faith does not guarantee political truth or effective governance.

And finally, let's not forget what can happen when political leaders begin to invoke God, Jesus, Allah, etc., as justification for certain policies. No, Buckley's slope is just too slippery to start down.

Looking Back, Looking Ahead
50th Anniversary Celebration
AJC Dallas Chapter
November 13, 1996

I love to get away from New York every once in a while. Don't get me wrong; it's a fascinating city and in the midst of a remarkable revitalization, but it's still quite a distinctive place.

Take the following conversation overheard between two nine-year olds standing in front of their East Side school one day and reported in the *New York Times*: "You'll never believe it. I found a condom on our terrace last night," said one. Replied the other: "No kidding, what's a terrace?"

Or a situation that happened to me while walking down Broadway with my son Danny. An elderly woman approached and, with a strong Yiddish-accented English, says to me, "What a good-looking boy you have! He must look exactly like your wife."

Or this true story with my wife. She wakes up with a start very early the other morning and announces: "Our new housecleaner, whom I hired to come once a week, starts today. I've got to clean the house before she arrives, or else she might quit on us."

That's New York for you. But tonight we're here to celebrate a milestone in Dallas, the AJC Chapter's fiftieth Anniversary, and I couldn't be more delighted to have been asked to share the evening with you.

The year was 1946. The United States had only the year before emerged triumphant, though at great cost of course, from the Second World War. America's world position was preeminent. America's self-confidence was riding high.

The country's population was 140 million, just under 10 percent of which was African American, with much smaller numbers of Hispanics and Asians. The minimum wage was seventy-five cents per hour; 8,000 homes had television sets; 108,000 immigrants were admitted that year.

In the U.S. Congress there were nine women, two African Americans, one Jew.

About a third of all women were in the workforce. There were fewer than 3,000 women lawyers in the entire country.

Less than 3 percent of white families with children under eighteen were headed by a woman. For African Americans, the figure was about 8 percent.

African American income was about 44 percent of that of whites.

The major leagues had not yet seen their first African American baseball player. The American military was still segregated, as it had of course been during the war, and was to remain until 1948 when President Truman issued an executive order.

The Supreme Court had not yet ruled that restrictive covenants could not be enforced in courts of law, nor had it yet proclaimed segregation in graduate and professional schools illegal. Those rulings would come two and four years later, respectively. And of course the landmark school desegregation case, *Brown v. Board of Education*, was still six years away.

Discrimination in public accommodations, employment, transportation, recreation, and education were all facts of life in many parts of the country, and they hadn't yet been addressed by the courts or the federal government. Enough of us in this room remember the separate toilets, the separate water fountains, the separate eating places, the separate seating—in other words, the separate and unequal country in which we lived.

The major universities of this country, including the eight Ivy League institutions, were all led by white, Christian men, and would be until 1970 when a Jew became president of Dartmouth.

So, too, the major corporations, the banks, the principal cultural and social institutions that formed the core power structure of this country.

And not that far from this city in March 1946, one of the greatest men of this century, perhaps the greatest, stood before an audience at Westminster College in Fulton, Missouri, and solemnly declared: "From Stettin in the Baltic to Trieste in the Adriatic, an iron curtain has descended across the Continent. Behind that line lie all the capitals of the ancient states of Central and Eastern Europe. Warsaw, Berlin, Prague, Vienna, Budapest, Belgrade, Bucharest, and Sofia, all these famous cities and the populations around them lie in what I must call the Soviet sphere . . ."

The speaker of course was the indomitable Winston Churchill, and he described a cold war that was to affect our domestic and international policy for the next forty-five years.

The world looks quite different today than it did fifty years ago, a great deal of it for the better. Enormous, even unimaginable, strides have been made in so many fields. Yes, a lot has changed in these fifty years since the Dallas Chapter of the American Jewish Committee was founded.

Wouldn't it be wonderful to come before this particular audience on this evening and suggest causality: that somehow the Chapter was created and, poof, fifty years later we can point to the long distance the country has traveled?

Not so simple, you say. I know, though I daresay that the American Jewish Committee and its Dallas Chapter have not been in the bleachers but on the playing field these past fifty years—ninety years in the case of the national organization—and we're proud of the role we've played, locally, nationally, even internationally, in at least some of the extraordinary changes that have taken place.

We take no credit—if credit is due—for the meteoric rise in the number of television sets from 8,000 to 93 million in these fifty years.

But if the U.S. Congress is just a bit more reflective of the face of America today than it once was . . .

If the last fifty years have seen a veritable revolution in the laws of this land concerning race, equal rights, and equal opportunity . . .

If women now comprise half or more of the entering classes of the nation's medical and law schools (and, if you're wondering, those 3,000 women lawyers in 1946 have now become over 200,000) . . .

If this country has become more generous and less ethnocentric in its immigration policy . . .

If this country shows more compassion and sensitivity in its refugee policy than it once did . . .

If the centers of political, economic, and cultural power in this country have begun to open up . . .

If this country has held together as a nation during these past five tumultuous decades while undergoing wrenching political, social, cultural, and demographic changes . . .

If this country has prevailed in the worldwide struggle with its communist adversaries and along the way strengthened still further its commitment, in word and in deed, to the principles of human rights, human decency, and human freedom . . .

I would propose to you that the American Jewish Committee and this Dallas Chapter have helped encourage these changes and, yes, helped manage these changes to ensure that that which unites us in this country—i.e., the centripetal forces—always far outweigh the centrifugal forces, those that would pull us apart.

I suspect that those who would wax nostalgic about the "good old times" in this country may be suffering from a selective memory syndrome or simply, as I do from time to time, confusing their own warm memories as a younger person—or perhaps their desire to be young once again—with a more utopian era.

Ah yes, to have my slice of savory New York pizza for fifteen cents and a Coke for a dime and then to go home and watch on television as Fred MacMurray played in *My Three Sons*.

No, I wouldn't trade 1996 for 1946 any more than I would trade 1946 for 1846. And I suspect the generations that follow us—I can't resist, those just behind us on that heavily trafficked bridge to the next century—will not want to trade 2046 for 1996 either because the trajectory of this country continues to be upward.

Too optimistic? Perhaps. It's true that in Soviet Russia an optimist was defined as someone "without all the facts." But I remain bullish on this continuing experiment we call America. I remain confident in the American people and their innate good sense and decency, moderation, and love of this country. And I continue to believe that proper attention to the unfinished business of America will only make us still stronger as a nation.

The greatness of this country has always been in its recognition that the task of forming a more perfect union is seen as a permanent work in progress; in its perception of itself as a standard-bearer for the prin-

ciples of human dignity, democracy, and the rule of law; and in its willingness to periodically engage in self-examination, confront flaws,
and, as a result, emerge stronger to sustain its unique calling.

But never for a moment can we allow ourselves complacency about
this country, or simply assume that there are inexorable forces at work
that will push us to ever greater heights. No, it doesn't work that way.
And no, not everyone shares the same agenda. No, for those good
forces to prevail, we must constantly remind ourselves that they are
us—the organizations and businesses, universities and civic associations, and, not least, individuals gathered here together this evening.
We are those forces, or at least a part of them, whose vision is of an
America democratic and strong, of an America open and whole. We
still have the power to write history, to continue on the remarkable and
unparalleled journey of this great country to become something still
better. But others also seek that authorship role and theirs is a narrower, harsher, more restrictive vision of this country.

To accomplish our goals over the next fifty years, to advance the
intertwined causes of human relations and pluralism, democracy and
social justice, we will have our work cut out for us.

We must always keep before us the proposition that in our hands has
been placed a sacred trust—the trust of that unique historical enterprise, the United States.

We must avoid doctrinal thinking—the kind of narrowness of vision
and deliberation that locks us into one particular school of thought or
another and prevents us from hearing reasoned views from other
thoughtful quarters. No one political camp has a lock on public policy
wisdom; surely the experience of the past thirty years alone has amply
demonstrated that simple but critically important fact.

We must constantly learn when to stand firm on our principles and
when to seek compromise.

We must remind ourselves, and those around us, that the complex
problems we as a country face defy simplistic solutions. They require
sober thought, not sloganeering; long-term resolve, not quick fixes or
sound bites.

Therefore, we should challenge those decision-makers who descend
to the lowest common denominator, driven by obsessions with polling

data and a media with a nanosecond attention span, to adopt instead a higher standard befitting the demands of our times and the intelligence of the American people.

Time does not permit a fuller explication, but let me set before you this evening, in summary fashion, six particularly compelling challenges in the years ahead, recognizing that this is far from an exhaustive list. And let me suggest that these six areas are precisely the areas which this audience, and audiences like it around the country, are best suited to address, each in its own way.

First is the challenge of managing the extraordinary sociodemographic changes afoot. Perhaps as never before, this country is literally changing its face. The white European population is continuing to decline as a percentage of the total population; and the percentages of Hispanics, Asians, and African American are growing, with still other groups emerging on the scene.

The business of keeping before us the ties that bind; making place at the American table for all our inhabitants, new and old; maintaining unity with diversity; combating manifestations of racism and other forms of bigotry, and strengthening mutual respect and mutual understanding will not be an easy one. It never has been easy; it won't get any easier in the years ahead. Daily, for example, we are reminded of the lingering hatreds that continue to exist in this land, though we should also draw satisfaction from the community of conscience, of which we are an integral part, that is quick to rise on almost every occasion.

Just to illustrate the demographic change in one way—the number of Asian Americans doubled during the 1970s, then doubled again during the 1980s. The 1990 census counted just over 7 million Asian-Americans, 2.9 percent of the population. It's estimated the total will reach 12 million in the year 2000 and almost 20 million by 2020.

New languages, new religions, new cultures, new traditions, new histories in our midst.

Dramatic change, sociologists remind us, often bring with them expressions of fear, anxiety, dislocation, insecurity, and anomie among those who feel most threatened by the changes. These expressions have to be monitored carefully. They also have to be addressed thoughtfully.

The second challenge is and will remain that of defining the role of government in our lives. Much was heard about this issue in the recent elections. I believe the debate over the appropriate role of government is entirely legitimate. But there are disturbing trends at hand that cannot be ignored and that bespeak an underlying doubt about governance of any sort in this country, and I'm not now speaking of the most extreme manifestation—the militia movement and its offshoots.

According to a recent comprehensive survey undertaken by the Gallup Organization for the University of Virginia, only 32 percent of Americans have a "great deal" or "quite a lot" of "confidence in the Federal government." Twenty-one percent expressed no confidence that "when the government decides to solve a problem, the problem will actually be solved."

In 1966, 41 percent of the population had "a great deal of confidence" in the presidency. Today, that figure is just 13 percent.

Again in 1966, 42 percent of the American population had "a great deal of confidence" in Congress. In 1996, this figure is just—please listen carefully—5 percent!

And eight out of ten Americans, according to the same survey, agree that "our country is run by a close network of special interests, public officials, and the media."

The conclusion of the study was as follows: "Whether confused, angry, resentful or indifferent, the vast majority of Americans (81 percent) resonates with the stinging indictment that political events these days seem more like theater or entertainment than like something to be taken seriously."

That's worrisome. The government, the presidency, the Congress, and public officials are held in low esteem. Voter turnout declined to 49 percent of eligible voters this November 5th, the lowest rate in the Western world and the lowest U.S. figure since 1924 despite commendable efforts to simplify registration. And, it should be added, these views cut across party, education, economic, and other lines. In sum, we have a potential long-term crisis on our hands, because many citizens could eventually conclude that no government—or an alternative form of government—is the best government. This, we know, would be a formula for unmitigated disaster.

And this brings me to my third, and closely connected, point. The ultimate health of democracy depends on confidence in government, yes. It also depends on an educated citizenry, an informed citizenry, a curious citizenry. In this extraordinary age of technological and communications revolution, more information is available, more readily, than ever before to anyone who seeks it and has time to digest it. And many are. Sadly, more are not.

I believe that too often the principal shapers of our views—especially the politicians and the media—are succumbing to a belief that we want less, not more; that we are more interested in being entertained than educated; that we are prepared to forgo content and context, history and geography, depth and discourse, in our unquenchable desire for instant gratification, tantalizing bells and whistles, manipulative gimmickry, the culture of narcissism—as the late critic Christopher Lasch called it in his 1979 book—the culture of complaint, the culture of consumerism, the constant barrage of images and noise, or whatever else is perceived as the craving du jour. Maybe they're right, but do they not also carry a good deal of the responsibility for our present situation?

Consider for a moment what Dan Rather, the CBS anchorman, said to a gathering of industry news executives:

"It's the ratings, stupid, don't you know? And they've got us putting more and more fuzz and wuzz on the air, cop-shot stuff, so as to compete not with other news programs but with entertainment programs (including those posing as news programs) for dead bodies, mayhem, lurid details. . . . Hire lookers, not writers. Do powder-puff, not probing interviews. Stay away from controversial subjects. . . . Make nice, not news. . . . We put videotape through a Cuisinart trying to come up with high-speed, MTV-style cross-cuts. And just to cover our assets, we give the best slots to gossip and prurience."

We've been silent too long. We need to speak out. We need more education, less entertainment; more eloquence, less drivel; more depth, less superficiality. In short, we need to restore the building blocks for an involved, engaged citizenry that is encouraged to participate actively in the business of this country and, in doing so, to strengthen the democratic fabric and fiber of this nation. Do our politicians and the media want this? Frankly, I'm far from certain that most do. I'm reminded of the famous dialogue when Socrates was accused by Meletus of being a corrupter of the young.

Socrates: Come hither, Meletus, and let me ask a question of you. You think a great deal about the improvement of youth?

Meletus: Yes, I do.

S: Tell the judges, then, who is their improver? . . .

M: The laws.

S: But that, good sir, is not my meaning. I want to know who the person is, who, in the first place, knows the laws?

M: The judges, Socrates, who are present in court.

S: What, do you mean to say, Meletus, that they are able to instruct and improve youth? . . . What, all of them, or some only and not others?

M: All of them.

S: By the goddess Hera, that is good news! There are plenty of improvers, then. And what do you say of the audience—do they improve them?

M: Yes, they do.

S: And the senators?

M: Yes, the senators improve them.

S: But perhaps the members of the assembly corrupt them? Or do they improve them?

M: They improve them.

S: Then every Athenian improves and elevates them; all with the exception of myself; and I alone am their corrupter? Is that what you affirm?

M: That is what I stoutly affirm.

S: I am very unfortunate if you are right. . . . Happy indeed would be the condition of youth if they had one corrupter only, and all the rest of the world were their improver.

No, as Socrates suggested, surely there is more than one corrupter of our youth and our society, and there aren't enough improvers. And in the final analysis, over time, this does damage to the resilience of our democratic well-being, a democracy premised on the active involvement of a concerned and informed citizenry.

Fourth, we as a country must find ways to manage the deep and growing divide over the proper role of religion in our society. Obviously, this is not unique to our country. Religion presents a great challenge—whether it is to be a force for uplifting the human spirit and contributing to the commonweal, as it most assuredly can, or whether it is to become a major fault line in our society, as we have seen occur elsewhere where battle lines are drawn and even blood is shed, all in the name of one religion's desire for supremacy over another.

What has always distinguished the United States has been the text of our Constitution and the principles of our Founding Fathers. Two basic tenets—freedom of worship and separation of church and state—were included in our basic documents and intended to be adhered to equally. Some would wish to lead us in one direction or the other, or perhaps even to amend the Constitution to reflect their own interpretations of religion and faith.

But I cling to the old notion, "If it ain't broke, don't fix it." And the Constitution ain't broke. And it doesn't need fixing either. Indeed, if America today is arguably the most religious country in the Western world, I believe that fact is not unconnected from the very constitutional protections governing our land. Precisely because of the absence of a state religion, or the state's interference with religion, or the state's effort to promote or discourage religion, religion has flourished here as nowhere else.

Visit the countries of Western Europe—such nations as Germany, Italy, Britain, and the Scandinavian countries, all of which have experienced the mix of religion and state—and see the hemorrhaging of religious affiliation and seek to understand why.

No, religion here flourishes, as it should. And each religion occupies, or should occupy, the same valued place in American society, with no special role in the public square, with no special sanction for or against from the government. Religion in this country is doing just fine. Let's leave it alone.

What's not doing quite as well, though, are the endemic problems of poverty, homelessness, hunger, crime and violence, drug addiction, teen-age pregnancy, joblessness in the inner cities, or the racial, social, and economic divides. The list of domestic crisis zones goes on, as you know no less well than I.

No, we're not doing nearly as well as we should on this front. For too long, these problems have been neglected, downplayed, demagogued, or highlighted only in election season. In the final analysis, as it has been said, our country will be judged not by how well we treat the best-off among us but rather the least well off.

We could do a better job. We must do a better job. Frankly, both compassion and self-interest demand it. It's true that government can't do it alone. But surely we can't do it alone either, not without government, and notwithstanding the vital, and I do mean vital, role played until now by business, community groups, churches, and synagogues. And government won't act, won't really act, I believe, unless we insist on its acting—not episodically, not rhetorically, but acting in a sustained, determined manner that overcomes ideological fixations and begins to restore hope to areas where today there is none. America can do better. We've seen what America can do when it sets it mind to it. We, too, can do better. And our voice must be heard loud and clear on these issues, always matched by our commitment.

And our last major challenge, as we face the next fifty years, is to understand that the world around us has changed so profoundly, so irreversibly, that, like it or not, America cannot extricate itself from the rest of the world or establish a fortress America, nor can it remove itself from engagement with other countries, indeed from its leadership of the free world. It cannot, it must not.

Foreign policy is not a favorite issue among the population, we are frequently reminded by the pollsters and the pundits. And it was all too evident in the second presidential debate this years when moderator Jim Lehrer had to prod a question on foreign policy out of the audience. But God help us if we seek to turn inward and adopt a policy of neoisolationism. History has taught us, if only we will take the time to study that history, that when American turns inward we have always later paid a very heavy price. When American turns inward, a vacuum is created and too quickly it is filled by aggressive and mischievous states whose aims are antithetical to our own.

So these, then, are some of the main challenges I see before us in our broadly defined field of human relations:

(1) continuously nurturing and tending to American pluralism to keep it robust;

(2) defending a role for government by restoring confidence in the role of government in our lives;

(3) strengthening democracy in America by strengthening our own levels of education and involvement in public affairs and demanding no less from those who shape the public sphere;

(4) keeping religion strong and the balance between freedom of religion and the separation of church and state in equilibrium;

(5) reminding ourselves of the unfinished and compelling social agenda here in our very midst;

(6) and bearing in mind that America cannot turn inward or create a false choice between internationalism and isolationism, for we are part of the larger world and have a role to play in ensuring the security and well-being of that larger world and, in turn, ourselves.

On this special evening, I salute the Dallas Chapter of the American Jewish Committee for five decades of making a difference; for five decades of synthesizing American ideals and Jewish values in the pursuit of American advancement and Jewish security; and for five decades of tapping the best in us all and believing fervently in the possibilities of repairing our fractured world. May the next fifty years be equally rewarding and productive.

Groundbreaking Ceremony*
Gay's Hill Baptist Church
Millen, Georgia
December 15, 1996

Reverend Baldwin, ladies and gentlemen, brothers and sisters,

Perhaps they're out there right now, maybe hiding behind that tree, or over in that field, or behind that car. I'm speaking of those who would commit such an act as burning a church. Maybe they're out there right now, watching us. I hope so.

*Inserted in the *Congressional Record* by Congressman Jack Kingston, March 12, 1997.

Perhaps they thought they had found an isolated church to burn down, a church no one would notice, much less care about.

They were wrong. This church is now at the center of the universe. It might as well be located in the middle of Times Square in New York, or between the White House and the Capitol building in Washington.

Perhaps they thought only Baptists would care.

They were wrong. It's not just Baptists who care. It's all caring people who care. And if this was an assault against Baptists, then all of us—of many religions—are today Baptists.

Perhaps they thought only African Americans would care.

They were wrong. It's not just African Americans who care. It's all caring people who care. And if this was an assault against African Americans, then all of us—of many races—are today African Americans.

Perhaps they thought only Christians would care.

They were wrong. It's not just Christians who care. It's all caring people who care. And if this was an assault against Christians, then all of us—of many faiths—are today Christians.

Perhaps they thought their hate would prevail.

They were wrong. Our love will. Our bonds—across race, religion, geography—will prevail. As we stand here today, hand in hand, arm in arm, shoulder to shoulder, we know that to be true.

Perhaps they thought destruction would prevail.

They were wrong. Construction will prevail. We are builders, not destroyers. The rebuilding of this church is but one example.

Perhaps they thought an exclusive vision of America would prevail.

They were wrong. An inclusive vision of America—of all its people and their rich diversity—will prevail. We reaffirm that vision today, as we must every day. An America where we will learn to live together as brothers and sisters, else we die together as fools, as the late Reverend King so poignantly stated.

Ladies and gentlemen, brothers and sisters, when we at the American Jewish Committee learned about the spate of church burnings, we wanted to extend a helping hand—not just in words, words can be quite cheap, but in deeds. We wanted to stand with those in pain and in need. We wanted to do something tangible.

For many of us, the site of church burnings was all too familiar. Near and far, we have witnessed many of our synagogues, far too many, go down in ashes—targets of hate. We have experienced the sense of fear, of vulnerability, of anger, and of isolation that comes with such tragedies. And we know what can happen when we are alone. Yes, we know.

For too long, we were alone, as you have been alone.

But no more. Enough. Many good people are waking up and want to be counted. You are not alone. We are not alone. Just this past week, for example, Jews around the world were celebrating the holiday of Hanukkah, the eight days marking the first recorded struggle for religious freedom, the freedom to be different. A Jewish family outside Philadelphia experienced a frightening event.

During the night, someone came, broke a window and destroyed the candelabra, the menorah as we call it, shining brightly in their window. But what happened next? By the end of that day, virtually every home in the immediate neighborhood, Christian and Jewish, had placed a menorah in their front window. And something very similar happened in Billings, Montana, three years earlier when thousands of Christian homes placed menorahs in their windows after a similar attack.

That's true faith, that's real brotherly and sisterly love.

No, none of us should be alone. None of us should ever again experience the fear of isolation. And none of us should ever again remain quiet or inactive at such moments. That would be akin to acquiescence, to defeat.

And that's why we wanted to help, to stand up and be counted, to affirm that we are all God's children, all created in the divine image. In doing so, we were motivated by the words of Samuel:

"The Lord declares to you that He, the Lord, will build a house for you. . . . He shall build a house for God's name. . . . Be pleased, therefore, to bless Your servant's house, that it may abide before You forever; for You, O Lord God, have spoken. May Your servant's house be blessed forever by Your blessing."

With me here today are a number of American Jewish Committee colleagues whom I'd like to ask to join me now. From Atlanta: Lois Frank, Steve Kleber, Sherry Frank, and Sunny Stern. From Philadelphia: Lisa Weinberger and Eric Kantor.

And though technically not a colleague, I'd also like to ask my seventeen-year-old son, Danny, to come up. I asked Danny if he would be here today because I wanted him to experience this day for himself and to draw strength and inspiration from it.

Reverend Baldwin, my colleagues and I at the American Jewish Committee said we wanted to do something tangible. As you know, we and the whole family of the American Jewish Committee undertook a fund-raising effort to help you and your congregation rebuild the Gay's Hill Baptist Church. I am pleased today to be able to give you these checks, totaling more than $87,000, that resulted from the effort.

And now, may I ask you all—Christian and Jew, black and white, we who seek to build, not destroy; to love, not hate; to heal, not wound—to join hands for a moment of prayer.

Our God and God of all generations, we rejoice at the gift of friendship and fellowship that is ours this day.

We ask Your blessing upon those who lead and serve this congregation.

Bless them in their endeavors to build a new House of Prayer.

Give special strength, wisdom, and courage to those who will labor to build this new House. Be with them in the days and months ahead.

And may they achieve the goal we all seek, the gift we Jews call Shalom, the gift of peace. And let us say, Amen.

Buddying Up to a Bigot
The Washington Post
March 15, 1997

Hypnotized by Louis Farrakhan's "kind words" and message of "self-help and moral values," Robert Novak ["Farrakhan and the GOP," op-ed, March 6] charitably calls the Nation of Islam leader a man trying to "transcend his past"—that is, his corrosive bigotry. Novak minimizes Farrakhan's history of invective by noting merely that he has been "accused" of anti-Semitism—a seemingly minor blemish he urges Republican leaders to overlook.

But Farrakhan's transgressions are not merely "accusations" to be proven at some point in the court of public opinion. Nor are they just a part of his past. Any recent issue of the Nation of Islam's newspaper, *The Final Call*, would clear up the doubt in Novak's mind about Farrakhan's bigotry. So, too, would his speeches to Nation of Islam minions, as well as remarks by Farrakhan's surrogates, all laden with vicious and pernicious slander not only about Jews but about whites, Catholics, homosexuals, and other groups. And Farrakhan's vigorous promotion of *The Secret Relationship Between Blacks and Jews: Vol. 1,* the Nation of Islam's book that outrageously accuses Jews of controlling the slave trade, should not distinguish him as a man of "kind words" or "moral values."

Jude Wanniski, who organized the recent Republican flirtation in Florida with Farrakhan, seems to be issuing the same naïve and careless advice he gave Jack Kemp during the 1996 elections: Buddy up to this "great" leader and you may win a few African American votes. The votes didn't come. But the mainstreaming of Farrakhan sadly began without any retraction of the bigoted and divisive positions that have been at the core of his worldview every bit as much as the self-help message so appealing to Novak. But you can't separate the two; it's a package deal, and history has taught us—or should have taught us—that such packages are highly dangerous, especially when influentials succumb to the bigot's charms.

As Novak acknowledges, Farrakhan "could risk support from his core constituency" if he discards his bigotry. Well, what does this say about Farrakhan's leadership skills and his sincerity about "transcending" his usual hate-filled rhetoric? Farrakhan has built himself into a box of bigotry. Either he can't get out of the box or, notwithstanding many recent opportunities to do so, he doesn't really want to.

Paul Robeson's Silence on Stalin's Anti-Semitism
New York Post
August 21, 1997

Eric Breindel's critique of *CommonQuest* ("Dialogue or denial?" op ed, July 31) does an injustice to the magazine.

Sponsored by Howard University and the American Jewish Committee (AJC), *CommonQuest* has gained national acclaim for its tough-minded explorations of black-Jewish relations and the larger subjects of race, diversity, and identity in the United States. Unfortunately, *Post* readers would never know this from Breindel's column, or that the magazine has featured such top writers as Richard Cohen, Glenn Loury, Jim Sleeper, and E. J. Dionne.

Breindel wonders why the American Jewish Committee might lend its name to this enterprise. Since its founding ninety-one years ago, AJC has always worked to fight against ethnic, religious, and racial hatred, and to seek to identify common ground, where it exists, among America's diverse groups as one means of combating hatred. This magazine supports that purpose.

Surprisingly, Breindel overlooks the fact that the AJC publishes another magazine, *Commentary*, which, like *CommonQuest*, enjoys full editorial independence and which he happens to admire. In both cases, AJC is interested in engaging serious people with serious ideas, whether we agree with all those ideas or not.

In his column, Breindel zeroes in on a few paragraphs of a two-page article by Paul Robeson Jr. Breindel writes that the article has the "virtue of being true"—it simply does not go far enough in exposing Robeson's father's involvement with communism. The tragic folly of many American left-wing intellectuals' romance with communism, Paul Robeson Sr. included, is entirely beyond dispute for us. That wasn't the aim of the piece, however. Nor, God forbid, was it to justify any attempt at historic revisionism of the abhorrent Soviet anti-Semitism in this period (and others), especially from an organization credited with pioneering the research exposing Stalin's war against the Jews. Rather, the aim was to look at the phenomenon of "cultural borrowing" between blacks and Jews, blacks and whites.

But alas, Breindel's target turns out to be larger—the magazine itself. He writes that "undertakings of this kind are doomed to failure." That is why he can dismiss as "nonsense" a magazine that has published some of the most powerful writing on race available today. That is why he can ignore the sum total of the first three issues and instead draw unfair conclusions from just a few paragraphs in one article.

Let readers of the *Post* judge for themselves. For more information about *CommonQuest*, write to: AJC, Box CQ, 165 East 56th St., New York, NY 10022.

Close State Gaps
The New York Times
October 15, 1998

James B. Jacob's argument against the enactment of hate-crime legislation (op-ed, Oct. 14) misses the mark. The American Jewish Committee believes that such legislation is necessary and effective.

Thousands of brutal acts are committed each year based upon the victim's race, religion, sexual orientation, or ethnicity.

While an overwhelming majority of states have enacted laws that provide heightened penalties for at least certain crimes motivated by prejudice, there remains a need for prosecution at the federal level if and when the state penalties are inadequate. Pending federal legislation would close these gaps by allowing for prosecution where interstate commerce is implicated and by covering categories of hate crimes often not covered by state law.

CNN Early Edition—
David Harris:
"There's No Quick Solution"
to Anti-Semitic Violence
August 12, 1999

• *Leon Harris, CNN Anchor:* The latest incident of gun violence was directed against Jews. It is the most recent of a string of attacks on Jews, African Americans, Asian Americans, and others.

Well, joining us this morning to talk about what can be done to stop the attacks is David Harris. He's executive director of the American Jewish Committee, and he joins us from our New York bureau.

Good morning, sir. I'd like to ask you if you see a wider conspiracy here. Do you see some sort of linkage between all of these events? I mean, we're just a few weeks away from seeing an event like this in Chicago.

• *David Harris, American Jewish Committee*: I think there is a common thread here that we've seen over the last several years. These are individuals and groups that are fueled by a common theology and a common ideology that seek to demonize, seek to vilify Jews and other minority groups in this country and, inspired by that theology and ideology, believe that violence is the answer. Ultimately, their aim is to create a white, Christian nation that has no Jews, no minorities living here whatsoever.

• *Leon Harris*: Well, let me ask this: What do you see then as the root of all this? Do you see the root being the Christianity or the racial angle?

• *David Harris*: I think it's a combination of things. You have people who are seized principally by racial ideology that in some respects mirrors Nazi ideology. And you have those who have created a distortion of Christian theology, taking the concept of Adam and Eve, for example, and asserting that the offspring of Adam and Eve are white Christians, whereas Jews and others are satanic forces who are not derived from the same common family and therefore are dehumanized people.

So you have a mixture, a very combustible and dangerous mixture of racial politics together with corrupt, demonic theology. And as we've seen in Los Angeles and elsewhere, that can be a lethal combination.

• *Leon Harris*: And I can tell you from my own personal experience, it's the kind of thing that people don't like to talk about openly. What do you think about, then, this other comment that's often thrown about when these things happen, that there may be for every single one Buford Furrow, ten to fifteen or twenty other sympathizers?

• *David Harris*: I think we have to face the fact that these are not simply lone operatives that we can react to when crimes are committed and then, within two or three days, begin to forget about them and go about our daily lives.

Again, there is a network here in the United States, and with the power of the Internet, the power of computers, the protection of laws that they hide behind, these groups now claim thousands of members across this country.

• *Leon Harris*: So then what's the best way to counter that?

• *David Harris*: Well, there's no magic bullet. There's no one quick solution, but there is a combination of things that have to be done.

For example, we have been calling for several years for congressional hearings on these groups. We have yet to see those hearings take place. Law enforcement needs to be strengthened on the local, state, and federal levels; the ability to monitor and track these groups has to be enhanced; and within the Christian churches there has to be an alertness to the fact that these Christian Identity groups are trying to penetrate mainstream Christian churches with their corrupt theology.

And lastly, I think all Americans have to understand that an assault on the Jewish community center in suburban Los Angeles is an assault not only on Jews, it's an assault on all of us. It's a challenge to the America we believe in. So it requires us to stand up together and to face this as a nation.

• *Leon Harris*: Well, since we haven't seen any mainstream Christian church leaders who have actively taken stands against this sort of thing, do you read anything into this, then, about the relations between Jews and Christians in this country?

• *David Harris*: No, I think relations between Jews and Christians have undergone a remarkable positive revolution in recent decades. It's been a great success story.

The problem is that there are small groups, cults, and sects that have taken Christianity and perverted it, and, in effect, established a new religion using the Christian name. Christians in this country need to stand up against this attempt to infiltrate and corrupt their own sacred doctrine.

• *Leon Harris*: David Harris of the American Jewish Committee, thank you very much for your time and your perspective this morning. Fascinating thoughts.

National Memorial Tribute for James Farmer
The Kennedy Center, Washington, D.C.
September 10, 1999

James Farmer was a man with a vision. Armed with that vision, a powerful mind, a stentorian voice, and a deeply compassionate heart, he helped dramatically alter the face of the United States. And even when, in his later years, he lost his sight, he never, ever, lost his vision. That vision was a guide and beacon for us; it was also a constant challenge for us to press ahead and to persevere with heads held high.

As the late Rabbi Stephen Wise, a friend of the civil rights movement, aptly put it: "Vision looks inward and becomes a duty. Vision looks outward and becomes aspiration. Vision looks upward and becomes faith."

When James Farmer was born in 1920, America was a country deeply divided along racial lines that were sustained by suspicion, ignorance, and hate, not to speak of gross and shameful inequality.

By the time he died two months ago, America had come a long way. Certainly we have learned that it's sometimes easier to change laws than to change hearts. But none of us should underestimate the distance traveled, even as our final objective sometimes seems frustratingly elusive.

On this century's journey, we were led by giants who never faltered, who never succumbed to despair, who rose up even after they were beaten down, and who unfailingly loved when they had every right to hate.

James Farmer was such a man. A hero of our time. A moral visionary with his eyes cast aloft and his feet planted firmly on the ground.

James Farmer's power was twofold. It lay in his unyielding insistence that this country fulfill the noblest aims of its founders, and it lay in his ability to inspire that change by appealing to the highest instincts of all those within earshot. By always remembering that the ultimate aim of the civil rights movement was in fact nothing less than the prophetic vision of peace, equality, and mutual respect, he never allowed himself to get swept away by the bitterness, even bloodiness, of the fight.

Let me quote Hyman Bookbinder, one of the American Jewish Committee's leaders in the historic civil rights struggle, when in 1994 he presented Mr. Farmer with our Public Service Award. James Farmer, Bookie said, "demonstrated that militancy, doggedness, and courage can reside in the same individual as civility, integrity, and tolerance."

It was this remarkable spirit that inspired people like the legendary Jewish scholar and civil rights activist, Rabbi Abraham Joshua Heschel, to say in 1963: "The plight of the Negro must become our most important concern. . . . It is the test of our integrity. . . . It is not enough for us to exhort the government. What we must do is set an example, not merely to acknowledge the Negro, but to welcome him, not grudgingly, but joyously, to take delight in enabling him to enjoy what is due him. . ."

Perhaps because James Farmer was a religious man who always felt a close spiritual link to God, he never failed to conjure up an image of a society that strove to tap the best in us all. In his own words, his fight "was not pressing toward the brink of violence, but for the peak of freedom."

Not only was James Farmer a towering figure of the century that is coming to a close, but also a herald for the century that is about to begin. His essential message, every bit as relevant today, can be summed up in the words he expressed upon accepting the American Jewish Committee honor: "It is not hate that has won our victories, it is brotherhood."

Let me speak for just a moment about the brotherhood between Jews and African Americans. I continue to believe profoundly in that notion.

African Americans and Jews have three fundamental options. We can yield to those strident voices who would have us in permanent conflict, while our common enemies look on in delight.

We can each go off on our own, asserting that we are separate communities with separate needs, but failing to make use of the proven dynamism of our past cooperation to achieve our goals, which are so often compatible, if not at times identical.

Or we can follow James Farmer's lead and stand together in solidarity and common purpose. Together, we become a powerful force of change. History has shown that time and again. Together, we represent a vision of a better America, an America that is both more just and more humane.

Let us not forget that whether we cooperate or not, we do share the same enemies. Who could fail to notice that anti-Semites invariably are also racists and that racists don't much like Jews either? The World Church of the Creator, an organization that claims killer Benjamin Smith of Chicago as a friend, sees no difference between the "inferior" black and Jewish races, and Smith, if you remember, was "color blind" when he killed an African American and an Asian American and wounded numerous Jews in July. Yes, our enemies remind us that what binds us is far more important than those occasional moments when we are apart.

Today, on the eve of the Jewish New Year, Rosh Hashanah—the day the world was born, we Jews are told—let us evoke the memory of James Farmer as we pay tribute to this man who so profoundly changed the course of our nation's history.

Truly, the man whose memory has summoned us here today embodied the words of Psalm 34:

> *Keep thy tongue from evil, and thy lips from speaking guile.*
> *Depart from evil, and do good; seek peace, and pursue it.*
> *The eyes of the Lord are upon the righteous, and his ears are open unto their cry.*
> *The face of the Lord is against them that do evil, to cut out the remembrance of them from the earth.*
> *The righteous cry, and the Lord heareth, and delivereth them out of all their troubles.*

May James Farmer's memory forever be a blessing, and may we all be ennobled by the example of his life.

10. LOOKING TO THE FUTURE OF AMERICAN JEWRY

Revitalization and Renewal:
The American Jewish Committee Confronts the 1990s
AJC's National Executive Council, St. Louis
October 25, 1990

The decision to take this job [i.e., AJC executive director] was not a simple one. It involved a number of professional and family considerations that were not easy to resolve. The other candidates for the position probably had no more ardent supporters than my wife and three children. Years ago, I considered entering the diplomatic service of the United States but rejected the idea largely because I couldn't see myself moving every three years—I didn't want to do that to my children. Little did I know that the Jewish community had its own version of the diplomatic service. This appointment entails the fifth move for my family in the eleven years since I first joined the American Jewish Committee.

There is a story about a Soviet Jew who emigrates to Israel but, after a few months, returns to the Soviet Union and complains to his former friends and neighbors about the climate, about the bureaucracy, about the traffic in Israel. In a few months, though, he returns to Israel and complains to his neighbors there about economic deprivation, communism, and bureaucracy in the Soviet Union. And thus he keeps going back and forth between the two countries. Finally, one of his friends says, "Abram, you complain about the Soviet Union and you complain about Israel, so why do you insist on going from one to the other?" Abram replies, "It's because I love the stopover in Vienna." In my case, it is the reverse. I love New York and I love Washington; it's the New Jersey Turnpike that I can't stand.

I am unhappy about the circumstances that brought me here at this particular time—a personal tragedy in the life of Ira Silverman that over the last two and a half years has seriously debilitated him, prompting his resignation. It is my fervent hope and prayer that Ira will recover fully and speedily so that, as a young and vibrant man with so much to offer the Jewish community, he will soon be back in our midst contributing to the AJC, the Jewish people, and American society.

I owe Ira my very first job at the American Jewish Committee. I was working in Vienna in 1978 when he and Jane came by to see the work we were doing in facilitating the emigration of Soviet Jews. And he said, "If you are ever in New York, why don't you drop by and come see me." Little did he or I know that I would take him up on it, and that the result would be a job working for Ira Silverman. All through the years that followed I have felt for him both profound respect and deep affection.

Our organization has recently gone through tumultuous times. What we have needed more than anything else has been a set of leaders with the skill to heal the wounds. We have been fortunate to have such leadership in the current lay ranks. . . . And the quality of the top leadership is a reflection of our members. And so I compliment the entire membership, both for their own role and for helping shape the top leadership of this organization.

Finally, I wish to thank the staff, my colleagues, people with whom I've worked, in some cases, for more than a decade. Through good times and bad, they've been supportive, they've been wonderful. The American Jewish Committee has the best staff anywhere. . . . Between the skills of our lay people and the talents of our staff, we have a very exciting agency.

I believe very deeply in this agency. It has consistently been ahead of its time. Over the years, the AJC has been the organization that defines the agenda, that frames the emerging issues for the Jewish community.

We helped define intergroup relations at a time when race and ethnicity were rarely matters of pride and positive identity.

We were the first to establish an office in Israel and the first to understand that the issue of American Jewish–Israeli relations is so important that it warrants, not just a few programs here and there, but a full-time institute.

We plunged into programming with Germany, at a time when it still wasn't terribly popular in the American Jewish community.

We were the agency that recognized the growing complexity of Jewish life and had the special research talents and unique insights to help attain an understanding of the American Jewish family in all its many manifestations.

We were in the forefront of the movement to rescue Soviet Jewry, whether in the 1950s when we helped define the subject through the research work of Solomon Schwartz, or earlier this year when we undertook the first survey ever of Soviet attitudes toward Jews.

We are doing pioneering work in the establishment of Jewish ties with the nations of the Pacific Rim. Our emphasis now is on work with Japan and Korea, and one day we hope to include China as well.

We work with the Vatican and the World Council of Churches and a whole range of church groups in the United States. We build bridges to them, bridges that are unique in the American Jewish community.

All in all, the American Jewish Committee is, in my view, the most thoughtful, most reflective Jewish organization anywhere. This truly is the Harvard of Jewish organizations.

I am often asked where we fit on the political spectrum. My answer is: the creative middle. Since we are a reflective organization, we are not necessarily predictable in how we deal with issues. The AJC is sufficiently dispassionate and courageous to take issues as they come.

We do our research thoroughly and then we develop policy positions. In doing so we try to blend many different perspectives, because the AJC membership itself reflects much of the range of American Jewish thinking. That is why, often after vigorous and healthy debate, we come up with the right answer—or close to it—on so many issues.

I also believe in the American Jewish Committee because it reaches beyond the Jewish community. We have worked tirelessly on behalf of Jews in the Soviet Union, yet we didn't walk away from Andrei Sakharov, a gentile, as some other Jewish organizations did when he was in internal exile, simply because he wasn't a Jew. And as concerned as we have been about Jewish refugees, we couldn't, wouldn't, turn our backs on Vietnamese or other Indochinese refugees. We put ourselves in their shoes and advocated the justice of their cause because it was the right thing to do.

This organization has had more than its share of difficulties of late. But we are not alone in that—so have many other organizations. Still, perhaps we ought to derive a certain pleasure from the attention that has been given us. Isn't it, in a way, flattering to be considered important enough that our problems are reported so widely?

Within a day or two of the offer of this job I saw a headline in the *Forward*: "AJC's Harris to Face Cash Crunch." I almost hoped they were talking about my personal finances, but they weren't. I still figured that if I hid the article and just used the headline there would be terrific advantages. Every time my children would ask for a new Ninja Turtle, I could simply hold up the headline. Every time I got another solicitation for a contribution, I could Xerox the headline and send it back. All kinds of possibilities. . . .

That article was not the only reason to worry. Along came Jacob Neusner to declare our death. Then came Seymour Lachman and Barry Kosmin in the *New York Times* telling us that we and some of our fellow organizations were in decline. And there were the sharp budget cuts and painful staff retrenchment. There was the persistent problem of articulating the elusive focus of the agency, the frustration that we couldn't somehow encapsulate it in one or two or three neat sentences. There was the dilution of our priorities by a proliferation of initiatives that made us look like an agency for each and every program under the sun. There were tensions between the national office and the field offices that created a sense of "them versus us."

We've had our problems. But I firmly believe that many, if not most of them, are behind us. And that is largely due to the courage of our leaders. It took courage to make the painful but, I believe, ultimately correct decisions about how to shape this agency and to position it for the next decade. The staff deserves equal credit for persevering over several very difficult months, keeping the agency on an even keel through stormy waters.

We've got our priorities in order now. We understand what our proper concerns ought to be and we will be there to act on them:

- We will be there on Israel, to do what we can to help ensure its safety, security, well-being, and democratic fiber.

- We will be there so long as a single Jew in Syria, Ethiopia, Romania, the Soviet Union—anywhere—feels in jeopardy.
- We will be there whenever extremism, racism, and of course anti-Semitism rear their ugly heads, whether in this country or overseas.
- We will be there to enrich the quality of Jewish life in this country so that there is something for us as Jews to live for and pass on to our children and grandchildren.
- We will be there trying to promote contact, communication, and understanding between Jews and the many other religious and ethnic groups in this country, because our mutual survival depends on our ability to walk and talk with one another.
- And we will be there to help ensure the continuous strength and resilience of this country's pluralistic society, which is so vitally important to our flourishing as Jews, indeed to the hopes of all mankind.

We know the strategies and tactics that will help achieve these goals. There is our research, which has been so important, so trailblazing, over many years. There is our coalition-building expertise. There are our media efforts—I don't think there has been another period in AJC's recent history when we have done so much in both the print and electronic media to get our message across. There are our more discreet forms of advocacy and diplomacy in the halls of power—in Washington, Jerusalem, Bonn, Moscow, and elsewhere. And we will continue to develop creative programming both in New York and in the field—and, as one who has visited each of the thirty-one chapters over the past several years, I stress that the field will continue to play a central role.

The American Jewish Committee will move ahead as a pioneering, activist organization. The fact that we are in it for the long haul often distinguishes us from other organizations. Rather than be part of a twenty-four-hour phenomenon, I want to be where patience and perseverance can yield results. We can point to such results. Here are just three examples:

We recently held a luncheon for the ambassador of Japan to the United States. This event was the product of more than three years of working with Japanese officials in the United States and Tokyo to build up their confidence in this organization. It was the first address by a Japanese ambassador in the United States to a Jewish audience in the history of Japanese–American relations. This might lead to better understanding between Japanese and Jews, and could influence Japan's Middle East policy.

A second example: our persistence and perseverance in dealing with Germany enabled us to produce, not only the best, but I dare say the *only* serious statement on German unification of *any* major American Jewish organization. I know that our statement was read, and taken seriously, by the highest German officials, both because of its content and also because the Germans know that the signatory, the American Jewish Committee, has been a responsible partner for more than a decade.

My final example is immigration and refugee policy. Not only has the AJC become a respected authority on the subject in this country, but it has also helped define American immigration policy. That is not something that happens overnight. It happens because of a long, deliberate, and committed effort on the part of lay and staff people. And that is the sort of work that we will continue to do.

• • • •

It is customary on occasions like this to talk about the influences on one's life. My family—my mother, my father, and my wife—have together experienced the three worst scourges faced by the Jewish people in the twentieth century. My mother was a refugee from the Soviet Union and then a refugee from occupied France. My father, who came from Berlin, was sent to Vienna in 1933 for his safety. And when Hitler took over Austria in 1938, he went to France, where he enlisted and ended up in a prisoner-of-war camp. My wife was forced to leave Libya, the ancestral homeland of her family. In 1967, during the Six-Day War, a mob of several hundred Arabs came with gasoline bombs planning to set fire to her home. There were eight small children in that house, my wife and her seven brothers and sisters.

So I have come to learn what communism means. I have learned what Nazism means. I have learned what Arab extremism means. . . .

And I have learned as well what freedom means and what Israel means.

When I was in Moscow a few months ago, I saw an Israeli consulate: no quotas, no waiting lines, no slammed doors for Jews fearful of the future and anxious to leave. That for me is the meaning of Israel.

I remember my first trip, as a teacher, to the Soviet Union in 1974. On Simchat Torah I decided to go to the Moscow synagogue. As I made my way there I wondered why I was doing this. There were surely no identified Jews left in the Soviet Union, I thought. There would probably be a sign placed by government authorities on the synagogue door saying, perhaps, "Closed for the Holiday." But something drove me on. I remember turning the corner, and suddenly I was stunned. The street was filled with thousands upon thousands of Jews who shouldn't have been, who weren't suppose to exist, who had been confined to the dustbin of history. They were trying to assert their Jewish connection and identity any way they could. I stood there tearful and transfixed because at that moment I understood our connectedness. I understood the bond between past, present, and future, and I understood as well our special responsibility never to take freedom for granted, to be vigilant to the plight of Jews in need.

I recall as well visiting Ethiopia in 1984 at the time of the famine when Operation Moses was beginning. I remember walking with some other American Jews across a dirt field in Gondar Province in northwestern Ethiopia in the middle of nowhere, I thought—when suddenly two black children approached, and, in better Hebrew than mine, with big smiles, asked, *Atem medabrim ivrit?*—"Do you speak Hebrew?" Here, 8,000 miles from New York, in the middle of Ethiopia, children spoke Hebrew. And again I felt the interconnectedness and understood our special responsibility. And—by the way—if I wasn't then persuaded that they were Jewish, when we got to the hut that was the synagogue, there was a tug at my sleeve and an Ethiopian Jew said in English, "Mister, do you want to come and see the other synagogue?" Then I was sure. Two synagogues in one tiny village! That way everyone could have one synagogue to attend, another to avoid. . . .

There have been three extraordinary chapters—indeed, three miracles—in contemporary Jewish history. The first was the creation of the

State of Israel. The second is the redemption of Soviet Jewry. And the third miracle is us: the miracle of American Jewry. We came here to the most powerful country on earth, a blessed country that has been good to us and, I would like to believe, to which we have been no less good.

Think about it. What if all of us had ended up elsewhere in the Diaspora? Would we have been able to take advantage of the opportunity to shape history the way we have here, in the United States, the greatest power in the world?

We, as an empowered community, have an extraordinary opportunity and an awesome responsibility. We must use our power, our access, in order to do good. To help fellow Jews in need. To advance human rights for all. To create a more tolerant society. To help shape a peaceful future for the world. The opportunity and the responsibility lie in our hands, yours and mine.

My great-aunt, Mila Racine, was a heroic member of the Jewish resistance in France who was captured by the Nazis while assisting elderly Jews to escape from occupied France into neutral Switzerland. She was killed just a few weeks before the war ended. In the barracks which she shared with Simone Weil and other French Jews, she had written on the wall: *N'oubliez pas*—"Don't forget." And I pledge to all of you, the American Jewish Committee cannot, will not, ever forget our history, our mission, our purpose, and our responsibility for a better tomorrow.

Jews in Dartmouth
Forward
February 9, 1996

Apropos the Jewish identity of James Freedman, the president of Dartmouth College, readers of the *Forward* may be interested to know that he was one of the fifteen distinguished participants to date in an ad series we have run in the *New York Times* and other general circulation papers under the title "What Being Jewish Means to Me" ("Featherman File," *Forward*, Jan. 19).

In his 400-word essay for the series, published in December 1994, he wrote, "By pursuing scholarship and learning, American Jews have preserved their identity, taught their children's children, made their mark on American life, and fortified the covenant between themselves and God." It was precisely this eloquent and forthright tone that led a number of readers to praise President Freedman's statement, citing the need for just such voices of Jewish renewal and commitment when the American Jewish community is buffeted by concerns of identity and continuity.

Interestingly, several of those contacting us noted that the Dartmouth connection was also significant. They pointed out that Dartmouth (not uniquely, of course) was once regarded as a campus with a strict quota on the admission of Jewish students; therefore, the fact that today it is led by a president who is willing to affirm so openly his Jewishness speaks volumes about the distance America—and American Jews—have traveled in this century.

As a related historical footnote, it is worth mentioning that Dartmouth was actually the first of the Ivy League colleges ever to name a Jew as president. John Kemeny assumed office in 1970. To young people today, that fact may seem surprising since many Jews have followed in the footsteps of Professor Kemeny, including Martin Meyerson, who became president of the University of Pennsylvania only a few months later, not to mention several current leaders of Ivy institutions. But to those of us old enough to remember a more restrictive era, these welcome changes bespeak a great deal about the mainstreaming of American Jewry.

Renewal or Decline: The Future of American Jewry
AJC 90th Annual Meeting, Washington, D.C.
May 9, 1996

Titles can be notoriously tricky. For example, consider the following titles which have appeared recently in newspapers: "Iraqi head seeks arms," "War dims hope for peace," "Miners refuse to work after death," and "Police to begin campaign to run down jaywalkers."

When we first began planning this Annual Meeting several months ago, I proposed the grandiose title "Renewal or Decline: The Future of American Jewry." It certainly seemed to fit with what we were planning. But a few weeks ago, when I sat down to write my remarks for today's session, I realized that the title merits not a twenty-minute speech but rather a week-long conference of rabbis, scholars, communal workers, and others meeting from early morning till late at night.

I ask you, therefore, to excuse my chutzpah and hope you'll indulge me as I offer some thoughts on this vast topic, recognizing from the outset that the discussion will necessarily be incomplete.

Ten years ago, a major debate about the future of American Jewry arose. Here's one perspective:

"Since the beginnings of Jewish Emancipation in the eighteenth century, Jews have feared an open society as much as they have welcomed and, indeed, fought for it. Consciously or unconsciously, Jews suspect that it has been anti-Semitism that has kept them a people and that the relative absence of anti-Semitism in the United States will dissolve their will."

So wrote Charles Silberman in his popular 1985 book, *A Certain People*. He went on to say that "Judaism is not seriously threatened by the new openness of American society. . . . In short, the end is not at hand; for all the talk about intermarriage and assimilation, Judaism is not about to disappear in the United States."

And here's the opposing perspective. Writing in *Commentary* that very same year, 1985, Professor Nathan Glazer argued: "Every American, it seems, is expected to be more: a Jew or a Christian, an Italian or a Pole, a Texan or a New Yorker. . . . In that respect, to be a Jew, particularly when the pejorative associations of the term have declined, is an easy thing. The fact that today's young Jews are less embarrassed about their Jewish identity does not mean, however, that the identity . . . exercises great influence over their behavior. It is likely to exercise even less over the behavior of their children."

Professor Glazer concluded his article by writing: "Less and less of the life of American Jews is derived from Jewish history, experience, culture, and religion. More and more of it is derived from the current and existing realities of American culture, American politics, and the general American religion. What this means for the future is that Jews will survive, yes, and perhaps even continue to identify themselves as Jews, but that little by way of custom, belief, or loyalty will be assumed as a result of their identity as Jews."

Six years ago, however, the nature of the debate changed dramatically. The National Jewish Population Study was issued and, for all its extraordinarily rich and multifaceted data, for many its legacy has been reduced to one stark finding—today more Jews, we are told, marry non-Jews than Jews.

For those who looked more closely there were other dark clouds overhead. We are disproportionately elderly and our fertility rate is low, below even replacement level. More than 1 million Jews no longer even consider themselves members of the Jewish faith. The conversion rate for the non-Jewish partner in a marriage is low and getting lower, under 10 percent. And Jewish children of mixed-marriages have been marrying a non-Jewish partner at a rate of over 90 percent.

Since the release of that 1990 study, the American Jewish community has been near panic. Are we destined to eventually disappear, or at the very least to be reduced to a bare shadow of our former selves in the decades ahead? Are there potentially successful strategies for arresting the decline, or is it simply to be a permanent *gevalt* and the occasional blue-ribbon commissions that meet and issue more or less predictable reports, while the ship sinks and we head toward inclusion on the "endangered species" list?

These are not idle questions. American Jewry is at a crossroads. The decisions we take now will affect the course of Jewish history. Thus, there can be no more important issues before us, the American Jewish Committee and the larger American Jewish community.

At the same time, without in anyway lapsing into Silberman's unbridled optimism, which would be misplaced, we also ought not swing to the other extreme either. There are extraordinary, and I use the word advisedly, extraordinary centers of Jewish energy and activity and commitment in this country. Wherever one looks, there are burgeoning Jewish day schools; synagogues in need of additional sanctuary and classroom space; new Judaic studies programs opening on ever more American campuses, not to mention the success of both Brandeis and Yeshiva universities; prospering organizations—old and new; manifold creative expressions in Jewish culture; and, not least, a far higher comfort level in blending the American and Jewish sources of our identity without feeling the need to modify one for the sake of the other, neither in our private nor, significantly, in our public lives.

Yes, in so many ways, this truly is a golden age for American Jewry, a Jewry as educated, as prosperous, as influential, as successful as any in Diaspora history. And we ought not lose sight of these accomplishments or simply give way to bottomless despair as we sort out where we go from here.

We ought not overlook either a remarkable essay written, appropriately enough, by a Brandeis scholar, the late Simon Rawidowicz, and entitled "Israel, the Ever-Dying People." Professor Rawidowicz, who passed away in 1957, wrote, and I quote: "He who studies Jewish history will readily discover that there was hardly a generation in the Diaspora period which did not consider itself the final link in Israel's chain. Each always saw before it the abyss ready to swallow it up. . . . Each generation grieved not only for itself but also for the great past which was going to disappear forever, as well as for the future of unborn generations who would never see the light of day."

So, the good news is that we surely are not the last link in the chain, far from it; the bad news, though, is that, due to intermarriage, a low conversion rate, low birthrate, and defection to other religions or no religion in what is increasingly the American marketplace of religions, our numbers appear destined to diminish; we are indeed hemorrhaging and not just numerically.

There is also an interrelated problem. Nathan Glazer was right. For too few of us, our Jewish identity really is serious business. For too few of us, as our own admired Steve Bayme appropriately reminds us, our level of Jewish literacy matches that of our general literacy.

I've long held a personal theory that there are six factors to explain American Jewish identity today, and that each of us is a composite of a few, or most, or even all, of these factors.

First, there is Judaism, our connection to a faith and to its values and beliefs, to its texts and tenets, to its life cycle and annual calendar.

Second, there is Zionism, our connection to a land, or, for some today, "Israelism."

Third, there is tribalism, or, perhaps more pleasing to the ear, peoplehood—a connection to a people, its history and culture, both past and present, here at home and around the world.

Fourth, there is anti-Semitism, our determination to preserve our identity not in spite of anti-Semitism but rather because of it, especially in the wake of the Shoah, the Holocaust.

Fifth, there is nostalgism, that warm mélange of the memory of a neighborhood, a particular smell, our grandparents' home on a holiday, or the heartwarming sound of an increasingly incomprehensible Yiddish word or expression.

And sixth, there is universalism, a sense that the fulfillment of our Jewish identity can best be achieved by seeking to repair our fractured world, *tikkun olam*, whether in the South Bronx or on an Apache reservation or in the struggle for Tibetan independence.

I believe that all these factors are important and, if embraced together, do create a wonderfully strong and enriching sense of being a Jew.

But I also believe that the latter three—anti-Semitism, nostalgism, and universalism—have too often served to replace, yes, to replace, the first three—the book, the land, and the people—as the principal sources of identity for some here in the United States, and that will not work.

Anti-Semitism, or the Holocaust specifically, cannot become the principal definer of our Jewish identity. It won't sell to our children, even if we wanted it to, and I don't believe we should want it to.

Nostalgism, by definition, fades with each new generation. The link today with the "world of our fathers" so richly depicted by Irving Howe is tenuous at best, and only getting more so with each passing year. Mel Brooks and matzo ball soup may be a prescription for an enjoyable evening but hardly for sustaining an identity.

Universalism, important as it is, cannot by itself guarantee Jewish identity from generation to generation. Jewish ethics do matter and are consequential, indeed central to the Jewish mission, but Jews today do not have a monopoly on ethical behavior and the pursuit of social justice, however disproportionately we may be represented in these endeavors and inspired by our tradition.

No, these three factors can only contribute to identity formation if they're juxtaposed with the first three—Judaism, Zionism, and peoplehood.

But Judaism, Zionism, and peoplehood as sources of primary Jewish identity are not without complications either. For one thing, many Jews are ambivalent about questions related to religion, faith, and God. They may go through the motions of some observance, out of habit or for the sake of the children or as a sign of respect for parents or grandparents, but don't really find salience in Judaism—and that mixed message is easily picked up by children. Of course, it's a sad reality that many adults, in other words many of us, are insufficiently learned in this area and therefore don't even realize what we might be missing with respect to Judaism's ability to provide meaningful guidance in today's world.

Our relationship with Israel, regrettably, is growing more, not less, detached. And the same can be said for Israel's relationship with us. I have believed this for some years and little I've seen of late changes my point of view. The reasons have been rehearsed too often to repeat in detail here. Suffice it to say that Israel, the sovereign state, and Israel, the land, are increasingly distant for many American Jews, two-thirds of whom have never visited it, more than 90 percent of whom cannot speak Hebrew, and many of whom believe that Israel, as an increasingly self-sufficient, powerful, and prosperous country, no longer needs American Jews in the ways it once did. And neither we nor the Israelis have really yet come up with enough compelling and wide-ranging new ways to replace the old, though it's vital we do so and certainly not beyond our grasp.

And there is our connection to a people, and here, too, we face our challenges. We can only celebrate the fact that the barriers against Jews, and others, have come tumbling down in the United States in our lifetimes, in no small measure due to the relentless efforts of the American Jewish Committee. It can be said: Jews have made it in America. Jews occupy positions in every significant corner of American life. Jews today go to just about any school or university, law firm, bank, corporation—you name it. And in doing so, Jews, it must be said, have contributed mightily to the greatness of this country.

We now bring up our children in an atmosphere of infinite possibilities, and we raise them to be tolerant and open-minded, fully participatory in American life. But many of us also seek to raise them along another track as well—the particularist. That's not easy in today's America, and I speak especially of the 90 percent of us who do not consider ourselves Orthodox. Not impossible, but far from easy. It can be difficult to draw boundaries for our children, or to have them draw boundaries for themselves.

So what do we do?

I believe the first challenge must, perforce, be directed at ourselves. In the end, there simply is no substitute for the individual and, by extension, the family, in this discussion. Some of us are serious about creating a Jewish environment in our own lives; more of us must become so. As a Jewish pluralist, I don't believe there is only one route to this goal; to the contrary, there are many.

Our synagogues must also strive to do still more. There are extraordinarily successful contemporary models of thriving synagogues— Reform, Reconstructionist, Conservative, and Orthodox—bursting at the seams not just on Yom Kippur but also on Shabbat, yet there are others that can barely scratch together a minyan, even in prospering Jewish areas, unless there is a special hook to draw congregants. We must all learn from the secrets of those successful models.

A good example is the synagogue in which I happened to have had my bar mitzvah, B'nai Jeshurun, a Conservative congregation on Manhattan's West Side. Shortly after my bar mitzvah, and I assume totally unrelated, a once thriving congregation came within a hair's breadth of extinction. Today, more than a thousand people, many of them young, attend a typical Shabbat service. And this is but one example. Another, close to the AJC home, is Or Zarua, the synagogue in New York founded by our own Mimi Alperin.

I am absolutely convinced of the synagogue's importance in the years ahead if we are to succeed. I am equally convinced that the synagogue has the potential to fulfill the two oft-sought quests of many American Jews, including younger American Jews—a sense of community and a sense of meaning and purpose for their lives.

In my many conversations with Jews around the country, often through AJC, I hear it again and again. We're looking for Jewish anchorages, they tell me, a synagogue, an AJC chapter, places where we can feel at home, places where we can feel welcome and comfortable and among people whose company we enjoy and cherish, people with whom we share something in common.

And equally, we're looking for answers to some pretty heady questions—the meaning and purpose of life, the ways of coping with life's surprises and tragedies, the route to spiritual fulfillment.

And younger American Jews often tell me they feel much more sure-footed as Americans than as Jews. Help us to explore our Jewish identity, one twentysomething young man told me, but first take the time to understand us. What worked for your generation may not so readily apply to us. Still, we want to be able to find answers, to plant roots, to build Jewish families, and to express ourselves as Jews, even as we eagerly continue our full and active participation in the larger civic society.

The biggest long-term challenge and opportunity, of course, is our youth. For an increasing number of Jewish families, day schools have become the option of choice, though as a percentage our day school attendance still lags far behind such countries as Australia and South Africa. For most Jewish kids, though, it is after-school Jewish education that they receive.

I'm sure I speak for at least some of you in saying that it is more a turnoff than a turn-on for many of the children who pass through it. Its negative impact can be long-lasting, even life-shaping.

And yet many of us send our children through the same process because we cling to the hope that the something they might gain is better than no attendance at all.

How many of us take the same level of interest in the religious education of our children as in their secular education? When my middle son, Michael, asked me to sit in on one Hebrew school class two weeks ago, actually because he thought he wasn't learning enough, the school director afterward told me I was the first parent to observe a class in the years she had been there. And I can't even take credit for the idea; it was Michael's.

Again, as in our personal and family lives, we have to make clear that the religious education of our children does matter to us, and that the learning environment must be appropriate, the teachers need to be fully qualified, and the emphasis has to be on creating a sense of awareness and depth, as well as excitement, in being a Jew.

The story, perhaps apocryphal, is told of a philosophy professor at the Sorbonne who gave a final exam to his 500 students. There was only one question on the exam, *Pourquoi*? "Why?" The students wrote furiously in their exam books. When the results were in, 498 had flunked; only 2 passed. One of the two had simply written in his exam book two words: *Pourquoi pas*? "Why not?" The second student who passed also wrote only two words: *Parce que*! "Because!"

Maybe some years ago it was enough for parents to be able to say "Because" or "Why not?" in response to the question "Why be Jewish?" Whether it was sufficient then or not, I know it's not going to get a passing grade today.

A few years ago, I went to meet a potential donor. The plan was to solicit him for a major gift to support our Jewish communal work. The gentleman said to us: "What are you at AJC doing to make my grandchildren Jewish?" The problem with the question was that it became increasingly clear from our conversation that he himself had failed to do enough, if anything at all, and was seeking to place the burden on institutions alone—AJC, synagogues, federations, you name it.

We cannot do it alone. None of the institutions can. Much though we can do, and we at AJC are and have been active on this front for over thirty years, we cannot substitute for the family—the nuclear and extended family—or, for that matter, for the rabbi and the synagogue. We can supplement their efforts, and indeed we do, but seldom can we simply replace them if they haven't done their job.

I have no illusions whatsoever about the magnitude of our twin challenges—stanching the numerical hemorrhaging and strengthening our Jewish understanding, knowledge, connection, and commitment. I live in a largely secular Jewish world, and I could spend the rest of the afternoon, and then some, talking anecdotally about the daunting, and I mean daunting, problems I encounter—and I'm sure you do, too—stemming from indifference, ignorance, cynicism, apathy, alienation, even downright hostility.

In fact, when I look around at the Jewish paths of at least some of my friends from high school, college, family, and neighborhood, I cannot help but shudder for our future.

But then I also see those many centers of Jewish strength and I know there really is hope, hope not borne of naïveté but rather of confidence in the resilience, durability, and determination of countless American Jews to continue this remarkable journey on which we embarked 3,600 years ago. And believe me, that hope outweighs the fear.

These Jews profoundly believe that the Jewish mission in the world is far from complete. They believe that there is a distinctive, irreplaceable message contained in Judaism. They believe in the Jewish people's covenantal relationship with God. They take to heart the words in Exodus: "You shall be to me a kingdom of priests and a holy nation." They believe in the joy and fulfillment to be found as part of the Jewish people, in the strengthened family that often results, and in the connection to community, a link that transcends borders and other man-made barriers.

In a word, from these people I see the unbroken chain. And I know that Professor Rawidowicz was right. "Israel," meaning the Jewish people, he wrote, "has indulged so much in the fear of its end, that its constant vision of the end helped it to overcome every crisis, to emerge from every threatening end as a living unit, though much wounded and reduced. In anticipating the end, it becomes its master. Thus no catastrophe could ever take this end-fearing people by surprise, so as to put it off balance, still less to obliterate it—as if Israel's incessant preparation for the end made this very end absolutely impossible."

To which I would add, it's time to stop talking simply about Jewish continuity or Jewish survival. In many ways, these terms have a ring of business-as-usual, almost of defeatism. Instead, it's time to begin talking about Jewish renewal. Examples of such renewal abound all around us—congregations, institutions, individuals. It's an extraordinarily exciting time to be a Jew, an American Jew, and it's not beyond our reach to convey that excitement.

And as we move forward, as a community, as an agency, we need to keep several questions squarely before us, questions which defy simplistic responses:

(1) Can we persuasively answer for ourselves, much less for others, the questions: Why be Jewish in this modern era? Why carry on this enterprise? Is it for its own sake alone, or is there a larger purpose? Can Judaism speak to the needs of the contemporary world?

(2) Can we meet the challenge of those seeking a sense of community? Can we satisfy the quest of those seeking a sense of spirituality—of meaning and purpose—in the Jewish world?

(3) Can we ensure that Israel retains a place of centrality in the consciousness of American Jewry and in our identity formation?

(4) Can we, if not prevent, at least slow, the deepening of the fault lines, especially denominational, in American Jewry, that threaten to further fractionate us and ultimately divide and weaken us as a people?

(5) Can we find successful strategies to welcome those intermarrieds who seek a link to the Jewish community and encourage their ever-closer connection, while maintaining Jewish distinctiveness?

(6) Can we successfully integrate the hundreds of thousands of Jewish newcomers who have arrived in the States over the past twenty-five years, principally from the Former Soviet Union, many of whom remain detached from Jewish life and who today comprise 10–15 percent of our total community?

(7) And despite slowly diminishing numbers and weakening identity at the periphery, as well as the emergence of other ethnic and religious groups claiming their share of what is ultimately a finite political pie, can we continue to maintain a high level of Jewish *qua* Jewish participation in American public affairs and successful advocacy on behalf of those issues at the core of our agenda?

We'll be there. AJC will maintain its leadership efforts, blessed by devoted lay people and talented staff. We will continue to bring together diverse people in the community, tapping into the best minds available, sponsoring research and publications, pursuing innovative programs that set an example for what can be done (e.g., our national college essay contest and the highly acclaimed ad series on Jewish identity), organizing national and chapter Judaic literacy seminars, emphasizing the ties that bind Jews all over the world, and focusing on the links between Israel and American Jewry.

Let it one day be written that we, fin-de-siècle American Jewry, faced with daunting challenges, tapped into the seemingly limitless reservoir of Jewish optimism and ingenuity and found the will to foster a sense of renewed Jewish purpose and connection, in this the most populous and prosperous Diaspora community in history.

AJC Insider's Letter I*
December 1998

The German philosopher Georg Friedrich Wilhelm Hegel (1770–1831) spoke of history as a dialectic—every thesis brings forth its own contradiction, its antithesis. The conflict between the two creates a synthesis. Since reality is dynamic, the synthesis becomes the new thesis, spawning yet another antithesis. And on it goes.

In thinking about American Jewish history in this century, there is something to be said for Hegel's analysis and, if we are correct, this discussion has considerable bearing on our work here at the American Jewish Committee. Let us explain.

From the turn of the century until 1924, American Jewry was largely, though not exclusively, defined by the millions of Jewish arrivals in this country: religious Jews, Zionists, Bundists, etc. Despite the considerable diversity among them, they were united by a very strong sense of Jewish identity. In other words, first and foremost they were Jews. Their identity came from within; it also came from their East European societies of origin that more often than not placed legal or social barriers in the path of their full emancipation or assimilation.

In line with Hegel's theory, this generation of Jewish immigrants gave rise to a second generation, i.e., the "antithesis," that was eager to become as American as possible, and believed that to do so, it was important, perhaps even necessary, to shed much of their parents' Jewishness.

At the time, this generation felt that a degree of choice had to be made between being an American and being a Jew, and for many it was an obvious call. Facing formidable systemic impediments to Jewish advancement, whether in select private schools or universities, corporate ladders or executive suites, desirable neighborhoods or well-connected social clubs, Jews worked doubly hard in their quest for full acceptance.

The "synthesis" came with the third generation of American Jews—the grandchildren of the immigrants. Exposed to two different models

*Cosigned with AJC's president, Bruce Ramer. Published in abridged form as an op-ed in the *Jewish Week*, September 24, 1999.

of Jewish identity within their own families—their parents' and their grandparents'—they created a new American Jewish identity. Some sociologists have described it as a civil religion.

Blessed with an America that by the late 1960s and early 1970s had largely dismantled the barriers to full participation in American life, this generation was less affected by anti-Semitism, less concerned therefore about the need to make choices between their American and Jewish selves.

Instead, they began to realize that the emerging America actually welcomed their "two selves," and they in turn, with growing confidence, started to assert publicly the congruity between American ideals and Jewish values.

To illustrate this dramatic evolution: Lionel Trilling became the first Jew granted tenure in the English Department at Columbia University. It didn't happen until the 1930s. Why? Previously, Jews weren't deemed capable of properly teaching the classics of the Western tradition at this distinguished university. That sounds preposterous today, but it clearly illustrates the roadblocks to Jewish upward mobility earlier this century.

It wasn't until 1970 that an Ivy League university named a Jew as president. Dartmouth took the first step, quickly followed by Penn. It wasn't that these universities were in search of a Jew, nor was it that Jews suddenly gained the qualifications to lead major American universities. No, the climate in American had begun to change and previously closed doors were beginning to open wide.

Jumping ahead, no one gives a second thought today to the naming of a Jew as a college or university president, and Ivy League faculties are estimated to be somewhere between one quarter and one-third Jewish. And as importantly, no one would even think to ask these Jews to compromise their Jewish identity as a price for appointment.

Living in this more propitious time, the third generation, then, took on an externalized form of Jewish identity, at least those who were determined to sustain their affiliation to the Jewish community.

Often more comfortable with their Jewishness than their parents were, and more self-confident about their place in America, they were nonetheless ill at ease with an emphasis on Jewish ritual and learning.

But they saw another means of expressing their identity—politics and social action.

Pro-Israel activism became a focal point for their identity. So, too, did support for the rescue of Jews in danger, especially in the Soviet Union. Grappling with the meaning of the Holocaust became another key element. Engagement in American domestic political battles, in the name of Jewish values, intensified. And aggressively combating manifestations of anti-Semitism, whether at home or abroad, was also a part of this new American Jewish identity.

Again, this was an understandable reaction to the atmosphere prevailing in America in the 1960s and 1970s. Jews felt secure enough about their place in America to speak out unabashedly, to petition the government, to seek coalition partners, and to call attention to particular concerns in ways previously shunned.

Those concerns included an Israel that faced two massive wars within six years (1967 and 1973); a Soviet Jewry movement that began to emerge post-1967 in the USSR and desperately needed outside support; a growing understanding of the enormity of the Holocaust after some two decades of near silence among the survivors; and a new assertiveness in taking on anti-Semitism, often masked in those days as anti-Zionism.

And now we come to the fourth generation of American Jews in this century. Again, Hegel is on to something when he speaks of the historical dialectic.

If many in the third generation tended to externalize their Jewish identity by focusing on the political challenges facing Jews and paying little more than lip service to issues of faith and spirituality, then the new generation shows every sign of changing that.

Israel's hold on the identity of American Jews is not nearly as strong among our young. Poll after poll reveals this point.

Thankfully, rescue efforts have been unimaginably successful. Those Jews seeking to leave Ethiopia and the countries of Eastern Europe and the Muslim world have largely been able to do so, creating new lives for themselves in Israel, North America, Western Europe, and Australia. At the moment, there are few Jews in immediate danger, though the situation in Russia—home to hundreds of thousands of Jews—warrants especially close monitoring.

The Holocaust continues to be an omnipresent and defining factor in the identity of American Jews, including the young, but surely that will recede with the passage of time and the eventual disappearance of the survivors and other eyewitnesses among us, much as we hope that, amid the current attention to the Holocaust, the importance of remembrance and education will be our enduring legacy for the future.

And if younger American Jews worry about the anti-Semitism of the Nation of Islam, the Religious Right, or the militia movements in the Northwest, it's only up to a point.

At the same time, these younger American Jews see few, if any, hurdles to their chosen paths in America. They feel they can study, work, and live where they wish.

Thus, committed younger American Jews aren't entirely served by the three previous models described above. Instead, they are creating a fourth model, in part at least as a reaction to the third model which they found devoid of spiritual content. They are focused on introducing more elements of Judaism into their personal and family lives.

Are they abandoning the classic Jewish political agenda? No, not entirely, though many may be less energized by it or possibly see a less compelling need to pursue it than their parents.

Are they in danger of turning inward, away from the larger American society? We doubt it, but they are looking for meaning in their lives through the manifold expressions of Judaism at work here. They believe that to sustain Judaism in America's extraordinarily tolerant and open atmosphere today, they will have to intensify their Jewish identity.

This new trend can be seen as well in Jewish young leadership circles. In our meetings with these groups, the yearning for more Jewish content is consistently present. To accommodate younger people, AJC chapters are adapting. At the same time, however, our chapters are appropriately emphasizing the importance of maintaining an active involvement in the public policy arena, even as they seek to accommodate this new paradigm.

We are not seers, but it's a safe bet that there will be a fifth generation of American Jews who will create their own distinctive identity, which will, in important respects, differ from the four models we've seen thus far. We can't foresee its contours, although it is entirely possible that it will consist of two radically different approaches to Judaism and Jewish identity.

One community will turn further inward, the other still more outward, accelerating trends we've recently witnessed. Such defining issues as criteria for membership in the Jewish people—i.e., who constitutes the Jewish community and, additionally, what constitutes legitimate Jewish practice—will be hotly contested, even more so than today.

It's already beginning to happen, and the possibility of a schism down the road—for all practical purposes, two Jewish peoples essentially linked only in the minds of anti-Semites who couldn't care less about the issues that divide us—can't be excluded.

We're doing our best to help forestall this eventuality, but we're under no illusion about the magnitude of the challenge. And we also recognize that the American Jewish Committee (and other Jewish agencies) may not be immune to such internal tensions. Indeed, managing these issues could well become one of the most difficult tasks facing lay and staff leadership in the period ahead.

But let us return to the present. There's a certain unsettling complacency that has begun to take hold about our place in America and even about our political clout.

Some prominent American Jews are reaching the conclusion that our place is assured for all time, and consequently are turning away from Jewish involvement, lured by other sectors of American life that once spurned, and now welcome, Jews. That's problematic enough. When combined with the growing inward quest described above, it could, over time, diminish our ability to grapple effectively with the external challenges which will surely confront us as American Jews.

What are these challenges? For one thing, the numbers. America continues to grow; the Jewish community does not. Whereas we were 4 percent of the American population just fifty years ago, today we are only slightly over 2 percent. And with our Jewish population likely to decline in the years ahead, both in absolute terms and as a proportion of the American population, the problem will only intensify.

In point of fact, American Jews haven't succeeded in the civic realm through numbers alone—whether regarding such priorities as U.S.-

Israel relations, church-state separation, rescue of endangered communities, or dismantling anti-Semitic barriers. Rather, it's been the power of ideas, the strength of coalitions, the growing willingness of Americans to listen, and the sophisticated political advocacy techniques that have made the difference.

But will these be sufficient in the years ahead? AJC is determined to ensure they will, but we need your help. We will need to call still more frequently on American Jews who have achieved high standing in their professional and civic pursuits, and who enjoy access, reach, and influence in public life.

More and more ethnic and religious groups, reflecting the rapidly changing face of America, are emerging and are on the road to achieving greater political power, often modeling their organizations and political advocacy on us, American Jews.

These groups seek to be heard, aim to influence the political process, and support domestic and international priorities that reflect their own community values. And why not? Who could begrudge them those very same rights that we have exercised so energetically? Yet, at the same time, there are implications for us.

We will have to be even better at the things we do well in order to be heard, if we are to have our views taken seriously by decision-makers. We will also have our work cut out for us as master coalition builders and passionate defenders of both the *pluribus* and the *unum* in our national motto.

To take but one example: Muslims today claim 6 million adherents in the United States. If so, they surpass the Jewish community in size. What is certain is that their numbers are increasing, due especially to immigration. What does this mean for Jews over the medium and long term? How will this change an America that has hitherto been defined as Judeo-Christian? What are the possible consequences for American foreign policy, and especially support for Israel, as some Muslim groups begin to organize more effectively and seek to flex their political muscle?

True, the Muslim community is by no means monolithic, but the politically active groups have been trying to soften America's commitment to Israel, decrease foreign aid to Israel, press for a more accommodating line on Iraq, and even, in some cases, urge greater sympathy for those who resort to violence in the name of Islam. The political clout isn't quite there yet, but the intent surely is. And with time, the challenge will only grow.

History keeps moving, and seldom in a linear path, as Hegel demonstrated. We can't afford to rest on the accomplishments of these past extraordinarily successful twenty-five years, when the American Jewish impact on this country has been breathtaking. Our domestic and international agenda, as American Jews, will continue to demand a core of deeply committed and influential individuals who are prepared to help us.

This becomes all the more critical when, due to our community's static numbers, growing complacency, an inward turn by some and the weakening of identity by others—coupled with the inevitable rise of many and diverse interest groups—the going may get just a bit tougher for us in the years to come.

In raising these issues, we wish to begin a discussion with the goal of preparing ourselves institutionally to meet the challenges ahead. One of AJC's greatest strengths over these past ninety-two years has been our uncanny knack for anticipating many major societal trends and, in response, adjusting the agency to most effectively grapple with their consequences.

With your continued involvement and support, we feel confident of our ability to continue to do so, and thus help the Jewish people go from strength to strength.

The Good News and the Bad
Presentation to AJC New York Chapter Annual Meeting
June 29, 1999

I'm so glad my mother was actually present to hear that wonderful introduction. Thank you, Diane Steinman, you caught me by surprise. I'm really at a loss for words, though if that gives you all hope that I'm going to sit down, you are, I'm afraid, wrong. I'm quite sure I will find something to say quickly enough. . . .

In 1975, I was working in Rome with the movement of Jewish refugees from Eastern Europe and the Soviet Union. I was asked by the director of the office if I would accompany several Russian Jews to Naples, where the American consulate was located. We took the train from Rome to Naples, left the train station, and hailed a taxi to the American consulate. The taxi raced off and went through a series of red lights. It took me a while to overcome my fear and summon my few words in Italian, but finally I did when he came to a screeching halt at an intersection where, believe it or not, the light was green. In my best Italian I turned to him and said: "Explain something to me. You've just gone through a dozen red lights, but here we are stopped at a green light. Why?" He turned around and looked at me as if it was the dumbest question he had been asked in his entire life, before saying, with a certain degree of condescension: "How do you expect me to go through the intersection on a green light when all the cars from the other side are going through on the red light?"

Why do I tell the story? As a matter of fact, I'm not sure. Why *do* I tell the story? Maybe someone can help me. No, no, there is a good reason, but I'll tell you one other story first, prompted by your encouraging response. You have to be careful the next time before you laugh.

It was in the same year. I actually had just arrived in Rome to take on this job. And I didn't speak a word of Italian then except for a few Italo-Americanisms like "pasta fassule," which of course doesn't exist in Italian. I had to find an apartment. So the office staff said to me: "David, all you need to know is one word in Italian. The word is *affittasi*. *Affittasi*, for those of you who don't speak Italian, means "for rent." "So go out, pick a neighborhood you like, walk along the streets, look for an *affittasi* sign, and knock on the door," I was told. So I picked a neighborhood and started walking with a certain degree of boldness, which completely belied my fear and anxiety. And finally I see the first *affittasi* sign. I go up to the front door and knock, and a concierge opens the door. With a big smile I point to the sign and say, "*Affittasi, affittasi*." She emphatically says, "*No*." I say, "*Si*." We go back and forth like this. Then she shrugs her shoulders, takes me by the arm, walks me down into the basement, and shows me a parking space in the garage and says, "*Affittasi.*" The small print on the placard actually was about a parking space for rent in that building!

This is how I began my career in Jewish life. And I've still been searching for the meaning of many things, just as I've been searching for the rules, which somehow don't always govern as neatly as they should, whether on Naples streets or in Jewish political life.

I would argue that there are three kinds of people in life. There are those who are prisoners of history, who believe as a result of their own experience or through their understanding of history that things cannot move forward. They, therefore, become paralyzed by their own experience with, or knowledge of, history. There are others, too many in fact, who are entirely indifferent to history, who know nothing about, and care not a whit for, the past. It is simply not part of their experience. Frankly, this is an increasingly dominant element in American culture. Then there is the third group, to which I aspire, who are in effect permanent students of history, seeking to understand the meaning and lessons of history, but who, at the same time, perhaps inspired by our Judaic tradition, believe that we can indeed move forward, perhaps even toward a messianic age.

My perspective on history does not begin with the Second World War, but was largely informed by it as a result of my date of birth and my particular family experience. But when I consider the condition of the Jewish people shortly after the war, a condition that you in this room know well, in some cases far better than I from firsthand experience, we must recognize that the Jewish people had reached the lowest point in our history. We had lost one-third of the Jewish people and two-thirds of European Jewry. The major centers of Jewish culture and learning and civilization lay in ruins. Hundreds of thousands of survivors were strewn across Europe, in many cases moving toward their ancestral homes only to be pushed out, told that Hitler should have completed the task. No one wanted to relinquish the houses, the furnishings, and the other belongings that had long since been seized by local inhabitants. Displaced persons in camps across Germany were too often without hope, family, or visas. We were a people without a state, a people entirely dependent on the goodwill of the world, and we had seen from 1939 until 1945 just how "extensive" that goodwill was.

And then I look at the Jewish people today, just a half a century later. We have experienced a previously unimaginable revolution in our condition. We ought to sit up and take notice of it. Too often, we are so mired in the "trees" of daily life that we fail to understand the remarkable shape of the "forest" that is now before us. I don't want to sound excessively optimistic, much less triumphalistic, but we are truly living in a golden age. No, not a fool's paradise, but a golden age.

Now it's tough for Jews to admit that. It goes against the grain. Henny Youngman once asked why Jews don't drink alcohol. His reply: Because Jews don't want to interfere with their suffering.

Lest you think that we are alone, the Irish poet William Butler Yeats once said that the Irish are comforted by the knowledge that even in moments of great happiness, tragedy lurks just around the corner.

We do have problems and I want to talk about them in just a minute. We're Jews, after all. But before addressing some of them, I simply want us to pause for a moment and recognize what has been achieved in these last fifty years. By whom? By us. How have we catapulted ourselves from the nadir of Jewish existence to the summit in the span of just five decades?

It is a remarkable story. It didn't happen entirely by divine design, I believe, nor did it occur simply because we wished it so. Rather, it unfolded because a group of individuals and institutions in this country and abroad determined that we must take our fate, the fate of the Jewish people, into our own hands. We must become the first line of defense and offense on behalf of our own collective interests. And we have succeeded far beyond what we ever might have imagined.

We have managed to create an unprecedented Diaspora community here, the likes of which have never before been seen, even in the best days of Weimar Germany or the golden age of Spain. We have witnessed the creation of the Jewish sovereign state, now fifty-one years old, whose survival was certainly not assured from its birth. And whatever the daily discussion and disagreement regarding Israel, we should never for a moment forget the miracle that is this land. Surely, it is something that we should all take enormous pride in—pride in everything from its sheer survival to its rapid social and economic development, from its celebration of democracy to its enactment and implementation of the Law of Return.

The rescue of Jews, to which I've devoted a fair part of my life, is another illustration of the increasing empowerment of world Jewry. I don't have to tell you the stories of the Evian Conference, nor of the unfilled immigration quotas here in the United States: 21,000 Jewish refugees admitted to this country during the war years, just over 10 percent of the permissible quota at the time. In other words, as much as 90 percent of the quota went unfilled during the war. And by the way, even that overall quota was low due to the restrictive immigration policies introduced in 1924.

Moreover, I don't have to tell this group about the U.S. and RAF bombers that came within literally kilometers of the Auschwitz industrial complex, yet didn't divert one single bomb to target a single rail line. Not one. The Allies determined that to deviate even for a moment from their war plan might prolong the war. And they persuaded the leadership of American Jewry that this was the right course. At the same time, respected newspapers like the *Boston Globe*, in 1942, often relegated stories on the Final Solution to back pages. On June 26, 1942, for example, a page 12 story was headlined "Mass Murders of Jews in Poland Pass 700,000 Mark." Page 12! The eminent historian Paul Johnson wrote that national surveys conducted in the United States during the war revealed that Jews were seen as a bigger threat to America than any other group after Japanese and Germans. And as of January 1943, according to a Gallup Poll, a majority of Americans did not believe reports that as many as 2 million European Jews had already been killed.

Now look what has happened. Take the Soviet Jewry campaign of some two decades and the Ethiopian Jewry effort of the 1980s. Not only have we managed to achieve the seemingly impossible task of rescue and resettlement, with the invaluable assistance of the U.S. government and the support of the American public, but also we have achieved something still more. We have transformed language and its very meaning.

In the Soviet campaign, when I was working in Rome and Vienna, we came across a number of people arriving in the West who turned out not to be Jewish at all, but simply pretended they were. The same takes place today. The German embassy in Baku, which is processing applications of Azerbaijani Jews wanting to move to Germany, discovered that more than two-thirds of the documents submitted are fraudulent, the German newsweekly *Der Spiegel* reported recently. It is not Jews who are applying, but people presenting themselves as Jews. Why? In the eyes of increasing numbers of people in the former Soviet Union, and similarly in Ethiopia, where I also had experience, it is the non-Jews today who believe that to be a Jew means a ticket to life, to rescue, to freedom, and to a new start, with the support of world Jewry.

It was sixty years ago that Jews were seeking as best they could to hide their identity or to create a new one in the remote hope of escaping the Nazi extermination policy. Imagine—in the span of just a few decades we have transformed the very meaning of being a Jew to the point where in the former Soviet Union people are paying literally thousands of dollars on the black market to acquire documents verifying that their mother was a *yevreyka* and their father a *yevrey*, "Jews." Imagine! Imagine similarly in Ethiopia, where Jews had for centuries been shunned, that some Muslims and Christians were trying to pass themselves off as Jews to escape the ravaging famine in that country in the mid-1980s and establish new lives abroad.

We have done it. You have done it. The American Jewish Committee has done it. The Claims Conference has done it. The Joint Distribution Committee has done it. UJA has done it. Others here have done it. And especially, of course, Israel has done it. Collectively, we have done it. *It didn't happen by itself.* And if I have one message this evening, it is to grasp the fact that we were able to become authors of our own history in this last half century, and in doing so, we succeeded beyond our wildest dreams. The proof is before us.

But lest we become too smug or self-satisfied by this litany of successes, we need to remember a simple fact—we are Jews. And we need to bear in mind that history doesn't stop. Rather, it is a dynamic process. We don't necessarily know in which directions it moves, but there is perpetual motion. Consequently, we need to stay ever alert and continue, as best we can, to influence those directions. Jews can ill afford complacency, now or ever.

What are some challenges we are likely to face? Let me start with my nightmare scenario. You know, Diane was extraordinarily gracious in her introduction, but had she simply introduced me as the CPW, "Chief Professional Worrier," for the American Jewish Committee, she would really have been on target. One of my responsibilities is to conjure up those possible scenarios of what might go wrong, not what will go right. If things go right, wonderful. But it's because things can, as we know all too well, get derailed that we need to be sure that organizations like the American Jewish Committee are alert, prepared, and adequately staffed and funded.

My nightmare scenario is really made up of four potentially interconnected elements. Number one, I worry about certain countries, especially in the Middle East, countries like Iran and Iraq, that are hellbent on acquiring weapons of mass destruction in any way they possibly can. And I ask myself, why? To what end? Presumably, to be used against foes. Foes near, Israel perhaps, foes farther away, perhaps in the West.

The second element is the collapse of the Soviet Union. Don't get me wrong, the collapse is good news. None of us could have dreamed of the implosion of the USSR. What is bad, though, is that we now have hundreds of thousands of scientists, engineers, and technicians who are underemployed, if not unemployed. There are those who have been unpaid for a very long time—from the security guards to top scientists. In this vast nuclear, chemical, biological, and defense establishment, there are people struggling to put food on the table and to provide for their children. Some, at least, are going to be vulnerable to tantalizing offers from outside—offers to move abroad, offers to look the other way while material is being taken, offers to assist with valuable information.

The third element is that Russia today, to a large degree, is a kleptocracy dominated by organized crime, and organized crime does not live by a code of ethics, at least not ours. Thus, the prospect for outsiders seeking to acquire individual talents or material via the organized crime network—or conversely, the network looking for prospective buyers—makes this scenario still more frighteningly realistic.

And fourth, for those of you who recall the Sarin attack by followers of the Aum Shinrikyo cult in a Tokyo subway in March 1995, you may remember that twelve people were killed and 5,000 others—I repeat, 5,000—were hospitalized. And disaster workers in Japan said that it could have been far worse.

Now, what happens when you have single-minded individuals, or ad hoc or organized groups, who want to wreak havoc and, in doing so, call attention to their cause? Too often, we have seen the result. We saw it in Tokyo, in Nairobi, in Dar-es-Salaam, at the World Trade Center, in Oklahoma City. We witnessed a variety of individuals, some of whom our intelligence services had previously not been aware of, determined to send a message in the most "explosive" way possible.

Who can preclude the possibility that this threat will only get worse with the growing availability of technology and weaponry? If even two of these elements come together, much less three or four, think of the challenges we in the West will have to face in the years ahead. In response, we need a strong United States that does not recoil from the permanent challenge of international leadership. We need a United States that doesn't ever yield to the false choice between an inward and outward looking country. In this era, no country, least of all ours, can attempt to turn its back and close itself off from the rest of the world.

History alone should have taught us that, of course. When we sought to retreat inward, a dangerous international vacuum quickly developed and we had to return to the world scene at much higher cost. Whether the issue is terrorism, or organized crime, or hate groups, or the environment, or labor, or energy, few issues today are strictly domestic or international. Increasingly, such issues inconveniently do not respect national borders. The United States must be prepared to continue to assert international leadership and to project and, if appropriate, use force. Otherwise, I fear, we shall face an ever more difficult road ahead.

That is one of the reasons why Kosovo became so important. Yes, perhaps among ourselves, we might disagree on objectives, methods, and the definition of success. But what needs to be said, I believe, is that this is the first time in modern history that nations have come together to launch a war solely and exclusively for the purpose of preventing human rights violations. I can think of no other such case. Did politicians and military planners foresee that hundred of thousands of Muslims would be expelled as a result of the war? Probably not. But then the law of unintended consequences has always operated in international politics. That said, the credibility of the Western nations and NATO was on the line, and an important precedent was established when a group of democratic countries declared that they would not accept such egregious human rights violations. A single standard? No. Were these countries equally motivated to act in Rwanda? No. Questions of color? Maybe. But frankly, I'd rather take a partial standard than no standard at all, and then attempt to build on it.

Lastly, as I look ahead, I worry about the continued state of anti-Semitism in the former Soviet Union. I hope many of you saw our full-page ad on the subject in the *New York Times* ten days ago, which was signed by ninety-nine of the hundred U.S. senators. (The lone holdout, if you're curious, was Nebraska's Senator Hagel, who sent a separate letter condemning Russian anti-Semitism.) We have a presidential election in Russia coming up in 2000. No one can predict its outcome, a far cry from the days when Russian election results were stored in a KGB safe years in advance. What I do know is that anti-anti-Semitism is not the stock-in-trade of most Russian politicians. Of some, perhaps. Of most, certainly not. And I know that in a country as convulsed and weakened as Russia is today, where, as just one illustration, the life expectancy is plummeting and a male born today in Russia can expect to live just fifty-eight years, an unpredictable and potentially dangerous situation lurks. Living in that situation are up to a million Jews, whose fate hangs in the balance.

And if we need another reminder of the persistence and resilience of anti-Semitism, look at Iran. There are thirteen Jews today who have been held incommunicado since Passover. The youngest of the thirteen, by the way, is only sixteen years old. Among them are teachers, a rabbi, a *mohel*, and a couple of students. They are to be tried in the so-called revolutionary courts, we are told, on charges of espionage on behalf of Israel and the United States. The usual sentence for such espionage is death. Tellingly, seventeen Iranian Jews have already been hanged since 1979. Tactically, the problem, in a word, is that we have virtually no leverage.

Within Iran, there is a raging power struggle between the more moderate elements, if you will, led by President Khatami, and the fundamentalist religious mullahs spearheaded by Ayatollah Khamenei. The United States has very little influence. What little clout there is lies principally in Europe and Japan.

AJC has, as you know, developed close ties with Japan and the countries of Europe, and we have been calling on our friends in capitals around the world to help us. Thankfully, many have. If there is to be a solution, it could well come from that web of European and Japanese governments and multinational companies that do business in Iran. And it is an extraordinarily interesting turn of history that it is principally Germany to which we have turned. Today, Germany is Israel's best friend on the European continent. No question about it. Susan Jaffe was just in Germany and I'm sure, Susie, that you heard this description from the Israeli ambassador in Bonn.

The Germans have told us in private meetings that they will make this a key bilateral issue with Tehran. That is a remarkable statement for a government to make. These are not, it must be noted, citizens of Germany, nor even citizens of the European Union. They are simply thirteen Jews who, not for the first time in Jewish history, became hostages. And here the world's third most powerful economy—and Germany to boot—has said that their plight is going to be a key factor in determining the overall bilateral climate with Tehran.

So, even given the daunting challenges of trying to help rescue these thirteen Iranian Jews, monitor the fate of one million Jews in Russia, and help forestall the nightmarish scenario of weapons of mass destruction in a region that should finally know the true meaning of the word peace, I confess I'm not entirely discouraged as we close the century.

We have come so far as a Jewish people in assuming responsibility for our own fate, so far as a growing family of staunchly democratic nations, and so far as an international community in enshrining human rights into our code of values, that there is every reason to be strengthened in our determination to face the inevitable challenges; in other words, to enter the next century and millennium with both optimism and fortitude.

11. THE AMERICAN JEWISH COMMITTEE

Every Day's a Marathon
AJC Journal
Winter 1989

I've always joked that the most difficult hours of my day are those spent getting our children dressed, fed, and out the door in time to catch their school or day camp bus. And that by the time I leave for work I've met the greatest challenge of the day. Now, however, in my position as the AJC's Washington representative, with its fast-paced tempo and nonstop schedule, I may have to reevaluate my early morning schedule as being the most difficult time of my day.

Not long ago I began my workday at one of the many coalition meetings in which the AJC actively participates. This one took place at the Armenian Assembly office in the shadow of Capitol Hill. It was attended by six of the principal immigrant and refugee agencies; AJC was the only Jewish organization present. The main topic of discussion was ironic indeed. Some Armenian groups were deeply troubled by the explosive growth in immigration of Soviet Armenians, and were looking for ways to stem the tide. Strange, I thought. Here were several advocacy groups whose very purpose was to find ways of increasing the numbers of refugees admitted into the United States, and we were faced with the unusual challenge of one ethnic community seeking ways to slow it down. Actually, they feared high levels of immigration would weaken their Armenian homeland. In their efforts to find ways to slow down migration and to have the United States reconsider its policy of defining Soviet Armenians as refugees, a basic clash of interests arose between us. It has always been our goal to have Soviet Jews defined as refugees by the government. The Armenians, on the other hand, were seeking to have the government reconsider its definition of Armenians as refugees and to make it more difficult to emigrate here. We were unable to reach any agreement.

I then rushed to the Democratic Committee Club for a luncheon meeting with a black member of Congress, which had been arranged by an AJC leader. It proved to be a very useful session. We discussed a number of issues, including black-Jewish relations, and we agreed that it was important for our respective communities to find ways to repair the damage done in recent months. We agreed that neither side wanted to abandon the partnership that had produced several landmark civil rights acts. The congressman noted, for example, that most black members of Congress have shown strong support for issues of primary concern to Jewish communities, including the U.S.-Israeli relationship and Soviet Jewry. Similarly, he was gratified that Jewish members of Congress were often in the forefront in the struggle against apartheid, and were supportive of emergency aid to famine-stricken areas and long-term programs for development and assistance in black Africa.

Even so, he confessed his concern about Israel since the Likud government came to power in 1977, and especially about events since the Palestinian uprising began in December 1987 in the West Bank and Gaza. Moreover, he continually returned to an issue that deeply troubled him: the purported relationship between Israel and South Africa, which was very offensive to the black community in this country. He urged that we do everything possible to convey to Israeli leaders the negative effect this could have. I tried to persuade him that the ties with South Africa had declined since the March 1987 Israeli cabinet decision to limit the relationship. I also made it clear that Israel was not among the nations—including Japan, West Germany, the United States, the United Kingdom, and Persian Gulf nations—who were the major investors and primary providers of oil technology and arms. My argument seemed to fall on deaf ears. Still, we agreed to remain in touch.

Then, off to yet another meeting at the State Department with a senior official. Our discussion revolved around reports that the United States was prepared to change its policy and permit Soviet Jews arriving in Israel to maintain their refugee status and remain eligible to enter the United States. An explosive rumor! The Israelis had already indicated that if it is true, it would be considered a hostile act. How could a Jew arriving in Israel be considered a refugee? Wouldn't such a move undermine the very notion of Zionism and the Jewish state? The official told me that the proposed changes had indeed been entered into the *Federal Register*, though the final decision would rest largely with Secretary of State George Shultz. Nevertheless, there was deep concern about Israeli efforts to redirect Soviet Jewish immigrants to Israel and thereby deny freedom of choice for emigrating Soviet Jews.

We discussed the feasibility of a two-track system: those with Israeli visas in the USSR would go directly to Israel, while others seeking to come to the United States could approach our embassy and request American visas. It wasn't clear, he added, whether the Soviet Union would agree to such a system or whether they would permit other than the immediate relatives of United States citizens/permanent residents to come here. The important question remains: Would those in the USSR without immediate relatives here have the right to leave for the United States rather than Israel?

It was already late afternoon when the meeting ended. Back at the office messages had piled up. A West European diplomat, who checked in from time to time on Middle Eastern issues, wanted to know whether we saw any changes emanating from the PLO leadership. He said that his government had been making a concerted effort in several Middle Eastern capitals to press the PLO for an open and unambiguous statement recognizing Israel's right to exist. He felt that there had been a few potentially encouraging signs and wanted to know whether we had heard anything. The only thing I could point to was the statement made by Abu Sharif at the Algerian summit meeting (subsequently reprinted in the *New York Times*) in which I found some positive elements, but it was unclear whether it reflected Abu Sharif's views alone or was endorsed by other senior PLO officials, including Arafat.

I then talked with two journalists, one Israeli and the other American, both anxious to get more information about the debate over Soviet Jews and their country of destination.

Judith Golub, our assistant Washington representative, started *her* day with an 8 a.m. breakfast with a coalition dealing with the genocide treaty. While the AJC has been in the forefront of this fight for many years, it was not until 1986 that the Senate finally passed a resolution of approval. However, until the Senate passes implementing legislation that would amend the U.S. Criminal Code to make genocide punishable under domestic law (as the House has already done), the United States will not become an official signatory to the treaty. Judy and the AJC's partners in the coalition reviewed Senate lists and agreed on a strategy to target those senators who had not yet become cosponsors of the Senate bill. The group also agreed to prevent in every way possible the inclusion of a death penalty amendment to the legislation, which would certainly provoke major debate and further stall passage of the bill.

Then she met at considerable length with two members of Congress on the issue of child care. AJC has played a very central, if unpublicized, role in seeking a compromise over the church–state issues in child care legislation. Judy has been in continous contact with members of Congress to ensure that the bill's provisions uphold church–state separation and civil rights policies. Churches and synagogues, which provide about one-third of all child care nationwide, would receive much of the funds under this act.

Even with our departure from the office, the day did not end. On the way home on Washington's Metro, a chance meeting with a key Senate aide gave me an opportunity to learn more about an upcoming Senate foreign aid appropriations vote.

A typical day? Actually, one of the unique qualities of this job is that no two days are quite alike, but each day is guaranteed to be busy, exciting, and challenging.

Presentation to the Board of Governors
St. Petersburg, Florida
February 2, 1990

It has been a very special relationship for me with the American Jewish Committee since I first came in 1979, hired, in fact, by Ira Silverman during his first incarnation, together with another new staffer, Gary Rubin. Gary and I began on the same day in 1979 and it is very fitting to note that we both left AJC in 1981, came back in 1984, and are both sitting here on this dais this evening.

I have been working with AJC because to me it is a unique and distinctive organization in Jewish and, indeed, public life. And one of the very special things for me is that AJC is a bifocal agency.

While for years during Shcharansky's imprisonment in the Soviet Union advocated in his behalf, we never recoiled from supporting Andrei Sakharov as well, though he was not a Jew and not involved in the refusenik movement. Presumably, some other Jewish organizations had a problem with that. And I was proud to work for an agency that in 1984 permitted me and others to travel to Ethiopia, just at the time when Operation Moses was beginning, to meet with Ethiopian Jews in the Gondar Province, but that insisted that if 8 million people were on the brink of famine in Ethiopia, we as Jews could not, dare not, turn our backs on the famine ravaging that country. And that just as we had been fighting—and Gary has been among the leaders in the fight—on behalf of refugee admissions for Jews from Iran, Romania, the Soviet Union, and elsewhere, when refugees began streaming out of Indochina in the late 1970s, we did not turn our backs on them. To the contrary, we became a lead agency in this country for their admission, struck by the humanitarian poignancy of the boat people. Perhaps we felt some historical similarities to another boat people, ourselves. All this has made the organization very special for me.

As I look ahead, I see five overarching issues that concern me as an American Jew.

First, the permanent challenge of Israel's security and quest for peace.

Second, the relationship between American Jews and Israel because that relationship is vital to both sides—indeed, we are inextricably linked—and yet it seems to me that the inexorable forces of history are pulling us apart. They are pulling us apart linguistically and culturally and in other ways as well. We have got to reverse that trend.

Third, every Jewish organization has to come up with some contribution to the question of why be Jewish. It's not enough that we assign it to some organizations. Rather, it is a task for each and every self-respecting American Jewish organization. Just as we have devoted time to the rescue of Jews overseas, just as we have helped create the National Conference on Soviet Jewry and the North American Conference on Ethiopian Jewry, it is time to talk about a national conference on American Jewry. We rightly have been talking about the rescue of 2 million Jews in the Soviet Union, but what about 2 million Jews in the United States who, statistics tell us, are on the verge of disappearing from our community? It is not enough to shrug our shoulders and say, yes, it's a problem, but others should take care of it. No, it is the responsibility of every organization to define for itself its unique and distinctive role in a task that is larger than any of us and yet so vital.

Fourth, forty-five years after the Holocaust, the challenge to us as American Jewish organizations to monitor and, yes, to rescue Jews abroad continues. Lest we have any doubt about that need, today's front-page story in the *New York Times* brings it home yet again: Anti-Semitism in the Soviet Union on the rise, Jews increasingly worried. We could have visualized that headline so many times over the past seventy, indeed 300 years, on Russian soil. And here it is again in 1990. What are we doing about it? What is our unique and distinct contribution when 10 to 15 percent of the world's Jews are threatened? And it goes beyond the Soviet Union, of course.

Fifth, and I will simply mention this because Gary has dwelt on it at some length and very eloquently: the social and political well-being of American Jewry in the context of a healthy and thriving America, an America committed to pluralism and to ever strengthening its democracy and democratic institutions.

An organization like our own has to look at each of these five broad issues and identify those areas where we can make a unique and distinct contribution.

Incidentally, even as we look ahead, let's take just a moment to pat ourselves on the back. Because in each of those five issues, AJC has proven yet again a prescient organization. On Israel, which was the first American Jewish organization to establish a full-time office in the State of Israel? It was AJC. And on American Jewish-Israeli relations, which was the first major American Jewish organization to establish an institute on that subject? It was AJC. And on the question of why be

Jewish, it was again AJC that pioneered in studies on the Jewish family, contributing so much to our knowledge and understanding in these areas. And on Soviet Jewry, I need not go through our agency's history, whether one begins in 1906 or in the early 1950s with the Solomon Schwarz studies on anti-Semitism in the Soviet Union. Or our own Richie Maass's contribution and the very founding of the National Conference on Soviet Jewry, due, at least in part, to a recognition by AJC of this emerging issue. And fifth, in the area of the social and political well-being of America, the list simply is too long to even begin to enumerate here.

What is it that we have done best in these areas? I would suggest that there are three things—things as valid in the 1990s as they were in the 1980s. The first is research and analysis. The second, and Gary again made reference to it, is our unique expertise as coalition builders. And the third is our advocacy, successful advocacy, relentless advocacy on these issues at the highest political and diplomatic levels, both in this country and abroad.

We have been, and continue to be, the Jewish community's think tank. We have been and continue to be the Jewish community's civil engineers and bridge builders. And we have been, and we can again reassert our primacy as, the Jewish community's crystal-ball gazers, the prescient organization that defines tomorrow's emerging issues.

What are some of the issues facing us on the international scene? Well, I guess Yogi Berra said it best: déjà vu all over again. The two most compelling issues for us today on the international scene remain events in the Soviet Union and the Middle East. Of course, when I speak of the Soviet Union I speak about anti-Semitism, emigration, religious and cultural development. And in neighboring Eastern Europe, we are presented with both opportunity and challenges.

Look at Israel for a moment. The foreign aid issue, the strategic relationship, interpreting Israel in the United States, preserving Israel's democratic fiber, the overall health of the American-Israeli relationship—none of these things can be taken for granted. If ever we could, we cannot now, and certainly the next decade will challenge us as never before. We have had credibility on Israel because we have done our homework; because we have always spoken candidly if discreetly;

because we've adopted our positions through a deliberative process that some would say is occasionally arthritic but, in the final analysis, tends to produce good, rational policy. We are taken seriously in places like Washington. Sholom Comay and other AJC leaders have gone back and forth to Washington, for meetings with John Sununu, Dan Quayle, Dick Schifter, John Kelly, John Bolton, and other key policy makers in the current administration and in administrations past. We have to continue this approach and do it even better.

When I look at Israel and issues down the road, there is one that Vice President Dan Quayle has focused on. That's the "Zionism equals racism" issue. To me, at least, there has been no greater act of verbal violence inflicted upon the Jewish people in the postwar period than the UN's passage of the "Zionism equals racism" resolution in 1975. Not only has it delegitimized the State of Israel, it has licensed thinly disguised anti-Semitism in many parts of the world. I wasn't here last night because I was debating the political counselor of the Soviet embassy in a public forum in Washington. And he was acknowledging the fact that, yes, there is some anti-Semitism in the USSR but he didn't know, frankly, what can be done about it. And someone in the audience stood up and said to him: What you can do about it is, first, to announce Soviet support for the repeal of the Zionism equals racism resolution. You have helped sanction anti-Semitism with that resolution.

AJC can play a very special role in this regard. What is it that we can do? What we have done best. Research and analysis. Intergroup relations work, because we can't achieve our goals alone. And diplomatic efforts *with follow up* because there are no quick solutions.

The difference we can make is persistence, nagging, nudging, pestering, perseverance. It's being there. We have begun to do it. And it's got to come together even better. We have begun to do it in the chapters with the consular visitations program, but it is still too episodic, and it is still a bit too unfocused. And we have begun to do it in Washington. Many of you participated in those twenty-two delegations to the embassies for meetings with ambassadors last May—countries from Morocco to Mozambique. No one else has been doing it. We can do it. We can make a difference.

Two days ago I was invited, together with Al Moses, to a meeting with the president of Kenya. And let me tell you, he takes the Jewish community seriously. He thinks that we can make a big difference in the life of Kenya. There is a lot that we can be doing to advance our interests as we involve ourselves more actively on the diplomatic front, as we press questions affecting Israel, the United Nations, and Soviet Jewry. And forgive me for name-dropping, but yesterday morning, together with the National Conference on Soviet Jewry and the Presidents Conference, I participated in a meeting with Larry Eagleburger, the deputy secretary of state. We were discussing specifically the question of Soviet anti-Semitism and its resurgence. And when we asked Eagleburger what could be done, he said to us, folks, you have done a terrific job in awakening the consciousness of the United States on Soviet Jewish issues, immigration, and anti-Semitism. But who is banging on the doors of the embassies of Spain, West Germany, France, Britain, who is traveling to their capitals, who is trying to awaken consciousness in those countries as well? We in the United States government cannot do it alone. That was Larry Eagleburger's advice to us just twenty-four hours ago.

And finally, it seems to me that as we approach the international questions facing us, whether in the Soviet Union, the Middle East, Eastern Europe, or other parts of the world, we have not been exploiting as many of our own talents and resources as we could be.

The Jewish Communal Affairs Department has done enormously good work on issues affecting everything from grandparenting to intermarriage, from Jewish identity to single-parent families. It doesn't only affect the American Jewish community. The British, the French, the Argentinians, the Brazilians, and others are not immune to such questions. Ask the Brazilian Jewish community what is their biggest problem today and they will tell you it is not anti-Semitism, it's Semitism. It's not forces from without seeking to challenge their legitimacy, but rather forces from within that no longer see relevance in continuing this extraordinary and fascinating, if ever challenging, Jewish saga. We have something to say within our building on Fifty-sixth Street. We have something that can be tailored for those communities that are seeking to hold on and to build from within. Let's use it.

The Interreligious Affairs Department as well has a lot to offer. And they have done a great deal—in the Vatican, in Israel, now in Poland. But there is even more that can be done. And as Eastern Europe opens up and the Soviet Union as well, the churches there will play an important role. Who is talking to them? Who has the experience and the tools to dialogue with Christian leaders? We have the experience. We have the tools. Again, it needs to be tailored. But we have something important to offer, which they might well need.

Our Research Department does such excellent studies measuring the pulse of American Jews, of American attitudes toward Jews. Are those problems unique to the United States? Of course not. Why aren't we sharing that experience with Jewish communities around the world that are equally interested in both their internal state of health and their societal position? We are now starting such a project with the Research Department to prove that it can be done. Where? In the Soviet Union looking at polling possibilities to measure the pulse of Soviet Jews and to determine attitudes of Soviet citizens toward Jews. And I wish I could have had that study's results yesterday for Secretary Eagleburger, because he sure needed it. And we are the agency that could provide it.

But this is really the message that I wanted to offer: as we look ahead, as we look within ourselves, and as we focus to some extent this weekend on our institutional weaknesses, our strengths are so considerable, both in our volunteer structure and our professional staff, that AJC's star shall burn brightly for a very long time to come.

Harris Updates
Forward
October 12, 1990

Imagine my surprise when I read your headline: "AJC's Harris to Face Cash Crunch" (Sept. 14). Prompted by this heart-stopper, I rushed to call my wife to alert her to the bad times ahead. She asked what's up. I told her I wasn't sure, but it was enough for me that the *Forward*, presumably based on "usually reliable sources," had printed the news.

It was only a few days later, at my wife's relentless urging, that I summoned up the courage to read your full article. Alas, I had gotten it all wrong. It wasn't about my personal finances at all. Rather, it was meant to be about AJC's. In point of fact, however, it was last spring's news, since overtaken by a number of positive developments.

AJC did go through a difficult period during the last program year, which involved some painful budget-cutting and staff reduction. As a consequence, the agency has been successfully streamlined, while AJC continues pioneering and vital work in those areas of importance to American Jewry: protecting Jewish security at home and abroad; enriching the quality of American Jewish life and thereby helping to insure Jewish (qua Jewish) continuity; and contributing to the well-being of American pluralism, which, in our view, is a *sine qua non* for ensuring the well-being of any minority, Jews included.

Identity Efforts
The Jewish Week
October 7, 1994

It was both surprising and disappointing that a recent column ("Rethinking Our Priorities," Between the Lines, Sept. 9–15), citing remarks by Edgar Bronfman, failed to distinguish the American Jewish Committee from other community relations agencies in calling on these organizations to focus greater attention on the daunting internal challenge of strengthening Jewish identity.

AJCommittee's pioneering work in this area over the past three decades—long before rising concerns about American Jewish demography and depth of commitment became such dominant themes—has been one of the principal features distinguishing it from sister organizations.

To cite but a few examples: AJCommittee established a Jewish Communal Affairs Department in 1963, which, through research, publications, and conferences, has helped diagnose major troubling trends in American Jewish life (including declining birth rates, increased intermarriage, diminished impact of the extended family on Jewish identity, etc.). To further bolster these efforts, we set up the Petschek

Jewish Family Center in 1982. That same year we also created the Institute on American Jewish–Israeli Relations; and more recently, we have added several new dimensions, such as an ad campaign (nine ads to date in the *New York Times* and several campus papers) featuring individuals discussing the meaning of being Jewish, a national essay contest on Jewish identity for college youth, Judaic literacy programs, and enhanced contact with all the major rabbinic groups to share our experiences in these areas.

Given the magnitude of the problems faced by an American Jewish community buffeted by high rates of intermarriage, low rates of conversion, and, among too many, weak education and involvement, it goes without saying that every institution needs to do more. But at the same time, to fail to acknowledge AJCommittee's significant and long-standing efforts in this vital area was a regrettable omission.

Not Just Liberal
The Jewish Week
August 18, 1995

In your otherwise perceptive and comprehensive profile of Robert Rifkind (Aug. 4), the American Jewish Committee, of which Mr. Rifkind is the new president, is described as a "liberal bastion."

The AJC, in fact, prides itself on attracting lay and staff members whose political views range across the spectrum of thoughtful opinion and who are drawn to the organization precisely because it welcomes such diversity and encourages serious debate on pressing policy issues.

Our leaders in recent years have included Democrats and Republicans, conservatives and liberals, as well as those who do not easily fall into any category. They have been united by a recognition that the answers to the challenges facing the Jewish people usually defy doctrinaire thinking, instead benefiting from vigorous and wide-ranging discussion.

As a result, a careful reading of our policy positions and public statements reveals a nonideological, nonreflexive approach that tailors individual responses to individual issues.

Mr. Rifkind is a proud heir to this AJC commitment to open-mindedness and rejection of simplistic political labels. It is a tradition we at AJC cherish as a singular agency strength.

David Roth:
In Memoriam
AJC Board of Governors
September 11, 1995

He joined the AJC staff twenty-seven years ago with the title of Assistant Area Director for the North Central Region, based in Chicago, having previously served brief stints with the National Labor Relations Board and the American Jewish Congress after attending graduate school at the University of Illinois.

Six months later, he passed his probationary period. Joel Ollander, his supervisor, wrote: "His work in our Executive Suite program, urban affairs, civil rights, has been outstanding. He quickly grasps the implications of these programs, familiarizes himself with the facts, and determines a course of action."

That work intensified and the responsibilities grew. A year later, his staff evaluation read, in part: "His research into police–community relations and his budding attempts to put together a meaningful coalition of powerful groups to change current police practices in Chicago hold out significant promise. And he will shortly bring to fruition a Chicago Consultation on Ethnicity which will be a major community-wide event. He has already successfully completed the complicated task of bringing a large number of Chapter members into an active relationship with various inner-city groups working directly on various aspects of urban affairs."

In recognition of these achievements and consistent with the growing priority attached by AJC to emerging ethnic issues and intergroup relations, in 1971 he was appointed to a new position as Midwest Coordinator of AJC's National Project on Ethnic America.

And so was launched the career of David Roth, a career that spanned twenty-seven years at AJC.

Tragically, that career ended abruptly with David's death, on July 29, at the age of fifty-five.

He had entered the hospital two weeks earlier for what he believed would be routine heart surgery. So unconcerned was he that up until the night before the actual surgery he was on the phone with his office, with me, and with others sharing ideas, discussing projects, dictating memos. Indeed, suggestive of David's exceptional commitment to his work, that very night he left eight separate messages on the voice mail for Denita, his secretary, the last at 4 a.m.

David never recovered from the surgery. Instead, he went into a coma and died twelve days later. He leaves his widow, Sandy, and his daughter, Abbie, seeking to find the strength to deal with the magnitude of their loss.

To us and to the world, David leaves an extraordinary legacy of the work to which he was devoted—the work of the National Affairs Department, the National Project on Ethnic America, the Institute on American Pluralism, the Illinois Ethnic Consultation, the Polish American–Jewish American Council, Project Ukraine, and the Ethnic Sharing models he developed for schools.

Shula Bahat, who spoke at David's funeral, described him so aptly: "He believed that this country is the greatest experience in history in pluralistic democracy, a place where the dreams of diverse people can be fulfilled. . . . David, whose life revolved around love and tolerance, could not tolerate intolerance. He knew that people can be taught and trained to understand difference, to accept and cherish difference until difference no longer makes any difference. He was ready to go to every corner of the world to convey this message: with George Szabad to Poland; with Andy Athens to Greece, Cyprus, and Israel; with Elie Lazarus to Washington; with Maynard and Elaine Wishner and Barbara and Howard Gilbert and Ron Weiner everywhere."

And as I wrote to Sandy, David's wife: "In an era when many Jews still view other groups with mistrust and suspicion, David was a bridge-builder, both architect and engineer, and the spans he constructed were by no means easily achieved. Trying to develop meaningful relationships with the Polish, Ukrainian, Lithuanian, and other communities, for example, is complicated, to say the least, in light of history. This did not, however, deter David. To the contrary, in his own determined and uniquely effective way, he set about planting the seeds of these relationships and then nurturing them, ever mindful of the pitfalls but convinced of the need. He was right, of course, and it is no overstatement to suggest that his contribution to advancing Jewish interests was historic."

David loved the American Jewish Committee. Per capita, year after year, he was the single most generous staff contributor to our annual campaign. Knowing his salary, I once asked him how he could afford such a substantial gift. His reply: "I can never adequately repay the AJC for all that it has given me over the years."

It is, of course, we who are in David's debt. He gave of his heart, his soul, his intellect. Those of us who were blessed to know him, who were touched by him in big ways and small, are forever the beneficiaries. And through the perpetuation of his ideals, especially his goal to improve understanding between diverse peoples, his memory will live on in the American Jewish Committee for generations to come.

Shanks Unfair to AJC
Moment
December 1995

Had Hershel Shanks chastised the American Jewish Committee for the food served at our Annual Dinner in May, about which he wrote in his August Perspective, I wouldn't have been surprised, much less offended. To the contrary, I would have wholeheartedly agreed. Had he chastised us for the length of the dinner program, that, too, wouldn't have hurt.

But to chastise us for a program that included President Bill Clinton, Senator Bob Dole, and Justice Ruth Bader Ginsburg but "no one who spoke about assimilation, intermarriage, lack of Jewish education, paucity of spiritual satisfaction, how to be Jewish in an open society"? Unfair!

The Annual Dinner, by its nature, has always emphasized external concerns. More than one-third of the 1,000 attendees were guests from the political, diplomatic, and civic communities.

Even so, though absent from Mr. Shanks's column, it was noteworthy that Alfred Moses, the U.S. ambassador to Romania (and AJC honorary president), used the occasion to focus on the threat to Jewish survival, "not because of persecution but because of assimilation. . . . If we are serious about the survival of the Jewish people here in the United States, we have to be serious about being Jewish, not only in name but in practice."

Had Mr. Shanks looked at our total program, of which the dinner was but one part, he would have seen a Jewish agency that assigns very high priority to the issues he identifies. The day before the dinner, AJC sponsored, in the *New York Times*, the thirteenth ad in our highly acclaimed series on the meaning of being Jewish, featuring a finalist in our annual college essay contest on the same topic; the contest winner was with us the same day for a plenary session on Jewish campus life. And a major theme of the entire gathering was the link among Jews worldwide.

In sum, to understand the totality of AJC's agenda requires attendance at more than one event in a three-day meeting, just as a full appreciation of *Moment* may require the reading of more than one article or even one issue.

Remarks
AJC Board of Governors Institute
Scottsdale, Arizona
February 2, 1996

Sholom Comay, of blessed memory, was right. As you may recall, he was firmly of the view that out of the difficult challenges this agency faced in the late 1980s would emerge a stronger, more focused organization that would rightfully reclaim its leadership role in the decade of the '90s.

Here we are, midway through the decade, and we instinctively know that Sholom, had he lived to this day, wouldn't have been so immodest as to say "I told you so," but rather might have nodded his head and smiled with satisfaction. For Sholom ignored Yogi Berra's advice— "When you come to a fork in the road, take it"—and understood the need to make choices, however difficult, and he—and you—chose well in St. Petersburg and thereafter.

The cover story in the *Baltimore Jewish Times*, a copy of which you have, noting that AJC is "one success story" in a fairly bleak communal landscape, offers additional confirmation.

I might add that the author of that story, Jim Besser, a very respected syndicated reporter—with impeccable judgment, of course—told me that, before submitting the piece to his editors, he had checked out his own conclusions about us with a number of informed observers, all of whom offered a similar assessment.

I need not rehearse for you the signs of our strength, of our success. I've done that elsewhere and in any case the evidence is before you. Suffice it to say that our vital signs are all strong—program, fund-raising, lay leadership, staff, chapters, spirit, and sense of purpose and mission.

It's precisely because we are in this position—and I probably ought to invoke some gesture here to keep away the evil eye—that I believe it appropriate, indeed necessary, for us to turn inward this weekend, more so than we usually do, and to give serious thought to the future.

This agency has been down and considered its future, and this agency has been up and considered its future, and isn't it a whole lot nicer to consider our future while being up? So, we do not look ahead driven by crisis, rather by opportunity.

The American Jewish landscape is changing rapidly. Consider:

First, the traditional issues we as a community have faced—and successfully at that—may have less claim on younger generations. Israel's safety, the rescue of endangered Jewish communities, anti-Semitic barriers, and the impact of the Holocaust have largely determined the Jewish agenda for several decades now. That could change. Bob Rifkind, I know, dealt with this picture in his customarily eloquent and provocative manner yesterday evening.

And speaking of Bob, let me pause here for just a moment to share the obvious—how blessed I've been these past five and a half years to work with not one, not two, but three truly exceptional presidents of this agency—Sholom, Al Moses, and Bob Rifkind. How lucky I am! How lucky this agency is to attract leaders of such unusual caliber and dedication.

Second, increasingly we are moving from addressing the external issues facing Jews to the internal issues—the existential issues—facing Jews: our own Jewish identity and literacy, the transmission of that precious heritage to our children, the nature of our relationship to Israel, the ties that bind us as Jews and those that divide us.

Third, partly in response to this changing agenda, and partly in response to the evolving nature of philanthropy, about which Morris Offit will speak tomorrow and whose remarks I eagerly anticipate, Jewish organizations are beginning to scramble more to justify their existence and to attract support in a highly competitive marketplace, where increasingly non-Jewish agencies—for example, universities, cultural institutions, and medical centers—are drawing substantial Jewish largesse. In some cases, though not enough, these Jewish organizations are considering merger, consolidation, or downsizing. The current merger discussions of the UJA, UIA, and CJF are one good example.

Fourth, younger American Jews, like their counterparts, are less likely to join organizations and to commit scarce time to them. And importantly, as Bob Rifkind has noted, many Jews are marrying later, having children later, and, in some cases, moving more frequently for career or lifestyle reasons. Further, as *Time* magazine has just reported, they are facing substantially higher relative costs than the generation that preceded them for housing and college, among other big-ticket items. Many therefore are either unable—or unwilling—to carve out the time, commitment, and financial support necessary for the level of involvement we've come to expect.

Does such a portrait of current trends, therefore, lead inevitably to pessimistic conclusions? No, not necessarily, but it does mean that a Jewish organization like AJC will continue to face the challenge of adapting to the times—a challenge we have handled quite skillfully over the years by constantly fine-tuning our agenda, identifying and training future leaders, expanding our membership base, assuring our financial well-being, and, with some delay, now coming to grips with the implications of the information and communications revolution.

The road ahead is not going to be easy. That's why we need to pause this weekend and, joined by several unusually qualified experts, put our heads together and begin a discussion—a serious discussion—on institution building.

Everyone in this room, as far as I'm concerned, has a Ph.D. in AJC Studies—a new major!—and has something to contribute to this discussion, to the questions we must ask ourselves. How, for example, do we more effectively communicate who we are and the extraordinary breadth and depth of what we do? How do we convey that the issues of tomorrow are those we're already at work on today and those of today already drew our attention yesterday?

How do we utilize more effectively the new technologies to achieve our programmatic and institutional aims? How do we attract attention to our deliberative method, nuanced message, and long-term strategy in a world increasingly driven, it seems, by instant gratification, quick takes, infinite information sources, five-second sound bites, and the glib and, at times, all-too-successful hucksters of the shrill, the sensational, the simplistic? How do we reach and touch those American Jews who no longer reside in the traditional urban/suburban areas where our thirty-two chapters function, but now live in wealthy enclaves along seashores and in mountainous regions?

And how do we broaden and deepen the base of financial support for this agency to ensure that we don't live so perilously from year to year? That we aren't so dangerously dependent on one plate dinner here and another there? How do we draw more younger people to our ranks and ensure future generations of leaders who will need to be every bit as bright and committed and generous and, when necessary, as tough as are our current leaders to face the times ahead?

How do we tap into an emerging Jewish renewal that is, I believe, beginning to occur among a numerically important segment of American Jewry, driven by a quest for community and spirituality? Even if fewer in number, the Jewish critical mass will be there. Our challenge will be to continue to find common ground with a key part of that critical mass.

I can assure you that we—the senior staff—are spending very long hours discussing precisely these issues and the range of options available. And the conceptualization of this Institute, done in characteristically close coordination with our officers, reflects an important step in that direction.

We need your involvement and we need your input, not only in these four days but in the weeks, months, and years ahead, for the challenges we are talking about, as you know so well, are not simply here today and gone tomorrow.

When my son Michael was three, he was asked in a nursery school class what he wanted to be when he grew up. Others in the class had answered "ballerina," "racing car driver," or "athlete." My son responded that when he grew up he wanted to be four!

I always admired that answer and in a way he is absolutely right. One day at a time, one year at a time. But an institution of the size and scope of AJC, operating in a rapidly changing and highly competitive environment, can't simply afford to proceed one year at a time. Eventually it won't work, eventually a bad year will befall us for any of many possible reasons. The admonition—"Never make predictions, especially about the future"—just doesn't apply. We have to make predictions; we have to plan; we have to position ourselves; we have to deepen our institutional strength if we are to continue to flourish.

I am absolutely convinced that this agency is unique both in its content and its method. The need for precisely this kind of agency—which blends the best of the American and Jewish traditions, which creates for many of us, I believe, a perfect harmony between the two essential elements of our identity, our American ideals and our Jewish values— will be ever more, not less, compelling to help our beloved country and our cherished Jewish community traverse the challenging terrain which lies ahead.

I want to be absolutely certain that there will be an American Jewish Committee, thriving and resilient, to provide the thoughtful, reasoned, and sophisticated strategies for those who follow us, your descendants and mine.

We have the opportunity to help assure that. Once again we turn to those who have best understood the genius of this agency, to those who have seen the central role played by this organization in some of the major issues of our times—from the veritable revolution in Christian–Jewish relations, to the essential end of structural anti-Semitism in this country, to the remarkable development of American pluralism. It is to you we again turn, to you who have already given so much of yourselves, of your time and of your resources.

Together we can lay the groundwork for the next glorious chapter in this agency's history, as we pursue the age-old dream of the perfectibility of the world.

Tribute to Leo Nevas
Congregation Beth El, Norwalk, Connecticut
May 19, 1996

Some occasions are truly special. This is one such occasion. And that's why I was so delighted to be invited by Joseph Schachter to participate this evening.

I first met Leo about fifteen years ago because of our mutual involvement with the American Jewish Committee, he as a lay member whose list of key leadership positions at the AJC would take all my allotted time here were I to read them to you, I as a junior professional.

It didn't take me very long to figure out that Leo was someone quite out of the ordinary. Not only did he obviously have the formula for the fountain of youth, and that would have been reason enough to stick close to him, but there was much more. Leo was a man of principles and, especially noteworthy and, I daresay, all too rare, a man who acted on those principles.

Since he's not a boastful man, it did take some time to figure out the layers of involvement of this unusual person, and I'm sure I haven't seen the half of it, but what I did come to see was quite remarkable.

I discovered a caring, knowledgeable Jew who has shared those values with his family and friends. And I discovered an ecumenical Jew who doesn't simply repeat a phrase like *am echad*, "one people," without necessarily meaning it or living it. He means it, and lives it. His record of involvement with, and generous support for, a range of Jewish religious institutions here in Connecticut is unparalleled.

I discovered a proud and courageous Jew who was willing to help break down barriers against Jews, especially those business and residential barriers that were at one time all too pervasive, and that are probably unimaginable to the younger people in this room, without forsaking one iota of his own identity.

I discovered a man deeply committed to Israel and to the well-being of fellow Jews around the world, and especially those in the former Soviet Union denied their fundamental rights to emigrate or to practice their religion. And again, he acted on those commitments.

He's spent more time in Israel than most of us; he's spoken and written on the subject, often defending Israel when it has come under attack in international settings. And he tenaciously stuck with the Soviet Jewry issue for years and years, never faltering in his desire to focus the world's attention on this egregious violation of human rights.

And that, of course, brings me to the broader subject of human rights, which, as we all know, has always been at the center of Leo's concerns. Embodying Hillel's invocation, "If I am only for myself, what am I?" Leo has devoted a major part of his life, through the American Jewish Committee, the International League for Human Rights, and the United Nations Association, to the struggle for universally accepted international human rights standards. Not just standards, by the way, but compliance as well.

International declarations and covenants on human rights are essential of course, but in and of themselves are insufficient. Without the implementation of the guarantees enshrined therein, these documents would be essentially meaningless. To make them work requires the constant energy of the world's democracies—and to get governments to speak out requires the vigilance, monitoring, and prodding of the nongovernmental community, the so-called NGOs. Leo has been at the forefront of such efforts for a very long time.

And now please allow me to say a few words to Leo's grandchildren, to the eight of you. Countless people who are not here this evening, who may never know your grandfather's name, who live in lands far and near—from Burma to China, from Ethiopia to South Africa—are today a bit freer, a bit more protected, a bit more confident that the world does care about them, because of this man. Your grandfather has taken the essential elements of Jewish teaching and sought to make a difference—in the lives of his fellow Jews, in the lives of his fellow human beings. That's who your grandfather is to the larger world.

Leo's put himself on the line in his work. It's not risk-free. To cite but one example: His activities in the Soviet Union involving the late

Nobel laureate Andrei Sakharov, his wife, Elena Bonner, and other Soviet activists, which epitomized Leo's dedication to the cause of human rights, entailed some danger. How many of you know that Leo had clothes specially tailored to facilitate the smuggling of important materials back and forth? That wasn't simply an impetuous James Bond lark; one didn't risk tangling with the KGB without a lot of forethought. But Leo went ahead because of the depth of his convictions. And he took those risks. And he was successful. And thank God he was unharmed.

We can only stand in awe of such people who are not content with simply being bystanders to the passage of history, but are determined to shape that history, and to do so for the principles of democracy, human rights, and individual dignity.

One is tempted to ask what the world would look like, what our country would look like, what our communities would look like, if there were more such indivduals like Leo in our midst. Sad to say, there are too few.

Still, enormous progress has been achieved on so many fronts over the past fifty years. With all of the challenges and, yes, tragedies that face us each day as we read the morning newspaper or watch the evening television news, we still know that we are living in an extraordinarily exciting and promising era, with the reach of freedom extended farther than ever before and with the possibilities of peaceful coexistence within the grasp of more and more countries.

Leo's life to date—and given his remarkable energy level, the many years ahead—are testament to the ability of one man to make an impact on this world of ours, inspired by his heritage, encouraged by a loving family, confident of the course on which he has set out.

Leo, I salute you tonight and wish you the continued success that has enriched us all.

So, What's in a Name Anyway?
Washington Jewish Week
July 25, 1996

Nine years ago, I had a letter in the *Washington Jewish Week* that began as follows: "I must share a problem which has plagued me much of my life—my name. No, don't misunderstand me. I really do like it. In fact, it's such a nice name that, according to the phone books, 23 others in my native Manhattan share it, 19 in my current home, Montgomery County, and 16 in the District of Columbia, where I work. And that's the problem.

"Actually, I've lost count of the number of times I've been asked: 'Are you the real David Harris?' Often, the questioner has David Harris, the former husband of Joan Baez and a well-known 1960s student activist, in mind. Or perhaps David Harris, the respected photographer. Or another one of my worthy namesakes."

At the time, there was yet another David Harris, who, like me, enjoyed submitting letters to the various Washington papers, including this one, which prompted the above-quoted paragraph. You see, the problem was his views were usually diametrically opposed to mine, which often got me in trouble.

So I left Washington and moved back to New York. Okay, there were other reasons, too, but I figured maybe I'd get a fresh start in the Big Apple.

Imagine my surprise, then, when we moved into our new home and unfamiliar mail began arriving—bills, cruise tickets, alumni solicitations—all addressed to, you guessed it, David Harris. Why?

It turns out that our next-door neighbor was none other than David Harris, a retired businessman, and the mailman was confused. (By the way, if you're curious, I returned the bills and solicitations but kept the cruise tickets.)

Having successfully persuaded this David Harris and his wife to move, I thought I might finally be home free, at least in my own personal and professional corner of the world, but alas, no such luck.

To my utter dismay, *Washington Jewish Week* just carried a story announcing the appointment of the new Washington representative of the American Jewish Congress. His name? David A. Harris.

Now this is really serious. It's not just the first and last names this time, but the middle initial as well, plus, *oy vay iz mir*, an organizational affiliation that shares the very same initials as my own.

What do I now do? Take credit for every intelligent statement he is sure to make? Suggest that we each use our social security number or date of birth every time our name appears somewhere? Or, best of all perhaps, lobby President Bill Clinton to quickly name him to a diplomatic post in Mongolia?

Yes, frankly, I prefer this idea. Otherwise, how could I ever claim I'm the "real" David Harris the next time someone in our overlapping worlds asks?

P.S. Seriously, good luck, David A. Harris, in your exciting new post (the one in Washington, that is, not Ulan Bator)!

Ruth Goddard's 95th Birthday Bash
New York
September 9, 1996

There is the story of the KGB agent, let's call her Irina Ivanova, who was trained in intelligence and sent to Tel Aviv with a new name, Sarah Goldberg. Her instructions were to rent an apartment, lead as normal a life as possible, and wait for another KGB agent to contact her with the code words "The roses are red."

Ivanova, now Sarah Goldberg, gets established in a Tel Aviv apartment building and several years pass with no contact.

One day, the KGB in Moscow, having decided to activate her, sends another agent, Boris Petrov, to Tel Aviv. Petrov arrives and heads straight for the apartment building, but alas, to his dismay, he sees three separate Sarah Goldbergs listed in the building directory.

Not having been given an apartment number, he has no choice but to risk it. Ringing the first Sarah Goldberg listed, he hears a woman's voice and he says, "The roses are red." The voice back replies: "Oh, you want Sarah Goldberg the Soviet spy. She's in apartment 4B."

The moral of this story, of course, is that there aren't many secrets in an intimate community like Israel. And there aren't all that many here in our own intimate community either. And on an occasion like this there shouldn't be and there probably won't be.

For Ruth Goddard is well known to each of us in this room. She's beloved by each of us. That's why we're here, and that's why there are those of you in this room who've flown long distances to be part of the celebration.

Each of us has been touched by Ruth, ennobled by her, enriched by her. Each of us has our own stories to tell. You remember the opening of that old TV program—what was it called, *The Naked City?*—"New York City, eight million people, eight million stories."

Well, here in this room are nearly three hundred people and I daresay three hundred stories that could be told about Ruth—about her absolutely unique combination of *yikhes* and *yiddishkeit*, of acumen and activism, of philanthropy and flair, of leadership and largesse, of courage, yes, real courage, and commitment, and not least, most certainly not least, of humanity and heart.

Much will be said about Ruth from this podium tonight and deservedly so. After all, this is a celebration of an extraordinary ninety-five years in the life of an individual who has always aspired to the challenge of the legendary Jewish philosopher, Spinoza—"To be what we are and to become what we are capable of becoming is the only worthy thing in life."

Speaking on behalf of the AJC staff, I want to talk directly to you, Ruth, for just a moment, though if others in this room overhear me I won't in the least mind.

I can only say, however inadequately, Ruth, that we are deeply, and I mean deeply, deeply grateful to you for the incalculably rich fifty years of involvement you have given us at every level, in every imaginable way:

- as a founder of the Women's Campaign Board, which has prospered so magnificently over the years with your continued leadership, often visible, sometimes invisible, but always there, always setting new goals, always believing there's still more that can be done with just a bit more effort on everyone's part;

- as a national vice president of AJC, the second woman, incidentally, ever to hold this honored post;
- as an honorary vice president, the first woman to be so recognized;
- as a long-standing member of the national Board of Governors;
- and many more titles too, but most importantly, as a constant voice of conscience, of candor—and, as all of you know Ruth well, you know that candor in Ruth's case is not an afterthought, it's her trademark. Hers is a voice of genuine and all-too-rare independence of mind and spirit.

Ruth, thank you for these fifty years and for the years yet to come. On behalf of all us on AJC's staff who've been honored to work with you, who've learned so much from you, who've been constantly challenged by you to ever greater heights of excellence, let me shout from the rooftops our heartfelt *mazel tov* on this joyous occasion.

And, though I said earlier there aren't many secrets around, let me share with you, Ruth, and all those gathered here this little secret: We're all looking forward to getting together with you for your hundredth as well, and lots of occasions in between.

Ruth, we love you.

On the Fifth Anniversary
of the AJC-Project Interchange Merger
AJC 91st Annual Meeting, Washington, D.C.
May 6, 1997

Six years ago, Debbie Berger, Project Interchange's longtime leader, came to me, a glint in her eye, and said she had an idea she wanted to discuss. And not only was I delighted with the opportunity presented to AJC by Debbie's initiative to merge our two organizations, but also I was deeply touched by the confidence she showed in

AJC becoming the permanent home of such a unique treasure as Project Interchange.

I hope and trust you will agree with me that we have justified the confidence of Debbie and her colleagues who made the decision at that time. To me, it's a natural fit. There is a shared, profound commitment to Israel; an unflinching dedication to strengthening U.S.-Israel relations; a confidence that Israel can and should be shown as it really is, that it will more than withstand the exposure to visitors of a range of viewpoints; and a recognition of the importance of dealing intelligently and sensitively with key sectors of political, ethnic, religious, and civic America. That's what AJC is all about; that's what Project Interchange is all about.

We marked our fifth anniversary earlier this year, and I feel as if Project Interchange has always been a central part of the AJC family and, frankly, can't imagine us without it.

As I wrote to Lisa Eisen, the project's executive director, just a few weeks ago to mark the auspicious occasion of our anniversary, and please excuse my hubris in quoting myself, though I understand it to be an especially common practice in Washington: "Project Interchange is an unquestioned jewel in the AJC crown. We could not be more proud of the essential work you do in advancing understanding of Israel among key American target groups, or the consummately professional manner in which the work is done. The preliminary results of the Project Interchange Seminar Participants Study ... provide impressive documentation on both counts.

"As we look ahead, the compelling need for Project Interchange surely remains undiminished; to the contrary, still more importance will be attached to the program. Working together, we shall do our utmost to ensure that Project Interchange remains fully able to meet the challenges before it and, in so doing, enjoys the support of the entire AJC international, national, and local network."

Project Interchange's reach has been enhanced substantially by the merger. Moreover, AJC's vital work concerning Israel, which is in fact without parallel in its breadth and depth, has taken a quantum leap forward as a result of this partnership. What lies ahead? Clearly, challenges, but opportunities as well.

For one thing, I want to be sure that each and every one of AJC's thirty-two chapters is directly involved in the seminars of Project Interchange and also in the follow-up with participants once a seminar is over. And that follow-up, of course, needs to sustain the Israel connection and, at the same time, widen and deepen the link to include other potentially overlapping areas of concern with AJC, most often in the domestic and intergroup arenas.

For another, I hope to see more and more AJC lay people, our members, become familiar with the Project Interchange program and seek opportunities for involvement, in addition to their other areas of AJC engagement. Many of these members, I believe, would find much satisfaction in participating in the Project Interchange effort; and knowing many of these members as I do, I am sure that Project Interchange would be the beneficiary of an ever greater pool of talent and commitment.

Third, it is my desire, and I've made no secret of it, to offer Project Interchange assistance with its year-to-year fund-raising efforts, including the longer term desirability of endowing major chunks of the program, if not the naming of the project itself. At this point, a word of praise, however insufficient, is certainly in order for Kathy Hiryok for her tenacious, if always elegant, efforts in the area of fund-raising.

Surely, there are potential benefactors out there who would find the program sufficiently attractive, tangible, and compelling to consider providing major support.

Just think, for half a million dollars, a donor could assure in perpetuity an annual seminar in Israel for ten distinguished Americans in a given field. That is a real contribution to the vital task of strengthening understanding and support for Israel in this country. I wish I were in a position to do it myself, so persuaded am I by my own words!

And fourth, I would like to see us sit down together and look at whether there are other programming ideas that might complement those already in existence. For example, is it logistically feasible to think about new initiatives, perhaps bringing to Israel influentials from third countries in which AJC has a stake, or possibly considering other emerging target groups in the United States that need exposure to Israel?

In this respect, I applaud Stanford Adelstein, who is, as you well know, a member of the AJC Board of Governors and vice chairman of the Project Interchange national board, for doing just that—identifying student body presidents from major Midwestern colleges and universities on the premise that they tend to show up disproportionately later in life in key political positions—and providing the financial means to conduct this program year after year. And this is of course but one example.

Since we are celebrating our sapphire anniversary this year, I thought about an appropriate gift to mark such an auspicious occasion. In the end, I came up with America's most successful contribution to gift-giving—the T-shirt! I wish time and production facilities had permitted a T-shirt for everyone in this room, but alas, I have but three to offer today and I would like to present them to three very deserving people—Debbie Berger, Lois Zoller, and Lisa Eisen. As you will see, the logo reads: "AJC and Project Interchange, The way a merger was meant to be!"

I wish you all a very productive and successful meeting today and hope you will understand if I cannot stay throughout. Like the proverbial Hungarian salami, I'm being sliced very thinly this week.

Tribute to Hyman Bookbinder[*]
AJC 91st Annual Meeting, Washington, D.C.
May 8, 1997

To a heathen who came to him to be converted on condition that he teach him the entire Torah "while standing on one foot," Rabbi Hillel, as we know, replied: "What is hateful to you, do not unto your neighbor; this is the entire Torah, all the rest is commentary."

To those who come to the American Jewish Committee and ask us to describe the organization in twenty-five words or less, often finding us tongue-tied in our inability to do so quite that succinctly, let me suggest that the next time you stand on one foot and reply: "The American

*Washington representative emeritus of the American Jewish Committee.

Jewish Committee is Hyman Bookbinder; all the rest, I can't resist saying, is *Commentary!*"

And indeed AJC is Bookie—larger than life Bookie; the Bookie who valiantly struggled back from a nightmarish medical ordeal; the permanently youthful Bookie; the ever engaged Bookie, whatever the issue; the Bookie who has always focused on both the universal and the particular and the nexus between the two; the Bookie who has never stopped dreaming of a better world or stopped working toward it; the Bookie ever mindful of history but never paralyzed by it; the Bookie who could with one hand call the secretary of defense and with the other stuff envelopes for our Soviet Jewry rally; the Bookie who could be in the White House one minute meeting top officials and be in front the next joining a demonstration; the Bookie who would make latkes for Hanukkah and walk the picket line at the South African embassy on Christmas Day; the Bookie talking Middle East policy at 3 p.m. in Israel and dancing on the tarmac of Ben-Gurion Airport at 3 a.m.

I am so thrilled that when we opened our new Washington office, we could name the conference center there in his honor as a permanent reminder of Bookie's presence in our midst and incalculable contribution to our work.

And I am so thrilled today that we can bestow this prestigious award, AJC's highest for its very own, on this truly extraordinary man, a man I am pleased and proud to call a mentor and a friend, a man all of us on the staff of AJC consider the role model of the Jewish communal professional.

Life Devoted to Protecting Rights of Jews
The New York Times
June 29, 1997

David A. Harris grew up on the West Side in Manhattan in the '50s hearing firsthand accounts from his father and mother and many aunts, uncles, and neighbors of their lives under communism and how they later escaped the Nazis.

Since 1990 Mr. Harris, 47 and a resident of Chappaqua, has been executive director of the American Jewish Committee and has worked on such issues as Jewish emigration from the former Soviet Union, preservation of Nazi death camps, reparations for Jewish victims of the Holocaust, and ways to prevent the sale of nuclear technology to terrorist countries.

Here are excerpts from a recent conversation with Mr. Harris:

Q. How did you get into this line of work?

A. All my relatives came from Europe and were either refugees once under communism or twice under communism and Nazism. My mother was from France, had come there from Moscow (with her family) to what they thought was safety; through the occupation of France, she hid and managed to escape with her family across the border to Spain and eventually reached the United States during the war. My father was born in Budapest, was raised in Berlin and Vienna, and joined the French Foreign Legion in 1940 because the French army would not accept him as a foreign Jew. When France fell in June 1940, he spent three years in a special Vichy regime camp in southern Algeria working in the coal mines, then managed to escape and came to Algiers. Eventually, the OSS—the American espionage service—got wind of a single-minded, native-speaking German Jew who was eager to go back behind enemy lines and fight the rest of the war there.

This is the kind of family I came from. My aunts and uncles and grandparents and neighbors each had similar stories. Happenstance played a role when I went to work for the American Field Service, an international educational exchange organization, after graduate school. While there from 1972 to '74, two things happened: I noticed the AFS program did not have Israel among the countries in the exchange program and found out this was the price the organization seemed willing to pay for the inclusion of Arab countries. The other thing was the 1973 Yom Kippur War. In the first days, Israel was pushed back, and suddenly many people, myself included, began to ask the previously unfathomable question: what if Israel were really destroyed? I realized it meant a great deal to me, so much so that I wanted to go to Israel to do what I could with the Israeli army. But they turned me down because I'm the sole surviving son—I didn't know they had some restrictions. Had I known, I would have lied.

Q. How did you get involved with Soviet Jewry?

A. About the same time, Soviet Jews began arriving in the United States as refugees. As a second job in the evening here in the city, I began to teach English as a foreign language to refugees and immigrants, and increasingly Russian Jews were among them. I was very much drawn to the Russian Jews and, in 1974, became a teacher in the Soviet Union in a U.S.-Soviet exchange program. I was drawn to the synagogues there because they became symbols of Jewish resistance. They also became gathering places for the KGB. I became more and more involved with families that invited me to their homes. As a result, I was eventually detained, and at the end of 1974 I was expelled from the country.

But that determined my career direction. In 1975 I began working in Rome, one of the two transit points in Europe for Soviet Jews. Rome had an additional benefit—I met my wife, who was a member of the small Libyan Jewish community that resettled in Rome after the Six-Day War.

Q. You were later denied a visa to Russia. Why?

A. In 1981 I was allowed back in to attend the Moscow International Book Fair, representing Jewish book publishers. We brought several thousand books, records, calendars in Hebrew, Yiddish, Russian, and English. At one point, we were being so heavily monitored by the KGB, which was seeking to restrict access to our small exhibit space, that I protested to the director of the book fair. We had a bit of a squabble. I was detained by the KGB upon my departure and was warned that I had violated rules and regulations and would not be allowed back.

Nine years later, as things began to ease up in the Soviet Union, I was allowed back in. Yet last year when I applied for a visa, thinking no more about it than if I were traveling to Canada, I was refused. The State Department made inquiries and was told it was due to my (past) political activity. Eventually, forty-five members of Congress wrote to Boris Yeltsin protesting it, and I got a visa this year.

Q. You are involved with issues relating to reparations for Nazi war victims. What aspect are you concerned with?

A. Our current focus is on the fact that the Jewish survivors of the Holocaust living in the former communist countries of Eastern Europe were never eligible for German pensions, unlike Jewish survivors living elsewhere. After the collapse of communism, we began to involve ourselves in this issue, seeking from the German government pensions comparable to survivors elsewhere. But to our surprise, we ran into a road block. They simply drew the line here. On top of this, we learned that veterans of the Third Reich from Eastern Europe who were wounded are eligible for pensions. So, believe it or not, you have real-life situations where the Jewish survivors of the Holocaust are receiving nothing, and their neighbors, the perpetrators, are receiving monthly checks from the German government. We grew so frustrated that we took out newspaper ads focusing on the injustice of this. The upper house in Germany recently adopted a law to drop pensions for Nazi war criminals. If that is enacted, it only addresses part of our concern.

Q. You are active in negotiations to preserve the Auschwitz-Birkenau death camp complex in Poland. Describe the problem.

A. You have the general problem in Europe of seeking to preserve the physical integrity of the concentration camps as permanent and lasting monuments and also ensuring that each of the camps will adequately convey the true history of what took place there. The history has often become highly politicized. For example, the camps in eastern Germany reflected an entirely different history because they were under communist rule. The communists wrote the history as if they were the principal victims.

In Auschwitz and Birkenau we have an additional problem. While Auschwitz has become synonymous with the Holocaust, it was actually the adjoining camp called Birkenau, otherwise known as Auschwitz II, which was the principal killing center for Jews. Over the years, religious symbols have been introduced into the camps by private (Polish Catholic) citizens or groups. The religious symbols have been largely crosses, but a few Stars of David have also been placed there. You have really a difficult and thorny issue: about 100,000 Polish Catholics were killed at Auschwitz by the Nazis and over 1 million Jews. In the Polish Catholic tradition, one honors death in part through religious symbols. But for Jews, to see those religious symbols—the crosses—on the killing fields of Birkenau is very problematic because it blurs distinctions and confuses, and, in some cases, quite frankly, it offends.

This has become a very sensitive issue, and it has blown up at times. About a year ago, Elie Wiesel said publicly, "Remove the crosses," which caused a great furor in Poland. You have the clash of two groups that both were victims of Nazism but cannot find a solution to how to mark or commemorate the deaths.

Q. What is your role?

A. An international group has been created that includes the American Jewish Committee. We were invited by the government of Poland to work together to find a solution. In March, four principal negotiators from the Jewish side, including myself, traveled to Warsaw and Auschwitz for three days of intensive meetings with local authorities and the people who live in the neighborhoods around the camps. The meetings have continued in Washington. The Jewish community is seeking the removal of all religious symbols. At the same time we are pressing for—and the Polish government has been very cooperative about this—a master plan to ensure the permanent preservation of the camps and to avoid in the future the kinds of controversies that have occurred. You may, for example, remember a proposal to build a super-market on the edge of Auschwitz.

I'm fairly optimistic that we will find a solution to the problems that now divide us.

AJC Insider's Letter II[*]
August 4, 1998

Since its founding in 1906, AJC has sought to make a difference.

As you well know, we work to shape American and international public policy and affect the course of Jewish history. To accomplish such ambitious goals, good intentions and a compelling mission statement are insufficient. A special mix of organizational traits is needed.

It takes dedicated leadership and talented staff; a long-term and sophisticated approach that recognizes the complexity and changing nature of issues; an awareness that issues always take precedence over institutional ego; a carefully calibrated balance between public advocacy and private diplomacy; ready access to officials in decision-mak-

*Cosigned with AJC's president, Bruce Ramer.

ing positions; high standing in the general community; the ability to build broad coalitions; and a reputation for integrity, credibility, and reason.

It won't surprise you that in listing these criteria, we have the American Jewish Committee very much in mind. These are precisely the attributes that explain why the *New York Times* referred to us as "the dean of American Jewish organizations," or why Reuters called us "one of the world's most influential Jewish organizations," or, most recently, why Leslie Wexner, chairman of The Limited, Inc., and a major Jewish philanthropist, described us as "the premier Jewish organization in the United States, if not the world."

Over the past fifty years alone, AJC has played a central role in addressing many of the most daunting and compelling issues of our time as Americans and Jews. In doing so, we have made a difference, a significant difference.

Space does not permit us to go into detail in this letter. But since we all sometimes run the risk of losing sight of the bigger picture, permit us to briefly recall several of the key issues where we've truly made a difference in the postwar era.

(1) The positive revolution in Christian-Jewish relations in this country and around the world, and the more recent promising efforts to forge ties with other major world religions;

(2) The marginalization of anti-Semitism in democratic societies, including, most notably, the removal of the systemic barriers to full Jewish participation in all arenas of American society, and the widespread recognition by American Jews today that the Diaspora experience in this country is entirely without precedent in the annals of Jewish history;

(3) The imprint of the Holocaust on the world's conscience, lest it otherwise over time be forgotten, relativized, trivialized, or denied, and the determination to seek some measure of justice, however inadequate, however belated, for the survivors;

(4) The introduction of international human rights standards—and the monitoring of those standards by governments, multilateral institutions, and nongovernmental organizations—in the wake of the horrors of the Second World War;

(5) The development of a remarkable network of ties between American Jewry and Israel, the two largest Jewish communities in the world, which, even with the occasional tensions, has had a profound and enduring impact on both sides of the ocean;

(6) The building of an unparalleled bilateral relationship between the United States and Israel and a high degree of American public support for that link;

(7) The rescue of endangered Jews in the former Soviet Union and other communist lands, in Ethiopia and Iran, and in Arab countries, sending the clear message that, contrary to the situation before 1945, no Jew anywhere in the world need ever feel alone or without support;

(8) An America actively promoting democracy, the rule of law, and human rights protections around the world, checking the threat of rogue states, seeking peaceful conflict resolution, and, when necessary, projecting military might and the resolve to use it;

(9) An America that has traveled light-years in this past half century in dismantling the legal and other barriers to full participation by all its citizens; an America that is more inclusive, more compassionate, and more genuinely pluralistic than it once was, even as it passes through seismic sociodemographic changes;

(10) An America that, despite periodic challenges, has managed to preserve the fundamental balance between the "establishment" and "separation" provisions in our Bill of Rights, ensuring, at the very same time, the unparalleled freedom of religion in America and the separation of church and state.

This country and the Jewish people have both come a very long way in this past half century. AJC can be justifiably proud of our role—in big ways and small, up front and behind the scenes—in working with policy makers, engaging in legislative and court battles, educating the Jewish and general publics, and helping forge the coalitions that achieved these landmark gains.

But, at the risk of stating the painfully obvious, there can be no room for complacency. With all the remarkable progress already achieved, we cannot let down our guard. Constant vigilance and initiative are required both to protect what has been accomplished and to expand upon it.

In the months ahead, we will be focusing in our letters, as we have in the past, on specific areas of AJC activity. On this occasion, though, against the backdrop of a particularly busy and productive period in the agency's life, we wanted to share with you several examples of our impact in a number of areas.

• When the new Israeli ambassador to the United Nations, Dore Gold, took up his post, he paid a visit to the White House. As he recounted the story to us, he asked a senior White House official about the role of American Jewry on the political scene here and how the administration took the pulse of the Jewish community. The response from the official, and we are quoting Ambassador Gold, was that "we watch carefully what the American Jewish Committee says and does."

• When the U.S. State Department called in all of its ambassadors from North Africa and the Middle East for a three-day conference on the region, together with top government officials based in Washington, one two-hour session was devoted to the role of the American Jewish and Arab communities in influencing decision-making. AJC was chosen to represent the American Jewish perspective.

• When the Educational Testing Service (home of the legendary SATs) convened an off-the-record two-day colloquium on the complex issues of testing, race, intergroup relations, and higher education, they invited just twenty people, including the presidents of Princeton University, the American Council on Education, the College Board, the National Urban League, the NAACP Legal Defense Fund, and a leader of AJC, the only Jewish organization asked to participate.

• When LULAC, the leading Latino organization in the United States, held its annual meeting in Dallas attended by 6,000 delegates, it was an AJC representative who was asked to speak, joined by representatives of the African American and Asian American communities, on the politics of unity and coalition-building.

• When Japanese Americans sought to organize an exhibit at Ellis Island on the internment of 120,000 Japanese Americans during World War II, and sparked controversy by referring to "America's concentration camps" in the title, AJC convened Jewish and Japanese American leaders, including Senator Daniel Inouye, to find an acceptable compromise. As a result of our successful efforts, AJC was accorded the honor of being the only non–Japanese American organization invited to speak at the gala opening of the exhibit.

• Consistent with our pioneering intergroup relations agenda, AJC's Belfer Center sponsored a day-long "ethnic summit" with the leadership of the rapidly growing Korean American community, and has scheduled a similar summit with the Latino leadership for this December.

• While many nations, including Argentina, Norway, and Switzerland, established historical commissions to examine their role in the Second World War and its aftermath, the three Baltic states— Estonia, Latvia, and Lithuania—balked. But with prodding from AJC—an organization trusted in the region in part because of our early support for Baltic independence—commissions have now been created. In fact, the formal government announcements not only cited the AJC effort but also stipulated a special consultative role for us.

• When Polish prime minister Jerzy Buzek came to Washington as a guest of Vice President Gore, the Polish leader, in his public remarks, singled out AJC for our vital support of NATO expansion to include the Czech Republic, Hungary, and Poland. Indeed, at the luncheon hosted by the vice president, AJC was the only national Jewish organization invited to attend.

• This close link with Poland also paid off when Poland, which traditionally follows the European Union's lead on UN voting, broke with the EU and became one of only fourteen countries unwilling to support the upgrading of the PLO's status at the UN. Poland's ambassador to the UN has privately noted AJC's role in his country's voting decision.

• When President Clinton visited Berlin in honor of the fiftieth anniversary of the Berlin Airlift, German chancellor Kohl, in his formal welcoming remarks to the president, cited the work of two organizations in building ties between Germany and the United States—the American Academy, a cultural organization devoted to German-American relations, and the AJC.

• Further on the diplomatic front, this summer has been anything but quiet. Among the many world leaders we have met with are the foreign ministers of Egypt and Qatar, the defense ministers of Germany and Greece, the immediate past prime minister of India, the mayor of

Berlin, the Swiss ambassador responsible for wartime claims, and delegations from Germany, Japan, and Poland.

• In the fall, we will be gearing up for our annual "diplomatic marathon" when world leaders come to New York for the opening of the UN General Assembly. Last year, we held forty-six private, bilateral meetings with presidents, prime ministers, and foreign ministers. Discussion topics included local Jewish communities, Israel, international terrorism, rogue states and nonconventional weapons proliferation, and human rights.

• Speaking of human rights, this is the fiftieth anniversary year of the signing of the Universal Declaration of Human Rights. AJC's Jacob Blaustein Institute for the Advancement of Human Rights has taken the lead, among a remarkable coalition of human rights and other civic agencies, in marking this auspicious occasion by educating the public about the importance of human rights advocacy. One result has been the publication of a critically acclaimed book, *In Your Hands*, which seeks to advance these goals. A copy was given to the First Lady, Hillary Clinton, at a ceremony in New York.

This small sample of our recent work indicates the broad scope and powerful impact of our agency. Our programs are designed to ensure that, in the next fifty years, we will build on the achievements of the past fifty—and indeed the past ninety-two.

Presentation to the AJC Budget Committee
New York
August 12, 1998

Ron Weiner has asked me to provide a larger context for your consideration of this year's budget submission. I'm pleased to do just that.

I'd like to use this occasion to review the five management goals that we established for ourselves eight years ago and that remain operative to this day. Each is reflected in one way or another in this budget, either directly or indirectly. Also, I'd like to talk more specifically about one or two elements of this particular budget because it's quite different from previous budgets, as you surely will have noticed.

First, when this management team came into place in 1990, our foremost goal was, unquestionably, to restore the financial stability of the organization. I need not review for this group the fiscal health or, should I say, ill health of the agency at the time. It is all too familiar to each of you. What is worth recalling, if only for a moment, is the critical role played by Shula Bahat, on the staff side, in ensuring the agency's successful navigation of those potentially lethal shoals.

What's the record been since 1990?

As the result of a synergistic lay–staff partnership reflecting a remarkably deep commitment to this agency, we have enjoyed eight consecutive years of campaign growth.

We have experienced eight consecutive years of expenses under budget.

Consequently, we have had eight consecutive years of budgets in balance or, for that matter, in surplus.

We are, as all of you know, entirely debt free and, in fact, became debt free two years ahead of the schedule established in the wake of St. Petersburg in 1990.

In addition, in the last several years we have received nearly $11 million in gifts to the organization outside our regular campaign, which has permitted us a certain amount of controlled growth in both programming and capital development.

Lastly, however we define "endowments," and it's clearly going to be an ongoing topic of discussion as illustrated by our review of it this month, the fact is you can see the encouraging direction in which we're headed. Increasing the restricted, temporarily restricted, and unrestricted endowment funds of AJC is a top priority, and, fortunately, we have progress to show on all three fronts.

The second goal has been to rebuild and enhance the agency's physical infrastructure with three particular objectives in mind: (a) increased safety and security of the facilities; (b) enhanced staff productivity and morale; and (c) improved institutional image consistent with the high-level nature of our work.

Eight years later, I can say that we have made significant strides.

We're more than halfway through the refurbishing of our headquarters building here in New York, made possible by a wonderful initial grant from Barbara and David Hirschhorn and the Blaustein Foundation. Incidentally, one of the things I'm most proud of in this refurbishing is that on the three working floors completed to date (third, seventh, and eighth), of the roughly fifty employees affected all but two have direct access to natural light.

Thanks to the generosity of Al Moses and his family, we have acquired a magnificently renovated building in the center of Jerusalem. Moreover, we now have appropriate representational offices in Washington, D.C.

And, of course, we have a ten-year, rent-free lease arrangement in the heart of the new Berlin.

We have moved those chapter offices that were located in once desirable but now deteriorating neighborhoods, where area directors feared walking after dark, even as far as the adjoining parking lot. It has been a high priority to ensure that our thirty-two chapter offices are located where our members live or work, so they are easily reached and in the safest possible settings.

The third goal has been to make a dent in that seemingly permanently vexing issue of why this organization was for so many years the best kept secret in Jewish life. Or, put most simply, why is it that so many people who should know what we do, don't?

We have invested heavily in explaining who we are to a broader audience, which obviously complements and reinforces our fund-raising, leadership development, membership, and political advocacy efforts. We think we've achieved some notable success in underscoring the centrality of our work to the well-being of American and world Jewry.

Our principal tools have been frequent advertisements in the *New York Times* and other leading media outlets (including cost-sharing incentives to the chapters to place ads locally), direct mail, the World Wide Web, annual reports, insider letters, the bimonthly *AJC Journal*, the AJC films produced by CBS that are now available, and both updated and new institutional publications.

By the way, I mentioned direct mail. Overcoming our inhibitions about direct mail, we launched an effort last December based on AJC's leadership regarding the United Nations/WEOG issue. We've since gained 12,000 new supporters, experienced a surprisingly high response rate of 3–4 percent, and turned a profit in the process. The potential for expanding our reach may be far greater than we had previously realized.

As we go forward, we're trying to understand the intersection of emerging opportunities in technology, marketing, media, and education, as elements of the new communications, and we are investing quite heavily in information technology throughout the agency.

In today's dramatically fast paced and rapidly changing world, how does an institution like ours most effectively reach people? How does it transmit images and messages in real time and in such a way that it stands out from the information overload and communications cacophony of our era?

To give you only one illustration, in a breakfast meeting that I had last December with Sandy Sigoloff, a member of our Board of Governors from Los Angeles and a professor at UCLA's School of Business, he told me that the school today is an entirely paperless institution. Moreover, he noted, young people entering the MBA program spend one month—prior to their first semester—in a special program on technology and graphic presentations. That's how important the school believes the visual element is now in the world of business.

By such cutting-edge standards, we are, may I say, slightly behind. I trust I can reveal that institutional secret to the people in this room. You won't jump ship, I'm sure, but the truth is we are behind. We are trying to catch up as best we can.

Those of you who were at the AJC capital budget meeting earlier this morning, for example, heard Shula report on our efforts to substantially upgrade our website. In the same spirit, in searching for a new public relations director we are looking for someone who not only has a traditional media orientation but also grasps these broader communications challenges and, yes, unparalleled opportunities.

One such opportunity, long overdue, is to reach important Jewish audiences in places where we do not now have chapters. How can we afford to write off increasingly large and important segments of the American Jewish community who no longer choose to live in one of our thirty-two chapter cities? Obviously, we neither can nor should.

Fourth, we have sought to sharpen our focus on the core issues that we as an agency believe are the defining issues for us as American Jews. Many of you will recall that in the '80s the agency began to drift. AJC became a bit like a magnetic field that was attracting everyone's favorite issue, to the point where we became so diverse as to become diffuse.

While we were certainly doing important work then, the organization—always a challenge, even in the best of times, to describe in a sound bite—no longer projected a central message or a defined set of priorities. We were spending as much or as little time on anti-Semitism, it seemed, as we were on some issues far removed from the core agenda. As a result, it was not always clear what we stood for or, I might add, how firmly we stood.

We have sought in the last eight years to sharpen our focus a great deal more—in the public image we project, the issues with which we grapple, and the allocation of staff resources.

To illustrate: If you have followed our ads over the last eight years, you've seen three overarching themes. One has been Israel and the Middle East, the second Jewish identity and renewal, and the third the struggle for pluralism and against intolerance, bigotry, and anti-Semitism. We've very consciously tried hard not to stray far from these three tracks.

And the last of our five management goals has been to avail ourselves of the possibilities for controlled growth, made possible both by the extra-campaign gifts received and recent budget surpluses.

Ron Weiner has encouraged us in this direction, especially in light of the impressive 1997–98 numbers. Therefore, you will see, as you go through the budget, an attempt to respond to this welcome turn of events.

We have placed special emphasis on two areas in particular. One is fund-raising, because we believe that our development efforts must stay ahead of program expansion, not the other way around, though, understandably, there's an interdependence between the two.

What are the growth-oriented fund-raising priorities? Three in particular—planned giving, major gifts, and regional expansion.

I don't have to speak to you about planned giving. As they say, it's a no-brainer. We've been slow off the mark. We had some trouble with staffing issues in the last couple of years. In this budget, we've devoted a lot of resources to planned giving because we recognize its enormous potential for an organization like ours.

Major gifts, again, is a no-brainer. We've had success. I mentioned the $11-million figure in the last several years, and it can, with nurturing, go still higher.

The third of the fund-raising goals is enhanced regionalization, because to a large degree there are untapped resources around the country, and also we are dangerously dependent now on the success of the New York campaign. While we've been very pleased with the steady upward trend in the New York campaign, the field, with very few exceptions, has not kept pace.

The second emphasis in this new budget is on chapters. Parenthetically, I should note that even in the worst of times we went to great lengths to protect the chapters. As a result, the chapter staff was proportionately far less affected by the St. Petersburg decisions than, say, the national program departments.

In the 1996–97 and 1997–98 budgets, we added one new professional staff position per annum in the field (Atlanta and New York). This year we have included two new professional positions. I suspect you will ask where, but I'd rather not comment on placement for the time being, except to say that the decision will be made, as always, only after close consultation with the Community Services Department.

The regionalization of fund-raising should be seen not only in development terms but also, if you will, as chapter "relief."

When a fund-raiser is added in Seattle, as is the case in this new budget, the chapter director will then be able to devote much more of her time to leadership and membership recruitment, program enrichment, political advocacy, and media relations—all the elements of a chapter director's job that run the risk of getting shortchanged because of the constant drumbeat of the importance of annual in-house events and plate dinners.

Once the regional fund-raising positions provided for in this new budget are filled, a total of thirteen of our thirty-two chapters will be covered in one way or another: Chicago and Los Angeles (with two fund-raisers each), Washington, Boston, Houston, and Dallas (the latter two share a fund-raiser), Boca Raton/Palm Beach and Miami (which will share a fund-raiser), Seattle, Sarasota/Tampa, New York (which is assisted by the New York Campaign), and Atlanta and New Jersey (both of which opted for a third professional staff member in lieu of a fund-raiser, with the chapter director agreeing to assume responsibility for an expanded campaign). Moreover, our Kansas City chapter is in a special arrangement with the local CRC that precludes separate fund-raising. In all, that's actually fourteen chapters.

I should add that the fund-raisers establish annual campaign goals in consultation with our department, and their job performances are measured largely by their ability to meet these goals.

Our management aim, however, is not necessarily the placement of a fund-raiser in each of our thirty-two chapters, though we don't preclude that either. It may well be more important to beef up certain offices, in Florida for instance, rather than mechanically placing fund-raisers in one AJC office after another. In other words, it may yield us a far greater return to have two or even three fund-raisers in a particular AJC office even if it means having no fund-raisers, for the foreseeable future, in another office.

Apart from the new positions created in fund-raising and the chapters, we have also allowed for some growth in programmatic staff.

We need the expertise to follow what's going on in the Arab and Muslim worlds, both here at home and abroad. We need the ability, largely missing until now, to begin to really sort out who's who and what's what in these worlds. We have to have some independent means of determining what groups and individuals are—and are not—appropriate dialogue and coalition partners.

We're also expanding our legislative operation in Washington. We are doing wonderfully effective work in this area, especially regarding domestic policy issues. This effort needs to be strengthened still further. With the new team of a legislative director, an assistant legislative director, and an administrative assistant, we're taking an important step in that direction. I would also point out that this unit works especially closely with the chapters in its advocacy initiatives.

Another way we've sought to extend our overall output is by out-sourcing more and more of our research and publications. In the past, much of it, though certainly not all, was done in house. No longer. This new approach has proved efficient and cost effective, and has been particularly felt in the international arena.

Finally in regard to our planned growth, I should say a word about our institutional partnerships. In an era of growing corporate mergers and strategic alliances, AJC must explore possible opportunities in our sector as well, all the more so in light of the dramatic changes at hand in the Jewish organizational world—downsizing, consolidations, mergers, shifts—including generational—in the patterns of Jewish giving, and the emergence of more "boutique" Jewish organizations.

It's virtually impossible these days to be a public speaker in America and avoid any reference to sports, so let me say that we're batting .600 on this front.

We successfully merged with Project Interchange and entered into fruitful partnerships with the London-based Institute for Jewish Policy Research (JPR) and the Australia/Israel Jewish Affairs Committee (AIJAC).

On the other hand, to my deep disappointment, we tried but failed to reach agreement with the American Jewish Congress and, less well known, we were engaged in serious talks with CLAL. The group, under the leadership of Rabbi Yitz Greenberg, ultimately decided, however, to link up with UJA. We will continue to be open to other possibilities, both here in the United States and overseas.

In closing, let me hasten to assure you that the fiscal prudence you have come to expect from this management team over the past eight years remains intact, even as we begin to reap the benefits of an improving financial picture.

It is never, not for a moment, far from our minds that 60–65 percent of our total budget is committed to human resources, which means that if for any reason our revenue should decline, it will not be long before it affects real people here. In these last eight years, we have tried very hard, very hard indeed, to preserve and protect jobs. Having experienced the painful impact of a 15 percent cut in staff as a result of the decisions taken at St. Petersburg, regrettably we know whereof we speak.

If I may say so, I think we've done a reasonably good job of protecting jobs. When we downsized a bit—and it was only a bit—in recent years, it was achieved largely through resignation or retirement rather than retrenchment.

Today AJC is, I believe, a lean, productive, focused, and effective organization that is poised for an exciting new chapter in its institutional life, as reflected in the budget before you.

Having survived its most difficult internal challenge in decades, AJC, through the determined efforts of the people in this room and beyond, dramatically bounced back, regaining its bearings, restoring its fiscal health, and recapturing its place in the top tier of American civic organizations. Given that experience and bearing in mind this agency's uncanny knack for anticipating and adjusting to changing times, I am very bullish indeed on our future.

Eulogy for Richard Maass
Congregation Kol Ami, White Plains, N.Y.
September 14, 1998

What a full and exceptional life he led. How blessed we all were to have known him. How many of us he touched.

Richie was a man of enduring passion and compassion, of unyielding—and lived—principles and ideals, of boundless energy and curiosity, of an all-too-rare grace, dignity, and charm.

He was a student of history, but not its captive. He believed in a better tomorrow and devoted his life to its realization.

Somehow, Richie, who dedicated himself to a myriad of organizations, causes, and issues—at one point in his life, Dolly told me, he was simultaneously involved with seventeen different groups—always managed to give his fullest to each.

I first met Richie in 1979. He was president of the American Jewish Committee. I was an entry-level professional. But I knew Richie's name long before I joined.

He was the founding chairman of the National Conference on Soviet Jewry in 1971, when I was a student. Richie helped galvanize people across this land and beyond—Jews and non-Jews alike—to stand in solidarity with those brave Soviet Jews. I was one of the galvanized. It was due to Richie's leadership.

By 1979, then, when I first met Richie, I felt myself in the presence of a modern-day legend. Soviet Jews were tenacious and determined, but they could not have succeeded alone.

Richie was at the helm in those first crucial years, enlisting the support of presidents, secretaries of state, senators, you name it. As a result, tens of thousands of Soviet Jews—ultimately, hundreds of thousands—were able to establish new lives in Israel, the United States, and other lands of freedom.

Richie was also president of AJC during a vitally important period, 1977 to 1980. One of his greatest hopes at the time was the Camp David process.

Richie cared deeply about Israel. As he said at an AJC dinner in 1978: "To me the reestablishment of an independent Jewish state in the land of Israel, after more than eighteen centuries following the Roman conquest, is a miracle of our times. Her continued survival and well-being come close to being a second miracle when we consider the fact that over the past thirty years there has not been one day during which Israel was at peace with her neighbors."

But in the final analysis, Israel's survival, Richie was convinced, rested both on its ability to achieve peace in a troubled region and to remain steadfastly committed to the values of democracy and respect for human rights, based, as he once said, "on the finest traditions of ethical and religious principles."

He yearned for peace, and for Israel to become, as he put it, "the messenger of peace unto the peoples of the world." And he devoted so much of his effort to that quest.

In his years as AJC's president, Richie, to his delight, also witnessed an American administration that finally elevated the struggle for universal international human rights—a struggle with which he was so closely identified in large measure through AJC's Jacob Blaustein Institute for the Advancement of Human Rights—to unprecedented heights.

Here at home, though, to his consternation as a lifelong advocate of civil rights and social justice, he saw a conservative backlash emerge in his beloved America that continues to the present.

"We are in imminent danger of canceling many of the social gains made during the past twenty years," he said at an AJC function in 1978. "Much of the so-called tax reform is initiated by elements who use code words to disguise their antipathy for the poor, the disfranchised, and minority groups in our society. The challenge to us is to educate the public about the real effects of such propositions before they succeed in destroying the fabric of American life."

In thinking about this wise and gentle man, with that resonant and ever-so-distinctive voice, the trademark bow tie, the sparkle in the eye, and the infectious smile, who never hesitated to speak out against those whose views he considered mean-spirited and callous, and who always held this country to the standard of its own highest aspirations, I am reminded of a quote from the late Rabbi Leo Baeck:

> One can always find warm hearts who in a glow of emotion would like to make the whole world happy but who have never attempted the sober experiment of bringing a real blessing to a single human being. It is easy to revel enthusiastically in one's love of man, but it is more difficult to do good to someone solely because he is a human being. When we are approached by a human being demanding his right, we cannot replace definite ethical actions by mere vague goodwill.

Throughout his lifetime, Richie Maass did not wait to be approached. He reached out. He reached out to fellow Jews in need, he reached out to non-Jews in need. He accomplished what too few of us can claim in our lifetimes—he made an indelible impact on the lives of so many people and institutions around him, both near and far.

Through them, through us, through everyone he touched, his spirit will live on.

Richie, we feel you here today, as we have felt your presence throughout our lives. We are grateful to you for showing us how life should be lived, for reminding us that we are all here for a purpose, and for teaching us, by your example, how one person can help repair our fractured world.

To Dolly, his dear wife and traveling companion on a fifty-five-year journey that witnessed the affirmation of mutual love and the thrill of mutual discovery until the very end, even as Richie's illness took its mounting toll; to Andy and Doug, his beloved sons of whom he was always so proud; and to all the members of the grieving family, let me express, on behalf of the AJC family, Richie's other family for five decades, our sympathy and our love.

Tribute to Sam Rabinove
AJC 93rd Annual Meeting, Washington, D.C.
May 4, 1999

In 1966, a forty-three-year-old attorney for the Allstate Insurance Company decided he wanted a change of working venue to allow him the possibility to grapple with societal issues he truly cared about affecting both this country and the Jewish community.

In supporting this idealist's application to AJC, Abe Rosenthal of the *New York Times* said he had known him since their time together at City College where he was a "terribly bright guy." Moreover, said Rosenthal, the applicant was a "first-class man and gentleman in every way," and "highly cultured" to boot. What he couldn't comment on, though, was our applicant's legal skills since, Rosenthal noted, "I've never had occasion to find out."

Convinced that AJC had found the right person to serve as director of our Legal Division in the Department of Civil Rights and Social Action, the late John Slawson, my distinguished predecessor, wrote to Sam Rabinove on December 9, 1966, offering him a job.

Sam accepted, at a pay cut from his Allstate job, I might note, and started on January 3, 1967. And so began a remarkable thirty-year career at the AJC, a career that, sadly, ended on June 20, 1997, when Sam formally retired.

A number of years ago, in a report Sam prepared on a private visit to New Zealand and Australia, he began with a joke, quite characteristic of him. The joke went as follows: An American Jewish writer traveled to Israel for the first time, planning to do a book on his visit.

Shortly after his arrival, he was interviewed by an Israeli reporter who asked him how recently he had arrived. His answer: "Yesterday." The reporter then asked him when he would be departing. His answer: "Tomorrow." The reporter then asked him whether he still intended to write a book about Israel. His answer: "Of course! It will be called *Israel: Yesterday, Today and Tomorrow.*"

I'm not going to deliver either a book-length or a three-day speech, tempted though I may be given the subject matter. But let me briefly mention four attributes of Sam that have particularly struck me over the many years I've been privileged to call him a colleague and friend.

The first is Sam's wisdom. He's not just bright, as Abe Rosenthal said, and the author of countless learned articles and essays, but much more rare, he's truly wise and, as such, richly deserves the title counsel and counselor.

Second, Sam is possessed of courage—the physical courage he displayed during four years of wartime service in the U.S. Navy and again since the onset of his debilitating stroke; and the moral courage he has displayed throughout his life, the courage of an independent mind unafraid to speak out and assert his position, but always in a manner designed to bring people closer together, not farther apart.

Third, compassion. Few people I have ever met care as much about people, especially the less fortunate, as Sam does. You know, there are those who seek to save humanity but couldn't care less about individuals. No, Sam cares every bit as much about real people as he does about larger societal issues affecting them.

And fourth, humility. Sam is in many ways a giant among us, yet to be with him is to be with a man of quiet dignity. Joe Klein, writing in the *New Yorker* about Tony Blair, the British prime minister, said he is a man of "ostentatious humility." Sam is just the opposite, a man of authentic humility. He has lived his life nobly, serving his country in its hour of need, always being there for his beloved wife and four children, pursuing the mandate from Deuteronomy, *Tsedek, tsedek, tirdof,* "Justice, justice shalt thou pursue," and yes, treating his neighbor as he would himself be treated.

We live in an era increasingly dominated by the culture of complaint, the culture of celebrity, the culture of self-indulgence, and the culture of instant gratification. Sam, however, embodies the enduring—and tireless—values recently highlighted in Tom Brokaw's book, *The Greatest Generation*, about the Depression and wartime generation. Brokaw wrote admiringly of that generation's values of duty, responsibility, service, modesty, and family—in other words, the values that really count, the values that capture Sam's essence.

Ralph Waldo Emerson wrote: "To leave the world a bit better, whether by a healthy child, a garden patch or a redeemed social condition, to know even one life has breathed easier because you have lived. This is to have succeeded." By this standard Sam has succeeded brilliantly. He has redeemed countless social conditions and made many lives breathe easier.

Sam, the American Jewish Committee owes you an enormous debt of gratitude no speech could ever adequately convey. Even more, the Jewish people, the American Constitution, which you have cherished and protected all your adult life, and countless disadvantaged individuals everywhere owe you that enormous debt of gratitude.

Sam, we salute you. Please come up here and accept a small token of our esteem and affection.

HIAS Masliansky Award Acceptance Speech
New York
June 8, 1999

In Exodus 12:49, it is written: "One law for the native and the stranger among you."

This principle is particularly apt today because it embodies the very spirit that inspires the work of HIAS (Hebrew Immigrant Aid Society). Your organization does not draw false distinctions between them and us, between Americans who have been here for longer and those newly arrived, between natives and strangers of any land. Rather, it believes that there are some inalienable rights and privileges to which all human beings are entitled and some conditions that none should have to tolerate.

Your extraordinary work aiding refugees throughout the world is a testament to human generosity and to the possibility of realizing this highest of human standards. Since 1880, HIAS has relieved the horrors of being a stranger for millions of people. It has, in effect, created homes for the homeless, providing the gift of a new life, building air, land, and water bridges for those fleeing persecution and seeking a safe haven and the chance for a new start. In creating those homes, it has itself become a household name for many.

HIAS has worked in the best spirit of both Jewish and American cultures. Its mission is derived from the Ethics of the Fathers, from the teaching *kol yisrael arevim zeh ba zeh* ("All Jews are responsible one for the other"), and from the words inscribed on the base of the Statue of Liberty: "Give me your tired, your poor, your huddled masses, yearning to breathe free."

Indeed, from the very start of the first massive wave of Jewish immigration from Eastern Europe, members of the Hebrew Immigrant Aid Society sent representatives to Ellis Island and other ports of entry to help welcome these new Americans—and to defend their rights.

It is because of your historic work that I am honored to be here today and to accept, in the name of the American Jewish Committee, the Masliansky Award from HIAS.

The American Jewish Committee and HIAS share a common spirit. It is the spirit of communal self-reliance, of grounded enlightenment, of belief in the possibility of a better tomorrow. Both our organizations pursue the same noble visions. Our work is complementary in every sense.

HIAS is there when homes turn inhospitable, as, sadly, they continue to do for some to this very day. You have been there—sometimes openly, sometimes quietly—to extend a guiding hand when and where it is called for, whether assisting refugees from Eastern Europe, North Africa, Iran, Ethiopia, or Indochina.

And AJC's mission is to improve the political and social landscape for Jews and other peoples through the promotion of democratic values, protection of basic human rights, and enhancement of mutual respect, so that all people can one day feel at home and at peace in their chosen place of residence, as we fortunately do here in the United

States today. Our firm and long-standing commitments to one standard of justice for all and to fair and generous immigration policies are rooted in that mission.

In sum, you and we share the view that America is good for newcomers and, equally, that newcomers are good for America.

The common history of HIAS and AJC actually begins in the early years of this century. The annals of our respective histories are replete with the same great names—Jacob Henry Schiff, Louis Marshall, Cyrus and Mayer Sulzberger, Cyrus Adler. These prominent American Jews understood two fundamental things.

They understood that the Jewish community had needs—needs that it would have to meet in large part by itself, for itself. Many of these needs were directly related to the influx of Jews to the United States from Russia and elsewhere in Eastern Europe, where there was a marked rise in anti-Semitism and a tidal wave of pogroms in the region.

And these men understood as well that the time had come for the Jewish community to participate actively and without inhibition in the public life of America.

To offer but one illustration of our overlapping histories, permit me to read from a letter from Louis Marshall, then president of the American Jewish Committee, to Secretary of State Charles E. Hughes, dated April 27, 1921:

"Personally I have felt greatly pained that, in a public document emanating from the State Department, there should have occurred expressions such as [those your department] has seen fit to transmit to Congress [in the report of April 16, 1921]. . . . [They] seem to single out for opprobrious reference the Jews who desire to migrate to the United States. . . . They are depicted as undesirable, as coming in great hordes, as being of low physical and mental standards, and as desirous of coming here, not to become useful and industrious members of the community in which they wish to live, but in search of 'an easier life.'"

Mr. Marshall goes on to counter the arguments in this State Department report in detail. One in particular is worth mentioning in the context of this morning: his response to attacks on HIAS.

"Let me pause here to make my comments," Marshall continued. "The Hebrew Sheltering and Immigrant Aid Society undoubtedly is rendering aid to those who desire to come to this country. It is not engaged in unlawfully assisting immigration. . . . On account of the confusion that existed abroad and the exploitation to which emigrants were subjected, [HIAS] sent abroad representatives to protect those who were to come to this country from the fraudulent devices which they were certain to encounter, and to minimize the hardships and delays that would otherwise have occurred. Every dollar expended by that society was furnished by the relatives of those who were to migrate to the United States. The society has rendered great assistance to the American consulates and has simplified their task. It receives no compensation for the services it renders and is a philanthropic institution in the best sense of the word."

Since those days of common battles, HIAS and AJC have continued their close cooperation on matters of immigration.

Together, we fought to end unreasonable and biased limits on immigration and to assure adequate entry slots for refugees—and we continue to do so today.

Together, we opposed the attempt to deny benefits for immigrants who had legally entered this country.

Together, we have worked—and continue to work—to help Jews, first in the Soviet Union, now in the countries of the former Soviet Union, to leave the too often inhospitable soil of that land if they so choose. Well over a million have come—a tribute to the success of our efforts. We have welcomed them in Israel, where they have become a significant factor in the national landscape, and we have welcomed them into this country, where their presence and impact are increasingly felt.

And most recently, both our organizations have been helping Kosovo Muslim refugees faced with brutalization and expulsion. AJC has raised over a million dollars from concerned members and friends for immediate relief, while HIAS has focused its energies on the challenging task of resettlement.

These and many more are the common objectives and projects that have repeatedly brought us together.

Before closing, I want to add a personal note because HIAS has played a very important role in my own life. This makes the occasion today still more meaningful. You see, it's a homecoming for me.

In 1973, I was moonlighting in New York as a teacher of English as a foreign language. Increasing numbers of Soviet Jews began showing up in our school. I was immediately drawn to them for reasons of family, language, culture, and Jewish solidarity. During coffee breaks, they would speak to me of their migration to the United States, via Vienna and Rome, and laud the assistance rendered by HIAS en route.

The next year, I had the unusual opportunity to live and teach in the Soviet Union on a government-to-government exchange program. Until being expelled by Soviet officials for political activities, I was deeply involved in the lives of many Soviet Jews, especially refusenik families.

Shaken by the sudden departure but determined to continue my involvement with the historic awakening of Soviet Jews, I remembered my students in New York and took a train to Rome. Without an appointment or even the name of anyone, I simply showed up at the HIAS office on Viale Regina Margherita and said I was a Russian-speaking American Jew who had been profoundly moved by my three-month experience in the USSR and was hoping to work with Soviet Jewish migrants. Shortly thereafter, I was hired by Irving Haber of the Geneva office and spent nearly two and a half years working with HIAS, first in Rome, then in Vienna.

They were difficult years, but, most of all, they were exhilarating and inspiring years. All of us in the HIAS frontline offices felt we were involved in an historic mission, an aboveground railroad to move Jews who had previously been thought lost to world Jewry, to new homes and new lives in freedom and safety. The workload was enormous, the security concerns were ever present, and the daily challenges of dealing with an extraordinarily diverse and complex refugee population were sometimes overwhelming.

I kept a diary in Vienna and reread it before coming here today. Let me briefly read one excerpt:

"August 29, 1978. There were dozens of Soviet Jews filling the corridor and only three of us at HIAS to deal with them. Each of the refugees wanted priority in the handling of his or her case, each person insisted there was a sick parent or child involved. Every time one of the three of us would go out into the corridor we would be surrounded by the refugees. *Molodoy paren, budtye lubyezny, pomogite nam* (Young man, be so kind and help us). *U menya k vam malenkaya prosba* (I have a small favor to ask you). *Kak ya mogu popast v San Francisco?* (How can I make my way to San Francisco?). And so on. It never ended, yet at the same time here were people in literally the first or second day of their new lives in the West, entirely unprepared, totally disoriented, still dazed from the departure experience, and hell-bent on protecting their families."

Inspiration, of course, came from many of the refugees themselves. So, too, from my HIAS colleagues in Rome and Vienna. They worked hard, unimaginably hard, and endured unrelenting pressure from a steady stream of people in need. They performed magnificently, with grace, efficiency, humor, and respect for the refugees. They are unsung heroes—people like Evi Eller, Suzy Hazan, Cathy Bottone, Ida Pompucci, Marita Dresner, Walter Hitchman, Marilla Haggiag, Sylvia Zimmaro, Gert Miller, Hedva Hassan, Dahlia Boukhobza, and Vera Morse—who made a substantial difference in the lives of fellow Jews.

They processed, counseled, and guided thousands upon thousands of refugees through the first critical steps of a new life in the West and facilitated their onward migration to permanent new homes. *Yad b'yad*, hand in hand we worked, *regel b'regel*, together we walked.

This encounter with HIAS also left two other enduring imprints on me. First, it persuaded me to pursue a career in Jewish communal work. Frankly, when I first arrived in Rome, I thought I might do the work for a couple of years and then, with that out of my system, go on and pursue a career in the State Department or UN. Instead, the HIAS experience convinced me that there could be no higher calling than a lifetime spent in the Jewish community. And since joining AJC in 1979, I've learned that there certainly is no shortage of compelling diplomatic and political challenges to grapple with in the context of our wide-ranging domestic and international agenda.

Second, it led to my marriage. Yes, that's right, to my marriage. Thanks to Hedva Hassan, my wonderful colleague in the HIAS office in Rome, I met my future wife, Giulietta, Hedva's cousin, in 1975. I'll save you the details, but trust me, it wouldn't have happened without HIAS.

Since leaving HIAS twenty years ago, I've never had a proper chance to express my appreciation for those wonderful years in Rome and Vienna, for launching me on my professional career, and for being the *shadchan*, the matchmaker, that made possible my marriage and family life. Allow me to voice that gratitude today, and to thank you once again for bestowing the prestigious Masliansky Award on the American Jewish Committee.